VIATOR

Medieval and Renaissance Studies

VOLUME 2

VIATOR

MEDIEVAL AND RENAISSANCE STUDIES

Volume 2 (1971)

PUBLISHED UNDER THE AUSPICES OF
THE CENTER FOR MEDIEVAL AND RENAISSANCE STUDIES
UNIVERSITY OF CALIFORNIA, LOS ANGELES

UNIVERSITY OF CALIFORNIA PRESS
BERKELEY, LOS ANGELES, LONDON 1971

VIATOR
Medieval and Renaissance Studies

Manuscripts should be addressed to the Editor, Center for Medieval and Renaissance Studies, University of California, Los Angeles, California 90024, U.S.A. *Viator* is open to contributions from all sources. Texts, illustrations, maps, diagrams, musical examples and the like, will be published when they are necessary to the documentation. Articles that have been, or soon will be, printed elsewhere in any language in substantially the same form are not acceptable.

Inquiries concerning subscriptions should be addressed to the University of California Press, 2223 Fulton Street, Berkeley, California 94720, or 25 West 45th Street, New York, New York 10036, U.S.A.

University of California Press
Berkeley and Los Angeles, California
University of California Press, Ltd.
London, England
Copyright © 1972 by The Regents of the University of California
ISBN: 0-520-01830-3
Library of Congress Catalog Card Number: 71-111417

CONTENTS

DÉCISIONS ET TEXTES CONSTANTINIENS DANS LES ŒUVRES D'EUSÈBE DE CÉSARÉE

•

par Clémence Dupont

Les Codes Théodosien et Justinien ne livrent qu'une partie des décisions constantiniennes. Leurs indications sont complétées par d'autres sources de renseignements: lois de Constantin même ou de ses successeurs rappelant des dispositions perdues, inscriptions, papyri, œuvres historiques, biographiques et religieuses. Parmi les auteurs de ces dernières, Eusèbe de Césarée occupe la première place. L'*Historia ecclesiastica* et la *Vita Constantini* fournissent de nombreuses indications; des textes y sont insérés et des décisions mentionnées. Or, à notre connaissance tout au moins, aucune étude systématique d'ensemble n'en a jamais été présentée. Elle offrirait cependant un triple intérêt, ferait mieux connaître la personnalité de Constantin, autoriserait une appréciation supplémentaire sur Eusèbe et deux de ses œuvres, inciterait à rechercher les raisons ayant fait éliminer du Code Théodosien tant de mesures constantiniennes.

L'exposé que nous présenterons suppose résolue une difficulté. L'*Historia ecclesiastica* ne soulève pas de controverse, tout au moins pour ce qui nous intéresse. Au contraire, la *Vita Constantini* a suscité des discussions passionnées.[1]

Deux tendances se sont manifestées. La première attribue à Eusèbe la *Vita* et juge authentique la quasi-totalité des textes qui y sont insérés. La

---

[1] Les travaux des auteurs sur la question sont très nombreux. Pour ne pas alourdir cette étude, nous renvoyons à l'article de Milton V. Anastos, "The Edict of Milan (313); a Defence of Its Traditional Authorship and Designation," *Revue des études byzantines* 25 (1967) (*Mélanges Venance Grumel* 2) 13-41; on trouvera p. 15 n. 3 une abondante bibliographie sur le sujet. On pourra aussi consulter l'ouvrage de B. Altaner, *Précis de patrologie*, adapté par H. Chirat (Mulhouse 1961) 336-343 et celui de M. R. Farina, *L'impero e l'imperatore cristiano in Eusebio di Cesarea, La prima teologia politica del cristianesimo* (Zurich 1966) 16-17. Enfin, pour certaines questions, le recours à l'ouvrage de J. R. Palanque, G. Bardy, P. de Labriolle, *Histoire de l'Église*, sous la direction de A. Fliche et V. Martin; vol. 3, *De la paix constantinienne à la mort de Théodose* (Paris 1950) sera toujours utile.

deuxième conteste en partie cette authenticité; de plus certains auteurs ont vu dans la *Vita* un récit remanié; dans l'opinion la plus radicale, Eusèbe ne l'aurait même pas rédigée.

Actuellement, la tendance conservatrice retrouve une nouvelle faveur. L'hypercritique qui s'était exercée sur plusieurs documents de la *Vita* a été très fortement ébranlée. Elle avait choisi pour cible particulière l'édit aux provinciaux de Palestine; or, il a été découvert qu'un passage de ce texte était reproduit dans le Papyrus londoniensis 878.[2] Dans son *Later Roman Empire* paru en 1964, M. Jones a catégoriquement admis l'authenticité de tous les édits ou lettres cités dans la *Vita*.[3]

Le rôle d'Eusèbe, et d'Eusèbe seul, dans la rédaction de la *Vita* est lui-même réaffirmé. Dans l'étude citée précédemment, M. Farina[4] reprenant l'opinion de Vittinghoff[5] écarte toute objection sur ces points; la *Vita* nous est parvenue sous le nom d'Eusèbe; elle doit être attribuée à cet écrivain jusqu'à preuve contraire; l'*onus probandi* doit peser sur les adversaires de cette présomption.

Nous adopterons dans ces pages l'attitude conservatrice. Eusèbe sera considéré comme l'auteur de la *Vita Constantini* et les textes qu'il livre seront utilisés. Nous écarterons toutefois l'*Oratio de pace* adressée au Concile de Nicée, œuvre de rhétorique religieuse et l'*Oratio ad coetum sanctorum*, transmise en appendice à la *Vita*, qui possède le même caractère.[6] La lettre à Sapor, roi des Perses, subira un sort identique; pour constituer un document diplomatique de portée pratique, elle aurait dû enregistrer, tout au moins proposer un accord; or, elle est strictement unilatérale; elle exalte le christianisme dont elle recommande les adeptes à la bienveillance du souverain.

Cet article comprendra quatre chapitres. Le premier étudiera les textes cités par Eusèbe, le second et le troisième, les allusions de l'auteur aux décisions constantiniennes; dans le dernier seront recherchées les raisons ayant fait écarter du Code Théodosien la quasi-totalité des indications fournies par l'évêque de Césarée.

---

[2] Cf. A. H. M. Jones, "Notes on the Genuineness of the Constantinian Documents in Eusebius' Life of Constantine," *The Journal of Ecclesiastical History* 5 (1954) 196-200 (avec un appendice de T. C. Skeat).

[3] A. H. M. Jones, *The Later Roman Empire* 1 (Oxford 1964) 77.

[4] Farina (n. 1 *supra*) 17.

[5] Friedrich Vittinghoff, "Eusebius als Verfasser der Vita Constantini," *Rheinisches Museum für Philologie* 96 (1953) 333.

[6] L'authenticité de cette *Oratio* est d'ailleurs contestée, même par des auteurs conservateurs. Cf. sur ce point, R. Farina (n. 1 *supra*) 15-16.

CHAPITRE I. LES TEXTES CONSTANTINIENS CITÉS PAR EUSÈBE

Plusieurs questions seront successivement examinées.

I. LE NOMBRE DES TEXTES

L'*Historia ecclesiastica* contient six documents, tous traduits du latin en grec: cinq épîtres de Constantin, plus les *litterae Constantini et Licinii* concernant les chrétiens.

La *Vita Constantini* livre seize textes (sans l'appendice). Nous en avons éliminé deux. Aucun d'entre eux ne figure dans le livre 1; ils se rencontrent aux livres 2(4), 3(7), et 4(3).

L'*Historia ecclesiastica* étudiant sous Constantin les années 312-325[7] et le livre 1 de la *Vita* la période antérieure à la guerre de 324, les documents transmis par les deux œuvres sont évidemment différents. Chaque groupe concerne une partie spéciale du règne de l'empereur. Tout se passe comme si l'auteur de la *Vita* avait voulu éviter la répétition d'indications déjà données dans l'*Historia*. Cette constatation corrobore l'opinion attribuant à Eusèbe la paternité des deux récits.

II. LES DESTINATAIRES

Les décisions signalées sont adressées à des personnalités ou à des groupements religieux.

A. LES TEXTES DE L'HISTORIA ECCLESIASTICA.

Dans l'*Historia ecclesiastica*, trois lettres ont pour destinataires des évêques: ceux de Rome (Miltiade),[8] de Carthage (Cécilien), de Syracuse (Chrestus). Deux mentionnent dans leur *inscriptio* le nom du proconsul d'Afrique, Anullinus.

Enfin, *Historia* 10.5.2-14 octroyant la liberté religieuse aux habitants de l'empire, fut envoyée à un fonctionnaire, vraisemblablement à un gouverneur; l'expression *devotio tua* qui lui est appliquée convient en effet à un chef de province; de plus une autre version du même texte, rapportée par Lactance,[9] est adressée au gouverneur de Bithynie.[10]

---

[7] Toutefois, *l'Historia ecclesiastica* ne dit rien du premier conflit entre Licinius et Constantin.

[8] Au nom de Miltiade est adjoint celui de Marc. Il s'agit pour les uns de l'évéque de Milan, Méroclès, pour d'autres d'un coadjuteur du pontife. Cf. sur la question Palanque et al. (n. 1 *supra*) 45.

[9] *De mortibus persecutorum* 48.

[10] *Historia ecclesiastica* (HE) 10.5.2-14 a été l'objet de multiples travaux et discussions. Nous ne pouvons entrer ici dans le détail des controverses. On trouvera dans l'article de M. Milton V. Anastos, précédemment cité les indications bibliographiques nécessaires pour un examen complet du problème.

Beaucoup plus embarrassante est la question de savoir si ce gouverneur était un agent de Constantin ou de Licinius. Les auteurs penchent pour la seconde hypothèse. J. Maurice a souligné l'absence dans le passage de Lactance du préambule figurant dans la version d'Eusèbe: il en a déduit que si le texte de Lactance représentait les *litterae Licinii*, celui d'Eusèbe correspondait aux *litterae Constantini*.[11] Cette théorie qui ne peut être prouvée de façon absolue paraît vraisemblable.

Deux constatations l'appuient:

En dehors du texte dont il est question, l'*Historia ecclesiastica* ne cite pour la période 312-325 que des lettres concernant l'Occident.

Eusèbe avertit ses lecteurs qu'il traduit ces épîtres du latin en grec. *Historia* 10.5, était donc originellement rédigé en latin.

Jusqu'à preuve contraire, nous croyons donc pouvoir considérer ce texte comme proprement constantinien.[12]

B. LES DOCUMENTS DE LA VITA CONSTANTINI.

Parmi les destinataires des documents de la *Vita*, les évêques sont en majorité. Parfois, il s'agit de chefs religieux nommément désignés: Macarius de Jérusalem (une fois),[13] Alexandre d'Alexandrie et son adversaire Arius (une fois),[14] Eusèbe de Césarée (trois fois).[15]

Parfois, il s'agit de groupes d'évêques. Ainsi, 3.52-53 est adressée à Macarius et aux chefs religieux de Palestine. D'après Eusèbe (2.45), la lettre qu'il reçoit (2.46) est aussi envoyée aux *antistites* de chaque église, mais la teneur de la missive prouve qu'Eusèbe pensait à ses collègues de l'Orient.[16] Enfin, une épître (3.17-20) fut expédiée à tous les évêques de l'empire. L'adresse, *ad ecclesias de synodo Nicaea*, est équivoque à un double titre: *ecclesias* semble viser les communautés chrétiennes mais l'expression διατάττειν ὀφείλετε montre qu'il s'agit en réalité des évêques. D'autre part, Eusèbe a lui-même déclaré que l'empereur écrivit à tous ceux *qui huic synodo minime interfuissent*; enfin, sous le nom d'*ecclesiae* peuvent être compris les groupe-

---

[11] J. Maurice, "Critique des textes d'Eusèbe et de Lactance relatifs à l'Édit de Milan, 313," *Bulletin de la Société nationale des antiquaires de France* (1913) 349-354; idem, "Note sur le préambule placé en tête de l'Édit de Milan," *Bulletin d'ancienne littérature et d'archéologie chrétiennes* (BALAC) 4 (1914) 45-47.

[12] Même si nous avions adopté un point de vue différent, nous aurions dû étudier HE 10.5. En effet, à cette époque, Constantin étant premier Auguste, toutes les lois publiées dans l'empire sont juridiquement des lois constantiniennes.

[13] *Vita Constantini* (VC) 3.30-32.

[14] VC 2.64-72.

[15] VC 3.61; 4.35-36.

[16] Dans les premières lignes, Constantin déclare en substance vouloir réparer pour les bâtiments cultuels catholiques les effets de la persécution licinienne.

ments de fidèles, mais aussi les évêques.[17] Une autre hésitation peut naître. P. Batiffol a nié l'authenticité de la lettre; de toute façon, elle aurait été envoyée aux seuls *antistites* de l'Orient car l'empereur déclare à ses correspondants qu'il ira célébrer avec eux la *sancta festivitas*.[18] Ayant admis au début de cet article l'exactitude de presque tous les textes livrés par la *Vita*, nous discuterons seulement la réflexion de Batiffol concernant les destinataires de l'épître. Trois arguments lui semblent opposables. Eusèbe, annonçant l'envoi de la lettre, ne distingue pas entre les évêques d'Orient et d'Occident;[19] reprenant son récit après avoir cité le texte, il précise: "*Hanc epistolam . . . in omnes provincias direxit*";[20] enfin, le concile de Nicée ayant été œcuménique, la communication de ses décisions ne peut avoir été réservée à un groupe de prélats. Reste le passage relevé par Batiffol. On pourra supposer que, dans l'exemplaire adressé aux évêques d'Orient, les conseillers ecclésiastiques du prince insérèrent la phrase apparemment restrictive. D'ailleurs, si l'on poussait à l'extrême l'argumentation de Batiffol, on devrait ajouter que la lettre concerna seulement quelques prélats orientaux; Constantin ne pouvait en effet rencontrer le jour de Pâques qu'un petit nombre d'entre eux.

Les synodes épiscopaux d'Antioche et de Tyr reçoivent des instructions du prince.[21]

Constantin s'adresse quatre fois à des groupes de sujets: les habitants d'Antioche,[22] les hérétiques,[23] les provinciaux de l'Orient;[24] II, 24-42 est en effet copié sur l'exemplaire authentique gardé par Eusèbe de l'édit aux provinciaux de Palestine; mais la dernière ligne de l'acte déclare: "*Proponatur in partibus Orientalibus nostris.*"

III. L'OBJET

Les documents cités traitent tous de questions religieuses. Le fait est normal pour ceux de l'*Historia*; il l'est aussi pour ceux de la *Vita* car, dans 1.11, Eusèbe avertit ses lecteurs qu'il rapportera *ea sola quae ad Dei cultum pertinent*.

A. LES TEXTES DE L'HISTORIA ECCLESIASTICA.

Les textes de l'*Historia* concernent la liberté religieuse et la situation des chrétiens, la convocation des synodes, et l'aide financière au clergé d'Afrique.

---

[17] Cf. sur tout ceci, PG 20.1079 n. 76.
[18] P. Batiffol, "Les documents de la Vita Constantini," BALAC (1914) 86-87.
[19] VC 3.16.
[20] VC 3.20.
[21] VC 3.62 et 4.42.
[22] VC 3.60.
[23] VC 3.64 et 65.
[24] VC 2.24-42 et 48-60.

1. *la liberté religieuse et la situation des chrétiens.*

Historia 10.5.2-14 garantit à tous les sujets la liberté religieuse; les lieux de culte des chrétiens, les propriétés ecclésiastiques seront restitués aux églises; les propriétaires dépossédés pourront obtenir de l'empereur une indemnité.

Ce texte est-il autonome ou dépend-il d'une disposition antérieure? *Historia* 9.9-12 rapporte que, peu après la défaite de Maxence, Constantin et Licinius promulguèrent d'un commun accord une loi très parfaite et complète concernant les chrétiens.

Peut-on voir dans *Historia* 10.5.2-14 cette *lex* qui aurait été expédiée à chaque gouverneur? Nous ne le pensons pas. *Historia* 10.5 se présente plutôt comme un ensemble d'instructions visant l'application d'une décision antérieure; la plupart des verbes y sont employés au passé; les empereurs rapportent ce qu'ils ont décidé, parlent d'une loi précédente.[25]

Il faut alors préciser la nature de l'acte transmis par Eusèbe. Apparemment il s'agirait d'un rescrit, rendu probablement sur consultation d'un fonctionnaire embarrassé. On lit en effet dans le texte: ἅτινα οὕτως ἀρέσκειν ἡμῖν ἀντιγράψαι ἀκόλουθον ἦν.[26] Peut être cependant ne faut-il pas attacher trop d'importance à ces termes. *Historia* 10.5 pourrait être un *mandatum* envoyé à tous les gouverneurs; d'ailleurs, même s'il fut un rescrit, il dut être expédié à tous ceux ayant intérêt à le connaître.

Une épître enjoint au proconsul d'Afrique, Anullinus, de faire restituer aux églises leurs propriétés. Par sa place dans l'*Historia ecclesiastica* (10.5.15-17), elle semble postérieure à celle que nous venons d'étudier. Son objet étant limité, M. Anastos incline à lui attribuer une date légèrement antérieure.[27] Une deuxième missive au même fonctionnaire exonère de *functio publica*, c'est-à-dire des charges municipales, les clercs de l'église catholique.[28]

2. *la convocation des synodes.*

Les deux lettres à Miltiade et à Chrestus ont un objet semblable. La première[29] prescrit au pape et à Marc de tenir un colloque auquel ils participeront avec trois prélats; l'évêque de Carthage, Cécilien, comparaîtra devant eux avec vingt évêques pris en nombre égal parmi ses partisans et adversaires. La lettre à Chrestus[30] est un exemplaire des convocations adressées à de nom-

---

[25] Ils ordonnent notamment la restitution des biens d'église ἐπὶ τῷ νόμῳ ὃν προειρήκαμεν.

[26] G. Bardy traduit de la façon suivante: "Ainsi, il était convenable qu'il nous plût de donner ce rescrit." G. Bardy, *Eusèbe de Césarée, Histoire Ecclésiastique* 3 (Paris 1958) 105.

[27] Anastos (n. 1 *supra*) 33.

[28] HE 10.7.

[29] HE 10.5.17-20.

[30] HE 10.5.21-24.

breux évêques de l'Occident. Les Donatistes, mécontents de la sentence prononcée à Rome, s'étaient plaints à l'empereur qui avait décidé la réunion, en août 314, d'un concile dans la ville d'Arles.

3. *l'aide financière au clergé d'Afrique.*

Cécilien, vers la même époque, avait été avisé que le prince mettait à sa disposition trois mille *folles* pour le clergé d'Afrique; ils devaient lui être remis par le *rationalis* d'Afrique et être partagés par Cécilien selon les instructions d'Hosius. De plus, Constantin prescrit à son correspondant de contacter les autorités civiles; elles prendront à l'égard des fauteurs de troubles les décisions que l'empereur leur a communiquées verbalement.[31]

B. LES DOCUMENTS DE LA VITA CONSTANTINI.

Plus nombreux que ceux de l'*Historia*, ils ont aussi des sujets plus variés.

1. *la liquidation des mesures anti-chrétiennes de Licinius.*

L'édit aux provinciaux de Palestine (2.24-42) abroge les mesures ayant, avant 324, frappé les chrétiens. Prendront fin pour eux exils, relégations, condamnations *ad metalla* et *ad opera publica*, servitude, appels injustifiés à la curie. La succession des martyrs, confesseurs, relégués, qui avait été accaparée par le fisc, retournera aux proches des victimes, en leur absence à l'église du lieu. Les occupants des fonds, maisons, jardins les restitueront mais pourront en garder les fruits; le fisc même n'échappera pas à ces règles. Les églises recouvreront les cimetières et les corps des martyrs. Si le fisc a vendu ou donné des biens d'églises, acheteurs ou donataires s'en dessaisiront. La loi se termine par une exhortation à honorer Dieu.

Elle devait sur le moment amener de grands bouleversements. Une disposition notamment se révéla grave de conséquences. L'enrôlement abusif des chrétiens dans les curies avait sans doute permis à Licinius de libérer des partisans qui avaient gagné l'armée ou les offices; la libération de ces décurions accentua la désertion des ordres municipaux; pour y parer, des mesures énergiques furent nécessaires et le Code Théodosien nous en a gardé le souvenir.

2. *la crise arienne.*

Elle provoque l'épître à Alexandre et Arius (2.64-72). Constantin, à peine vainqueur de Licinius, demande aux adversaires de se réconcilier; pour les y amener, il minimise la portée de leur controverse; instruit par l'affaire donatiste, il veut à tout prix enrayer un nouveau conflit religieux dont il ne soupçonne pas encore la gravité ni les répercussions.

---

[31] HE 10.6.

Après le concile de Nicée, les évêques qui n'avaient pu y assister reçurent une lettre du prince communiquant ses décisions. En fait, celle livrée par Eusèbe (3.17-20) concerne presque uniquement les prescriptions sur la date de la *festivitas Paschae*.

En 335, au synode de Tyr, Constantin enjoindra de rétablir la paix religieuse toujours troublée par la question arienne (4.42).

3. *les hérésies.*

Contre la multitude des hérésies répandues dans l'empire, Constantin réagit. La constitution *adversus haereticos* (3.64, 65) énumère plusieurs sectes, mais ajoute: *omnes denique qui haereses.* . . .

Elle poursuit un double but: empêcher la diffusion des erreurs, ramener à la vérité les égarés. Pour atteindre ces objectifs, deux mesures sont édictées: l'interdiction des réunions, la confiscation des lieux de culte publics et privés; s'il s'agit d'oratoires, ils iront à l'église catholique; sinon, ils seront adjugés publiquement.

4. *la construction d'églises.*

Eusèbe et les évêques d'Orient sont invités à bâtir des églises, à réparer et agrandir celles déjà existantes; l'aide de l'autorité civile pourra être requise.[32]

Macarius de Jérusalem reçoit des instructions pour faire construire la basilique du Saint-Sépulcre avec la collaboration des agents du prince.[33] Comme ses collègues de Palestine, l'empereur l'entretient du site biblique de Mambré; il évoque les actes impies se passant dans le Lieu Saint et les déclare pour l'avenir passibles de mort; les évêques collaboreront pour leur répression avec les pouvoirs publics en signalant au prince les coupables; une basilique sera érigée à Mambré.[34]

5. *les intérêts spirituels des habitants de Constantinople.*

Pour les satisfaire, une lettre est envoyée à Eusèbe;[35] il fera confectionner cinquante *codices* contenant les Saintes Écritures; le *rationalis* du diocèse a reçu des instructions et procurera les matériaux nécessaires pour ce travail. La demande atteste l'activité du *scriptorium* adjoint à la bibliothèque de Césarée et la réputation dont il jouissait.

6. *la désignation de l'évêque d'Antioche.*

La déposition d'Eustathe d'Antioche avait provoqué des troubles sérieux dans la ville. Constantin écrit trois lettres au sujet de sa succession: l'une

[32] VC 2.46.
[33] VC 3.30-32.
[34] VC 3.52-53.
[35] VC 4.36.

aux *Antiocheni* leur demande de ne pas réclamer le chef de Césarée;[36] la seconde loue Eusèbe d'avoir récusé le siège d'Antioche;[37] la troisième s'adresse au synode réuni dans la cité pour qu'il écarte Eusèbe et lui propose deux excellents candidats.[38]

7. *les exhortations religieuses aux provinciaux de l'Orient.*

Un édit aux provinciaux de l'Orient traite notamment du culte des idoles, rassure les païens, loue le vrai Dieu, invite les populations à fuir le mal et à pratiquer la vertu.[39]

8. *la louange d'Eusèbe pour son Oratio de Pascha.*

Elle nous est connu par 4.35 et ne présente qu'un intérêt religieux.

IV. RÉFLEXIONS GÉNÉRALES

Elles concernent les destinataires, les causes de promulgation et le domaine d'application des dispositions étudiées.

A. LES DESTINATAIRES.

Dans l'*Historia ecclesiastica*, tous les destinataires sont des Occidentaux. Dans la *Vita*, la quasi-totalité habite l'Orient; seuls, deux groupes de personnes, les évêques absents de Nicée, les hérétiques, résident dans les deux parties de l'empire.

L'explication est facile pour les textes de l'*Historia*. Eusèbe n'a sans doute pas voulu citer de documents venant de Licinius, devenu persécuteur des chrétiens[40] et dont les lois avaient été abrogées.

Dans la *Vita*, deux périodes sont à distinguer. Pour les années 312-324, le biographe de Constantin n'avait pas à livrer des textes liciniens; il ne voulut pas d'autre part rééditer les décisions occidentales transmises par l'*Historia*. Pour l'époque 324-337, il a sans doute préféré rapporter des dispositions qu'il pouvait connaître facilement comme évêque d'Orient et ami du prince; d'autre part, la majorité des événements religieux se passe alors en Orient.

[36] VC 3.60.
[37] VC 3.61.
[38] VC 3.62.
[39] VC 2.48-60.
[40] Nous partageons l'opinion selon laquelle, dès la conférence de Milan, Licinius exerça en fait dans ses états le pouvoir législatif, la première guerre civile amenant juridiquement le partage de l'empire à cet égard. Nous reviendrons sur la question dans un travail ultérieur.

B. LES CAUSES DE PROMULGATION.

La question est la suivante. Les textes cités par Eusèbe présentent-ils un caractère occasionnel? Expriment-ils au contraire des conceptions personnelles du prince et sont-ils, de ce fait, indépendants de la pression des événements?

Une réflexion préliminaire sera faite. Certes, les circonstances historiques et religieuses de l'époque jouèrent un rôle important dans l'apparition des décisions étudiées; mais, le plus souvent, elles ont simplement offert à l'empereur la possibilité de montrer aux sujets ses tendances et sa volonté; elles n'ont pas eu un rôle déterminant.

Ainsi, la victoire de 324 permit à Constantin de publier l'édit aux provinciaux de l'Orient; la loi reste cependant avant tout une mesure de protection du christianisme, conforme à la pensée religieuse du prince.

La crise arienne, sa gravité en Orient, sont comparables aux événements militaires; elles permettent au prince de manifester son tempérament, désireux de concorde et de paix.

Au contraire, le déroulement de pratiques impies à Mambré, les lettres à Constantin sur ce sujet, sont l'occasion au sens restreint du mot, de l'épître aux évêques de Palestine.

Cette distinction étant admise, on constatera que, parmi les textes étudiés, une minorité seulement présente un caractère ocasionnel. Semblent rentrer dans cette catégorie, outre la missive citée, les lettres à Miltiade et à Chrestus— Constantin déclare intervenir à la suite de rapports d'Anullinus ou de plaintes des donatistes—les trois épîtres liées à l'affaire d'Antioche et celle louant le discours pascal d'Eusèbe.

La lettre *Alexandro et Ario* prête à discussion. Si la tentative impériale de concilier les adversaires avait réussi, l'affaire arienne eût pu être classée et l'épître eût été qualifiée d'occasionnelle. Peut-être faut-il lui attribuer ce caractère, bien qu'elle s'intègre dans les documents concernant l'arianisme.

Les autres textes nous semblent exprimer la volonté d'établir un état ou le vrai Dieu sera honoré, le christianisme favorisé, le paganisme en recul, voire disparu, et la concorde religieuse établie.

C. LE DOMAINE D'APPLICATION.

Ce domaine est extrêmement varié. Parmi les textes de l'*Historia ecclesiastica*, cinq révèlent leur domaine d'application, particulier dans deux cas, général dans les autres.

L'aide financière promise à Cécilien concerne le clergé d'Afrique, de Numidie et des Mauritanies. Les *litterae* sur la liberté religieuse expliquent et développent une loi antérieure visant tous les sujets de l'empire. Les missives à Miltiade et à Chrestus semblent théoriquement valoir pour leur seul destinataire; mais, d'autres prélats ayant reçu des instructions identiques, nous leur attribuerons la valeur du litige donastiste examiné à Rome et Arles. Embarrassante est la lettre à Anullinus dispensant les clercs de *functio publica*; elle est explicitement édictée pour le Proconsulaire; or, le 31 octobre 313, Code Théodosien 16.2.1, au destinataire inconnu, mentionne la violation du privilège. Admettons—ce n'est pas sûr—qu'il s'agisse du successeur d'Anullinus. Mais, le 21 octobre 313, 16.2.2,[41] envoyé au gouverneur de Lucanie et *Brittium* traite aussi de l'exemption des clercs et paraît également faire allusion à sa méconnaissance. Il semble donc qu'il y eut plusieurs dispositions semblables adressées aux gouverneurs d'Occident.

Reste la première lettre à Anullinus, sans doute antérieure à celle sur la liberté religieuse. Elle fut peut-être édictée pour toute l'Afrique ou pour le Proconsulaire mais elle devint rapidement inutile avec la promulgation du texte qui, indiscutablement, visait l'empire.

Parmi les documents de la *Vita Constantini*, cinq concernent un prélat ou Alexandre et Arius, un les évêques d'une province, un les prélats de l'Orient, deux des conciles, un les habitants d'une ville, deux les Orientaux et un les hérétiques.

Le plus souvent, lettres ou édits indiquent la sphère de leur application, précisent qu'ils visent telle ou telle personnalité.

Un texte seulement était valable pour l'empire; les autres ne pouvaient s'appliquer qu'à une région ou à l'ensemble de l'Orient, ou encore à des évêques de cette partie de l'état. Le nombre restreint de textes ayant valeur générale est évident. Cependant, on ne peut déceler chez le prince aucun désir de créer pour l'ancien domaine de Licinius un particularisme quelconque. En réalité, les textes de la *Vita* traitent de questions propres à l'Orient ou veulent aligner la situation des nouveaux territoires sur celle de l'Occident.

CHAPITRE II. LES DÉCISIONS CONSTANTINIENNES MENTIONNÉES PAR EUSÈBE NE FIGURANT PAS DANS LES CODES.

Les allusions aux décisions de Constantin non insérées dans les codes se trouvent essentiellement dans la *Vita Constantini*. Toutefois, l'*Historia ecclesiastica* ne peut être négligée.

I. L'HISTORIA ECCLESIASTICA.

Les renseignements fournis par ce récit sont très rares mais l'un est de particulière importance.

[41] Sur la date de ce texte, apparemment de 319, cf. O. Seeck, *Regesten der Kaiser und Päpste für die Jahre 311 Bis 476 n. Chr.; Vorarbeit zu einer Prosopographie der christlichen Kaiserzeit* (Stuttgart 1919) 55, 161.

Eusèbe (9.9) rapporte qu'après la défaite de Maxence, Constantin et Licinius promulguèrent tous deux, d'un seul consentement, une loi τελειώ-
τατον et πληρέστατα favorable aux chrétiens. De ce passage résulte ex-
pressément la collaboration des deux empereurs à la disposition. Si l'on
admet que ἐπὶ τούτοις indique une date très voisine de la victoire du Pont
Milvius, que d'octobre 312 à juin 313—époque où Licinius afficha à Nicomédie
ses lettres sur la liberté religieuse[42]—le seul lieu de rencontre des princes fut
Milan, on verra dans la loi relatée par Eusèbe celle connue sous le nom d'Édit
de Milan. Après un examen sérieux du texte eusébien et de son contexte,
il nous semble impossible de maintenir l'adhésion donnée dans l'introduction
de notre thèse[43] à la théorie de Grégoire. Déclarer qu'il y eut à Milan de simples entretiens entre Constantin et Licinius, dont ce dernier seul publia les
résultats en Orient, se heurte aux termes employés par Eusèbe νόμον, ἀμφω,
μιᾷ βουλῇ καὶ γνώμῃ.

C'est cette loi dont l'exécution sera prescrite à un fonctionnaire, probablement un gouverneur, dont l'*Historia ecclesiastica*, 10.5 rapporte le texte.[44]

On peut discuter sur le lieu de promulgation de la décision mais Milan
paraît le seul acceptable.

Les autres passages de l'*Historia* mentionnant des mesures constantiniennes perdues sont négligeables. Pour les périodes suivant la chute de Maxi-
min et celle de Licinius nous apprenons que furent rendues des *leges* favorables
aux chrétiens.[45] L'expression, trop vague, n'autorise aucune déduction; de
plus, nous connaissons des lois de Constantin qui, après 311 et 324, avanta-
gèrent les chrétiens; quant à celles de Licinius, elles ne nous intéressent pas.

II. LA VITA CONSTANTINI.

A. LES DIFFICULTÉS.

Les difficultés que nous rencontrerons ont essentiellement deux causes.

1. *Eusèbe est un biographe, un panégyriste.* Au cours de son récit, il mentionne des mesures prises par Constantin, sans en préciser toujours l'époque
de promulgation.

2. *Eusèbe n'est pas un juriste.* Il est parfois difficile de déterminer si les
décisions qu'il rapporte constituèrent de véritables lois. L'usage notamment
des termes *jubere, jussio* est équivoque. Indiquent-ils l'exercice du pouvoir

---

[42] Cf. Lactance, *De mortibus persecutorum* 48.2-12.

[43] *Les constitutions de Constantin et le droit privé au début du IVe siècle: Les personnes*
(Lille 1937) = Réimpression anastatique par la maison l'"Erma" di Bretschneider (Rome
1968) 16. Sur ces points, n. b. Anastos (n. 1 *supra*) 23 ss.

[44] Cf. 3 *supra*.

[45] HE 10.2 et 9.

législatif ou un ordre immédiatement exécutoire, épuisant en une fois ses effets? D'après *Vita* 1.43, le prince ordonna de secourir les mendiants du forum: à première vue, la disposition sera exclue des actes législatifs; mais le Code Théodosien a gardé deux constitutions[46] en faveur des pauvres d'Italie et d'Afrique; la mesure concernant les miséreux de Rome a pu constituer une loi. Il est aussi parfois difficile de déterminer si un sujet déterminé donna lieu à un ou plusieurs textes. Des dispositions connexes ont pu être réunies dans une seule décision; d'autres, sur un même thème, adressées à plusieurs personnes, furent peut-être des exemplaires différents d'une seule loi.

Ces difficultés influenceront notre attitude; elle sera large dans la présentation des décisions de Constantin, nuancée dans l'appréciation de leur caractère.

B. LE NOMBRE DES DÉCISIONS.

Ce nombre ne peut être déterminé avec précision. Le premier livre rapporte quatre dispositions (ou séries de dispositions), le deuxième cinq, le troisième vingt six, le quatrième seize. Les deux derniers livres sont donc les plus intéressants pour nous.

L'explication est simple. Le livre 1 traite entre autres de la période 312-324; quant au livre 4, il expose notamment la législation de Constantin, sans égard à sa chronologie.

C. L'OBJET.

Les décisions mentionnées par Eusèbe se rapportent à cinq thèmes.

1. *la liquidation du régime de Maxence.*

Eusèbe cite le rappel des relégués, la libération *a vinculis*, les restitutions aux personnes spoliées. Furent-elles comprises dans une seule loi? L'auteur parle de lettres impériales. *Litterae* désignant souvent un acte unique, nous croyons qu'il y eut à la fin de 312, pour toutes les victimes de Maxence, une constitution analogue à celle promulguée en 324 en faveur des chrétiens de l'Orient.[47]

A la même époque, Constantin publia deux constitutions pour faire cesser la délation, séquelle indirecte du régime disparu. Elles figurent au Code Théodosien[48] alors qu'Eusèbe n'en dit rien. Le silence du biographe se comprend; ces lois répriment des abus commis par les sujets de Constantin et non par le prince déchu.

---

[46] Code Théodosien (CT) 11.27.1-2.
[47] Cf. *supra* 5, 7, 11.
[48] CT 10.10.2, 1er décembre 312 (sur la date de ce texte, cf. Seeck, n. 41 *supra*, 50, 160) et 10.10.1, 18 janvier 313.

2. *le christianisme.*

Très nombreuses, d'objet varié, les mesures sur ce thème se succèdent de 312 à 337.

a. Les décisions impériales et les conciles.

i. La réunion des synodes.

Vita 1.44 déclare "... *ministrorum Dei concilia congregavit* ..." Dans la suite du récit, Eusèbe ne dit rien des réunions de Rome et d'Arles, alors que l'*Historia ecclesiastica* livre les missives reçues à cette occasion par Miltiade et Chrestus;[49] il signale au contraire la convocation des assemblées de Nicée et de Tyr,[50] sans y joindre les lettres d'invitation adressées aux prélats[51] ou l'ordre donnée aux évêques réunis à Tyr de gagner Jérusalem;[52] il ne mentionne pas à propos du concile de Nicée que le lieu des séances avait d'abord été fixé à Ancyre en Galatie.[53]

En convoquant les chefs des églises, Constantin exerçait-il le pouvoir législatif? Il semblerait logique qu'une décision générale eût précédé les invitations personnelles; affichée dans les cités épiscopales, tout au moins au lieu de la résidence impériale, elle eût en somme constitué une loi. Mais les indications d'Eusèbe ne permettent pas d'affirmer l'existence d'une telle mesure; dans la *Vita*, comme dans les épîtres à Miltiade et Chrestus, l'ordre de réunion est toujours lié aux lettres envoyées aux évêques.

ii. Les sentences des synodes *Vita* 3.23 et 4.27 indiquent soit une décision particulière, soit l'attitude générale du prince.

Vita 3.23 concerne l'une des péripéties de l'affaire arienne. Constantin écrivit aux Égyptiens, leur signifia par lettre la sentence arbitrale qu'il venait de prononcer et confirma les décisions du synode.[54] L'intitulé de 3.23 porte "*Quomodo ad Aegyptios scripserit* ..." mais, du corps du chapitre, résulte que l'empereur écrivit à ceux qu'il avait auparavant convoqués et dont il avait arbitré le conflit.[55] D'autre part, nous possédons deux lettres du souverain ne figurant pas dans Eusèbe; l'une est adressée à l'église d'Alexandrie, l'autre à Arius et aux Ariens;[56] aucune ne correspond aux indications du biographe.

---

[49] Cf. *supra* 3, 6, 10, 11.

[50] VC 3.6; 4.41.

[51] La lettre au Synode de Tyr livrée par VC 3.42 s'adresse aux évêques déjà réunis.

[52] VC 3.43.

[53] Cf. sur ce point, J. Hefele, *Histoire des conciles*, trad. H. Leclercq, 1.1 (Paris 1907) 403-404.

[54] Il s'agit du synode de Nicée.

[55] On a invoqué ce passage en faveur d'une deuxième session du concile de Nicée. L'hypothèse ne semble pas pouvoir être retenue. Nous renvoyons pour cette question, à Palanque et al. (n. 1 *supra*) 100.

[56] Cf. PL 8, 507-518.

D'après 4.27, le prince confirma de son autorité les sentences des conciles *"adeo ut provinciarum rectoribus non liceret episcoporum decreta rescindere. . . ."* Ce membre de phrase est instructif. Nous avons bien des textes de Constantin approuvant les dispositions de tel ou tel synode; mais ils sont adressés à des personnalités ou communautés chrétiennes; d'autre part, ils mentionnent des décisions de caractère essentiellement religieux. Par la *Vita*, nous devinons que des instructions furent envoyées aux gouverneurs sur les matières de leur ressort.

En imposant à ses agents le respect des mesures conciliaires, Constantin transformait en lois de l'état celles de l'Église. La portée de cet acte était considérable.

b. Le dimanche et les jours de fête.

Trois chapitres de la *Vita Constantini*, 4.18, 19, et 23, rapportent cinq décisions sur cette question. Elles correspondent sans doute à trois ou quatre lois.

D'après 4.18, tous les sujets de l'empire chômeront le dimanche et même le samedi. Les militaires chrétiens recevront le temps nécessaire pour vaquer à leurs oraisons.

Une autre loi signalée par 4.19 enjoint aux soldats païens de prier la Divinité le dimanche, en utilisant une formule distribuée dans les camps.

Enfin 4.23 avertit qu'une loi envoyée aux gouverneurs leur prescrivit de vénérer le dimanche; il ajoute que ces fonctionnaires, par ordre du prince, célébraient aussi les fêtes ecclésiastiques et celles des martyrs.

Faut-il voir, dans ces décisions une allusion à Code Justinien 3.12.2 et Code Théodosien 2.8.1 affichées en mars et juillet 321 par l'*agens vices praefectorum praetorio* Helpidius,[57] qui imposaient le repos dominical aux juges et aux populations urbaines? Nous ne le pensons pas et cela pour trois raisons:

La date des mesures mentionnées par Eusèbe est inconnue; elles figurent en effet dans un passage de la *Vita* où l'auteur expose la législation de Constantin, sans égard à la chronologie. Mais Sozomène qui rapporte certaines d'entre elles les situe, d'après le contexte de son *Historia ecclesiastica* 1.8, après la soumission de l'Orient.

Les destinataires des mesures rapportées dans les Codes et la *Vita* sont différents. Helpidius, fonctionnaire civil, ne peut avoir reçu des instructions concernant les militaires. D'autre part, 4.23 parle d'une loi envoyée aux gouverneurs de province et non à un *agens vices praefectorum praetorio*.

Les codes n'ont gardé aucun souvenir de la célébration du samedi, mentionnée par Eusèbe mais aussi par Sozomène.

---

[57] Contrairement à Seeck (n. 41 *supra*) 61, 62, 171, nous pensons qu'il s'agit de lois différentes et non de fragments d'une même disposition. Cf. sur ce point mon article "Constantin et la préfecture d'Italie," *Études offertes à Jean Macqueron* (Aix-en-Provence 1970) 259. La question est d'ailleurs sans importance pour cet exposé.

Nous conclurons. Après sa victoire de 324, Constantin étendit à l'Orient la législation de 321, mais il la compléta par plusieurs dispositions visant le repos du samedi et l'invitation à prier Dieu. *Vita* 4.18, 19, et 23 peuvent donc être étudiées dans cette section concernant les allusions aux décisions ne figurant pas dans les Codes.

c. La représentation impériale.

D'après 4.15, l'empereur ordonna que ses monnaies d'or et statues le représentent dans l'attitude de la prière. Il défendit la dédicace de ses statues dans les temples des idoles (4.16).

d. La gravure des armes.

Le signe de la croix devait figurer sur les armes des soldats (4.21).

e. Les constructions d'églises.

Les décisions en ce secteur furent très nombreuses. L'une fut générale, d'autres particulières.

i. Selon *Vita* 2.45, une loi prescrivit de bâtir des églises. Eusèbe dit ensuite que l'empereur écrivit aux gouverneurs de provinces pour les aviser de cet ordre et leur donner des instructions en vue du financement des travaux; il s'adressa de même aux évêques. Le biographe cite alors le texte de la lettre qu'il reçut à cette occasion.[58]

Une décision de ce genre avait-elle été édictée après la chute de Maxence? *Vita* 1.42 montre en effet Constantin érigeant de ses deniers des sanctuaires et agrandissant ceux déjà existants. On ne peut rien affirmer sur ce point.

ii. Les décisions particulières concernent des églises nommément désignées. La première est celle du Saint-Sépulcre à Jérusalem (3.30-32). Pour son édification il y eut un ordre de détruire le temple bâti sur le Lieu Saint et d'en évacuer matériaux et décombres (3.27), des constitutions sur la construction du nouveau sanctuaire (3.29), une lettre aux gouverneurs relative aux frais (3.29), une lettre à l'évêque de Jérusalem qui nous est parvenue;[59] elle révèle l'existence d'instructions à l'*agens vices praefectorum* Dracilianus et d'une épître au *praeses* de Palestine sur la question des murailles. Les autres églises mentionnées sont celles de Nicomédie et d'Antioche (3.50), de Mambré (outre la lettre à Macarius,[60] il y eut des instructions aux gouverneurs [3.51]), la basilique d'Héliopolis (3.58), des églises à Constantinople (3.48), notamment celles des apôtres (3.58).

f. Les exhortations religieuses.

Constantin (3.24) écrivit plusieurs fois aux évêques et aux populations *ad ecclesiarum Dei utilitatem*; les évêques furent exhortés à propager la louange de la divine religion (3.63).

---

[58] Cf. n. 32 *supra.*
[59] Cf. n. 13 *supra.*
[60] Cf. 8 *supra.*

3. *les hérétiques.*

La constitution *adversus haereticos* fut précédée ou accompagnée d'instructions aux gouverneurs de provinces. Nous aurions volontiers considéré le texte de l'une et des autres comme des exemplaires différents d'une même loi. La façon dont s'exprime Eusèbe appuie cependant l'idée de décisions distinctes.

4. *le paganisme.*

Les mesures à son égard figurent aux livres 2, 3, et 4. Leur interprétation est difficile car Eusèbe revient à plusieurs reprises sur les mêmes sujets. Elles se répartissent en quatre groupes:

a. L'interdiction des sacrifices et du culte des idoles. D'après 2.45 une loi interdit les sacrifices du culte des idoles. Sont visés l'érection de statues, le recours à la divination, l'immolation de victimes.

Vita 4.23 déclare: "A tous les habitants de l'empire étaient fermées les portes du culte des idoles et tout genre de sacrifice prohibé."

Vita 4.25 revient sur la question. "Par de nombreuses lois et constitutions, sacrifices aux idoles, érection de statues, consultation de devins furent interdits à tous."

Enfin *Vita* 3.48 signale la décision prise en ce domaine pour Constantinople.

Faut-il supposer qu'il y eut sous Constantin plusieurs dispositions concernant les sacrifices... etc? Le témoignage de 4.25 est difficilement récusable. On peut ainsi écarter l'argument inverse qui serait tiré du Code Théodosien 16.10.2 (341); dans cette décision Constant évoque "la" loi de son père ayant interdit les sacrifices. On supposera que la résistance aux mesures frappant les pratiques païennes en avait rendu nécessaire la réitération;[61] Constant aurait rappelé la dernière disposition paternelle.

L'objet des prohibitions constantiniennes ne peut être comparé à celui du Code Théodosien 9.16.1-2 qui, avant 324, frappèrent l'haruspicine pratiquée dans les maisons particulières. Eusèbe ne distingue pas le culte privé du culte public.

Quant à la sanction appuyant les interdictions, elle n'est pas mentionnée dans la *Vita*.

Apparemment les mesures de Constantin visèrent les deux parties de l'empire; mais 4.25 unit aux lois sur les idoles, devins..., la décision de 325 prohibant les combats de gladiateurs; or, celle-ci insérée au Code Théodosien 15.12.1 à l'adresse du *vicarius Orientis* Maximus, dut concerner l'Orient seul; après sa promulgation, Constantin autorise en effet le *munus gladiatorium*

---

[61] La répétition au Bas Empire des lois contre les sacrifices païens atteste cette résistance (Cf. CT 16.10.2 et ss.).

dans la cité italienne d'Hispellum.[62] Cependant, l'application en Occident de
la législation constantinienne sur les sacrifices résulte du Code Théodosien
16.10.2; Constant qui rappelle en 341 la loi de son père régnait sur l'Occident.

   b. La destruction des temples.

   Vita 3.54 est intitulé *Fana et simulacra ubique diruta*. Eusèbe y rapporte
des faits qui se déroulèrent de son temps et le sort infligé aux temples et aux
idoles.

   Le biographe relate aussi la destruction de sanctuaires dans certaines villes
Aphaca et Heliopolis en Phénicie,[63] Aegis en Cilicie.[64] Nous avons déjà signalé celles effectuées à Jérusalem.[65] Pour la destruction des *simulacra* et
de l'autel de Mambré, le *comes* Acacius reçut des lettres de l'empereur (3.52).
A Constantina et dans certaines provinces, le zèle spontané des habitants
se manifesta.[66]

   La question est de savoir si une loi générale fut édictée en la matière.
Godefroy qui l'admet a exposé les divergences des historiens du Bas-Empire
sur ce point;[67] il semble difficile de ne pas se rallier à cette opinion[68] devant
le témoignage de la Chronique de Saint-Jérôme pour l'année 331 *"Edicto
Constantini gentilium templa subversa sunt"*.[69] Le même auteur a trouvé un
écho de la mesure constantinienne dans le Code Théodosien 9.17.2 adressé
en 349 par Constant à Limenius, alors préfet de la ville et du prétoire.[70] Son
raisonnement, vraisemblable, entraîne la conclusion que la disposition visa
non seulement l'Orient mais aussi l'Occident.

   c. Constantin et les fonctionnaires.

   Peu après la mort de Licinius,[71] les gouverneurs adonnés à la superstition
grecque reçurent la défense d'offrir des sacrifices païens; la même loi concerna
leurs supérieurs et les préfets du prétoire.

---

[62] Cf. *Corpus inscriptionum latinarum* 11.5265, postérieur à la mort de Crispus (326).
Sur ce rescrit, très étudié, on consultera notamment M. de Dominicis, "Il rescritto di Costantino agli Umbri, Nuovi osservazioni," *Bullettino del Istituto di diritto romano* 65 (1962)
173-191; "Un intervento legislativo di Costantino in materia religiosa," *Revue internationale
des droits de l'antiquité* 10 (1963) 199-211; J. Gascou, "Le rescrit d'Hispellum," *Mélanges
d'archéologie et d'histoire* 79 (1967) 609-659.

[63] VC 3.55 et 58.

[64] VC 3.56.

[65] Cf. 16 *supra*.

[66] VC 4.39.

[67] J. Godefroy, *Codex Theodosianus cum perpetuis commentariis Jacobi Gothofredi*, editio
nova (Leipzig 1736-1745), Commentaire de CT 16.10.2.

[68] *Contra*, Palanque et al. (n.1 *supra*) 179-180; A. Piganiol, *L'empereur Constantin* (Paris
1933) 184.

[69] PG 19.587-588.

[70] Pour ne pas alourdir cet exposé, nous renvoyons au commentaire de J. Godefroy (n. 67
supra) sur CT 9.17.2.

[71] Ceci résulte de la place de 2.44 dans la *Vita Constantini*.

Les termes superstition grecque sont embarrassants; ils peuvent viser les pratiques des sectes orientales; Constantin aurait alors légiféré pour les fonctionnaires de l'Orient; l'idée est appuyée par le fait que la victoire de 324 amena certainement des changements dans le personnel administratif de l'Orient; la disposition précitée put naître à cette occasion. Il serait cependant bizarre que les fonctionnaires occidentaux aient échappé à la mesure. Avait-elle été déjà édictée antérieurement pour eux? Nous n'avons aucune indication sur ce point.

d. La prohibition des pratiques immorales.

Constantin interdit l'immoralité sévissant à Héliopolis et, sur ce point, adressa des *institutiones* aux habitants;[72] de même, il supprima les prêtres impurs du Nil.[73]

5. *l'humanité et la philanthropie.*

L'aide aux mendiants du forum[74] édictée après la chute de Maxence donna peut-être lieu à une loi. L'injonction aux soldats d'épargner leurs adversaires vaincus, lors de la campagne contre Licinius,[75] fut certainement affichée dans les camps. *Vita* 3.22 signale l'ordre de distribuer de l'argent aux populations pour les vicennales de l'empereur; d'après 3.58, des largesses furent octroyées aux pauvres d'Héliopolis; 4.28 parle de sommes d'argent allouées aux veuves, aux pauvres et aux pupilles.

Ces actes s'ajoutent à ceux d'ordre religieux qui aident Eusèbe à donner de Constantin l'image d'un prince chrétien; ils pourraient tout autant caractériser un souverain philanthrope et humanitaire; aussi avons-nous préféré les classer sous une rubrique spéciale.

6. *les institutions laïques.*

Les allusions aux lois concernant ces institutions sont très rares, étant donné l'avertissement de l'auteur dans *Vita* 1.11.[76]

Une décision concerne les impôts. Constantin remit aux possesseurs le quart de l'impôt foncier; d'après 4.2, il y eut deux dispositions successives, l'une accordant le dégrèvement, l'autre confirmant ce bénéfice pour les contribuables et leur postérité.

La portée réelle de ce passage ressort nettement si on le compare à celui d'*Historia* 10.8: "Il (Licinius) inventa des milliers d'accusations contre les nations soumises, toutes sortes d'exactions à payer en or et en argent, de nouveaux arpentages de terres et des amendes très profitables infligées à

---

[72] VC 3.58.
[73] VC 4.25.
[74] VC 1.43.
[75] VC 2.13.
[76] Cf. 5 *supra.*

des hommes qui n'étaient plus à la campagne mais qui étaient morts depuis longtemps."[77] Dans la *Vita* comme dans l'*Historia*, parmi les multiples dispositions de caractère religieux est rapportée une mesure touchant l'impôt foncier; la loi de Constantin correspond à celle de Licinius dont elle semble la réparation; *Vita* 4.2 est donc vraisemblablement une mesure de liquidation du régime licinien, édictée pour l'Orient.

Trois décisions ont trait à la nomination des villes. Byzance s'appellera Constantinople (3.48) et l'emporium de Gaza, érigé en cité, Constantia;[78] une ville créée en Phénicie prendra le nom de Constantina.[79] Eusèbe ne précise pas que des lois furent alors édictées mais on peut présumer leur existence. En effet, Socrate, parlant de la désignation de Constantinople, ajoute "*utque nova Roma vocaretur, lege sanxit*" (Constantinus).[80] Certes, il s'agit là d'une décision spéciale, concernant la nouvelle capitale; cependant, toute désignation de cité se fit probablement par une loi.

Un acte important sur le plan constitutionnel sera mentionné; toutefois, il ne donna pas lieu à exercice du pouvoir législatif. Constantin divisa son empire entre ses trois fils *velut paternam haereditatem* (*Vita* 4.51). Juridiquement parlant, il y eut donc une sorte de *divisio inter liberos*, acte auquel tout *paterfamilias* pouvait recourir. Par ce procédé, qui dut sembler naturel aux contemporains, Constantin écartait les principes posés par Dioclétien pour la succession à l'empire; l'hérédité dynastique était introduite.

Nous terminerons ce passage, en évoquant des dispositions de caractère international. *Vita* 4.6 rapporte les circonstances dans lesquelles Constantin vint à l'aide des Sarmates. Les Scythes leur ayant déclaré la guerre, les Sarmates armèrent leurs esclaves; après la victoire, ceux-ci se tournèrent contre leurs anciens maîtres qui recoururent à Constantin; le souverain les reçut dans l'empire; suivant leurs capacités, il les enrôla dans l'armée ou leur assigna les subsides nécessaires pour cultiver les champs. Eusèbe ajoute que la même attitude fut observée à l'égard de plusieurs nations barbares.

D. RÉFLEXIONS GÉNÉRALES.

1. *les destinataires.*

a. Ils sont mal connus.

Très souvent, Eusèbe ne les nomme pas. Sur la cinquantaine de dispositions (ou séries de dispositions)[81] rapportées, une vingtaine seulement indi-

---

[77] Trad. G. Bardy, (n. 26 *supra*) 115.

[78] VC 4.38.

[79] VC 4.39.

[80] HE 1.16.

[81] Constituent par exemple pour nous une série de dispositions les lettres exclusivement religieuses mentionnées par 3.24 et adressées aux évêques et aux populations.

quent leurs destinataires.[82] Dans plusieurs autres cas des suppositions peuvent être faites. Ainsi estimera-t-on que la loi dénommant une cité fut adressée aux habitants de la ville et que l'ordre aux militaires de sanctifier le dimanche le fut aux soldats; mais ils peuvent tout aussi bien avoir été envoyés à l'*ordo* municipal ou aux officiers; aussi ne ferons nous aucun état de ces dispositions.

b. Les destinataires que nous connaissons appartiennent à trois catégories.

Les dignitaires ou groupes nommément désignés sont toujours des Orientaux.

i. Les évêques.

Les évêques apparaissent dans *Vita* 2.23[83] et 45, 3.6, 24, et 63, 4.14, 41, et 43. Leur mention est naturellement plus fréquente que dans les codes, vu le caractère religieux des mesures mentionnées dans la *Vita*. Le pontife de Rome ne semble pas encore pour Constantin jouer un rôle primordial.

Si l'on excepte les convocations aux conciles, les demandes adressées aux chefs des églises sont d'ordre général: prier pour l'empereur, rétablir la concorde, agir *ad laudem divinae religionis propagandam*. Mais les évêques reçurent aussi certainement des lettres d'objet pratique.

ii. Les fonctionnaires.

Les fonctionnaires sont essentiellement les gouverneurs; font exception l'*agens vices praefectorum praetorio*. Dracilianus et le *comes* Acacius. Ces constatations n'autorisent aucune conclusion en faveur ou à l'encontre du souci de la hiérarchie administrative chez Constantin.

La mention d'Acacius et de Dracilianus est sans importance. Le premier est un de ces agents extraordinaires, hors cadre, envoyés sous Constantin dans les provinces pour enquêter et faire des rapports au souverain.[84] Le second est bien un supérieur des gouverneurs et vicaires;[85] mais le véritable sens de la hiérarchie aurait commandé l'envoi à Dracilianus seul des instructions impériales; au contraire, Constantin écrivit aussi au gouverneur de Palestine et Eusèbe mentionne des ordres aux *rectores* de l'Orient.

En s'adressant surtout aux chefs des provinces le souverain ne manifeste pas un manque de considération pour les fonctionnaires supérieurs, notamment pour les préfets du prétoire. En effet:

---

[82] Nous éliminons les cas où l'aureur déclare: Constantin promulgua d'innombrables lois, ou emploie une expression équivalente (cfr 4.27 et 55). Ce laconisme exclut obligatoirement toute indication sur les destinataires.

[83] Si l'on donne à *ecclesiae* le sens d'évêques.

[84] Ce n'est pas Acace mais la *socrus* du prince qui le prévint des pratiques impies se déroulant à Mambré.

[85] Dans des articles antérieurs, nous avons considéré les *agentes vices praefectorum praetorio* comme des représentants exceptionnels des préfets du prétoire.

La plupart des décisions mentionnées sont rendues après la victoire sur Licinius, époque où la préfecture régionale n'est pas encore bien établie.

Sauf celle rapportée dans 4.23, elles concernent des événements de caractère local.

iii. Les populations.

Deux cas précis seuls nous sont connus. D'après *Vita* 3.58, des *institutiones* écrites furent envoyées aux *gentiles* d'Héliopolis et, selon 4.25, Constantin s'adressa *ad Aegyptios et Alexandrinos*. Mais, d'innombrables décisions ayant été expédiées *ad plebes*,[86] on trouvera dans la *Vita* une confirmation des renseignements fournis par les Codes. Comme il arrive souvent dans les gouvernements personnels, l'empereur, en certaines occasions, entrait directement en relation avec ses sujets pour leur communiquer ses instructions.

2. *les causes de promulgation.*

Peu de dispositions présentent un caractère vraiment occasionnel; la plupart trahissent le dessein d'imprimer à l'état, dans certains secteurs, une orientation déterminée.

a. Les décisions exprimant un plan de Constantin.

Les objectifs visés, rarement indiqués de façon explicite dans la *Vita*, se déduisent du récit d'Eusèbe et de la teneur des dispositions.

L'empereur veut notamment:

Restituer aux victimes des tyrans le statut normal des citoyens de l'empire; faire disparaître le paganisme (d'où les mesures d'ordre général sur les idoles, les sacrifices, les temples); assurer le culte du vrai Dieu par la construction d'églises et la sanctification du dimanche; faire régner entre les chrétiens l'unité et la paix (la convocation des conciles de Nicée ou de Tyr, la constitution *adversus haereticos* n'ont pas d'autre but); proclamer devant tous ses sentiments personnels en se faisant représenter dans une attitude pieuse; manifester aux sujets et même aux ennemis de l'empire la bienveillance et l'humanité du souverain (les remises d'impôts, certaines largesses du prince, le respect des ennemis vaincus témoignent de cette intention).

b. Les décisions de caractère occasionnel.

Certaines mesures rentrent dans la ligne de conduite générale de Constantin; mais elles sont liées à des circonstances parvenues à la connaissance du souverain. Nous rangerons dans cette catégorie:

Celles prohibant l'immoralité ou la superstition en certains lieux et prescrivant dans ce but la destruction d'édifices païens nommément désignés; celles octroyant des libéralités dans des circonstances exceptionnelles; les décisions concernant les Sarmates; l'ordre au synode de Tyr de gagner Jérusalem.

---

[86] VC 3.24.

3. le domaine d'application.

Un certain équilibre semble réalisé entre les textes d'application générale et ceux valables pour une partie de l'empire. Une décision adressée à tous les évêques ou à tous les gouverneurs est générale, bien que chaque exemplaire concerne un seul ressort. Malheureusement, les indications d'Eusèbe sont parfois inexactes. Annonçant certaines dispositions qu'il cite *in extenso*, Eusèbe est enclin à présenter comme générales des mesures édictées seulement pour l'Orient.[87] Ne peut-on supposer que, résumant certaines dispositions de Constantin sans en communiquer le texte, il a la même tendance? Nous l'avons présumé pour *Vita* 4.2,[88] mais il y eut sans doute d'autres cas. La véritable question est de savoir si, en légiférant, Constantin voulut instaurer pour l'Orient un particularisme quelconque ou aligner la situation de ses nouveaux domaines sur celle de l'Occident.

Presque toutes les dispositions valables pour un ressort restreint révèlent essentiellement par leur objet ce caractère particulier. Rentrent parmi elles les décisions sur la construction de tel ou tel sanctuaire, la destruction de certains temples, la répression de pratiques idolâtres en des lieux donnés, la nomination des villes, l'ordre d'aider les mendiants du forum, les convocations d'évêques à des synodes restreints, les mesures concernant les Sarmates, l'injonction d'épargner les soldats de Licinius.

Le caractère général de plusieurs dispositions résulte (a) de leur objet ou du texte de la *Vita*; pour d'autres (b), il faut recourir au raisonnement et interpréter le récit d'Eusèbe. Du premier groupe (a) font partie une douzaine de décisions. Les lettres liquidant les effets du régime de Maxence sont affichées *ubique*, les convocations pour le concile de Nicée envoyées aux évêques de tous lieux. Personne ne pourra sacrifier aux idoles; temples et *simulacra* sont détruits partout. La sanctification du dimanche et du samedi concerne tous les sujets de l'empire; l'octroi de loisirs aux militaires chrétiens pour prier le dimanche suit une phrase parlant de l'*omnis exercitus* et la loi prescrivant l'oraison le même jour aux soldats païens ne fait aucune exception. Traitant de l'effigie impériale sur les monnaies d'or, Eusèbe précise que ces monnaies ont cours *per universum orbem romanum*.

Par le raisonnement (b) se verront attribuer le caractère général la demande aux évêques de prier pour le prince, l'ordre aux gouverneurs de respecter les décrets synodaux, et toutes les instructions ayant accompagné la constitution contre les hérétiques de l'empire.[89] Quant aux dispositions

---

[87] A propos des édits aux provinciaux de l'Orient (2.24-42, 48-60) il signale des lettres envoyées dans toutes les provinces ou *ad universos provinciales* (2.23 et 47); les épîtres aux évêques d'Orient concernant la construction des églises, sont présentées comme adressées aux *antistites cuius loci ecclesiarum*.

[88] Cf. 19-20 *supra*.

[89] Nous avons mentionné *supra*, l'hésitation soulevée par VC 3.64.

signalées au pluriel de façon générique et vague[90] elles peuvent avoir été, suivant les cas, générales ou particulières.

4. *la non insertion par Eusèbe du texte de ces décisions.*

a. Les décisions mentionnées dans *l'Historia ecclesiastica.*

Une seule pose un problème. Si, comme nous l'avons admis, une loi commune des empereurs précéda les lettres impériales sur la liberté religieuse, Eusèbe aurait dû nous livrer cette loi et non le texte relatif à son exécution. La difficulté sera facilement résolue. Évêque lui-même, Eusèbe, par ses relations, pouvait facilement connaître les missives adressées aux prélats. On supposera également que des collègues complaisants, notamment celui de Carthage, lui transmirent les épîtres envoyées à Anullinus et au gouverneur anonyme, bien connues des milieux religieux en raison de leur caractère. Rien n'établit au contraire qu'Eusèbe ait eu accès aux archives officielles et surtout au dépôt central de l'Occident.

b. Les décisions mentionnées dans la *Vita Constantini.*

La *Vita Constantini* révèle (3.24) le motif ayant incité Eusèbe à exclure certains textes. L'auteur passera sous silence de nombreuses lettres pour ne pas briser le cours de son récit. Si, dans ce but, le biographe évite de mentionner tant de mesures constantiniennes, *a fortiori* dut-il éliminer quantité de textes et se borner à les résumer.

A première vue cependant, il semblera bizarre qu'Eusèbe ne cite pas les *litterae* liquidant le régime de Maxence, alors qu'il livre l'édit de 324 aux provinciaux de l'Orient. On remarquera que le biographe avait reçu personnellement un exemplaire de cet édit; au contraire, il n'a dû connaître les lettres de 312 que par des comptes-rendus.

CHAPITRE III. LES ALLUSIONS D'EUSÈBE À DES CONSTITUTIONS FIGURANT DANS LES CODES.

Ces allusions sont très rares. Les codes ont recueilli de nombreuses lois civiles de Constantin, au sens large du terme; or, de telles décisions sont en principe exclues des récits d'Eusèbe. La *Vita Constantini* en mentionne cependant quatre; deux concernent les successions, la troisième les Juifs, la quatrième les combats de gladiateurs.

I. LES SUCCESSIONS

Vita 4.26 expose longuement l'abrogation partielle des lois caducaires puis, en quelques lignes, la suppression du formalisme dans les testaments. Eusèbe

---

[90] Cf. VC 3.1, octroi d'honneurs aux chefs des églises *"edictis ac legibus propositis"*; VC 3.24 lettres innombrables aux évêques et aux populations; VC 4.28, aide financière aux veuves, pupilles et pauvres.

souligne l'accord de la première mesure avec la conception chrétienne du célibat; il loue de la seconde la façon dont elle respecte la volonté des mourants.

II. LES JUIFS

D'après *Vita* 4.27, Constantin interdit aux Juifs d'avoir des esclaves chrétiens; le *servus* sera libéré et le maître puni d'une amende. Ce passage diffère du Code Théodosien 16.8.22 (415), où Théodose signale la même loi dans les termes suivants: "Si un esclave chrétien est retenu par un Juif, selon la loi de Constantin, il sera mancipé à l'Église." Les sanctions indiquées sont donc différentes.

Pour Godefroy,[91] Théodose aurait rappelé non un texte de Constantin, mais la loi de Constance[92] prohibant sous peine de confiscation générale l'achat —et non plus la possession—d'esclaves chrétiens par les Juifs. J. Gaudemet conteste cette opinion; Constance ne prévoit pas l'attribution des *servi* à l'Église; et la confusion de noms, acceptable pour Théodose, est inconcevable pour Eusèbe; l'auteur suppose alors que Constantin avait interdit l'achat des esclaves chrétiens; Théodose, si l'on consulte d'autres lois de ce prince, aurait visé la même opération.[93]

Deux questions se posent donc: la nature de l'acte prohibé par Constantin, la sanction frappant les contrevenants. Sur le premier point, il semble prudent de garder les indications concordantes d'Eusèbe et de Théodose;[94] l'interdiction du législateur visait la détention des esclaves chrétiens par les Juifs. Sur le second point règne l'obscurité; on pourra supposer que, pour un même délit, des circonstances différentes entraînaient une variation de la peine; il ne s'agit évidemment que d'une hypothèse.

III. LES COMBATS DE GLADIATEURS

Dans *Vita* 4.25, Eusèbe rappelle l'interdiction par Constantin des combats de gladiateurs. La décision est connue par le Code Théodosien 15.12.1 adressée en 325 au vicaire d'Orient Maximus. L'expression d'Eusèbe est générale et la loi semble donc avoir concerné l'empire. Cependant, nous l'avons signalé, une inscription fait connaître un rescrit de Constantin, postérieur à

[91] Commentaire de CT 16.8.22.

[92] CT 16.9.2.

[93] Cf. "La législation religieuse de Constantin," *Revue d'histoire de l'Église de France* 33 (1947) 57-59.

[94] La décision de Constant, le véritable auteur de la loi selon Seeck (n. 41 *supra*) 187, peut s'expliquer comme suit: En 339, il n'y avait plus en fait d'esclaves chrétiens chez les Juifs. Constant voulut alors prohiber l'acte le plus courant qui eut pu faire renaître la situation antérieure à la loi de Constantin.

la mort de Crispus (326), autorisant le *munus gladiatorium* dans la cité italienne d'Hispellum.[95] On présumera donc que la loi *ad Maximum* visa seulement les régions orientales.

Chapitre IV. Les indications d'Eusèbe et le Code Théosodien.

La plupart des indications d'Eusèbe n'ont pas trouvé place dans le Code Théodosien. Après avoir signalé des raisons inexactes ou partielles qui pourraient en être données, j'essaierai de dégager une explication qui rende compte de la quasi-totalité des omissions.

I. les raisons inexactes ou partielles.

Le texte des mesures citées ou rapportées par Eusèbe ne serait pas parvenu aux compilateurs. Ceci ne peut valoir que pour un nombre limité de cas.

Plusieurs décisions avaient pour destinataires des évêques. La raison est sans valeur. Le Code Théodosien contient maintes lois adressées à des chefs de communautés chrétiennes ou juives.

Des dispositions concernaient strictement une personnalité. Le motif est valable mais ne peut expliquer que certaines omissions.

La quasi-totalité des mesures était de caractère religieux. Ceci n'a pu entraîner l'élimination que de prescriptions et textes purement édifiants car le livre 16 du Code Théodosien a recueilli de multiples lois concernant la religion.

Maintes décisions avaient un domaine géographique d'application très restreint. La raison est sans valeur; les constitutions générales édictées pour certains lieux pouvaient figurer dans le Code.

II. essai d'explication générale.

Cette explication pourrait découler simultanément de la mission donnée aux compilateurs et de la façon dont elle fut exécutée.

A. la mission des compilateurs.

D'après le Code Théodosien 1.1.6 (435) les compilateurs devaient:

1. Recueillir toutes les constitutions générales et édictales, émises et affichées de Constantin à 435 dans certaines provinces et certains lieux.

---

[95] Cf. 23 *supra*.

2. D'après leur objet, les répartir en titres, à l'intérieur desquels l'ordre serait chronologique.

3. Le cas échéant, les scinder en chapitres placés dans différents titres.

4. Les abréger, compléter, modifier pour en faire ressortir nettement le contenu.

Le but des trois dernières prescriptions n'était pas explicitement énoncé. La dernière phrase du Code Théodosien 1.1.6 le révèle. A dater de la promulgation du Code, seules s'appliqueront dans les jugements et affaires, les lois insérées dans le recueil ou émises après sa publication. L'œuvre devait donc avoir un caractère pratique et faciliter notamment le travail des juges.

B. L'EXÉCUTION DE CETTE MISSION.

Les compilateurs ont bien compris leur mission et, en présence des textes eusébiens, l'ont exécutée avec intelligence.

1. Ils ont éliminé textes et décisions ne constituant pas des *leges*—exemple la lettre à Alexandre et Arius, celle à Eusèbe pour son *Oratio Paschae*—et ceux dont le destinataire (évêque ou fonctionnaire) était chargé d'une mission restreinte déterminée (construction d'une église, destruction d'un temple).

2. Pour présenter un recueil utile aux praticiens, ils ont écarté textes et décisions:

> leur semblant inutiles. Les mesures antérieures à Constantin étaient exclues des codes; celles les abrogeant ou réparant leurs conséquences le furent également. Ainsi négligea-t-on les *litterae* supprimant les effets du régime de Maxence, la loi sur la liberté religieuse et les instructions subséquentes à un gouverneur, la lettre au proconsul Anullinus, prescrivant des restitutions aux églises.
> Les dispositions infirmant lois et rescrits illégitimes de Licinius avaient trouvé place dans le Code Théodosien 15.14.1 et 3; l'édit aux provinciaux de l'Orient parut inutile.
> sans action sur les institutions: lettres *ad ecclesias* après le synode de Nicée, exhortations religieuses, octroi occasionnel de largesses impériales.
> ne pouvant donner lieu à un procès: demande de prier pour l'empereur,[96] érection d'une ville en cité et nomination de localités, décrets sur la représentation impériale, enrôlement des Sarmates parmi les soldats ou colons, ordres concernant la sanctification du dimanche et du samedi.[97] La défense de sacrifier adressée aux adminis-

---

[96] Nous la classons sous cette rubrique et non sous la précédente; sans effet pratique sur les institutions, elle marque cependant la volonté du prince de mobiliser les évêques au service de la prospérité du prince et donc de l'état.

[97] On peut ajouter qu'ils étaient sans action sur les institutions. Au contraire, les décisions sur le repos dominical ayant des répercussions économiques et juridiques trouvèrent place dans les codes.

trateurs peut rentrer dans cette catégorie, les infractions commises ayant dû être connues non des juges ordinaires mais des chefs de service ou de l'empereur.

3. Pour présenter un recueil facilement consultable et donc relativement concis, ils ont supprimé des textes et décisions utiles aux juges du quatrième siècle mais non à ceux de leur époque. Ainsi ont disparu les mesures réprimant ou supprimant l'immoralité et l'idolâtrie en certains lieux. Le même motif pourrait expliquer la suppression de la loi générale sur les sacrifices, rappelée par Constant en 341. On ne peut toutefois exagérer la valeur du désir de brièveté des compilateurs; l'étude du Code Théodosien, du livre 16 en particulier, montre l'existence de nombreuses redites, la présence de plusieurs lois sur un même sujet. Il reste donc à rechercher la raison qui a fait éliminer telle ou telle disposition plutôt que telle autre. Si les compilateurs ont voulu faciliter le travail des praticiens, ils ont dû écarter de préférence des textes anciens; les lois constantiniennes auraient ainsi fait l'objet d'une discrimination plus sévère que celles de ses successeurs et surtout de Théodose. Il nous est impossible actuellement d'apporter la preuve de cette suggestion.

III. LES TEXTES ET DÉCISIONS EXCEPTIONNELS.

Leur élimination des codes semble injustifiable par la raison précédemment indiquée. Nous essaierons de trouver une explication de leur omission.

A. La lettre au proconsul d'Afrique, dispensant le clergé catholique de *functio publica*. D'autres lois de Constantin sur la question figurent au Code Théodosien, adressées parfois à des gouverneurs moins élevés que le proconsul dans la hiérarchie administrative. Les compilateurs ayant éliminé la première épître à Anullinus, la seconde a pu l'être avec elle.

B. La constitution *adversus hæreticos* et le *praeceptum* aux gouverneurs sur la même question. On notera qu'aucune sanction n'était prévue contre les hérétiques. D'autre part la confiscation des lieux de culte n'a peut-être pas soulevé de difficultés après son exécution par les autorités de police. Cependant l'incorporation dans le code des décisions signalées eût paru normale.

C. La loi générale sur la destruction des temples. Certes, comme la disposition sur les sacrifices, elle était rendue inutile par une loi ultérieure prescrivant la fermeture des temples *omnibus locis atque urbibus universis*;[98] toutefois, Constance ne rappelle pas ici la loi de son père, ce qui rend l'exclusion moins compréhensible.

D. LA REMISE D'IMPÔT FONCIER.

Tout acte de ce genre, même déclaré perpétuel par son auteur, est toujours provisoire; le souci de brièveté semblerait donc expliquer la non insertion.

---

[98] CT 16.10.4 (346, 354? pour Mommsen; 356 selon Seeck).

Mais les compilateurs ont accepté dans leur recueil des dispositions du même genre. On peut recourir à l'idée d'une perte de la décision ou au manque de soin des commissaires de Théodose.

CONCLUSIONS

Les conclusions présentées à la fin de cet exposé concernent Eusèbe et son œuvre, Constantin, la composition du Code Théodosien.

I. EUSÈBE ET SON ŒUVRE.

A. L'HISTORIA ECCLESIASTICA ET LA VITA CONSTANTINI PARAISSENT RÉDIGÉES PAR UN MÊME AUTEUR.

En dépit de leur caractère différent, l'une complète heureusement les indications de l'autre.

Aucun des textes transmis par la première ne figure dans la seconde. D'autre part, la *Vita* mentionne peu de décisions antérieures à la soumission de l'Orient; elle ne signale même pas l'existence des dispositions de 312-313 sur la liberté religieuse. Au contraire, elle détaille avec complaisance les décisions publiées de 325 à 337. Il semble que l'auteur du panégyrique veuille éviter de répéter des indications déjà données dans l'*Historia*.

B. LES SOURCES DE RENSEIGNEMENTS D'EUSÈBE PARAISSENT PRINCIPALEMENT, SINON EXCLUSIVEMENT, DE CARACTÈRE ECCLÉSIASTIQUE.

Parmi les textes livrés par Eusèbe, trois seulement sont adressés à des fonctionnaires civils. Dans l'ensemble les destinataires sont des prélats ou des populations; l'empereur leur communique ses ordres et souhaits sur des questions religieuses. Ainsi, pour l'Église du Saint-Sépulcre, nous possédons la lettre à l'évêque de Jérusalem mais non les épîtres ou instructions envoyées à Dracilianus et à certains gouverneurs. Il semble qu'Eusèbe ait surtout consulté les archives épiscopales et non les dépôts officiels; la copie des trois lettres aux fonctionnaires occidentaux a pu lui être communiquée par un collègue.

C. LA VÉRACITÉ D'EUSÈBE.

Deux affirmations paraissent autorisées.

1. *les indications de l'historien sont exactes.*

L'auteur livre surtout des renseignements qu'un évêque d'Orient était en mesure de connaître et de bien comprendre. Ses contemporains pouvaient confronter la concordance de son œuvre avec la réalité et il ne se serait pas exposé à leur contradiction.

L'exactitude de ses indications est parfois bien établie. On comparera le texte de certaines lois connues par les codes et la version des mêmes décisions offertes par Eusèbe. L'abrogation partielle des lois caducaires, la suppression du formalisme testamentaire, sont fidèlement rapportées dans la *Vita*. Si Eusèbe et Théodose évoquent différemment la disposition de Constantin sur les Juifs et les esclaves chrétiens, on ne peut a priori déclarer l'un moins véridique que l'autre. Tous deux ont sans doute exposé partiellement la question.

2. *les indications d'Eusèbe sont incomplètes.*

Le biographe écarte intentionnellement de son récit la quasi-totalité des lois civiles de Constantin et même des mesures de caractère religieux, parfois relatées par d'autres historiens. En cela, il ne peut être accusé de manquer à la vérité. Tout auteur est libre de limiter son sujet et d'éviter la rédaction d'une œuvre trop longue.

Par contre, on pourra reprocher à Eusèbe des omissions qui faussent la vision d'ensemble. Dans tel ou tel secteur de la réglementation, il indique une décision permettant de louer le prince; il passe, au contraire, sous silence d'autres mesures défavorables à son héros. Ainsi, parlant de la réduction du cens, il se garde de mentionner la création des *collationes glebalis et lustralis*.

Mais une telle attitude était un peu normale dans une biographie qui est en même temps un panégyrique respectant les règles existant au IVe siècle pour ce genre d'ouvrage. Il appartient au lecteur de rester clairvoyant et de rechercher la vérité qui se trouve sous la louange.

II. CONSTANTIN

Les indications d'Eusèbe permettent de mieux apprécier cet empereur comme législateur et comme prince chrétien.

A. CONSTANTIN LÉGISLATEUR.

L'*Historia ecclesiastica* et la *Vita Constantini* nous documentent sur une partie de la législation de Constantin qui n'a pas été recueillie dans les Codes.

Son abondance, sa prolixité même, tiennent en partie à la confusion totale des pouvoirs dans les mains du souverain. La notion de loi n'y gagne d'ailleurs pas en précision; ce qui, actuellement, nous paraît exercice du pouvoir réglementaire, rentrait alors dans un concept très large de *lex*. On se rappellera l'affirmation d'Ulpien; "*Quod placuit principi habet legis vigorem.*" De simples questions concernant la vie locale et journalière pouvaient donner lieu à l'intervention du souverain.

Cette législation dans la majorité des cas ne semble pas occasionnelle. Si l'empereur se prononce parfois, à la suite de rapports qui lui sont parvenus ou d'événements particuliers il ne se laisse pas mener par les circonstances. De grands objectifs inspirent des dispositions apparemment disparates ou échelonnées dans le temps. Favoriser le christianisme, assurer le culte dû à la divinité, supprimer les dissensions religieuses, lutter contre le paganisme. telles sont les intentions qui expliquent la promulgation de nombreuses lois, Les circonstances historiques fournissent simplement le cadre dans lequel s'exerce la volonté du prince. Certes, parfois des faits particuliers se produisent, qui amènent Constantin à légiférer, mais, bien plus souvent, il intervient de lui-même, pour appliquer un plan de réforme mûrement élaboré.

Les décisions rapportées par Eusèbe sont à la fois de portée générale et locale. Celles valables pour l'empire, ou tout au moins pour l'Orient après l'échec de Licinius, nous ont paru nombreuses. Toutefois, beaucoup concernent une localité—ou ses habitants—certains groupes d'individus. La constatation est d'autant plus intéressante que les codes nous ont transmis peu de textes appartenant à cette catégorie. Parfois l'empereur s'adresse à un individu sur un sujet particulier, mais Constantin ne semble pas avoir été l'objet d'une requête ou d'une consultation.

Nous ferons une dernière remarque. Sur certaines questions l'empereur contacte plusieurs personnes ou groupes de personnes de caractère différent. Pour les constructions d'églises, il alerte évêques et gouverneurs, s'il s'agit de réprimer les pratiques impies de Mambré, il avise Acacius et les évêques de Palestine. La constitution *adversus haereticos* est assortie d'instructions aux *praesides provinciarum*. En somme, dès que la volonté du prince réquiert pour son exécution l'aide de l'autorité publique, les agents du pouvoir sont personnellement avertis. On peut d'ailleurs supposer que si la décision avait un caractère religieux, le texte envoyé à ces derniers différait de celui adressé aux évêques. En ce cas, le même sujet donna lieu non à des exemplaires distincts mais à des versions différentes.

B. CONSTANTIN PRINCE CHRÉTIEN.

Le but d'Eusèbe dans la *Vita* est de montrer en Constantin le prince converti et de tracer l'idéal du monarque chrétien. Faisant abstraction des intentions d'Eusèbe, nous constaterons simplement les faits. La possibilité d'un récit exposant tant de décisions de caractère religieux est par elle-même caractéristique. Le prince qui édicta ces dispositions, ne fut certainement pas indifférent.

La question véritable est de savoir si l'attitude de Constantin fut celle d'un habile politicien ou d'un chrétien véritable. Mais un politicien aurait-il heurté les habitudes ancestrales des païens, appauvri les curies orientales par la libération des chrétiens, prescrit la restitution des biens des églises, de la succession des martyrs et confesseurs? Il eût peut-être confisqué les trésors des temples, mais non englouti des sommes considérables dans les constructions d'édifices chrétiens.

Le groupement dans la *Vita* de nombreuses mesures de Constantin favorables au christianisme prend ainsi une valeur beaucoup plus grande qu'une présentation dans des œuvres dispersées venant d'un même auteur et surtout d'auteurs différents.

III. LA COMPOSITION DU CODE THÉODOSIEN

La comparaison des indications fournies par Eusèbe et par le Code Théodosien atteste simultanément l'obéissance des compilateurs et leur initiative intelligente: l'obéissance, car ils ont éliminé les textes et décisions ne présentant pas le caractère de *leges*; l'initiative intelligente, car, devant réaliser une œuvre pratique, ils ont très largement écarté ce qui ne pouvait servir aux juges et aux plaideurs de leur temps.

La constatation de cette attitude autorise une remarque. Il serait intéressant de rechercher dans le Code Théodosien la mention des constitutions perdues et les raisons ayant amené leur disparition. On pourrait alors juger si l'omission de certaines dispositions peut être attribuée à la réflexion des compilateurs. Un sujet d'étude se présente ainsi à ceux qui s'intéressent au Code Théodosien et à ses rédacteurs.

Chargée de recherche au C.N.R.S., Paris
80 rue Jean sans Peur
59 Lille (Nord), France

THE SHAPING OF THE EARLY MEDIEVAL PRINCIPALITY AS A TYPE OF NON-ROYAL RULERSHIP

•

by Herwig Wolfram

We have to ask what a given ruler says of himself; we have to seek what one might label his "self-manifestation," if we want to obtain a methodologically reliable answer to the question, "what is a ruler?".[1] In addition to this, it is certainly very useful to learn what other people say of a given ruler, especially when this ruler is not a king, that is to say not the recognized head of a kingdom.[2]

Between Julian the Apostate's autobiography and that of Charles IV there exists little evidence that the rulers used the literary media to speak of, and about, themselves.[3] Many, if not the overwhelming majority of them, were illiterate: a literary education was just one form, and not the only form, of education. Literary sources, helpful and illustrative though they may be, however, do not provide us with the politically and philosophically relevant formulas we are looking for. It is primarily the diplomatic sources, such as the diplomas, charters, administrative acts, legal texts, and laws, that we have to investigate. These sources usually contain a specific formula, which the diplomatists call *intitulatio, suscription* or simply, though inexactly, *title*.[4]

---

[1] H. Wolfram, *Intitulatio I: Lateinische Königs- und Fürstentitel bis zum Ende des 8. Jahrhunderts*, Mitteilungen des Instituts für österreichische Geschichtsforschung (MIÖG) supp. 21 (1967) 9ff. I wish to thank Professor Howard Kaminsky, University of Washington, Seattle, for having offered me the opportunity for a thoroughgoing discussion of the present article in a faculty-student seminar that he conduced in Seattle on 24 April 1969.

[2] K. Brunner will investigate this problem in *Intitulatio II*, which is due to appear as a continuation of the aforementioned book (see n. 1 above). Cf. Wolfram 136ff., where I dealt with the nomenclature of the Late-Merovingian aristocracy.

[3] *Karoli IV. imperatoris Romanorum vita ab eo ipso conscripta*, ed. Walther Bulst in the series Editiones Heidelbergenses 16 (Heidelberg 1950). Julian's *Commentaries* on his Gallic campaigns are praised by, and partly known through, Libanius and Eunapius but are not now extant; see *The Works of the Emperor Julian*, ed. W. C. Wright, Loeb Classical Library, ed. 4, 1 (London 1962) viii. Cf. Georg Misch, *Geschichte der Autobiographie*, 4 vols., ed. 3 (Bern 1950ff.).

[4] Wolfram, Intitulatio (n. 1 above) 22ff.

Here, the individual who issues a document states his name, title, and sometimes divine authorization. Certainly, this person, briefly called issuer, did not write that formula by himself. There was always a scribe or clerk around who was charged with this duty, which had to be fulfilled in keeping with the traditional rules of a chancery. Nevertheless, there is enough evidence that it was not the chancery nor a given individual scribe who devised the issuer's *intitulatio* without being controlled by the latter. It was the issuer himself who said the decisive last word about the phrasing and contents of the *intitulatio* formula. It was really a self-manifestation of the ruler-issuer, as can be clearly shown, for instance, by comparing the political events of the second half of the eighth century with the rapid change of the Frankish kingly *intitulatio* under Charles the Great.[5] I would go even further and apply to the ruler's *intitulatio* the question that the "priests and Levites of Jerusalem" put to John the Baptist (John 1.22f.), In this very "Quid dicis de teipso?" formula the abridgment of a whole political or even theological program had to be laid down, as, for instance, a title such as *Carolus gratia Dei rex Francorum et Langobardorum atque patricius Romanorum* would indicate.[6]

I am prepared to concede that in process of time, maybe by the end of the twelfth century, when the spread of writing increased the traditionally scarce diplomatic sources to a formerly inconceivable degree, the value of the *intitulatio* formula as the ruler's self-manifestation decreased at the time. I am not quite sure about this problem at the moment; yet I could imagine that the methodological approach to the late medieval *intitulatio* would have to be a different one. For the early medieval titles, however, it is in my opinion correct and even necessary to insist upon their political, theoretical and even theological relevance.

If we can accept this general assessment of the formula we are prepared to take the next step. The *intitulatio* is not the only place in a document where politically relevant terminology appears; other parts of a document have to be related to the wording of the *intitulatio*, as do other texts, even literary sources, which have a bearing on its shape.

The third step to be taken is to ask the questions: what is the terminology involved; what is the title of a nonroyal ruler over a *regnum*; what does a quasi-king say of himself when he does not dare to use the title *rex*?

It was part of the common political heritage which the Latin-Germanic kings had taken over from the Roman emperors that each of them was the *princeps* or *dominus* of a *regnum*, which could also be called *terra* or *patria*. For instance, *gens vel patria Gotorum* meant nothing else but the Visigothic

---

[5] *Ibid.* 206ff.
[6] *Ibid.* 225ff.

kingdom in Spain.[7] Similar expressions were used with the Franks and Lombards alike. For reasons upon which I slightly touched on an earlier occasion, the Anglo-Saxon institutional situation was so different from that on the Continent that here I must skip its investigation.[8] This seems to be necessary because the imported Latin vocabulary could give the false impression that a comparable situation existed in England and on the Continent.[9]

For the Continental Latin kingdoms, as one would label the successor states of the Empire, the formulas *rex qui et princeps gentis* or *rex qui et dominus*, that is to say, *terrae, patriae vel regni* were politically relevant.[10] Most kings of the Barbarian Invasions, and the very few who survived this holocaust, had not only replaced the emperor as *princeps et dominus*, if only in a given part of the Roman Empire, but also and above all an outdated type of tribal king who vanished with the destruction of the traditional tribal structure.[11] The settlement on Roman soil and the establishment of kingdoms allowed the formation of new peoples and completely new political entities. The political tradition of the prevailing ethnic element or ruling class might have been age-old, pre-Christian and wrapped up in the abolished tribal system, for this tradition was sacred and long-lived. But it cannot conceal the fact that the kingdoms on Roman soil formed new peoples, new ethnic systems, and new or at least strongly modified upper classes.[12] We know, moreover, that kings heavily stressed the latter process by virtually wiping out their relatives and all members of royal families within their zone of influence, in order to destroy any potential pretender to their positions.

---

[7] Cf. *Lex Visigothorum* 2.1.8, ed. K. Zeumer, MGH Leges nationum 1.1 (Hannover 1902) 54. See Wolfram (n. 1 above) 70. Cf. O. Brunner, *Land und Herrschaft*, ed. 4 (Vienna 1959) 188f., and annotations.

[8] Wolfram, "The Shaping of the Early Medieval Kingdom," *Viator* 1 (1971) 1-24. Cf. Wolfram, *Intitulatio* (n. 1 above) 18f.

[9] Take, for instance, the terminology used in a grant by Aethelbald, King of Mercia and of the *Sutangli*, 736; there, the titles *subregulus, dux* and *comes* come in, although nobody can really pretend that this political vocabulary had anything to do with its equivalent on the Continent. The Frankish *dux*, for instance, is the result of an institutional development that derives from both Roman and Germanic roots alike, whereas the Anglo-Saxon *dux* is a Latin word for an Anglo-Saxon type of leading position. See *Chartae latinae antiquiores*, ed. Albert Bruckner and Robert Marichal, 3 (Lausanne 1963) n°. 183. Cf. Wolfram, *Intitulatio* 145f., n. 27.

[10] Wolfram, *Intitulatio* 69f., 104ff., 148f.

[11] Wolfram, "The Shaping" (n. 8 above) 15ff.

[12] My remark does by no means interfere with the conclusive results of Franz Irsigler, *Untersuchungen zur Geschichte des frühfränkischen Adels*, Rheinisches Archiv 70 (Bonn, 1969), 253ff. I would just like to stress my conviction that the Frankish nobility from, say, the end of the sixth century onward came to be a new body social and politic, consisting of both the Roman senatorial aristocracy and Teutonic noblemen alike. Cf. K. F. Werner, "Bedeutende Adelsfamilien im Reich Karls des Grossen," *Karl der Grosse* 1 (Düssemdorf 1965) 86ff.

The best evidence for this stems from Gregory of Tours's *History of the Franks*, where Clovis is quoted as saying: "Woe unto me who remain as a traveler among strangers, and have none of my kin to help me in the evil day"; whereupon Gregory adds the wise judgment: "But he did not thus allude to their death out of grief, but craftily, to see if he could bring to light some new relative to kill." This passage ends Gregory's account of the killing of four Frankish kings who were Clovis's kinsmen.[13] Despite this systematic extirpation, the next generations after Clovis could still continue in this friendly activity.[14]

Beside the threat from defeated but still existing royal families, and despite the formerly inconceivable success of the Migrations-kings, there was the possibility that any outstanding leader of a warrior retinue, a *dux* in the word of Tacitus,[15] could become king and directly replace the new tribal king. We have to realize that the centrifugal forces that dismembered the Roman Empire did not stop working with its fall. A king like Clovis, for instance, had to cope with the same trends and tendencies in Gaul and Germania as did the Roman emperors decades and centuries earlier.[16] His great advantage was, however, that he could concentrate on a smaller territorial unit than the empire had been and use a very successful army, the *exercitus Francorum* which stood for the Frankish people. So he and his successors not only had the power of monopolizing their kingship in their own Merovingian family but also restrained the right of organizing an effective warrior retinue strong enough to become the nucleus of a rival kingship.[17]

The Lombard kingdom in Italy, in contrast had been given up and then re-established by the *duces*, the nonroyal warlords who had finally come to realize that the Lombard people needed a kingdom to survive as a political entity that included their own positions. Consequently, however, the Lombard kingdom of the sixth and seventh centuries was weak and never really able to create a stable dynasty strong enough to expand its domination over

---

[13] Gregory of Tours, *Historia Francorum* 2.42, ed. Bruno Krusch and Wilhelm Levison, MGH Script. rer. merov., ed. 2 (Hannover 1951) 1.92f.

[14] *Ibid.* 3.14 (110). Erich Zöllner, *Geschichte der Franken*, Geschichte der deutschen Stämme (München 1970) 126.

[15] Tacitus, *Germania*, 7; cf. Wolfram, "The Shaping" (n. 8 above) 7.

[16] Werner (n. 12 above) 89f.

[17] Zöllner (n. 14 above) 137f. By the phrase "restrained the right of organizing an effective warrior retinue" I do not mean that the Frankish aristocracy of the late fifth and sixth centuries had no bodies of retainers at all (cf. Irsigler, n. 12 above, 228ff., who rightly points out the contrary). I just wanted to say that those retinues could not compete with the royal *antrustiones* as far as these two centuries were concerned. Zöllner (n. 14 above) 112ff., and D. Claude, "Zu Fragen frühfränkischer Verfassungsgeschichte," *Zeitschrift für Rechtsgeschichte, germanistische Abteilung* 83 (Weimar 1966) 273, and above all Irsigler (n. 12 above) dealt with the difficult topic "Frankish aristocracy" most recently.

the *duces*, above all over the Lombard duchies of Benevento and Spoleto. It was not before the beginning of the eighth century that the Lombard kingdom could overcome the built-in deficiency of its foundation; the Lombard kings stemmed more often than not from the *dux*-stratum that had created the kingdom.[18]

The Visigoths in Spain did not allow the establishment of a sacred royal family such as the Merovingians. The *duces* had still the chance to become kings, naturally one after the other, since the *morbus gothicus*, as Frankish historiographers described the disease of the Gothic kings, namely getting killed or at least deposed by their own people, was always endemic. Yet or maybe therefore, particularistic tendencies are not known before the last third of the seventh century, when the Gallic remains of the realm were close to becoming an independent kingdom.[19]

The most momentous shift in the political spectrum, however, occurred in seventh-century Frankland when a divided and probably decaying royal family could no longer effectively prevent the upper class from becoming an actually ruling class.[20] It was exactly this political atmosphere that created the beginnings of the Frankish, and to some extent the European, nonroyal rulerships. At that time the credibility of the formula *rex qui et princeps Francorum* was destroyed. Yet since the long-haired Merovingian kings embodied an ecclesiasticized tribal charisma, which even obvious ineffectiveness could not abolish, the dynasty was not to be replaced until 751.[21] But the formula *dux qui et princeps Francorum* could be established, with a shadowy figurehead of a Merovingian king still around.[22] Our textbooks describe this historical phenomenon as the "Rise of the Carolingian Mayors of the Palace," or *duces* of Austrasia, which ended up in the royal unction of Pippin III, Charles the Great's father, as new King of the Franks. We know that this process took more than three generations; but it is easily overlooked that this long period could have been decisively shortened if Grimoald's attempt to replace the ineffective and powerless long-haired kings in 661 or 662 had met with permanent success.[23] Shocked by the stout resistance of their peers and the obviously poor support by the "people," who were in awe of their

[18] As to the history of the Lombards, one still must rely on L. M. Hartmann, *Geschichte Italiens im Mittelalter* 2.1.2 (Gotha 1900-1903). C. Brühl's new edition of the diplomas of the Lombard kings promises to provide us with a profound revision of the Lombard history.

[19] As to *morbus gothicus* or rather *Gothorum* see H. Messmer, *Hispania-Idee und Gotenmythos*, in the series Geist und Werk der Zeiten 5 (Zürich 1960) 66ff. On the particularistic tendencies in the Visigothic kingdom in 673, see Wolfram, *Intitulatio* 70f.

[20] Werner (n. 12 above) 92ff. Wolfram, *Intitulatio* 112ff.

[21] J. M. Wallace-Hadrill, *The Long-Haired Kings* (London 1962) 231ff., esp. 243ff.

[22] Wolfram, *Intitulatio* 149ff.

[23] Wallace-Hadrill (n. 21 above) 234ff.

sacred kings, the Carolingians switched over to a policy of a gradual and very cautiously prepared take-over. So it was not before the year 742 that a Carolingian major-domo used the formula *dux et princeps Francorum* in front of the *servi Dei et optimates mei. . . qui in regno meo sunt.*[24] Yet, the previous history of *dux et princeps Francorum* can be essentially and formally traced to the end of the seventh century, probably to the decades after Pippin II's victory at Tertry in 687 when he defeated his last serious Frankish rival.[25] Therefore, we can conclude that despite Grimoald's catastrophe in 661 or 662, the next generation of his family provided if not the *rex et princeps Francorum* at least the *dux et princeps Francorum* who ruled over the *regnum Francorum.*

What should we understand by this term *regnum Francorum* on the verge of the seventh century? It means nothing else than the *tria regna*, the three kingdoms of Neustria, Austrasia, and Burgundy, which actually constituted the *regnum Francorum* more as a "Frankish commonwealth" than as single kingdom. This plurality of Frankish kingdoms had been institutionalized and stressed by numerous divisions of the greater *regnum Francorum* among the male members of the Merovingian family. More often than not, those three parts of the *regnum Francorum* built the base upon which a Frankish *pars regni* came to be constituted.[26]

By 700, the *tria regna* actually stood under the Carolingian sway. While Carloman, Charles the Great's uncle, had the aforementioned *intitulatio* formulated, the *tria regna* had successfully expanded. Within another forty years of Carolingian princely policy, the practically independent Alsatian *dux* and his Thuringian counterpart, both successors of former Frankish officials invested by Merovingian Kings around 650, had vanished. The Frisians had no longer a king, in the sense in which Anglo-Saxon sources had interpreted the kingly qualities of the Frisian *dux*. The Swabians were crush-

---

[24] Wolfram, *Intitulatio* 137ff.

[25] J. F. Böhmer and Engelbert Mühlbacher, *Regesta imperii*, ed. 2, I (Innsbruck 1908) nᵒ. 4f. There is strong evidence that soon after the events of 687 the title *princeps* was first used for the Carolingian mayor of the palace, certainly in opposition to the Merovingian king: see Wolfram, MIÖG 76 (1968) 214.

[26] Werner (n. 12 above) 92ff. Wolfram, *Intitulatio* 114, 157. E. Ewig, "Die fränkischen Teilungen und Teilreiche, 511-613," *Akademie der Wissenschaften und der Literatur in Mainz, Abhandlungen der geistes- und sozialwissenschaftlichen Klasse* (Mainz 1952) 651ff., and "Die fränkischen Teilreiche im 7. Jahrhundert, 613-714," *Trierer Zeitschrift für Geschichte* 22 (Trier 1953) 85ff. The later two treatises are still by far the best descriptions of the topic. They are supposed to appear as a book in a revised edition soon.

[27] Ewig, "Die fränkischen Teilreiche," 85ff. W. Schlesinger, "Lord and Follower in Germanic Institutional History," *Lordship and Community in Medieval Europe*, ed. F. L. Cheyette (New York 1968) 00. B. Gebhardt and H. Grundmann, *Handbuch der Deutschen Geschichte*, ed. 8, I (Stuttgart 1954-60) 121ff. Wallace-Hadrill (n. 21 above) 239ff.

ingly defeated and were soon to lose their ducal family the members of which had appeared as independent rulers a generation earlier, although they owed their position to their investiture as Frankish officials. Even in the most outlying districts of the "multi-regnal" *regnum Francorum*, in Aquitaine and Bavaria, the Carolingian influence was growing considerably. The last Merovingian king had died five years before, and was not yet succeeded by another member of the sacred, long-haired family.[27]

But at this very moment, the old opposition forced the Carolingians to reverse their policy and to suffer a setback at the hands of their enemies. A Merovingian had to become king, and when Carloman's younger brother Pippin III repeated the formula *dux et princeps Francorum* in 744, he no longer spoke of his *regnum*.[28]

Who was this opposition, evidently strong enough to impose upon the Carolingians a policy that they did not like? This opposition consisted of those people who considered the Carolingians to be no more than their peers, if not social upstarts, who tried "to prevent them from obeying their Merovingian kings as they were wont to do since time immemorial."[29] The leaders of this aristocratic opposition were no doubt the Agilolfingians in Swabia and Bavaria and the ducal family of Aquitaine.[30]

Although there remains no diplomatic evidence which would show the self-manifestation of the latter, contemporary papal and Carolingian sources alike prove the assumption that the ducal family of Aquitaine possessed the principate over Aquitaine, that is to say they were the *principes Aquitanorum*.[31] This principate can be traced back to the second half of the seventh century when the Frankish "dux Lupus" established a quasi-royal government over the "Romani" of the former Roman provinces Aquitania I and II.[32] There is evidence that Lupus's accession fell in the same year that the Gothic *dux* Paulus tried to establish Languedoc as an independent kingdom. Paulus failed, because he proclaimed himself king.[33] Certainly, Frankish sources denounced Lupus's accession also as an usurpation of royal rights.[34] But diplomatic sources show that Lupus kept theoretically recognizing a

---

[28] Wolfram, *Intitulatio* 139f.

[29] *Erchanberti breviarium regum Francorum*, MGH Script. 2 (1829) 328.

[30] See n. 29. E. Zöllner, "Die Herkunft der Agilolfinger," *Zur Geschichte der Bayern*, Wege der Forschung 60 (Darmstadt 1965) 131f.; H. Löwe, "Bonifatius und die bayerisch-fränkische Spannung," Wege der Forschung 285f., 294ff.; Wolfram, "Das Fürstentum Tassilos III, Herzogs der Bayern," *Mitteilungen der Gesellschaft für Salzburger Landeskunde* 108 (Salzburg 1968) 178f.

[31] Wolfram, *Intitulatio* 156f.

[32] *Ibid.* 114f., 156f.

[33] *Ibid.* 70f.

[34] *Ibid.* 142 n. 11.

Merovingian as his superior, as his *princeps*.[35] Lupus remained a *fidelis*, a faithful in theory so that he could easily overcome the verbal attacks on part of the Franks who had virtually to give up the whole southwestern part of Gaul.[36] The Merovingian king and his major-domo had no legal pretext to interfere. We shall see that this very theoretical construction is a typical product of Frankish politics and was to become even more important in the ninth and tenth than it had been in the seventh and eighth centuries.

After about three generations of "homerule," the new body politic, called *principatus, ducatus,* or *regnum Aquitanorum*, created a new tribal entity with a native political consciousness. The *Romani* of the territories and former Roman provinces south of the Loire River, who had up to then been just a legal unity which lived according to its provincial Gothic-Roman law, started thinking of themselves as a political unity which adopted a new "national" name. By about 750, the former *Romani* had finally become *Aquitani*. It was the very unifying "force of statehood" that had inaugurated and completed this process.[37]

In this particular case, the concept "statehood" means a *regnum* created by a non-Merovingian Frankish official, called *dux*, who used the Frankish political structure to organize a body politic. This was no longer dependent on the Merovingian kings and their government, although theoretically the new *regnum* did not separate from the greater *regnum Francorum*. I consider this compromise to be a genuine Frankish speciality which, for one, did justice to the principle that a successful warleader, a *dux*, was allowed and supposed to replace an ineffective "national" king as *princeps regni*. On the other hand, by refraining from becoming "kings" themselves in the technical and legal sense, these *principes-duces* avoided the built-in centrifugal forces of that principle that made them *the* first (*furisto, Fürst*) of a *regnum*. At the same time, they avoided being outlawed as unfaithful, *infideles*, which would have been the signal for their peers to fall upon them under the pretext of supporting the king.[38]

The process of establishing nonroyal rulership was by no means limited to Aquitaine nor to the seventh century. By 700, Frisia, Swabia, Alsace, Thuringia, and Bavaria were political entities built more or less on the lines of the aforementioned principate of Aquitaine.[39] The Carolingians tried to

---

[35] *Ibid.* 125f.

[36] Werner (n. 12 above) 123ff.

[37] Wolfram, *Intitulatio* 114f.

[38] J. Dhondt, *Études sur la naissance des principautés territoriales en France, IXe-Xe siècle* (Brugge 1948) 213; Werner 123ff.

[39] For the understanding of this most important phenomenon I am deeply obliged to the helpful cooperation with K. F. Werner whose forthcoming book, *Die Entstehung des Fürstentums, 7.-10. Jahrhundert; Studien zur fränkischen Reichsstruktur und zur Geschichte*

reverse this development; but they did not destroy the new *regna*. It was only the independent dynasties that they could deprive of their power.[40] After 850 and above all from 887 onward, when the last Carolingian, who theoretically held the whole empire under his sway, was deposed for his in-effectiveness,[41] the seventh century process was revitalized. Certainly, there were new families and mostly new entities to become organized as *regna* ruled by nonroyal *principes*. We encounter again Aquitaine, Bavaria, and Swabia. But there are also Gothia-Septimania (Languedoc), Burgundy, (German) Franconia, Saxony, Flanders, Normandy, Brittany, (French) Francia (Ile-de-France), Lorraine and Gascony.[42] The latter might have had genuine indigenous origins. In Brittany, native traditions certainly provided the main impulse in the making of the duchy, although the final impact was initiated by the Breton Nominoë who was at the same time a Frankish count of the ninth-century type.[43]

Certainly, this description contains much interpretation of a very contro-versial topic. I am attempting to refute the whole hallowed doctrine of the difference between the beginnings of the West-Frankish, "French", *princi-pautés territoriales*, and the East-Frankish, "German," stem-duchies. I have refuted the doctrine of the difference between the French *nationalités ré-gionales* and the allegedly "age-old" political consciousness of the coeval German tribes. Certainly, their names had already appeared during the Migrations. Yet, their political, institutional, and biological structures had more often than not thoroughly changed. I have, moreover, refuted the basic difference between the so-called *älteres Stammesfürstentum* and *jüngeres Stammesfürstentum*, since I consider the duchies before and after Charlemagne to have been basically the same Frankish institution, although, of course, I do not overlook the differences in detail. I am also implying that both the French *nationalités régionales* and the German tribes of the ninth and tenth centuries were not the cause but the result of the dismemberment of the Carolingian Empire which, despite all its efforts, finally could not stop that dismemberment that had originated with the late Merovingian *regnum Francorum* two centuries before.

In sum: The *nationalités régionales* of the French Middle Ages and the tribes of the German side of the Rhine River were created by princes who

---

des nichtköniglichen Herrschertums (Munich, Wilhelm Fink), will throw much light upon this issue. K. Brunner will deal with the same topic in *Intitulatio II*, laying, however, stress upon the princely and ducal titles involved: cf. n. 2 above; Wolfram, *Intitulatio* 113ff., 142ff.

[40] Wolfram, "Tassilo III" (n. 30 above) 179, and *Intitulatio* (n. 1 above) 221f.

[41] Böhmer-Mühlbacher (n. 25 above) no. 1765ab.

[42] See n. 39 above.

[43] See n. 39 above, and Dhondt (n. 38 above) 84ff.

could connect the Frankish political and military organization forms with varying tribal traditions of mostly legal and socioeconomic nature.[44]

But let us once more return to the eighth century, prepared to have a glance at the other outlying duchies of the fading Merovingian period. In the first half of the eighth century, the ducal families of Swabia and Bavaria had the same ancestors and took pride in being Agilolfingians. It is not quite clear as yet whether or not this powerful clan derived from the old Burgundian royal family. We know, however, that their political tradition came from those venerable origins.[45] The Agilolfingians had been a noble family whose core-land must have been Burgundy, who then spread all over the eastern part of the Merovingian *regna*, and even crossed the border of Frankland. Agilolfingians were kings of the Lombards for almost 80 years from the mid-seventh century onward. Members of this family had been invested by the Merovingian kings in Bavaria probably by the sixth century, and at an unknown but certainly much later date in Swabia. I believe 624 to be the first secure date for the inveterate conflict between Agilolfingians and Carolingians. From then onward the former were always prepared to fight the latter as upstarts without tradition.[46] Compare, for instance, the personal names of both families with each other. On the one hand, *Garibald*, *Tassilo*, *Odilo*, and *Theodo* were names worthy of royal persons. On the other hand, one has *Pippin*—nobody can tell what this emotional gemination is supposed to mean—then *Karl*, a name that is akin to Old Saxon *ceorl* which means *freeman*, and *Karlmann*, which is just a duplication, a rather unimaginative variation of *Karl*. Little wonder that Charlemagne himself tried to measure up to the status of a royal family by giving his son Louis-Clovis the name of the famous founder of the Merovingian dynasty.[47]

Despite their "better" origins, the Agilolfingians along with other noble families were more and more losing ground while the Carolingians progressed. Finally, Bavaria came to be the last stronghold of the formerly most powerful family.

Yet, only a few months before Carloman claimed to be the *dux et princeps Francorum*, he and his brother Pippin were deeply scandalized by the fact that their sister did not share their innate animosity and left Frankland for Bavaria to marry Odilo the Agilolfingian princelike *dux Bavariorum*.[48]

---

[44] See n. 39.

[45] Wolfram, "Tassilo III" (n. 30 above) 178. Werner, (n. 12 above) 108, differs from Zöllner (n. 30 above) 108ff., upon the question whether this family derived from the old Burgundian royal family actually or ideologically.

[46] Wolfram, "Tassilo III" 79; Werner (n. 12 above) 107ff.; E. Hlawitschka, "Die Vorfahren Karls des Grossen," *Karl der Grosse* (Düsseldorf 1965) 51ff., 56ff.

[47] Werner 107ff.; Zöllner (n. 30 above) 110ff.; E. Förstemann, *Altdeutsches Namenbuch* (Bonn 1900) 299f., 359f., 855ff.

[48] Wolfram, "Tassilo III" 158f.

The offspring of that detested marriage was Tassilo III. He reigned over the Bavarians for forty years until Charlemagne, who was then the lord of the whole of Latin Continental Europe, could finally destroy him and take vengeance upon him for more than 160 years of Agilolfingian resistance.[49] Tassilo's diplomatic documents show that he took pains to keep up with the political development in Frankland. Except for the title *rex* itself, which he never used, the wording of Tassilo's *intitulatio* literally followed the pattern of the new Carolingian royal title. Tassilo was a *princeps regni*; he was the lord of "his" territorial church lately established by Boniface himself, and he invested counts by his own hand. He was hailed *novus Constantinus* as only Charlemagne was at this time, and he had his son christened and anointed by the pope in a ceremony that had just been introduced for the Carolingians to guarantee the dangerous transition from their principate to their kingship. Moreover, Tassilo married King Desiderius's daughter when the Lombard kingdom had arrived at the peak of its power and reputation in Europe. And he was the brother-in-law of another nonroyal ruler, the *princeps-dux gentis Langobardorum* in Benevento. Tassilo's fall in 788 included that of his family, which came to be imprisoned in several monasteries throughout Francia. But Tassilo's *regnum* survived. Thus Charlemagne repeated simply the policy already applied to Aquitaine.[50]

The first war Charlemagne had to wage as a young king was the inherited *bellum Aquitanicum*.[51] He succeeded in abolishing the ducal family, but not the *regnum Aquitanorum*, which he recognized as such hardly more than a decade later when he invested his little son Louis as *rex Aquitanorum*.[52] The same held true for the Bavarian kingdom. It was not divided into a plurality of counties as a superficial reading of Einhard would perhaps make one believe. Instead, it remained as an entity under the control of men who were both faithful to Charlemagne and relatives of the deposed duke. Louis the Pious, the former *rex Aquitanorum*, finally gave the *regnum Bavariorum* its king in the person of first his son Lothair and then of Louis whom the textbooks call the German.[53]

It is almost a commonplace that the Carolingian empire was a centralized state, relatively well organized in more than 300 counties,[54] which was only

[49] *Ibid.* 177-79.

[50] Werner (n. 12 above) 111ff. Wolfram, *Intitulatio* 157, 170ff., esp. 181ff.

[51] Einhard, *Vita Karoli magni* 5, ed. G. Waitz, MGH Script. rer. germ. in usum scholarum (Hannover 1911) 7.

[52] Wolfram, *Intitulatio* 222f.; Cf. Einhard, *Vita* 5.

[53] Wolfram, *Intitulatio* 223. Böhmer-Mühlbacher (n. 25 above) nos. 528a, 1338c.

[54] Werner (n. 12 above) 122, rightly criticizes this obsolete opinion, which is still held by N. Zacour, *An Introduction to Medieval Institutions* (New York 1969) 102ff., whereas E. Klebel, "Herzogtümer und Marken bis 900," *Die Entstehung des Deutschen Reiches*, Wege der Forschung (Darmstadt 1956) 91, or *Deutsches Archiv* 2 (Weimar 1938) 52, has

to be thrown into chaos and aristocratic anarchy by the inefficiency of a
pious hypocrite. But how do the two just mentioned *regna* fit into this picture? Furthermore, there were not just two *regna* as such recognized by,
and incorporated in, the *regnum Francorum*. From 774 on, there existed
the Frankish *regnum Langobardorum* which Charlemagne himself had recognized in his new title *rex Francorum et Langobardorum*, and which he had
organized as a subrealm in 781 when he invested his son Pippin as another
rex Langobardorum.[55] And there was the *regnum Neustriae*, obtained around
790 by Charlemagne's oldest son and heir apparent, Charles, who unfortunately died in 811. When this King Charles built up his kingdom, the concept
Neustria started changing or had already considerably changed. It finally
shrank to connotate that part of Francia which lay between the Loire and
the Seine.[56] This kingdom, which by the way was no *ad hoc* creation, advanced
the process that finally led to the dismemberment of Francia proper into
four and even more parts. These parts were Neustria, whose tradition was
continued by the Normans; Francia in the narrow sense of the word, the
Frankish country between the Seine and the Ardennes, which during the
tenth century lost Flanders and became virtually limited to the Ile de France,
the political base of the Capetian dukes and kings alike; then Lorraine, the
regnum quondam Lotharii, called after the second Lothair, King of Lorraine
(855-869), and again an example of the importance of political decisions in
establishing statehood; finally Franconia along the Main river, the German
duchy, which was to enable the East-Frankish German kingdom to remain
theoretically a *regnum Francorum*.[57]

The development that I have just described took place mostly between 850
and 950, but it was Charlemagne himself who, if he did not start it, at least
did not fight it. How can we explain this seemingly contradictory policy
of the architect of the Carolingian Empire? Again, diplomatic sources provide
the clue to its understanding. It was neither Pippin's nor his greater son's
policy to destroy what has been called the "regna-structure" of the fading
Merovingian Kingdom. They simply fought the incumbents of the *regna*
who possessed them in virtue of their own "age-old" rights as heirlooms
of their ancestors, confirmed by the tribal law, as is evident with the

clearly shown and proven the contrary. As to the figure "more than 300 counties" see
J. Flach, *Les origines de l'ancienne France* (Paris 1886) 165.

[55] Wolfram, *Intitulatio* 220ff., 224.

[56] *Annales sancti Amandi*, ad annum 789, MGH Script. 1 (Hannover 1826) 12. Cf. Dhondt,
(n. 38 above) 100. Wolfram, *Intitulatio* 206.

[57] E. Ewig, "Descriptio Franciae," *Karl der Grosse* 143. E. Hlawitschka, *Lotharingien
und das Reich an der Schwelle der deutschen Geschichte*, MGH Schriftenreihe 21 (Stuttgart
1968) 15ff. Dhondt (n. 38 above) 81ff. W. Schlesinger, "Die Auflösung des Karlsreiches,"
Karl der Grosse 1.852ff., and above all, K. F. Werner in his forthcoming book (see n. 39).

Bavarian Agilolfingians.[58] I am of the opinion that it was this very recognition of the *regna*-structure based upon already shaped or still growing tribal or national entities, which actually allowed the Carolingians to build their Empire.[59] Of course, the Frankish army was irresistible at the moment; but without the support of the *gentes adquisitae*, of the "acquired peoples" as the sources had it,[60] the most glorious victory was almost in vain. For instance, the Frankish army defeated the Bavarians in 725, 728, 743, 749, and 787. But the Bavarian dukes survived all these bloodless defeats, until feudal policy mainly based upon feudal law and the factional strife among the Bavarians themselves allowed the Frankish King to build up a strong Frankish party in Bavaria by means of which he could oust Tassilo, the ducal family, and its followers in 788.[61] The same held true for the Saxons whom Charlemagne had to fight for more than 30 years. All his numerous victories over this people did not meet with decisive success until the Saxon aristocracy sided with the Franks in fear of the growing strength of the so-called freemen (*Gemeinfreien*).[62] The best way, certainly, to attain the support of a *gens adquisita* was to recognize its tribal or "national" entity in the form of a *regnum*. Like the Late Roman Empire, so the Carolingian Empire contained a plurality of *regna*.[63]

We must clarify or rather define this word *regnum*. The Merovingian kings divided the Frankish greater *regnum* into as many separate Frankish *regna* as they had sons living. Moreover, during the seventh century it became more and more common and necessary to establish subrealms for the heirs apparent while the fathers were still living.[64] These different types of *regna* could attach to local political traditions or more often create the political commonalty of a given area. The Carolingians had to follow their predecessors in this policy, imposed upon them by the sacred law of heritage. Therefore, we have to reckon with a threefold meaning of *regnum*: (1) *regnum* in the sense of *Regnum Francorum*; (2) *regnum* in the sense of *pars regni Francorum*, as evidenced in 741 or 768, when Carloman and Peppin, and Charlemagne and Carloman II respectively shared in the *regnum Francorum*; and (3) *regnum* in the sense of subrealm, *provincia*, *regio*, *patria*, as for instance, evidenced

---

[58] Wolfram, "Tassilo III" 173. About the anti-Carolingian aspects of this very law see Löwe (n. 30 above) 294ff.

[59] Wolfram, *Intitulatio* 222-224.

[60] *Ibid.* 157, n. 7.

[61] Wolfram, "Tassilo III" 163, 161f., 171-173.

[62] M. Lintzel, "Der sächsische Stammesstaat und seine Eroberung," *Entstehung und Verfassung des Sachsenstammes*, Wege der Forschung 50 (Darmstadt 1967) 198ff.

[63] Werner (n. 12 above) 122. Wolfram, *Intitulatio* 35.

[64] G. Eiten, *Das Unterkönigtum im Reiche der Merowinger und Karolinger*, Heidelberger Abhandlungen zur mittleren und neueren Geschichte 18 (Heidelberg 1907) 16f.

by the *regnum Aquitanorum* of Louis the Pious and the *regnum Bavariorum* of Louis the German.[65]

Thus far, I have mainly dealt with seventh- and eighth-century principalities, although enough allusions to the later development may already have made clear that I consider the ninth- and tenth-century principalities merely to have been the continuation of the former. Certainly, the *principes regni* had little or nothing to do genealogically with the defeated and destroyed ducal families of former times. Moreover, the people who lived in the older type of principalities had more often than not changed, too. New tribal entities emerged, more locally and territorially oriented, in fact, but still considered to be tribal units in theory. In other words, the Capetian duke of Francia called himself "*dux Francorum*"; his counterparts in Aquitaine, *dux Aquitanorum*; in Bavaria, *dux Bavariorum*, and so on. Yet, despite the particular changes, which I would never deny, the rise of the new *principes regni* occurred along the same lines as it did centuries earlier.[66]

But before I enter the final chapter of my topic, I would like to mention the only nonroyal princely dynasty in Europe which actually survived the Carolingian Empire. From 715 to 774, the diplomatic records of the powerful Lombard Dukes of Benevento bear the proud and certainly much older title *Nos domnus vir gloriosissimus (nomen) summus dux gentis Langobardorum*. The kings of the barbarian invasions inherited the titles both of *princeps* and *dominus* from their political model, the Roman emperors. Thus far, we have investigated how *princeps* could be adopted by nonroyal rulers. Certainly, *princeps* was the more important title. In Italy, however, it was *dom[i]nus* that became part of a princely duke's title. The Lombard duke of Spoleto tried to imitate his more successful colleague in Benevento. And it is true that both duchies virtually remained outside of the proper Lombard kingdom. After 774, when this realm collapsed and was incorporated into the growing Carolingian Empire, Spoleto fell victim to the impact of both papal and Frankish pressure. The duke of Benevento, no longer hindered by a *rex et princeps gentis Langobardorum*, assumed the title *princeps*. It proves my theory of the value of *dominus* that *princeps* replaced not only *dux* but *dominus* alike. Despite heavy attacks from all sides, from Franks, Arabs, and Byzantines, this genuine Lombard principality survived as a

---

[65] For this scheme, I draw upon K. F. Werner, as n. 39 above indicates.

[66] Dhondt (n. 38 above) 217ff., 285ff.; K. Reindel, "Bayern unter den Luitpoldingern," *Handbuch der bayerischen Geschichte* (Munich 1967) 206ff.; F. Prinz, "Das Herzogtum der Luitpoldinger," *Handbuch der bayerischen Geschichte* 295ff. It goes without saying that Werner will deal with this topic as well as K. Brunner (see n. 39 above).

bufferstate between East and West, even when it came to be divided, to build the nucleus of the Italian Norman state.[67]

When the Carolingians were still major-domos, they used the Frankish aristocracy, that is to say their peers some generations earlier, for missions all over Europe unless these nobles resisted them as the Swabian and Bavarian Agilolfingians did. The transfer of nobles, as holders of offices and benefices, from one part of the *regnum Francorum* to another effected a deep change in the structure of a great many of the aristocratic clans. It goes without saying that Charlemagne's reign increased the need for Franks all over Europe. Eventually, a purely provincial aristocracy, tied to its inherited estates and traditional patterns, turned into a European aristocracy, the so-called Carolingian imperial aristocracy. A stream of noblemen poured out from Austrasia, the heartland of Carolingian power, into the other parts of the Kingdom.[68] These newcomers fused with the local families into a new aristocracy, in Bavaria as well as in Italy, in Saxonia as well as in Aquitaine. For instance, the ancestors of the Capetians, the kings of France after 987, were newcomers from the central Rhine valley, settling then in Neustria and Francia around Paris.[69]

Certainly, among these newcomers there were not only men of lowly origins; usually, the contrary was true. We find mainly those members of the Merovingian-Frankish elite who made up their minds in time to support the apparently irresistible rise of the Carolingians, whom they followed as their feudal lords and kings of the Franks. This aristocracy first had a vested interest in maintaining the universality of the empire. The struggles among Charlemagne's grandsons and great-grandsons, however, occurred against the background of Viking and Saracen invasions; the affliction was soon to be increased by the Hungarian horsemen, so that virtually no place within the large Frankish commonwealth was safe any more. The inability of most of the Carolingian kings and emperors to protect their kingdoms against the external enemy led to a situation somewhat similar to that in which the Carolingians had risen themselves, two hundred years earlier. The members of the imperial aristocracy, moreover, had to decide whom of the Carolingians to follow. Their services came to be highly honored by each of the potential lords. So, the new upper class took rather quick advantage of the dismemberment and internal strife in concentrating their power in a given *regnum*

---

[67] Wolfram, *Intitulatio* 185ff. E. Cornides will cover the later development (from 774 onward) in *Intitulatio II*.

[68] H. Fichtenau, *The Carolingian Empire* (Oxford 1957) 110. Cf. E. Hlawitschka, *Franken, Alemannen, Bayern und Burgunder in Oberitalien, 774-962* (Freiburg im Breisgau 1960).

[69] Werner, "Untersuchungen zur Frühzeit des französischen Fürstentums," *Welt als Geschichte* 19 (Stuttgart 1959) 168f. n. 90. Flach (n. 54 above) 3 (1904) 199, speaks of the Saxon origins of the Capetians.

of the empire. Some of them could even rise to become the nonroyal heads of those *regna*, again called *principes*, that is to say of a people or simply of a *regnum*.[70]

Such a new *princeps regni* was not only the most ruthless collector of counties in a given *regnum*,[71] but he had to prove himself prepared and able to protect and organize this *regnum* as an efficient body politic. Odo, count of Paris, defended the city against the Normans. His success backed his principate over Neustria and expanded it over Francia (Ile-de-France) to some extent. Odo finally received a sort of personal kingship which can be understood as a direct principate over Neustria and Francia plus indirect overlordship over Burgundy and Aquitaine, if we are allowed to neglect Brittany and Gascony.[72] Arnulf of Bavaria alone was able to defeat and come to terms with the Hungarians after the catastrophes of Pressburg-Bratislava in 907 where his father fell, and of Augsburg in 910 when the Carolingian king himself was defeated.[73]

The rise of this new stratum of Carolingian officials to an eventual ruling class was accompanied by an interesting terminological "confusion." The famous foundation charter for Cluny was issued by William the Pious of Aquitaine who called himself *comes et dux* in 910, after having used several variations of this title form, among which we even find *comes, marchio atque dux* (898).[74] Beside this threefold *intitulatio*, *princeps* and *dux gentis* could have been used also.[75] How can we explain this?

Charlemagne defeated the ducal families and of necessity suppressed the titles *dux* or even *princeps* for their king-likeness. The princely *regna*, however, were recognized by him as such and even upgraded by the investiture of real kings in the persons of Carolingian offspring. But this policy neither occurred automatically nor materialized everywhere. In contrast, while the "county organization" of the empire might have been relatively efficient in the core-land, it was certainly too weak to provide sufficient protection on the borders. "Super-counts" in charge of a plurality of counties had to be invested. To avoid all kinds of inconvenient allusions to former princely titles and to measure up to the classical renewal, such an official, such a "super-count" came to be called *praefectus limitis*. In Bavaria, a *praefectus limitis* was in charge of the whole *regnum*. Little wonder that less official sources soon started calling him *praefectus provinciae* or *dux*, again. Officially the artificial "literary" term *praefectus limitis* was replaced by the Latinized German-Frankish

---

[70] See n. 39 above. Werner (n. 69 above) 163ff.; Dhondt (n. 38 above) 234ff.
[71] Dhondt 34f.
[72] Dhondt 100ff., cf. 45ff.
[73] Reindel (n. 66 above) 210.
[74] W. Kienast, *Der Herzogstitel in Frankreich und Deutschland*, (Munich 1968) 169.
[75] *Ibid*. 169ff.

term *marchio* (from *mark, march*, i. e. border). For the next generation, this word was obviously prevailing. Then the word *marchio* remained but with a new meaning. Now, each "supercount" no matter where in the Frankish commonwealth, was called *marchio*. In fact, *marchio* came to name the new non-Carolingian and nonroyal *princeps regni* for a while. After 900, almost in the same year, the *princeps regni* in Aquitaine, in Burgundy, and in Bavaria used the title type *Dei gratia dux* (*princeps*) *gentis*, which was evidently modeled after the royal title. Yet, the Carolingian chanceries east and west of the Rhine river continued calling those self-styled *duces-principes* simply *marchiones et comites*. The new royal dynasties, however, who were to replace the Carolingian kings, had to recognize the *dux-princeps* title as a matter of fact.[76]

The princes around 900 were *comites* as incumbments of counties, *marchiones* as holders of a plurality of counties, both in keeping with the official Carolingian policy. But they had also become *duces* by the way of fact. *Dux* by this time definitely meant *heritoho, herzog*, leader of the army, that is to say leader of the people under arms. The Carolingian kings were no longer able to fulfil this task. Possessing the most powerful position in a given *regnum*, the greatest number of counties, and having proven himself a successful leader of the army of the *regnum*, the *dux-marchio-comes* had become the *princeps regni*, or, since the army was the "people," the *dux gentis* or *princeps gentis*.

The last question which almost automatically rises is: Why did they not try to become real kings? I have already touched upon this issue, but it is important enough to discuss more completely.

In 887, Charles the Fat was deposed for inability and disease; these legal reasons were confirmed by ecclesiastical theory as well as by the Teutonic right of resistance.[77] In 888, some of the nonroyal non-Carolingian *principes regni* tried to proclaim their kingship.[78] Very few of them succeeded, however. Much more successful was the way shown by Bernard Plantevelue, William the Pious's father, some years earlier, who remained faithful to the Carolingian king and was able, therefore, to become the most powerful magnate in southern France;[79] this goal was never reached either by Bernard of Gothia or even by Boso of Burgundy, who either proclaimed themselves kings or at

---

[76] Kienast (n. 14 above) 43ff., who heavily relies on the fundamental article of J. Dhondt, "Le titre du marquis à l'époque carolingienne," *Archivum latinitatis medii Aevi* 19 (Brussels 1946) 407ff.

[77] F. Kern, *Gottesgnadentum und Widerstandsrecht*, ed. 2 (Darmstadt 1954) 318. An English translation of the first edition that appeared in 1914, *Kingship and Law in the Middle Ages*, by S. B. Chrimes (Oxford 1948), is now obsolete.

[78] Regino of Prüm, *Chronicon*, ad annum 888, ed. F. Kurze, MGH Script. rer. Germ. in usum scholarum (Hannover 1890) 128-31.

[79] Dhondt (n. 38 above) 240ff.

least behaved as such.[80] It was actually the faithful, *fideles*, who dismembered the Frankish empire, not the unfaithful usurpers, *infideles*. For despite his lack of power to be an over-all efficient king, the Carolingian king was still powerful enough to curb the unfaithful who had broken their feudal oaths.[81] To fight them, he would always find enough support from men who, otherwise, could not care less about the king's glory and honor. The very powerful Arnulf of Bavaria, for instance, had to flee his duchy twice from the king to whom he did not want to swear feudal allegiance.[32]

In sum, it did not pay off to become king, except in the long run for the Capetians who possessed Francia proper with all its Carolingian resources and traditions, and for the Saxon kings who could make the world believe that they continued the Carolingian-Frankish tradition in Aachen as well as in Pavia and Rome.[83] It was the latter who came to be powerful enough to repeat Charlemagne's policy toward the principalities in a modified form, which was so effective, in the end that it definitely broke those principalities based upon a tribal body politic. In the West, however, the rising French principalities maintained the status of their incumbents much longer. They were still heads of the church in their *regna*, decided upon their basically hereditary succession, possessed the former royal domains, intermarried with royal families, were supreme judges in their *regna*, were lords of the former royal vassals, feudal lords of counts, bishops, abbots. It was at their courts that the cultural life, the political and socioeconomic organization were initiated and concentrated. The West-Frankish principalities were the almost forgotten cradle of France, of French culture, French litterature, and above all of French and European religous renewal. The Truce-of-God movement was inaugurated by the church of the duke of Aquitaine, and the monastery of Cluny was founded neither by an emperor nor by a king, neither by a pope nor by a bishop, but by William the Pious, the first to call himself by God's grace duke of the Aquitanians.[84] On the other hand, the Neustrian-Norman *regnum-ducatus* provided the base from which the Normans conquered Eng-

---

[80] *Ibid.*, cf 213.

[81] See n. 38 above.

[82] Reindel (n. 66 above) 211.

[83] H. Beumann, "Grab und Thron Karls des Grossen zu Aachen," *Karl der Grosse* (Düsseldorf 1967) 9ff., and K. Hauck, "Die Ottonen und Aachen, 876 bis 936," *Karl der Grosse* 4.39ff., are dealing with the Carolingian tradition east of the Rhine. As to the "French" counterpart see J. F. Lemarignier, *Le gouvernement royal aux premiers temps capétiens, 987-1108* (Paris 1964) 37ff. R. Fawtier, *Les Capétiens et la France*, (Paris 1942), has been recently translated into English as *The Capetian Kings of France*, by L. Butler and R. J. Adam (New York 1966), but this book does not meet the standards of modern research; Cf. Werner, "Die Legitimität der Kapetinger und die Entstehung des 'Reditus regni Francorum ad stirpem Karoli,'" *Welt als Geschichte* 17 (Stuttgart 1952) 203ff.

[84] See the list of titles given by J. Flach (n. 54 above) 4 (1917) 507 n. 20.

land and Southern Italy where they modified the feudal system along the lines of logic, and achieved feudal immediacy for the king. Flanders, finally, became the cradle of modern industry and commerce and another center of cultural life.[85]

The efforts and achievements of those bodies politic are unjustly overlooked by a "king-centered" historiography, which is interested too exclusively in the modern, centralized, and unifying Leviathan—the modern state.

[85] Werner, "Untersuchungen zur Frühzeit des französischen Fürstentums," *Welt als Geschichte* 18 (Stuttgart 1958) 256ff.

University of Vienna
A-1010 Vienna 1
Austria

THE LEGIMUS SUBSCRIPTION OF CHARLES THE BALD AND THE QUESTION OF BYZANTINE INFLUENCE

•

by Michael D. Metzger

The *Legimus* subscription that appears on seven surviving diplomas of Charles the Bald[1] has long interested students of diplomatics. It has always been treated, however, as evidence contributing to the understanding of some other distinct, though related, questions, such as the dating of the celebrated Byzantine imperial letter preserved at Paris,[2] or the origins of the gold bulla of Charlemagne.[3] Unfortunately, such investigations have often been based on inadequate knowledge of the position of the *Legimus* subscription within Carolingian royal diplomatics in general and within the acts of Charles the Bald in particular.[4]

---

[1] Georges Tessier et al., *Receuil des actes de Charles II le Chauve, roi de France*, (Actes), 1: *840-860* (Paris 1943); 2: *861-877* (Paris 1952); 3: *Introduction et table* (Paris 1955) no. 167 (a copy), 22 August 854; no. 239 (a copy), 23 April 862; no. 338 (original), August 866-April 870; no. 364 (original), 12 May 872; no. 378 (original), 19 March 875; no. 413 (original), [September] 876; no. 425 (original), 5 May 877.

[2] Immediately after the discovery of this famous piece of papyrus by the Maurists in 1693-1694, Mabillon linked its subscription to the *Legimus* of the acts of Charles the Bald; all later scholars have followed his lead. Cf. H. Omont, "Lettre grecque sur papyrus émanée de la chancellerie impériale de Constantinople et conservée aux Archives nationales," *Revue archéologique* 3.19 (1892) 384-393; K. Brandi, "Der byzantinische Kaiserbrief aus St. Denis und die Schrift der frühmittelalterlichen Kanzleien; diplomatisch-paläographische Untersuchungen zur Geschichte der Beziehungen zwischen Byzanz und dem Abendlande, vornehmlich in fränkischer Zeit," *Archiv für Urkundenforschung* 1 (1908) 5-86; W. Ohnsorge, "Das Kaiserbündnis von 842-844 gegen die Sarazenen, Datum, Inhalt und politische Bedeutung des 'Kaiserbriefes aus St. Denis,'" *Abendland und Byzanz, Gesammelte Aufsätze zur Geschichte der byzantinisch-abendländischen Beziehungen und des Kaisertums* (Darmstadt 1958) 131-183.

[3] Cf. P. Bonenfant, "L'influence byzantine sur les diplômes des Carolingiens," *Annuaire de l'Institut de philologie et d'histoire orientales et slaves* 11 (1951) (= *Mélanges Henri Grégoire* 3) 61-77; W. Ohnsorge, "*Legimus*, Die von Byzanz übernommene Vollzugsform der Metallsiegeldiplome Karls des Grossen." *Abendland und Byzanz* 50-63; P. E. Schramm, "*Legimus* auf Karolingischen Urkunden und die Kaiserbullen Karls des Grossen und Ludwigs des Frommen," *Herrschaftszeichen und Staatsymbolik* 1, MGH Schriften 13.1 (Stuttgart 1954) 297-302.

[4] M. Jusselin, in his study "La chancellerie de Charles le Chauve d'après les notes tironiennes," *Le moyen âge* 33 (1922) 18-19, has pointed out that to understand the Tironian

In 1936 Georges Tessier noted the appearance of a *Legimus* subscription in a seventeenth century copy of a diploma issued by Louis the Pious on 22 February 839.[5] This was a renewal of a diploma, previously granted to a certain Jew, Gaudiocus, and his two sons, guaranteeing them full possession and ownership of their property. This diploma was of further interest in that it lacked a monogram, its legend, and a subscription by the chancery. The *Legimus* was the only subscription it bore.

Other scholars, prompted by this discovery and influenced by the corroboration formula of this diploma: "et ut haec auctoritas . . . inviolabilem . . . obtineat firmitatem more nostra eam subterscribere et de bulla nostra jussimus assignari," have concluded that the *Legimus* subscription appeared on certain acts of Charlemagne.[6] Similarly, P. Bonenfant has suggested that one surviving issue of Lothar I originally bore a *Legimus* subscription.[7] More recently W. Ohnsorge has also maintained that this subscription was used by the chancery of Lothar I. He drew this conclusion from the existence of a copy, bearing a *Legimus* subscription, of a tenth century forgery of an issue of Lothar I.[8]

While there are elements in these latter attributions which are debatable, the following conclusions appear to be reasonable. The *Legimus* subscription was probably introduced into Carolingian usage under Charlemagne, whose reign produced much innovation within Carolingian diplomatic practice.[9] It does not appear to have been used very frequently, and it seems to have been connected in some way with the gold bulla.

------

notes that appear in the acts of Charles the Bald, it is necessary to place them in the context of their use in all Carolingian issues; until the publication of the critical edition of the acts of Louis the Pious research in these areas will produce only tentative results.

[5] G. Tessier, "*Legimus*," *Bibliothèque de l'École des chartes* 97 (1936) 245-246.

[6] It would appear that the chancery of Charlemagne had adopted the *Legimus* subscription by 803; cf. Bonenfant 71; Ohnsorge, "*Legimus*" 52; Schramm 299; F. Dölger, "Byzanz und das Abendland vor den Kreuzzügen, Forschungsbericht über das ganze Gebiet (mit Ausnahme von Wirtschaft, Handel, Verkehr und Kunst)," *ΠΑΡΑΣΠΟΡΑ, 30 Aufsätze zur Geschichte, Kultur und Sprache des byzantinischen Reiches* (Ettal 1961) 82.

[7] Bonenfant 74 n. 1. The diploma in question is no. 51 in the recent edition by T. Schieffer (MGH Dipl. Karol. 3: *Lotharii I et Lotharii II diplomata*).

[8] W. Ohnsorge, "Ein Deperditum Kaiser Lothars I mit Legimus-Ausfertigung von 842," *Konstantinopel und der Okzident, Gesammelte Aufsätze zur Geschichte der byzantinisch-abendländischen Beziehungen und des Kaisertums* (Darmstadt 1966) 163-170; for a different, perhaps more plausible, interpretation of this piece cf. Schieffer no. 141.

[9] The addition of the monogram, the bulla, the verbal invocation, the devotion or legitimization formula within the *Intitulatio*, etc., cf. G. Tessier, *Diplomatique royale française* (Paris 1962) 80ff. For the milieu that encouraged this imitation of things Roman-Byzantine cf. H. Bresslau, "Internationale Beziehungen im Urkundenwesen des Mittelalters," *Archiv für Urkundenforschung* 6 (1918) 22ff.

It is against this background that the *Legimus* subscription of Charles the Bald must be studied. The frequency of its use hardly increased during his reign; of the more than four hundred surviving acts of Charles the Bald, only seven are known to have borne the *Legimus*. These are dated during the years 854 to 877. For placing this usage of the chancery of Charles the Bald within the tradition of Carolingian diplomatics, the first example is of central importance.[10] It is dated 22 August 854 and was issued at Tours. It confirms and renews all the possessions and immunities of the monastery of Saint Martin of Tours whose records were destroyed when the monastery was burned by the Vikings.[11] It is recognized by the notary Bartholomeus who had been active in the chancery of Louis the Pious.[12] It may have borne a gold bulla.[13]

To this the witness of the remaining six diplomas bearing the *Legimus* may be added. They involve major grants to various monasteries and churches. Three of them definitely bore gold bullas.[14] The *Legimus* and its accompanying crosses, or cross, were in red ink.[15] In two of them the king's personal intervention in the issue, *Domnus rex fieri jussit*, is noted in the Tironian notes within the ruche.[16] All of this indicates that, within the chancery of Charles the Bald, the red *Legimus*, like the gold bulla,[17] was part of the form of an especially solemn issue.[18] None of this implies anything more than a continuation and development of the practices of his predecessors.[19]

---

[10] Actes no. 167.

[11] 8 November 853, cf. *Annales bertiniani*, ed. Waitz 53, cited in Actes 1.438.

[12] Actes 3.65ff.; Jusselin 5.

[13] Actes 1.439-440; but note that Actes 3.142 attributes a gold bulla to this diploma only by analogy with diplomas that bear a *Legimus* subscription and a gold bulla.

[14] Actes 3.141-142.

[15] The only other instances of the use of red ink by the chancery of Charles the Bald occur in diplomas nos. 413 and 425, both issued after his imperial coronation, in which the monogram is also in red ink. On the significance of the red ink cf. Brandi 15ff.; F. Dölger, "Der Kodikellos des Christodulos in Palermo; ein bisher unerkannter Typus der byzantinischen Kaiserurkunde," *Byzantinische Diplomatik, 20 Aufsätze zum Urkundenwesen der Byzantiner* (Ettal 1956) 13ff.; Dölger, "Die Kaiserurkunde der Byzantiner als Ausdruck ihrer politischen Anschauungen," *Byzanz und die europäische Staatenwelt, Ausgewählte Vorträge und Aufsätze* (Ettal 1953) 29; and most recently Dölger and Johannes Karayannopulos, *Byzantinische Urkundenlehre, Erster Abschnitt: Die Kaiserurkunden* (Munich 1968) 28-30 (= *Byzantinisches Handbuch im Rahmen des Handbuchs der Altertumswissenschaft*, hereafter BUL).

[16] Actes nos. 338, 378; on the significance of this cf. Jusselin 19ff., esp. 35 and Actes 3.102.

[17] Cf. Actes 3.142 on the possibility of the apposition of a gold bulla to a diploma not subscribed with *Legimus*.

[18] There is no indication that the *Legimus* was a royal autograph as it was on occasion in Byzantium; cf. Actes 3.182-183; G. Tessier, *Diplomatique royale française* 93-94.

[19] Carolingian diplomatic practices were not static. Charlemagne's reign was, as noted (n. 9 above), very innovative; the chancery of Louis the Pious adapted the inherited prac-

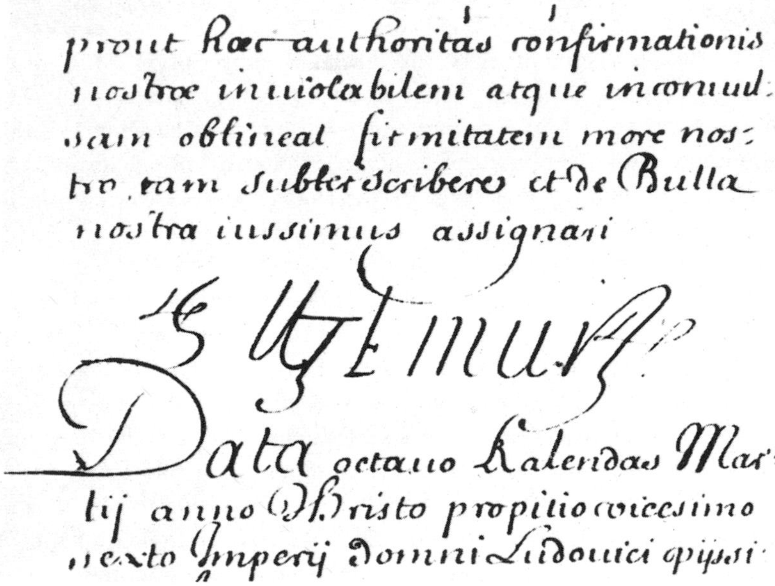

prout hæc authoritas confirmationis
nostræ inuiolabilem atque inconuul-
sam obtineat firmitatem more nostro tam subterscribere et de Bulla
nostra iussimus assignari

Vgemus

Data octauo Kalendas Mar-
tij anno Christo propitio uicesimo
sexto Imperij Domni Lidouici pijssi

Fig. 1. Capot's copy of the diploma of Louis the Pious
(Collection Doat, vol. 66, fol. 39)

Fig. 2. Montfaucon's tracing of the imperial letter (Paris,
Bibl. Nat., MS lat. 11909, fol. 169)

FIG. 3. No. 239, 23 April 862

FIG. 4. No. 338, August 866–April 870

FIG. 5. No. 364, 12 May 872

FIG. 6. No. 425, 5 May 877

It has been stated that there was no continuation of the Carolingian tradition within the chancery of Charles the Bald, at least with respect to the *Legimus* subscription, and that the archives of Louis the Pious passed into the control of Lothar I.[20] Even apart from the complicated question of Carolingian archives, this assertion would appear difficult to justify. At the death of Louis the Pious certain of his chancery officials passed into the service of Lothar I, others into that of Charles the Bald. Meginarius, the chief notary of Louis the Pious, and the aforementioned Bartholomeus, the notary who recognized the first *Legimus* issue of Charles the Bald which has been preserved, joined the service of Charles the Bald.[21] This fact alone provides for the continuation of a living tradition within the chancery of Charles the Bald;[22] it is not necessary to accept the contention that Louis the Pious spent the winter of 839/40 arranging the administration of his favorite son.[23]

But where does this leave the relationship between the *Legimus* of Charles the Bald and that of the Byzantine imperial letter preserved at Paris? The connection between the two was first suggested by Mabillon.[24] It was based on the paleographic similarity between the *Legimus* of the imperial letter and that of the acts of Charles the Bald.[25] But there is another explanation for this similarity, one that does not require the direct dependence of one upon the other. If the *Legimus* subscription of Louis the Pious (LP; see

---

tices to its own circumstances; a similar process of adaptation took place in the chancery of Charles the Bald. The verbal invocation might be taken as an example of this process. It was introduced under Charlemagne; a different form of it was adopted by Louis the Pious; and a third form appears in the issue of Charles the Bald. This type of variation is sufficient to explain the fact that, although the only surviving copy of a *Legimus* issue of Louis the Pious bears neither a monogram, its legend, nor a chancery subscription, the surviving *Legimus* issues of Charles the Bald have all three.

[20] Ohnsorge, "*Legimus*" 56: "In der Kanzlei Karls des Kahlen bestand also keinerlei Tradition hinsichtlich einer Ausfertigung von Diplomen mit Legimus. Das ist nicht verwunderlich. Das Archiv Ludwigs des Frommen war an Lothar I übergangen."

[21] Jusselin 4-10; Actes 3.54-57, 65-67.

[22] For the notaries as guardians of the tradition cf. Jusselin 4; for examples of Meginarius and Bartholomeus continuing the traditions of the chancery of Louis the Pious cf. Actes 3.66.

[23] P. Grierson, "Hugues de Saint-Bertin: était-il archichapelain de Charles le Chauve?" *Le moyen âge* 44 (1934) 251.

[24] Omont 386.

[25] Brandi 8-9: "Diese Legimus in den Urkunden Karls d. K. von 862-877 sind nun die einzigen und noch dazu sehr unsicheren Daten aus der älteren Überlieferungsgeschichte unseres Papyrus; unsicher, weil das rote Legimus nach byzantinischen Muster auch auf irgend eine andere Kaiserurkunde zurückgehen kann; einzig, weil keine ältere Kopie, keine archivalische Notiz über die Zeit Mabillons zurückführt." This judicious comment was made before the discovery of the *Legimus* subscription of Louis the Pious or the *Legimus* issue of 854.

fig. 1),[26] that of the imperial letter (I; see fig. 2),[27] and that of the issues of Charles the Bald (CB; see figs. 3-6),[28] are compared, there appears to be a greater similarity between LP and I than between either of them and any of CB. Therefore it would seem as likely that CB depends on LP as on I. This possibility has been noted before; but it was argued that the initial crosses of CB reflected the initial cross of I and not that of LP.[29] This seems a bit tendentious, especially since LP is preserved in a copy, not a tracing, and the entire form of the initial cross in I is not preserved.[30]

The most attractive solution would be to have LP depend on I and then it would not matter which of the two CB depended on. Unfortunately, this solution is chronologically impossible. LP, as noted above, is dated 22 February 839. I is dated 6 May 841,[31] or 6 May 843.[32] In either case the similarity of LP and I is not due to any direct relationship. The simplest explanation for their similarity, then, is that LP is dependent on some other Byzantine issue that bears a *Legimus* subscription written by the same careful hand[33] as that of I. Such a Byzantine issue could date from the period between 820 and 856 during which Theoctistus occupied the office of ἐπὶ τοῦ κανικλείου.[34] There were Byzantine embassies to Louis the Pious in 824, 827, and 833.[35] Any one of these could have provided the model for

---

[26] Fig. 1, a reproduction of the copy made by Gratien Capot in 1668, after W. Ohnsorge, "*Legimus*" Plate I.

[27] Fig. 2, a reproduction of the tracing made by the Maurist Montfaucon, after W. Ohnsorge, "*Legimus*" Plate II; for a photograph of the original see BUL Tafel 3.

[28] Unfortunately I did not have access to the facsimiles of the *Legimus* issue of Charles the Bald. F. Lot et P. Lauer, *Diplomata karolinorum: Recueil de reproductions en fac-similé des actes des souverains carolingiens conservés dans les archives et bibliothèques de France* (Paris 1936ff.) 5.7, 10, 11, 20; E. Monaci, *Archivio paleografico italiano* 51 (vol. 9) 103. I have reproduced the facsimiles of four *Legimus* subscriptions of Charles the Bald published by Omont 391.

[29] Ohnsorge, "*Legimus*" 58ff.

[30] This latter point is even clearer if one examines the photograph of I published in BUL (Tafel 3). The difference in the formation of the final loop of the cross bar in the initial cross, given the kind of transmission involved in LP, will not support a very heavy structure of argumentation; cf. Ohnsorge, "*Legimus*" 60.

[31] Dölger in his review of Ohnsorge, "Kaiserbündnis," *Byzantinische Zeitschrift* 48 (1955) 469.

[32] Ohnsorge, "Kaiserbündnis" 165.

[33] Cf. Ohnsorge, "*Legimus*" 58.

[34] On the position of Theoctistus cf. Ohnsorge, "*Legimus*" 58ff.; Dölger, "Kodikellos" 52ff. For the inner workings of the Byzantine chancery cf. Dölger, "Die byzantinische und die mittelalterliche serbische Herrscherkanzlei," *Actes du XIIe congrès international d'études byzantines, Ochride 10-16 septembre, 1961* 1 (Belgrade 1963) 83-103, esp. 83-86; BUL 57-66, esp. 66.

[35] Bonenfant 388; Brandi 29-30; Dölger, *Regesten der Kaiserurkunden des oströmischen Reiches von 565-1453*, Corpus der griechischen Urkunden des Mittelalters und der neueren Zeit, Reihe A: Regesten, Abteilung 1: *Regesten der Kaiserurkunden des oströmischen Reiches* (Munich 1924) nos. 408, 413, 429.

the *Legimus* subscription that appeared on the diploma of Louis the Pious dated 22 February 839.

This argument opens the possibility that the *Legimus* of Charles the Bald could depend on some other Byzantine issue bearing the *Legimus* of Theoctistus; however, such a speculative solution is not required. If the paleographic similarity between the *Legimus* subscription of Louis the Pious and that of Charles the Bald is added to the continuity of personnel which existed between their chanceries, the obvious conclusion is that the *Legimus* subscription, as used by the chancery of Charles the Bald, in its form as well as in its significance, is merely a continuation and development of the practice of the chancery of Louis the Pious. The paleographic similarity between the *Legimus* of this tradition and that appearing on the imperial letter is a result of their common origin, which is ultimately the form of *Legimus* produced by the Byzantine official Theoctistus. It would appear, then, that Byzantine influence reached the court of Charles the Bald through the chancery of Louis the Pious.

Department of History
University of California
Los Angeles, California 90024, U.S.A.

MUHTASIB AND MUSTASAF:
A CASE STUDY OF INSTITUTIONAL DIFFUSION

•

by Thomas F. Glick

Recent studies of the Spanish Middle Ages have stressed Spain's crucial role as a receiver and transmitter of elements of Islamic culture. Indeed, the question of how much influence the culture of the Muslims had upon that of Christian Spaniards has divided Spanish historians into two opposing camps. The majority view is that associated with Claudio Sánchez-Albornoz and is subscribed to by most incumbents (many of them his disciples) of medieval history chairs in Spanish universities today. This view insists upon the paramountcy of Visigothic traditions and institutions in medieval Spain, stresses eternally Spanish characteristics of Iberians, Hispano-Romans and Visigoths, and on a theoretical level may be described as static and anti-behaviorist in that the possibility of any but superficial culture change in the indigenous population through contact with Muslims is structurally denied. It suffices to mention that Sánchez-Albornoz believes that culture descends in the blood line, by processes similar to, or identical with, those of biological heredity.[1] It should be noted, moreover, that this antibehaviorist approach manifests the selective biases of traditional Spanish ethnocentricity: it admits dynamic and profound interchange between Hispano-Roman and Visi-

---

[1] Sánchez-Albornoz's views of medieval Spanish culture are set forth in *España : un enigma histórico*, 2 vols. (Buenos Aires, 1956). For his views on "heredity," see the extraordinary exchange between Sánchez-Albornoz and S. M. Stern at the 1964 Spoleto conference. Stern took Sánchez-Albornoz to task for categorically ascribing certain psychological traits of Hispano-Muslims to an indigenous inheritance. Sánchez-Albornoz replied that Stern had succombed to the dangers of over-specialization "en négligeant. . . comme indigne d'un historien l'étude de la projection de l'hérédité idiosyncrasique de chaque communauté historique dans la lignée nationale." In the same rejoinder he said further: "Mais il serait vain de nier que tout homme porte en lui cette trinité formée: par sa propre équation per-sonelle, vitale et psychologique, *par l'hérédité de sa lignée c'est à dire de son peuple*, et par l'emprise de l'univers culturel où se déroule son existence." (Emphasis mine.) Discussion in *L'Occidente e l'Islam nell'alto medioevo*, 2 vols. (Spoleto 1965) 1.384.

gothic cultures but denies the same dynamics, the same processes and mechanisms of cultural change, where Islamic and Jewish cultures are concerned.

The behaviorist approach is characterized by the admission that cultural processes affect all peoples, not just some. The leading figure in this camp is Américo Castro whose classic, *The Structure of Spanish History*, presents a dynamic view of cultural interchange in the Spanish Middle Ages based, however, more upon Castro's insightful and highly informed intuitions than upon a systematic and scientific theory of cultural change. In an article with Oriol Pi-Sunyer I have suggested that the anthropological theory of acculturation offers a sound theoretical basis for the explanation of problems raised in the Castro—Sánchez-Albornoz debate.[2] I accept as a working hypothesis that two different cultures in a situation of intimate and prolonged contact will give rise to a distinct daughter culture, partaking of elements of both parents. I can agree with Castro's critics that non-Islamic elements outweigh Islamic elements in the resultant cultural mix. But the heart of the matter is qualitative, not quantitative, and the rejection of the profound, if selective, impact of Islamic upon Spanish culture entails the rejection, or at the very least ignorance, of mechanisms of cultural change and exchange which have been observed in dozens of analogous situations of culture contact.

This article presents a case study of cultural borrowing in the area of municipal institutions, as a complement and parallel to such literary studies as Castro's brilliant exposition of the Islamic roots of the *Libro de buen amor*[3] or to technological monographs like Oliver Asín's treatise on the water system of Madrid.[4] I do not assert that all, or even most, medieval Spanish institutions bear a strong Islamic imprint. But I believe that institutions, no less than literary works, scientific ideas, or technological systems, modes of dress, speech, or behavior, are subject to the same kind of comparative analysis.[5]

Institutions are more than the sum of administrative, juridical, and organizational elements that compose them. They also have distinctive styles and are elaborated in discrete traditions that are just as susceptible to historical analysis as are the individual component elements. I am proposing,

---

[2] Thomas F. Glick and Oriol Pi-Sunyer, "Acculturation as an Explanatory Concept in Spanish History," *Comparative Studies in Society and History* 11 (1969) 136-154. See discussion of Castro on pp. 146-147.

[3] Américo Castro, *The Structure of Spanish History* (Princeton 1954), chap. 12.

[4] Jaime Oliver Asín, *Historia del nombre "Madrid"* (Madrid 1959).

[5] As a model for the comparative study of a Spanish institution, Julián Ribera, *Origenes del justicia de Aragon* (Zaragoza 1897). See also my study of the Islamic antecedents of the irrigation system of Valencia, both in its technological and institutional aspects, *Irrigation and Society in Medieval Valencia* (Cambridge, Mass. 1970) part two.

therefore, an approach that is, first, necessarily comparative and, second, more functional than has been the case in Spanish institutional history that has been narrowly legalistic and formalistic in orientation. Moreover, I believe that such an approach, founded on a dynamic view of cultural change and interchange, is one that will lead to a more accurate and realistic picture of Spanish town life and institutions in the Middle Ages.

The subject of this essay is one tradition of municipal adminstration— a tradition whose chief characteristic was the uniting under a single magistracy of all the service functions of civic administration. These functions fall into two categories, the first embracing the economic activities of the city, the second, those aspects of urban life having to do with public health, safety, and morality. I will follow this tradition from its origin in ancient Greece through successive transformations in Islamic and Spanish cultures, in hopes of learning something of the processes of cultural diffusion—how ideas and institutions are transmitted from one culture to another—and acculturation —how one culture assimilates elements of another and creates a new and distinctive cultural synthesis.

From agoranomos to ṣaḥib al-sūq.—In classical Athens and in other cities of the Hellenic world, the direction of the affairs of the marketplace was entrusted to officers called *agoranomoi*, whose duties were described by Plato and Aristotle.[6] They were charged, first, with the physical condition of the market place and with the inspection of the shops of the various tradesmen. They checked the accuracy of weights and measures;[7] assured that articles offered for sale were fairly priced, pure and unadulterated; and protected consumers in all of their dealings with the tradesmen and artisans.[8]

Other services characteristic of municipal concern for public welfare were entrusted to the *astynomoi*. These officials enforced building codes and those concerned with sewage and rubbish; saw to the cleanliness of streets and public buildings; served as general arbiters of public morals; and intervened in the settlement of labor disputes.[9]

---

[6] Plato, *Laws* 8.849 (*agoranomos*); *Laws* 6.759; *Laws* 8.847 (*astynomos*), in *The Collected Dialogues of Plato*, ed. Edith Hamilton and Huntington Cairns (New York 1961). Aristotle, *Politics* 6.8. and 7.12; *Athenian Republic* 50.1 (*agoranomos*); *Politics* 6.8 and *Athenian Republic* 50.2 (*astynomos*), in *The Works of Aristotle*, ed. W. D. Ross, 10 (Oxford 1921).

[7] Aristotle also designated ten commissioners of weights and measures, called *metronomoi* (*Athenian Republic* 50.2), but their functions eventually devolved upon the *agoranomoi*.

[8] On the general attributes of the *agoranomos*, see Gustave Glotz, *Ancient Greece at Work* (New York 1926) 296; Richard Häderli, "Die Hellenischen Astynomen und Agoranomen vornehmlich in alten Athen," *Jahrbücher für classische Philologie*, Supplementband 15 (1887) 47-94; A. H. M. Jones, *The Greek City from Alexander to Justinian* (Oxford 1940) 216-217; David Magie, *Roman Rule in Asia Minor*, 2 vols. (Princeton 1950) 1.60-61.

[9] On the duties of the *astynomos*, see Glotz 296; Häderli; and Jones 213-215.

The offices of *agoranomos* and *astynomos* were known throughout the Hellenic world, as numerous inscriptions attest,[10] and in late classical times the two offices tended to merge, the functions of the *astynomos* devolving upon the *agoranomoi*, especially in smaller towns.[11] The overlapping of jurisdictions was the natural result of the amorphous nature of the *agora*, a term that often designated a considerable district extending beyond the strict confines of the market square. The *astynomos*, who in classical times had some jurisdiction over matters of commercial cheating, was eased out of this jurisdiction in the Imperial Age and replaced by the *agoranomos*.[12] In some cities, such as Sparta, there had never been any *astynomoi* at all.

In the Hellenistic period the *agoranomos* gained additional power and jurisdiction. A new division of labor required a more direct use of governmental power, and thus "the *agoranomoi* no longer confined themselves to inspecting weights and measures [but] fixed compulsory units for each class of goods" and set prices.[13] Numerous inscriptions from Antonine times cite *agoranomoi*, several indicating astynomic functions such as construction of pavement.

The classical *agoranomos* carried out in the first century A. D. basically the same functions as those attributed to the office in the fifth century B. C. But in the Roman period the entire character of the office changed, owing to the influence of the Roman *aedilitas*. Along with the general transformation of Greek political life, the civic offices of *agoranomos* and *astynomos* were transformed as the result of an effort to bring them into line with existing Roman offices. The *agoranomos* was made equal to the *aedilis*, just as the *strategos* came to be a *praetor*. Polybius and Plautus translated *aedilis* by *agoranomos*, and later, when the Greek states fell under Roman rule, the offices themselves were transformed.[14] The aedile had three functions: the *cura urbis* (involving streets, traffic, water supply, and the market), the *cura annonae* (grain supply), and—its most typical function—the *cura ludorum sollemnium*. As a general test, therefore, the complete aedilization of the office can be assumed when the *agoranomos* is seen sponsoring games.

By 100 B. C., a leveling of instutitions had occurred. Thus Athens had two *agoranomoi*, instead of the classical ten, and no *astynomoi* at all. In the reign of Marcus Aurelius, inscriptions attribute game-giving functions to the *agoranomos*, who in one instance was styled *agoranomos kouroullios*, on the model of the curule aedile.

---

[10] See the article "Agoranomos" in C. Daremberg and E. Saglio, *Dictionnaire des antiquités grecques et romaines* (Paris 1873) 155; and Häderli, passim.

[11] Jones 215, 349 (especially 349 n. 10—astynomic functions of *agoranomoi*).

[12] Häderli 50.

[13] Glotz 297.

[14] Häderli 61-64.

Inscriptions mentioning *astynomoi* do not, after the second century A. D., appear to be talking about the ancient Hellenic magistracy. By the second century the *agoranomoi* had become completely aedilized, and the office by now was largely honorific, just like the contemporary Roman aedilate. In the fourth century the aedilate disappeared entirely in Rome; and, as far as I can determine, the third century is the last in which Greek inscriptions mentioning *agoranomoi* appear.

Arabists are generally agreed that the antecedent of the Islamic *muḥtasib* is the Greek, Hellenistic, or Byzantine *agoranomos*.[15] Indeed, the classical *agoranomos* and the *muḥtasib* are strikingly similar, but the gap of several centuries between the last agoranomic inscriptions and the full development of the *muḥtasib* is too wide to permit proof of institutional continuity. Rather than correlating the functions of the two offices in full development, it seems more logical to establish a connection between the moribund *agoranomos* and the nascent *muḥtasib*, to find, that is, an office in the pre-Islamic East with characteristics of the proto-*muḥtasib* (the *ṣāḥib al-sūq*) not present in the classical Greek office, while yet retaining the Greek name. Such an office undoubtedly existed, but there is no record of its existence in the records of Byzantine municipal administration.[16]

The clue to the transitional office lies among the Semitic communities of Syria and Mesapotamia. A third-century inscription of Palmyra[17] evokes some interesting associations. A *strategos*, Julius Aurelius Zabdilah, was described as chief of the market, in which capacity he had spent large sums. The inscription is bilingual and the Aramaic translation of the Greek *ago-ranomesanta* ("the one who was *agoranomos*") reads *wa-hū rab šūq*. The title *rab šūq* offers a splendid model for the Arabic *ṣāḥib al-sūq*. Indeed, the very

---

[15] M. Gaudefroy-Demombynes, "Un magistrat musulman: le Mohtasib," *Journal des savants* (1947) 36; *idem, Muslim Institutions* (London 1950) 154-155; G. E. von Grunebaum, *Islam ; Essays in the Nature and Growth of a Cultural Tradition* (New York 1961) 137 n. 4; *idem, Medieval Islam*, ed. 2 (Chicago 1961) 355.

[16] After the third century A.D., eastern Roman municipal magistracies, the *agoranomos* included, became collegiate, annual, and probably elective (A. H. M. Jones, "The Urbanization of the Iturean Principality," *Journal of Roman Studies* 21 [1931] 270-271); the fourth-century *agoranomos* of Antioch was no longer a magistrate proper, but a curial (Paul Petit, *Libanius* [Paris 1955] 74). In third- and fourth-century Egypt, the *agoranomos* became a liturgical official; his duties were divided with another official, the *logistes*, and later were assumed by another official, the *ekdikos*; there was a curule *agoranomos* and a non-curule one, neither of whom resembled the classical *agoranomos* (Pierre Jouguet, *La vie municipale dans l'Égypte romaine* [Paris 1911] 328-334; J. Grafton Milne, *A History of Egypt under Roman Rule*, ed. 3 [London 1924] 132).

[17] J. Cantineau, *Inventaire des inscriptions de Palmyre* 3.22 (Beirut 1930) 28-31; also, G. A. Cooke, *A Text-Book of North Semitic Inscriptions* (Oxford 1903) 278-281. See also, J. G. Fevrier, *Essai sur l'histoire politique et économique de Palmyre* (Paris 1931) 97.

word *sūq* is, in Arabic, a loanword from Aramaic,[18] the type of market found in Syria having been unknown to the ancient Arabians.[19]

Yet it was not in the Byzantine empire that the Semitic *agoranomos* enjoyed its greatest flowering, but in the more easterly domain of the Persian Sasanians. Numerous references to fourth-century Jewish *agoranomoi* can be found in the Talmud, as well as in other rabbinic literature such as the *Midrashim* and *Tosefta*.[20] These officials were not—it should be stressed—imperial magistrates, but rather communal officials, appointed by the Exilarch as market supervisors, who presided over the commercial life of the Jewish communities.[21] The local officer apparently functioned in the traditional Greek fashion (although without astynomic duties), only complementing municipal legislation with religious law, or perhaps even substituting the latter for the former completely. There is no reason to doubt that this communal official survived up to the time of the Arab conquest. The Arabs would then have encountered in such communities a market inspector, called *agoranomos* or *rab šūq*, functioning not as the grand magistrate of olden days, nor as a liturgical magistracy of the empire, but rather as a local, communal official, occupied only with the affairs of the market place, and enforcing regulations of inspection and control based not upon Greek or Persian imperial legislation, but upon law of a canonic or religious nature. These characteristics place this official far closer to the Umayyad *ṣāḥib al-sūq* than to the Greek whose name he bore. Strikingly, the Babylonian Talmud yields evidence of an *agoranomos* among local *Arab* communities. In *Baba Kamma* 98a an *agoranomos* is described as "Arabian," indicating that fourth-century Arabs living in the Euphrates area has a market officer modeled in some fashion on the *agoranomos*. It seems probable, then, that the *muḥtasib* was the succesor not of a Greek magistrate but of a native official of the eastern Semitic communities.

---

[18] Siegmund Fraenkel, *Die Aramaischen Fremdwörter in Arabischen* (Leiden 1886) 186-187. Cooke 288 points out that *šūq* of the Old Testament and *Targum* meant street; in the *Talmud* it means "broad place," "market."

[19] Cf. Gaudefroy-Demombynes, "Un magistrat musulman" (n. 15 above) 37, on Meccan markets.

[20] See the Jerusalem Talmud, *Baba Bathra* 5.14, *Le Talmud de Jerusalem*, ed. M. Schwab (Paris 1888) commenting on Deuteronomy 25.15 ("Thou shalt have a full and just weight"). In the Babylonian Talmud, ed. I. Epstein (London 1935), *agoranomoi* are mentioned in *'Abodah Zarah* 58a; *Baba Bathra* 89a; and *Baba Kamma* 98a. Note also that by the mid-third century *agoranomoi* had disappeared from Byzantine imperial administration in Palestine (Häderli, n. 8 above, 66 n. 19).

[21] See the discussion in Jacob Neusner, *A History of the Jews in Babylonia 2: The Early Sasanian Period* (Leiden 1966) 112-114. I am indebted to Mr. Benjamin Braude for this reference as well as for pointing out to me that there are numerous questions of interpretation yet to be cleared up with regard to the Jewish *agoranomos* and the apparent difference in the office's attributes in Palestine and Babylonia, respectively.

From ṣāḥib al-sūq to muḥtasib.—The history of municipal administration in the East during the 150 years following the Arab conquest is somewhat mysterious. In formerly Byzantine territories Hellenistic forms of administration are thought to have survived into the Islamic era,[22] to be superseded completely only with the "Islamization" of government under the ʿAbbāsid caliphs.

The earliest sources—the *Akhbār al-Quḍāt* of Waki and the *Aḥkam al-Sūq* of Yaḥya b. ʿUmar—mention a ṣāḥib al-sūq ("master of the market"), as do the legal writings of Malik and his disciples.[23] Although the ṣāḥib al-sūq was primarily a market officer, he did have some astynomic functions outside of the market as well.[24]

The eastern ṣāḥib al-sūq was replaced by the official called the *muḥtasib* soon after the fall of the Umayyad Caliphate. But in Al-Andalus the transition was much slower. Owing to the origin of its rulers, the institutions of Islamic Spain from the eighth to the eleventh century were Umayyad, that is, Syrian in nature.[25] The general diffusion of the office of *muḥtasib* in Spain was delayed,[26] and yet the titles given the Andalusí *sūq* magistrates betray a curious mixture of Umayyad and ʿAbbāsid forms.

Ibn al-Abbār (1198-1260) reported that the emir Hishām b. ʿAbd al-Raḥmān (ruled 788-796) assigned to Futays b. Sulaymān the function of *sūq*, which was the name given in Spain to the *ḥisba*.[27] The same author in his *Kitāb al-Takmila li'l-Kitāb al-Ṣila* mentioned two other personages of the same epoch who held this office. The first, Idris b. Yaḥya, is referred to as "*walī* of the *ḥisba* in the market" (*walī al-ḥisba bi'l-sūq*).[28] Similarly,

---

[22] Gaudefroy-Demombynes, "Un magistrat musulman" (n. 15 above) 36; and the same author, "Sur les origines de la justice musulmane," *Mélanges René Dussaud* (Paris 1939) 2.819ff.

[23] M. Talbi, "Quelques données sur la vie sociale en occident musulman," *Arabica* 1 (1954) 299-300; E. García Gómez, "Unas 'Ordenanzas del Zoco' del siglo IX," *Al-Andalus* 22 (1957) 253-316.

[24] For example, enforcement of regulations regarding ditches around one's house and doors facing on dead-end streets (García Gómez 291-292).

[25] See Gaudefroy-Demombynes, "Un magistrat musulman," (n. 15 above) 36.

[26] Of the Andalusí *ḥisba* manuals (see n. 36 below), the treatise of Al-Saqaṭī was written in the late eleventh or early twelfth century; that of ibn ʿAbdūn in the twelfth; and al-Jarsīfī's manual not earlier than 1278. The book of ibn ʿAbd al-Raʾūf would appear to be an earlier exception. J. D. Latham ("The Interpretation of ibn ʿAbd al-Raʾūf on Nikāḥ," author's typescript) dates it "not earlier than the second half of the ninth century." According to G. Colin and E. Lévi-Provençal, *Un manuel hispanique de ḥisba* (Paris 1931) v n. 2, the ṣāḥib al-sūq was current throughout the eras of the Umayyads and the Party Kingdoms. The term *muḥtasib* became current in the eleventh century.

[27] Émile Tyan, *Histoire de l'organisation judiciaire en pays d'Islam*, ed. 2 (Leiden 1960) 623.

[28] Ibn al-Abbār, *Takmila kitāb al-ṣila*, ed. Francisco Codera (Madrid 1887-1889) 1.149.

Abu Muḥammad ʿAbd al-Wāḥid b. ʿAbd al-Salam was *walī* of the *ḥisba* of the *sūq* in his town (*walī ḥisbat al-sūq bi-baladi-hi*).[29]

The term *ḥisba* (from which *muḥtasib* is derived) usually referred to the duty of every Muslim to "promote good and discourage evil."[30] It seems clear, however, that *ḥisba* in fact functioned on two levels, a theoretical or philosophical one, and a practical one. Êmile Tyan is careful to make this distinction, pointing out that, in spite of the theoretical definition of *ḥisba* which indicates that its concern extended to all of man's activities, in practice "it did not pass the limits of an ordinary institution of administration and police."[31] It is in this light that the expression *walī al-ḥisba bi'l-sūq* must be understood.

In speaking of a time nearer his own than that of the two above-mentioned *walīs*, ibn al-Abbār also mentioned an eleventh-century Valencian official who was "governor of the administration of the *sūq*" (*walī khuṭṭat al-sūq*),[32] *khuṭṭat* in this instance having the same sense as *ḥisba* in the expression *walī ḥisbat al-sūq*. The twelfth-century author, ibn Bashkuwal [Pascual], described a tenth-century personage as having been named "to the function of the *ḥisba*, which is known among us as *wilāyat al-sūq*." To Andalusí Muslims, at least through the twelfth century, *ḥisba* and *wilāyat* or *khuṭṭat al-sūq* were synonymous, indicating that *ḥisba* was understood in its practical, administrative connotation, rather than a philosophical one.

Until the reign of ʿAbd al-Raḥmān II (822-852), the *ṣāḥib al-sūq* was the only municipal magistrate in Al-Andalus charged with the direction of urban police and the administration of civil justice in cases involving common law. This emir created several new magistracies—two *shurṭa* bureaus for urban police and the *ṣaḥib al-madīna*, a city prefect[33]—but the *ṣāḥib*, or *walī*, *al-sūq* continued in the exercise of most of his functions and remained a most powerful official.[34]

---

[29] *Ibid.* 364.

[30] On philosophical and religious aspects of *ḥisba*, see C. Cahen and M. Talbi, "Ḥisba," in *Encyclopedia of Islam*, ed. 2 (Leiden 1960-) 3.485-489; Gaudefroy-Demombynes, *Muslim Institutions* (n. 15 above) 154-155; G. E. von Grunebaum, *Islam* (n. 15 above) 152; and Joseph Schacht, "The Law," *Unity and Variety in Muslim Civilization*, ed. G. E. von Grunebaum (Chicago 1955) 75.

[31] Tyan (n. 27 above) 631. The more theoretical moral aspects of the *ḥisba* were characteristic of the eastern tradition, whereas western *ḥisba* was more practically oriented (*ibid.* 621 n. 1).

[32] "Apéndice a la edición Codera de la 'Tecmila' de Aben al-Abbār," *Miscelánea de estudios y textos árabes*, ed. M. Alarcón and A. González Palencia (Madrid 1915) 352.

[33] E. Lévi-Provençal, *España musulmana hasta la caída del califato de Córdoba*, tr. E. Garcia Gómez, *Historia de España* 4, ed. 2, ed. R. Menéndez Pidal (Madrid 1957) 165-166.

[34] Al-Khushanī (d. 971) recounts two anecdotes concerning the office of *walī al-sūq* in mid-ninth-century Córdoba. In the first, Ibrahīm b. Ḥusain b. Khālid, market magistrate of Córdoba (*kāna ʿalā sūq qurṭuba*) in 232 H., near the end of the reign of ʿAbd al-Raḥmān

Even after the common appearance of the *muḥtasib* in the eleventh century, the Umayyad and ʿAbbāsid terms continued to coexist.

There are two sources for the duties of the *muḥtasib*: the Books of *Ḥisba* (or *adab al-muḥtasib*)—manuals of ordinances regulating urban life—and discussions of the office in general legal and historical treatises. These two sources give somewhat different views of the office.

The *adab al-muḥtasib* is exceedingly difficult to characterize. In one author's view, it is the urban literature *par excellence*, "regulating the conduct of the *homo islamicus* in the essential situations of his everyday life." To another scholar, the books are little more than catalogues of nuisances that are controlled by the *muḥtasib*.[35] Indeed, it is hard to accept as completely representative of medieval Islamic town life the pigeon-fanciers, herbalists, quacks, and other uncommon types who populate the pages of *ḥisba* manuals.[36]

The descriptions by historians also have limitations. The *muḥtasib* was a colorful and distinctive figure who easily lent himself to folkloric, somewhat stylized anecdotes concerning the life of the market place. Nevertheless,

---

II, pronounced a sentence against certain merchants, causing their shops to be razed. In the second, the *wali al-sūq* of Córdoba during the reign of Muḥammad (852-886), Ibrahīm b. Ḥusain b. ʿĀṣim, was authorized to execute the punishments of amputation and crucifixion without the ruler's authority. See al-Khushanī, *Historia de los jueces de Córdoba* (*Kitāb al-Quḍāt bi-Qurṭuba*), ed. and trans. Julián Ribera (Madrid 1914) text 99, 178-179; trans. 121, 220-222. Similar in tone are two incidents recounted by al-Faradī (962-1013) as having taken place during the reign of the same Emir Muḥammad. In each case the *wali al-sūq* is described as dealing violent blows to wrongdoers. See al-Faradī, *Tarīkh ʿulamāʿ al-Andalus*, ed. F. Codera (Madrid, 1890) 98, 303.

[35] Latham (n. 26 above); Wilhelm Hönerbach, "Das Zunft- und Marktwesen und seine verwaltung im heutigen Tetuan," *Die Welt des Islams* 4 (1956) 112.

[36] The following Andalusī manuals have been published: (1) Treatise of ibn ʿAbd al-Raʾūf: text, E. Lévi-Provençal, *Trois traités hispaniques de ḥisba* (Cairo 1955) 67-116; trans. Rachel Arie, "Traduction annotée et comentée des traités de ḥisba d'ibn ʿAbd al-Raʾūf et de Umar al-Garsīfī," *Hesperis-Tamuda* 1 (1960) 5-38, 199-214, 349-388; see also n. 25 above. (2) Treatise of ibn ʿAbdūn: text, E. Lévi-Provençal, "Le traité d'ibn ʿAbdūn," *Journal Asiatique* 224 (1934) 177-299, and in the same author's *Trois traités* 3-65; trans. F. Gabrieli, "Il trattato censorio di ibn ʿAbdūn sul buon governo di Siviglia," *Rendiconti Accadémia dei Lincei* 6.11 (1935) 878-935, Lévi-Provençal, *Séville musulmane au début du XIIᵉ siècle* (Paris 1947), and Lévi-Provençal and García Gómez, *Sevilla a comienzos del siglo XII: El tratado de ibn Abdūn* (Madrid 1948). (3) Treatise of al-Jarsīfī: text, Lévi-Provençal, *Trois traités* 117-128; trans. G. M. Wickens, "Al-Jarsīfī on the Ḥisba," *Islamic Quarterly* 3 (1956) 176-187, and Rachel Arie, "Traduction annotée"; commentary, J. D. Latham, "Observations on the text and translation of al-Jarsīfī's Treatise on ʿḤisba,'" *Journal of Semitic Studies* 5 (Manchester 1960) 124-143, and G. M. Wickens "[Corrections to] al-Jarsīfī on the Ḥisba," *Islamic Quaterly* 4 (1957) 95. (4) Treatise of al-Saqaṭī: text, Colin and Lévi-Provençal, *Un manuel hispanique de Ḥisba* (n. 26 above); trans. Pedro Chalmeta Gendrón, "El ʿKitāb fī ādāb al-ḥisba' (Libro del buen gobierno del zoco) de al-Saqaṭī," *Al Andalus* 32 (1967) 125-162, 359-397 ; 33 (1968) 143-195.

since the historian is selective and is expected to report only the salient features of the office, the record is perhaps a more reliable picture of the *muḥtasib* as he actually was. In discussing the duties of the *muḥtasib*, I shall, in the interests of space, describe the office only as it existed in the western Islamic tradition.[37]

Agoranomic functions.—The earliest ordinances preserved are those of Yaḥya ibn ʿUmar, a ninth-century Maliki scholar who was born in Jaen but who spent many years in Kairawan. These regulations refer preponderantly to the market place, to make it so safe that even "the sick man and the old woman" might go there without being cheated.[38] Equity in the market was sought, first, by a constant surveillance of weights and measures and, second, by prevention of the adulteration of products, particularly foodstuffs.

Later descriptions by western Muslim historians confirm the central role of the *muḥtasib* as chiefly a market officer. The most complete and most often cited description is that of al-Maqqarī[39] (d. 1631), which he copied from the thirteenth-century historian, ibn Sa'id:

> And in regard to the office of *iḥtisāb*, certainly among [the Andalusis] it is held by men of learning and wisdom, as if its holder were a *qāḍī*. And the custom in it is that he proceeds personally overseeing the markets, along with his assistants. And his balance, with which he weighs bread, [is] in the hand of one of his assistants, because bread among [the Andalusis] is determined in weight; for a quarter of a *dirham* [one can buy] a loaf of a determined weight, and likewise for an eighth. [This procedure has the advantage that] owing to the public safety, the buyer might send a small boy or a defenseless slave-girl [to buy for him], and in what they bring him from the market they are equal with [one who is an] expert in the

[37] The basic eastern *ḥisba* texts are ibn al-Ukhuwwa, *Maʿālim al-Qurba fī Aḥkām al-Ḥisba*, ed. R. Levy (London 1938); al-Shaizarī, *Nihāyat al-Rutbah fī Talab al-Ḥisba* (Cairo 1946); and R. B. Serjeant, "A Zaidi Manual of Ḥisbah of the Third Century (H)," *Rivista degli studi orientali* 28 (1953) 1-34.

[38] García Gómez, "Ordenanzas del Zoco" 299.

[39] There are several other descriptions of *muḥtasibs* by Magribi and Andalusí authors. See ibn Khaldūn, *Muqaddimah*, trans. F. Rosenthal, 3 vols. (New York 1958) 3.462-463; and the sarcastic letter of ibn al-Khaṭīb (1313-1374) to a *muḥtasib* of Malaga (text in Maqquarī, *Nafḥ al-Ṭib*, Cairo 1949, 8.274-275, trans. Fernando de la Granja, "La carta de felicitación de ibn al-Jaṭīb a un almotacen malagueño," *Al-Andalus* 26 (1961) 471-475. Ibn Khaldūn mentions both economic and astynomic functions, but ibn al-Khaṭīb's letter indicates that the duties of the *muḥtasib* were confined to the market place. See also Leo the African's description of the "Governour of the Shambles" of sixteenth-century Fez in a contemporary English translation: Leo Africanus, *The History and Description of Africa*, trans. John Pory, ed. Robert Brown (London 1896) 2.434. A better translation can be found in Jean-Léon l'Africain, *Description de l'Afrique*, trans. A. Epaulard (Paris 1956) 1.195-196.

knowledge of weights. Likewise, meat has on it a sheet with its price. And the butcher would not dare to sell it in disregard of what the *muḥtasib* has fixed on the tag.[40] And he can hardly hide his false-hood, for indeed the *muḥtasib* secretly sends to him a small boy or girl so that one of the two might buy from him. Then the *muḥtasib* checks, and if he finds an error, he gauges in this his comport-ment with people, Do not ask what befalls an offender in such a case, for if he does it often and does not repent after being flogged and receiving public reprobation in the markets, he is expelled from the city.[41]

Astynomic functions—The *muḥtasib* was not only concerned with the market but with cleaning the streets, enforcing building codes, and caring for the general concerns of public health. One western author, ibn Farḥūn (d. 1397) described the *muḥtasib's* function as purely astynomic in nature: "As for the authority of the *ḥisba*, it falls short of the *qaḍā'* in the establish-ment of all rules, but [the *muḥtasib*] passes judgment upon outside skylights between houses and upon the construction of stone benches in the streets, because that is what pertains to the *ḥisba*."[42]

Closely related to the purely astynomic functions were those of a religious and moral nature. The *muḥtasib* had to enforce upon the public the ritual obligations of Islamic law, see to the upkeep and public used of the mosques, direct the traffic around the mosques, and oversee the propriety of public behavior, particularly between the sexes.[43]

The *muḥtasib* exercised general surveillance over the craft guilds and in larger towns designated an *amīn* or inspector to supervise each profession.[44]

Jurisdiction.—The *ḥisba* was a sub-jurisdiction of the *qaḍā'*, and the *muḥtasib* was therefore subordinate to, and often appointed by, the *qāḍī*. There were significant differences between the judicial process of the two officials, however. The most important attribute of the *muḥtasib* was that he could initiate actions against wrongdoers. Ibn Farḥūn observed that "the *muḥtasib* is greater than the *qāḍī* through the fact that he turns his attention to the search for things which are forbidden, if they are not apparent to the *qāḍī*. As for the *qāḍī*, he does not judge except in what is submitted to him."[45] The *muḥtasib* could act only in cases where there was a clear and obvious

---

[40] Cf. R. Dozy, *Supplément aux dictionnaires arabes*, 2 vols., ed. 2 (Leiden 1927) 1.478: "au dessous du poids indiqué par le Mohtesib sur le morceau de papier."

[41] Maqqarī, *Nafḥ al-Ṭīb*, reprinted in M. Asín Palacios, *Crestomatía de árabe literal* (Madrid 1959) 34-35.

[42] Ibn Farḥūn, *Tabṣirat al-Ḥukkām* (Cairo 1958) 1.19.

[43] Arie (n. 36 above) 22; Cahen and Talbi (n. 30 above) 487.

[44] Cahen and Talbi 488.

[45] Ibn Farḥūn (n. 42 above) 1.19; see also Tyan (n. 27 above) 646.

wrong. He could not deal with claims that did not result from wrongful acts, regardless of their magnitude, and even then, he could only act on admitted liability. If the misdeed were disputed he could not act, for only the *qāḍī* was empowered to hear evidence and administer an oath. The *muḥtasib's* judicial process was completely oral; once testimony or evidence had to be received in writing, the matter was beyond his jurisdiction.[46]

The *muḥtasib's* jurisdiction was *ratione materiae* and only rarely geographical. Therefore the office was particularly susceptible to jurisdictional disputes with other municipal officials, particularly the *ṣāḥib al-shurṭa* and *ṣāḥib al-madīna*.

The enforcement procedure and methods of punishment of the *muḥtasib* were most distinctive. There were no fines exacted (which immediately distinguished the *muḥtasib* from both his Greek antecedents and Spanish derivatives); rather, punishment was inflicted on the wrongdoer's person or merchandise. The *muḥtasib* could inflict a simple reprimand, or beating, a promenade around the marketplace (the wrongdoer proclaiming his misdeed aloud), deportation from the city, confiscation of property, or closure of the shop.[47]

In cases of fraud or adulteration of merchandise, a penalty was exacted upon the goods themselves, as well as on the owner, as indicated in an Andalusí *ḥisba* manual:

> The effect of condemnation shall be apparent either by mixing, where mixing can be carried out easily; or by breaking what must be broken; or by pouring away; so that his punishment is [effective] in the goods [themselves]; or, by distributing in charity.
> The original [position] was that punishment would be [effective] in the article [itself]: the Prophet . . . ordered the overturning of cooking-pots in which captured meat had been boiled before a division had been made.[48]

Our purpose here has not been to provide an exhaustive study of *ḥisba* and the office of *muḥtasib* but simply to provide background for comparison with the derivative Spanish offices, now to be described.

From muḥtasib to mustasaf—The viability and versatility of the *ḥisba*, and of its administrator, the *muḥtasib*, find a most striking illustration in the thoroughness and ease with which these were taken over in the municipal and princely administration of certain medieval Christian states, specifically those bordering on Dār al-Islām. The *muḥtasib*, in fact, proved such an adap-

---

[46] H. F. Amedroz, "The Ḥisba Jurisdiction in the *A ḥkām* [al-] *Sulṭāniyya* of Māwardi," *Journal of the Royal Asiatic Society* (1916) 78-79, 91-92, 100; ibn al-Ukhuwwa (n. 37 above) 91-92 (trans.).

[47] Tyan (n. 27 above) 648-650.

[48] Wickens (n. 36 above) 184, 186.

table office that it served the needs of all who sought to regulate town life,
whether kings, barons, or town councilmen. There was no great difference
either in procedure or in function between the Islamic and Christian officials.
With the single important exception of the collecting of money fines by Christian
officials, the offices were much the same in both cultures. Here I shall discuss the development of Christian *muḥtasibs* in Spain, where circumstances
provided for a prolonged intermingling of two cultures. As a postscript, I cite
similar officials in the Latin kingdom of Jerusalem and in Frankish Cyprus.

The tenth century in Christian Spain was marked by an upswing in commercial activity, involving the establishment of weekly markets in towns
such as León which had become more than mere centers of local supply.
Nothing is known of the administration of these markets before the eleventh
century. Probably the count exercised jurisdiction over the markets of his
county, appointing an agent to collect market taxes. The common Western
European *iudex fori* was known in Navarre (as well as a *senior mercati* in
Pamplona [1087] and an *alcalde del mercat* [1247]). No such officers were
known in Castile or León.[49]

In eleventh-century León, however, there emerged a new and distinctive
official—the *zabazoque* or *zavazaure*—derived from an Islamic model. As a
result of natural concern for the economic life of the town, local councils delegated men to act as judges or inspectors of the market.[50] Thus, the Fuero of
León (1020) provided that "all butchers with the agreement of the council
may sell by weight pig-, goat-, ram-, or cow-meat and may give a meal to
the council along with the *zavazoures*."[51]

Zabazoque is derived from Arabic, *ṣāḥib al-sūq*.[52] The diffusion of the title
and office was no doubt effected through the agency of mozarabs immigrating
northwards to the Asturo-Leonese kingdom.[53]

In the twelfth century, the *zabazoque* was supplanted by the *almotacen*,
derived from the *muḥtasib*. From this time on the *almotacen* in the Castilian
orbit, and—somewhat later—the *mustasaf* in the Mediterranean towns, were
widely diffused.[54]

---

[49] Luis G. de Valdeavellano, "El mercado: apuntes para su estudio en León y Castilla
durante la edad media," *Anuario de historia del derecho español* 8 (1931) 320-326.

[50] Valdeavellano, *Historia de España*, ed. 2 (Madrid 1959) 1.2.481-482.

[51] Valdeavellano, "El mercado" (n. 49 above) 321 n. 364: "omnes carnizarii cum consensu
concilii, carnem porcinam, ircinam, arietnam, bacunam, per pensum vendant, et dent pran-
dium concilio una cum zavazoures," The fines set for disturbances within the market in
the same Fuero were not collected by the *zabazoque*, however, but by an agent of the king
(*persolvat sagioni regis*); *ibid.* 322.

[52] Leopoldo de Eguílaz y Yanguas, *Glosario etimológico de las palabras españolas de orígen
oriental* (Granada 1886) 371.

[53] Valdeavellano, (n. 50 above) 1.2.107.

[54] For the etymology of Castilian and Catalan derivatives from Arabic, *muḥtasib*, see

The *almotacen* was not only in charge of weights and measures but oversaw the activities of most of the urban tradesmen. The Fuero of Zorita de los Canes (thirteenth century) stipulated that the *almotacen* ought to supervise all the measures of bread, wine, oil, and salt; weights and measures; and butchers, bakers, oil dealers, store and tavern keepers, fishmongers, tile makers, carpenters, and other tradesmen.[55] He took his oath from the council, definitely putting him in the ranks of municipal officials. Compared to the wealth of documentation concerning the *mustasaf*, detailed information concerning the early *almotacen* is scarce. (There is no body of legal literature peculiar to the *almotacen*.) He seems not to have had any religious or moral police functions, but simply economic ones. Finally, the *almotacen* does not seem to have had the widespread acceptance in Castile which the *mustasaf* had in Valencia; the *almotacen* was not the sole officer entrusted with agoranomic and astynomic functions.[56]

The reason for the incomplete development of the *almotacen*, as compared with its Valencian homologue, was, first, the earlier date of its diffusion. The Islamic institutions that diffused into León in the eleventh century were less highly evolved than those adopted in thirteenth-century Valencia. Secondly, the circumstances of the diffusion were markedly different. The Leonese learned of the office from immigrant mozarabs, whereas the Valencan situation was one of direct continuity with Islamic municipal administration. For these reasons León and Castile acquired a *ṣāḥib al-sūq* but not a fully developed *muḥtasib*.

It was on the eastern coast, especially the kingdom of Valencia, that a Christian *muḥtasib* reached full development. Soon after the conquest of Valencia in 1238, James I named Raymond Deslluch of Zaragoza to be the first Christian *mustasaf* of the city.[57]

Antoni M. Alcover, *Diccionari català-valencià-balear*, 10 vols. (Palma 1930-1962) 7.618; J. Corominas, *Diccionario crítico etimológico de la lengua castellana*, 4 vols. (Bern 1954) 1.159; Eguílaz y Yanguas, *Glosario* (n. 52 above) 237, 241; Eero K. Neuvonen, *Los arabismos del español del siglo XIII* (Helsinki 1941) 93-94; and Arnald Steiger, *Contribución a la fonética del hispano-árabe* (Madrid 1932) 110 (*ba* losing sonority and changing to *f*) and 265 (interior *ḥa* dropping out).

[55] Valdeavellano (n. 49 above) 324 n. 377.

[56] *Ibid.* 323. Royal officials, called *alcaldes*, *merinos*, or *sayones*, also intervened in market affairs in Castile as collectors of fines, police, and even as inspectors of weights and measures.

[57] Francisco Sevillano Colom, *Valencia urbana medieval a través del oficio del mustaçaf* (Valencia 1957) 23. See the description of Deslluch in the *Trovas de Mossen Jaime Febrer* (Valencia 1967) 245:

> Nomená lo Rey del pes é medida
> A Ramon Deslluch primer mustasaf . . .
> Aqueste prengué sobre camp d'or
> Un pes de romana, per poder millor
> Igualar la cosa que á cascú sels deu,
> Segons té lo preu, dantli lo que es seu.

The "Book of the *Mustasaf*" of Valencia contains ordinances dating from 1293, when the records of the municipal council began to be collected in the Manuals de Consell. In the late fourteenth century, regulation specifically involving the jurisdiction of the *mustasaf* were culled from the larger corpus and written down in *Llibres del mustasaf*, a genre of legal compilation which became common in the towns of Valencia and Catalonia.[58]

The duties and functions of the Valencian *mustasaf* fell into the same categories as those of the *muḥtasib*: the agoranomic, the astynomic, the religious and moral, and those concerned with the supervision of guilds.

Agoranomic functions.—The keystone of the magistracy remained, as it had been since ancient times, the preserving of accurate weights and measures. Thus, at the beginning of his administration, each new *mustasaf* had "to demand and receive from last year's *mustasaf* the standard measures of wine and oil, the balances . . . the standard of the cubit, and the balances for weighing meat . . . and all the other accouterments which pertain to the office of *mustasaf*."[59] Indeed, the fair weight and measure have always been the symbols of commercial equity.[60]

The *mustasaf* had universal authority over all who dealt in foodstuffs and consumer goods. Judging by the number of regulations, supervision of weavers, bakers, and butchers was extremely strict and exacting. Although he did not actually fix prices, the *mustasaf* saw that the prices established

---

[58] On the *Llibres del mustasaf*, for Castellón de la Plana, see Francisco A. Roca Traver, "El mustaçaf de Castellón y el Libre de la Mustaçaffia," *Boletín de la Sociedad Castellonense de Cultura* (BSCC) 28 (1952) 455-492; for Igualada, see Gabriel Castellà y Raich, *Llibre de la mostaçaferia: Ordinacions de la Vila d'Igualada, segles XIV-XVI* (Igualada 1954); for Palma, see Antonio Pons, *Libre del mostassaf de Mallorca* (Palma 1949); for Valencia, see Francisco Almela y Vives, "El 'Libro del Mustaçaf' y la vida en la ciudad de Valencia a mediados del siglo XVI," BSCC 25 (1949) 1-24; Sevillano Colom (n. 57 above); for Vich, see Arcadio Garcia, "El 'Llibre del mustaçaf' de Vich," *Ausa* (Vich 1955) 2.18-24; for Vila de Catí, see Joan Puig, "El libre del mustaçaf de la Vila de Catí," BSCC 28 (1952) 85-93.

[59] Sevillano Colom, *Valencia urbana* (n. 57 above) 175.

[60] The balance has always been the symbol of *agoranomos*, *muḥtasib*, and *mustasaf* alike. See Jaume Roig's description of a fifteenth-century *mustasaf*, *Spill o libre de consells*, ed. R. Miquel y Planas (Barcelona 1929-1950), lines 7478-7485:

> Lo Mustaçaf,
> sos balançes,
> hi van de mes:
> ans daforar,
> solen mostrar
> triat millor;
> ab aquell for
> ne val sotil.

by municipal ordinances (and recorded in the "Book of the *Mustasaf*") were rigorously adhered to.[61]

Astynomic functions.—Astynomic duties of the *mustasaf* are found in full flower. The regulations stated that "the *mustasaf* watches over . . . and takes care that the roads of the city do not become narrower nor worsen in condition, and that sewage and dung be not put in the streets . . . or in other places within the walls."[62] He was in charge of everything that had to do with building, maintenance, or repair of edifices. The regulations described in minute detail the various types of disputes which could arise from new construction, and only the *mustasaf* was empowered to solve them: "The *mustasaf* by his office ought to go and see and determine the disputes which exist by the nature of the works, and [to see] what the works are, and to give right judgment to the parties, summarily and openly."[63] Some of these building ordinances have a decidedly oriental flavor (indicating the presence of a Muslim population in the town, or at least the residue of Islamic building habits and tastes). One could not, for example, build a window or a flat roof that overlooked a neighbor's house.

All those duties pertaining to sanitation and public health were within the jurisdiction of the *mustasaf*, especially as regards drinking water. There were fines for those who watered their animals at public fountains or who otherwise befouled public water.[64]

Religious and moral functions.—The *mustasaf* literature was most explicit in regard to duties of a religious or moral nature. The *mustasaf* was in charge of the spiritual as well as the physical health of the community, at least in its public manifestations.

Laws providing for the cessation of work on Sundays or holidays were standard in this legislation, and the *mustasaf* was the enforcing officer. Mills, for example, could not run from Saturday vespers through Sunday vespers, and if they did the millers must lose all the grain that they had milled during that time. Further, no oven might function on Sundays or on Good Friday, "so that with all reverence that day of Sunday (or Holy Friday) might be celebrated by all—Christian, Jews, and Saracens."[65]

Moral regulations were particularly in evidence in the duties of Catalan *mustasafs*. The *mustasaf* of Igualada was empowered to impose a fine of twenty *sous* upon any who spoke against Jesus Christ or Mary, or who said

---

[61] Note the price scales for bread and wine (Sevillano Colom, *Valencia urbana* (n. 57 above) 179-181, 182-184). Likewise, the *muḥtasib* generally only checked prices but had no authority to fix them (Cahen and Talbi, n. 30 above, 488).

[62] Sevillano Colom, *Valencia urbana* 178.

[63] *Ibid* 199.

[64] Castellà y Raich (n. 58 above) 53.

[65] Sevillano Colom 203-204.

that they had no power, or who spoke maliciously against God. The Igualada official could impose a similar fine on anyone calling a married woman "cuckold, damsel, whelp, whore, bitch, burro, sow, or other similar vile or denigrating words."[66]

Seventeenth-century documents record that the *mustasaf* of Sabadell, Damiá Llobet, fined a businessman for carrying cloth from a fulling mill on Sunday; the same official fined a tinker for going to Barcelona with a wagonload of kettles on the day of Saint Luke.[67]

Authority over guilds.—The *mustasaf* exercised authority over the craftsmen, and thus over the quality of merchandise, through elected officials of each guild. Thus, he was required "at the beginning of his administration to demand and require the merchants, the heads of trades, arts, and crafts of the city of Valencia that each elect among themselves two virtuous men of their group, or art, or craft, who would swear to guard against and prohibit the doing of any fraud or falsehood by one or several of his trade, art, or craft."[68] If they found such frauds, they were to make the same known to the *mustasaf*, "so that frauds and wrongdoings might be punished" and fines meted out.

The election of two representatives of each trade, called *veedors* (inspectors), was stipulated in a privilege of James I in 1270.[69] These inspectors had no judicial function but acted only in the capacity of experts advising the *mustasaf*.[70] The relationship between *mustasaf* and *veedor* parallels that between *muḥtasib* and *amīn*.

Jurisdiction—The way in which the *mustasaf* judged cases was peculiarly Islamic and was recognized as such at the time. James II of Aragon alluded to this tradition in a charter of 1316:

> We understand on behalf of the masters of the city of Valencia that anciently, earlier than the time of the conquest, it was the custom of this city that the *mustasaf*, summarily and openly, not having received in writing petition or opinion, but by hearing the statements of the disputants concerning the management of works, doors, windows, rain water, medial walls, roads, or other similar disputes, decides by himself or, should doubts occur to him, with

[66] Castellà y Raich 3, 113.

[67] Archivo de la Corona de Aragón, Real Patrimonio, Sig. 1686 (*Cuentas de los mustasafes*): "Item a xviii de dit mes de octubre ha rebut dit Mostassaph de Jacques Calderer, habitant en la vila de Sabadell, quatre sous, y son per averlo trobat lo die de St. Lluch anave a Barcelona ab una carrega de calderes."

[68] Sevillano Colom, *Valencia urbana* 175.

[69] *Ibid* 176.

[70] *Ibid* 218.

the advice of the jurates and of other masters of the city and of others who were [formerly] mustasafs.[71]

Just like the muḥtasib, the mustasaf could initiate a judicial process without one of the disputants seeking justice from him. He not only decided the case summarily, at the place of commission, but executed his own decision as well. This ideal combination of powers was admirably attuned to the pace and demands of economic life.[72]

The method of exacting punishment was precisely that characteristic of the muḥtasib, with the addition of a fine:

> If once or twice bread be found of insufficient weight, that bread will be broken to pieces, at the rate of three loaves per punishment; but if it be found insufficient a third time, the bread . . . will be broken to pieces and lost [to the baker], and she will give as fine five *sous*; and if she cannot give them, the baker will be placed in the pillory in her nightshirt only . . . and will suffer no other punishment to her person or possessions.[73]

Similarly, should a weaver fail to weave the requisite number of threads into the highest grade cloth, he not only was fined but his loom was burned.[74] In the making of rope shoes, if the product did not contain the required complement of stitches and loops of cords, the shoes were burned.[75] So also, wine and milk that had been mixed with water were to be poured out on the ground. Resistance or disobedience to the mustasaf merited imprisonment, but corporal punishment was not customary.[76]

---

[71] *Ibid* 201. The privilege authorizing the office of mustasaf in Vich (1366) also is explicit in regard to oral process ("non receptis in scriptis peticione . . . et ea omnia determinent et decidant verbo tantum"); see Arcadio Garcia, "La actuación procesal del mustaçaf," *Ausa* 2 (1955-56) 307.

[72] Garcia 308 breaks down the informal procedure of mustasaf into stages: first, the pertinent parties gathered in the office of the mustasaf, or at the place where the claim originated; then, the disputants told their stories, and the mustasaf called for whatever testimony or proofs he deemed necessary; sentence was then passed without further ado, in the same place and at the same time, and—in Vich—in the presence of a notary. The notary would not defeat the purposes of oral process; he would record the fines (see n. 67 above) but would not write down any testimony or evidence. An identical procedure was described to me by the khalīfa al-muḥtasib of Tetuan in 1962, except that no notary was present at the hearing.

[73] Sevillano Colom, *Valencia urbana* 182.

[64] *Ibid*. 213.

[75] *Ibid*. 234.

[76] *Ibid*. 280. The council of Valencia wrote to its counterpart in Barcelona in 1371 that "as for corporal punishment, we say to you that we do not know nor find that ever such has happened." But the councillors admitted that the mustasaf did have this power.

The *mustasafs* of Valencia and other towns governed according to the Fueros of Valencia were annually elected officers of the municipality, chosen by lot.[77] In Valencia, the *mustasaf* was one of the nine principal magistrates of the city, as illustrated by his position in the processional order for state occasions.[78] No one in the city was exempt from the *mustasaf's* jurisdiction, as the council of Valencia stated in a reply to a letter concerning the office sent by the council of Barcelona in 1371:

> Likewise you request clarification as to whether any person be exempt from [the jurisdiction of] said office or whether it is general to all people of whatever condition, law, or office; and in this regard you specifically mention clerics, moneyers, Jews, and Saracens. We reply to you that said office is so general that it provides for no exemption for said persons or others, for it is common to all persons, ecclesiastical and secular, of whatever law, office, condition, or status, foreigners or citizens.[79]

Even though other officials were forbidden to interfere in the *mustasaf's* jurisdiction, the nature of the office and its involvement in cases *ratione materiae* meant that the *mustasaf* would in fact come into frequent jurisdictional disputes with other judicial and executive authorities. No matter how specific the regulations, the inevitable *et aliorum consimilium* of the privileges allowed him to broaden his jurisdiction by analogy and, by the same token, other officials just as easily trespassed the imprecise limits of his own jurisdiction. In Valencia, most of the *mustasaf's* jurisdictional disputes were with the Civil Justiciar.[80] Moreover in Valencia, owing to situations arising from irrigation canals, the *mustasaf* was frequently embroiled with irrigation officials. Irrigation water flowing onto roads was a problem for the *cequiers*—irrigation officials—of the various canals; but the roads, their cleanliness, and suitability for pedestrians were a typical astynonic concern of the *mustasaf*. In 1396 the council was informed that the roads had been befouled owing to the neglect of the *cequiers* and that the *mustasaf* was too busy to enforce the regulations. It was decided to appoint some special road guards, the *mustasaf* to have charge of the appointment.[81] The canal of Na Rovella flowed directly through the city and furnished water to the shops of numerous tradesmen, such as weavers and tanners. Insofar as they were users of water,

---

[77] Sevillano Colom, "De la institutión del mustaçaf de Barcelona, de Mallorca y de Valencia," *Anuario de historia del derecho español* 23 (1953) 530.

[78] *Ibid.* 535. Two jurates came first along with the Criminal Justiciar, then two more jurates and the Civil Justiciar, then the two remaining jurates and the *mustasaf*.

[79] Sevillano Colom, *Valencia urbana* (n. 57 above) 279.

[80] *Ibid.* 394.

[81] Archivo Municipal de Valencia, Manuals de Consell, 21, fol. 40 (14 August 1396).

these artisans were under the jurisdiction of the *cequier* of Na Rovella and ultimately the governor of the kingdom; but as industrial producers and tradesmen, they had to submit to the *mustasaf*. In a case of 1414 it was held that the *cequier* and *mustasaf* had joint jurisdiction over the problems of the canal and the governor, none.[82] The matter was further complicated in the case of mills. Mills were considered *regalia* and hence were under the jurisdiction of the royal bailiff; but as water users the millers were responsible to the *cequiers*, and as producers of flour or participants in the textile industry, they answered to the *mustasaf*.

The *mustasaf* of Valencia was the model for the establishment of the office in other cities. Doubtless in many of the larger towns of the kingeom there was some continuity with the preconquest Islamic administration. In other, smaller towns the office was diffused through a process that has been called the "territorialization" of the Fueros,[83] whereby the law of Valencia, capital, was adopted in all parts of the realm.

Another secondary diffusion, from Valencia to Catalonia, was the result of a quite different process. In this case the king deliberately created the office of *mustasaf* in order to improve local administration. Thus, *mustasafs* were established by royal privilege in such cities as Barcelona (1339) and Villafranca de Panadés (1390).[84]

Once implanted, the *mustasafia* was as successful in Catalonia as it was in Valencia and continued in force until the office was abolished throughout eastern Spain when, at the beginning of the eighteenth century, the Bourbons revoked the Fueros of the lands of Aragon.[85]

The *mustasaf*, then, was a carbon copy of the *muḥtasib* whom he emulated in duties, judicial procedure, and jurisdiction.[86] Indeed, in those crafts—and there were many—whose technologies were derived from the Islamic world the *mustasaf* continued to encforce exactly the same regulations as Andalusí *muḥtasibs* had centuries before. To cite only one example, the specifications for manufacturing cork-soled shoes, called *alcorques*, were the

---

[82] Archivo del Reino de Valencia, Gobernación, 2209, 30th hand, fol. 47v (7 December 1414).

[83] See Manuel Dualde Serrano, *Fori antiqui valentiae* (Madrid 1950-1967) xii n. 5.

[84] Sevillano Colom, "Institución del mustaçaf" (n. 77 above) 531-532; Próspero Bofarull y Mascaró, *Colección de documentos inéditos del Archivo General de la Corona de Aragón*, 8.325.

[85] Even after the disappearance of the official, the books of the *Mustasaf* continued to remain in vigor for many years—until the end of the century in Palma. See *Capitols per lo exercici de la jurisdicció del Magnifich Mostesaph, decretats per su Illustrissima del Señor Virrey à XXXI Agost de MDCLXXVIII* [1678], Madrid, En la Imprenta Real, any 1796.

[86] Certain aspects of the *mustasaf's* jurisdiction, such as the implementation of religious strictures that obviously had nothing to do with Islam, are examples of stimulus or idea diffusion; see A. L. Kroeber, "Stimulus Diffusion," *American Anthropologist* 42 (1940) 1-20.

same in the *Book of Ḥisba* composed by the Malagan *muḥtasib* al-Saqaṭī in the eleventh century as in the fourteenth-century regulations of the *mustasaf* of Valencia.[87]

To recapitulate: the two aspects of municipal services, economic and sanitary-moral, were first united in the late classical *agoranomos* who assumed the duties of the *astynomos*. A market officer of the local Semitic communities of the Near East, with attenuated jurisdiction, became the model for the Umayyad *ṣāḥib al-sūq*. Although the *ṣāḥib al- sūq* was replaced by a more specifically Islamic official—the *muḥtasib*—in early ʿAbbāsid times, there was a lag in institutional transition in Al-Andalus which was reflected in the adoption of a *ṣāḥib al-sūq* in the Asturo-Leonese kingdom. The fully developed *muḥtasib* was the model and direct antecedent of the Valencian *mustasaf*, which first appeared in the thirteenth century. From Valencia, the office was diffused again, throughout the kingdom of Valencia by the uniform imposition of the Fueros, and into Catalonia by direct royal action.

The diffusion of *ḥisba* was not limited to the Islamic West. Two other medieval Christian states, in close contact with the Islamic world—Tyre and Cyprus—also developed Latinized *muḥtasibs*.

Tyre was divided into three quarters, two ruled by the King of Jerusalem and one by the Venetians. The king, however, imposed the jurisdiction of a *muḥtasib* upon the entire city, causing complaints by the Venetians and finally the designation of their own *muḥtasib*. Thus, in 1243 the bailiff of the Venetians in Syria, Marsiglio Giorgio, wrote to the Doge:

> The king who was [reigning] at that time,[88] or the bailiff who had the power of the kingdom unjustly, reserved a portion and imposed a tax upon all those of our quarter who sold wine, oil, candles, and meat and who were apothecaries selling spices and other goods, which [taxes] are collected in all our lordship and jurisdiction. Any tax is imposed on the city of Tyre on the grounds that it pertains to the said citizens in common, but not if our consent and that of our viscount is withheld. And in our quarter we impose and exact taxes freely, just as the king in his two parts imposes and exacts. And let it be known that in the time of the aforementioned King John, a certain [officer] was established who was called *matasep*, which in our language is called justiciar, who imposed taxes and exacted them in our quarter as well as in his two parts; and this has lasted up to our time. But now, by the grace of God, we have set ours

---

[87] Jaime Oliver Asín, "'Quercus' en la España musulmana," *Al-Andalus* 24 (1959) 138 n. 2. The comparison of the *adab al-muḥtasib* and *Llibres del mustasaf*, craft by craft, is a fertile field for further research.

[88] Jean de Brienne. See W. Heyd, *Histoire du commerce du Levant au moyen-âge* (Amsterdam 1959) 1.336.

over our quarter, John of Palermo by name, a Venetian, who does all the aforementioned things as we command and lay down.[89]

The description of the Cyprus official gives a more precise definition of the duties of the office:

> The office of *mathessep* is that he ought to go in the morning to the market places, that is to say, to the butcher shop and where bread and wine and other things are sold, and to see to it that no fraud be done by the sellers and regraters, and that bread be not lacking at the market place . . . . [And he should see to] the weight of the bread; [and he ought] to mind the things which are sold at a fixed price, particularly bread and wine, flesh and fish, according to the ordinance publicly promulgated. And then he ought to make a turn through the town, looking out for the above-mentioned things and [seeing] that no misdemeanors be done, such as rapes and thefts and brawls, which he ought to find and resolve.[90]

The *mathessep* of Cyprus carried out the market and moral-police functions characteristic of all *muḥtasibs*. He appears not to have had the power of summary punishment, however, but had instead to bring offenders before the viscount.[91] The office survived into the time of Venetian rule (1489-1570), when the *mathiessep* [sic] was entrusted with the "superintendence of the markets, prices, and correctional police."[92]

The *muḥtasib* would appear to have been admirably suited to the requirements of medieval town life. The office, amoeba-like, filled up jurisdictional voids created by the original lack of definition in Islamic law. Europeans of various cultures, it has been seen, were quick to adopt the office and make it serve different social needs admirably. Yet there is evidence that in the Islamic world itself the office of *muḥtasib* was less than a full success. As early as the eleventh century al-Mawardī reported that although the early imams had executed the duties of the *ḥisba* for the common good, "the office declined in the people's estimation when rulers neglected it and conferred it on men of no repute whose object was to profit and get bribes."[93] The formerly prestigious office had become in the fifteenth-century Mamluk kingdom a minor office, an easy prey to venality and corruption.[94]

---

[89] G. L. Tafel and G. M. Thomas, *Urkunden zur Alteren Handels- und Staatsgeschichte der Republik Venedig* (Vienna 1856) 2.359-360.

[90] *Assizes de Jerusalem* 2: *Abrege*, ed. Beugnot (Paris 1843) 243. Beugnot thought that *mathessep* was a corruption of Greek, *mathetes*, "disciple," since the *mathessep* was an adjunct of the viscount (note b).

[91] *Ibid.* 244.

[92] S. Romanin, *Storia documentata di Venezia* (Venice 1857) 6.281.

[93] Amedroz (n. 46 above) 101.

[94] Ira Lapidus, *Muslim Cities in the Later Middle Ages* (Cambridge, Mass. 1967) 147, 275.

How is this contrast between the healthy vitality of the borrowed Christian institution and decadent Islamic one to be explained? My impression is that the answer lies in the different natures of European and Islamic towns and the way they were ruled. In the Islamic system, characterized by G. E. von Grunebaum as "theocratic authoritarianism," power was derived from above. Further, when one considers that there was no distinction made in Islamic law between municipal jurisdictions, it becomes clear how Islamic cities were unable to develop municipal institutions that had enough internal consistency to survive the tenure of a weak or corrupt incumbent.[95] All of the municipal magistracies derived from the *qaḍā* were susceptible to jurisdictional ambivalence that even in the best of times made their authority hard to impose unequivocally.

In contrast, the medieval European city-state, those of eastern Spain included, elaborated a system of municipal government which, in its mature form in the thirteenth and fourteenth centuries, allowed a rather broad "popular" participation in the formation of public policy, which lent the power of consensual authority to the elected magistrates.[96] Compared to the relative lack of civic spirit in the Islamic world, the cohesive nature of urban life in Europe made the daily chores of governance easier to carry out. In addition, the European towns developed a comprehensive body of distinctively urban law, interpreted by urban lawyers and tried in urban courts, which gave the town offices—the derived "ḥisba" jurisdiction included—a much more formal quality than their Islamic counterparts had. As grounds for further comparative study, it might also be suggested that the role of economic life in the value systems of European and Muslim townsmen differed substantially. There is a distinct strain in medieval European thought that commerce is an aspect of life which, for the good of both public weal and men's souls, must be controlled by public authority (witness the strictures on usury). One does not notice in Islamic political thought any such compulsion, beyond the constraints of simple morality, to trammel commerce for the good of men's souls (e.g., the antipathy to price-fixing). Further study, relating these broad areas of social and economic value systems to individual institutions, will add much to our understanding of medieval urban life.[97]

---

[95] See G. E. von Grunebaum, *Medieval Islam* (Chicago 1946, repr. 1961) 166-167.

[96] See John H. Mundy and Peter Riesenberg, *The Medieval Town* (Princeton 1958) 86-87

[97] Too recent for detailed analysis in this paper is Benjamin R. Foster's article, "Agoranomos and Muḥtasib," *Journal of Economic and Social History of the Orient*, 13 (1970), 128-144. Foster surveys the literature of market inspection in the Near East prior to the Islamic conquests, but he fails to explore the possibility of transitional, nonimperial officials in the native communities—to my mind, the only avenue of research capable of yielding any new insights into this institutional transition.

Department of History
University of Texas
Austin, Texas 78712, U.S.A.

THE LITERARY MAGIC OF "WIð FÆRSTICE"

•

by Howell D. Chickering, Jr.

In the past the literary worth of the Anglo-Saxon poetic charms has usually been defined as the degree to which they appear to contain relics of pre-Christian Germanic customs, beliefs, and narratives.[1] *Wið Færstice* or "Against A Sudden Stitch" (i. e., rheumatic pain), one of the three or four charms apparently richest in pagan references, has often been admired for its literary qualities. Kemp Malone spoke for most students of the charms when he called it "a little masterpiece of its kind."[2]

---

[1] The twelve charms commonly regarded as poetry are edited by E. V. K. Dobbie, *The Anglo-Saxon Minor Poems*, The Anglo-Saxon Poetic Records 6 (New York 1942) 116-128. The text of *Wið Færstice* is quoted from Dobbie's edition, 122-123. The most useful collection of all the charms, prose and poetry, is by Godfrid Storms, *Anglo-Saxon Magic* (The Hague 1948). Other collections are by J. H. G. Grattan and Charles Singer, *Anglo-Saxon Magic and Medicine* (Oxford 1952); Felix Grendon, "The Anglo-Saxon Charms," *Journal of American Folklore* (*JAF*) 22 (1909) 105-237; and T. O. Cockayne, *Leechdoms, Wortcunning, and Starcraft of Early England*, Rolls Series, 3 vols. (London 1864-1866) reissued with an introduction by Charles Singer (London 1961). An excellent bibliography to 1961 is found in Wilfrid Bonser, *The Medical Background of Anglo-Saxon England* (London 1963) XVII-XXXV. Discussion of the place of the charms in early medieval medical practice may be found in Bonser 13-113; Grattan and Singer, pt. 1 (3-94); Lynn Thorndike, *A History of Magic and Experimental Science* 1 (New York 1923) 719-741.

The idea that the older and more pagan a charm, the better it is, is implicit in Storms's system of classification: "We start with those that may be regarded as of true Germanic origin, free from classical or Christian influences" (129). Most of the poetical charms occur early in his list; *Wið Færstice* is no. 2. Francis P. Magoun, Jr., makes a similar judgment about "der geistige Wert" of the charms in offering us "einen kostbaren, sonst unerreichbaren Blick" into the earlier Anglo-Saxon era, in "Zu den ae. Zaubersprüchen," *Archiv* 171 (1937) 17. The shortcomings of the general approach of using "the unknowable unknown" to date and explain the known, and the history of the attitudes behind it, have been traced by E. G. Stanley in "The Search for Anglo-Saxon Paganism," *Notes and Queries*, n. s. 11 (1964) 205-209, 242-250, 282-287, 324-331; 12 (1965) 9-17, 203-207, 285-293, 322-327.

[2] Kemp Malone, "The Old English Period (to 1100)," *A Literary History of England*, ed. A. C. Baugh (New York 1948) 42. The charm is also discussed by E. E. Wardale, *Chapters on Old English Literature* (London 1935) 23-25; C. W. Kennedy, *The Earliest English Poetry: A Critical Survey* (London 1943) 8-10; S. B. Greenfield, *A Critical History of Old English Literature* (New York 1965) 193-196; C. L. Wrenn, *A Study of Old English Literature* (London 1967) 166-169.

Wið færstice feferfuige and seo reade netele, ðe þurh ærn inwyxð, and
wegbrade; wyll in buteran.
    Hlude wæran hy, la, hlude,   ða hy ofer þone hlæw ridan,
    Wæran anmode,   ða hy ofer land ridan.
5 Scyld ðu ðe nu, þu ðysne nið   genesan mote.
    Ut, lytel spere,   gif her inne sie!
    Stod under linde,   under leohtum scylde,
    Þær ða mihtigan wif   hyra mægen beræddon
    And hy gyllende   garas sændan;
10 Ic him oðerne   eft wille sændan,
    Fleogende flane   forane togeanes.
    Ut, lytel spere,   gif hit her inne sy!
    Sæt smið,   sloh seax lytel,
    * * * iserna,   wundrum swiðe.
15 Ut, lytel spere,   gif her inne sy!
    Syx smiðas sætan,   wælspera worhtan.
    Ut, spere,   næs in, spere!
    Gif her inne sy   isernes dæl,
    hægtessan geweorc,   hit sceal gemyltan.
20 Gif ðu wære on fell scoten   oððe wære on flæsc scoten
    Oððe wære on blod scoten
    Oððe wære on lið scoten,   næfre ne sy ðin lif atæsed;
    Gif hit wære esa gescot   oððe hit wære ylfa gescot
    Oððe hit wære hægtessan gescot,   nu ic wille ðin helpan.
25 Þis ðe to bote esa gescotes,   ðis ðe to bote ylfa gescotes,
    Ðis ðe to bote hægtessan gescotes;   ic ðin wille helpan.
    Fleoh þær * * *   on fyrgenheafde.
    Hal westu,   helpe ðin drihten!
Nim þonne þæt seax, ado on wætan.

[Against a sudden stitch, feverfew and the red nettle that grows into the
house and waybroad: boil in butter.
    Loud were they, lo, loud, when they rode over the mound,
    Were resolute (of one fierce mind) when they rode over the ground.
5 Shield yourself now, that you may escape this evil.
    Out, little spear, if you be in here!
    (He, or I) stood under linden-wood, under a light shield,
    Where the mighty women talked up their strength
    And sent their screaming spears.
10 I want to send them back another,
    A flying arrow, from the forefront, against them.
    Out, little spear, if it be in here!
    A smith sat, struck a little knife,
    * * * of irons, exceptionnally strong.
15 Out, little spear, if you be in here!
    Six smiths sat, worked war-spears (slaughter-spears).

Out, spear, not in, spear!
If a piece of iron be here within,
Work of witch, it must melt away (*or* heat must melt it).
20 If you were shot in the skin, or were shot in the flesh,
Or were shot in the blood,
Or were shot in the body, never may your life be injured.
If it were the shot of gods, or it were the shot of elves,
Or it were the shot of witch, now I will be your help.
25 This be thy remedy for the shot of gods, this thy remedy for the shot
of elves,
This thy remedy for the shot of witch; I will be your help.
Fly away there * * * to the mountaintop!
Be well! God be your help!
Take then the knife, plunge it in the liquid.]

The first seventeen lines of the poem (lines 3-19), couched in a mysterious elevated style, constitute its principal claim to Malone's description. But what is its kind, and why is it a masterpiece? Commentators disagree about the exact nature of the narrative allusions in this so-called "epic introduction." Opinion is divided over whether the "mighty women" are *wæl-cyrige* in the sense of Valkyries, that is, Woden's "choosers of the slain," or simply witches; whether or not the riders in lines 3-4 are members of Woden's Wild Hunt; and whether the smith in line 13 is Weland. More important, there is no convincing explanation of what kind of defensive magic is used in this "epic introduction."[3] In fact, it could be said that this charm epitomizes the methodological difficulties that literary scholars face in dealing with an Anglo-Saxon anthropological document. These difficulties are increased when its purpose is primarily medicinal, and when its antiquity, paganism, and textual integrity can vary with their own assumptions.[4] It is possible

[3] The only full-length article on the charm is Wilhelm Horn, "Der altenglische Zauberspruch gegen den Hexenschuss," *Probleme der Englischen Sprache und Kultur: Festschrift Johannes Hoops*, ed. Wolfgang Keller (Heidelberg 1925) 88-104. He claims that the first seventeen lines are older than the rest, and that the whole charm gains its force mainly from the power of iron, in most cultures, to break spells and protect against spirits. He sees a progression in the strength of the iron weapons referred to: arrow, little knife, little spear, war-spear. Other explanations are discussed below.

[4] The standard modern reference work on Germanic heathen religion is Jan de Vries, *Altgermanische Religionsgeschichte*, Grundriss der germanischen Philologie 12.1-2 (Berlin 1956-1957). The early Continental evidence is discussed in 1.83-164. For an account of Anglo-Saxon heathenism from an older point of view, see E. A. Phillipson, *Germanisches Heidentum bei den Angelsachsen* (Leipzig 1929). The principal documentary and place-name evidence is given by Sir Frank Stenton, in *Anglo-Saxon England*, ed. 2 (Oxford 1947) 96-103; further place-names have been adduced by Margaret Gelling, "Place-Names and Anglo-Saxon Paganism," *University of Birmingham Historical Journal* 7 (1962) 7-26. E.O.G. Turville-Petre lucidly discusses the difficulties of using the Old Norse literary sour-

that the usual treatment of this "epic introduction" has impeded both our literary and anthropological understanding of *Wið Færstice*. In what follows, I first argue that the concept itself needs re-examination. Then (section II) I explore the possible kinds of supernatural power available to the users of this charm, using the comparative method so far as Anglo-Saxon cultural history allows. It is important to acknowledge what cannot be known about the historical and sociological context of such a charm before trying to describe its magic.[5] A careful examination of the pagan allusions section (III) suggests that there probably is no epic or mythic narrative behind this murky, portentous "introduction." Rather, the literary value of these lines is more

---

ces comparatively in *Myth and Religion of the North: The Religion of Ancient Scandinavia* (New York 1964) 1-34. One can see the highly inferential nature of the study of Anglo-Saxon paganism by comparing J. S. Ryan, "Othin in England," *Folklore* 74 (1963) 460-480, with Audrey L. Meaney, "Woden in England: A Reconsideration of the Evidence," *Folklore* 77 (1966) 105-115.

The manuscripts of the charms date from the tenth to the twelfth centuries: see the articles listed under "Folklore: Charms, Headings to Charms and Directions for their Use," in N. R. Ker, *Catalogue of Manuscripts containing Anglo-Saxon* (Oxford 1957) 523. The dating of the contents of the charms has been more variable. For instance, Storms asserts that "the charm formulas are the oldest relics of Anglo-Saxon and Germanic literature. Some of them antedate *Widsið* by hundreds, in certain cases perhaps by thousands of years" (11). The extant texts are often considered diluted or distorted versions of older charms, as in Hilda R. Ellis Davidson, *Gods and Myths of Northern Europe* (Baltimore 1964) 63, and Gustav Ehrismann, *Geschichte der Deutschen Literatur bis zum Ausgang des Mittelalters* 1 (Munich 1918) 48. Magoun (n. 1 above) points out the steep difficulties in reconstructing these faded (*verblasst*) remains, but does not regard them as insuperable.

Recently Karl Schneider, "Die strophischen Strukturen und heidnisch-religiösen Elemente der ae. Zauberspruchgruppe 'wið þēofðe,'" *Festschrift zum 75. Geburtstag von Theodore Spira*, ed. H. Viebrock and W. Erzgraber (Heidelberg 1961) 38-56, has given new life to the older reconstructive approach by free emendation and rearrangement of the texts. But the textual integrity of Old English poetical texts, in the absence of positive paleographical evidence to the contrary, is now generally accepted. Dobbie (85) defends the unity of the two parts of *Wið Færstice* against older interpretations; the integrity of other questionable texts has been upheld by J. A. Burrow, "An Approach to the *Dream of the Rood*," *Neophilologus* 43 (1959) 130; Kemp Malone, "Notes on Gnomic Poem B of the Exeter Book," *Medium Aevum (MA)* 12 (1943) 65-67; and R. MacGregor Dawson, "The Structure of the Old English Gnomic Poems," *Journal of English Germanic Philology* 61 (1962) 14-22.

[5] The very definition of a charm may need to vary with its cultural context. For instance, Thomas A. Sebeok adopts J. Grimm's definition of charms as *Segen*, "Formulas in use outside the Church, of both Christian and non-Christian sort, to which a supernatural effect and indeed mostly one of a protecting, healing kind is ascribed," "The Structure and Content of Cheremis Charms," *Language in Culture and Society*, ed. Dell Hymes (New York 1964) 356. Harold L. Klagstad, Jr., "Great Russian Charm Structure," *Indiana Slavic Studies* 2 (1958) 135 and 142-143 n. 2, rejects this definition "on a functional basis" and prefers Potebnja's "a verbal representation of the comparison of a given or purposely produced phenomenon with one which is desired, having as its aim the production of the latter."

comprehensible when they are seen as a dramatic verbal performance, in which the very act of saying creates its own magic. This is often casually said to be true of all verbal magic, but usually on the basis of disputable abstract theories about "the primacy of the word" in "the primitive mind" instead of upon the actual features of the words that might create their primacy.[6] In section IV, I try to show how the magic and poetry of these lines are the same. Not every act of magical saying is a masterpiece of its kind.

I

The "epic introduction," which is found almost exclusively in poetic charms, has usually been defined as a mythological or epic precedent for the curing of the ailment at hand. Felix Grendon describes it thus: "Among the earliest Indo-European charms, the actual conjuration of the disease-spirit was preceded by a short narrative, in epic manner, of deeds performed by some god or hero. . . . In the two Old High German and in many of the Hindu incantations, it will be observed that the recitation of the mythological precedent frequently concludes with a precise formula, supposedly uttered by the deity or hero who appears in the incident. The potency of a phrase having been proved by its use under supernatural auspices, the conjurer believes that recital of the same formula will insure the attainment of his end." Grendon applies the term to the beginning of *Wið Færstice* as does Storms, who also compares it to the Second Merseburg charm.[7] In this view, the concluding formula would be the strophic refrain, *Ut, lytel spere, gif her inne sie!* (lines 6, 12, 15), while *Stod* (line 7), which can be either first or third person, would be translated as "he stood," referring to the hero or god who had withstood the attack of *ða mihtigan wif* and their *gyllende garas* in the mythic story. The magician would take his power from this figure, just as

---

[6] For a skeptical critique of anthropological theories about primitive religion and mentality, see E. E. Evans-Pritchard, *Theories of Primitive Religion* (Oxford 1965).

[7] Grendon 110-112, 114; Storms 144-145 (see n. 1 above). The grounds for comparison of thematic elements among the charms in the Indo-European languages were established by Adalbert Kuhn, "Indische und Germanische Segensprüche," *Zeitschrift für vergleichende Sprachforschung* 13 (1863-64) 49-80, 113-157. Grendon notes that "charms with narrative passages in heroic style may be found also in Celtic, Slavonic, and Greco-Italic languages, and also in the Finno-Ugric group" (111-112). John Abercrombie, in *The Pre- and Proto-Historic Finns . . . with the Magic Songs of the West Finns*, 2 vols. (London 1898) 2.42 has noted that in the Lettish charms sometimes just "the recitation of the story was itself sufficient for the purpose of banishing the evil." He prints four versions of one charm against a stitch caused by magic arrows that has a long narrative introduction similar to *Wið Færstice* (1.335-342).

the widespread Anglo-Saxon charm against theft of cattle takes its power
from Christ:

> Bæðleem hatte seo buruh   þe Crist on acænned wæs,
> Seo is gemærsod   geond ealne middangeard;
> Swa þyos dæd for monnum   mære gewurþe
> Þurh þa haligan Cristes rode![8]

This too is considered an "epic introduction," and Grattan and Singer explain it thus: "The magician narrates a sacred event thought to bear some
analogy to that with which he is faced. The meaning is that, as the birth-
place of Christ and His crucifixion are known everywhere, so may the cattle-
theft be made manifest" (183 n. 1).

These explanations treat the introductory narration as a magical analogy.
This treatment is dependent upon a larger notion of the kind of magic presumably at work, and that notion is clearly Frazer's "homeopathic," which
"is founded on the association of ideas by similarity."[9] But to classify the
"epic introduction" as homeopathic magic does not take us very far in explaining the interplay in *Wið Færstice* between the "mythical" references
and the strophic refrain, which has a suspicious look of ritual. Nor does
this explanation consider the total curative situation—especially the conjurer himself and the relation between the herb concoction and the words
of the charm. Frazer has little to say about verbal magic, even when treating "The Public Expulsion of Evils" in *The Scapegoat*.[10]

A more recent anthropologist of religion, Gerardus van der Leeuw, has
tried to provide a comprehensive explanation for the "epic introduction"
in his article, "Die sogenannte 'epische Einleitung' der Zauberformeln,"[11]
where he treats it not as the magic of analogy but as part of the actual event
that the magician wishes to bring about. In van der Leeuw's argument the
magic ritual is seen as though it were a religious rite. Using mainly Egyptian and Indian examples, he argues that narrative references to events in
the semihistorical or mythical past take on a present reality in such charms.

---

[8] "For Loss of Cattle," no. 5 in Dobbie 123, lines 3-6; repeated in substance in Dobbie
no. 10.

[9] Sir James Frazer, *The Magic Art and the Evolution of Kings* 1 (London 1911) 52-54;
pt. 1 of *The Golden Bough*.

[10] Pt. 7 of *The Golden Bough* (London 1914) 109-169.

[11] Gerardus van der Leeuw, "Die sogenannte 'epische Einleitung' der Zauberformeln,"
Zeitschrift für Religionspsychologie 6 (1933) 161-180. For a brief account of van der Leeuw's
conception of magic and its dependence on Freud's notion of "omnipotence of thought,"
that is, a presumed similarity between neurotic thinking and primitive mentality, see Evans-
Pritchard (n. 6 above) 41ff. Claude Lévi-Strauss, "The Sorcerer and His Magic," *Structural Anthropology* (New York 1963), assumes a similar psychological analogy.

This would mean, in this charm, that the withstanding of the attack and the sending back of a spear should not be regarded as a story fragment, but as part of the charm rite. In van der Leeuw's view, it is this representational aspect of the charm that contains its magic and causes the repetition of the events in the myth.[12] For *Wið Færstice* this would mean that *stod* should be translated as "*I* stood under linden-wood" rather than "he." Morton W. Bloomfield appears to follow van der Leeuw's conception of such charms when he so translates the verb, and suggests that the speaker of this charm "is taking up the mask of a mythological or heroic character," and that "the magician identifies himself" with the narrative episode.[13]

This view gives us a coherent passage recited by a single speaker at one time and place. Such an explanation has the important advantage of emphasizing the words of the charm and the role of the magician who says them, yet it also puts a difficult twist on both, since if we wish to know what, or who, the magician "becomes" when he "identifies with" this episode, we must first know what the episode is, and that, as Bloomfield says, "is not clear to us" (540). Unless we can assume some lost story, we are bound within a circular definition of the meaning of the ritual. There is a second difficulty, too, in that this explanation is purely psychological and defines the function of this part of the charm only in relation to the magician's mind. It would be better if an explanation of its allusive meanings did not depend upon such an unknown as the Anglo-Saxon exorcist's own understanding of his magic.

There are no such difficulties in understanding the second part of the charm (usually taken as lines 20 and following). Scholars generally agree that it has a simple serial structure of a widespread type. The anatomical catalogue, the *ðis ðe to bote* triplet answering the triplet of possible causes, and the "throwing away" action at the end all have many analogies in other healing charms, such as the Anglo-Saxon "For Delayed Birth" (Dobbie, no 6) and the Second Merseburg charm.[14] However, in the first part of the charm no two scholars have seen the same likeness. For Grendon, the apparent narrative interjected between the conjuring refrains is a story of earlier retaliations by the exorcist; that is, simple defensive magic by analogy. For Storms it is a story of the origin of the pain and a testimony of the exorcist's personal mana gained through his learning "the origins of things." For Skemp it is a fragmented story that stage by stage, gives the true secret name to the *spere*: a naming charm that proceeds by an alternate naming of the object and its

---

[12] Van der Leeuw, especially 171-175.

[13] M. W. Bloomfield, "The Form of *Deor*," *Publications of the Modern Language Association* 79 (1964) 540.

[14] The possible connection of such series (often triplets) with the Old Icelandic *ljóðaháttr* is explored by F. P. Magoun, Jr., "Strophische Überreste in den altenglischen Zaubersprüchen," *Englische Studien* 72 (1937) 1-6.

ancestry.[15] Taken at face value, the lines could possess all these qualities and more. Their affinities with other types of charm do not let us settle on a single structural type, quite apart from the theoretical difficulties of so typing Anglo-Saxon charms.[16]

The obvious alternative to a structural comparison would be an analysis of the role of the charm in its immediate cultural context. We do not, however, know enough about the physical setting and social meaning of such charm performances to arrive at a Functionalist or a Contextualist explanation of this "epic introduction."[17] This seriously hampers a modern anthropological approach to this charm, since, after E. E. Evans-Pritchard's classic study, *Witchcraft, Oracles, and Magic Among the Azande* (1937), most cultural anthropologists agree that any full explanation of magic must include its total social context.[18]

With so many contexts lacking, let us assume that the particulars of the charm itself contain its magic. This assumption is based on current anthropological thinking about magic as a world-wide phenomenon. Magical operations may be defined very simply as stereotyped formulas or actions that influence events in the physical world. To a believer in magic, this "physical world" includes supernatural causation, invisible mental forces, and the like. Magic is itself a force in this world, rather than an invocation of deific forces from a world elsewhere (as in the usual definition of the "epic introduction"). As Lévi-Strauss puts it : "Magical operations [to the magically-minded man] appear to him as additions to the objective order of the universe. They are part of the sequence of natural events."[19] The believer in magic does not have to have a special primitive mentality; to him the use of a magical technique or material is as scientific as the use of a lever to move a rock. Each must be used correctly for its force to produce the desired result. Given this

[15] Grendon 214, Storms 144-149 (see n. 1 above); A. R. Skemp, "The Old English Charms," *Modern Language Review* 7 (1911) 289-292.

[16] For a discussion of the possibilities and problems of structual analysis in folklore and linguistics, see Sebeok (n. 5 above) 357-359.

[17] On the importance of contextual information in the nanalysis fo folk texts, see Alan Dundes, "Texts, Texture, and Context," *Southwest Folklore Quarterly* 27 (1964) 251-265, and Roger D. Abrahams, "Introductory Remarks to a Rhetorical Theory of Folklore," JAF 81 (1968) 143-158.

[18] For the current anthropological approach, see John Middleton, *Magic, Witchcraft, and Curing* (Garden City 1967) x. When a clear context is lacking, as it is for this ancient text, the tendency has been for folklore scholars to fall back on an older definition of magic which polarizes it against religion or science, and which characterizes magic as either a pseudoscience or pseudoreligion occurring at an early stage in the history of the culture. Some difficulties in these tendentious definitions, even as held by the great theorists Tylor, Frazer, Durkheim, and Malinowski, have been suggested by Murray and Rosalie Wax in "The Notion of Magic," *Current Anthropology* 4 (1963) 495-518.

[19] Claude Lévi-Strauss, *The Savage Mind* (Chicago 1966) 220-221.

definition, the question of the charm's meaning now becomes: what are the magical forces in it and how are they used? We can look at the magician, the poetic text, and the herbal rite. Herbs are treated in many Anglo-Saxon charms and recipes as though they had inherent magical powers of protection and alleviation. These powers, to which I will return below, are not clearly distinguished from what we should call their nonmagical medicinal qualities. The power of the magician is a more complicated question.

II

Little is clear about the sort of person who could be expected to speak this charm. There is no sure way of determining whether he would be a professional physician (OE, *læce*), a pagan magician, a Christian priest or exorcist, or an ordinary layman. We have no account of leeches as a class of person, but must infer their activities from recipes, prescriptions, and passing references. Leeches probably were literate, but manuscript drawings do not show them as tonsured, and usually the depiction is copied from classical sources. "Of the status and character of these men," write Grattan and Singer, "we know almost nothing" (17). The term *læce-seax* "leech's knife," which occurs in Alfred's translation of Gregory's *Cura Pastoralis* as a rendering of *ferrum medicinale* (Bonser 98) may indicate a forerunner of the familiar barber-physician who bled the sick. Such a person, however, might as easily have been a pagan warlock using a sacred knife among those unconverted whose socio-religious rituals, such as eating and dancing upon graves, and horse sacrifice, are damned as devil-worship and the work of witches in Ælfric's homilies and the Penitentials.[20] In contrast, the leech in Bede's *Ecclesiastical History* who cured the scabby head of the dumb youth blessed with speech by Bishop John of Hexham (5.2) and the physicians who could not cure a tumor on the eyelid of the monk at Dacre (subsequently cured by the hairs of Saint Cuthbert's head (4.32) must have been attached to monasteries in some capacity. Probably most healers were male; we do not read of female leeches, while witches and their evil spells are mentioned frequently (warlocks only very infrequently).[21] But beyond this we cannot go: the religion, training, and social status of the magician are unknown. Any combination of social and personal traits is likely.

---

[20] Contemporary references to such magical practices are described by Bonser (n. 1 above) 118-129, 145-153, and are examined critically by Jane Crawford, "Evidences for Witchcraft in Anglo-Saxon England" MA 32 (1963) 99-116.

[21] See Maria Brie, "Über die ags. Bezeichnung des wortes Zauberer," *Englische Studien* 41 (1909) 20-27.

It might well be that any person could say such a charm, and that its efficacy depends on a power obtained solely through herbal and verbal magics, not through a particular person's mana. In describing the Finnish charms, some of which show thematic and structual affinities with the Anglo-Saxon, John Abercrombie notes that any ordinary Finn could be his own wizard in Lönnrot's day. F. P. Magoun, Jr., in his article debunking "heroic exorcism" in *Beowulf*, argues that it is unlikely that Anglo-Saxon magicians had shamanistic powers.[22] Evans-Pritchard very plainly distinguishes magic from witchcraft by the fact that magic can be learned and that its power is located in its techniques and materials, while witches possess a special psychical power that can affect others without the aid of rites and spells.[23] But we cannot transfer this distinction from Zandeland in the 1920s to Northern Europe in the Dark Ages without first determining what kind of immanent personal power or mana the Germanic peoples believed in. This question is largely a matter of degrees of belief, according to Jan de Vries.[24] The gradations are most evident in Old Norse. To take only one example from the gods' end of the scale, Oðin, who is the clearest example of a Germanic shaman, had obvious deific powers when he practiced *galdr*, a secret verbal magic of transformation. At the human level, witches or *vǫlva* who praticed *seiðr*, the most malevolent sort of magic, had lesser but considerable power of a demonic sort. Personal mana as it is currently defined[25] was expressed by *ásmegin*, *megin*, *máttr*, which refer to a supernatural strength or blessedness that is not godlike or witchlike.[26] These words have the Old English cognates *mægen* "strength" and *miht* "power, might."[27] *Beowulf*, for instance, who is blessed with the *mægen* of thirty men in his handgrip, and is favored by God in battle, clearly possesses Anglo-Saxon

[22] Abercrombie (n. 7 above) 2.45. F. P. Magoun, Jn, "Zum heroischen Exorzismus des Beowulfsepos," *Arkiv för nordisk Filologi* 54 (1939) 215-228.

[23] E. E. Evans-Pritschard, *Witchcraft. Oracles, and Magic among the Azande* (London 1937) 387. This distinction is followed, for example, by William A. Lessa and Evon Z. Vogt, *Reader in Comparative Religion: An Anthropological Approach*, ed. 2 (New York 1965) 299.

[24] De Vries (n. 4 above) 1.276. De Vries uses Codrington's definition of mana in his discussion of "Macht und Kraft" (1.275-335).

[25] Evans-Pritchard, *Theories* (n. 6 above) 110, notes that anthropologists have changed their definition of this concept from Codrington's "vague impersonal force, a sort of ether or electricity which was distributed in persons and things" to "an efficaciousness (with the allied meaning of truth) of spiritual power derived from gods or ghosts, usually through persons, especially chiefs—a grace or virtue which enables persons to ensure success in human undertakings."

[26] Old Norse examples are given in de Vries (n. 4 above) 1.275-279 and Turville-Petre (n. 4 above) 64-65.

[27] See F. P. Magoun, Jr., "Some Survivals of Pagan Belief in Anglo-Saxon England," *Harvard Theological Review* 40 (1947) 33-46

mana. However, unlike the case for Old Norse beliefs, there is no Anglo-Saxon evidence to my knowledge that makes a man's *mægen* the effective cause of his magic. Evans-Pritchard's distinction appears to hold good for the Anglo-Saxons, but this may be only because so little is known about their charm-sayers.

Lastly, the power of the words in the charm: if they can in fact be regarded as only magical, then they are efficacious formulas with their own physical force and do not invoke religious aid. But since some other Anglo-Saxon charms, notably *Æcerbot*, combine incantation with prayer, this "epic introduction" may somehow ask for power from above.[28] We cannot be sure unless we can precisely define the nature of its allusions. And we cannot logically exclude the possibility that there may have been an intrinsic magic in the person using the charm; it is simply that it cannot be demonstrated. Since the text is our only sure evidence, we may look for the magic of the charm in the verbal and herbal rites. Presumably, since the words are not runes and show no signs of being used in an amulet, the spell was spoken aloud to gain its magical power, and was used with the herbal rite.

Given these limitations, how can we determine the meaning of these rites from both the anthropological and literary standpoints? We need an approach that will respect the totality of effect gained by using both magics, yet one that will also treat the verbal charm as poetry. Because the words probably had no power unless said aloud and had to be linked with the herbal rite, and because in actual practice all the actions of the charm would be joined only in the person of the magician, perhaps the most fruitful means of analyzing the text is the literary notion of the "speaker" or "voice" of the poem. This metaphorical personage is the reader's inferential construction, an imaginary character who may be thought to say and perform the charm. For the student of magic, the advantage of this imagined speaker is that his person combines all the charm's magical parts and presents them for our inspection, but as a concept to be analyzed, not as a shadowy, historically undefinable magician. Further, when a literary critic sees such a speaker in a text making dramatic verbal gestures, he often calls the whole gesture "the rhetorical performance." The notion of a speaker can therefore lead to a literary definition of this charm's magic as its rhetorical force. By this use of "rhetoric," derived from Klagstad and Kenneth Burke, I mean the *goal-directedness* of the magical gesture, the way it is organized toward an expected result, and not its verbal beauty or argumentative organization.[29] The total rhetoric of the charm will then include the unliterary

---

[28] See Bruce A. Rosenberg, "The Meaning of *Æcerbot*," JAF 79 (1966 suppl.) 428-436.

[29] Harold Klagstad (n. 5 above) and Kenneth Burke, *The Philosophy of Literary Form* (Baton Rouge, La. 1941) 5. Burke notes that even simple assertions of fact may have this kind of tendentiousness. If a Hottentot states that his race is superior to all others, "the

physical magic along with the poetic chant. The complete charm's "rhetorical force," so defined, will be the "science" that controls natural events
in the magical world.

Viewing the charm this way casts a new light on its structure. First, the
charm does not have the unity of structure that we ordinarily see in the rhetoric of written works. Despite its unity of purpose, it falls into two distinct
parts, distinguished by differences in audience and style of attack, although
the transition (lines 18-21) is blurred so as to obscure the shift. In the first
part, the spear is addressed intermittently (line 5 adresses the patient),
and in the second part the patient is addressed (with the exception of line
27, addressed to the spear). These two parts are held together only by a
unity of practical purpose and the similarity of the references to the "spear"
and the "shot" (or "arrow"). The repetition of lines 15b and 18a, and the
transitional appearance of lines 18-19, the audience of which is uncertain,
might be thought of as formal elements that unify the charm.

> Ut, lytel spere,   gif her inne sy!
> Syx smiðas sætan,   wælspera worhtan.
> Ut, spere,   næs in, spere!
> Gif her inne sy   isernes dæl,
> Hægtessan geweorc,   hit sceal gemyltan. (15-19)

But these lines are better understood as the characteristic "narrowing" of
phonological and syntactical elements in goal-seeking statements, such as
Klagstad found in the Great Russian oral charms (139-142). There is extensive comparative evidence, especially in the Finnish charms, that when
charms are extemporaneous oral performances, the composition of a charm
for a given ailment can vary widely in the selection of its themes, from singer
to singer, so long as the themes, unrelated in themselves, all apply to the
purpose at hand.[30] Without pronouncing upon the unknowable circumstances of its actual composition, I might point out that no elements in this particular Anglo-Saxon charm depend upon a knowledge of writing or runes,
unlike many shorter, more unified charms in Storms's collection. Perhaps
we should not assume any aesthetic necessity in this apparent thematic unity.

It is also likely that the themes of the "spear" and the "shot" are only
generally similar. No commentator sees the "narrative allusions" that sur-
round the "spear" refrain in the first half as references to the "elf-shot" in

---

facts of the historical assertion here are but a strategy of inducement (apparently describing the *scene* for the action of a drama, they are themselves a dramatic *act prodding to a
further dramatic act*)."

[30] Abercrombie (n. 7 above) 2.2-6, and F. P. Magoun, Jr., trans., *The Kalevala, or Poems
of the Kaleva District, Compiled by Elias Lönnrot* (Cambridge, Mass. 1963) XVII-XVIII.

the second half. Probably we should not even classify the whole charm as "against elf-shot" as do Bonser (158-160) and Grattan and Singer (175). It must be granted that *der Alpenschuss* is the broadest Northern European folk tradition of supernatural missiles causing illness,[31] and that they are often called arrows or darts (= *lytel spere*?); but in the second part of the charm "elves" are only one of the three equivalent evil forces that are named.[32] One might as well title the charm "Against Witch-shot" in the light of the supernatural women in the first part, the transitional reference to *hægtessan geweorc* (line 19), and *haegtessan gescot* (lines 24, 26) in the second part. Such a title would be an equally incomplete designation of the possible sources of the pain. Even if we accept Bonser's translation of *færstice* as "sudden puncture" (160-161), we cannot settle whether the puncture is due to elves or to witches (assuming for the moment the "mighty women" are in fact witches). Hence we cannot speak of "a unified theme" other than the shooting pain itself. In short, we may conclude that the curative focus of the text is more general than the specifying words of either part would suggest. It is even possible that the only unity here is the continuity of a single goal-directed gesture.

An investigation of the botanical and magical properties of the herbs shows that the accompanying herbal magic also has a general focus. The *reade netele* has been identified as *Urtica Dioica*, the common, bigsting, or great nettle, a hairy perennial with no medicinal value.[33] *Feferfuige* is the

---

[31] De Vries (n. 4 above) 1.296-298; Storms (n. 1 above) 142.

[32] Bonser (n. 1 above) 158, treats the genitive plural *esa* as "of the Æsir" and sees the three sources of the "shot" named in lines 23-24 as "the descending stages of powers." However, they are probably of roughly equal force. The form *esa* appears nowhere else in Anglo-Saxon, and its stem, *ōs* "god," is not a clear equivalent in cultural meaning to its cognate, Old Norse *áss*. F. P. Magoun, Jr., in his review of Storms, *Speculum* 28 (1953) 208, warns that "*Æsir* is far too specific for OE *esa*, better rendered 'divine beings'; one must be wary in projecting on to the Anglo-Saxon scene Old Scandinavian, specifically Icelandic concepts and procedures . . . of which many are perhaps quite late and specifically Scandinavian." The *esa* and *ylfa* in line 23 are probably equivalent since they match the stock alliteration *alfar ok æsir* in Old Norse mythological poetry (e. g., *Voluspá* st. 48); they may even be a late stereotyped borrowing from Old Norse (cf. n. 14 above). It is more likely the *esa* here are on the level of the *ylfa*, and not vice versa (as suggested by Turville-Petre, n. 4 above, 231) since elsewhere in Germanic folk belief elves commonly cause bewitchment, not cosmic harm. The *hægtessan* of line 24 has supernatural powers of similar strength (see section III below). In this context the most likely translation of *esa gescot* would be "the shot of spirits."

[33] F. P. Magoun, Jr., (n. 1 above) 19, and his review of Storms (n. 32 above) 207-208. The following identifications and properties of centaury and plantain have been ascertained from Grattan and Singer; the Anglo-Saxon version of the *Herbarium* of Apuleius, in Cockayne (n. 1 above) vol. 1; Cockayne's discussions in "Saxon Names of Plants Collected" (vol. 3); T. F. Thiselton-Dyer, *The Folk-Lore of Plants* (New York 1889); Edith Grey Wheelwright, *The Physiek Garden: Medicinal Plants and their History* (Boston 1935); Encyclopædia Brittanica (Chicago 1969).

antipyretic formerly called "feverfew," *Erythraea Centaurium*, or common
centaury. *Wegbrade* or "way-broad" is some member of the plantain family.
The seeds of one variety of plantain, *Plantago indica*, yield the demulcent
Psyllium, while the most common, *Plantago major*, called "the mother of
worts" in the Nine Herbs Charm, is an astringent used since Pliny's time
for broken skin and wounds. Medically, then, these herbs would be helpful
only for fever, sore throat, or lacerations. Magically, however, the nettle
and the black heads of the ribwort plantain (*Plantago lanceolata*) resemble
spears or arrows in shape. If the feverfew in the charm were centaury, it
too might have had magical value because its seeds are in the shape of small
spindles. It is possible that all three herbs were thought to attarct the *lytel
spere* by similarities of shape. This is so common a characteristic of herbal
magic in Europe that Renaissance herbalists elevated it to the "doctrine
of signatures."[34] In short these herbs offer a broad spectrum of curative
properties: feverfew as an antipyretic against rheumatic pain; plantain as
a staunching agent for the invisible wound by the *spere*; and the nettle, plantain, and the *seax* at the end of the charm each as some kind of sympathetic
magic. Against this view of a general focus, it could be argued from Bonser's position that the three herbs appear together principally because each
is a specific against elf-shot, since in several other charms and recipes they
are used against maladies caused by elves or "flying venoms." But there
is such a variety of uses for these herbs that it seems more accurate to say
that they were thought of as having efficacy against a class of poorly defined internal pains and respiratory ailments, only some of which were caused
by elves or other evil forces in the air.[35] The conclusion to be drawn, if we
are to avoid the dangers of circular explanation, is that these three herbs
were used for all their properties at once: their sharp shapes, medicinal value, and traditional associations with elves and venoms.

---

[34] See Agnes Arber, *Herbals*: *Their Origin and Evolution*, ed. 2 (Cambridge 1938) 247-
263).

[35] Plantain and feverfew turn up again in Storms, no. 17, part D, against the elf-disease
(jaundice?) (226), but these herbs are not used in the recipe for "Salve Against Elf-Shot,"
Storms, no. 20 (244-247). Feverfew was used also against *þeor*, which Grattan and Singer
identify as a bronchial malady (110 n. 2), and for fever, which was sometimes thought of
as an elf riding the sick person (see Grimm, *Deutsche Mythologie* 2 [1876] 966: *Ynglinga
Tal* chap. 16). Plantain was also used for fever (Grattan and Singer 199); in recipes for
"heartache" (Bonser 404); and against one of the undefined "flying venoms" in the Nine
Herbs charm. There the "red nettle" is apparently used against another flying venom
in lines 16-17, possibly also 27-29, though the nomenclature is confused (*stiðe, wergula*).
Elsewhere the nettle is good against *þeor* and eruptive rash (Grattan and Singer 119, 165).
Unless all these ailments were thought to have a single magical cause, such as elves, it
would appear that the three herbs occur together in this charm because each is in itself
generally appropriate for the case.

When we look further at the physical rite of plunging the knife into the hot liquid (*wætan*) of herbs boiled in butter, we cannot distinguish whether its magical force was homeopathic or contagious, because we are not told what else is done with the mixture and the knife. It might be contagious magic in which the spearlike herbs were softened by boiling, to soften the internal spear, or the boiling might have been to make the herbs edible. The charm might simply end with *ado on wætan* as a final conquering gesture, or the knife might be thrust in the liquid to coat it before applying it to the stitch sympathetically (here the heat would have medicinal value). Or the knife might be used to make symbolic cuts, or even for subsequent surgery. There are analogies for all these possibilities, and no way to decide between them. In this respect, our ignorance of the specific rite keeps our own focus general. However, so far as we can determine for the herbs themselves, their curative powers are as generally focused as the verbal charm.

III

The broad curative focus of the charm is an important point to keep in mind when examining the possible sources of magical power in the "narrative allusions" of the first part. Generality of reference is not the kind of ambiguity literary students have been taught to admire, but it is an important characteristic of many classes of magical speech, as is its converse, specific naming references, such as those in the second part of this charm. This peculiar generality is one key to the nature of the speaker's magical and poetic powers in the first part. But before demonstrating how those powers are fused in a single rhetorical performance, we must squarely face the question whether the "narrative allusions" themselves somehow manipulate or invoke supernatural powers.

First it should be noted that none of these allusions has been identified with an extant Germanic epic or myth. If they could be linked to a known story, it would be prima-facie evidence for a genuine "epic introduction." But there is little scholarly agreement even about the meaning of individual references. The first allusion, lines 3-4, is to the Wild Hunt of Woden, say Grendon and Ryan; Skemp, however, calls these loud riders "wind-demons." Although they are grammatically sexless, most commentators go on to connect this "they" (*hy*) with the mighty women of lines 7-9. The women have been called Woden's *wæl-cyrige* by Kennedy, Wardale, and Ryan; ordinary human "witches" by Wrenn, Bonser, and Skemp; and less certainly "female spirits" or "supernatural women" by Greenfield, Malone, Storms, and Hilda Davidson. There is a possibility, perhaps, that they are an Anglo-Saxon analogue to the ON *dísir*, since those female tutelary spirits were sometimes more closely connected with elves dwelling in dead-mounds than with

Oðin's Valkyries, and *hlæw* clearly means a burial mound.[36] But it is not possible to connect any of the 'elf-' compounds in Old English with burial mounds,[37] and another chance to simplify and clarify the picture behind both parts of the charm disappears. Storms connects the evil power of the women with the *hlæw* (145), but if this were so we could only conjecture whether they maliciously awaken the power of elves in mounds by riding over them, or gain their power directly from the dead, or are themselves spirits of the dead.

Perhaps a contemporary hearer of the charm was meant to wander among these possibilities. The precise nature of the women must remain uncertain, although they probably are not Valkyries of the late variety. If, despite the charm's looseness of structure, we can connect them with references in the second part, we might consider them *hægtessan* (line 19), ordinarily translated as "witches" (cf. Ger. *Hexen*). Yet the precise history of *hægtis* cannot be clearly traced from the Anglo-Saxon glossaries. Frequently it glosses one of the terms for the Furies, but sometimes *pythonissa*; in a few cases the Furies are glossed as *wæl-cyrige*.[38] If the charm were composed late, all its reference to females might blend a conception of human witches with the supernatural "choosers of the slain." If it were early, the "mighty women" might be "followers of Woden, but not yet promoted to their important part in the ordering of Valhalla" (Crawford 105). Their mana may be indicated by the words *mihtigan* and *hyra mægen beræddon*. These references to their "strength" might suggest they exercise witchcraft by an inborn psychic force, but they do too much to be witches in the strict definition. The verb *beræddon* bears this out: they "plan" or "talk up" their strength. They might, therefore, perform a particular rite by their loud riding and noisy spears, and gain their *mægen* through magical means. If we look for religious analogies, it can be argued that much of the charm hangs together curiously. Both the riding and spears are associated with the cult of Woden, and the throwing of spears strongly recalls the Scandinavian practice of dedicating the deaths of enemy troops to Oðin by throwing a spear over their heads before battle. It might be supposed that in lines 10-11 the exorcist is resisting the power of the mighty women to choose the slain, by saying that he will throw a spear back against them. If so, this can be added

---

[36] See Turville-Petre (n. 4 above) 221-224, 230-231, and Ellis Davidson (n. 4 above) 154-157.

[37] See R. A. Peters, "OE *Ælf, -Ælf, Ælfen, -Ælfen*," *Philological Quarterly* 42 (1963) 250-257; there are no "elf-" compounds with the element *-hlæw-*; such likely looking words as *dūn-ælfen* and *munt-ælfen* are glosses for Latin *castalides* and *oreades*.

[38] Brie (n. 21 above) 25-27; Crawford (n. 20 above) 106; N. K. Chadwick, "The Monsters and Beowulf," *The Anglo-Saxons: Studies . . . presented to Bruce Dickins*, ed. Peter Clemoes (London 1959) 175 n. 5.

to the other types of defensive magic here, although due to the ambiguity of *stod* we cannot know if they "choose" the exorcist or the patient. We may note that the penultimate poetic line in the charm, *Fleoh þær * * * on fyrgenheafde*, while badly corrupt, apparently means "Fly away there to the mountaintop"; and, further, that in English place names as well as Wulfstan's version of *De Falsis Dies* Woden, or Oðon, was connected with mountaintops.[39] It might be that in conjuring the "piece of iron within" "away to the mountaintop" the exorcist is sending it back to one of the powers from which it came. Thus we can, if we please, posit a fairly coherent set of references throughout the charm to magical practices and beliefs related to Woden.

But there are two objections to accepting this explanation as an "epic introduction." First, the very difficulty of identifying the nature of the agents in the narrative suggests that a deliberately vague range of reference was intended. Second, these practices in themselves do not constitute a "myth" in the more scrupulous definitions of the term: one of the "traditional tales of the deeds of . . . supernatural or superhuman beings. That is, when we say *myth* we shall mean a *story* of a certain kind."[40] The practices behind the allusions appear frequently enough in Scandinavian accounts, but only as aspect of the cult of Oðin, and not as stories about him or his followers. Nor is there an account of a magician or warrior-hero resisting members of a Woden cult, to which the exorcist could compare himself.

While these objections do not absolutely rule out the possibility of mythic references, there may be a more likely explanation for the narrative quality of the charm. Any narrative coherence may come from the speaker being the main character in what little story there is. What looks like a set of mythic allusions may instead be an especially successful invention of the circumstances in which the speaker gains his magical power. The story may occur only in the present time of the charm, and its meaning may simply bè that the speaker gains control over the *lytel spere* by imagining, and living within, this fragmented narrative of bad magic, and then successfully resisting its malevolence. When we see further that the vexing references to the smiths can be plausibly explained as also part of the speaker's magical practice, we can conclude that the possibility of a mythical story as a source of the speaker's power is extremely unlikely. It is more likely that the imaginative force of his magical practice, that is, the literary power in the texture of the words, creates the special magic of the charm.

---

[39] There was a ninth-century *Wodnes beorg* in Wiltshire, for instance. See Dorothy Behturum, *The Homilies of Wulfstan* (Oxford 1957) 223, 338.

[40] Joseph Fontenrose, *The Ritual Theory of Myth*, University of California Folklore Studies 18 (Berkeley 1966) 54. See also William Bascom, "The Forms of Folklore: Prose Narratives," JAF 78 (1965) 3-20.

The smith in line 13 who "sat, struck a little knife, / [word lost] of irons, exceptionally strong,"[41] has been as Weland by Grendon, and Kennedy and Storms extend this identification to suggest that Weland and his two bro- thers of the *Volundarkviða* are referred to by *Syx smiðas* (line 16), the *syx* being due to alliteration.[42] Magoun, who is willing to see "pagan remains" wherever possible, regards both these inferences as "dangerous."[43] A re- ference to Weland in a charm whose most nearly identifiable allusions are Wodenistic seems unlikely when we recall that Weland and Woden do not appear together either as opponents or allies in Scandinavian or English story. Nonetheless, while no Germanic legend is in plain sight here, it may be that simply to say "smith" in a charm was to invoke Weland somehow. This question cannot be settled with certainty. We can, however, reach a conclusion about the magical valence of the smiths. Scholars have been divided on this question, because the allusion is so vague. Wrenn (168) thinks the smiths are bad magic, "at their wicked work" against the exorcist, while Grendon and Storms see them hammering good magical weapons for him. Skemp (290-292) splits the valence between a good smith in lines 13-14 and kad "elf-smiths" in line 16, and transposes the two passages. He argues first for a series of three successful resistances by the exorcist against "wind- demons," "sorceresses" and "smiðas," and equates these with the *es*, *hæg- tessan*, and *ylfe* of the second half of the charm. Second, he argues for the *seax lytel* as forged in magical reply and then applied, covered with salve, to each part of the body named in the catalogue in the second half. Although the text should not be transposed so freely and the equation of the two triple series seems quite forced, Skemp's notion of how the "little knife" might be used is very plausible, and comparative information about this kind of physical magic lets us more certainly assign a positive magical value to both the *seax lytel* and the *wælsperu*.

Although the directions for plunging the knife into the hot salve—*Nim þonne þaet seax, ado on wætan*—come after the poetical charm has been com- pleted, and *þonne* appears to call for a clear temporal sequence, the direc- tions for physical magic throughout the Anglo-Saxon charms are typically as abbreviated as the verbal magic is lengthy and repetitive. Wrenn reports that the practice of "setting the blade of a knife covered in butter to a bruise" can still be found in England today, and *þonne* may merely represent an af- terthought. I would not want to insist on the exact coordination of the phys-

---

[41] So Dobbie 213, following Rieger's emendation of *wund* to *wundrum*. Sweet in his *Reader* emends instead to *isernē[e]* and translates "wounded with iron." Grendon (n. 1 above) 165, translates the unemended line as "with iron (blows) sore wounded," meaning "beaten with hammers."

[42] Grendon 214; Kennedy (n. 2 above) 10; Storms (n. 1 above) 146.

[43] Magoun, review of Storms (n. 32 above) 208.

ical and verbal magic, however, because it makes a neater explanation than the evidence offers, and forces a strained meaning on *þonne*. It is enough, for my argument, that the definite article *þæt* in *þæt seax* may have an anteced- ent. This suggests that the knife forged by the smith in line 13 may be linked to the physical magic, whenever it may occur. This connection is strength- ened by the probability that *hit* (line 19) means *hyt* "heat" as in *Beowulf* 2649 (so Dobbie), rather than "it," and by the likelihood that the butter salve would be hot, since it has been boiled (*wyll*). If we do not transpose the two "smith" references, we can then settle the positive valence of the second reference by looking again at the implement, not the maker. Like *þæt seax*, these "slaughter-spears" are alluded to earlier, in the word *oðerne* (line 10) "another," which if we follow Dobbie's confident interpretation (212) re- fers to an understood *gar* "spear", followed by the poetic variation *fleogende flane* "a flying arrow, dart." The six smiths can then be taken to fashion the spears with which the exorcist earlier wished to threaten the "mighty women." Since knives used in charms occasionally were invested with ma- gical powers, as in charm no. 22 in Storms (248-251), the visible knife used in the final physical action may be thematically linked to the magician's imaginary spears in the verbal charm.

This explanation of the "smith" passages still does not let us infer the exact magical use of the knife. The connection between the verbal and physical magic remains general. Yet such an explanation seems more plaus- ible than the assumption that there is an unknown story about smiths behind the charm. Further, if we take it as a generally focused rhetorical performance in which the allusions exist only for the goal they are meant to influence, with their meaning entirely within the span of their saying, then we can see how its magical and poetical strategies are the same. Such a self-creating verbal magic must make a strong aural impression, moment to moment, by the hum of its generalized implication. In this kind of magic a vague focus, at times verging on incoherence, goes hand in hand with repetition and phonolog- ical narrowing (for example, *Syx smiðas sætan*) to create the sense that the speaker is in the very act of finding and repeating words of mystery. While the words themselves are vivid phrases, the act of their discovery is unfocused in regard to its audience, so far as I can tell, since it is not clear in line 15 whether the exorcist is addressing himself, reminding the patient of his powers, or addressing the spear. The context is so general that the mode of adress may be threefold, and in this breadth of possibility lies its magical strength.

IV

Now let us examine how the verbal magic of the first part of *Wið Færstice* arises from the tones of the lines themselves, that is, from the imagined speaker's

sense of his situation. He differs from most poetic speakers in that he is
in a practical goal-seeking situation, and one where words create the need
in him and his audience for more words until his goal is reached. The whole
charm prods itself onward to create the physical effect of healing the stitch.
Thus the more the speaker says *Ut lytel spere*, the more powerful this healing command becomes. But mere repetition would not create an effective
literary magic, as can be seen from the dreary series of *Crux Christi* repeti-
tions in the two poetical charms for loss of cattle (Dobbie, nos. 5 and 10).
It is the speaker's uncanny wielding of the lines between the refrain that
creates the special rhetorical force in the charm. Much of the power of the
intervening lines lies in their generally applicable vagueness, but even more
depends on other aspects of their style. How much less effect the first two
lines would have if they culminated a five-line description of riders. But
they stand as a beginning: an abrupt, beheaded entry into a seeming account by the speaker. At first it appears that this plunges *in medias res*,
but there is no *res* from the past behind "Loud they were, so loud, when they
rode over the mound." There is only the assumption of power, at the moment of utterance, by a speaker who deliberately, dramatically, mystifies
his listener by his very first words. We learn only that the riders are "loud"
and "resolute"—a single vivid impression of danger—and yet he crooningly
repeats the phrase *ofer . . . ridan* as though overheard wondering to himself
about something he knows or sees. Then in the third line he frightens his
patient by turning suddenly to address him directly, and implicitly connects him with the riders: "Shield yourself, [so that?] you may come through
this evil (or conflict)." With even greater abruptness, the speaker then commands the little spear to leave: *Ut, lytel spere, gif her inne sie!* (line 6). This
is a redirection of attitude toward a new audience, just as sharp as the previous "Shield yourself," but now in a tone at once soothing to the patient
and peremptory to the spear. Thus far in the charm's saying, the only connection between the three different utterances, addressed to three different
audiences, is the speaker's performance. Its supple dramatic turning and
firm control of pace make his power as a speaker as clear as his references
are vague (for example, "Shield yourself" against what from the riders?
—the *spere* has not yet been mentioned). The very act of suddenly shifting
creates a psychic rhythm in which the speaker's verbal gestures are the sole
determining power in the speaker-audience situation. His words and the
belief in the real presence of their referents are fused in this state of mind;
distinctions are lost, and rapport and magic result.[44]

---

[44] Eric A. Havelock, *Preface to Plato* (Cambridge, Mass. 1963), offers the best general
argument for the existence of such a state of mind resulting from literary performances
in a predominantly oral culture.

This inward rhythm of the curative situation is a function of the mutual belief held by exorcist and patient, and it can be perceived by modern readers only as a literary effect. Even so, we can see that it continues to grow in power through the first half of the charm. The speaker immediately shifts again, and begins another bit of "narrative" (lines 7-11). The grammatical ambiguity of *Stod* (line 7) at first seems resolved toward "*he* stood under the shield," meaning the patient, from the previous "Shield yourself," but then as one encounters lines 10 and 11, it seems to have referred to the speaker himself. This vagueness of reference, asyntactic and atemporal, may be meant to have an empathetic effect, as though the speaker were saying, "We are in this together, I as much as you, and I will protect you," but it is not certain that this is a purposeful ambiguity. A more direct effect of the shift into a warlike confrontation is the sense that the speaker is courageous and clear-eyed in his appraisal of the danger. There is less mystery in these few details than in lines 3-4. Again they are sketchy but vivid, and in lines 7-9 the speaker's tone is closest to the noble, impersonal descriptive voice in Old English heroic poetry. There is internal repetition, as there was in lines 3-4, but now it comes in the more elevated mode of a variation upon the shield (7), and in the reappearance of the noise of *beræddon* in the *gyllende* spear: as the mighty women shout out, so their spears scream as they fly through the air. The nuance of calm epic strength in the speaker's voice then changes immediately into hectoring invective as he boasts in line 10 that he wants to reply to the women. The confident promise of what he will do to them is tinged with the kind of arrogance found in *Brunanburh*, and this ready shift in tone of voice, after the vivid glimpse of supernatural danger, increases his power. What began with a preterite (*Stod*) turns into the present tense of *wille sændan*. Possibly the composer of the charm used the preterite in all four allusions only because it seemed a more elevated diction, as though referring to the traditional past. Certainly the imaginative force of this second brief account lies all in the strength of the bullying tone the speaker takes toward what his own words have made a real and present danger.

On the heels of this jeering comes the refrain, and the timing of its return at this point is admirable. The suspenseful scene the speaker has created around himself and his listener heightens his command so that *Ut* in line 12 seems virtually to erupt through his self-dramatization, in order to thrust at the listener's pain once more. His knowledge and scene-setting have now become synonymous with the language of command. As the refrain in line 12 forces another redirection of attention upon us, we can see that lines 7-11 were directed at the internal spear-pain as much as was the refrain. That is, the whole statement of the part of the charm, so far as it is addressed to the spear, can be generally couched as "I am in power and I command you." This double assertion is really only one magical command, but the speaker cannot say it with any potency in a single phrase. His chant must rock him and his listener into this state of power by the continuous, abrupt shifting of his attention and tone of voice. This incantation is much more complex than the hymnlike solemnity of many charms.

The pace at which the refrain is repeated quickens until the very shifting between the two "smith" passages and the refrain becomes a kind of curative focus itself, at the exact point in the charm (lines 13ff.) where we are least certain of the nominal references. It is noteworthy that the refrain is more rapid after the knife is mentioned in line 13, which is short, heavy, and metrically extraordinary. The newly invocative tone of the *Sæt smið* lines (13-14) provides the most ponderously mysterious moment so far, and perhaps from this we should infer that now the speaker's power is great enough to begin the cure. Possibly the knife is now physically produced. After the wrenching command of the refrain is repeated again in line 15, the speaker threatens the pain anew with the reference to his slaughter-spears, and his power is so strong that in the next line he changes the refrain to a more colloquial, peremptory phrase: *Ut, spere, næs in, spere!* A slightly self-important solemnity can be heard in lines 18-19: the *gif her inne sy* clause, now shifted to the on-verse, begins to sound like the conditional of an Authority, and not, as before, both a command and a quest for power. Then the speaker fades away as a poetic voice in lines 20 following, and becomes a rather toneless actor in the actual curative drama. As he does, his verbal performance becomes more simplified and less interesting as poetry.

Although we do not know the full context of the cure, we may be sure that neither charmer nor charmed would say that the verbal charm fell off in magical power in its second half. But, because as modern readers we bring only an aesthetic appreciation to the charm, not a real belief, we can only perceive the literary force of its verbal magic. Claims might be made for the charm as a unified whole and of equal literary power throughout, but they would have to be overingenious and would not, I think, answer to the experience of reading the charm as a poetic performance. Many Old English poems are best admired for their parts, not as wholes, and it is praise enough if a literary response to the first part of this charm places a reader firmly within its magical power.[45]

[45] My grateful acknowledgements to Professor Charles Adams, University of Massachusetts, and Professor Robert S. Cox, Rice University, for valuable advice and criticism during the preparation of this article.

Department of English
Amherst College
Amherst, Massachusetts 01002, U.S.A.

INGELD AND CHRIST: A MEDIEVAL PROBLEM

•

by Robert Levine

Students of *Beowulf* are familiar with the notion that the poem can be read as an attempt to answer Alcuin's question, "Quid Hinieldus cum Christo?" (What has Ingeld to do with Christ?).[1] More than two centuries later, a similar complaint was registered by a certain Meinhard against Bishop Gunter of Bamberg: "Numquam ille Augustinum, numquam ille Gregorium recolit, semper ille Attalam, semper Amalungum et cetera idgenus portare [or, pro tempore] tractat."[2] Both Alcuin and Meinhard clearly see secular heroism and Christian principles as mutually exclusive ideals; for them, the physically active, pridefully and violently assertive, materialistic and frequently murderous pagan hero cannot be reconciled with the gentle, humbly submissive protagonist of the New Testament, whose most glorious act is to allow himself to be killed. Christ's "passion" is, of course paradigmatically, as well as etymologically "passive."

Not every medieval mind, however, found Christ and Ingeld irreconcilable; a variety of responses to Alcuin's question may be seen imaginatively articulated in a number of medieval vernacular heroic works, ranging from the *Nibelungenlied's* total rejection of the possibilities of a reconciliation between Christ and Ingeld, through the ambiguous, tentative, undogmatic resolutions made in *Beowulf* and *Njal saga*, to the naively positive assertion of reconciliation made, more devotionally than imaginatively, by the *Roland* poet.

Early in the fifth century, Prudentius combines Christ and Ingeld in his *Psychomachia*, in a way that would seem to have been designed explicitly to avoid offending the Alcuinian sensibility; in his poem Prudentius attributes heroic glory not to an individual human figure, but to blatantly labeled personifications of abstract virtues. Consequently, Sobriety can smash Luxury in the teeth, and add insult to injury by pointing out the poetic justice of

---

[1] J. R. R. Tolkien is probably responsible for the currency of the notion; see his "Beowulf: The Monsters and the Critics," *An Anthology of Beowulf Criticism*, ed. Lewis E. Nicholson (Notre Dame 1963) 84.

[2] As quoted in Carl Erdmann, "Fabulae curiales," *Zeitschrift fur deutsches Altertum und deutsche Literatur* 63 (1936) 88-89.

her action, without leaving herself open to charges of *superbia*, since her *gab*, or *beotword*, as well as her actions, do credit not to an Ingeld figure, but to an abstract quality (lines 417-431):

> Addit Sobrietas vulnus letale iacenti,
> Coniciens silicem rupis de parte molarem,
> Hunc vexilliferae quoniam fors obtulit ictum,
> Spicula nulla manu sed belli insigne gerenti.
> Casus agit saxum, medii spiramen ut oris
> Frangeret et recavo misceret labra palato.
> Dentibus introrsum resolutis, lingua resectam
> Dilaniata gulam frustis cum sanguinis inplet.
> Insolitis dapibus crudescit guttur, et ossa
> Conliquefacta vorans removit quas hauserat offas.
> "Ebibe iam proprium post pocula multa cruorem",
> Virgo ait increpitans, sint haec tibi fercula tandem
> Tristia praeteriti nimiis pro dulcibus aevi:
> Lascivas vitae inlecebras gustatus amarae
> Mortis et horrifico sapor ultimus asperet haustu ![3]

In this passage, however, as well as in the *Psychomachia* as a whole, Prudentius complicates the reconciliation of Christ and Ingeld both by showing an elaborate interest in gore, and by coloring the passage with echoes of Vergil; Lavarenne offers line 420 as an echo of *Aeneid* 8.683 and 12.289, and he characterizes the *Psychomachia* generally as "ce pastiche du style virgilien."[4]

Vergil created difficulties for many Christian lovers of poetry; a passage from Augustine's *Confessions* is one of the more famous statements of a common predicament:

> Nam utique meliores, quia certiores, erant primae illae litterae, quibus fiebat in me et factum est et habeo, iilud, ut et legam, si quid scriptum invenio, et scribam ipse, si quid volo, quam illae, quibus tenere cogebar Aeneae nescio cuius errores oblitus errorum meorum et plorare Didonem mortuam, quia se occidit ab amore, cum interea me ipsum in his a te morientem, deus, vita mea, siccis oculis ferrem miserrimus.[5]

For Augustine, then, at least in this passage, the study of pagan literature is opposed to the study of the Bible; like Alcuin, he thinks in terms of ex-

---

[3] *Psychomachia* 417-431, ed. M. Lavarenne, *Prudence* 3 (Paris 1963) 65.
[4] *Ibid.* 12.
[5] *Confessions* 1.13, ed. Joseph Trabucco (Paris 1960) 30.

clusive, irreconcilable opposites, a *sens* emphasized in the above passage by the symmetrical rhetorico-syntactical structures Augustine chooses.

Augustine, of course, is only one of many early Christians for whom a choice between pagan and Christian literature seemed necessary; Jerome's problem, to choose between Christ and Cicero, is the other famous example. Prudentius, then, by combining Christ, Ingeld, and Vergil, created a problem at once doctrinal and aesthetic; recent critical response to the poem suggests that Prudentius's solution to the problem was not entirely satisfactory. Lavarenne speaks of "la terrible faute de gout qui consiste à représenter les vertus cruelles et bavardes," and his response substantially agrees with that of J. H. Thomson: "The zest with which Prudentius . . . dwells on the gruesome details of slaughter often obscures the fact that the poem has a religious purpose."[6] Although he gives flesh and fleshly deeds somewhat too literally to his personified abstractions, Prudentius keeps his poem more in a devotional than in an imaginative mode,[7] as the conclusion to the encounter between Patience and Wrath demonstrates; Patience literally infuriates Wrath to death (lines 145-161):

> Ira ubi truncati mucronis fragmina vidit,
> Et procul in partes ensem crepuisse minutas,
> Iam capulum retinente manu sine pondere ferri,
> Mentis inops ebur infelix decorisque pudendi
> Perfida signa abicit, monumentaque tristia longe
> Spernit, at ad proprium succenditur effera letum.
> Missile de multis, quae frustra sparserat, unum
> Pulvere de campi perversos sumit in usus:
> Rasile figit humi lignum, ac se cuspide versa
> Perfodit, et calido pulmonen vulnere transit.
> Quam superadsistens Patientia: "Vicimus," inquit,
> "Exultans vitium solita virtute, sine ullo
> Sanguinis ac vitae discimine; lex habet istud
> Nostra genus belli, furias omnemque malorum
> Militiam et rabidas tolerando extinguere vires.
> Ipsa sibi est hostis vesania, seque furendo
> Interimit, moriturque suis Ira ignea telis."

Unlike Sobriety, Patience has been able to keep her hands clean, but in the process, Prudentius has sacrificed the imaginative to the moral faculty. Seven

---

[6] Lavarenne (n. 3 above) 12; for an elaborate apology for Prudentius' technique, see Christian Gnilka, *Studien zur Psychomachia des Prudentius* (Wiesbaden 1963) 51-81, in which Gnilka appeals to *das Vergeltungsprinzip, das Talionsprinzip*, and to Dante. Intellectual justification, however, does not always correspond with aesthetic justification.

[7] The distinction between imaginative and devotional is C. S. Lewis's; *Allegory of Love* (Oxford 1958) 356.

hundred years later, in another battle of vices and virtues, Alanus de Insulis seems to have profited by Prudentius's folly; in the *Anti-Claudianus*,
zeugma and asyndeton dispose of the task of describing the activities of the
more blatantly restrained virtues:

> Pugnat in Excessum Moderantia, Sobria Fastum
> Aggreditur Ratio, Poenam Tolerantia, Luxum
> Sobrietas; sed pugna favet virtutibus, harum
> Defendit partem victoria, vincitur ergo
> Fastus, Luxus abit, cessat Gula, Crapula cedit.[8]

Prudentius's error seems to have been the decision to ignore a truth with
which he shows himself to have been familiar toward the end of the *Psychomachia*: "Non simplex natura hominis [sc. est] . . . spiritibus pugnant variis
lux atque tenebrae, Distantesque animat duplex substantia vires" (lines 904,
909-910).

   Not every attempt to combine Ingeld and Christ produces even the complexity of the *Psychomachia*; in the ninth century, Angilbert's lament for
Lothair makes the combination for the purpose of simple panegyric:

> Ecce olim velut Iudas salvatorem tradidit,
> sic te, rex, tuique duces tradiderunt gladio;
> esto cantus, ne frauderis agnus lupo previo.[9]

The Christlike analogy that Angilbert is emphasizing here, however, concerns betrayal and death, without any element of triumph.

   The most elaborate attempt to assert the validity of combining Christ
and Ingeld is the *Song of Roland*, in which the hero is more complex than
the personification of an abstract quality, and in which the poet chooses
a genre more complex, at least in Aristotelian terms, than a lyric panegyric.
In addition, *Roland* contains a notion of the *duplex substantia* of reality,
if not of man; the opposition noticed most frequently by critics is a variation
of the *topos* of *sapientia et fortitudo*, and occurs in the poem as a formula
Rollant est proz e Oliver est sage (line 1093, *inter alia*). A contrast more specifically relevant to what I have been talking about is represented by another
virtually formulaic line (1015): *Paien unt tort e chrestiens unt dreit*.[10] This
particular over-simplification, that pagans are categorically wrong and Christians categorically right, reflects a general characteristic of the poem which
Auerbach has pointed out:

---

[8] PL 210.512.
[9] Ed. E. Dummler, *Poetae latini aevi carolini* 2.137.
[10] All references to *Roland* are to Joseph Bédier's edition (Paris 1937).

The subject of the *Chanson de Roland* is narrow, and for the men who figure in it nothing of fundamental significance is problematic. All the categories of this life and the next are unambiguous, immutable, fixed in rigid formulations. . . . Temptation is there, to be sure, but there is no realm of problem. . . . Rigid, narrow, and unproblematic schematization is originally completely alien to the Christian concept of reality. It is true, to be sure, that the rigidifying process is furthered to a considerable degree by the figural interpretation of real events, which, as Christianity became established and spread, grew increasingly influential and which, in its treatment of actual events, dissolved their content of reality, leaving them only their content of meaning. As dogma was established, as the Church's task became more and more a matter of organization, its problem that of winning over peoples completely unprepared and unacquainted with Christian principles, figural interpretation must inevitably become a simple rigid scheme.[11]

Auerbach suggests that the poet has sacrificed a sufficiently complex sense of reality in order to convey a specific meaning; like Prudentius, then, the *Roland* poet has created a poem that is more devotional than imaginative. Certainly laisses 175-176 support Auerbach's suggestion, by presenting if not an abstract, at least a highly "figural" Roland:

> Co sent Rollant de sun tens n'i ad plus:
> Devers Espaigne est un pui agut,
> A l'une main si ad sun piz batud:
> "Deus, meie culpe vers les tues vertuz
> De mes pecchez, des granz e des menuz,
> que jo ai fait des l'ure que nez fui
> Tresqu'a cest jur que ci sui consout!"
> Sun destre guant en ad vers Deu tendut.
> Angles del ciel i descendent a lui.
> Li quens Rollant se jut desuz un pin;
> Envers Espaigne en ad turnet sun vis.
> De plusurs choses a remembrer li prist,
> De tantes teres cum li bers cnnquist,
> De dulce France, des humes de sun lign,
> De Carlemagne, sun seignor, kil nurrit;
> Ne poet muer n'en plurt e ne suspirt.
> Mais lui meisme ne volt mettre en ubli,
> Cleimet sa culpe, si priet Deu mercit:
> "Veire Patene, ki unkes ne mentis,
> Seint Lazaron de mort resurnexis
> E Daniel des leons guaresis,
> Guaris de mei l'anme de tuz perilz
> Pur les pecchez que en ma vie fis!"

> Sun destre guant a Deu en puroffrit.
> Seint Gabriel de sa main l'ad pris.
> Desur sun braz teneit le chef enclin;
> Juntes ses mains est alet a sa fin.
> Deus tramist sun angle Cherubin
> E seint Michel del Peril;
> Ensembl' od els sent Gabriel i vint.
> L'anme del cunte portent en pareis.   (2366-2396)

In this passage, Roland begins his speech with the *mea culpa* of the *Confiteor*, sees himself prefigured both in the Old Testament and in the New, performs a series of gestures by means of which he seems to become iconographical before our very eyes, and is assumed, though not bodily, into heaven by three angels. Even Roland's diction contributes to the devotional effect of the scene: *Patene* (line 2384) is usually glossed as *imago paterna*; Gaston Paris's response to this line is relevant: "On pense à ces colossales images de Dieu le père, à ces 'majestés' en mosaïque, qui remplissent le fond des absides ou les voûtes des coupoles dans les églises byzantines."[12]

That Roland should receive a saint's reward for his efficacy as a killer is a bit troublesome, though explicable in terms of what became Christian dogma. Patristic discussions of the justification for war continued uninterruptedly throughout the Middle Ages; going on a Crusade, of course, could be a way of doing penance. Perhaps the most formidable intellectual consideration of the problem is in Thomas Aquinas's *Summa theologica*; the three requirements for a just Christian warrior are *auctoritas principis*, *causa justa*, and *intentio bellantium recta*.[13] As the Old French poet presents him, Roland certainly fulfills all three of the Angelic Doctor's requirements, although, as Auerbach suggests, he fulfills them in a way closer to the demands of dogma than to those of art.

One of the figures in the *Song of Roland*, however, cannot be disposed of with similar dogmatic neatness; Archbishop Turpin is troublesome. Aquinas deals at some length with the problem of clerical warriors, and concludes that Christ and Ingeld are unequivocally irreconcilable in the figure of a priest: "Onmes clericorum ordines ordinantur ad altaris ministerium, in quo sub sacramento repraesentatur passio Christi, secundum illud (1 Corinth. 11.26) *quotiescumque manducabitis panem hunc, et calicem bibetis, mortem Domini annuntiabitis, donce veniat.* Et ideo non competit eis occidere vel effundere sanguinem, sed magis esse paratos ad propriam sanguinis ef-

---

[11] Erich Auerbach, *Mimesis* (Garden City 1957) 96, 97, 104.

[12] Quoted in *La Chanson de Roland*, ed. T. A. Jenkins (Boston 1924) 173-174.

[13] Thomas Aquinas, *Summa theologica*, Secunda Secundae, Quaestio 40, Articulus 1, n. 14, Articulus 2 (Bari 1868) 4.292 (also see n. 15).

fusionem pro Christo, ut imitentur opere quod gerunt ministerio."[14] Aquinas argues that the clergy may offer spiritual assistance to soldiers fighting
for a just cause; Turpin certainly offers such assistance in laisse 89 and 115,
but elsewhere he certainly violates the biblical injunction, "Arma militiae
nostrae non carnalia sunt, sed potentia Dei" (2 Corinthians 10.4).   In laisse 114, for example, the poet describes Turpin's charge (providing incidentally a miniature handbook of equitation), which results in the violent death
of the pagan, Abisme:

> Turpins i fiert, ki nient ne l'esparignet,
> Enpres sun colp ne qui qu'un dener vaillet,
> Le cors li trenchet très l'un costet qu'a l'altre,
> Que mort l'abat en une voide place.
> Dient Franceis "Ci ad grant vasselage!
> En l'arcevesque est bon la croce salve." (1504-1509)

The battle humor of the fictional French in this passage suggests that they
are not troubled, but merely amused, by the combination of Christ and Ingeld in the figure of Archbishop Turpin. A bit later, when Malquiant kills
Anseis, Turpin avenges his peer:

> Par le camp vait Turpin, li arcevesque.
> Tel coronet ne chantat unches messe
> Ki de sun cors feist tantes proecces.
> Dist al paien: "Deus tut mal te tramette!
> Tel as ocis dunt al coer me regrette."
> Sun bon ceval i ad fait esdemettre,
> Si l'ad ferut sur l'escut de Tulette
> Que mort l'abat desur l'herbe verte. (1605-1612)

Clearly, Turpin does not conform to Aquinas's notion of proper clerical con-
duct in battle, a notion, incidentally, which did not originate with Aquinas;
Vanderpol cites passages from Ambrose, Pope Nicholas I, Pope Innocent
I, the first Council of Toledo, and others, all of which indicate a strong tra-
dition of Catholic thought condemning killer priests.[15]
    More difficult to accept than the contradiction inherent in the figure of
Turpin is that inherent in Charles's evangelical technique; having conquered
Sargossa, the emperor offers his vanquished foes a clear choice:

> Li reis creit en Deu, faire voelt sun servise,
> E si evesque les eves beneissent,

[14] *Ibid.* 295-296.
[15] Alfred Vanderpol, *La doctrine scolastique du droit de guerre* (Paris 1919) 121ff.

> Meinent paien entesqu'al baptiserie:
> S'or i ad cel qui Carle cuntredie,
> Il le fait prendre o ardeir ou ocire.
> Baptizet sund asez plus de .C. milie
> Veir chrestien. (3666-3672)

Exactly how *veir* such *chrestien* could be presents no problem for the *Roland* poet.

The *Song of Roland*, then, offers a solution to the problem of combining Ingeld and Christ which is both intellectually and aesthetically less than satisfying, perhaps, as Auerbach suggests, because the poet lacked the sense that he was dealing with a problem at all. Although the poem has been called an epic, its racist, jingoistic, and hagiographic elements certainly create a poem entirely unlike the *Aeneid*, to which it bears some formal resemblances.[16] Vergil never sees things as starkly categorically right or wrong as the *Roland* poet; his famous sense of *lacrimae rerum* is too strong for such oversimplifications, as the sorrowful words of Aeneas after he has killed Lausus, indicate:

> Quid tibi nunc, miserande puer, pro laudibus istis,
> Quid pius Aeneas tanta dabit indole dignum?
> Arma, quibus laetatus, habe tua; teque parentum
> Manibus et cineri, si qua est ea cura, remitto.
> Hoc tamen infelix miseram solabere mortem:
> Aeneae magni dextra cadis. (10.825-830)

Vergil's awareness of the complexity of morality, and even his *caritas*, are greater than the awareness and *caritas* of the Christian poet of the *Song of Roland*.

Devotional poetry, however, need not necessarily lack a sense of the problematic in combining Ingeld and Christ. Composed in the ninth century, the Old English *Andreas*, deals with a recognized Christian saint, and yet provides a number of problematic moments for Andreas, during the most dramatic of which he compares himself to Christ (lines 1401-1428):

> Næfre ic geferde   mid frean willan
> Under heofonhwealfe   heardran drohtnoþ,
> Þær ic dryntnes æ   deman sceolde.
> Sint me leoþu tolocen,   lic sare gebrocen,
> Banhus blodfag,   benne weallaþ,
> Seonodolg swatige.   Hwæt, þu sigora weard,

---

[16] The comparison is developed by W. Tavernier, in *Zeitschrift für französische Sprache und Literatur* 36.76ff.

Dryhten hælend,   on dæges tide
Mid Judeum   geomor wurde
Þa þu of gealgan,   god lifigende,
Fyrnweorca frea,   to fæder cleopodest,
Cininga wuldor,   on cwaede þus:
"Ic þe, fæder engla,   frignan wille,
Lifes leohtfruma,   hwæt forlætest þu me?"
Ond ic nu þry dagas   þolian sceolde
Wælgrim witu.   Bidde ic, weoroda god,
Þæt ic gast minne   agifan mote,
Sawla symbelgifa,   on þines sylfes hand.
Þu þæt gehete   þurh þin halig word,
Þæt þu us twelfe   trymman ongunne,
Þæt us heterofa   hild ne gesceode,
Ne lices dæl   lungre oþþeoded,
Ne synu ne ban   on swaþe lagon,
Ne loc of heafde   to forlore wurde,
Gif we þine lare   læstan woldon.
Nu sint sionwe toslopen,   is min swat adropen,
Licgaþ æfter lande   locas todrifene,
Fex on foldan.   Is me feorhgedal
Leofre mycle   þonne þeos lifcearo.[17]

Andreas's suffering, as martyr and spiritual *heterofa*, is subsequently relieved by God, who sends a flood to drown his disciple's cannibal tormentors. Then, presumably to show the *duplex substantia* of divinity, which exercises *caritas* as well as *justitia*, God brings the dead men, at Andreas's request, back to life. Andreas's own double nature, as warrior and as a type of Christ, is explicitly, even blatantly present in the text of the poem.

A less explicitly Christian killer, in a poem whose resemblances to *Andreas* have often been noted, *Beowulf* is a good example of a nondogmatic, tentative, unschematic attempt to solve the problem of combining Ingeld and Christ. Not everyone, however senses such ambiguities in Beowulf; Maurice McNamee has no difficulty in seeing Beowulf as Christ, particularly in the battle scene with Grendel's mother:

> To an audience familiar with this symbolic meaning of immersion into emersion from waters infested by the powers of hell and purified by the powers of God, it would have been natural to see in Beowulf's descent into the serpent-infested mere and his triumphant ascent from those waters purified of their serpents a symbolic representation of the death and burial and of the resurrection of

---

[17] *The Vercelli Book*, ed. G. P. Krapp (New York 1961) 42.

Christ, and, in the purification of the waters, a symbol of the redemption of man from the poisonous powers of evil . . . sufficient
clue for such an interpretation would have been provided for such
an audience by the explicit identification of Grendel's dam and
Grendel himself with the powers of evil.[18]

Passages with rich, vaguely archetypal elements such as the one Father
McNamee is talking about lend themselves fairly easily to patristic exegisis, but the results of such exegisis sometimes suggest that the poetry is functioning as a set of circus animals in the mind of the exegete. Some very attractive examples of such ringmastership present themselves in a fourteenth-
century poem, the *Ovide moralisé*, for example, and some of them are sug-
gestively relevant to Father McNamee's remarks.

When Aeneas descends to hell, the poet explains (14.978-984):

Par Eneas puis droitement
Noter le piteuz Rambeour,
Le debonaire Sauveour.
Le fil Dieu, qui deigne[r] venir
Des cieulz en terre, et devenir
Vrais homs, e enfers visiter,
Pour ses amis d'enfer giter. (14.9)[19]

When Orpheus descends to hell, the poet offers a similar explication: (11.178-
183):

Orpheus denote à delivre
Jhesu Christ, parole devine,
Le douctour de bone doctrine
Qui par sa predicacion
Avoit de mainte nacion
La gent atraite et convertie. (11.1)

The *Ovide moralisé* poet offers a similarly ingenious explication for the des-
cent of Pirithous and Theseus (7.2037ff.), and manages an extraordinarily
violent yoking of opposites in 13.931ff. where Ajax and Ulysses are said to
represent Saint John and Christ, respectively.

The poet's ingenious ability to find any number of Ingelds to be Christ
is a historical curiosity, and may produce some aesthetic pleasure for us,
but his exegesis certainly cannot be considered to have much to do with
the poem Ovid wrote. Similarly, Father McNamee seems to mistake a re-

---

[18] M. B. McNamee, "*Beowulf*—an Allegory of Salvation?" ed. Nicholson (n. 1 above)
341. For another extravagantly patristic exegesis see n. 44 below.

[19] References to *Ovide moralisé* are to C. de Boer's reprinted edition, 5 vols. (Wiesbaden
1966).

semblance for an identity, possibly because his remarks were intended for
a polemical context. Critics have occupied themselves for many years in
a discussion of the extent to which *Beowulf* is a Christian or a pagan poem.
Father McNamee's position represents one pole, F. A. Blackburn's "*Beowulf* is essentially a heathen poem" represents the other.[20] Neither position
seems compelling, however, since *Beowulf* is a poem, not an argument. Perhaps the most satisfying position is represented by J. A. A. Tolkien's remarks about the poem: "It is a poem by a learned man, writing of old times,
who looking back on the heroism and sorrow feels in them something permanent and something symbolical. So far from being a confused semi-pa-
gan—historically unlikely for a man of this sort in the period—he brought
probably *first* to his task a knowledge of Christian poetry, especially that
of the Caedmon school, and especially *Genesis*."[21] Tolkien focuses his attention on the poem as an imaginative work, in which the poet attempts
paradoxical combinations: "And in the poem I think we may observe not
confusion, a half-hearted and muddled business, but a fusion that has occurred *at a given point* of contact between old and new, a product of thought
and deep emotion."[22]

Other critics have also described *Beowulf* in terms of paradoxical combinations. Robert Kaske, for example, says: "I believe that in the *sapientia
et fortitudo* theme itself we may find the "precise point at which an imagination, pondering old and new, was kindled"—that the poet has used this old
ideal as an area of synthesis between Christianity and Germanic paganism.
In a broad way, he seems first to draw on both traditions primarily as they
relate to *sapientia et fortitudo*, and secondly, within this circumscribed area,
he seems to emphasize those aspects of each tradition that can be made reasonably compatible with the viewpoint of the other—somewhat like Dante's
more complex synthesis of classical and Christian morality in the *Inferno*."[23]
As a result of examining three sets of opposites, Herbert Wright concludes:
"He [the *Beowulf* poet] has no meticulous design, worked out with mathematical precision from start to finish. The three groups of opposites that
have been examined are seen to intersect but not to coincide; and though
they contribute to a fundamental unity, as the poem advances, with the
deepening of the elegiac strain, sorrow gets the upper hand, and all else is
subordinate."[24]

[20] F. A. Blackburn, "The Christian Coloring in the *Beowulf*," ed. Nicholson (n. 1 above)
1.

[21] Tolkien (n. 1 above) 78.

[22] *Ibid.* 70.

[23] R. E. Kaske, "*Sapientia et Fortitudo* as the Controlling Theme of *Beowulf*," ed. Ni-
ckolson (n. 1 above) 273.

[24] *Ibid.* 267.

Analyzing works of literature in terms of paradoxical combinations is, of course, by now a fashionable critical employment. The remarks of Tolkien, Kaske, and Wright, however, suggest that *Beowulf* offers particularly rich material for such analyses, principally, I think, because the *Beowulf* poet, unlike the *Roland* poet, does not sacrifice imaginative possibilities for devotional exigencies.

The lines that follow the slaying of Grendel's mother illustrate the *Beowulf* poet's ability to suggest rather than to schematize lines 1605b-1611):

> þe þæt sweord ongan
> æfter heaþoswate   hildegicelum.
> Wigbil wanian;   þæt wæs wundra sum,
> Þæt hit eal gemealt   ise gelicost,
> Þonne forstes bend   Fæder onlæteþ,
> Onwindeþ wælrapas,   se geweald hafaþ
> Sæla ond mæla;   þæt is soþ Metod.[25]

In this striking combination of heroic, folk, and Christian elements, the poet suggests an analogy between the melting of the sword and the seasonal miracle God performs by seeing to it that spring follows winter. God's presence in the universe, then, for the *Beowulf* poet can be felt in the course of natural events, but for the *Roland* poet God's presence in the universe can only be represented by a literal break in the natural course of events, by making the earth quake, and by paralysing the sun. Aelfric's remarks at the end of the tenth century on the tawdry sensationalism of miracles help illustrate the contrast between the two poets:

> Fela wundra worhte God, and dæghwamlice wyrcð, ac ða wundra sind swiðe awacode on manna gesihðe, forðon ðe hi sind swiðe gewunelice. Mare wundor is þæt God Aelmihtig ælce dæg getealne middangeard, and gewissað þa godan, þonne þæt wundor waere, þæt He ða gefylde fif ðusend manna mid fif hlafum.[26]

As a result of the *Beowulf* poet's less schematic, less artificial notion of the nature of reality, no contradictions as blatant as those produced, for example, by the figure of Archbishop Turpin in *Roland*, exist in any of the characters in *Beowulf*. Although the characters and incidents are pre-Christian, the poet makes use of what has been called "Christian coloring," and consequently manages, intentionally or otherwise, to follow Gregory's advice about putting pagan material to Christian use:

[25] References to *Beowulf* are to Klaeber"'s edition (New York 1950).
[26] *An Old English Anthology*, ed. W. F. Bolton (Evanston 1966) 75.

We have been giving careful thought to the affairs of the English, and have come to the conclusion that the temples of the idols
in that country should on no account be destroyed. He is to destroy the idols, but the temples themselves are to be aspersed with
holy water, altars set up, and relics enclosed in them. For if these
temples are well built, they are to be purified from devil-worship,
and dedicated to the service of the true God. And since they have
a custom of sacrificing many oxen to devils, let some other seolem-
nity be substituted in its place, such as a day of Dedication or the
Festivals of the holy martyrs whose relics are enshrined there. On
such occasions they might well construct shelters of boughs for
themselves around the churches that were once temples, and celebrate the solemnity with devout feasting. They are no longer to
sacrifice beasts to the Devil, but they may kill them for food to
the praise of God, and give thanks to the Giver of all gifts for His
bounty. If the people are allowed some worldly pleasures in this
way, they will more readily come to desire the joys of the spirit.
For it is certainly impossible to eradicate all errors from obstinate
minds at one stroke, and whoever wishes to climb to a moun-
tain top climbs gradually step by step, and not in one leap.[27]

Gregory's practical advice suggests that one who has a strong feeling for
the spirit can accommodate the possible ambiguities of the letter; Alcuin's
response would then seem unduly rigid. Leo Spitzer has suggested that the
difference between Ambrose and Augustine may be characterized roughly
as a contrast between an inclusive and an exclusive sensibility; Alcuin and
Gregory would seem to illustrate the same contrast.[28] Alcuin sees a problem,
where Gregory and the *Beowulf* poet find a compassable ambiguity.

A very strong feeling for the positive aspects of heroic values, combined
with an equally strong feeling for the transitoriness of the same values gives
Beowulf its unique quality. In the same speech, Hrothgar can say:

> Blaed is araered
> Geond widwegas,   wine min Beowulf
> Ðin ofer þeoda gehwylce.   Eal þu hit geþyldum healdest,
> Maegen mid modes snyttrum.   (1703b-1706a)

and subsequently add:

> Nu is þines maegnes blaed
> Ane hwile;   eft sona bið,
> Þaet þec adl oððe ecg   eafoþes getwæfe,

---

[27] Bede, *A History of the English Church and People*, trans. Leo Sherley-Price (Penguin
1960) 86-87.

[28] See Leo Spitzer, *Classical and Christian Ideas of World Harmony* (Baltimore 1963)
32-33.

Oððe fyres feng, oððe flodes wylm,
Oððe gripe meces,   oððe gares fliht,
Oððe atol yldo;   oððe eagena bearhtm
Foriteð ond forsweorce;   semninga bið
Þaet ðec, dryhtguma,   deað   oferswyðeð.   (1761b-1768)

Like Chaucer in the *Troilus*, then, the *Beowulf* poet presents the phenomenal world with positive intensity, while simultaneously attempting to
create a feeling in his audience (or to articulate his own feeling) for a structure that transcends and in a sense negates the values of the phenomenal
world. Also like Chaucer in the *Troilus*, he creates a poem whose imaginative
life cancels out, for many readers, the possible homiletic intentions.

At this point, the *Nibelungenlied* may provide, with its unequivocal rejection of the possibilities of a reconciliation between Ingeld and Christ,
a contrast that will make clearer the extent to which *Beowulf* represents a
tentative, ambiguous response to the problem of such a reconciliation.[29] The
opening stanza of the *Nibelungenlied* lays out a series of antinomies that
create, instead of ambiguity, an explicitly articulated awareness of the limitations of the phenomenal world:

Uns ist in alten maeren   wunders vil geseit
Von helden lobebaeren,   von grozer arebeit,
Von frouden, hochgeziten,   von weinen und von klagen
Von kuener recken striten   muget ir nu wunder hoeren sagen.[30]

That joy is followed by sadness is of course the central commonplace of the
De contemptu mundi tradition, which might be considered a series of variations on Proverbs 16: "Extrema gaudii luctus occupat."[31] In this particular stanza the *Nibelungenlied* poet has made use of prosodic and syntactical
patterns to emphasize his Stoic horror of heroic activities. Several other
examples of the expression of this commonplace, also reinforced by parallel
prosodic and syntactical patterns, occur in the first *Aventiure*: in the second
stanza the poet says about Kriemhild that "si wart ein scoene wîp. dar umbe
muosen degene vil verliesen den lîp"—great physical beauty leads to great
physical destruction. In the sixth stanza the poet connects heroic nobility
with inevitable tragic destruction:

---

[29] For the most precise argument of the sense in which the *Nibelungenlied* is a criticism
of heroic values (among others), see Gottfried Weber, *Das Nibelungenlied, Problem und
Idee* (Stuttgart 1963), and particularly his "Schlussmeditation" (195-198).

[30] References to the *Nibelungenlied* are to stanzas in the edition by Karl Bartsch, revised
by Helmut de Boor (Wiesbaden 1959).

[31] For a convenient description of the *De casibus* tradition, see Willard Farnham, *The
Medieval Heritage of Elizabethan Tragedy* (Berkeley 1936).

In diente von ir landen   vil stolziu ritterscaft
Mit lobelîchen eren   unz an ir endes zît.
Si stûrben sît jaemerliche   von zweier edelen frouwen nît.

Toward the end of the first *Aventiure*, Kriemhild and her mother, Vote, discuss the meaning of Kriemhild's first dream (stanzas 14-15):

Den troum si dô sagete   ir muoter Uotèn.
Sine kundes niht besceiden   baz der guoten:
"Der valke den du ziuhest,   das ist sin [e]del man.
In welle got behüeten,   du muost in sciere vloren hân."
"Waz saget ir mit von manne, viel liebiu muoter mîn?
Âne recken minne   sô wil ich immer sîn.
Sus scoen ich wil belîben   unz an mînen tôt,
Daz ich von mannes minne   sol gewinnen nimmer nôt."

Although Kriemhild's response is to be taken as a dramatic statement, and not necessarily as a statement of the poet's view of things, her sense of the connection between love and disaster proves to be accurate in the course of the poem. Her use of the word *nôt* also echoes one of the central themes of the poem, the ineluctable workings of fate, the overwhelming force of Necessity. "*Nôt*" is of course literally the last word in the text, as we have it, and such is the force of the notion of necessity in the poem, that the alternative title of *Nibelungennôt* has frequently been prefixed to it. In addition, one of the hypothetical sources of the *Nibelungelied* is a poem usually known as *Diu Nôt*.[32]

Necessity is used in the poem in the sense of a universal limiting force, and in the sense of human compulsion; when Giselher offers to try to make up for the death of Sifrid, Kriemhild replies: "des waere Kriemhilde nôt (stanza 1080)." Relentlessly, the *Nibelungenlied* poet pursues his notion that heroic values *necessarily* lead to the destruction of human ones, as the concluding two stanzas and the final word of the poem clearly assert:

Diu vil michel êre   was dâ gelegen tôt.
Die liute heten alle   jâmer unde nôt.
Mit leide was verendet   des kuniges hôhgezît.
Als ie diu liebe leide   z'aller jungeste gît.
Ine kan iu niht beschieden,   waz sider dâ geschach:
Wan ritter under vrouwen   weinen man da sach,
Dar zuo die edeln knehte,   ir lieben friunde tôt.
Hie hât daz maere ein ende: daz ist der Nibelunge nôt.

---

[32] See Weber (n. 29 above) 245-249, for his excursus on *nôt*.

In addition to its diction and rhetoric, the poem's two central trap scenes emphasize the poet's sense of the compulsive destructiveness of heroic values; Sifrid's entrapment and death ends the first part of the poem, and the destruction of the Burgundians and most of their hosts ends the second part of the poem.

Trying for the darkest ironies possible, the *Nibelungenlied* poet shows Hagen killing Sifrid at a spring, conventionally a source of life:

> Der brunne der was küele,   lûter une guot. . .
> Dâ der herre Sîfrit   ob dem brunnen tranc,
> Er schôz in durch das kriuze,   daz von der wunden spranc
> Daz bluot im von dem herzen   vaste an die Hagenen wât.
> (979, 981)

The *kriuze* is the mark Kriemhild has made to protect Sifrid, and possibly the poet also wants some of the resonance that would result from the audiences' Christian associations with *kriuze*, a cross. The notion of violated nature is further emphasized when the poet tells us that flowers were wet with Sifrid's blood: "Die bluomen allenthalben von bluote wurden naz" (998).

Associating his death with violated nature also supports Sifrid's mythic overtones in the poem; the Burgundians are killed in a hall, traditionally symbolic of civilization, in a treacherous, most uncivilized encounter with Etzel's men. Thus, the *Nibelungenlied* poet has structured his poem to convey very vividly the sense that purely heroic values lead to the destruction both of nature and of civilization.

The most startingly gruesome illustration of the destruction of civilized values is in the final trap, a dark parody of heroic Gemütlichkeit and possibly also of the Eucharist, represented by the Burgundian's enforced vampirism:

> Ir einer sprach dar inne: "wir müezen ligen tôt.
> Was hilfet uns das grüezen,   daz uns der künec enbôt?
> Mir tuot von starker hitze   der durst sô rehte wê,
> Des waen mîn leben schiere   in disen sorgen zergê."
> Dô sprach von Tronege Hagene: "ir edeln ritter guot,
> Swen twinge durstes nôt,   der trinke hie daz bluot.
> Daz ist in solher hitze   noch bezzer danne wîn.
> Ez enmac an disen zîten   et nû niht bezzer gesîn."
> Dô gie der recken einer   da er einen tôten vant.
> Er kniete im zuo der wunden,   den helm er ab gebant,
> Dô begonde er trinken   daz vliezende bluot.
> Swie ungewon ers waere,   ez dûhte in groezlîchen guot.
> "Nu lôn iu got, her Hagene",   sprach der müede man,
> "Daz ich von iuwer lêre   sô wol getrunken hân.
> Mir ist noch vil selten   geschenket bezzer wîn.
> Lebe ich deheine wîle,   ich sol iu immer waege sîn." (2113-2116)

In addition to violating the decorum of nature, civilization, and the *comitatus* feast, the relentless pursuit of heroic values also perverts the erotic relationships in the poem: Brunhild is an amazon, Kriemhild metamorphoses from a *minnecliche meide* into a Medea figure. Wealhtheow or Alde la bele would not survive long in the world of the Nibelungs.

Despite the blatantly antiheroic attitudes that the poet expresses, not everyone agrees that the *Nibelungenlied* is a Christian poem. A. T. Hatto goes to what seem to me perverse lengths to deny Christianity to the poem: "Although we must assume that the *Nibelungelied* was written by a Christian poet for Christian audiences, and that he leaves loose ends for thoughtful Christians to take up if they so please, the mood which the poem induced was not a Christian mood, and the result is not a Christian poem."[33] His statement is reminiscent of the kind of statement occasionally made in the not too distant past about Shakespeare's *Lear*, and suggests a rigidly narrow notion of what the possibilities of a Christian imagination are. Certainly the *Nibelungenlied* poet's horror at the values of heroic society corresponds to Alcuin's horror, and is intensified by the poet's awareness of the relevance of his subject to his own time and place. As Gottfried Weber has said: "Was also der Nibelungenautor wunschmässig erstrebt, ist ganz gewiss nicht das spezifisch Heideische am Germanischen, ebensowenig aber etwa auch eine gegenwartsnahe Art von mittelalterlichem Neuheidentum. Sondern seine Position wird klar bezeichnet durch eine höchst problematische Spannung zwischen dem Heldischen und dem für ihn im Nebelhaften bleibenden Christlich-Göttlichen."[34]

Like *Beowulf*, the *Nibelungenlied* has long supplied critics with material to argue for or against the notion that it is a Christian poem. Even without considering Weber's formidable arguments, the poem seems obviously and utterly Christian. The overall movement from joy to grief, from the top of the wheel of Fortune to the bottom, certainly fits the notion of tragedy repetitively referred to by that repository of Christian clichés, Chaucer's Monk:

> For hym that folweth al this world of prees,
> Er he be war, is ofte yleyed ful lowe.[35]

That the poet has substituted a church for a stream as the setting for the flyting of Brunhild and Kriemhild also suggests a feeling for specifically Christian dark ironies.

---

[33] Arthur Thomas Hatto, *The Nibelungenlied* (Baltimore 1965) 343.
[34] Weber (n. 29 above) 178.
[35] *Canterbury Tales* 7.2137-2138, ed. F. N. Robinson (Cambridge, Mass. 1957) 191.

In addition to the canibalistic parody of the Eucharist, the meeting of Brunhild and Kriemhild at church, and the general correspondance of the poem to the *De Casibus* tradition, the figure of Dietrich von Berne, the historical Theodoric, may also have some Christian significance. Of the heroic figures in the poem, Dietrich survives in the most admirable fashion at the end of the poem. Theodoric, though an Arian, was associated with religious tolerance, a tradition that is reflected in a thirteenth-century poetic description of him piously lamenting his dead companions:

> Ich bite iuch, muoter unde meit,
> Kunegin von himmelrich,
> Daz ir bedenket miniu leit![36]

Another tradition, however, represents him as an enemy of the church; after Theodoric has imprisoned the Pope, the *Kaiserchronik* records:

> Die cristen dô clageten
> Daz si verlorn habeten
> Ir maister alsô lieben,
> Dô rach si got sciere,
> Want er die cristen hête gelaidiget
> Dô wart im vor gote vertailet,
> Vil manige daz sâhen,
> Daz in die tievel nâmen,
> Si vuorten in in den berch ze Vulcân
> Daz gebôt in sancte Johannes der hailige man,
> Der brinnet er unz an dem jungisten tac,
> Daz im niemen gehelfen nemac.[37]

Dietrich in the *Nibelungenlied*, however, is unambiguously decent, as the lament he recites for his fallen men indicates:

> "Und sint erstorben   alle mîne man,
> Sô hât mîn got vergezzen,   ich armer Dietrîch.
> Ich was ein künec hêre,   vil gewaltic unde rîch."
> "Wie kinde ez sich gefüegen,"   sprach aber Dietrîch,
> "Daz si alle sint erstorben,   die helde lobelîch,
> Von dem strîtmüeden,   die doch heten nôt?
> Wan durch mîn ungelücke,   in waere vremde noch der tôt...
> "Owê, lieber Wolfhart, sol ich dich hân verlorn,
> So mac mich balde riuwen   daz ich ie wart geborn!

[36] George Zink, *Le Cycle de Dietrich* (Paris 1953) 112-113.
[37] *Kaiserchronik*, ed. Edward Schröder (Hanover 1892) 1.1.337.

Sigestap und Wolfwîn   und ouch Wolfprant!
Wer sol mir danne helfen   in der Amelunge lant?
Helpfrîch der vil küene,   und ist mir der erslagen
Gêrbart und Wîchart,   wie solde ich die verklagen?
Daz ist an mînen vreuden   mir der leste tac.
Owê daz vor leide   nieman sterben nemac!" (2319-2320,
2319-2323)

Like Andreas, Dietrich feels abandoned by God, like Charlemagne he articulates his grief in terms of *ubi sunt* rhetoric[38] (as he does in the passage from the *Battle of Ravenna* quoted above); in addition, he places himself in the *De casibus* tradition, wishes for death, like Job and Oedipus, and echoes the *Nibelungelied* poet's preoccupation with *nôt*. Dietrich is then an extremely complex figure, or *figura*, in a Christian poem, who nevertheless does not represent an attempt to combine Christ and Ingeld. Instead, Dietrich represents the *Nibelungenlied* poet's notion of an heroic paradigm, as Weber has asserted: "Denn kein Zweifel kann weiterhin darüber obwalten, dass die Dietrîch-Gestalt von ihrem Schöpfer als eine geschlossene und ganzheitliche gedacht ist, dass Ethos und metaphysisches Meinen letztlich in ihr zusammenstimmen, dass ritterliche Züge und heldische Geistesart zu neuer Einheit in Dîetrich von Bern zusammenwachsen sollten."[39] But the *Nibelungenlied* poet, as Weber points out, is careful not to give Dietrich any transcendent qualities, because, I think, he, like Alcuin, saw no possibilities for combining Ingeld and Christ.

The most violent combination of Ingeld and Christ in medieval literature is in *Njal-Saga*, when Kari and his men discover the partially burned body of Skarp-hedin, the saga's leading killer:

Þá leituðu þeir Skarpheðins. Þar vísuðu heimamenn til, sem þeir Flosi hofðu vísuna heyrt kveðna, ok var þar ekjan fallin at gaflaðinu ok þaer maelti Hjalti, at til skyldi grafa. Sið an gerðu þeir svá ok fundu þar likama Skarpheðins, ok hafði hann staðit upp við gaflaðit, ok váru brunnir foetr af honum mjok svá neðan til knjá, en allt annat óbrunnit á honum. Hann hafði bitit á kampi sínum. Augu hans váru opin ok óþút in. Hann hafði rekit øxina í gaflaðit svá fast, at gengit hafði allt upp á mið jan fetann, ok var ekkidignuð. Síðan var hann ut borinn ok øxin; Hjalti tók upp øxina ok maelti: "Þetta er fágaett vápn, ok munu fáir bera mega." Kari maelti: "sé ek mann til, hverr bera skal øxina." "Hverr er sá?" segir Hjalti. "Þorgeirr skorargeirr," segir Kari, "er ek aetla ná mestan vera í þeiri aett." Þá var Skarpheðinn foerðr af klaeðum, því at þau

---

[38] See *Roland* 2402ff.
[39] Weber (n. 29 above) 169.

varu ekki brunnin. Hann hafði lagit hendr sínar í kross ok á ofan
ina hoegri, en tvá díla fundu þeir á honum, annan meðal herðanna,
en annan á brjostinu, ok var hvárrtveggi brenndr í kross, ok aetluðu menn, at hann mundi sik sjálfr brennt hafa. Allir menn mael-
tu þat, at betra þoetti hjá Skarpheðni dauðum en aetluðu, því at
engi maðr hraeddisk hann.[40]

Skarp-Hedin literally makes himself into a *figura* combining Christ and Ingeld, but in the light of Skarp-Hedin's past brutality, the *figura* seems gro-
tesque. Of all the killers in the saga, Skarp-hedin seems the most cold-blood-
ed, least self-conscious, and certainly least guilt-conscious. Gunnar, on the
other hand, a kind of Dietrich figure, shows the kind of hesitancy about
killing that one might reasonably expect of a Christian, but he is exiled and
killed before Christianity enters either Iceland or *Njalssaga*. Skarp-Hedin's
apparently self-inflicted stigmata suggest that *Njala's* author had an ironic
awareness of the sense in which Christianity first came to Iceland. Earlier
in the saga, Thangbrand, the first successful Christian missionary to Iceland, demonstrates an evangelical technique roughly equivalent to that of
Turpin and Charlemagne. Instead of undergoing the passion of a martyr,
Thangbrand beats his pagan opponents to death, or, with the assistance
of white magic like an Old Testament prophet, he causes the earth to open
up and swallow them. The only element in the scene clearly drawn from
the New Testament is Thangbrand's crucifix, which he uses quite literally
as a shield against the assaults of his enemies.[41]

---

[40] *Brennu-Njals Saga*, ed. Einnar O. Sveinsenn (Reykjavik 1954) 343-344.
　　　Then they looked for Sharp-Hedin. The servants showed them the place where
　　Flosi and his men had heard the verse uttered. The roof had collapsed there beside
　　the gable wall, and that was where Hjalti told them to dig. They did so, and
　　found the body of Skarp-Hedin. He had himself upright against the wall; his legs
　　were almost burnt off below the knees, but the rest of him was unburnt. He had
　　bitten hard on his lip. His eyes were open but not swollen. He had driven his axe
　　into the gable with such violence that half the full depth of the blade was buried
　　in the wall, and the metal had not softened. His body was carried out, with the
　　axe. Hjalti picked up the axe and said, "this is a rare weapon. Few could wield
　　it." "I know the man to wield it," said Kari. "Who is that?" asked Hjalti. "Thor-
　　geir Skorar-Geir," replied Kari. "He is outstanding member of that family now."
　　They stripped Skarp-Hedin's body, for the clothes has not been burnt off. He
　　had crossed his arms, with the right one over the left. They found two marks on
　　his body, one between the shoulders, the other on his chest, both of them burn
　　marks in the shape of a cross; they came to the conclusion that he had branded
　　them on himself. They all agreed that they found it less uncomfortable to see Skarp-
　　Hedin dead than they had expected; for no one felt any fear of him.
Njal's Saga, Trans. Magnus Magnusson and Hermann Palsson (Penguin, 1960). Some of the
delicate equivocation of "ok aetluu menn" is lost by translating "they came to the conclusion."
[41] Sveinsenn (n. 40 above) chap. 101.

Other, less grotesquely ironic combinations of Christ and Ingeld occur in medieval literature, particularly in Arthurian material. In the thirteenth-century *Prose Lancelot*, a strikingly precise combination occurs, as R. S. Loomis has observed; when Galahad is introduced with the greeting, "pais soit o vous":

> The author, let us observe, has subtly imparted a Christian flavor to the pagan myth by introducing details from the gospel of St. John. Twice, when the disciples were gathered together after the Resurrection, Jesus entered, though the doors were closed and stood among them; and greeted them with the words "Peace be with you!" By borrowing these two details from one of the most awe-inspiring appearances of Christ after His death, the author created precisely the right atmosphere for the arrival of the Christ-knight Galahad.[42]

By the fourteenth century, the combination of Christ and Ingeld seems to offer no great difficulties; William Matthews points out such a combination in the alliterative *Morte Arthure*:

> The poet chose to make both his Arthur and his Mordred regard Gawain dead as Christ crucified, and from his own bitterness over Gawain's self-immolation and the passionate lyricism of his own lament it may be suspected that he himself looked on his hero as a type of the Saviour. But if Mordred's fear that his part in the catastrophe has been a Judas role has the poet's support, the parallelisms between Joseph of Arimathea's proceedings and Arthur's do not make the king a type of Joseph. When Arthur finds Gawain's corpse, pierced through and stained with blood, his sorrow surpasses anything proper to the death of a mortal man, and his kinghts rebukingly suggest a more fitting object:
> Be knyghtly of contenaunce, als a kyng scholde,
> And leue siche clamoure for Cristes lufe of heuen (3979-3980)
> But Arthur's grief is the passion of one who sees before him both an embodiment of Christ and the tragic result of his own guilt. Catching up the corpse, he kisses the leaden lips, fainting under the stress of his emotion:
> Than sweltes the swete kynge and in swoun fallis,
> Swafres vp swiftely, and swetly hym kysses,
> Till his burliche berde was blody beronnen,
> Alls he had bestes birtenede and broghte owt of life (3969-3972)

---

[42] Roger Sherman Loomis, *The Development of Arthurian Romance* (New York 1964).

The blood guilt symbolized in this gesture is made explicit in the king's next words: "He es sakles supprysede for syn of myn one!" And if the guiltless Gawain is a type of the sinless Christ, the sin of Arthur can only be the sin of imperial war that had brought Gawain to his death.

It is this two-fold parallelism, Gawain-Christ and Arthur-Alexander, that lends to the last part of *Morte Arthure* its pitiful irony. Arthur is committed to the Alexandrian logic of his vow in the original war council, but his last prayer in battle is an anguished wish that God had cast him in the role of Christ:

> "Qwythen hade Dryghttyn destaynede at his dere wille,
> þat he hade demyd e todaye, to dy for 3ow alle!
> That had I leuer than be lorde all my lyfe tyme
> Off all, þat Alexandere aughte, qwhills he in erther lengede."[43]

Neither Loomis's remarks nor Matthews's represents a fanciful allegorization like that of Father McNamee's reading of Beowulf's battle with Grendel's mother. Loomis's reading is supported both by the diction of the passage, and by the numerous allegories supplied for his material by the author of the *Prose Lancelot*; Matthews's support is present in the passage that I have just quoted from his book.[44]

Spenser's Saint George, Guyon, Arthur, and Cervantes's Don Quixote are, of course, the final, exhaustive elaborations of the technique of bestowing Christlike attributes on Ingeld.

An alternative technique, that of bestowing Ingeldlike attributes on Christ, was also popular.[45] Perhaps the original suggestion for the technique comes from Matthew 10.34, where Christ tells his apostles: "I have not come to bring peace, but a sword." In the Apocryphal Gospel of Nicodemus Christ harrows hell in a warlike fashion, and the many medieval paraphrases, dramatizations and elaborations of the Harrowing of Hell develop the notion of Christ the warrior. Perhaps the most famous example is towards the end of *Piers Plowman*:

---

[43] William Matthews, *The Tragedy of Arthur* (Berkely 1960) 149-150.

[44] The Green Knight, in *Gawain and the Green Knight*, has been interpreted as an Ingeld-Christ figure in a patristical exegete's tour-de-force by Hans Schnyder: "In the sequence of our story the appearance of the Green Knight would consequently herald the manifestation of divine interference in the course of world events. The Green Knight might in that case be accepted as the word of God and—on a different allegorical level—anagogically as Christ." *Sir Gawain and the Green Knight* (Bern 1961) 41.

[45] See Wilbur Gaffney, "The Allegory of the Christ-Knight in *Piers* Plowman," *Publications of the Modern Language Association* 46 (1931) 155-168, and Rosemary Woolf, "The Theme of Christ, the Lover-Knight in Medieval English Literature," *Review of English Studies* 13 (1962) 1-16.

> *Liberum-dei-arbitrium* for love hath undertake
> That this Jesus of his gentrice shal jouste in Pers armes
> In his helm and in his haberjon, *humana natura*,
> That Christ be nat yknowe for *consummatus deus*;
> In Peres plates the Plouhman this prikiare shal ryde,
> For no dynt shal hym dere as *in deitate patris*.[46]

In this complex passage, Langland has combined Christ, Ingeld, Piers, and a number of theological abstractions without confusing imaginative and devotional categories: all the schemes and tropes of *alta fantasia* may be legitimately employed in the impossible task of describing divinity. A striking modern use of the Christ-Ingeld *topos* is Wilfred Owen's "Soldier's Dream," in which Owen despairingly opposes God and Christ, suggesting a kind of ultimate biblical disharmony:

> I dreamed kind Jesus fouled the big-gun gears;
> And caused a permanent stoppage in all bolts;
> And buckled with a smile Mausers and Celts;
> And rusted every bayonet with His tears.
> And there were no more bombs, or ours or Theirs,
> Not even an old flint-lock, nor even a pikel.
> But God was vexed, and gave all power to Michael;
> And when I woke he's seen to our repairs.

In addition to giving Christ Ingeldlike qualities, some medieval authors give him simultaneously the qualities of a courtly lover, as in the following passage from the thirteenth-century *Ancren Riwle*:

A leafdi wes mid hire fan biset al abuten, hire lond al destruet, ant heo al poure, inwið an eorðene castel. A mihti kinges luue wes þah biturnd upon hire, swa unimete swiðe þet he for wohlech sende hire his sonden. an efter oðer, ofte somet monie; sende hire beaw-belez baðe feole ant feire, sucurs of liveneð. help of his hehe hird to halden hire castel. Hee underfeng al as on unrecheles, ant swa wes heardi-heortet þet hire luue ne mahte he neaver beo þe neorre. Hwet wult to mare? He com himseolf on ende; schawde hire his feire neb, as þe þe wes of alle men feherest to bihalden; spec se swiðe swoteliche, ant wordes se murie, þat ha mahten deade arearen to liue; wrahte feole wundres ant dude muchele meistries biuoren hire ehsihðe; schawde hire his mihte; talde hire of his kinedom; bead to makien hire cwen of al þet he ahte.

Al þis ne heold nawt. Nes þis hoker wunder? For heo nes neauer wurðe forte beon his þuften. Ah swa, þurh his deboneirte, luue hefde

---

[46] *Piers Plowman* C 20-24, ed. W. W. Skeat (Oxford 1886) 1.521, 523.

ouercumen him þet he seide on ende: "Dame, þu art iweorret, ant
þine van beoð se stronge þet tu ne maht nanesweis wiðute mi succurs
edfleon hare honden, þet ha ne don þe to scheome deað efter al
þi weane. Ich chulle, for þe luue of þe, neome þet feht upo me ant
arudde þe of ham þe þi deað secheð. Ich wat þah to soðe þet Ich
schal bituhen ham neomen deað es wunde; andt Ich hit wulle heorte-
liche, forte ofgan þin heorte. Nu þenne biseche Ich þe, for þe luue
þet Ich cuðe þe, þet tu luuvie me, lanhure efter þe ilke dede dead
hwen þu naldest lives." þes king dude al þus—arudde hire of all
hire van, ant wes himseolf to wundre ituket ant islein on ende,
þurh miracle aras þah from deaðe to liue. Nere þeos ilke leafdi of uue-
les cunnes kunde, 3ef ha ouer alle þing ne luuede him herefter?

þes king is Jesu, Godes sune, þet al o þise wise wohede ure sawle
þe deolfen hefden biset.[47]

Miss Woolf supplies other medieval examples in her article; the commonplace continued through the Renaissance—its most famous reoccurence is
probably "Batter my heart, three-personed God," in which Donne intensifies
the *topos* with a sense of urgent personal guilt, and with an hysterical sense
of sexuality. The combination of Christ, Ingeld, and Eros, particularly in
Tristan, *Parzifal*, and *Troilus*, however, deserves to be treated in a separate
paper.

Merely combining Christ and Ingeld presented a considerable range of
problems; successful solutions were achieved, I think, by the poets who in-
tuited a notion of art articulated by Graham Hough: "Since the immediate
conformity of the sensibility to the moral imperative is generally approved
in our culture there is a strong critical inclination to make the poets conform
in this way. I think we should be more willing to recognize unresolved
tensions. It is one of the missions of the poet to retain them. It is not what
Milton meant, but perhaps that is one of the reasons that they are better
teachers than Scotus or Aquinas."[48]

---

[47] *Early Middle English Verse and Prose*, ed. J. A. W. Bennett and G. V. Smithers (Oxford 1966) 239-240.

[48] Graham Hough, *A Preface to the Fairy Queen* (New York 1963) 165-166.

Department of English
Boston University
236 Bay State Road
Boston, Massachusetts 02215, U.S.A.

FEUDAL WAR AND MONASTIC PEACE:
CLUNIAC LITURGY AS RITUAL AGGRESSION*

•

by Barbara H. Rosenwein

"The length of time [spent] continuously observing the daily round was so great, the persistence of the church offices especially was so protracted, that in the very heat of the Crab or the Lion [that is, summer], when the days are longer, hardly half an hour out of the entire day remained in which the brothers could talk in the cloister."[1] Thus did Peter Damian describe the liturgy at the monastery of Cluny. He was not alone in commenting on its length. In 1083 a Cluniac monk named Ulrich made an observation very similar to Peter's:

> Often indeed before all can get to their places in the cloister and one of the brothers utter a single word, the bell for vespers is sounded, and that is the end of talking . . . After vespers comes supper; after supper comes the supper of the servers; after the supper of the servers comes the office for the dead; after the office comes the collation, and so on to compline.[2]

Later in the same work Ulrich spoke of the lessons, which were "so long . . . [that] they were no less burdensome to hear than a lump of lead is wont to

* I wish to thank Professors Karl F. Morrison, who read and commented on this paper in manuscript, and Philip S. Holzman, who advised me on its psychoanalytic aspects. I am particularly indebted to Professor Lester K. Little for his assistance at every phase of its development.

[1] Peter Damian, *Epistolae* 6.5, PL 144.380: "Nam tanta erat in servandi ordinis continua jugitate prolixitas; tanta praesertim in ecclesiasticis officiis protelabatur instantia, ut in ipso cancri, sive leonis aestu, cum longiores sunt dies, vix per totum diem unius saltem vacaret horae dimidium, quo fratribus in claustro licuisset miscere colloquium."

[2] Ulrich, *Antiquiores consuetudines cluniacensis monasterii* (hereafter Ulrich) 1.18, PL 149.668: "Saepius namque priusquam omnes in claustro consideant, et aliquis fratrum vel unum verbum faciat, pulsatur signum ad vesperas, et ecce ibi finis loquendi . . . Post vesperas, coena; post coenam, coena servitorum; post coenam servitorum, officium pro defunctis; post officium, collatio, et ita ad completorium."

be to carry."[3] Even a modern historian has ended his study of Cluny's liturgy on a note of awe at the sheer amount: "in his liturgy the Cluniac monk practiced to a heroic degree the 'pray without ceasing' of the Gospel."[4]

A mere list of the number of additions which the Cluniacs[5] made to the liturgy prescribed by Benedict of Nursia is striking.[6] No wonder the historian of Cluny has sometimes considered a description of the liturgy task enough. But the liturgy requires explanation as well. A problem of this sort can be attacked on several levels: theological, sociological, even psychological. Much work from a theological and sociological point of view has already been done; in contrast, psychological aspects have been largely neglected. In this essay an attempt is made to integrate these approaches. The author has gratefully drawn upon the work of other historians for theological and sociological explanations; the studies of psychoanalytic thinkers have been used to shed light on the psychological aspects of the problem. While historians have occasionally applied psychoanalytic methods to biography, remarkably little has been done to use them in understanding broad historical movements. This essay, in which such an application is attempted, can therefore generate only tentative hypotheses. It is an early effort in a new methodology.

I

The liturgy of Cluny is described by several Cluniac monks in writings extending in date from the end of the tenth to the late eleventh century.[7] Al-

---

[3] *Ibid.* 1.41, PL 149.687-688: "Tam prolixas lectiones . . . non minus graves essent ad audiendum quam massa plubea fore solet ad portandum."

[4] Philibert Schmitz, "La liturgie de Cluny," *Spiritualità cluniacense*, Convegni del Centro di studi sulla spiritualità medievale 2 (Todi 1960) 99.

[5] The definition of a "Cluniac" house is difficult to formulate. In general there were three sorts of monasteries that might be termed Cluniac: those belonging to the order (but not necessarily influenced by Cluny in their customs), those adopting the customs of Cluny but remaining independent, and those practicing modified Cluniac customs. In this essay, which relies mainly on an exploration of Cluny herself to shed light on the "Cluniac" phenomenon, the thesis presented should hold best for monasteries following Cluny's way of life whether technically in the order or not, less for monasteries that followed modified Cluniac customs, and not at all when applied to houses whose customs were uninfluenced by or, indeed, opposed to Cluny's.

[6] See the list (Table I, below). Some scholars have argued that the importance of the additions has been exaggerated; see Jean Leclercq, "Pour une histoire de la vie à Cluny," *Revue d'histoire ecclésiastique* 57 (1962) 801-805, and see Noreen Hunt, *Cluny under Saint Hugh 1049-1106* (London 1967) 99ff. and see below, at nn. 42ff.

[7] For the earliest Cluniac customaries see Bruno Albers, "Le plus ancient coutumier de Cluny," *Revue benedictine* 20 (1903) 174-184 and *Consuetudines monasticae* 2, ed. Bruno Albers (Monte Cassino 1905) 1-61. For a customary now known to be Cluniac (see A. Wilmart, "Le convent et la bibliothèque du Cluny vers le milieu du xiᵉ siècle," *Revue Mabillon*

though liturgical practices were modified over the years, these changes did
not represent radical departures from preceding practices, but rather evolved
organically. When Ulrich wrote his survey of the liturgy at Cluny, he indicated that the various psalms and collects sung for the dead had increased
with time, but the basic practice of singing psalms and collects for the dead
had not changed;[8] at the same time, some practices had diminished. Ulrich
tells how Abbot Majolus, noticing that the liturgy on Sundays and feasts
of twelve lessons was very burdensome for the brothers, alleviated their
task by substituting in the place of the office of the dead two psalms to be
sung after every hour.[9] The later customaries, therefore, should give an
indication of the kind of liturgy that Cluny had from its foundation. By
the eleventh century details, of course, had changed; but the basic characteristics of the liturgy remained the same.

Nevertheless this hypothesis of continuity in Cluniac customs has sometimes been challenged. Since the earliest extant Cluniac customaries date
from the late tenth century, some scholars have claimed that the customs
of Cluny at the time of its foundation were not like those resulting from later
accretions but rather were faithfully patterned on the rules of Benedict of
Aniane.[10] In point of fact, however, the liturgical additions practiced at
Benedict's monastery at Inden[11] were very similar to those found in later Cluniac customaries. Benedict established the recitation of the Gradual Psalms
before nocturnes[12] and probably also introduced a daily office of the dead.[13]
In Ulrich's day these two practices have become known as Cluniac customs.

---

11 [1921] 89-124) and written 1042-1043 see *Consuetudines farfenses* in *Consuetudines monasticae* 1, ed. Bruno Albers (Stuttgart 1900). There are two customaries from Saint Hugh's
time: Bernard, *Ordo cluniacensis* (hereafter Bernard) in *Vetus disciplina monastica*, ed.
Marquard Herrgott (Paris 1726) 134-364 was written c. 1075 and revised in 1084-1086.
See Kassius Hallinger, "Cluny's Bräuche zur Zeit Hugos des Grossen (1049-1109). Pro-
legomena zur Neuherausgabe des Bernhard und Udalrich von Kluny," *Zeitschrift der Sa-
vigny-Stiftung für Rechtsgeschichte*, kanonistische Abteilung 45 (1959) 99-139. Ulrich's
customary (n. 2 above) was written c. 1083 for the abbot of Hirsau, who wanted to pattern
the life of his monastery upon the Cluniac example.

8 For evidence that the number of psalms had grown through the years see Ulrich 1.3,
PL 149.647.

9 Ulrich 1.4, PL 149.648: "Quod cernens sanctus Majolus aliquando fratribus esse maxime in tali die onerosum, pro ipso officio constituit ut post singulas horas duo psalmi di-
cerentur."

10 See, for example, Ernst Sackur, *Die Cluniacenser in ihrer kirchlichen und allgemein-
geschichtlichen Wirksamkeit bis zur mitte des elften Jahrhunderts*, 2 vols. (Halle 1892) 1.50
n. 1.

11 A description of these practices can be found in Ardo, *Vita Benedicti Abbatis Anianen-
sis* 38-39, MGH Script. 15.216-217.

12 *Ibid.* 38.

13 *Capitula monachorum ad Augiam directa* 11, Herrgott (n. 7 above) 21: "ut defunctorum vigilia hoc modo ab eis [the monks at Inden] celebratur."

There were, it seems, few unprecedented customs at Cluny. In the last quarter of the ninth century, while Berno was abbot at Baume, the monks at Baume sang some 138 psalms per day,[14] a considerable addition to the 40 psalms per day prescribed by Benedict of Nursia.[15] Since Berno subsequently became the first abbot of Cluny (in 910)[16] he probably brought with him some of the practices of Baume. In the time of Saint Hugh the psalmody at Cluny was, quantitatively at least, essentially unchanged; Ulrich mentions some 170 psalms to be sung daily.[17] Hallinger and others have maintained that historical precedents for all of the details of Cluny's liturgy may be found at such monasteries as Reichenau, Saint Gall, and Attigny as well as in the works of Benedict of Aniane.[18] This thesis seems plausible, although detailed research on it has not yet been carried out. Why indeed should Cluny's liturgy have sprung forth fully blown in 910? Rather, all indications point to a slow development that saw its birth in the works of Benedict of Aniane and progressed unevenly until at last it was institutionalized at Cluny. In some ways Benedict of Aniane was ahead of his generation. Many of his additions to the liturgy met with opposition from his contemporaries.[19] Only as time passed did these additions become more popular, and only in the tenth century were they finally incorporated systematically into monastic life at Cluny.

Therefore, although precedents to Cluniac liturgy can be found and discussed fruitfully, the problem still remains to explain "how such liturgical practices of sometimes diverse origin ever came together and came to be observed with special intensity in Cluniac monasticism, and to interpret the significance of this remarkable phenomenon."[20]

---

[14] John of Salerno, *Vita sancti Odonis* (hereafter John) 1.32, PL 133.57: "Etenim in quotidianis diebus, inter diei noctisque cursus, cxxxviii canebant psalmos." See also the English translation in *St. Odo of Cluny; being the Life of St. Odo of Cluny by John of Salerno and the Life of St. Gerald of Aurillac by St. Odo*, trans. and ed. Dom Gerard Sitwell (London 1958) 33.

[15] For the *Rule* see Rudolph Hanslik, ed., *Benedicti Regula*, Corpus scriptorum ecclesiasticorum latinorum (CSEL) 15.

[16] This is the traditional date for the founding of Cluny. It has been challenged by Guy de Valous, who proposes 909 in "Cluny, l'Abbaye et l'Ordre," *Dictionnaire d'histoire et de géographie ecclésiastique* 73.40, but his arguments are not completely convincing (see Kenneth John Conant, *Cluny: les églises et la maison du chef d'ordre*, Cambridge 1968, 34 n. 57).

[17] See Table I below.

[18] Kassius Hallinger, "Neue Fragen der Reformgeschichtlichen Forschung," *Archiv für mittelrheinische Kirchengeschichte* 9 (1957) 1-32. See also the arguments of Schmitz (n. 4 above) 91 and of Hunt (n. 6 above) 106.

[19] Significantly, one of these controversial practices was the office of the dead, which later played a role of great importance at Cluny. See Edmund Bishop, *Liturgica historica* (Oxford 1918) 215, for an elaboration of this point.

[20] Cinzio Violante, "Il monaschesimo cluniacense di fronte al mondo politico ed ecclesiastico (secoli x e xi)," *Spiritualità cluniacense* (n. 4 above) 158-159 n. 9.

For this task the first requirement is to establish a full and detailed account of Cluniac liturgy. In Table I a typical liturgical "day" at Cluny is set forth.[21] To the right of it, for comparison, is the liturgical day as prescribed by Benedict of Nursia in his *Rule*.[22] The *opus Dei* of Benedict was still used as the core of Cluny's liturgy and to it were added various new practices. For example, the office of nocturns was sung at Cluny exactly as the *Rule* enjoined; but before the office proper the Cluniacs sang the gradual psalms, and after the office proper they added further prayers, psalms, and other liturgical acts. In Table I the office proper is indicated by capital letters and the Cluniac additions are indicated in lower case type. The typical day as set out by Benedict consisted of 3 1/2 hours for the *opus Dei*, 4 hours for reading, 6 1/2 hours for work, and 8 1/2 hours for sleep.[23] The table makes clear that at Cluny most of the daytime was spent in the *opus Dei*.

Aside from the formal liturgical practices indicated in this list, Cluniac liturgy and life exhibited what has been called a "ritualism" perhaps no less essential.[24] The rites at Cluny were accompanied by elaborate and rich ceremonial. Splended garments and liturgical vessels were so dazzling that one recent historian has seen in this pomp the major significance of Cluny's liturgy.[25] In addition, Cluny ceremonialized all aspects of life in the monastery. When the monks were excused from the liturgy in order to perform various tasks in the monastery they were expected, as far as possible, to continue the prayers and the offices that their brothers were chanting in the church.[26] Moreover, the most banal acts of everyday life took on a quasi-liturgical form. When the monks awakened in the morning, put on their clothes, sat, or ate, they did so in strictly prescribed ways at specifically appointed times.[27]

---

[21] Table I is patterned after a table compiled by Hunt (n. 6 above) 101-103.

[22] The calculations for the *Rule* are taken from David Knowles, "The Monastic Horarium 970-1120," *Downside Review* 51 (1933) 706-725.

[23] These are the figures of Edward Cuthbert Butler, *Benedictine Monachism* (Cambridge 1924) 297.

[24] The term was first used in an unpublished letter by Edmund Bishop and is later used in Butler (n. 23 above) 296.

[25] Ernst Werner, *Die gesellschaftlichen Grundlagen der Klosterreform im 11. Jahrhundert* (Berlin 1953).

[26] See for example how the cooks participated in the liturgy: Ulrich 2.35, PL 149.726-727.

[27] For waking see Ulrich 2.10, PL 149.706, for dressing 2.13, PL 149.707, for sitting, 2.11, PL 149.706, for eating, 2.23 PL 149.711.

TABLE I

THE MONASTIC "DAY" AT CLUNY[a]

Cluny[b]	Rule
Gradual Psalms [Plus the last 17 psalms][c]	

NOCTURNS   2:30 A.M. NOCTURNS

Prayers of 14 verses   3:30 Reading

Psalm 50

4 psalms called *familiares* (6, 19, 69, 141)[d]

[2 psalms said prostrate]

Procession to church of Saint Mary (Psalms 84 and 86)

Matins of All Saints

Matins of the Dead

Psalms 43, 78, 93

Gradual Psalms

Psalms 98, 22

Interval for private prayer

[a] This reconstructed "day" is based primarily on Ulrich 1.1-4 (PL 149.643-648); but see also Bernard (n. 7 above) 2.283-364. Neither of these documents provides a completely clear description of the liturgy. Hunt (n. 6 above) 100 has already observed in this connection that "historians emerge with very different conclusions from the same material."

[b] The following, being a "typical" day in the winter, is modified in numerous ways for different feasts and seasons. It is incomplete as a description of the liturgy because it omits, for the sake of brevity, the collects and lessons which the Cluniacs added and which Ulrich described in great detail. For collects see Ulrich 1.5 (648-649); for lessons, 1.1 (643-645).

[c] Brackets ([ ]) indicate a Lenten practice only. There is some discrepancy among commentators concerning these extra psalms. Ulrich indicates that psalms 119-150 are sung before nocturns at Lent, and that psalms 119-133 are sung before nocturns at all other times. J. B. L. Tolhurst, in his edition of *The Monastic Breviary of Hyde Abbey* 6 (London 1942) 64 points out that psalms 119-133 are the gradual psalms, introduced by Benedict of Aniane, and sung in three parts, each part for a particular intention. At Cluny the intentions were as follows: five psalms were sung for "our brothers and other departed faithful," five for "us ourselves," five for "the kings and all our *familiares* still living."—Ulrich 1.5 (PL 149.648). Tolhurst goes on to say that these gradual Psalms have often (wrongly) been confused with the *trina oratio*, which is based principally on the seven penitential psalms (Tolhurst 57). In fact the problem is often one of conflicting nomenclature. The "old" *trina oratio* is the same as the gradual psalms; the "new" *trina oratio*, introduced after Benedict of Aniane's time, contains the penitential psalms. Hence Schmitz (n. 4 above) 87 says that the Cluniacs sang the *trina oratio* before nocturns. But Hunt (n. 6 above) 101 states that both the *trina oratio* and the last 32 psalms were sung before nocturns during the winter while the *trina oratio* was sung alone during the summer.

[d] The *psalmi familiares* were chanted for lay benefactors and friends of the monastery.

Cluny[b]	*Rule*
MATINS	5:00 **MATINS**
Prayers of 14 verses [up to 20 verses]	5:45 Reading
Psalm 50	
4 extra psalms	
4 *familiares* (31, 85, 69, 141)	
[2 psalms said prostrate]	
Sleep	
PRIME	6:30 **PRIME**
Prayers of 31 verses	7:00 Reading
Psalm 50	
Athanasian Creed	
4 *familiares* (37, 22, 69, 141)	
[2 psalms said prostrate]	
7 penitential psalms (6, 31, 37, 50, 101, 129, 142)	
Litany	
[Psalms 69, 120, 122, 42]	
Chapter	
Psalms 5, 6, 114, 151, 129, 142	
Talk, reading, tasks, "private" Masses	
TERCE	8:15 **TERCE**
Prayers of 14 verses	8:30 Work
Psalm 50	
4 *familiares* (56, 12, 69, 141)	
[2 psalms said prostrate]	
Missa matutinalis (Mass for Dead)	
Reading	
SEXT	12 Noon **SEXT**
Prayers of 14 verses	12:15 P.M. Work
Psalm 50	
4 *familiares* (101, 66, 69, 141)	
[2 psalms said prostrate]	
Litany	
Missa major	
Dinner	
Psalm 50	

[b] See p. 134.

NONE	2:15 NONE
Prayers of 14 verses	2:30 Dinner
Psalm 50	3:00 Reading
4 *familiares* (129, 78, 69, 141)	
[2 psalms said prostrate]	
VESPERS	4:15 VESPERS
Prayers of 14 verses [up to 20 verses]	collation
Psalm 50	
4 extra psalms	
4 *familiares* (142, 83, 69, 141)	
[4 psalms said prostrate]	
Procession to church of Saint Mary (2 psalms)	
Vespers of All Saints	
Vespers of the Dead	
Supper	
Psalm 50	
Psalms 119, 3	
Vigils of the Dead	
COMPLINE	5:00 COMPLINE
Prayers of 17 verses	
2 extra psalms	
9 psalms (69, 12, 120, 50, 12, 42, 66, 126, 129)	
Retire	

II

What have modern historians made of all this? Henri Pignot, the first historian to attempt a comprehensive history of Cluny, described the liturgy, remarked upon its length, and indicated some of the ritualism in the rest of Cluniac life.[28] But he did not attempt to explain these characteristics except to remark that the spiritual aspect of monasticism was emphasized over the physical; in other words, the *opus Dei* was more important than manual labor.[29]

Pignot's work was superseded by that of Ernst Sackur, whose pioneer research on Cluny has served as the foundation of more modern studies. His study emphasized Cluny as a center of reforming activities. Cluny, he

---

[28] Henri Pignot, *Histoire de l'ordre de Cluny*, 3 vols. (Autun 1868).
[29] *Ibid.* 2.269.

argued, was directly or indirectly responsible for the total European monastic reform of the tenth and eleventh centuries. Only in connection with this reforming activity did Cluniac liturgy take on significance.

The Viking invasions had left in their wake, Sackur argued, almost total social dislocation. Men reacted by blaming themselves; a deep sense of sinfulness penetrated all social groups. But the group to feel its sinfulness in sharpest relief was that of the lay nobility. Its members sought atonement by establishing monasteries where the regular life would be followed conscientiously. The broken thread of Benedict of Aniane's monastic reforms was once again picked up by the tenth-century reformers, and Cluny was established along the lines set out by Benedict a century earlier. The liturgy at Cluny too, Sackur maintained, was at first modeled upon the Anianian program and could be explained as such. Only when attempting to describe the motivations of the landed nobility to give up their property to make way for monastic foundations of the Cluniac stamp did Sackur concern himself with "the continual prayers and masses of the Cluniac monks for the cure of souls of the dead and living."[30] Thus the needs of the secular nobility explained the liturgy at Cluny, for these men needed the comfort and hope of monastic intercession for their souls in order to assuage their feelings of sinfulness and their fear of the end of the world, the Last Judgment, and eternal damnation.[31] The monks at Cluny provided this intercession.

Sackur had painted a picture of the Cluniacs in a setting of universal and purely spiritual reform. Reaction toward his work came from two sides;[32] one group of historians attempted to show that the Cluniac reform movement was hardly "spiritual" in nature, while the other group attempted to show that it was hardly universal. Brackmann, for example, pointed to

---

[30] Sackur (n. 10 above) 2.228.

[31] This view is further supported in Georg Schreiber, *Gemeinschaften des Mittelalters* in *Gesammelte Abhandlungen* 1 (Regensberg 1948) 101-125. See also P. W. Jorden, *Das cluniazensische Totengedächtniswesen* in *Münsterische Beiträge zur Theologie* 15 (Münster 1930) 47ff., who concludes that "Blütezeiten des Ordens waren auch immer Blütezeiten des Totengedächtniswesens und umgekehrt" (112). The observations in H. E. J. Cowdrey, "Unions and Confraternity with Cluny," *Journal of Ecclesiastical History* 16 (1965) 152-162 are also relevant. But for evidence that much of the intercession was on behalf of the souls of dead Cluniac monks, see Joachim Wollasch, "Die Überlieferung cluniacensischen Totengedächtnisses," pt. 2 of Karl Schmid and J. Wollasch, "Die Gemeinschaft der Lebenden und Verstorbenen in Zeugnisses des Mittelalters," *Frühmittelalterliche Studien: Jahrbuch des Instituts für Frühmittelalterforschung der Universität Münster* 1, ed. Karl Hauck (Berlin 1967) 294-401, especially 398.

[32] Not all later work, of course, was a reaction. A work more anecdotal in nature but still much in the Sackur tradition is L. Smith, *The Early History of the Monastery of Cluny* (London 1920). See also her work covering a later period, *Cluny in the Eleventh and Twelfth Centuries* (London 1930). Unlike Sackur, Smith's major emphasis was on the history of Cluny itself rather than on the Cluniac monastic movement as a whole.

the many worldly contacts the Cluniacs had and stressed their political acumen.[33] With this emphasis, interest in the monastery focused on its external and worldly activities, while the importance of Cluniac life inside the cloister was minimized. Hallinger, attacking the other cornerstone of Sackur's study, pointed to the varieties of thought and practice that could be discerned within the reform movements of the tenth and eleventh centuries.[34] He stressed that there were non-Cluniac reform movements, and that these were just as legitimate and serious as the one at Cluny. By carefully detailing all the differences between Gorze and Cluny, he showed that Gorze had been the center of a different kind of reform. Instead of richness and elaboration, Gorze stressed asceticism and simplicity. Liturgy at Gorze was in agreement with the rest of its life style: it was simple and unadorned.

Neither of these approaches led to much thought on the problem of Cluniac liturgy. But concurrent with Brackmann and Hallinger was another group of historians who were convinced that "the best judgements of Cluny's external history are those which rest on sound research concerning Cluny itself."[35] These historians set about to understand Cluny internally, and here, of course, the problem of liturgy loomed large. One of the earliest works of this sort was a study by Joan Evans on the everyday life of the Cluniacs.[36] Evan's work, conceived without "thesis to maintain nor theory to develop,"[37] made no attempt to explain why the Cluniacs lived the way she so vividly

---

[33] Albert Brackmann, "Die politische Wirkung der kluniazensischen Bewegung," *Historische Zeitschrift* 139 (1929) 34-47. For the problem of Cluny's relationship to the Investiture Controversy see in particular Theodor Schieffer, "Cluny et la querelle des Investitures," *Revue historique* 225 (1961) 47-72 and Hartmut Hoffmann, "Von Cluny zum Investiturstreit," *Archiv für Kulturgeschichte* 45 (1963) 165-209.

[34] Kassius Hallinger, *Gorze-Kluny* in *Studia Anselmiana* 22-25 (Rome 1951). Guy de Valous had already pointed out that "la réforme lorraine, celle de Fleury, les tendances et la propagande d'un Guillaume de Volpiano en Italie, d'un Richard de Saint-Vannes, d'un Popon de Stavelot ou d'un Gérard du Brogne n'ont que des rapports lointain avec le movement clunisien." *L'Abbaye de Cluny: les monastères clunisiens*, vol. 1 of *Le monachisme clunisien: Des origines au XVᵉ siècle: Vie intérieure des monastères et organisation de l'ordre*, Archives de la France monastique 39 (Ligugé 1935) vi. On the question of Gorze-Cluny see Theodor Schieffer, "Cluniazensische oder gorzische Reformbewegung?" *Archiv für mittelrheinische Kirchengeschichte* 4 (1952) 24-44. See also Jean Leclercq, "Cluny fut-il ennemi de la culture?" *Revue Mabillon* 47 (1957) 172-182.

[35] Hunt (n. 6 above) 2. Because of its great attention to the details of life inside the monastery, the first volume of Valous's work (n. 34 above) belongs in this category. See also the studies on Cluniac spirituality, in particular Kassius Hallinger, "Zur geistigen Welt der Anfänge Klunys," *Deutsches Archiv* 10 (1954) 417-445; French translation: "Le climat spirituel des premiers temps de Cluny," *Revue Mabillon* 45-46 (1955-56) 117-140. See also Étienne Delaruelle, "L'idée de croisade dans la littérature clunisienne du xiᵉ siècle et l'abbaye de Moissac," *Annales du Midi* 75 (1963) 419-440.

[36] Joan Evans, *Monastic Life at Cluny, 910-1157* (London 1931).

[37] *Ibid.* Preface.

described. Similarly, the more recent work of Philibert Schmitz put major emphasis on a detailed description of the liturgy and stressed its historical precedents. In a brief attempt to explain Cluny's unusual emphasis on liturgy, Schmitz mentioned a thesis previously presented by Butler:[38] the monks, who no longer worked at manual labor, had to be kept occupied in some way. The *opus Dei* was the most convenient and natural part of the day to be expanded, and so eventually the liturgy increased in importance.

Ernst Werner attempted to provide a more comprehensive explanation of the liturgy.[39] He argued that Cluny consciously adopted Byzantine liturgical practices because of their pomp and splendor.[40] This magnificent and elaborate liturgy was imported because the Cluniacs, members of the noble class, needed a kind of liturgy that would dazzle the masses and turn them away from the lure of anti-materialistic Manichean heretical movements which, according to Werner, flourished in the eleventh century. For Werner these movements were a manifestation of lower-class opposition to the ruling class. The ruling class made a conscious and premeditated attempt to re-establish its prestige through the foundation of Cluny.

One of the most recent publications on Cluny, a study by Noreen Hunt, maintains that the length and novelty of the liturgy have been exaggerated. "Far from being unique, [Cluny's] timetable was typical of the black monks' horarium in the tenth and eleventh centuries. If anything, Cluny followed rather than led the tendency to protract and elaborate the structure of the liturgy."[41]

This argument adds a new dimension to Hallinger's point that the liturgy of Cluny had many precedents.[42] The most striking case in point is the office of Our Lady which, as Cabrol points out, was adopted at Einsiedeln between 970 and 995 and soon after was incorporated into the liturgy of monasteries in Italy.[43] Long before this office was introduced at Cluny, it had become part of the liturgy at Reichenau, Saint Gall, and Corbie.[44] Only in the twelfth century did Cluny finally adopt the office of Our Lady; even then it was probably limited to the infirmary. Cabrol, however, has concluded from this information not that Cluny had a shorter liturgy than other monasteries but rather that its own liturgy was so interminable that nothing more could be added.[45]

---

[38] Butler (n. 23 above) 296.

[39] Werner (n. 25 above). And see the critique of his work by Hallinger (n. 18 above).

[40] Werner (n. 25 above) 82-87, esp. 84.

[41] Hunt (n. 6 above) 106.

[42] See n. 18 above.

[43] *Dictionnaire d'archéologie chrétienne et de liturgie* (DACL) 12.2013.

[44] Hallinger (n. 18 above) 23.

[45] DACL 12.2013. Peter the Venerable said of this office: Quia ejus horae in conventu publico propter fratrum numerositatem, et officiorum multiplicitatem, brevitate temporis prohibente cantari non poterant. Peter the Venerable *Statuta* 60, PL 189, 1041-1042.

Perhaps most decisive for Hunt's new perspective is her use of new criteria to define liturgy. As we have seen, historians have traditionally included the ritualism pervading all activities at Cluny as a part of the liturgy. For Hunt the liturgy is strictly the religious practices that occur inside the church. Thus she argues:

> Most important of all in considering the community horarium is the question of how many followed it anyway. The amount of evidence for the monks being elsewhere or otherwise employed during the liturgy is sufficient to allow the conclusion that it was never hard for those whose work made it difficult to attend the full community round to get exemption.[46]

Despite these points, Hunt agrees that "the fact that the liturgy was paramount and occupied most of the monks' time is unlikely to be disproved by further study"[47]

III

The Cluniacs themselves suggested an explanation of their liturgy. After Ulrich listed the seven collects to be said at the matins of the dead he continued:

> The first [collect] is for brothers who died recently . . . the second is for the anniversary [of the death] of those named at chapter; the third is for all our dead familiars; the fourth for dead brothers; the fifth for all buried in our cemetery; the sixth for our sisters and our other female familiars; the seventh for all departed faithful.[48]

The collects are not the only parts of the liturgy sung for a particular intention. The morning mass (*Missa matutinalis*) is sung "for the dead."[49] An office "for the dead" is performed every day in the morning and evening.[50]

---

[46] Hunt (n. 6 above) 108. Much groundwork for this assertion was laid by Leclercq (n. 6 above) 795-797, 807.

[47] Hunt (n. 6 above) 109.

[48] Ulrich 1.5, PL 149.649: "Prima [collecta] est pro fratribus nuper defunctis . . . secunda pro anniversario in capitulo, recitatorum; tertia pro cunctis familiaribus nostris defunctis; quarta pro defunctis fratribus; quinta pro omnibus in loco nostro sepultis; sexta pro nostris sororibus et aliis feminis familiaribus nostris; septima pro omnibus fidelibus defunctis.

[49] Ibid. 1.9, PL 149.652-653.

[50] For matins of the dead see *ibid*. 1.3, PL 149. 646; for vespers of the dead, 1.3, PL 149. 647.

The gradual psalms sung before nocturns are divided into three parts, each sung for a particular category of Christians.[51] The fiftieth psalm, the *Miserere*, is sung "for our dead abbots" after each office.[52] The same is true of many of the other psalms. The four psalms added after each hour (two after compline) are sung "for our familiars."[53] One of these four, Psalm 141, is also specifically sung "for the departed faithful."[54] During Lent, after the four psalms for familiars are sung at prime, four more psalms are sung, one of which, Psalm 42, is "for the departed faithful."[55] Directly after this, at chapter, six psalms are sung for brothers who recently died.[56]

The majority of the intentions are connected with the dead in one way or another,[57] but there are several notable exceptions to this rule. At the major mass, for example, the "fourth [collect] is for kings and other princes, the fifth for bishops and our abbots, the sixth for our familiars, the seventh for the kings of Spain."[58]

Thus the Cluniacs explain their liturgy by its intention. Each collect, each psalm, is added "for" (meaning "for the benefit of") someone, specifically for someone's soul. The liturgy is almost entirely geared to intercession. Sackur had noted the importance of this concept in the liturgy, but he had approached it from the viewpoint of those receiving the benefit of the intercession, rather than from the viewpoint of the monks.[59] What can it mean for monks to spend their day praying for the salvation of the souls of dead men?[60]

The answer can be found in the following two legends set down by the Cluniac monk Jotsaldus in the eleventh century. The first tells of a monk who was traveling homeward and met a hermit who told him:

> There are places near us belching out from themselves the very strong heat of fire, in which the souls of sinners undergo diverse

---

[51] See Table I, n. c.

[52] Ulrich 1.2, PL 149.645.

[53] *Ibid.*

[54] *Ibid.*

[55] *Ibid.* 1.3, PL 149.647.

[56] *Ibid.*

[57] For the importance of prayers for the dead in Cluny's liturgical practices see Jorden (n. 31 above) and Wollasch (n. 31 above) 389-405. Cowdrey, (n. 31 above) also points to the confraters who received prayers for their souls while still alive.

[58] Ulrich 1.6, PL 149.651: "Quarta est pro regibus aliisque principibus; quinta pro episcopis et abbatibus nostris; sexta pro familiaribus nostris; septima pro regibus Hispaniarum."

[59] The intercessionary nature of the liturgy was also noted by Schreiber, Jorden, Wollasch, and Cowdrey (see n. 31 above).

[60] Jorden (n. 31 above) 104 suggested it was a matter of survival for the Cluniacs. No one would have supported them if they could not expect to receive in exchange prayers for their soul.

punishments for a fixed time by the manifest judgment of God. Indeed a multitude of demons were [*sic*] appointed ever to renew their torments. They, restoring [the souls'] punishments from day to day, heap up more and more intolerable sorrows. Nevertheless, I very often heard [the demons] lamenting, and making not a few complaints, that, due to the prayers of religious men and almsgiving to the poor, which are taking place throughout diverse holy places, often the souls of the damned were being freed from their punishments through God's mercy. You should know that among others they chiefly made mention and greatest complaint about the members of the Cluniac congregation and its abbot. On account of this, if you return home safely, I admonish you for the love of God to make known all these things which you have heard from me to the aforesaid congregation, and on my behalf bid that they devote themselves more and more to prayers, vigils, and almsgiving for the redemption of souls placed in punishment, so that by these things gladness may be multiplied in heaven and harm and sorrow may be inflicted on the devil. . .

[The monk returned home and told Odilo and the brothers the story.] Upon hearing it, they felt not a little astonishment with the greatest joy of heart. They gave thanks to the Lord, added prayers to prayers, applied alms to alms, and were eager to labor earnestly for the redemption of the dead. Therefore on that occasion the blessed Father [Odilo] formulated a general proposal for all his monasteries: that just as the feast of All Saints is performed at the beginning of the November calendar, so too on the following day a memorial was to be performed for the redemption of the souls of all the faithful in general. Masses with psalms and almsgiving were to be celebrated privately and publicly; alms were to be given in various ways to all the poor who came, so that through these things the adversary would lament more and more to appear a failure to himself and on the contrary the Christian laboring in this with the hope of mercy would rejoice.[61]

---

[61] Jotsaldus *De vita et virtutibus sancti Odilonis Abbatis* 2.13, PL 142.926-927 : Vicina loca sunt nobis, ex semetipsis manifesto Dei judicio, gravissima eructantia ignis incendia, in quibus animae peccatorum ad tempus statutum diversa luunt supplicia. Sunt vero ad eorum semper renovanda tormenta multitudo daemonum deputata, qui eorum poenas de die in diem restaurantes, intolerabiles magis ac magis exaggerant dolores. Quos tamen saepius audivi lamentantes, et non parvam querimoniam facientes, quia orationibus religiosorum hominum, et eleemosynis pauperum, quae fiunt per diversa loca sanctorum, multoties per Dei misericordiam ab eorum poenis liberarentur animae damnatorum. Inter caetera vero mentionem et maximam querimoniam noveris illos praecipue fecisse de illa Cluniacensi congregatione, et ipsius abbate. Quapropter per Deum te admoneo, si ad tuos cum prosperitate habueris reditum, ut haec omnia quae a me audisti nota facias praedictae congregationi, et ex mea parte denunties, quatenus magis ac magis insistant orationibus,

Thus is the origin of All Soul's Day explained.

The second legend has a similar theme:

> At one time lord Benedict [VIII], most outstanding among the nobility of Rome, most prudent in character, and, with respect to the worldly summit he attained, most apt in urban affairs, presided over the apostolic see. He used to love the blessed Odilo with a pure affection and honor him with the greatest devotion; and as often as the blessed man [Odilo] might enter his presence by the walls of Rome, he gave him what he needed with great generosity. Therefore, when the course of his mortal life was at last completed, he yielded his body to the earth and his soul to the power on high. . . .
>
> Much time had passed when the soul of the aforementioned leader, not having attained the society of eternal light, underwent penal judgment for [sins] committed. When, behold, merciful and compassionate God wanted to show, as a sign of the merit of blessed Odilo, both the punishment of that man [Benedict] and the gift of his own great benevolence. For the spirit of the aforementioned leader then appeared in a revelation to John, bishop of Porto, and to two others, whose names I forget, revealing to them what things were being done to [Benedict]: namely, that he was being held not in the brightness of light but in the shadow of punishments. And therefore [Benedict] advises that they go to his brother [Pope John XIX] and that he very quickly send an embassy to pious Odilo, for the celestial judgment decreed that by [Odilo's] suffrage [Benedict] would be released from his torments. Therefore, when darkness has diminished, the beholders of the vision go to the pope, and they make known what had been enjoined upon them. . . .

---

vigiliis et eleemosynis pro requie [*Thuan.*, redemptione] animarum in poenis positarum, ut per haec gaudium multiplicetur in coelo, et damnum sive luctus inferatur diabolo. [The monk returned home and told Odilo and the brothers the story]. . . . Quod audientes, admirationem non parvam cum maxima cordis laetitia sumpserunt, Domino gratias egerunt, orationes orationibus addiderunt, eleemosynas eleemosynis apposuerunt, et pro requie defunctorum instanter laborare studuerunt. Hac igitur occasione sanctus Pater generale propositum per omnia monasteria sua constituit, ut sicut in capite Kalendarum Novembrium festivitas agitur Omnium Sanctorum, ita etiam in sequenti die, memoria generaliter ageretur pro requie omnium fidelium animarum; privatim et publice missae cum psalmis et eleemosynis celebrarentur, omnibus supervenientibus pauperibus eleemosyna multipliciter daretur: quatenus per haec jacturam sibi provenire magis ac magis doleret adversarius, et e contrario gratularetur sub spe misericordiae in hoc laborans Christianus." See also this legend as reported by Rudolfus Glaber. The hermit in this version says: "Scito . . . prae cunctis Romani orbis illud [Cluny] valere praecipue in liberatione animarum a daemonica dominatione." He attributes this to the constant masses the Cluniacs celebrate. Rudolfus Glaber *Historiarum sui temporis libri quinque* 5.1, PL 142.692.

[The pope sends a letter to Odilo telling him what happened.] And so, carefully reading the letter which had been delivered, [Odilo] calls together the noble senate of monks and tells everything gravely. The profundity of his wisdom is clear, and he reflects upon many things, and he exhorts lest such a message be underestimated. Thereupon he bids that the offering of prayers and gifts of charity be solemnly performed for the liberation of the leader of all. The elders receive with joy the light burden of charity; publicly and privately they appeal to the ears of the benevolent Creator with pious prayers. A similar service is discharged according to the precepts of the father not only in that monastery but wherever a dependent community of brothers was standing.

Now the interval of established limit was coming to a close because so many prayers and oblations and generous almsgiving had penetrated the entrance to the divine mercy . . . [An elderly monk at Cluny has a vision.] He saw a certain person of striking elegance enter the cloister of the monastery with a great train of attendants and reach the chapter house where lord Odilo was seated with the blessed senate, and [he saw] the man bend his knees humbly before the father. When the brother asked who that shining figure was, he learned [it was] the lord Roman Pope Benedict, bishop of the first see, who referred to the acts of mercy for his liberation and the fact that through the intervention of lord Odilo and the brothers he had escaped frightful chaos and had flown to high beatitude. Awakening from these visions, and retaining the visual and auditory memories with tenacity, when day dawns he tells everyone in turn. Then the blessed senate leaps up and with the pious father shouts prayers of jubilation to the eternal majesty.[62]

---

[62] Jotsaldus 2.14, PL 142.927-929: "Praeerat quondam apostolicae sedi senior Benedictus, in romana nobilitate praecipuus, prudenti ingenio solertissimus, et quantum ad mundanum culmen attinet, urbanis causis aptissimus. Qui beatum Odilonem clara affectione diligebat, et summo studio excolebat: et quoties arcis Romanae moeniis sui praesentiam vir beatus intulisset, larga liberalitate necessitudinem juvamen exhibebat. Hic ergo mortalis vitae curriculo jam decurso, corpus terrae animam supernae remisit potestati. . . . Multum tempus effluxerat cum praenominati praesulis anima, non adepta lucis aeternae consortium, luebat pro commissis poenale judicium: cum ecce clementis Dei miseratio ad significandum beati Odilonis meritum, manifestare voluit et poenam illius hominis, et donum suae immensae pietatis. Apparuit namque spiritus jam dicti praesulis in revelatione Joanni Portuensi episcopo, et aliis duobus, quorum nomina non recolo, indicans eis quae circa se gererentur; quia videlicet non splendore lucis, sed poenarum teneretur in umbris. Monet itaque ut eant ad fratrem et ocius pio Odiloni legationem dirigat: ipsius enim suffragiis destinavit superna censura illum eripi a tormentis. Recedentibus ergo tenebris, hujus visionis conspectores papam adeunt, quae injuncta fuerat sibi edicunt. . . . [The pope sends a letter to Odilo telling him what happened.] Delatam itaque epistolam perlegens, convocat nobilem monachorum senatum, et seriatim cuncta perorat. Aperit profunda sapientiae suae, multaque replicat, et ne talis legatio parvipendatur exorat. Dein praecipit

We learn from these legends that Cluniac liturgy found its theological meaning in "a drama enacted between Heaven and Hell."[63] Intercession was a weapon with which to fight the devil, to thwart his progress in his great war with God, and to help God win his rights over the souls of men.[64] It was the most a man could do. Born, by the sin of Adam, under the lordship of the devil, man was generally doomed to passivity while the forces of good and evil battled for his soul. Only in the monastery, the place where the holiest Christian life was followed, could the kingdom of the devil be impeded and the kingdom of heaven helped to expand. And therefore, with their liturgy striking the blows, the Cluniacs fought the devil for God.

IV

If Cluniac liturgy was a kind of battle, there was no novelty in the fact. The earliest *milites Christi* had been the martyrs, but when Christianity became acceptable, the living martyrdom of the monastery became the home of God's soldiers.[65] And if the monks, disdainful of the world, were the soldiers of Christ, then the ordinary soldier, the *miles saecularis*, was the servant of his passions for wealth and glory. We learn that Saint Martin found the

---

ut libamina precum et dationes eleemosynarum pro generalis praesulis liberatione solemniter peragantur. Suscipiunt ergo seniores gratanter onus leve charitatis, publice et privatim aures pii Conditoris devotis precibus appellant. Nec tantum in eodem coenobio, sed ubicunque fratrum coetus manebat diffusus, praecepto Patris similis persolvitur famulatus. Jam praefixi termini spatium complebatur, cum tot preces et oblationes, atque eleemosynarum largitates aditum divinae benignitatis penetraverant. . . . [An elderly monk at Cluny has a vision.] Videbat namque quamdam personam decore conspicuo cum multo agmine candidatorum intrare monasterii claustrum, et usque ad capitulum, ubi domnus Odilo cum sacro senatu residebat, pervenisse, et ad ejusdem Patris genua caput humiliter flexisse. Cumque frater ille requireret quaenam illa fulgida esset persona, didicit domnum Benedictum papam Romanum, primae sedis episcopum, referentem gratiarum actiones pro sua liberatione, quod domni Odilonis et fratrum interventu immane chaos evasisset, et ad supernam beatitudinem evolasset. His visis, expergiscens frater a somno, et tenaci memoria visa et audita retinens, die relucente cuncta per ordinem narrat. Tripudiat tunc sacer senatus, et cum pio Patre aeternae majestati personant vota jubilationis."

[63] R. W. Southern, *The Making of the Middle Ages* (New Haven 1953) 235. The theological summary here derives largely from pp. 234-236. For a dissenting point of view see Hallinger (n. 35 above) 430ff.

[64] Valous (n. 34 above) 330 notes: "Les malédictions des psaumes étaient un exutoire pour leurs sentiments réfrénes et ils pouvaient en faire un libre usage contre leurs adversaires spirituels: les démons !" And Delaruelle observes that: "Si la vocation des clunisiens est différent de celle des *milites*, elle est aussi de style héroïque; mais il s'agit de lutter contre le démon" (n. 35 above) 428 n. 29.

[65] The following discussion borrows much from Carl Erdmann, *Die Entstehung des Kreuzzugsgedankens*, Forschungen zur Kirchen- und Geistesgeschichte 4 (Stuttgart 1935).

army incompatible with his belief in Christ: "I am Christ's soldier; I am not allowed to fight."[66] Sulpicius Severus, Martin's biographer, implies that the soldier was unchristian because he was in a profession that practiced killing:

> For Christ could not rightly have granted any other victory for the benefit of His own soldier than one in which the enemy were beaten bloodlessly and no man had to die.[67]

There were few holy men who could be found to disagree. The few saints of the early Middle Ages involved in military life—Saint Sebastian and Saint Maur, for example—seem to have become saints in spite of rather than because of their profession.[68] Saint Odo of Cluny, though he found out only later that he had been dedicated to Saint Martin, nevertheless imitated Martin's distaste for the military life:

> And my father began, as time passed, to take me out of ecclesiastical life and to direct me to military exercises. For this purpose he sent me to serve [as a page] in the household of Count William [of Aquitaine]. Gradually I abandoned the study of letters and began to be occupied with the duty of hunting and fowling. Then almighty God . . . began to terrify me in dreams and to show how prone my life was to evil, and he turned all my hunting into [a source of] fatigue. For the more I applied myself to those sorts of sports, the more I returned mournful, unsuccessful, and overcome with fatigue.[69]

In time such attitudes crystalized into the prevalent position of Western churchmen on war and warriors which lasted until about the year 1000. Thus during the Carolingian period a religious thinker like Jonas of Orleans (d. 844) set forth formally a distaste for the military similar to that expressed

---

[66] Sulpicius Severus, *Vita sancti Martini* 4, CSEL 1.114: "Christi ego miles sum: pugnare mihi non licet."

[67] *Ibid.*, CSEL 1.114-115: "neque enim aliam pro milite suo Christus debuit praestare victoriam, quam ut subactis sine sanguine hostibus nemo moreretur." The translation given here is from "The Life of St. Martin," *The Western Fathers*, trans. and ed. F. R. Hoare (New York 1954) 16.

[68] Erdmann, (n. 65 above) 11-12.

[69] John 1.8, PL 133.47: "Coepitque pater meus per incrementa temporum, me ab ecclesiastico subtrahere ordine, et militaribus exercitiis applicare; qua de re, intra domum Guillelmi me tradidit serviturum Comiti. Relictis tandem literarum studiis, venatorum, aucupumque coepi deservire officiis. Sed omnipotens Deus . . . coepit me in somnis terrere, et vita meam pronam ad malum ostendere ; sed insuper totam meam venationem vertebat in fatigationem. Nam quanto amplius me ingerebam hujuscemodi lusibus, tanto rediebam moerens sine omni effectu et fatigatione confossus."

in the *Life of Saint Martin* four hundred years earlier. According to Jonas a soldier could never live a moral life; he must avoid doing such things as robbing and plundering, but there was no positive action he could take which would allow him to live as a good Christian.[70] Hincmar of Reims (d. 882) only echoed his views.[71] A Carolingian military sermon was harsher: "killing in battle was considered a defilement for which penance had to be done."[72] Even killing the enemy in open warfare had to be atoned for by forty days of penance.[73] And later, in the tenth and early eleventh centuries, churchmen like Burchard of Worms (d. 1025) and Fulbert of Chartres (d. 1028) continued to write that a soldier who killed a man in battle violated the commandment of God and had to do penance accordingly.[74]

Quite different were the traditional Germanic ideas about warfare. To the tribe, the warrior had been a hero, the battle a test of courage and an opportunity for glory, the soldier's ethic of loyalty to his leader the highest moral value, and warfare in general the *Lebenselement* of the culture.[75] Such an attitude could not easily be reconciled with Christian, pacifist ideals; but with the progressive Christianization of Gaul and Germany, an accommodation, however tenuous, was inevitable.

The reign of Charles the Great (771-814) marked a crucial period in the rapprochement between Christianity and the Germanic peoples. From the court at Aachen emerged a renascence of Christian, classical culture that affected the entire realm, and for the first time Christianity and its values became integrated into the life of the landed aristocracy in the North. The harmonization of the new and imported habits, ideas, and values of classical Christian culture with those of the Franks extended to the notion of the "Germanic kingdom" for this concept now had to be expanded to coincide with the new role Charlemagne had assumed as emperor and ally of the pope. With the interests of ecclesiastical and secular authorities merged as never before in the West, it was inevitable that the power of the secular realm, and the manifestation of this power in war, would be reassessed by churchmen. And thus, while Jonas and Hincmar were writing about the "unholy warrior," others began to elaborate the notion of a "holy war."[76]

As the secular arm of the church, Charles was the protector of Christianity. And as the wielder of the secular sword, his duty was to extend Christianity

---

[70] Jonas of Orleans, *De institutione laicale*, PL 106.121ff.

[71] Hincmar of Reims, *De coercendis militum rapinis*, PL 125.953-956.

[72] Erdmann (n. 65 above) 14.

[73] *Ibid.*

[74] *Ibid.* 71-72.

[75] *Ibid.* 16.

[76] Augustine, of course, had introduced the concept of a *"bellum Deo auctore"* in the fifth century; his was limited to wars against heretics. After the seventh century, however, the virtual disappearance of heresy in the West made Augustine's notion superfluous.

to all unbelievers. Church spokesmen kept pace with secular practice: they invoked the protection of the saints in battle and prayed for victory.[77]

But the holiness of the war extended only to the ruler who declared it, not to the individual soldiers who fought in it. In the old German *Ludwigs-lied* of 881 the king who fights the heathen Normans is fighting for God and God rewards him with victory, but his men can claim only earthly rewards.[78] Churchmen too might see merit in a war but they could not condone the actual fighting even in the most righteous of wars. The matter was compli-cated by the fact that the bishops and abbots of the Carolingian Empire were also feudal lords and could not avoid becoming involved in worldly political matters such as warfare; but as long as they themselves did not carry arms (so the teaching went) they were absolved from the moral conse-quences of participating in war.

Even this doctrine had to be changed in the face of the Viking invasions. The defense of churches and monasteries during this period of crisis could not be left to royal authority, for the king was simply not strong enough to provide protection.[79] Royal authority soon broke down altogether under the onslaught, and defense became the job of members of the old landowning class who were rich enough to support a coterie of knights and to build them-selves strong fortified castles.[80] The Viking invasions hastened the transfer of "the attributes of government from the hands of the king into those of territorial princes in France and Italy and, though to a lesser degree, into those of the dukes of Germany."[81] The former royal vassals, the count, mar-grave, or duke, who had been endowed with large and rich *honores* now com-pleted their movement toward independence of the king and became petty rulers themselves. Their claim to this position being of doubtful legitima-cy, they maintained themselves simply by the exercise of power, and ulti-mately this meant success in war.

When the nobility fought against the barbarian invaders, the church looked kindly on its activities, and there was little cause for pangs of conscience. The notion of a "holy warrior" was slowly being formed; the fighter in a defensive war was becoming a hero. When some clerics themselves joined in the fray, saints were said to fight on their side. They were protecting

---

[77] Erdmann (n. 65 above) 20.

[78] *Ibid.* 21.

[79] See Lucien Musset, *Les invasions: le second assaut contre l'Europe chrétienne (VIIe-XIe siècles)*, Nouvelle Clio (Paris 1965) 158ff.

[80] *Ibid.* 162ff.

[81] F. L. Ganshof, *Feudalism*, trans. Philip Grierson, ed. 3 (New York 1961) 58-59. See also Joseph R. Strayer, "Feudalism in Western Europe," in *Feudalism in History*, ed. Rus-ton Coulborn (Princeton 1956) 22ff., and Marc Bloch, *Feudal Society*, trans. L. A. Manyon (Chicago 1961) 160ff.

God's churches and He would reward them. But the idea remained that the war had to be fought against heathens and had to be strictly defensive.[82]

The theories of the churchmen about war were not spun forth in the isolation of the cloister, unnoticed and unheeded. They were living ideas, and they affected prevailing values just as they were themselves a product of their times. The interests of churchmen and secular rulers were closely entwined; one individual often played both these roles at once. For this reason, some of the warfare in which the petty rulers engaged raised problems of conscience. Since the weak central authority could not stop a lord from encroaching on nearby lands, neighbors fought and plundered eachother during, and even long after, the Viking invasions.[83] But unlike the Vikings, these neighbors were Christians, and prevalent Christian values dictated against such fighting.[84]

The dilemma this situation produced for the landed classes could not easily be resolved. Their very position in life was a source for pangs of conscience and feelings of guilt. Carloman, the son of Louis the Stammerer, echoed the prevalent feelings well when he said that the Viking invasions were God's punishment for the sins of the nobility:

> It grieves us deeply that [certain statutes and capitula], since sins impede [them] and the evils of perverse men abound, become worthless beyond measure and seem virtually void, especially those which were promulgated by the holy Fathers and confirmed by Christian kings by virtue of their regal authority against the evil of rapine and plundering. For this venom has so spread and scattered everywhere far and wide that everyone, infected and corrupted in body and soul, as it were sponetaneously, now sinfully

---

[82] Erdmann (n. 65 above) 22-24, 26-27.

[83] This was the problem confronting Odo's model knight, Saint Gerald of Aurillac. He was most unwilling to use armed force against those who plundered his property. But even he was sometimes forced to do so. Odo explains: "Aliquoties autem cum inevitabilis ei praeliandi necessitas incumberet, suis imperiosa voce praecepit mucronibus gladiorum retroactis, hastas in antea dirigentes pugnarent." Odo, De vita S. Geraldi auriliacensis comitis 1.8, PL 133.646. In this awkward and virtually defenseless manner, Gerald managed to win his battles bloodlessly: "Ita protectus a Deo sit, ut gladium suum . . . numquam humano sanguine cruentaverit" (647). The story points up the anxieties felt about defending; but there is no reason to doubt that attackers may also have felt some pangs of conscience. Their aggressive acts may well have been, at least sometimes, merely attempts to survive. See Georges Duby, Le société aux XIe et XIIe siècles dans la région mâconnaise (Paris 1953) 53-60, on the impoverishment of the Burgundian landholders between 950 and 1000 owing in part to pious donations, in part to land partitioned through inheritance.

[84] Similarly, Christian values prevented much fighting. See Duby (n. 83 above) 196: "Seules, des considérations morales contiennent la turbulence des riches: la foi et le serment sont les soutiens de la paix."

takes advantage of this great wickedness and deadly malady, not
considering what Paul says (or, rather, omnipotent God through
him): "Robbers shall not inherit the Kingdom of God" (1 Cor 6.10).
Nor [do they consider] what the apostle says elsewhere, that if
we eat and consume ourselves—that is, if we plunder each other—
we shall soon be left desolate. Thus is fulfilled in us, or rather through
us, what omnipotent God admonishes through the prophet Isaiah,
saying: "They shall eat every man the flesh of his own arm" (Isa.
9.20), that is, he will plunder the property of his own brother. For
he who takes his neighbor's property, from which [the neighbor's]
life ought to be supported, eats the flesh and drinks the blood of
his own arm. Thus it is no wonder if the heathens and foreign tribes
dominate us and take our temporal goods when some [of us] take
by force from our own neighbor what [our neighbor] must live on.
. . . We plunder our brothers and therefore the heathens justly rob
us and our property. How shall we be able to march confidently
against our enemies and the enemies of the holy church of God
when the plunder of poor men lies in our house; and not only lies
at home but indeed very often it happens that certain men march
against the host with a belly full of plunder? And how shall we be
able to conquer our enemies when the blood of our brothers drips
from our mouth and our hands are full of blood and our shoulders are
burdened with the weight of misery and plunder, and our entire
spiritual and physical strength is weakened?[85]

---

[85] Carloman, *Capitula apud Vernis palatium* (March 884), MGH Leges 1.551: "Graviter
et moleste ferimus, quod [quaedam statuta et capitula] peccatis impedientibus et malitiis
perversorum hominum exuberantibus, ultra modum vilescunt atque pene adnullata existunt, praecipue illa quae contra malum rapinae et depraedationis a sanctis patribus sunt
promulgata, et a christianissimis regibus auctoritate regia confirmata. Siquidem ita passim longe lateque hoc venenum diffusum et dispersum est, ut quasi libere iam male abu-
tantur omnes infecti et corrupti corpore et anima hoc tam sceleratissimo atque mortifero
morbo, non recogitantes hoc quod Paulus dicit, immo Deus omnipotens per ipsum: *Ra-
paces regnum Dei non possidebunt*. Neque illud quod alibi apostolus ait, quia si nosmetip-
sos comedimus et consumimus, id est, depraedamur, cito deficiemus. Completur ergo in
nobis, immo per nos, quod omnipotens Deus per Isaiam prophetam improperat dicens:
Unusquisque carnem brachii sui vorabit, id est, substantiam fratris sui diripiet. Carnem
enim brachii sui devorat, et sanguinem brachii sui bibit, qui substantiam proximi sui tollit,
unde caro sustentari debuit. Non est autem mirum, si pagani et exterae nationes nobis
dominantur nobisque bona temporalia tollunt, dum unusquisque proximo suo per vim tollit
unde vivere debet.... Nos vero praedamur fratres nostros, et idcirco pagani merito nos
nostramque substantiam depraedantur. Quomodo igitur securi poterimus pergere contra
inimicos sanctae Dei ecclesiae et nostros, cum rapina pauperis inclusa est in domo nostra?
et non solum domi reclusa est, verum etiam plerumque evenit, ut pleno ventre rapina in
hostem quidam proficiscantur. Et quomodo poterimus inimicos nostros devincere, cum
sanguis fratrum nostrorum ab ore nostro distillat, et manus nostrae plenae sunt sanguine,
et brachia pondere miseriarum et rapinarum gravantur, totaque virtus animi corporisque
debilitatur?"

A man like Fulk Nerra (987-1040), one of the more successful of the new breed of rulers, fought against the Christian counts of Brittany and Blois. But to atone for his sins he went to Jerusalem three times. As Southern has pointed out:

> He and his contemporary Duke of Normandy were the greatest of the pilgrims who set on foot the movement to Jerusalem. In them the alternation of headlong violence with abrupt acts of remorse and atonement, which characterises the early feudal age, has its full play.[86]

Only the members of the upper classes could feel the conflict in sharp relief.[87] The lower classes had little to do with fighting. Documents connected with the Peace of God in France illustrate this point: they separate lay society into two groups, *milites et rustici*, knights and peasants, defining each by its relation to arms.[88] "The laity were divided into two categories: those whom it was necessary to defend and those whose aggressive tendancies it was necessary to repress."[89] When Bishop Jordan of Limoges excommunicated a number of nobles for breaking the peace, he anathematized their arms and horses,[90] "that is to say, the instruments of their turbulence and the symbols of their social position."[91] In contrast, several documents speak of merchants, pilgrims, noble ladies, and peasants in the same breath; they have in common only their defenseless condition. Of course peasants did at times pick up arms and fight in the host; but, at least in Burgundy and France, they probably did not think of themselves as warriors,[92] nor did

---

[86] Southern (n. 63 above) 86.

[87] The upper classes had one common characteristic: their members were warriors and fought on horseback. Thus they were often considered one class: "The word 'knight,' which had become almost synonymous with vassal, became also the equivalent of 'noble,'" Bloch (n. 81 above) 291.

[88] Georges Duby, "Les laïcs et la paix de Dieu," *I laici nella "Societas christiana" dei secoli XI e XII*, Atti della terza Settimana internazionale di studio Mendola, 21-27 agosto 1965, *Miscellanea del Centro di studi medioevali* 5 (Milan 1968) 454.

[89] *Ibid.* 453.

[90] Ludwig Huberti, *Studien zur Rechtsgeschichte der Gottesfrieden und Landfrieden*, Zur Rechtsgeschichte der Friedenssatzungen im Mittelalter 1 (Ansbach 1892) 214: "maledicta arma eorum et caballi illorum."

[91] Duby (n. 88 above) 454.

[92] In speaking of the peasants in the region of Mâcon ca. 980, Duby (n. 83 above) 108, observes that "déjà le service d'armes permanent n'est plus exigé que des francs les plus riches, seuls capables de combattre à cheval; les pauvres forment une réserve territoriale levée seulement en cas d'invasion et, hors les brèves alertes où les campagnes voisines sont directement menacées, leurs obligations militaires se résolvent en contributions matérielles, fournitures d'approvisionnement ou corvées d'entretien des forteresses."

the rest of society see them in that role. Adalbero of Laon was not alone in pointing out that medieval society was composed of three groups: those who pray, those who fight, and those who work.[93]

Those who prayed were the monks, but not necessarily the diocesan clerics, for the life of the secular clergy had been absorbed to a remarkable degree into lay life. Priests had been carrying arms since the Viking invasions. The only really religious life was the monastic. Abbo of Fleury, for example, divided society into three groups defined by closeness to God: first the monk then the cleric, finally the laity.[94]

Thus the conflict between being a Christian and being a knight was first fully made clear during the reign of Charlemagne; it became more painful for sensitive members of the upper classes when the breakup of royal authority forced them to violate Christian precepts for the life of a knight; it was finally resolved in the concept of the Christian knight, the Crusader. During that period in which the conflict chafed men most, that is, after the Viking invasions and before the First Crusade, the monastery of Cluny flourished and reached the height of its development. Was this simply a coincidence? On one level, at least, it clearly was not: members of Cluny were for the most part also members of the nobility; supporters of Cluny were from the same class. "Without any doubt the aristocratic element predominated there entirely."[95] Sackur and others have pointed out how the inner perception of sinfulness on the part of the nobility was the exciting cause of the Cluniac monastic reform movement and of the intercessionary liturgy performed there. We have seen that feelings of sinfulness at least in part stemmed from conflicts over fighting Christians. Perhaps the connections can be pulled together more tightly.

---

[93] Adalbero of Laon, *Carmen ad Robertum regem Francorum* 297-298, PL 141.782 : "Triplex Dei ergo domus est, quae creditur una; Nunc orant alii, pugnant, aliique laborant." For other instances of this theme see Paul Guilhiermoz, *Essay sur l'origine de la noblesse en France au moyen âge* (Paris 1902) 370-373 and Jacques Le Goff, "Note sur société tripartie, idéologie monarchique et renouveau économique dans la chrétienté du IXᵉ au XIIᵉ siècle, "*L'Europe aux IXᵉ-XIᵉ siècles: Aux origines des États nationaux*, ed. Tadeusz Manteuffel and Aleksander Gieysztor (Warsaw 1968) 63-71.

[94] Abbo of Fleury, *Apologeticus*, PL 139.463ff.

[95] Schieffer (n. 33 above) 51-52. He continues: "Il est fréquemment question de comtes et de princes qui se faisaient moines à Cluny. Sur ce point, même les chartes sont éloquentes: nous y lisons que des moines qui entraient dans l'ordre faisaient don au monastère de leurs propriétés, ce qui laisse supposer que la plupart d'entre eux appartenaient à la noblesse terrienne." See also Johannes Fechter, *Cluny, Adel und Volk. Studien über das Verhältnis des Klosters zu den Ständen (910-1156)*. Inaugural dissertation, University of Tübingen (Stuttgart 1966) 1-15.

V

The conflict between Christianity and knighthood is from one point of view a conflict between values and aggressive impulses. Men of the nobility were raised from boyhood to express their aggression in military exercises and warfare; but at the same time they were taught values that commanded an end to such behavior. Since children began military exercises at about the age of seven,[96] this conflict was inherent in child-rearing practices themselves. It could have been, and probably was for many, a source of anxiety. This is even more apparent when viewed at a personal level. For example, the child might, like Saint Hugh of Cluny, be torn by his mother's desire to see him enter a monastery and his father's ambitions for the boy's military career. Since these were the only careers open to a nobleman, the conflict could not be resolved by entering an emotionally neutral profession.

This limitation in the social and institutional alternatives offered to aristocrats by the first feudal age raises an interesting point. The individual in this society was faced with the problem of adaptation to a social order that offered relatively few acceptable modes of behavior. How could an individual in this society handle prohibitions of aggression? For the nobility, aggression in the first feudal age was institutionalized almost exclusively in fighting; the competitive life of the burgher, the *disputatio* of the schoolmaster,[97] and the militant religious activity of the Crusader were outlets for aggression that became common only in the twelfth century. The young nobleman who felt that his fighting was wrong faced the necessity of controlling his aggressive impulses in some way. Some men, such as Fulk Nerra, handled this task by a constant alternation between unmitigated expression of aggression and spells of total contrition and penance. Others could hardly be satisfied with such contradictory behavior.

Aggression is controlled, in both animals and man, by the ritualization of its expression.[98] The ritual confines the impulse, makes it predictable, and renders it relatively harmless. This observation, shared by the ethologist and psychoanalyst alike, cannot, of course, explain a historical phenomenon. Human ritual, however, uses—indeed must use—existing or acceptable social institutions. In the first feudal age these institutions were relatively limited. Yet there was one mode of behavior which presented the kind of repetitive and ritualized activity that could appropriately be

[96] See Philippe Ariès, *Centuries of Childhood. A Social History of Family Life*, trans. R. Baldick (New York, 1962) 365ff., and Bloch (n. 81 above) 225.

[97] As Abelard put it, "Trophaeis bellorum conflictus praetuli disputationum." See "Abelard's Letter of Consolation to a Friend (*Historia Calamitatum*)," ed. J. T. Muckle, *Medieval Studies* 12 (1950) 175-176.

[98] For a recent treatment of this point see Erik H. Erikson, *Gandhi's Truth: On the Origins of Militant Nonviolence* (New York 1969) 423-436.

utilized by individuals who felt an internal conflict between their social role as fighters and their religious duty as Christians: monastic liturgy. Although of relatively modest proportions before Cluny, this liturgy was nevertheless a highly developed and venerated activity in the first feudal age. A monastic life filled with liturgy could bind aggression by ritualizing it and at the same time allow for the expression of the highest religious aspirations.

The result was Cluniac liturgy. It allowed aggression to be displaced from the real world to the supernatural.[99] The monks fought the devil instead of men and they freed souls from him in their war of liberation. But even in disguise the aggression was recognizable. The curious satire of Adalbero of Laon, which has caused either much displeasure or much glee in historians of Cluny, is a case in point.[100] Adalbero described the Cluniac monk as a knight. This satirical jab has been cited to support the position that Cluniac monks mixed with the world of the knights.[101] But a further interpretation is possible: that the life of the Cluniac monk even inside the cloister was unconsciously a ritualized re-enactment of the life of the knight.

The length of the liturgy served many purposes. As Schmitz and Butler have pointed out, it kept the day occupied. Moreover, it kept the day occupied with an activity that enjoyed the highest regard in society at large and which could express the most devout piety of the monks. From a psychoanalytic point of view it functioned still another way: it defended aginst the surfacing of unacceptable impulses. The warfare that broke out among the members of Cluny during the abbacy of Pontius (1109-1122) indicates how easily these impulses might manifest themselves. The way of life at the monastery had continually to fight against their emergence. This also is one explanation for the ritualism of Cluniac activities unrelated to the *opus Dei*. The fact that the liturgy needed to be carried on all day attests to the importance of the conlict and the strength of the opposing impulses.

Of course many of the men (or young children!) who joined the Cluniac monastery did so for personal reasons unrelated to its liturgy. For example, they may have been dedicated to Cluny by their parents; or they may have desired the prestige that such a move would bring to them. Such considerations should not invalidate any conclusions about unconscious motivations.

---

[99] The impulse does not disappear when controls are placed upon it; rather the result is a compromise expression of both aspects. Thus, from the psychoanalytic view, Cluniac liturgy has two components: the aggressive aspect (fighting the devil and saving souls) and the prohibitive aspect (the ritualized nature of the liturgy and its projection of aggression onto the supernatural, thus rendering it harmless in this world).

[100] Adalbero of Laon (n. 93 above) 1-430, PL 141.771-786. Sackur's comment on the satire was "Die ganz Erzählung ist für uns ein Rätsel" (n. 10 above) 2.94. He concludes that it must mirror opposition to Cluny by various other parts of society.

[101] This is the view of Erdmann (n. 65 above) 62ff.

VI

Psychoanalytic methodology can link the two disparate phenomena of military aggressiveness and lengthy ritual through a number of clinically derived hypotheses. But, because of its very function, the liturgy's relationship with this aggression must be disguised. Were the connections more readily apparent, the liturgy would cease to serve its purpose since it was meant to suppress the very aggression for which it provided an outlet.[102] The connection between the Cluniac mentality and military aggression, however, can be demonstrated directly and explicitly through a bit corroborating historical evidence: the peace movement.

Although the data are limited, it seems that the *Pax* and *Treuga Dei* were sponsored and actively promoted by the Cluniacs as well as other churchmen.[103] The first phase (the *Pax Dei*) began with the Synod of Charroux (989) and ended in the second quarter of the eleventh century. During this period the *Pax* was directed towards protecting the unarmed members of society (including, of course, the monks and unarmed clerics who initiated the movement). It "tended solely to contain military violence within a sector of the Christian population consisting of men who carried the sword and shield and who went about on horseback."[104] In other words, the *Pax* did not condemn private warfare between two armed individuals, but rather attempted to limit the radius of warring activity. We should expect however, given the intensity of feeling against fighting outlined above, a more radical position on the matter. Such is found in the *Treuga Dei*.

The *Treuga Dei* began around 1020 in southern France. It, too, was initiated by the clergy; indeed it originated as a reform movement designed to

---

[102] The charters of donation to Cluny are only slightly more eloquent on this matter. For example, one begins by saying that men ought to hasten "ad tranquillitatis portum que nemo sustinet naufragium, valeamus pervenire. Quo non pervenitur nisi prius hic sua quis larga manu tribuat operariis Christi in vinea ipsius laborantibus, quatinus eorum precibus una cum eis adipisci mereatur supernum gaudium." A. Bernard and A. Bruel, *Recueil des Chartes de l'Abbaye de Cluny* 4, Collection de documents inédits 18 no. 3111. Cowdrey (n. 31 above) 153 observes, "In the charters of Cluny men often stated that they were moved to add to St. Peter's patrimony there [Cluny had been dedicated to Saint Peter and Saint Paul] in order that they might have a part in the prayers of the monks."

[103] Duby (n. 88 above) 448, has noted: "L'initiative... semble bien être venue des évêques et des supérieurs des monastères, notamment de l'abbé Odilon de Cluny"; and further (451): "C'était du moins le vœu de la portion du haut clergé qui n'était pas trop contaminée par les pratiques simoniaques et notamment dans l'église monastique, de ceux qui étaient touchés par le mouvement clunisien, particulièrement actif à l'époque même et dans les provinces où se propageaient les idées de paix." Much of the discussion below follows Duby's article. For a discussion of the scanty nature of the evidence, see Fechter (n. 95 above) 95.

[104] Duby (n. 88 above) 455.

prevent clerics from bearing arms. But soon it was directed towards the laity as well. Abstinance from warfare at certain specified periods now became a penance for sins, the sins, indeed, of fighting itself. "War is said to be a source of sin. It is a pleasure which one ought to refuse."[105] Thus the documents themselves impute an instinctual nature to the pleasures of aggression, the "joys of combat and pillage":[106]

> In the eyes of the part of the clergy placed at the forefront of the reform movement, to combat, to carry arms and use them, began to be considered, at the end of the tenth century, as a defilement of the same magnitude as the taste for money and the sexual act.[107]

It is significant that the earliest expressions of these new sentiments occured in Burgundy.[108]

The attempts on the part of Cluniacs to stop knights from fighting is, from the psychological point of view, an extension of their attempt to keep themselves from fighting. This is a change from the early days of Cluny. In the first half of the tenth century the liturgy alone was used to control aggression. By the first quarter of the eleventh century this was clearly not enough. Perhaps the reason is that the strictures against fighting were becoming more and more vehement. The evilness of fighting was not compared to the evilness of sexual pleasures until the end of the tenth century. These reinforced demands could well have made the liturgy seem an inadequate solution.[109] Thus the aggression in all of society was now tackled. The Cluniacs attempted to impose on their peers what they evidently had not quite succeeded in imposing on themselves.

In putting a stop to warfare at certain specified times of the week and year (and thereby ritualizing its expression), the sponsors of the peace movement managed, paradoxically, to Christianize the fighting that occurred at permissible times. The *Treuga Dei*, in fact, led inevitably to the sacralization of warfare and paved the way for the Crusader. Given this new outlet for aggression justified by the peace movement, why should Cluniac monasteries have continued to attract men from the nobility? The answer is that the sacralization of warfare was a gradual process. The first quarter of the eleventh century saw the very earliest, and by no means very widespread efforts to curtail the number of days on which a knight could fight. There

---

[105] *Ibid.* 458.

[106] *Ibid.*

[107] *Ibid.* 456.

[108] *Ibid.* 458.

[109] Psychoanalysts also speak of the "return of the repressed." The aggressive impulses, in this view, must have been so powerful as to require new as well as renewed attempts at control.

was no automatic justification of his position as warrior. On the contrary, the documents speak of his sins, not his virtues. To become virtuous he must become like the monk, that is, give up his arms. The position of the monk, then, is still morally superior to that of the knight, even if the knight conforms to the *Treuga*. The evolution of the knight from unjustified warrior to sanctified Crusader did not occur immediately; its final recognition came only in 1096 with the First Crusade itself. Thus, during some indeterminate period of the *Treuga Dei*, a man beset by the conflict between his aggressiveness and his devoutness might well still seek out the Cluniac monastery.[110] Clearly, the new outlet provided by the peace movement attracted many men; by the time of the First Crusade it might indeed be said to rival Cluny, for with the First Crusade Cluniac importance and influence began to decline. Although Cluniac monasticism by no means disappeared, the religious leadership of the twelfth century came from such new centers of spirituality as Cîteaux and was rooted in new historical circumstances and values.[111]

After the First Crusade, the theme of the battle between God and Devil no longer dominated theological reflection nor satisfied the emotional needs of the crusading generations.[112] Men could fight now without internal conflict; there was no need for them to project their fantasies onto the supernatural and to enter only vicariously into a war fought between Heaven and Hell. Cluniac liturgy, which had allowed men the closest substitute to actual participation in that eternal war now began to lose its attraction upon the sensitive members of Western knighthood; men went off to Jerusalem or Cîteaux instead.[113] The day of Cluniac liturgy was past.

[110] Delaruelle (n. 35 above) discusses in detail the antiwar stance of Cluniac writings, even late into Hugh's abbacy.

[111] For a discussion of the new circumstances in the twelfth century and their relationship to the rise of a new spirituality see M. -D. Chenu, "Monks, Canons, and Laymen in Search of the Apostolic Life," *Nature, Man, and Society in the Twelfth Century; Essays on New Theological Perspectives in the Latin West,* ed. and trans. J. Taylor and L. K. Little (Chicago 1968) 202-238; and see the forthcoming study by Lester K. Little.

[112] See R. W. Southern (n. 63 above) 219ff.

[113] Saint Bernard, in writing for permission for a canon who had taken the vow to go to the Holy Land to remain at Cîteaux instead, says of the canon: "Stantes sunt jam pedes ejus in atriis Jerusalem. . . . Et, si vultis scire, Clara-Vallis est. Ipsa est Jerusalem, ei quae in coelis est" Bernard, *Epistola* 64, PL 182.169-170. For further discussion of the relationship of Cîteaux to the Second Crusade and the crusading ideal in general see E. Willems, "Cîteaux et la seconde croisade," *Revue d'histoire ecclésiastique* 49 (1954) 116-151; and Giles Constable, "The Second Crusade as seen by Contemporaries,"*Traditio* 9 (1953) 213-280.

Department of History
Loyola University
Chicago, Illinois 60626, U.S.A.

THE GUILLEMS OF MONTPELLIER:
A SOCIOLOGICAL APPRAISAL

•

by Archibald R. Lewis

The Cartulary of the Guillems of Montpellier presents an unusually full record of the activities of a noble family of southern France between the last decades of the eleventh century and the earliest years of the thirteenth. Only the *Cartulary of the Trencavels* of Beziers, still unpublished, or the *Liber feudorum* of the Counts of Barcelona can be compared to it;[1] and each of these is much less complete. The Cartulary is preserved primarily because after 1204 most of the heritage of the Guillems was taken over by the commune or town of Montpellier in a corporate sense. Since the town wished to exercise rights that originally were those of its noble seigneurs, it was to the advantage of the townsmen to preserve intact the record of those rights and privileges which were contained in the Cartulary.

We should begin by describing who the Guillems were before attempting to analyze the contents of their Cartulary. Though there is a mention of a certain Guy (who was presumably the first Guillem) in a charter dating from the year 985, a document that tells how he was given a grant of land by the Count of Melgueil,[2] we know next to nothing about the first four generations of this family. Guillem II, who was presumably head of the family between 1019 and 1025, Guillem III, the husband of a certain Beliardis and holder of a similar position between 1025 and 1058, and Guillem IV, Ermengarde's sponse and head of the Guillems between 1058 and 1068, are shadowy figures.[3] Except for some agreements concerning castles in the Montpellier region which involved Guillem IV in 1059,[4] no charters in the

---

[1] For the Barcelona comital family records see *Liber feudorum maior*, ed. F. Miguel Rossell, 2 vols. (Barcelona 1945-1947). More typical of the scattered nature of surviving documents relating to a noble family of this period are those gathered together in M. Fazy, *Les origines du Bourbonnais*, 2 vols. (Moulins 1924).

[2] *Liber instrumentorum memorialium: Cartulaire des Guillems*, ed. A. Germain (Montpellier 1884) no. 70 (hereafter *Cart. des Guillems*, followed by number of document).

[3] See Germain's Introduction to the above Cartulary, especially pp. xi-xxiii for an account of these first three Guillems.

[4] For the castle of Pouget see *Cart. des Guillems* 480-484. For that of Saint-Pons de Mauchiens *Ibid.* 529.

Cartulary originate with them. This is not surprising for this was a period when the entire region of Languedoc where this family held its lands was becoming militarized and feudalized as new castles arose which were controlled by a special class of warlike castellans.[5] The Guillems were obviously such a family, at first indistinguishable from scores of others for whom we have a record in the Midi and nearby Catalonia.[6]

Then things change as the next Guillem, whom we know as Guillem V succeeds his father in 1068 and continues to head the family until 1120 or 1121. We find in the Cartulary a good deal of information concerning this Guillem—information added to knowledge derived from other sources of the period. He married Ermissende, a daughter of Count Peter of Melgueil, his overlord, and as a result became a kinsman of Count Raymond of Saint Gilles, Count Peter's brother-in-law.[7] He became an ally of Count Raymond who took him under his protection[8] at the moment when this able scion of the Toulousain house was busy creating a principality in this part of the Midi.[9] He even accompanied Raymond on the First Crusade and distinguished himself in the capture of Jerusalem.[10] Even earlier than this, in 1090, he had established special relationships between his family and both the bishops of Maguelonne and the papacy,[11] connections that, as we will note, were to last until the end of his line. Finally it was this Guillem who in 1114 accompanied the count of Barcelona on an expedition against the Muslims of Majorca—one in which Pisa participated—and thus began a long and important relationship between the Guillems and this nearby comital house. All of this sufficiently enhanced his position that in 1120 his daughter Guillamette was married to his nearby overlord and kinsmen, Count Bernard of Melgueil.[12]

---

[5] On the appearance of this class of castellans in the Midi see A. Lewis, *The Development of Southern Franch and Catalan Society, 718-1050* (Austin 1965) 287-314.

[6] For a general view of how such families operated see G. Duby, *La société aux XIe et XIIe siècles dans la région mâconnaise* (Paris 1953) 170-245 and L. Genicot "La noblesse au moyen-âge dans l'ancienne France: contuinuité, rupture ou évolution," *Comparative Studies in Society and Culture* 5 (Ann Arbor 1962). For a family early in this period in Catalonia see P. Bonnassie "Une famille de la campagne barcelonaise et ses activités économiques aux alentours de l'An Mil," *Annales du Midi* 16 (1964) 261-297 and also W. Wightman, *The Lacy Family in England and Normandy, 1066-1194* (Oxford 1966).

[7] See Germain's Introduction (n. 2 above) on this mariage and its local implications as well as *Cart. des Guillems* 78.

[8] *Cart. des Guillems* 78. It is worth nothing that this charter seems to have no mention of any homage or feudal relationship as such.

[9] On Raymond's development of this principality in Languedoc see J. and L. Hill, *Raymond IV de Saint-Gilles* (Toulouse 1959) 7-22.

[10] *Ibid* 114-119.

[11] *Cart. des Guillems* 41. This homage was renewed in 1110 (*ibid.* 42).

[12] The document which tells us of this marriage and which mentions a dowry of seven thousand *solidi*, is clearly a nonfeudal agreement or *convenientia* between equals (*ibid* 59).

Yet despite such evidence of Guillem V's growing influence, the Cartulary shows him less powerful at Montpellier itself than one might think—at the very time when this seat of his authority was beginning to become a commercial center of some importance. For instance, one finds few charters that mention castles under his control outside Montpellier, and in 1090 when the "Men of Montpellier" negotiated a trade treaty with nearby Narbonne, Guillem V did not sign the agreement. Instead a rival family of Montpellier, the Aimons, who served as hereditary *vicars* or *viguiers*,[13] took the lead in these negotations. Perhaps, as has been suggested, Guillem V was still only "primus inter pares" among the nobility of Montpellier and the nearby region.[14]

In 1121 Guillem V was succeeded by his son Guillem VI. This latter, who lived until 1149, further developed the close relationship between his house and the counts of Barcelona, who soon were to become kings of Aragon as well. This explains why Guillem VI married a Catalan noblewoman, Sybila,[15] and why he was assisted by the count and the Genoese, Barcelona's allies, when he suppressed a revolt of his bourgeois of Montpellier between 1141 and 1143—a revolt in which the latter were attempting to set up a commune.[16] Thanks to this alliance also Guillem VI helped the Catalans and Genoese capture Tortosa in 1146; the city was then given to one of his sons as co-lord.[17] Throughout these years close relationships were also maintained with the papacy amounting almost to a formal alliance,[18] but such was not the case with Guillem VI's nearby kinsman and direct overlord, the count of Melgueil, or even the more distant count of Toulouse.[19] By now the Guil-

---

[13] *Ibid.* 169. On the power of this family of Viguiers who possessed a castle within the walls of the town as well as holding the office of Viguier for Montpellieret, the bishop of of Maguelonne's section of Montpellier, as shown in the Cartulary record, see A. Lewis, "Seigneurial Administration in Twelfth-Century Montpellier," *Speculum* 22 (1947) 564-567.

[14] See B. Gaillard "La condition féodale de Montpellier," *Mémoirs de la Société archéologique et historique de Montpellier* 2.8 (1927) 348-349.

[15] *Cart. des Guillems.* 126, 127.

[16] See Lewis, (n. 13 above) 568 for an analysis of the Cartulary record of this revolt and also *Chronique romane* in *Petit Thalamus* (*Société archéologique de Montpellier* 1836) 329. See also A. Lewis, "Town Government in Twelfth-Century Montpellier," *Speculum* 22 (1947) 59.

[17] For an overall view of the rivalry between the houses of Barcelona and Toulouse during these years in which the Guillems deserted the Toulousain party and joined that of Barcelona see C. Higounet, "Un grand chapitre de l'histoire du xiie siècle. La rivalité des maisons de Toulouse et de Barcelone pour la préponderance méridionale," *Mélanges Louis Halphen* (Paris 1951) 313-322.

[18] The Cartulary contains a number of documents showing this close relationship between Guillem VI and Pope Anacletus II (1121-1149). *Cart. des Guillems* 3, 8-16.

[19] One major source of friction between the Guillems and their nearby overlords, the Count of Melgueil (who belonged to the Toulousian party), was Guillem VI's control of the mint

lems were definitely part of the Aragonese party in the Midi. Finally, on the more local level, we find this Guillem extending his influence over a whole series of nearby castles, whose castellans took a general oath of loyalty to him in 1130[20] and again in 1147.[21] The Cartulary also contains a series of more detailed special agreements concerning those castles dating from this period.[22]

When Guillem VI died in 1149, his son Guillem VII succeeded him and continued to head the family until 1179. He was influential enough as a lord to be able to win the hand of Matilda, a sister of Duke Eudes II of Burgundy[23]—which perhaps reflects as well the trading interests of Montpellier's merchants north towards the fairs of Champagne. Guillem VII, however, remained a loyal adherent of the Aragonese party in Languedoc and in his will made the count protector of his family and their holdings[24]. He also kept the accustomed close relationship of his house with the papacy, especially during the pontificate of Alexander III,[25] and made agreements with both the Pisans and Genoese with whom Montpellier had intimate commercial ties.[26] With the counts of Toulouse relations remained more strained, even

---

of Melgueil. In 1125 the latter, in making peace with Count Bernard of Melgueil, secured the promise that the Count would not debase this coinage (*ibid*. 65). Two years later in 1130 Guillem VI promised not to issue this coinage on his own authority (*ibid*. 68, 69). Other agreements covering these same points were made in 1132 (*ibid*. 71), in 1135 (*ibid*. 72, 73), and in 1145-1146 (*ibid*. 75-77).

[20] *Ibid*. 142, 151.

[21] *Ibid*. 158. This new oath of loyalty seems to have been exacted following the supression of the revolt of 1141-1143, an event that may well have loosened the bonds of loyalty which linked nobles inside and outside the town to their Guillem overlords. On this situation see Lewis, (n. 13 above) 567-568 and Lewis (n. 16 above) 62.

[22] For evidence of castles outside Montpellier controlled by the Guillems in this period, some with more degree of control than others, one finds much in the Cartulary record. For Castlenau see *Cart. des Guillems* 308, 309. For Montferrier, 314-325. For Pignan, *ibid*. 403-409, 406-409. For Coronsec, *ibid*. 425-427. For Frontignan, *ibid*. 443. For Valmale, *ibid*. 454-459. For Pouget (belonging to Guillem of Omelas, a brother of Guillem VI) *ibid*. 527-528. For Saint-Pons de Mauchiens, *ibid*. 530.

[23] See the marriage agreement between Guillem VII and Matilda of Burgundy, *ibid*. 129.

[24] Concerning Toulousain-Aragonese rivalry during the period see Higounet (n. 17 above). The will of Guillem VII, dating from 1172, which makes the King of Aragon the protector of his family, lands and rights, is found in the Cartulary, *ibid*. 96. So is that of his brother Gui Guerregrat, a loyal member of the Aragonese party, which dates from 1177-1178 (*ibid*. 97). Though Guillem VII refers to himself in his will as *homo* of the King of Aragon, we have no record of any homage of a formal sort.

[25] There are records of homages to Bishops of Maguelonne and the Pope in 1152 and 1161 (*ibid*. 46, 47). Other charters dating from this period stressing special Papal protection for Guillem VII and the merchants and commerce of Montpellier date from 1162, 1165, and 1169 (*ibid*. 19, 23, 21-22).

[26] See A. Germain, *Histoire du Commerce de Montpellier*, 2 vols. (Montpellier 1881) 10-31, and *Cart. des Guillems* 21-22, 202-203.

though in 1164 an agreement between the lord of Montpellier and Count
Raymond V was negotiated—one, however, which did not specify any homage.[27] When the count of Toulouse, however, became count of Melgueil as
well, in 1174 Guillem VII thought it wise to do homage to him as overlord
of some of his domains[28] a though how important he thought this act was
is problematical. By the time of his death the Cartulary reveals that he had
come into possession of many more castles in the region near Montpellier
than his father had controlled,[29] and in 1149 he exacted a general oath of
allegiance from the castellans of these fortresses.[30]

Guillem VII's son Guillem VIII succeeded him in 1179 and in 1181 made
a remarkable and, as it turned out, disastrous marriage. This was to Eudocia, a Byzantine princess who was the niece of the emperor Manuel Comnenus. Eudocia had expected to marry the king of Aragon, but when she
arrived for the nuptials she found him already married. Chivalrously Guillem VIII, loyal to his Aragonese ties, then married her himself. The union
proved an unhappy one. Eudocia was able to produce only a girl, named
Marie, as an heir to the Guillem lands. When the Angeli took over the Byzantine empire from the Comneni in 1185, she had little else to offer her husband. In 1186 Guillem VIII put her away and the next year married a certain Agnes of Castille who was a relative of the queen of Aragon.[31] From
this time until his death in 1202, he make every effort to get both the church
and his powerful neighbors and townsmen to accept the legality of this second marriage and recognized his son by his second wife, Guillem IX, as
heir to his possessions, thereby excluding Marie, his daughter by Eudocia.
With this in mind he not only made great efforts to enlist the popes on his

[27] *Ibid.* 79.

[28] *Ibid.* 81. He and his brother still remained loyal to the Aragonese party in the Midi
according to their wills. *Ibid.* 96, 97.

[29] In addition to the castles mentioned in n. 23 over which the Guillems had a measure
of control, Guillem VI expanded his authority over additional fortresses during this period,
according to the Cartulary: Saint-Felix of Substantion in 1171, a gift of Guillem VII to
his brother Gui Guerregrat (*ibid.* 311); Santeragues in 1168 (*ibid.* 312-313); Miréval between
1161 and 1165 (under the control of Guillem VII's Omelas kinsmen), finally sold to them
outright in 1171 (*ibid.* 339-344); Castries (owned by Guillem VI's brother, Guillem of Tortosa since 1158-1159 according to *ibid.* 392, 393, 395 bought along with its rirghts soon there
after by Guillem VII (*ibid.* 397, 400); Clermont in 1160-1161 (*ibid.* 534-536); Nebian in
1160 (*ibid.* 538, 539); a castle and domains owned by Gauclem of Claret in 1159 (*ibid.* 566-
568).

[30] *Ibid.* 151, 142.

[31] See Germain's Introduction (*ibid.* xxiv) for the best account of this marriage. Eudocia, however, was a niece of the Emperor Manuel Comnenus, not a daughter as Germain
states.

side, especially Innocent III,[32] and the kings of Aragon, but in 1090[33] and 1094[34] did homage to the count of Toulouse for some of his castles and other possessions.

In addition to mending his fences with the papacy and the houses of Aragon and Toulouse, Guillem VIII also made a great effort to consolidate his position at home. He purchased from the Aimon family their rights to the vicarage of Montpellier and Montpellieret, the bishop of Maguelonne's section of the town.[35] He consolidated his hold over nearby castles and their castellans by negotiating a series of intricate agreements[36] and in 1190 required them to swear a general oath of loyalty to him.[37] Most important of all, he seems to have made an attempt to establish his rights over the town of Montpellier on a firm basis by carefully listing the *censives* and *alberga* that were owed him on a monetary basis by the *milites* and bourgeois who lived within

[32] See the record of homages to Bishop of Maguelonne and the Pope dating from 1184 and 1193 (*ibid*. 48, 49). For special privileges granted Montpellier's lord in 1191 by Celestine III see *ibid*. 24. Pope Innocent III's relations with Guillem VIII were particularly close, in part because he wished to enlist his aid against the Cathar heretics in the Midi between 1199 and 1201 (*ibid*. 25-28), 32-35, 37-39). But Innocent neither recognized the validity of Guillem VIII's second marriage nor agreed to disinherit his eldest daughter Marie.

[33] As Count of Melgueil Raymond V of Toulouse was now important enough to be conciliated and considered as a serious threat to Guillem VIII's power. See homage of 1190 for details (*ibid*. 87).

[34] This record of homage to Raymond VI of Toulouse (Raymond V's heir) dating from 1194 suggests a closer relationship. For instance, in it Guillem VIII had his rights over the castles of Frontignan and Oomelas confirmed by his overlord (*ibid*. 89). Other privilege and rights are mentioned in *ibid*. 90, 91. By this time Tortosa, which had earlier been divided between the Genoese, Guillem of Tortosa, and the count of Barcelona, was completely in the latters hands and was so longer held in part by the Guillems as a fief.

[35] Sometime during the course of the twelfth century, probably during the lifetime of Guillem VII, the Guillems got control of the vicarage of Montpellieret (formerly belonging to the Aimons) as a fief from the Bishops of Nîmes (*ibid*. 50-51). In 1197 and 1201 Guillem VIII purchased all the rights of their Viguiers, the Aimons, over their own section of the town (*ibid*. 123, 119). For a full account of this purchase based on Cartulary records and its significance, which left the Guillems without noble rivals within the town, see Lewis, "Seigneurial Administration" (n. 13 above) 568.

[36] The new castles etc., over which Guillem VIII seems to have established varying degrees of control are: Lattes in 1201 (*Cart. des Guilllems* 304); Palude, purchased in 1202 (*ibid*. 406); the honors of Peter of Cersacio in Lattes, purchased in 1200 (*ibid*. 307); Vaguières in 1197 (*ibid*. 315); Montbazin in 1190 (*ibid*. 435); Valmale in 1197 (reacquired?;) *ibid*. 448); Omelas in 1199-1200 (sale of last rights; *ibid*. 465-466); The city of Agde (portions of it) in 1185 and 1189 (*ibid*. 469, 470, 473); Loupian in 1189, 1190-1191 and 1194-1195 (in accords with the viscounts of Beziers; *ibid*. 474-477); Paulan and Poussan in 1183-1184 (*ibid*. 494 and later agreements); Tressan in 1200 (*ibid*. 565); Frontignan in 1202 (*ibid*. 569-570); domains of the noble Ebrard family in Montpellier in 1194 (*ibid*. 238).

[37] *Ibid*. 124. For a list of nobles living in the town who owe homage to the Guillems—a list probably dating from the time of Guillem VIII—see *ibid*. 246, 248.

its walls.[38] Also he issued, just before his death, the first version of the well-known *Coutumes* of Montpellier[39] and in *de facto* fashion recognized the right of Montpellier's citizens to have their own board of consuls.[40]

All this turned out to be in vain. Ultimately Pope Innocent III proved unwilling to recognize the legality of Guillem VIII's second marriage and to deprive his elder daughter, Marie, of her rights as the heir of the Guillems. Futhermore, Marie herself strengthened her claims by marrying, as her third husband, Peter II, king of Aragon, who now had a vested interest in seeing that his wife gain her Guillem heritage for herself. In addition to all this the townsmen of Montpellier, eager to have their rights to a consulate formally recognized, wavered in their loyalty to the young Guillem IX. The result was that Guillem VIII's will was put aside and his children by his second wife were deprived of their inheritance. The lands and rights of the Guillems came into the possession of the House of Aragon shortly after 1204 and remained Aragonese until the middle of the fourteenth century.[41]

But much more emerges about the Guillems from the cartulary record than what has been related above. First of all we can see in the development of this family proof of its growing power and importance in the society of the time. From a marriage by Guillem V with the daughter of his weak overlord, and one by Guillem VI with a relatively unimportant Catalan aristocrat, we observe their progress to Guillem VII's marriage with a member of the ducal family of Burgundy and Guillem VIII's marrying into the imperial house of Byzantium and the royal house of Castile, with his daughter Marie becoming Queen of Aragon and the mother of the great Jaime the Conqueror. The story of the Guillems is one successful social mobility.[42]

---

[38] Lists of *alberga* owed by town *milites* and burgesses to the Guillems and of *censives* owed by nonnobles, probably dating from 1190, are found in *ibid.* 249-273, and 276-283. Their significance is discussed in Lewis (n. 13 above) 572-573.

[39] For provisions of the *Coutume*, dating from 1190, found in the Cartulary see *Cart. des Guillems* 239, 244. On their significance see Lewis (n. 16 above) 64. For the full form of the *Coutume* as it was written down in 1204 or 1205 see the *Petit Thalamus* (n. 16 above).

[40] The will of Guillem VIII, dating from 1202, contains provisions that represent a tacit recognition of consuls in the town of Montpellier (*Cart. des Guillems* 99). For a discussion of the development of this body which finally appeared in an official form by 1205 see Lewis (n. 16 above) 58-64.

[41] See Lewis (n. 16 above) 64-67 for the details of how Marie and her husband, Peter II of Aragon, finally took over as lords of Montpellier after 1202.

[42] The universal desire of scions of noble families to marry well and so to rise in the social world is dealt with in a recent article by Duby, which, though it deals essentially with northern France, reflects the Midi as well. See G. Duby, "Dans le France du Nord-Ouest: au XII siècle: les "jeunes" dans la société aristocratique," *Annales, économies-sociétés-civilisations* 19 (1964). For accounts of similar family alliances among the nobles of a somewhat earlier period see Lewis, *Southern French and Catalan Society* (n. 5 above) 337-35 and Bonnassie, "Une famille" (n. 6 above).

Second, when we carefully examine the Cartulary record of this family we grasp the realities of feudal power in the Midi during the late eleventh and twelfth centuries. The Guillems were tied by formal bonds of vassalage to their co-seigneurs of Montpellier, the bishops of Maguelonne, and the near-by counts of Melgueil. But much more important were the nonfeudal or semifeudal arrangements that linked them to the more powerful kings of Aragon,[43] the papacy[44] and, at times, the counts of Toulouse.[45] Their ties with the latter did not become formally feudal until 1174 and even then, judging from the record, were of minor importance to them. On the upper level of power politics in this part of France it is hard to believe that eudalism ever operated at all as a viable system. Indeed, if there was a supreme over-lord of southern France during the period covered by this paper it was the pope rather than the distant kings of France who are only mentioned in the documents of the Cartulary as a method of dating documents by their reigns.[46]

But ties of a feudal nature were not only extremely fragile or even non-existant on the upper level of society, to judge by what the Cartulary re-veals concerning the links of the Guillems to the papacy, the kings of Ara-gon, the counts of Toulouse, the counts of Melgueil and the bishops of Mague-lonne; they were equally ambigious on the lower level. There was no ef-fective second level of feudalism in this part of France: Witness the tangled story of the relationship between the Guillems and the Aimon family, who were the vicars of Montpellier before Guillem VIII bought them out in 1197 and 1201.[47] The Aimons, though vassals of the Guillems, led the bourgeois revolt of 1141-1143, which lost them their castle in the town.[48] For a period they controlled the bourgeois militia of Montpellier.[49] They were anything but loyal vassals, and although Guillem VI, Guillem VII, and Guillem VIII exacted general oaths of loyalty from nearby castellans in 1130,[50] 1147,[51]

---

[43] See especially the wills of Guillem VII and Gui Guerregrat which date respectively from 1172 and 1177-1178, *Cart. des Guillems* 96, 97.

[44] One could cite much evidence of this from the Cartulary already alluded to in the notes. But see especially *ibid*. 7, 12, 14, 19, 22, 23, 26-28.

[45] Especially that early charter of Raymond IV of Saint-Gilles which dates from 1070 (*ibid*. 78).) See also the *convenientia* between Guillem VII and Count Raymond V dating from 1164 (*Ibid*. 79).

[46] On the very early development of this special Papal relationship with nobles of South-ern France, as early as 909, see A. Lewis "Count Gerald of Aurillac and Feudalism in South Central France in the Early Tenth Century" in *Traditio* 20 (1964) 58 and, later on, Lewis (n. 5 above) 191-192, 335-336.

[47] *Cart. des Guillems* 123, 119.

[48] See Cartulary evidence summed up in Lewis (n. 13 above) 564-568.

[49] *Ibid*. 565.

[50] *Cart. des. Guillems* 142.

[51] *Ibid*. 151.

1149,[52] and 1190[53] according to the cartualry, detailed examination of scores of agreements covering individual castles and castellans shows a bewildering variety of ties. Some charters reveal "franc fiefs" or fiefs which owed no service,[54] some show castles jointly owned by Guillems and castellans,[55] some are *convenientia* or agreements that are not really feudal.[56] And the duties, largely military, which both *milites* and bourgeois who resided inside the town walls owed them, turn out often to have been simply the duty of making certain money payments, judging from the twelfth-century Cartulary record, a kind of *scutage* or *tallage*.[57] If we look below the surface, then, of the information that this Cartulary provides, we can hardly feel that the Guillems operated in a feudal fashion towards their dependants any more than they did when they confronted their noble betters, even though they may have attempted to establish some system of feudalistic loyalties in regard to such dependants.

Last of all, and by no means least important the Cartulary of the Guillems shows how important money was to this family, who were, in fact, embued with a businessman's psychology. Their power from the start tested on a financial base that came from their ability to tax the resources of a rising town with a growing long-range commerce. Quite early Guillem V managed to get control of the mint of Melgueil which provided the towns currency.[58] After he did so, he kept constant the value of the coinage issued by this

[52] *Ibid.* 158.

[53] *Ibid.* 124.

[54] One can find a general discussion of such *franc* fiefs, which is based on much evidence found in the Cartulary of the Guillems in H. Richardot, "Francs Fiefs: essai sur l'exemption totale ou partielle de fief," *Revue historique de droit français et étranger* 13 (1935). See also E. Magnou-Nortier ""Fidélité et Féodalité méridional d'après les serments de Fidélité (x^e- début xiie siècle)," *Les Structures sociales de l'Aquitaine, du Languedoc et de l'Espagne au premier âge féodal* (Paris 1969).

[55] Among many examples see charters explaining the status of the castle of Frontignan (*Cart. des Guillems* 431, 439), or Omelas (*ibid.* 548, 549); or Clermont (*inid.* 534-537).

[56] See as an example the charter of 1144 relating to the castle of Gignac (*ibid.* 532. For a discussion of this kind of agreement and its relationship to feudal ones see P. Ourliac "La'convenientia," *Études d'histoire du droit privé offertes à Pierre Petot* (Paris 1959) 413-22, and also P. Bonnassie "Les conventions féodales dans la Catalogue du xie siècle," *Les Structures* (n. 54 above).

[57] See especially *Cart. des Guillems* 254-261 as well as 272-276. A few lists of *alberga*, probably representing those from rural areas outside the walls of Montpellier, are expressed in payments in kind rather than money (*ibid.* 250-253).

[58] In 1120 Guillem VI got control of the mint of Melguiel on a mortgage basis as part of a marriage agreement between his daughter, Guillamette and Count Bernard IV of Melgueil, paying 7000 *solidi* for it (*ibid.* 59). This document, incidentally, is a *convenientia*. As early as 1103, however, Guillem V and Count Raymond of Melgueil, Bernard's father, had reached an agreement on how this mint would operate.

mint,[59] and late in the twelfth century he struck a special gold coin for trade with Muslim marts in the western mediterranean.[60] Money figures prominently in all the wills left by members of this family and in all marriage agreements.[61] Careful attention is paid to commercial interests when agreements are made with Pisans and Genoese, and charters show the popes taking the merchants of Montpellier under their express protection[62] The Guillem extended their holdings inside and outside the town by purchase rather than force, and the lists of twelfth-century *cênsives* and *alberga* that the cartulary provides to us are almost always expressed in monetary terms.[63] The Guillems seem to be good businessmen who succeeded because of their ability to accumulate hard cash. They help to disabuse us of the common notion that a noble family of this period, at least in the Midi, held to values different from those current among bourgeois merchants.

There is much else, of course, which can be learned from the cartulary of the Guillems. Here we glimpse the spread of Roman law throughout the Midi[64] and get a chance to understand aspects of private law as revealed in

[59] After this date we find a series of charters relating to agreements between the Guillems and the counts of Melgueil on keeping the value of Melgorian money, the town's currency, unchanged, etc. These charters date from 1128, 1130, 1135, 1145-1146, and 1188-1190 (*ibid.* 65-69, 71-77, 87).

[60] *Ibid.* 170, dating from 1194.

[61] Among these wills are those of Guillem V, dating from 1121, Guillem VI dating from 1146, Guillem VII dating from 1172, and Guillem VIII dating from 1202 (*ibid.* 94, 96, 99). See especially the dowry arrangements of Guillamette in 1120 and of Tiburge of Omelas, a Guillem relative, in 1191 (*ibid.* 59, 561).

[62] Some of these purchases include: the castle of Pouget in 1129 (*ibid.* 477); Santeragues in 1147-48 (*ibid.* 313); Castries in 158 (*ibid.* 306); the rights of the Ébrards in 1194 (*ibid.* 238); and the rights of the Viguier family of Aimons in 1197 and 1201 (*ibid.* 123, 119). One should contrast this urban seigneury and the rights and authority assembled by the Guillems, however, with the quite different contemporary rural seigneury of Forez described in E. Perroy "La seigneurie de Saint-Bonnet le Château," *Annales du Midi* 18 (1966) 285-295.

[63] For fuller discussions of this development, based in part on documents found in this Cartulary, especially the *Coutume of 1190* (*Cart. des Guillems* 239, 244) as well as the wills and marriage agreements of the Guillems see A. Gouron, "Les étapes de la pénétration du droit romain au xııe siècle dans l'ancienne Septimanie," *Annales du Midi* 69 (1957) and "Diffusion des consulats méridionaux et expansion du droit romain aux xııe et xıııe siècles," *Bibliothèque de l'École des Chartes* 121 (1963). See also P. Tisset, "Placentin et son enseignement à Montpellier," *Recueils des mémoirs et travaux de la Société d'histoire du droit des pays de droit écrit* 3 (Montpellier 1951).

[64] These wills not only include those of Guillem V, VI, VII and VIII, mentioned earlier, but a number of others such as that of Gui Guerregrat (brother of Guillem VII) which dates from 1177-1178, and of Bourgondion (brother of Guillem VIII), which dates from 1182 (*Cart. des Guillems* 97, 98). The Cartulary also contains two wills of Aimon Viguiers, that of Bernard-Guillem dating from 1119 and that of Raymond-Aimon dating from 1182 (*ibid.* 102, 116). Other wills of important noble lords and ladies of the region found here

a series of marriage agreements and wills.[65] Seigneurial administration, especially that in the realm of finance, can be deduced from an abundant documentation not yet examined carefully enough by scholars[66] and from much else as well. Yet perhaps it is possible to sum up the value of this Cartulary in a few words. Here stands revealed, in the growth of a family from castellan to seigneur to a house concerned with royal marriage alliances, the proof that in southern France during this period social upward mobility was easy, ties and loyalty were weak, and money was all important.

---

include those of Girondes of the Castle of Pouget, dating from 1059, of Pierre Guillem Ébrard of Montpellier, dating from 1136, of Dalmace of the castle of Castries, dating from 1145, and of Emessende of Castries, dating from 1157 (*ibid.* 482, 225, 394, 395).

[65] Equally important are the records of marriage agreements in the Cartulary, not only those of Guillem V, VI, and VII with their wives and daughters, already mentioned, but also one relating to Marie, eldest daughter of Guillem VIII, dating from 1197 (*ibid.* 205). Two other marriage agreements of noble ladies found here are one for Tiburge of Omelas, dating from 1149, and another for a second Tiburge of Omelas, dating from 1191 (*ibid.* 551, 561).

For a general discussion of the private law represented by these and other wills and marriage agreements of the Midi see the little known work of J. Hilaire, *Le régime des biens entre époux dans la région de Montpellier du début du XIIIe siècle à la fin du XVIe siècle* (Montpellier 1957).

[66] See Lewis, (n. 13 above) for a fuller discussion of administration by the Guillems, especially the development of the office of *bajalus* and that of the notary. For other areas of administration see Lewis, (n. 16 above).

Department of History
University of Massachusetts
Amherst, Massachusetts 01003, U.S.A.

CULTURAL CLIMATES AND TECHNOLOGICAL ADVANCE IN THE MIDDLE AGES

•

by Lynn White, jr.

To establish facts, and the more obvious relations among facts, has never satisfied the consciences of historians. We are driven to ask not only what happened but also why it happened. Historical explanation, of course, is seldom a matter of one billiard ball striking another, of "causes" in the narrow sense. It is much more often a process of gradual illumination of the fact to be explained by gathering around it other facts that, like lamps, seem to throw light on it. At last the historian arrives at a sense that the central fact on which he is focusing has become intelligible.

In 1959 when I finished the manuscript of a book on medieval technology,[1] I was painfully aware of its greatest defect: it identifies and describes a few major aspects of the unprecedented technological activity that occurred in the medieval West, but it fails to explain the phenomenon observed. To tell the truth, I was much more sure of the *what* than the *why*. Four years later I had become bold enough to publish a preliminary inventory of possible reasons, not all of equal weight but none mutually exclusive, for medieval technological advance.[2] This is not, however, the sort of problem that stands still. The present state of scholarship demands a new effort to understand it.

I

There is much to be understood. The technological creativity of medieval Europe is one of the resonant facts of history.[3] Beginning obscurely as early

---

[1] *Medieval Technology and Social Change* (Oxford 1962), hereafter *Med. Techn.*

[2] "What Accelerated Technological Progress in the Western Middle Ages?" in *Scientific Change*, ed. Alistair C. Crombie (London 1963) 272-291.

[3] The most comprehensive survey of medieval European technology is that by Bertrand Gille in *Histoire générale des techniques*, ed. Maurice Daumas, 1 (Paris 1962) 429-598, and 2 (1965) 2-139. See also Friedrich Klemm, *Der Beitrag des Mittelalters zur Entwicklung der abendländischen Technik* (*Beiträge zur Geschichte der Wissenschaft und der Technik* 2, Wiesbaden 1961), and my "The Expansion of Technology, 500-1500 A. D." in *The Fontana Economic History of Europe* ed. Carlo M. Cipolla, 1, chapter 4 (London 1969 issued as pamphlet).

as the sixth century, within three hundred years the northern peasantry created a novel agricultural system that, in proportion to expenditure of human labor, was probably the most productive in the world.[4] In the eighth century the Franks revolutionized their methods of warfare, and thereafter their descendants consistently maintained the initiative in improving military technology, as distinct from military organization. From about the year 1000 onward—although the movement was foreshadowed in the ninth century—the West produced new labor-saving mechanical devices and explored new applications of power to production, thus providing the industrial basis for burgher capitalism. Starting in the sixth century, but particularly after 1200, Europe led in the development of ship design and the nautical arts.

While the medieval West's cousinly cultures, Byzantium and Islam, long remained more sophisticated in most other respects, in technology they were laggards as compared with Europe. Only contemporary China—from which the West borrowed much[5]—could compare with Europe in inventiveness and eagerness for useful novelties. The emergence of the mechanical clock in the second quarter of the fourteenth century, however, by enlarging the number of craftsmen skilled in making and correlating moving metal parts in machines, led in Europe to heightened activity that soon gave to the Occident a clear technical superiority even over China.

Romans had been no less predatory than were Europeans of the late Middle Ages, but the Caesars were so ill equipped that they could not extend their rapacity greatly beyond the basin of the Mediterranean. By 1492, however, Europe had developed an agricultural base, an industrial capacity, a superiority in arms, and a skill in voyaging the ocean which enabled it to explore, conquer, loot, and colonize the rest of the globe during the next four centuries and more. This unification of world history was a unique event. Its implementation, and that of the Imperialist Age, 1500-1950, was provided largely by the Middle Ages.

Moreover, modern technology is the extrapolation of that of the Western Middle Ages not merely in detail but also in the spirit that infuses it. The later thirteenth century in Europe marks the moment of crisis in the history of mankind's relation to the natural evironment: it produced "the invention of invention" of which the practical effects were soon felt. The earlier record of technology around the globe is scattered and often lacking in continuity; it recounts a generally slow accumulation of isolated specific inventions,

---

[4] The salutary effect of this upon the standards of living among German peasants in the eleventh century is shown in my "The Life of the Silent Majority," in *Life and Thought in the Early Middle Ages* ed. Robert S. Hoyt (Minneapolis 1967) 85-100.

[5] No student of European technology can neglect Joseph Needham, *Science and Civilization in China*, 4 vols. in 6 to date (Cambridge, Eng. 1954-1970).

their spread and elaboration. But in the Middle Ages, in Europe alone, invention became a total and coherent project.[6] From the later Middle Ages onward, world technology was increasingly European technology.

Technicians at that time in large numbers[7] began to consider systematically all the imaginable ways of solving a problem. About 1260, the Franciscan Roger Bacon, pondering transportation, confidently prophesied an age of automobiles, submarines, and airplanes.[8] Since arrow wounds were then a medical problem, about 1267 Theodoric, successively bishop of Bitonto and Cervia, in his treatise on surgery noted that for the extraction of arrows "quotidie enim instrumentum novum, et modus novus, solertia et ingenio medici invenitur."[9] Clocks were a great problem, and proposals for their improvement were frequent before the solution was found. On the basis of the recently introduced Chinese mariner's compass, and inspired by the novel Hindu concept of perpetual motion, in 1269 Roger Bacon's friend, the military engineer Peter of Maricourt, proposed a magnetic clock to replace all others.[10] In 1271 Robert the Englishman, talking about plans for a weight-driven clock, admitted that the problem of the escapement had not been entirely conquered, but he was confident that it would be.[11] Almost at the same moment, at the court of Alfonso el Sabio of Castile, Rabbi Isaac ben Sid of Toledo described not only new kinds of waterclocks, which he claimed to be much better than any earlier models; he also depicted as an absolute novelty a weight-driven clock with a mercury brake.[12] Indeed, this was a fairly practical solution for the escapement, as a subsequent tradition of such clocks shows.[13] Before 1313 someone invented the sandglass.[14] But

---

[6] For a complex example of this coherence, see an inventory of the ways, between ca. 1010 and ca. 1480, in which Western technicians utilized the velocity, resistence and pressure of air, in my "The Invention of the Parachute," *Technology and Culture* 9 (1968) 462-467, and "Medieval Uses of Air," *Scientific American* 222 (Aug. 1970) 92-100.

[7] About 1235 Villard of Honnecourt, and in 1269 Peter of Maricourt, independently inform us that many men are arguing and laboring to the point of exhaustion to produce *perpetua mobilia*; *Villard de Honnecourt: Kritische Gesamtausgabe*, ed. H. R. Hahnloser (Vienna 1935) pl. 9; Peter of Maricourt, *Epistola de magnete* in *Rara magnetica 1269-1559*, ed. Gustave Hellmann (Berlin 1896) 11.

[8] *De secretis operibus*, chap. 4, in *Opera queadam hactenus inedita*, ed. J. S. Brewer (London 1859) 533.

[9] *Chirurgia* 1.22, appended to Guy de Chauliac, *Ars chirurgica* (Venice 1546) fol. 143.

[10] See my "Tibet, India and Malaya as Sources of Western Medieval Technology," *American Historical Review* 65 (1960) 522-526.

[11] Lynn Thorndike, "Invention of the Mechanical Clock about 1271 A.D.," *Speculum* 16 (1941) 242-243.

[12] *Libros del saber de astronomia del rey D. Alfonso de Castilla*, ed. M. Rico y Sinobas (Madrid 1866) 4.67-76.

[13] Silvio A. Bedini, "The Compartmented Cylindrical Clepsydra," *Technology and Culture* 3 (1962) 115-141.

[14] *Med. Techn.* 165-166.

technicians labored from the 1260s until the 1330s before the true mechanical clock was invented.[15]

In a sermon on repentance preached at Santa Maria Novella in Florence on 23 February 1306, the Dominican Fra Giordano of Pisa, while providing our best evidence of the invention of eyeglasses in the 1280s, incidentally sang the praises of the recent invention of invention. "Not all the arts," he said, "have been found; we shall never see an end of finding them. Every day one could discover a new art . . . indeed they are being found all the time. It is not twenty years since there was discovered the art of making spectacles which help you to see well, and which is one of the best and most necessary in the world. And that is such a short time ago that a new art, which never before existed, was invented . . . I myself saw the man who discovered and practiced it, and I talked with him."[16]

By the early fourteenth century, then, Europe showed not only an unmatched dynamism in technology: it also arrived at a technological attitude toward problem solving which was to become of inestimable importance for the human condition. The profound contrast between this aspect of the

[15] The intensity and diversity of the search is indicated by the fact that, almost simultaneously, inventors reached two related solutions: the verge and the wheel escapement; Ernst Zinner, *Die ältesten Räderuhren* (Bamberg 1939) 26. The use of geared weight-operated striking trains in clepsydras by the thirteenth century, and the assimilation of the vocabulary of the water clock to the mechanical clock, make difficult exact dating of the invention of the latter; cf. *Med. Techn.* 124. The earliest firm date is 1341 when Galvano Fïamma, *De gestis Azonis vicecomitis*, ed. L. A. Muratori, *Rerum italicarum scriptores* 12 (Milan 1728) 1038, tells of the invention in Milan of mills run neither by water nor by wind "sed per pondera contra pondera sicut fieri solet in horologiis. Et sunt ibi rotae multae, et non est opus, nisi unius pueri. . . . Nec umquam in Italia tali opus fuit adinventum, *licet per multos exquisitum*" (italics added). The middle 1330s however, seem indicated by the fact that in 1338 a party of six Venetian merchants left for India taking a clock and an automatic fountain as their most valuable merchandise. In Delhi the Muslim Sultan paid to them the fantastic sum of 200,000 bezants "tam pro rellogio quam pro fontanella et aliis rebus dicte societatis"; Robert A. Lopez, "L'extrême frontière du commerce de l'Europe médiévale," *Moyen âge* 69 (1963) 488 n. 16. To command such a price, this clock must have been a great novelty, almost certainly weight-driven and escapement-controlled, since Islam was entirely familiar with elaborate water clocks, as is shown by Eilhard Wiedemann and F. Hauser, "Über die Uhren im Bereich der islamische Kultur," *Nova acta* (Halle) 100.5 (1915) 1-272.

[16] "Non sono però trovate tutte. Di trovare arti non si verrebbe a fine mai. Ognedì se ne potrebbe trovare una dell'arti . . . e sempre se ne trovano delle nuove. Non è ancora xx anni che si trovò l'arte di fare gli occhiali, che fanno vedere bene, ch' è una delle migliori arti e delle piu necessarie che'l mondo abbia: ed è cosi poco che si trovò arte novella che mai non fu. . . . Io vidi colui che prima la trovò e fece, e favellagli"; Enrico Narducci, *Tre prediche inedite del b. Giordano da Rivalto* (Rome 1857) 59-60, an offprint from *Giornale arcadico di scienze, lettere ed arti* 146 (1857) 125-126. Edward Rosen, "The Invention of Eyeglasses," *Journal of the History of Medicine and Allied Sciences* 11 (1956) 13-46, 183-218, clarifies the context.

Occident and the relative passivity toward technology in the Near East is the more significant because Byzantium, Islam, and the Western world were related societies, all in great measure, but in varying proportions, built of elements found in the Greek and Semitic legacies from Antiquity. The fact that thirteenth-century theologians in Cairo, Constantinople, and Paris were all commenting on Aristotle helps us to grasp the unity of the triune Middle Ages. The fact that in the time of Saint Thomas Aquinas labor-saving machinery was little developed in the Near East and concern for invention was minimal, whereas in the West a new sort of engineering[17] was being pursued with an enthusiasm amounting to passion, helps us to understand why the Occidental third of the Middle Ages generated what we call the modern world.

II

This technological thrust of the medieval West does not yield easily to explanation. Necessity is not the mother of invention,[18] since all necessities are common to mankind living in similar natural environments. A necessity becomes historically operative only when it is felt to be a necessity, and after prior technological development makes possible a new solution. Even then, what seems needed and feasible to one culture may be a matter of indifference to another.

For example, the lands of medieval Islam were generally so arid that, even where there was enough water for agriculture, the flow of streams was too scanty or sporadic to operate many mills to grind grain. Windmills were an "obvious" solution, since dry country is notoriously windy because sparsity of vegetation helps to generate air currents. And in fact in the tenth century of our era[19] the first functional windmills appeared in eastern Iran and Afghanistan, rotating on vertical axles. Here, surely, the Muslim world had discovered an answer to its "need" for mechanical power. But did Islam feel that need with any intensity? There is no evidence that the windmill of Sejistan ever spread to the rest of Islam: claims for windmills in Muslim Spain have not been substantiated.[20] In 1185, on the other hand, the hori-

---

[17] The word "engineer" first appears in 1170 and is very common in the thirteenth century; see *Med. Techn.* 160.

[18] I have not been able to trace this misconception earlier than the late 1120s when Hugh of Saint Victor, *Didascalicon* 1.9, ed. Charles H. Buttimer (Washington 1939) 17, cites a proverb of which scholars have not found the source: "Ingeniosa fames omnes excuderit artes." In 6.14 (p. 130) Hugh comes closer to the modern phrasing: "propter necessitatem inventa est mechanica."

[19] For the controversy over the date see *Med. Techn.* 86 n. 7.

[20] *Ibid.* 161; *Isis* 58 (1967) 249. To judge by the distinction achieved in Yuan China by immigrant Muslim engineers (see Herbert Franke, "Westöstliche Beziehungen im Zeit-

zontal-axle windmill appeared independently in Yorkshire,[21] seemingly invented by analogy with the Vitruvian watermill, and it spread over Europe almost explosively.[22] Within seven years it had been taken to Syria by German crusaders. Yet fourteen years after that, writing at Edessa in 1206, the leading Arabic author on engineering, al-Jazarī, remarks that the notion of mills driven by the wind is nonsense: the wind is too fickle to power such a machine.[23]

Late medieval Byzantium, although ruling a dwindling area, was economically still fairly prosperous and continued to be amazingly vigorous in the arts and in religious speculation. Its resilience fills one with admiration. But, like the Muslims, the Greeks of that age were not particularly concerned to improve their technology.[24] About 1444 Cardinal Bessarion, a learned Byzantine cleric who had emigrated to Italy, wrote to the Despot of the Morea[25] urging him to strengthen himself against the Turks by sending young men to the West to learn the mechanic arts. He was impressed by improved Western glass,[26] textiles, weapons, and ships. What most amazed him, however, was the spectacle of water wheels operating both sawmills and the bellows of blast furnaces. Yet in the Occident at that time there was no novelty in these: the first lumber mill appears at Evreux in 1204, and the first water-

alter der Mongolenherrschaft," *Saeculum* 19 [1968] 99-100), Islamic technology must have been more dynamic than the present deplorable state of scholarship would indicate. The best, but inadequate, survey is that by Gaston Wiet, Vadime Elisséeff, and Philippe Wolff "L'évolution des techniques dans le monde musulman au moyen âge," *Cahiers d'histoire mondial* 6 (1960-61) 15-44.

[21] *Med. Techn.* 87.

[22] By about 1322 a monk at Saint Mary's of Pipewell in Northamptonshire complains that one of the chief reasons for deforestation is the search for long timbers for the vanes of windmills: "et quot virgae molendinorum venticorum dabantur in temporibus diversorum abbatum nemo novit nisi Deus"; W. Dugdale, *Monasticon anglicanum*, ed. 2 (London 1682) 1.816.

[23] E. Wiedemann, "Die Konstruktion von Springbrunnen durch muslimische Gelehrte, in *Festschrift zur Feier des hundertjährigen Bestehens des Wetterauischen Gesellschaft für die gesamte Naturkunde zu Hanau*, ed. C. Lucanus (Hanau 1908) 36.

[24] K. Vogel's admirable chapter on Byzantine technology in the *Cambridge Medieval History*, ed. 2, 4.2 (1967) 299-305, and bibliography 465-470, indicates little motion after the seventh century.

[25] Alex G. Keller, "A Byzantine Admirer of 'Western' Progress: Cardinal Bessarion," *Cambridge Historical Journal* 11 (1955) 343-348.

[26] A symptom of European initiative is not only the fact that in this period Western glass was being widely exported to the Near East, but also that the Venetians, and probably the glass-masters of Barcelona likewise, were manufacturing mosque lamps for that market decorated both with Western floral designs and with pious Koranic inscriptions, sometimes garbled; R. J. Charleston, "The Import of Venetian Glass into the Near East, 15th-16th Century," in *Annales du 3e Congrès International d'étude historique du verre, Damas 1964* (Liège 1968) 158-168.

powered blast furnace in 1384 at Liège.[27]   In much of Greece there were ever-running streams operating flour mills.   Nor were medieval Greeks and Latins ignorant of each other.   The essential fact is that they acted differently because they had differing notions on how it was important to act.   In the medieval East, whether Byzantine or Islamic, technological innovation was not considered important.   It involved no sense of necessity.   Bessarion's letter shows that by 1444 he personally had become Latinized in more than his religion.

There have been efforts to refine the idea of necessity by relating the vitality of medieval Western technology either to the disappearance of slavery or to an alleged labor shortage that placed a premium on increasing the productivity of labor, whether agricultural or industrial.

Unfortunately the present state of scholarship in the comparative sociology of the various medieval subcultures does not permit assured generalization.   For example, as regards slavery in Byzantium, one would assume that the military victories of Romanus I, Nicephorus II Phocas, and John I must have increased the supply of slaves from the ninth into the eleventh centuries.   However, we do not yet know the extent to which slave labor was used in Byzantine industry[28] and consequently how it may have affected inventiveness in that area.   About Antiquity we are somewhat better informed, and what we know does not confirm all modern presuppositions.   In certain contexts slavery does not appear to be an obstacle to technological advance.   The Hellenistic and early Imperial periods witnessed both the apogee of the ancient slave economy and the most rapid advances not only in engineering but also in basic inventions such as glass blowing.[29]   In contrast, the urban artisan class both in Byzantium and in medieval Islam seems, as in the West, to have consisted largely of free men; yet the Near East, unlike Europe, did not make the transition from craftsmanship to widespread industrial production.

There is scanty but interesting evidence that in late Roman times scarcity of manpower was, in fact, an occasional stimulus to invention;[30] but it would appear that the antitechnological attitudes of the ruling class—a bent of

---

[27] Bradford B. Blaine, *The Application of Water-Power to Industry during the Middle Ages*, Ph. D. dissertation, University of California, Los Angeles (1966) 155, 134-135.

[28] Anne Hadjinicolaou-Marava, *Recherches sur la vie des esclaves dans le mond byzantin* (Athens 1950) 114.

[29] See the thoughtful discussion by Ludwig Edelstein, "New Interpretations of Ancient Science," *Journal of the History of Ideas* 13 (1952) 579-585: he concludes that the obstacles to the wide application even of those inventions lay less in social conditions than in "the basic values underlying ancient life." In particular, Edelstein notes, p. 584, that in Antiquity there was no sense that technological advance was approved by the gods.

[30] H. W. Pleket, "Technology and Society in the Graeco-Roman World," *Acta historica neerlandica* 2 (1967) 15-16.

mind propagated from generation to generation by an almost exclusively rhetorical education—made such proposals abortive.[31] In Europe until the late thirteenth century[32] the movement of assarting indicates that there was probably more land available than there were hands to cultivate it, and this may have been one of the stimuli to the improvement of agricultural methods which was so notable in the West. Yet over the world and throughout history many peoples faced with untapped resources have been slow in developing methods of exploiting them.

At the level of concrete facts it is difficult to interpret technological history from its social context. The emergence of the water mill, the first mechanical application of inanimate power, is an event of prime significance. It appears almost simultaneously, in the first century before Christ, in three widely separated regions: Jutland, northern Anatolia, and China.[33] Are we to assume that in early Germanic Scandinavia, in the Pontus of Mithradates, and in the Yellow River Valley of the Han dynasty, social relationships were so similar as to evoke, in a single inspired generation, the notion of replacing human muscle with the force of water? Similarly the cannon, a complex invention harnessing the expanding forces of gasses by means of a metal tube to propel a missile, is found first at Florence in 1326, in England in 1327,[34] and in China in 1332.[35] Are we to believe that in the early fourteenth century conditions in Italy and England on the one hand, and in Yuan China on the other, were so alike that a major innovation in the art of war was socially necessary, or at least appropriate? It is far simpler, and more consonant with the present state of the evidence, to hold that technology, like art, religion, or social forms themselves, enjoys a certain autonomy in its development, and that diffusion is sometimes swift among very different societies.

The history of papermaking likewise illustrates the difficulty of explaining technological growth as a function of social relations. Paper was invented in China, and, after A.D. 751, when the Caliph's armies captured some papermakers in Samarkand, it spread throughout Islam because it was cheaper than either papyrus or parchment. By about 1050 the Byzantines were using imported Muslim paper both for documents and for books. It is curious that there is no present evidence that medieval Greece ever manufactured its own paper: in the thirteenth and fourteenth centuries its source of supply

---

[31] Ibid. 17-24.

[32] *Med. Techn.* 67 n. 4.

[33] Ibid. 80-81.

[34] Carlo M. Cipolla, *Guns and Sails in the Early Phase of European Expansion, 1400-1700* (London 1965) 21, 32.

[35] L. C. Goodrich, "Early Cannon in China," *Isis* 55 (1964) 193-195.

shifted increasingly from Islam to Italy.[36] The first indication of paper in the Occident is a Greek charter granted in 1101-1102 by Countess Adelasia of Norman Sicily;[37] this paper was probably imported. Despite assertions to the contrary regarding Játiva in Valencia in the middle of the twelfth century,[38] there is no proof that the production of pulp for paper was ever mechanized in Islam. In startling contrast, the first paper factory known to us in the West—it was already in operation by 1276 near Fabriano—[39] was a *mill*, using water power for pulping. So likewise was the second, in 1280 at Játiva,[40] now under Aragonese rule. There is no independent evidence that labor was scarcer in Italy or in Christian Spain at that time than it was in Islam. In the present state of historical research, the ardor for advancing technology which is observed in the medieval West cannot be explained, save marginally, by social conditions, although it is clear that technological changes were occasionally a factor in social change.[41]

In the twentieth century, new technology is composed so largely of engineering applications of scientific discoveries that we tend to assume a similar relation in the past. In fact, however, until a little more than a century ago there was small connection between science, which was a theoretical effort to understand nature, and technology, which was an empirical attempt to use nature.[42] For nearly five hundred years the world's greatest scientists wrote in Arabic, yet a flourishing science contributed nothing to the slow advance of technology in Islam. By the late thirteenth century the scientific movement in the West, which had begun in the eleventh century with a wave of translations from Greek and Arabic, had seized the global primacy that it still holds. Yet while some individuals at that time, like Roger Bacon, were concerned with both science and technology, their science does not seem to have enriched technology.[43] The slight connection was the

[36] J. Irigoin, "Les premiers manuscrits grecs écrits sur papier et le problème du bombycin," *Scriptorum* 4 (1950) 194-204, and "Les débuts de l'emploi du papier à Byzance," *Byzantinische Zeitschrift* 46 (1953) 314-319.

[37] E. Caspar, *Roger II* (Innsbruck 1904) 482, 561.

[38] E. g. in *A History of Technology* ed. Charles Singer *et al.*, 3 (Oxford 1957) 412.

[39] Aurelio Zonghi, "Le antiche carte fabrianesi," in *Monumenta chartae papyraceae historiam illustrantia*, ed. E. J. Labarre, 3 (Hilversum 1960) 114. Irigoin, in *Scriptorium* 4 (1950) 197 concludes that Italian paper was already being exported to Byzantium by 1255. Whereas Islamic paper never shows watermarks, the lively entrepreneurship of Westerners is indicated by the appearance of such trademarks in Italian paper by the 1280s; Irigoin, 194.

[40] Augustin Blanchet, *Essai sur l'histoire du papier et de sa fabrication* (Paris 1900) 52-53.

[41] Cf. *Med. Techn.*, passim.

[42] See my "Pumps and Pendula: Galileo and Technology," in *Galileo Reappraised*, ed. Carlo L. Golino (Berkeley 1966) 96-110.

[43] The idea that systematic scientific research can help to advance broad areas of technology is first clearly formulated in 1450 by Nicholas of Cusa in *De staticis experimentis* which

reverse: technology was advanced by supplying instrumentation for scientists, most notably the mechanical clock as an aid to medical astrologers.[44]

Still other hypotheses may be offered to account for the permeative technological interest of the medieval West. It has been shown in detail[45] that change leads to further change. In the early Middle Ages the West was much more deeply shaken by invasions and turmoil than were the lands of the Near East. Can this trauma have made the Occident more open to change than the Orient? Perhaps; but this does not explain why the West's penchant for change should have expressed itself so early and so notably in technology rather than in other kinds of activity.

Again: I myself once toyed with the notion[46] that since under Roman rule the Celts showed themselves to be fairly inventive, the vigor of medieval technology may have been simply an amplification of a cultural condition preexistent in Gaul. Perhaps; but this merely transfers the medieval enigma to the Roman age without illuminating it.

III

Clearly, along such paths we have little chance of reaching a satisfactory historical understanding of our problem. To find an explanation for this distinctive quality in the Western Middle Ages we must try to relate it to the general cultural climate of those centuries and places.

Unfortunately the scholarly discovery of the significance of technological advance in medieval life is so recent that it has not yet been assimilated to our normal image of the period. Moreover historians, like most humanists except archaeologists and art historians, are word-bound and therefore find it hard to appraise an activity like technology which has not usually left its traces in writing. In literate societies like those of the Middle Ages which place a high value on ancient texts, contemporary actualities are often obscured by words that are a prized ornamental veneer drawn from obsolete

---

is Bk. 4 of *Idiota*, ed. Ludwig Baur (Leipzig 1937); a complete French translation is available in Maurice de Gandillac, *Œuvres choisies de Nicolaus de Cues* (Paris 1942) 328-354, who notes (328 n. 166) that in the Vitruvius Strasbourg editions of 1543 and 1550, to which this dialogue is appended, the two participants, named Orator and Profanus in the original, are renamed Philosophus and Mechanicus. Throughout the conversation Mechanicus generally holds the initiative in proposing scientific experiments that might have useful applications in medicine, pharmacy, metallurgy, gem polishing, materials analysis, forecasting the weather, making bells and organ pipes, and perfecting ships and military engines.

[44] *Technology and Culture* 10 (1969) 439-441.

[45] Margaret Hodgen, *Change and History: A Study of Dated Distributions of Technological Innovations in England, A.D. 1000-1899* (New York 1952).

[46] "What Accelerated Technological Progress." (n. 2 above) 280-282.

but revered tradition. Historians trying to understand the cultural climate of an epoch recognize that the degree and style of an era's respect for written tradition is a major element in its climate. The extent, however, to which the verbal repertory of each age may have been self-deceptive, or else inadequate for expressing reality, is not always pondered.

As compared with words, nonsymbolic actions are usually functional rather than decorative. Since many such actions are related to the state and trend of a society's technology, technologies and changes in them offer a useful means of judging how far written records reveal or distort the true state of a cultural climate. There is thus a feedback between our understanding of technology and our interpretation of the general context to which technology is integral.

Items borrowed by a culture offer simpler case studies than those originated within it since they involve no internal genetic problems.

The quality of life in central Java contemporary with Charlemagne may be judged by one of the world's most evocative monuments, Barabuḍur. The enormous Buddhist stupa presents a panorama of bas-reliefs[47] illustrating a world of much elegance, but one remarkably restricted in its technical methods. Only the ships that gave contact with India, whence most of old Indonesian civilization was derived, were in any way advanced, and these vessels were presumably built on Indian models. It may be significant of cultural values that the sole technical novelty that seems traceable to Java at that time is in the arts: the fiddle bow.[48]

Despite this innovation, instrumental music in the East Indies has continued to be primarily percussive. Carried westward on the currents of the spice trade, however, the musical bow, still with a very curved stick, reached Europe about 980[49] where it spread and developed speedily. In order to equalized tensions along the entire length of the bowstring and thus produce a uniform and smooth tone, the stick in Europe was progressively flattened. In early twelfth-century France the first form of the "frog" appeared as a link between the lower part of the stick and the bowstring, thus greatly im-

---

[47] Nicolaas J. Krom, *Barabudur: Archaeological Description*, 2 vols. of text, 3 of plates (The Hague 1927-1931).

[48] Mantle Hood, "The Effect of Medieval Technology on Musical Style in the Orient," *Selected Reports* of the Institute of Ethnomusicology, University of California, Los Angeles, 1 (1970) 147-170. The evidence is not conclusive but is strong: the *surendro*, a type of five-tone gamelan orchestra which distinctively includes a bowed lute, was known in eighth-century Java. Francis W. Galpin, "The Violin Bow," in *The Legacy of India*, ed. G. T. Garratt (Oxford 1937), 331-334, provides no early dating from India. Bowed instruments were introduced to China perhaps as late as the Yuan dynasty; cf. H. G. Farmer, "Reciprocal Influences in Music 'twixt the Far and Middle East," *Journal of the Royal Asiatic Society* (1934) 327-342.

[49] Curt Sachs, *History of Musical Istruments* (New York 1940) 275.

proving the musical possibilities of bowed instruments.[50] By the later Middle
Ages the bow, probably Javanese and certainly Asian in origin, had acquired
the dominance of Western instrumental music which it retains today.

No medieval text documents with explicit words the amazing openness
of the medieval European mind to borrowings from alien cultures,[51] or shows
contemporary awareness of Europe's capacity to exploit and elaborate such
borrowings far beyond the level achieved in the lands that generated them.
The Indic concept of perpetual motion which in India was doubtless a symbol of karma, and which in Islam was a curiosity, fostered in the Occident
a generalized concept of a cosmos full of forces waiting to be used mechanically
by man.[52] What Europe did to Chinese paper manufacturing has already
been mentioned. India originated the stirrup and China developed it, but
Charles Martel's army was the first to realize its full implication for warfare[53].
Gunpowder was Chinese, but the Near East, India, and ultimately Japan
received artillery and firearms not from China but from the West.[54] Let
us consider one example of such a borrowing, and its consequences, in more
detail.

There has long been discussion, among architectural historians, of possible
Asian contributions to the genesis of Gothic architecture. The idea generally
has been rejected, particularly among the French.[55] The still dominant view
that gothic architecture was spontaneously born of the efforts of medieval
engineers to cope with the structural necessities of romanesque vaulting
shows, however, misunderstanding of the nature of diffusion and of the not
infrequent ability of a fairly simple item borrowed from an alien culture
to "trigger" much more elaborate creations in the borrowing culture, especially if the intrusive idea answers a felt need.

In the late tenth and eleventh centuries, for reasons that are far from clear,
the height of Europe's new churches was steadily increased. The lateral

[50] Hans Heinz Dräger, *Die Entwicklung des Streichbogens und seine Anwendung in Eu-
ropa* (Berlin 1935) 25-26.

[51] I attempt a brief inventory of such items, only a minority of which were technological, in "Medieval Borrowings from Further Asia," *Medieval and Renaissance Studies* 5:
*Proceedings of the Southeastern Institute for Medieval and Renaissance Studies, Summer
1969*, ed. O. B. Hardison, Jr. (Chapel Hill 1971) 3-26.

[52] See n. 10 above. The earliest repudiation of the feasibility of perpetual motion appears
on the first page of Leonardo's unfinished treatise on machine design: see Ladislao Reti,
"The Two Unpublished Manuscripts of Leonardo da Vinci in the Biblioteca Nacional of
Madrid", *Burlington Magazine* 110 (1968) 17.

[53] *Med. Techn.* 1-28.

[54] *Ibid.* 163-164; also Delmer M. Brown, "The Impact of Firearms on Japanese Warfare,"
Far Eastern Quarterly 7 (1948) 238-253.

[55] E.g., André Godard's discussion of "l'origine de l'architecture française du moyen-
âge" in "Voûtes iraniennes," *Āthār-é Īrān: Annales du service archéologique de l'Iran* 4
(1949) 239-256, and *Art de l'Iran* (Paris 1962) 266ff.

thrust of semicircular vaults demanded massive walls and buttresses; the loftier the vaults, the thicker the lower masonry that was required. In those days all quarrying and stone cutting was manual, and land transport was fearfully expensive, although less so than in Roman times.[56] What could be done to reduce the quantity of masonry needed for a church of the desired height? Moreover, the ground plans of great churches were becoming more elaborate with ambulatories, radial chapels, and the like. Semicircular vaulting could not easily be tailored to cover such irregular areas. Fortunately, to solve such problems a new idea came out of the East at the moment when Europe's architects most needed it.

The ogival arch, sometimes combined with pointed vaulting, is first found in Buddhist India about the second century after Christ.[57] It was used by the Sasanians, whose influence apparently brought it to Syria by A.D. 561.[58] The pointed arch, with vaults, appears at Ramla in Palestine in 789[59] and by the later ninth century was common in Muslim Egypt.[60] Thence it moved by about 1000 to Amalfi, a city intimately connected with Fatimite Egypt,[61]

---

[56] *Med. Techn.* 66.

[57] Although the present state of Indic studies does not permit definite statements about the priority of pointed arches among various sites, a growing opinion is expressed by Dietrich Brandenburg, *Islamische Baukunst in Ägypten* (Berlin 1966) 49, that the ogive began "in der frühesten buddhistischen Kunst Indiens, kam von dort nach dem zentralen Hochasien und von da nach dem Irak und Ägypten." This type of arch probably originated as a purely decorative form for gable ends in wooden structures; cf. a Kushan relief of the second century after Christ at Mathurā in John Rosenfield, *The Dynastic Arts of the Kushans* (Berkeley 1967) fig. 29. Small masonry pointed arches appear about the same time at Kauśambi; G. R. Sharma, "Kuṣāṅa Architecture with Special Reference to Kauśāmbi (India)," in *Kuṣāṇa Studies*, ed. G. R. Sharma (Allahabad 1968) 18-19, fig. 4 (3). Also of the second century is a pointed vaulted niche at the Buddhist monastery of Takht-i-Bāhi; Benjamin Rowland, *The Art and Architecture of India*, ed. 3, (Baltimore 1967) pl 42a. Alexander Cunningham, *Mahābodhi* (London 1892) 85, believed that the spectacular pointed arches and vaulting at this greatest of Buddhist shrines are later than the original Kushan (second century) construction; the evidence, as indicated by Rowland 98, 291, pl. 52b, is ambiguous. In any case the Gupta Hindu temple of the fifth century at Bhītārgāoṅ (Rowland fig. 20) with pointed vaulting antedates any known Iranian evidence of such construction; Rowland fig. 20 and J. P. Vogel, "The Temple of Bhītārgāoṅ, *"Archaeological Survey of India, Annual Report* (1908-1909) 5-16, pl. 3, 4.

[58] Arthur U. Pope, "Possible Iranian Contributions to the Beginning of Gothic Architecture," in *Beiträge zur Kunstgeschichte Asiens in Memoriam Ernst Diez* (Istanbul 1960) 20.

[59] Brandenburg (n. 57 above) 49.

[60] One of the earliest appearances in Egypt is in the shaft of the Nilometer (A.D. 866 or 861) built by an architect from Fergana; Pope (n. 58 above) 20.

[61] Cf. A. O. Citarella, "The Relations of Amalfi with the Arab World before the Crusades," *Speculum* 42 (1967) 299-312. Evidence of the pointed arch in Amalfi about 1000 has been available for more than three decades in the very dilatory restoration of the Old Cathedral, but has not been published. I myself saw some of the earliest discoveries in 1933.

and by 1071 a porch with pointed arches and pointed vaults graced Abbot Desiderius's new church at Monte Cassino.[62] Considering that the most remarkable monk there under Desiderius's abbacy was Constantine the African (died 1087), a native of North Africa who was the first great translator of Arabic science into Latin[63] and who dedicated his version of the *Pantegni* of 'Alī ibn 'Abbās (died 994) to Desiderius,[64] there is nothing surprising in the appearance of an architectural borrowing from Islam at that time and place.

Structurally the Monte Cassino porch was no more adventurous than its Near Eastern prototypes: it was, in Kenneth Conant's happy phrase, "a bit of chic."[65] The great technological advance involving the pointed arch occurred not in Italy but in Burgundy. In 1080 Abbot Hugh of Cluny visited Monte Cassino, and there either he or his engineers,[66] then working on the design of an enormous new church being planned for Cluny, realized that pointed arches and pointed vaults offered the key to solving the chief problems with which romanesque architects had been contending. As a result of their insight, the church at Cluny, begun in 1088 and effectively finished in 1120, contained 196 pointed arches with more in the high vault.[67] The new Cluny was the most conspicuous church of northern Europe. In 1130 Abbot Suger of the French royal abbey of Saint-Denis visited it. Between 1135 and 1144 he and his engineers produced at Saint-Denis what is usually regarded as the first true gothic church. In doing so they realized the full possibilities inherent in the novel Cluniac development of oriental architectural ideas.

Nothing is more characteristically and superbly medieval than Saint-Denis, and no monument of the twelfth century has been more often cited by historical meteorologists studying the cultural climate of that age. Yet an

---

[62] Kenneth J. Conant, *Carolingian and Romanesque Architecture, 800 to 1200* (Baltimore 1959) 223 and pl. 8 A, corrects and amplifies an earlier drawing published in conjunction with Henry M. Willard in *Speculum* 10 (1935) 144-146, pl. 1; see their article, below 203-209.

[63] See Paul O. Kristeller, "The School of Salerno," *Bulletin of the History of Medicine* 17 (1954) 151-153.

[64] The text of the dedication is best found in Constantine the African, *L'arte universale della medicina* (*Pantegni*) 1.1, ed. Marco T. Malatto and Umberto de Martini (Rome 1961) 37.

[65] Kenneth J. Conant, *A Brief Commentary on Early Medieval Church Architecture* (Baltimore 1942) 8.

[66] Jacques Stennon, "Hézelon de Liège, architecte de Cluny III," in *Mélanges offerts à René Crozet*, ed. P. Gallois and Y. J. Riou (Poitiers 1966) 1.345-358 fails to prove his thesis: the extant evidence indicates that Hezelo may have been the major fund-raiser, not the architect, of the great church at Cluny.

[67] Kenneth J. Conant, "The Pointed Arch: Orient to Occident," *Palaeologia* (Osaka) 7 (1959) 36.

essential quality of its achievement has been overlooked: that in creating this glorious synthesis of engineering and esthetics, the black-robed Benedictines of Saint-Denis were the vigorous heirs of russet-garbed Buddhist monks in India a millennium earlier.[68]

Apart from students of folklore—which of all the humanistic disciplines has the broadest geographic and sociological horizons—medievalists have been reluctant to recognize cultural connections over such distances. On its slow journey from India, however, the ogive travelled in much company. Since the middle of the eleventh century, shortly before Desiderius built his porch, a Christianized life of Buddha, transmitted from Sanskrit to Arabic, perhaps through a Manichean Turkic version, and thence through Georgian and Greek into Latin, had been circulating widely in the West, with the result that Buddha, slightly masked[69] as the ascetic Indian prince Josaphat (that is, Boddhisatva), was increasingly revered as a saint whose festival is on 27 November.[70] About 1110, as Cluny was approaching completion, the Arabic-speaking Jewish convert Petrus Alfonsi included in his very popular *Disciplina clericalis* many of the animal fables of the *Pañcatantra* which had made their way from Sanskrit through Pahlavi and Syriac into Arabic.[71] In 1138, while Saint-Denis was rising, Indic numerals appeared for the first time in the West on a coin of Roger II of Sicily.[72] In 1149, five years after Saint-Denis was finished, Robert of Chester, revising some Arabic astronomical tables to the coordinates of London, introduced into Latin

[68] So far as I can discover, no one in the Middle Ages spoke of gothic engineering as providing economies in construction. The proof that many were in fact aware of this virtue of the new style—which was quickly lost in the immense new elaboration of gothic carving, clustered pillars and the like—is that the austere order of Cistercians who hotly denounced the extravagances of Cluniac churches and permitted no towers or ornaments of any sort on their own (see François Bucher, "Cistercian Architectural Purism," *Comparative Studies in Society and History*, 3 [1960] 89-105) after an intial hesitation seized upon the gothic way of building and spread it over Europe. Hanno Hahn, *Die frühe Kirchenbaukunst der Zisterzienser* (Berlin 1957) 254-258, who holds that the usual image of the Cistercians as "missionaries of the gothic" is overdrawn, fails to distinguish gothic structure from gothic embellishment. The early Cistercian gothic churches achieved the stark beauty of pure functionalism in a period when the dominant trend of gothic towards lavish ornament was developing, as Hahn correctly indicates, in the cathedrals of northern France.

[69] The first Western suspicion that Josaphat was Buddha appears in a gloss inserted into a text of Marco Polo about 1446; cf. A. C. Moule and P. Pelliot, *Marco Polo: Description of the World* (London 1938) 1.410.

[70] See David M. Lang's introduction to [St. John Damascene] *Barlaam and Joasaph* (Cambridge, Mass. 1967).

[71] *Disciplina clericalis*, ed. Alfons Hilka and Werner Söderhjelm (*Acta Societatis scientiarum fennicae* 38.4, Helsingfors 1911); Haim Schwarzbaum, "International Folklore Motifs in Petrus Alfonsi's *Disciplina clericalis*," *Sefarad* 21 (1961) 267-299; 22 (1962) 17-59, 321-344; 23 (1963) 54-73.

[72] Lynn Thorndike, "The Relation between Byzantine and Western Science and Pseudo-Science before 1350," *Janus* 51 (1964) 18.

the Indian trigonometric concept of the sine function (in Latin *sinus*),[73] which word, by a series of mistranslations and transliterations, is derived from the Sanskrit term for sine.[74] In 1154, a decade after the completion of Saint-Denis, a Cistercian monk of Clairvaux named Lawrence who was returning from Rome, with the aid of two boys and many saints drove a herd of ten Indic buffaloes—creatures never before seen in northern parts—across the Alps to Clairvaux where they promptly propagated and spread "ex eo loco per multas jam provincias."[75] The inspired engineering of the new gothic architecture was part of a larger pattern of Eurasian relationships which was far more than technological and which we have scarcely begun to understand.

Medieval Europe's capacity for gathering and expanding insights and elements drawn from the most distant and unexpected sources is a major characteristic of its culture which, on the one hand, is underscored by the study of technology and which, on the other hand, helps to explain the vigor of that technology. Despite difficulties of travel and communication, medieval European technicians had autennae delicately adjusted to catch the vibrations of every promising novelty, however distant. If since 1500 global technology has become increasingly that of the Occident, the reason is not only the inventiveness of medieval Europe but also the fact that by 1498, when Vasco da Gama reached Calicut, Europe had already absorbed and adapted to its use a great part of the other technologies of Eurasia. The culture of the medieval West was unique in the receptivity of its climate to transplants, although the verbal statements of medieval men would not lead us to such an estimate of their mentality.

What a society does about technology is influenced by casual borrowings from other cultures, although the extent and uses of these borrowings are reciprocally affected by attitudes towards technological change. Fundamentally, however, such attitudes depend upon what people in a society think about their personal relation to nature, their destiny, and how it is good to act. These are religious questions.

IV

The most thoughtful analysis of the presuppositions of Western technology has been provided by a medieval historian, Ernst Benz[76] of the University of Marburg. Study of Buddhism and personal experience of it in Japan

[73] Charles H. Haskins, *Studies in the History of Mediaeval Science*, ed. 2 (Cambridge, Mass. 1927) 123.

[74] H. Hankel, *Zur Geschichte der Mathematik in Altertum und Mittelalter*, ed. 2 (Hildesheim 1965) 280-281.

[75] Herbertus, *De miraculis* 2.30, PL 185.1341.

[76] "Fondamenti cristiani della tecnica occidentale," in *Technica e casistica*, ed. Enrico Castelli (Rome 1964) 241-263. A more popular presentation of his thesis is contained in the chapter, "The Christian Expectation of the End of Time and the Idea of Technical

—especially of the anti-technological impulses in Zen[77]—led him to find the genesis of Europe's technological advance in Christian beliefs and attitudes. The Christian Creator God, the architect of the cosmos and the potter who shaped man from clay in his own image, commands man to rule the world and to help to fulfill the divine will in it as a creative cooperator with him. History, far from being cyclical as it is in most religions, in Christianity is unique and unilinear; it is accelarating toward a spiritual goal; there is no time to lose; therefore, work, including manual work, is an essential and pressing form of worship. Moreover, matter was created for a spiritual purpose and it is neither to be transcended nor despised: the dogmas of the incarnation and of the resurrection of the flesh vouch for this. The sense that intelligent craftsmanship is shown in the world's design, and that we participate in the divine by being ourselves good artisans; the conviction that we follow God's example when we use substance for righteous ends, that time must be saved because every moment is a unique psychic opportunity: these are characteristics of the Judeo-Christian view of reality and of destiny. They are alien to all the other major religions except Islam, which belongs to the same spiritual phylum, and possibly Zoroastranism, a related species. Since in Hellenistic times and in China there were notable and sometimes rapid advances in engineering, Christianity obviously is not essential to technological dynamism. What Benz suggests, nevertheless, is that Christianity provided, historically in Europe, a set of assumptions, a cultural climate, unusually favorable to technological advance.

One may expand Benz's thesis somewhat. In 1956 Robert Forbes[78] of Leyden and Samuel Sambursky[79] of Jerusalem simultaneously pointed out

---

Progress," in his *Evolution and Christain Hope*: *Man's Concept of the Future from the Early Fathers to Teilhard de Chardin* (Garden City 1966) 121-142.

[77] More research is needed on the relations of Buddhism to technology: the former is divided into many sects, which may have different influences. In the sixteenth century the Japanese were eager and metallurgically equipped to adopt European types of firearms from the Dutch and Portugese; see Brown's article, n. 54 above. In sharp contrast to the Chinese, in the nineteenth century they rapidly absorbed Western technology. Both in the sixteenth and the nineteenth centuries Buddhism would seem to have played a greater psychic role in Japan than in China. The considerable literature on the differential reactions of China and Japan towards Western technology (see particularly the thoughtful essay of Marion J. Levy, Jr., "Contrasting Factors in the Modernization of China and Japan," *Economic Development and Cultural Change* 2 [1953] 236-253) generally concludes that the essence of the divergence lies in the mentality of the aggressive feudal aristocracy of Japan as compared to that of the Confucian bureaucracy of China. Confucianism, however, cannot be considered inherently anti-technological: the Sung dunasty, the great age of Neo-Confucianism, produced achievements in engineering in which Confucian scholars participated; cf. Joseph Needham, Wang Ling, and Derek J. Price, *Heavenly Clockwork*: *The Great Astronomical Clocks of Medieval China* (Cambridge, Eng. 1960) esp. 129-130.

[78] "Power," in *History of Technology*, ed. Charles Singer et al. (Oxford 1956) 2.606.

[79] *The Physical World of the Greeks* (New York 1956) 241. As is emphasized by W. J.

that Christianity, by destroying classical animism, brought about a basic change in the attitude toward natural objects and opened the way for their rational and unabashed use for human ends. Saints, angels and demons were very real to the Christian, but the *genius loci*, the spirit inherent in a place or object, was no longer present to be placated if disturbed.

Undoubtedly also, there has been an element of Christian compassion motivating the development of power machinery and labor-saving devices: as early as the sixth century an abbot in Gaul, troubled by the sight of his monks grinding grain in querns, built a water mill, "hoc opere laborem monachorum relevans."[80] Pity, however, is not exclusively a Christian virtue: Antipater's pagan poem, which is our second document for the existence of water mills in the ancient Mediterranean, celebrates the new machine as harnessing the water nymphs to save the aching backs of slave women.[81]

Benz has pointed a direction by which historians can make intelligible the technological dynamism of the Middle Ages. His hypothesis, however, is defective because he fails to recognized that the Greek church held the fundamentals of the Christian faith as ardently as did the Latin, yet after Kallinikos's invention of Greek fire just before 673[82] the highly civilized regions dominated by Eastern Orthodoxy were unadventurous in technology. If, as Benz believes, the vigor of Western medieval technology is an expression of religion, the sources of that dynamism must be found less in the broader aspects of Christianity than in the distinctive qualities and moods that differentiate Occidental from Byzantine Christian piety.

It may seem ludicrous to claim that the distillation of alcohol,[83] the trebuchet,[84] the functional button,[85] the suction pump,[86] the wire-drawing

Verdenius, "Science grecque et science moderne," *Revue philosophique* 152 (1962) 329-331, lower-class animism was sophisticated into a deification of the cosmos among the educated which made intellectuals as reluctant as artisans to use mechanics to compel nature to submit to human wishes.

[80] Gregory of Tours, *Vitae patrum* 18.2, ed. B. Krusch, MGH *Script. rer. merov.* 1 (Hanover 1885) 735.

[81] *Anthologia palatina graeca*, 9.418, ed. H. Stadtmueller (Leipzig 1906) 3.402-403.

[82] M. Mercier, *Le feu grégois* (Paris 1952) 14.

[83] Ca. 1150, in Italy; cf. Robert J. Forbes, *A Short History of the Art of Distillation* (Leyden 1948) 87-89.

[84] Ca. 1199; *Med. Techn.* 102 n. 5.

[85] Some buttons were used in Central Asia, Iran, and Greece in Antiquity for ornament, but apparently not for warmth. The functional button, fastening overlapping edges of cloth, is first found ca. 1235 on the "Adamspforte" of Bamberg cathedral, and in 1239 on a closely related relief at Bassenheim; cf. Erwin Panofsky, *Deutsche Plastik des 11. bis 13 Jahrhundert* (Munich 1924) pl. 74; H. Schnitzler, "Ein unbekanntes Reiterrelief aus dem Kreise des Naumburger Meisters," *Zeitschrift des Deutschen Vereins für Kunstwissenschaft* 1 (1935) 413 fig. 13.

[86] Ca. 1440, in Italy; Sheldon Shapiro, "The Origin of the Suction Pump," *Technology and Culture* 5 (1964) 566-574.

mill,[87] and the myriad other medieval inventions are ultimately *gesta Christi* where Christ was worshiped with a Latin accent. Nevertheless, the processes of the human mind are so curious that our judgment of the forces that produced Western technology must be based upon what appear to be the relevant facts even when the result contains elements of irony. Since people are often comic, so also history may be.

Historians of spirituality have long been aware of a basic contrast of to-nality between the two great segments of Christendom which surely affected the development of their respective technologies. The Greeks have generally held that sin is ignorance and that salvation comes by illumination. The Latins have asserted that sin is vice, and that rebirth comes by disciplining the will to do good works. The Greek saint is normally a contemplative; the Western saint, an activist.

This difference, largely subliminal, emerges clearly in the iconography of the Creator God. During the first Christian millennium, in both East and West, God at the moment of creation is represented in passive majesty, ac-tualizing the cosmos by pure power of thought, Platonically. Then, shortly after the year 1000, a Gospel book was produced at Winchester which made a great innovation: inspired by Wisdom 11.20, "Omnia in mensura et nu-mero et pondere disposuisti," the monastic illuminator showed the hand of God—now the master craftsman—holding scales, a carpenter's square, and a pair of compasses.[88] This new representation spread and, probably under the influence of Proverbs 8.27, "certe lege et gyro vallabat abyssus," the scales and square were eliminated leaving only the compasses—the nor-mal medieval and renaissance symbol of the engineer—held in God's hand. This tradition, which culminated in William Blake's "Ancient of Days,"[89] was never adopted in the Eastern Church. It was the perfect expression of Western voluntarism, but it violated Greek intellectualist sensibilities about God's nature.

As medieval machine design became more intricate, God the builder de-veloped into God the mechanic. The term "machina mundi" is at least as old as Lucretius, but was rejected on religious grounds by Arnobius Afer. By the thirteenth century, however, it was commonly used by Latin clerical scientists and had strongly affirmative overtones.[90] The first to foreshadow the Deist concept of the clockmaker God was Nicole Oresme who died as

---

[87] The first secure evidence is a drawing, 1489-1494, by Dürer; Friedrich Lippmann, *Zeichnungen von Albrecht Dürer* 1 (Berlin 1873) pl. 4.

[88] Erwin Panofsky and Fritz Saxl, *Dürer's "Melencolia I"* (Leipzig 1923) 67 n. 3.

[89] A. Blunt, "Blake's 'Ancient Days': The Symbolism of the Compass," *Journal of the Warburg Institute* 2 (1938-39) 53-63.

[90] *Med. Techn.* 174.

bishop of Lisieux in 1382. He proposed that, to prevent the celestial spheres from accelerating as they turned, the Creator had provided the equivalent of a clock's escapement mechanism to keep them rotating at a constant speed.[91] The subsequent success of the simile indicates the direction of Europe's thought about God, nature and man.

Students of the history of scriptural exegesis are as helpful as art historians in laying bare structures of values that lie so deep that they are not often verbalized explicitly. For our purposes the varying treatments of Luke 10.38-42, the Mary-Martha episode, are full of meaning. Since the time of Origen at least, the Greek East has invariably assumed that Martha represents the active and Mary the contemplative life, and that Christ's rebuke to Martha validates the superiority of the contemplative over the active.[92] In the West, however, a quite different style of exegesis emerges early. Saint Ambrose, once himself a Roman official and now a bishop, feels that the sisters of Bethany are symbols of *actio* and *intentio*: both are essential, and one cannot rightly be considered better than the other.[93] Then Saint Augustine, a revolutionary in so many ways, entirely subverts the Greek exegesis, the structure of values inherent in it, and, one must add, the literal meaning of Christ's words. To him, Mary and Martha represent two stages in the perfect life: Martha, the life of the soul in time and space; Mary, in eternity. "In Martha erat imago praesentium, in Maria futurorum. Quod agebat Martha, ibi sumus; quod agebat Maria, hoc speramus."[94] Yet, since we mortals dwell in time and not eternity, we must be Marthas, troubled about many things, rather than Marys.

The Middle Ages grew increasingly restless over this pericope. In the middle of the twelfth century Richard of Saint Victor, while acquiescing in Christ's praise of Mary's choice on the Augustinian ground that contemplation anticipates our heavenly condition, nevertheless shows by his phrasing where

[91] "Excepté la violence, c'est aucunement semblable quant un homme a fait un horloge et il le lesse aler et estre meu par soi. Ainsi lessa Dieu les cielz estr meuz continuellment"; Nicole Oresme, *Le livre du ciel et du monde* 2.2, ed. Albert D. Menut and Alexander L. Denomy (Madison 1968) 288.

[92] T. Camelot, "Action et contemplation dans la tradition chrétienne," *La vie spirituelle* 78 (1948) 275. That the cultural climate of Semitic Christianity was in this particular closer to that of the West than of the Greek world is indicated by the fact that Saint Ephraem Syrus, writing in Syriac and almost uninfluenced by Platonic prejudices, adopts elaborate stratagems to avoid valuing Martha's activism below Mary's contemplation: see I. Hausherr, "Utrum sanctus Ephraem Mariam plus aequo anteposuerit," *Orientalia christiana* 30 (1933) 153-163.

[93] D. A. Csànyi, "Otima pars," *Studia monastica* 2 (1960) 56-57.

[94] Saint Augustine, *Sermo* 104.4, cited by A. M. de la Bonnardière," Marthe et Marie, figures de l'église d'après saint Augustin, " *La vie spirituelle* 86 (1952) 425.

his own sympathies lie: "Intenta erat Maria quomodo pasceretur a Domino; intenta erat Martha quomodo pasceret Dominum. Haec convivium parat Domino; in convivio Domini illa jam delectatur."[95] Two hundred years later the European affirmation of the primacy of action reaches almost absurd heights in one of Meister Eckhart's vernacular sermons on this text.[96] Martha, the older and wiser sister, fears lest the adolescent Mary may become so ecstatic in contemplation that she will not mature spiritually by realizing that action is essential to holiness. Christ's apparent rebuke to Martha and praise for Mary are, in Eckhart's opinion, the exact reverse: they are his way of telling the perceptive Martha not to be troubled by Mary's sentimental condition; she will grow out of it. The Greek Church could not have produced, much less tolerated, such a sermon. The mood of activism which Eckhart reflects surely fostered technological growth in the West.

Some degree of respect for manual labor is, along with activism, integral to massive technological development. It was generally lacking, at least among the literate classes, in the Greco-Roman world.[97] The Jews, however, considered God's command to labor six days of the week to be as binding as that to rest on the seventh.[98] In the late third century, massive conversions of pagans to Christianity around the eastern Mediterranean threatened to corrupt the Church, and quite naturally a few zealots tried to purify it by returning to its primitive, that is Jewish, tradition. One result was monasticism, which from the beginning asserted the originally Jewish thesis that work is worhip, indeed, that it is an essential kind of worship. With considerable constancy the monks of both East and West continued through the Middle Ages to work with their hands.[99] Many of them likewise were

---

[95] Richard of Saint Victor, *Liber exceptionum* 2.14.5, ed. Jean Chatillon (Paris 1958) 504.

[96] *Deutsche Predigten und Traktate*, ed. and trans. Josef Quint (Munich 1955) 280-289.

[97] Cf. Moses I. Finley, "Technical Innovation and Economic Progress in the Ancient World," *Economic History Review* 18 (1965) 44. Before the impact of the monastic ethic was fully felt, moral aversion to hard work was still found in the Christian West; see my "The Iconography of *Temperantia* and the Virtuousness of Technology" in *Action and Conviction in Early Modern Europe*: *Essays in Memory of E. H. Harbison*, ed. T. K. Rabb and J. E. Seigel (Princeton 1969) 198-199.

[98] S. Kalischer, "Die Wertschätzung der Arbeit in Bibel und Talmud," in *Judaica*: *Festschrift zu Hermann Cohens siebzigstem Geburtstage* (Berlin 1912) 583.

[99] The Greek ascetics may, in fact, have been even more steadily devoted to manual labor than the Latin: see P. McNulty and B. Hamilton, "Orientale lumen et magistra latinitas: Greek Influences on Western Monasticism (900-1100)," in *Le millénaire du Mont Athos, 963-1963* (Chevetogne 1963) esp. 187, 192, 212. One reason for this was that monastic reform movements in the West, combating what was regarded as corruption arising from worldly entanglements, elaborated Benedictine liturgies from the ninth century onward to the point where there was little time left for labor; cf. P. Schmitz, "L'influence de saint Benoît d'Aniane dans l'histoire de l'Ordre de saint Benoît," *Settimane di studio*

well read; indeed, for centuries monks were the most learned men of the West. This combination of education with pratical work would seem theoretically, by joining head and hand, to provide communities in the monasteries where technological innovation would thrive. Yet the contrast in this respect between the sons of Saint Basil and those of Saint Benedict is notable.

One voice of dissent in the West may illuminate the basic situation. The sole instance in Christian monasticism of an antipathy toward the mechanic arts appears in *Scholica graecarum glossarum* by Martin of Laon (died 875) who derives *mechanicus* not from μηχανικός but from μοιχός "adulterer": "Moechus est adulter alterius thorum furtim polluens. Inde a maecho dicitur mechanica ars, ingeniosa atque subtilissima et paene quomodo facta vel administrata sit invisibilis in tantum, ut etiam visum conspicientium quodam modo furetur, dum non facile penetratur eius ingeniositas."[100] Martin was an immigrant Irish monk. The rule of Saint Columba is the only monastic code of East or West in which manual labor is regarded as pure penance for sin, unconnected with prayer and praise.[101] Moreover this etymogy offered by Martin is the only Western occurence of the Heronic concept of technology as primarily producing machines to deceive and awe the populace: one among several indications of connections between early Christian Ireland and the Greek culture of Alexandria.[102] Yet this Irish mediation

---

del Centro Italiano di Studi sull'Alto Medioevo 5: *Il monachesimo* (Spoleto 1957) 401-415. The result was the development of *conversi*, lay brothers designated primarily for manual labor and distinguished from the choir monks whose prime duty was *opus Dei*. K. Hallinger, "Woher kammen die Laienbruder?", *Analecta sacri ordinis cisterciensis* 12 (1956) 38, shows that such *conversi* were found in many Western abbeys in the eleventh century, but not at Cluny before 1100. Greek monasticism never developed such specialized worker monks; cf. P. de Meester, *De monachico statu iuxta disciplinam byzantinam* (Vatican 1942) 93-95.

[100] Max L. W. Laistner, "Notes on Greek from the Lectures of a Ninth-Century Monastery Teacher," *Bulletin of the John Rylands Library* 7 (1922-1923) 439. Martin's etymology was remembered by Hugh of Saint Victor, *Epitome Dindimi in philosophiam*, ed. Roger Baron, *Traditio* 11 (1955) 112, who speaks of *mechanica* as "adulterina" but notes (p. 111) that "de interpretationibus vero nominum pauca deducimus."

[101] E. Delaruelle, "Le travail dans les règles monastiques occidentales du IVe au IXe siècle," *Journal de psychologie normale et pathologique* 41 (1948) 61.

[102] Early in the seventh century an Alexandrian merchant took a ship loaded with grain to Christian Celtic Cornwall and returned to Egypt with a cargo of tin: Leontius, *Vita sancti Joannis Eleemosynarii* (d. 616), PG 93.1624-1625. About 800 the *Martyrology of Oengus the Culdee*, ed. Whitley Stokes (London 1905) 86, 80, remembers an Egyptian monk, who from the context seems to have died in Ireland. A litany of the tenth-eleventh century remembers seven Egyptian monks buried at Disert Uilaig; Charles Plummer, *Irish Litanies* (London 1925) 64. These were presumably part of the massive emigration of the Greek Orthodox elite from Egypt resulting from the Persian and Muslim conquests in the early seventh century, on which see my *Latin Monasticism in Norman Sicily* (Cambridge, Mass.

of Greek secular alienation from labor and technology was to have small influence in the West.

Part of the reason for this differential development between Latin and Greek monasticism lies in the fact that in the Byzantine world a literate laity continued to preserve the worldly aspects of high culture, with the result that Greek monks felt able to devote themselves more exclusively to sacred studies. In the West, the level of civilization for a time sank so disastrously that the monks assumed almost sole responsibility for preserving and encouraging all aspects of culture, profane as well as churchly.[103] Thus in the Occident monks tended to be more deeply involved in secular matters than in the East. The Slavic and Germanic regions into which the missionary monks of each Church penetrated were equally primitive. The Greek evangelists were very theological in their emphasis, and their labors were almost entirely religious. The Benedictines, however, concerned themselves less with doctrine than with ethics, and carried with them not merely a new religion but also new practical arts.[104]

1938, repr. 1968) 16-26. Most commentators on Egyptian influence in Ireland have supposed that it was transmitted at second hand through abbeys in southern Gaul. However, Margaret Schlauch, "On Conall Corc and the Relations of Old Ireland with the Orient," *Journal of Celtic Studies* 1 (1950) 152-166, has collected literary materials known from Coptic, Ethiopic, and Christian Arabic sources, but resting on vanished Greek writings, which appear in Ireland long before they are found elsewhere in Europe. Miss Schlauch misunderstands the nature of the seventh-century migration from Egypt: it consisted not of Monophysite Copts, who would have found the West inhospitable, but of Melchite Greeks fleeing Coptic hatred.

[103] Benedictine libraries often contained a considerable group of secular works; cf. C L. W. Laistner, *Thought and Letters in Western Europe, A.D. 500 to 900* (Ithaca 1957) 228-235. The only regional survey of Greek monastic libraries known to me—that made in 1457 of the seventy-eight foundations in Calabria before there is any indication that their holdings were being looted by neo-Hellenic enthusiasts from the North—lists some sixteen hundred MSS of which only five are secular: two Homers (one a fragment), the *Hecuba* of Euripides, a part of Aristophanes, and Galen's treaise on medications; moreover, of these the four literary MSS are found in two abbeys, Seminara and Mesiano, which were no more than twenty miles apart; see *Le "Liber visitationis" d'Athanase Chalkeopoulos (1457-1458)*, ed. M. H. Laurent and A. Guillou, Studi e testi 206 (Vatican 1960) 47, 107, 111.

[104] See the provocative essay of Richard E. Sullivan, "Early Medieval Missionary Activity: A Comparative Study of Eastern and Western Methods," *Church History* 22 (1954) 17-35. Byzantine lack of interest in technological advance infected the waters with which their Slavic converts were baptized. Novgorod, for example, was a great and free republic of merchants in constant commerce with the west; one might expect, on sociological grounds, technological movement there. Yet, on the basis of recent excavations in the city, Michael W. Thompson, *Novgorod the Great* (London 1967) xvii, remarks that "In the tenth century there was perhaps little to choose between the two, but already in the twelfth century Russian and western societies were widely separated, because the former avoided innovation and the latter welcomed it. We do not appreciate how innovating western medi-

This monastic technical tradition finds its greatest written expression in *De diversis artibus* produced by a theologically sophisticated and technologically learned German Benedictine, Theophilus, in 1122-1123.[105] It is a religiously motivated codification of all the skills available for the embellishment of a church, from the enameling of chalices and the painting of shrines to the making of organ pipes and the casting of great bells for the tower. In Theophilus's mechanisms the first flywheels appear; he is the first to record a new and cheaper way of making glass, which largely accounts for the expansion of glazed windows in his time; he is the first to mention a wire-drawing plate and likewise the first to describe the tinning of iron by immersion,[106] a technique that continued in use until the Japanese capture of Malaya in 1941 caused such a scarcity of tin elsewhere that the electrolytic process was developed.

Theophilus was not exceptional in his interests. In his contemporary life of Saint Bernard, Abbot Arnold of Bonneval pictures the rebuilding of Clairvaux in 1136 without mentioning the church but with a delighted account of all the abbey's waterpowered machines for milling, fulling, tanning, blacksmithing, and other industries.[107] Another quite independent monastic

eval society was until we can put it beside a part of Europe which was virtually static." The judgement is just in relation to technology, but Novgorod proved itself very original in painting and the forms, as distinct from the structural methods, of architecture.

[105] *De diuersis artibus*, ed. C. R. Dodwell (London 1961). Cyril Stanley Smith and John G. Hawthorne, *On Divers Arts: The Treatise of Theophilus* (Chicago 1963) have provided an excellent English translation and learned notes on the basis of Dodwell's revised text. For the date, see my "Theophilus redivivus," *Technology and Culture* 5 (1964) 226-230. Benoît Lacroix, "Travailleurs manuels du moyen âge roman: leur spiritualité," in *Mélanges Crozet*, (n. 66 above) 1.523-529, believes that in the twelfth century the Benedictine sense of religious dedication in labor—at least in the building of churches—spread to the laity. There is danger of exaggeration: there is exhilaration simply from participating in great works. A quatrain of 1110-1120 inscribed on the sarcophagus of Buschetto, architect of the new cathedral at Pisa (which was as much a product of civic pride as of faith) indicates that Buschetto was admired more for his engineering skill than for his pious construction or its beauty:

   Quod vix mille boum possent iuga iuncta movere,
   Et quod vix potuit per mare ferre ratis,
   Busketi nisu quod erat mirabile visu,
   Dena puellarum turba levabit onus.

Cited by Craig B. Fisher, "The Pisan Clergy and the Awakening of Historical Interest in a Medieval Commune," *Studies in Medieval and Renaissance History* 3 (1966) 177 n. 92.

[106] Ernest S. Hedges, *Tin in Social and Economic History* (New York 1964) 107, 161.

[107] *S. Bernardi vita prima* 2.5.31, PL 185:285. "Abundantibus sumptibus, conductis festinanter operariis, ipse fratres per omnia incumbebant operibus. Alii cadebant ligna, alii lapides conquadrabant, alii muros struebant, alii diffusis limitibus partiebantur fluvium, et extollebant saltus aquarum ad molas. Sed et fullones, et pistores, et coriarii, et fabri, aliique artifices, congruas aptabant suis operibus machinas, ut scaturiret et prodiret, ubicumque opportunum esset, in omni domo subterraneis canalibus deductus rivus ultro ebulliens."

description of Clairvaux in the same period shows the same enthusiasms: the author is particularly taken by an automatic flour sifter attached to the flourmill; he makes a little monkish joke, saying that the stamps of the fulling mill have remitted the penalty for the sins of the fullers; then he thanks God that such machines can alleviate the oppressive labors of both man and beast; and at last he offers a picture of the abstract power of water flowing through the abbey seeking every task: "coquendis, cribrandis, vertendis, terendis, rigandis, lavandis, molendis, molliendis, suum sine contradictione praestans obsequium."[108]

Nor was the commitment of Western ascetics to holy labor confined to crafts and mechanized industry: it extended to major engineering. In 1248, for example, while giving the decayed abbey of Lorsch to a community of Premonstratensian canons, the archbishop of Mainz says of them: "Invenimus viros iuxta cor nostrum. . . . Hii etenim non tantum religionis immaculate et vite habent testimonium sancte sed eciam in viis parandis, aqueductibus extruendis, paludibus exsiccandis, quibus monasterium in illa vicina nimium pergravatur, et generaliter in arte mechanica exercitati sunt non modicum et periti."[109] Thus far no similar documents have been produced from the entire Orthodox Church.

The 1120s, in which Theophilius produced his *De diversis artibus*, witnessed a moment of change in Europe's attitude towards manual labor and technology. Theophilus himself was concerned solely with the dignity of the technical arts in the life of a monk. Some of his ascetic contemporaries made labor the prime act of religion: Abbot Rupert of Deutz (died 1130) rebukes fanatics who spurn liturgical worship and "qui in opere manuum fere totam spem suam ponunt."[110] But at that time the concept of "religion" was broadening and spreading from the monastic to the lay life, particularly through channels provided by the newly vitalized groups of regular canons.[111] It was spiritually essential to transfer dignity explicitly from monastic labor to labor in the world outside the cloister.

---

[108] *Descriptio positionis seu situationis monasterii Claravallensis*, PL 185.570-571. The fulling mill "pedes ligneos (nam hoc nomen saltuoso fullonum negotio magis videtur congruere) alternatim elevans atque deponens, gravi labore fullones absolvit: et si joculare quidpiam licet interserere seriis, peccati eorum poenas absolvit. Deus bone, quanta pauperibus tuis procuras solatia, ne abundantiore tristitia absorbeantur! Quanta poenitentibus poenae alleviamenta dispensas, ne laboris violentia nonnumquam fortassis opprimantur! Nam quot equorum dorsa frangeret, quot hominum fatigaret brachia labor, a quo nos sine labore amnis ille gratiosus absolvit?"

[109] *Acta imperii inedita*, ed. E. Winkelmann, 2 (Innsbruck 1885) 724 no. 1041.

[110] *In s. Benedicti regulam* 3.10, PL 170:517.

[111] See M. D. Chenu, "Moines, clercs, laïcs au carrefour de la vie évangélique (xiie siècle)," *Revue d'histoire ecclésiastique* 49 (1954) 59-89.

This task was undertaken by the Victorines in Paris.[112] At the end of *De civitate Dei*, Saint Augustine discusses technology in a mood of complete ambivalence: he exclaims over the ingenuity and variety of the arts, but considers many of them "superfluas, immo et periculosas perniciosasque"; medicaments and skills of healing are cancelled by "tot genera venenorum, tot armorum, tot machinamentorum."[113] In the face of Augustine's vast authority, Hugh of Saint Victor, one of the most original minds of the Middle Ages and, like Theophilus, a German, very deliberately developed a new and affirmative attitude toward technology.

His first effort was made in the early 1120s in the form of a curious dialogue on the nature and scope of philosophy in which Hugh's alter ego is none other than Dindimus, the leader of the Indian Brahmins who had long been regarded in the West as "instinctive" Christians, living saintly lives without the grace of revelation.[114] His intent is clear: to provide a secular schematization of all human knowledge which, for the first time, includes the mechanic arts. On Hugh's behalf Dindimus argues vehemently against the purists who would narrow the concept of philosophy to exclude not only mechanics but also grammar and logic: "conati sunt scindere et lacerare corpus universum [philosophie] ne membra sibi coherent, quia pulchritudinem totius non viderunt."[115] The unity of philosophy arises from its function of remedying man's three basic defects: ignorance, vice, and physical weakness. Speculation provides truth; ethics aids virtue; technology supports our bodily needs; recently logic or semantics (including grammar) has been added to philosophy to give it clarity and elegance of expression.[116] Of these, *mechanica* is the least in dignity; yet it is integral to philosophy not as regards its practice but because of the wisdom inherent in it.[117]

In the later 1120s Hugh expanded and elaborated his concept of the nature and elements of philosophy in his influential *Didascalicon*: at least 88 manuscripts of it are extant, of which not fewer than 50 are of the twelfth and

---

[112] Peter Sternagel, *Die artes mechanicae im Mittelalter: Begriffs- und Bedeutungsgeschichte bis zum Ende des 13. Jahrhunderts* (Regensburg 1966). In disagreement with Benz, Maurice de Gandillac, "Place et signification de la technique dans le monde médiéval," in *Tecnica e casistica*, ed. Enrico Castelli (Rome 1964) 273 n. 7, correctly asserts the contrast between Saint Augustine's and the Victorines' positions toward technology.

[113] Augustini, *De civ. Dei* 22.24, *Corpus christianorum, series latina* 48 (Turnholt 1955) 848-849.

[114] Cf. George Boas, *Essays in Primitivism and Related Ideas in the Middle Ages* (Baltimore 1947) 140-151.

[115] Hugh of Saint Victor, ed. Baron (n. 100 above) 113, 115-116. It is significant that Dindimus is likewise Hugh's spokesman in his *De grammatica* (*ibid.* 92).

[116] *Ibid.* 110.

[117] *Ibid.* 111.

thirteenth centuries.[118] Between 1153 and 1162 Richard of Saint Victor,
probably a Scot, in his widely read *Liber exceptionum*, repeated and reinforced
Hugh's fourfold division of the intellectual life.[119] Naturally both Hugh and
Richard recongnized that, in the hierarchical society of their day, inclusion
of the mechanic arts in a total scheme of knowledge might not be cordially
received, so they disclaimed any revolutionary intent. Things like architecture and agriculture are proper topics for theorizing by a philosopher, but
the doing of them is different: "agriculturae ratio philosophi est, administra-
tio rustici."[120] Nevertheless, by giving an unprecendented psychic dignity
and speculative interest to the mechanic arts, the Victorines provided one
of the theses for an egalitarian movement which, centuries later, spread east-
ward to destroy a great part of the less flexible Orthodox Church.

A development akin to the Benedictine and Victorine sense of the significance of technology was the increasing Western acceptance of mechanisms
as aids to the spiritual life. The Church Fathers, both Greek and Latin, had
passionately opposed the use of all musical instruments, including the organ.[121]
While in Byzantium organs habitually graced secular ceremonies, the Greek
Church forbade them in its liturgies, insisting that only the unaccompanied
human voice can worthily praise God.[122] Yet in the later tenth century,
in the cathedral at Winchester where, about the same time, the iconography
of the Creator God holding scales, square, and compasses appeared, Benedictines installed the first giant organ: 70 men pumped 26 bellows supplying
400 pipes.[123] Before the invention of the mechanical clock the organ was the
most complex machine. In sharp contrast to the East, great organs became
integral in the West first to processions, interludes, and the like, but, by
the middle of the twelfth century, they were admitted to the central act
of divine service, the Mass.[124] A hundred years later, in the mystery plays

[118] Ed. Buttimer (n. 18 above) viii. For the study of this text the annotations by Jerome Taylor in his translation (New York 1961) are fundamental.

[119] Richard of Saint Victor (n. 95 above) 105-106.

[120] Hugh of Saint Victor, *Didascalicon* 1.4 (n. 18 above) 11; cf. Richard of Saint Victor,
Liber exceptionum 4.23 (n. 95 above) 111.

[121] James McKinnon, "The Meaning of the Patristic Polemic against Musical Instruments," *Current Musicology* (1965) 69-82.

[122] Egon Wellesz, *History of Byzantine Music and Hymnography*, ed. 2 (Oxford 1961)
105-108; 366; cf. Jean Perrot, *L'orgue de ses origines hellénistiques à la fin du XIIIe siècle*
(Paris 1965) 211 n. 5, 215.

[123] *Frithegodi monachi Breviloquium vitae beati Wilfredi, et Wulfstani cantoris Narratio
metrica de sancto Swithuno* ed. Alistair Campbell (Zurich 1950) 69-70, lines 141-170.

[124] Edmund A. Bowles, "The Organ in the Medieval Liturgical Service" *Revue belge de
musicologie* 16 (1962) 13-29. Even in the West no instrument save the organ was admitted
to the Mass until the fifteenth century when trumpets began to announce the elevation
of the Host; *idem*, "Were Musical Instruments Used in the Liturgical Service during the
Middle Ages?", *Galpin Society Journal* 10 (1957) 40-56. This would indicate that, to the
West, a higher degree of mechanization involved higher spirituality.

that by that time were presented outside the churches, an organ was the indispensable accompaniment of any representation of Paradise;[125] indeed, it became almost a symbol of Heaven.

In a separate building outside Hagia Sophia, Justinian placed a clepsydra and sundials, [126] but clocks were never permitted within or on Eastern churches: to place them there would have contaminated eternity with time. As soon, however, as the mechanical clock was invented in the West, it quickly spread not only to the towers of Latin churches but also to their interiors, often as astronomical planetaria designed to demonstrate visually the godly order of the cosmos.[127] Clearly, by the later Middle Ages, Western men felt psychically compatible with machines.

And not simply in religious contexts: the *Mittelalterliche Hausbuch*, a German manuscript of *circa* 1480, shows a garden enclosed in which garlanded youths and maidens are sporting about a fountain, while at the right, quite unobscured, appears the waterpowered force-pump that operates the fountain.[128] To the Middle Ages all the arts, including the mechanic arts, were a part of the good life—*teste* Leonardo. Modern suspicion of technology is a reversion to the ambivalence of Saint Augustine.

The earliest indication that men thought advancing technology to be an aspect of Christian virtue appears in the Utrecht *Psalter*, illuminated near Rheims *circa* 830, almost certainly by a Benedictine monk. The illustration of Psalm 63 (64) shows an armed confrontation between a small body of the Righteous, led by King David himself, and a distressingly larger host of the Ungodly. In each camp a sword is being sharpened conspicuously. The Evildoers are content to use an old-fashioned whetstone. The Godly, however, are employing the first crank recorded outside China to rotate the first grindstone known anywhere.[129] Obviously the artist is telling us that technological advance is God's will.

---

[125] Henri Lavoix, "La musique au siècle de Saint Louis," in Gaston Raynaud, *Recueil de motets français des XIIe et XIIIe siècles* (Paris 1883) 2.351.

[126] E. H. Swift, *Hagia Sophia* (New York 1940) 180.

[127] *Med. Techn.* 124-125.

[128] *Das Mittelalterliche Hausbuch*, ed. H. T. Bossert and W. F. Storck (Leipzig 1912) pl. 31-32. Edgar Wind, *Pagan Mysteries in the Renaissance* (London 1958) 96, notes that renaissance emblem books place "next to the classical columns and sirens, diamonds and laurels, salamanders, porcupines and unicorns ... the new waterwheels, bellows, catapults, rockets, bombards and barbacanes. ... Nature is man writ large; hence if forces in nature produce miraculous effects when they are harnessed, collected and propitiously released, they can set an example for the forces in man."

[129] *The Utrecht Psalter*, ed. Ernest DeWald (Princeton, 1932) pl. 58. I am grateful to Bruce Spiegelberg of Colby College for introducing me in 1966 to the total implication of this miniature, although as early as *Speculum* 15 (1940) 153 I had noted its purely mechanical novelties.

About 1450 European intellectuals began to become aware of technological progress not as a project (as indicated above, this came in the late thirteenth century) but as an historic and happy fact, when Giovanni Tortelli, a humanist at the papal court, composed an essay listing, and rejoicing over, new inventions unknown to the ancients.[130] At almost that moment the artists of Burgundy reaffirmed the thesis of the illuminator of the Utrecht *Psalter* that an advancing technology is morally salutary: they clothed Temperance, who had displaced Charity as the chief Virtue, with major symbols of late medieval inventiveness. On her head she wore a mechanical clock, produced some 120 years earlier; in her right hand she held eyeglasses, invented, as we have noted (above, 174) in the 1280s as the greatest boon to the mature and presbyopic intellectual; she stood on a tower windmill, which first appeared in the 1390s and which was the most spectacular power machine of that era.[131] To the artists who painted those pictures, and to their patrons —clerical, aristocratic and burgher—it was axiomatic that man was serving God by serving himself in the technological mastery of nature. Because medieval men believed this, they devoted themselves in great numbers and with enthusiasm to the process of invention.

Probably there were forces other than the religious which stimulated technological progress during the Middle Ages. The tradition of illustrated calendars has been secular. Their usual pattern from Roman times until the ninth century showed the months as static personifications holding symbolic attributes. This convention continued unbroken in Byzantium. Among the Franks, however, by 830 a new form appeared which set the style for the rest of the Middle Ages in the West. The pictures now show active scenes: plowing, haying, the harvesting of grain, wood chopping, men knocking acorns from oaks so that pigs can eat them, pig slaughtering.[132] The new illustrations breathe a coerciveness towards nature which is, indeed, consonant with Christianity but which may have arisen independently. Man and nature are two things, and man is master. Technological aggression, rather than reverent coexistence, is now man's posture toward nature.

Such aggression is the normal Western Christian attitude toward nature.[133] It may be that the emergence of this stance in the Carolingian age can be

---

[130] Alex G. Keller, "A Renaissance Humanist Looks at 'New' Inventions: the Article 'Horologium' in Giovanni Tortelli's *De orthographia*," *Technology and Culture* 11 (1970) 345-365.

[131] See my "Iconography of *Temperantia*" (n. 97 above).

[132] Henri Stern, *Le calendrier de 354* (Paris 1953) 356-357, and his "Poésies et représentations carolingiens et byzantins des mois," *Revue archéologique* 46 (1955) 164-166.

[133] The brief effort of Saint Francis to institute a democracy of all creatures was quickly terminated; cf. my "The Historical Roots of Our Ecologic Crisis," *Science* 155 (1967) 1203-1207, reprinted in my *Machina ex Deo: Essays in the Dynamism of Western Culture* (Cambridge, Mass. 1968).

explained apart from religion. Slightly before that time a basic change in agricultural methods had occurred in Northern Europe,[134] especially between the Loire and the Rhine, the heartland of the Frankish Empire. As early as the sixth century a new heavy plow began to spread from the Slavic East. It was far more efficient than the earlier light plow, but in place of a pair of oxen it normally required as many as eight, at least in newly cleared or sticky soil. No peasant owned eight oxen. The only way to power such a plow was to organize several peasants to pool their oxen, and to distribute plowed strips to them in proportion to their contribution. Previously land had been parceled to peasants in allotments sufficient to support a family equipped with two oxen and a light plow. The assumption was subsistence farming, plus enough surplus to pay rent. Now, however, with the heavy plow and the pooling of oxen the standard of land division was not human need but rather the capacity of a new power machine to till the soil. No more profound reversal of the peasant's relation to the land can be imagined. Formerly he had been part of nature; now he became an exploiter of nature. This alteration of attitudes might be guessed from the heavy plow itself. The iconography of the new calendars confirms the change. Neither the heavy plow nor the new style of calendar was known in Byzantium. In historical analysis, even of a very religious era, we cannot credit to religion, any more than to social relations or to any other single element in culture, absolute sovereignty over every aspect of life.

Nevertheless, it can scarcely be coincidence that the miniature in the Utrecht *Psalter* (816-834) which announces the morality of technological advance appeared simultaneously with, and in the same region as, the new style of calendar illustration (shortly before 830). It can scarcely be coincidence that in 826 Louis the Pious, who, as a contemporary remarks, was always eager to introduce to his realm "illa quae ante se inusitata erant,"[135] commissioned a Venetian priest named George, who had learned his skills presumably in Byzantium, to construct the first organ built in the medieval West for secular use in his palace,[136] and that from Aachen organs spread so quickly among the churches of South Germany that in 873 Pope John VIII wrote to Freising to secure both an organ and an organist.[137] Many forces shaped the Middle Ages, but of these the most powerful was religion.

The Semitization of the Greco-Roman *oikoumene*, which was accomplished in the fourth century by the victory of Christianity, marks the most drastic change of world view, both among intellectuals and among the common people, that, before our own time, has ever been experienced by a major

---

[134] *Med. Techn.* 39-78.

[135] *Vita Hludovici imperatoris* 40, ed. G. H. Pertz in MGH Script. 2.629.

[136] Perrot (n. 122 above) 276 seq.

[137] *Epp. Johannis VIII*, ed. E. Caspar in MGH Epistolae Karolini aevi 5.287.

culture. In China the indigenous Confucian-Taoist symbiosis was supplemented, not displaced, by Indic Buddhism. In India itself, Vedic Brahmanism slowly broadened and diversified to engulf all rivals except the Islamic intrusion that was totally unassimilable and which produced two societies in tragic confrontation. The Muslim annexation of the southern shores of the Mediterranean had no such result because, as Dante rightly saw (*Inferno* 28.22-31), Muhammad was a Judeo-Christian schismatic, not the founder of a new religion. In the regions thus overrun, the faith of the *Koran* confirmed basic Jewish views of the nature of time, the cosmos, and destiny which had already been spread at all levels of society by Christianity, Judaism's daughter.

The historians' habit of terminating what we call ancient history with the chaos of the third and early fourth centuries in which Christianity rose to dominance is not arbitrary: it recognizes a major alteration in the cultural climate of classical civilization. During the Middle Ages, both Eastern and Western, this new religion was the essential novelty and stimulus to innovation as well as to the decay of some forms of creativity which had thrived in the Greco-Roman world. It is, therefore, not surprising that so many religious and parareligious phenomena illuminate both the high rate of technological advance in the West, and, by contrast, its slow pace in the Byzantine world.

No great religion is an entirely uniform species. As Christianity spread it accommodated to local circumstances but it likewise developed spontaneous genetic mutations which as yet cannot be explained by Lamarckian adaptation to preexisting cultural climates: to an extraordinary degree, medieval religion created the climate of its environment. Part of the fascination of the Middle Ages lies in the observation, within an essential unity extending from Greenland to the Jaxartes, of the variety of cultural subclimates that can often be interpreted according to regional variants in the temper of religion. The slight but significant differences between Greek and Latin piety in this period help not only to make historically intelligible the accomplishment of the medieval West in technology but likewise to expose the psychic foundations of our modern technology which rests on that achievement.

Department of History
University of California
Los Angeles, California 90024, U.S.A.

EARLY EXAMPLES OF THE POINTED ARCH AND VAULT
IN ROMANESQUE ARCHITECTURE

•

by Kenneth John Conant
in collaboration with Henry M. Willard

The destroyed abbey church of Cluny was one of the most splendid buildings of the Romanesque period. It was the largest Romanesque church, the largest monastic church, and the largest French church, built on the grandest scale —602 Roman feet in length, 262 in width at the great transept, and 100 in height to the crown of the vault. It was an innovative building—its main portal was the first one of great size with elaborate sculptural decoration, and the carvings of the sanctuary columns constituted one of the first really extensive sculptural ensembles with a lucid iconographical theme. The structure of the church involved about 200 pointed arches, and there were 64 bays of pointed groin vaulting, both of these features being novel in church architecture (fig. 1, well exemplified also at Autun, Fig. 2).

It is natural to ask questions about the genesis of this building, for which the preliminary studies and other preparations were complete in 1088; a dedication of altars occurred in the chevet in 1095; by 1106 the eastern half of the five-aisled nave was in service, and its entire 250-foot length—a magnificent processional space—was completed and vaulted by 1120.[1] The representative character of the church (for it set forth the full capability of Romanesque architecture better than any other building) was probably due to the great abbot, Hugh (ordained 1049, d. 1109) who had for forty years journeyed in France, Spain, Switzerland, Germany, and Italy. Interested in architecture, he had seen the greatest buildings, many of them Roman; indeed, he had authorized a considerable number of important build-

[1] Consult K. J. Conant, *Cluny: Les Églises et la Maison du Chef d'Ordre*, The Mediaeval Academy of America (Cambridge, Mass. 1968). The matter of the date is debated in two very critical articles in the *Bulletin Monumental* 126 (1968) 235-322 and 127 (1969) 183-186. I have replied in *Speculum* 45 (1970) 1-39 and in the *Gazette des Beaux Arts* 75 (112e année, no. 1212, January 1970) 1-10. It will be seen that our critic is not appropriately trained in engineering and architecture to deal with the problems of an immense enterprise like the reconstruction of Cluny. He accepts the conventional dating of the "école officiele" in Paris, which to us seems fossilized.

ings himself, for Cluny and the priories. The first architect of the great church (Cluny III)—its Anthemius, so to speak—was Gunzo, a retired abbot from the Franche Comté. The builder architect was Hezelo, a brilliant canon of Liège, who became a monk at Cluny and devoted himself to this noble structure for some forty years, until his death (1123).

While the fact that these architects came from terre d'Empire accounts in some measure for the grandeur of the building, and the report that Hezelo was a mathematician suggests the origin of its sophisticated layout, one would not naturally expect, in their work, the cusping or the pointed arches and vaults that were such conspicuously novel decorative and structural features in the design of Cluny III. The cusping was perhaps inspired from Muslim Spain. As an explanation of the pointed arches and vaults in Cluny III, we propose the long-continued and close relationship between Cluny and Montecassino, for Montecassino, through Amalfi, was in contact with North Africa, where the pointed arch had been effectively used for more than two centuries.

The relationship between Cluny and Montecassino was especially strong in the days of Abbot Hugh's personal friend, Frederick of Lorraine (later Pope Stephen IX, 1057-1058). Abbot Hugh visited Montecassino, the ranking Benedictine house, in 1083—in the time of Abbot Desiderius (1058-1086; he was Pope Victor III, 1086-1087). Cluny had second rank among the Benedictine abbeys, after Montecassino, and Abbot Hugh must have seen something of the other abbots in Rome, even before their election to the papacy. Clearly, there existed a channel of influence from Montecassino to Cluny.

Leo of Ostia's chronicle of Montecassino[2] includes a succinct and orderly account of the construction and embellishment of the monastery as rebuilt by Abbot Desiderius. It includes also a well-known reference to the remarkable group of technicians gathered and trained at Montecassino as craftsmen in stone, wood, stucco, bronze, ivory, gold, and silver, with some help from Byzantine (perhaps also from Muslim) experts. There is mention, also, of actual objects imported from the Eastern capital. The principal church at Montecassino was built between 1066 and 1071. By 1075 an atrium and an outer portico with two pylons had been added.

The dimensions of the church plan given by Leo of Ostia have been corroborated by the careful excavations of Dom Angelo Pantoni, O.S.B., of Mon-

---

[2] The reference to *lambardi* and Amalfitans comes in one version of Leo's manuscript: *Leonis Marsicani et Petri Diaconi chronica monasterii casinensis*, ed. W. Wattenbach, MGH Script. 7.551H. The rebuilding of the church and monastery buildings is described on pages 716 to 728. Reference to *lambardi* and Amalfitans is in a footnote on 717. Another footnote, on 718, recounts that Desiderius "manda en Costentinobble [*sic*] et en Alixandre pour homes grex et sarrazins," apparently for pavement work (Ainé [*sic*] = Amatus of Montecassino, 3.49). Constantine "the African," a monk of Montecassino, was not connected with the architecture as far as we know.

tecassino, who has elucidated the earlier history of the site by a scrupulous study of the texts and the remains. Dom Angelo received Dr. Henry M. Willard and me in the most kindly fashion when we came, long before the destruction, to gather data on the relationship of the much-rebuilt prewar church to the Desiderian original. We were not treated as interlopers; on the contrary, Dom Angelo generously helped us in every possible way. Dr. Willard studied related buildings in the region, and collected a considerable body of useful collateral information at Sant'Angelo in Formis, Amalfi, also Salerno, Minuto, and Aquino (which gave its name to Saint Thomas Aquinas)—all near Amalfi.[3]

Most unfortunately the older, tenth-, eleventh-, and twelfth-century cathedral of Amalfi has been closed for many years, and the study of it, made long ago (1931?) has never, to our knowledge, been made available. It is a complex building, several times rebuilt, but in our opinion there are interesting traces *or reflections* of eleventh-century construction in existence still. We have made a sketch restoration on the basis of Dr. Willard's photographs (fig. 8 shows only a wall section and typical bays).

Amalfi is of interest to us because of the pointed arches in the building and the probability that oriental influences brought the pointed form to Amalfi at a fairly early date. One forgets that Amalfi was a widely-ramified maritime republic from the tenth century on, with Tunisia close, and a station in Cairo, an influential capital, where there are remarkable examples of early pointed-arch construction. In the Christian states there was clearly some emulation of the Muslims—a phenomenon resembling the chinoiserie of the eighteenth century, which was generated in the same way. It is an attractive hypothesis, which we accept, that these Muslim influences played on the art of Amalfi during the great age of the Republic and not merely (as some think) after the city was subdued by the Siculo-Normans. It should be noted also that the Amalfitans had a station at San Germano, very close indeed to Montecassino.

If we are correct, the fact that Desiderius's famous abbey church at Montecassino was constructed by *lambardi* and Amalfitans has very great importance.[4] The *lambardi* may have been local men, for the Beneventan duchy itself was old Lombard territory. The Amalfitan connection may have had something to do with the station at San Germano.

The Amalfitan builders would naturally have been responsible for any pointed arches or vaults. Before the destruction I myself measured the pointed vault of the pylon or tower-chapel of Saint Michael, dedicated in 1075, and

---

[3] Dom Angelo Pantoni, "Problemi archeologici cassinesi" *Revista di archeologia cristiana* 16 (1939) 271-288. The proposed solutions of 1939 were largely corroborated by Dom Angelo's postwar excavations; see "Il Sepolcro di San Benedetto," *Miscellanea Cassinese* 27.

[4] See n. 2 above.

still possessing one of the bulls-eye windows that are reported as numerous in the Desiderian design (fig. 3, 4, 5). The corresponding chapel of Saint Peter had an ordinary groin vault, slightly crowned, and the date of the masonry here was less certain, though a bulls-eye still survived (fig. 3, 5, 10).[5] The pointed vault of the Chapel of Saint Michael raises a presumption that the arches of the adjoining portico must have been pointed, because the bays, while nearly or fully as deep as the square interiors of the towers, were much narrower (2m.65 by 4m.00$\pm$) so that pointed longitudinal arches were structurally most appropriate.

This portico between the two towers had five arches or vaults, according to Leo of Ostia, and a similar portico is referred to as the vestibule of the abbey church. The remaining three walks of the atrium were not vaulted, and is not quite certain that the vestibule was completely vaulted in masonry; lateral vaults in stucco are possible.

According to Leo, both porticoes had *fornices spiculi*, an ambiguous term that suggests the presence of pointed arches, pointed vaults, or both. The ambiguity arises because in this text, as often elsewhere, *fornix* may refer to an arch, or to a vault compartment that is, of course, connected with an arch, or to both. *Spiculi* is also ambiguous; *spiculum*, literally a spear, may imply either a lanceolate opening (shaped like a spearhead) or, in a derivative meaning, the projecting arrises of a vault. In the latter case, the vaults are called groin vaults in English, or in French *voûtes d'arêtes*, which is a strict equivalent for *fornices spiculi*.

The term groin vault implies nothing as to the plan, which may be square, as in the Michael Chapel that I measured; it may be oblong, as in the individual vaulted bays at Montecassino; in Gothic times it is often trapezoidal or rounded. Nor does the term groin vault imply anything as to arch shapes, which may be stilted or not, semicircular, semielliptical, parabolic, pointed, mitered—and indeed combinations of these shapes. Where the bays are oblong, the resulting vault surfaces are simplest and most practical to build, as well as pleasantest to look at, if the short sides of the bays have pointed arches. This is a valid reason for believing that the porticoes at Montecassino had pointed arches, especially since, as noted, the arches in the Michael chapel adjoining the outer portico were pointed (fig. 10).[6] The same is true

---

[5] See n. 3 above. The sides of the tower-chapel interiors all measured within a few centimeters (either way) of 4 meters. The vault severies in the church vestibule measured 3m. 30 by 3m.85 to 4m.55. An argument for round arches here and vaults like those of the chapel of Saint Peter (despite the oblong shape) is the fact that the four atrium porticoes are called "twins" by Leo and the fact that the arches of the portico in the painting at Sant' Angelo are rounded ("finger-shaped"). As already noted, in the outer portico at Montecassino the severies measured 2m.65 by 4m.00, which surely implies pointed arches in any case. See n. 10 below.

[6] See n. 5 above.

of the portico of Sant'Angelo in Formis, a priory of Montecassino, which must, in some measure, represent the Mother House, though it is later in date (fig. 7).

Groin vaults at Cluny (figs. 1, 9a, and 9b), Autun (fig. 2), Montecassino (fig. 10), Sant'Angelo in Formis (figs. 7 and 12) and certain Muslim vaults (such as those at the mosque of Mahdia, the Zirite capital in Tunisia, fig. 11)—all pointed—have for functional reasons a peculiar shape. Though rounded off at the base, the arrises are nearly straight over a large part of their length, as are the elements of the vault surface, so that the centering could be built up as a criss-cross of four planks, each rounded off a little at each end, and rising (one from each corner) to a mitre at the highest point (fig. 9b). The planks sustained the flat centering boards, and the imprint of one of these remains in the surviving vault at Cluny (fig. 9a). This type of vault is well exemplified in the aisles at Autun (about 1125-1135, fig. 2) and in the vaulted porticoes at Mahdia (921, vaults later; fig. 11).

It cannot be proved that Mahdia is in the direct line of this development, but the pointed arches and straight-arris groin vaults at Mahdia are, at the very least, important collateral examples. They cover a portico on the west side of the entrance court. Georges Marçais, finding earlier groin vaults only in practical works like cisterns, accepted these as the earliest in a mosque, and in fact their form is rather archaic—a local interpretation, perhaps, of Roman vaulting. Alexandre Lézine ascribed the pointed arches to the eleventh century builders. The Berber invasion, during which Kairouan was destroyed (1057) had grave consequences for Mahdia, and appears to have cut off this development.[7] Crusaders captured Mahdia in 1088.

How strong is the evidence that links these Muslim vaults to Italy and Burgundy? First, this type of vault does not occur systematically outside of Burgundy. As between Autun and Cluny there is no possible doubt of connections: they are evidenced in the ecclesiastical history, the architecture, and the sculpture. Autun was begun as Cluny was being finished.

As between Cluny and Montecassino the case is very strong. The vast rebuilding of the monastery was begun (about 1077), when the chief works at Montecassino were being finished, and the exceptional group of technicians trained under Desiderius, (beginning about 1066-1071), could have been drawn upon for Cluny. Several cloisters had been built at Montecassino, and there were two or three to build at Cluny between 1077 and 1088. Painting flourished

---

[7] Consult Georges Marçais, *L'Architecture Musulmane d'Occident* (Paris 1954) 126; also two titles in the series Archéologie méditerranéenne, published with the aid of the Centre National de Recherche Scientifique, Alexandre Lézine being the author in both cases: *Architecture de l'Ifriqiya—Recherches sur les monuments aghlabides* (Paris 1966) 135, fig. 56, and *Mahdïya—Recherches d'archéologie islamique* (Paris 1965) 71, fig. 29, 30, 39, 70, 71, 72.

in this period at Montecassino, and there is still a Cassinese imprint on the frescoes, Cluniac in style, but framed by a pointed horseshoe arch, at Berzé-la-Ville near Cluny, dated about 1105. Meanwhile the refectory at Cluny had been built (about 1080) and it was embellished by a vast fresco of the Last Judgment which inevitably recalls the Last Judgment at Sant'Angelo in Formis and brings to mind Abbot Hugh's visit to Montecassino in 1083, with the possibility that Cassinese painters were sent to Cluny. The visit of Abbot Hugh and one of his engineers, or a Cassinese specialist sent to Cluny, would account for the pointed vaulting in the abbey church. This possibility receives a curious confirmation in the bulls-eyes—like those of the chapels of 1075 at Montecassino (fig. 3)—which existed under the pointed vaults of the aisles beside the sanctuary at Cluny (fig. 1). This part of the church at Cluny was erected by 1093.[8]

Sant'Angelo in Formis was a priory of Montecassino, and in the church proper there is an acceptable representative of the church at Montecassino. It is natural to suppose that the portico, though later, was also thence inspired.

In our hypothetical restorations of Montecassino (figs. 3, 4, and 5) we show the porticoes with the arch shape which we actually found in the Chapel of Saint Michael (fig. 10). This shape is much more elegant than that at Sant'Angelo or Minuto, and it corresponds with the shape in the lower (and consequently older) parts of the cathedral of Amalfi (fig. 8), as it should if the builders came from Amalfi;[9] and moreover it resembles that of the pointed arches at Mahdia in North Africa, if we except the slight swelling, to horseshoe shape, at Mahdia. *The fact that the pointed arch and the straight-arris groin vault occur together at Mahdia,* as they do, *is a powerful argument for the oriental origin of this combination, which occurs so rarely in Christian architecture.*

The portrait of Abbot Desiderius in the apse at Sant'Angelo in Formis (fig. 6) inevitably comes into the discussion. The church model held by the abbot symbolically represents Sant'Angelo, but it is conflated with elements representative of Montecassino. The tower is to the north, as at Montecassino. The tower at Sant'Angelo was as yet unbuilt, and, unlike Montecassino, it had no intermediate stage (probably a guard room, because Leo says that it was substantially built, and he calls it both *campanile* and *arx*; fig. 4). When the portrait was painted during the lifetime of Desiderius, the portico of Sant'Angelo had not yet been built in its present form and it seems certain that the painter drew on the forms that already existed at Montecassino. We accept this interpretation, despite the lack of positive documentary evidence.

[8] See n. 1 above.
[9] See n. 2 above.

In the painting the arches of the church portico are finger-shaped rather than pointed (fig. 6). Such arches exist at Minuto and at La Cava in a different context, but these are not elegant designs, and finger-shaped arches would not give a good vault shape, or combine well with the round-arched lateral porticoes of the atrium at Montecassino. We therefore ascribe the painted finger-shaped arches of Sant'Angelo to inadvertence or artistic license.[10]

The finger-shaped arches would be even more infelicitous in the oblong bays of the outer portico at Montecassino. Here the portico was doubtless narrowed to the known width of the approach stair, above which it stood handsomely between the pylon towers. The outer portico and the tower of Saint Michael by themselves support the hypothesis that pointed arches were known, used, and admired at Montecassino by 1075. Thus, despite the lack of specific documents, we may confidently call Montecassino an eleventh-century steppingstone between Muslim Africa and the Romanesque north, where the pointed arch was so widely employed and so dramatically developed in the twelfth and thirteenth centuries.

[10] The finger-shaped form occurs at La Cava and at Minuto, but not very systematically, and some of the examples at La Cava are pointed. At Minuto, in the vault, what would otherwise be pointed arches are abruptly rounded over just short of the crown. Minuto has a bulls-eye in the tower, recalling Montecassino.

K. J. C.
274 Grove Street
Wellesley, Massachusetts 02181, U.S.A.

H. M. W.
c/o Mrs. John Manteiga
3802 Arbutus Avenue
Baltimore, Maryland 21207, U.S.A.

Fig. 1. The Sanctuary of Cluny III, built 1088–1093

Fig. 2. Aisle vaulting of the Cathedral of
Autun, built about 1125–1135

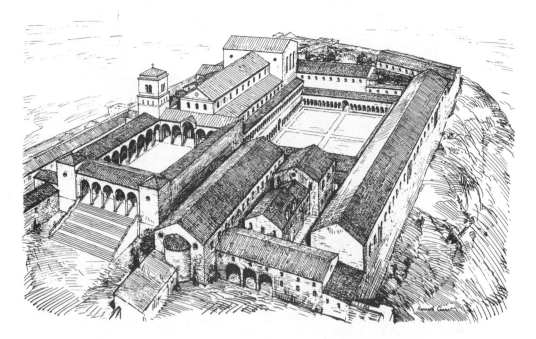

Fig. 3. Cavalier restoration of the medieval Abbey of Montecassino, largely rebuilt 1066–1086

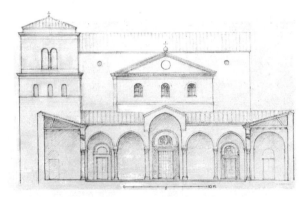

Fig. 4
Elevation of the Abbey church,
showing the inner portico
("vestibule"), 1066–1071 or 1075.
The spiral columns are based
on the painting at Sant'Angelo,
and may be fanciful

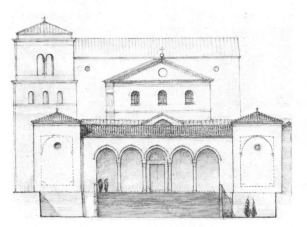

Fig. 5.
Elevation of the Abbey church
showing the outer portico
and towers, 1066–1075

FIG. 6. Desiderius and Church model: fresco in the apse of Sant'Angelo in Formis, before 1088

FIG. 7. Sant'Angelo in Formis, west view

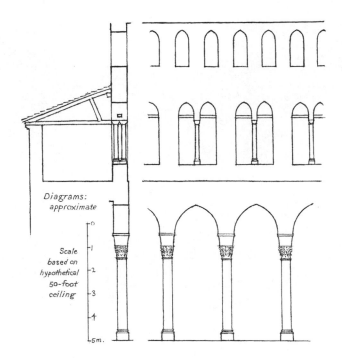

0
1
2
3
4
5 m.

FIG. 8. Amalfi — Old cathedral, sketch restoration of wall section and typical bays. The church probably includes eleventh-century elements, actual or derivative

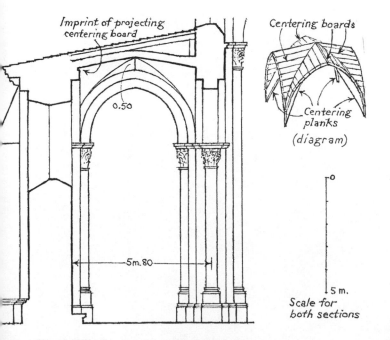

Imprint of projecting centering board

0.50

5m.80

Centering boards

Centering planks (diagram)

0

5 m.
Scale for both sections

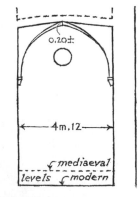

0.20±

4m.12

mediaeval levels modern

FIG. 10. Section of Chapel of Saint Michael, Montecassino, 1075. Measured by K. J. C. before the destruction

FIG. 9a. Cluny III — Section of existing aisle bay, ilt about 1100

FIG. 9b. Diagram of scheme for centering of aisle bay of Cluny III

FIG. 11. Mahdia, Tunisia—West aisle of Court of the Mosque. Before 990? More probably eleventh century

FIG. 12. Vault of the portico of Sant'Angelo in Formis. Eleventh—twelfth century

EARLY ROMANESQUE BOOK-ILLUSTRATION IN ENGLAND; THE DATES OF THE PIERPONT MORGAN "VITAE SANCTI EDMUNDI" AND THE BURY BIBLE

•

by Rodney M. Thomson

Fifty years and more after the Norman Conquest submerged the native An-glo-Saxon style of book-illustration without at first replacing it, extensively-decorated volumes made a fresh appearance in England with a series of sump-tuous liturgical codices.[1] The earliest and most influential of these were made at the great Benedictine houses of Saint Albans and Bury Saint Ed-munds. The Saint Albans book is a Psalter; one of the Bury volumes con-tains two Lives of Saint Edmund, and the other the first part of a great Bi-ble.[2] All have foliated and historiated initials as well as full-page miniatures, featuring rich, opaque body-color.[3] They exhibit an entirely new style of decoration, already at an assured and confident stage of development; some-thing it owes to the older "Winchester" school and to Norman illumination,[4] but its most revolutionary and characteristic features are the result of new elements, principally Byzantine—whether via the Continent or southern

My thanks to my colleagues Mr J. O. Ward and Professor R. I. and Mrs. Jack, who kind-ly read this article in typescript and offered valuable criticism and advice. On the specialized subject of coinage evidence I must acknowledge the invaluable assistence of Mr. C. Pitch-fork.

[1] For these developments see especially O. Pächt, *The Rise of Pictorial Narrative in Twelfth Century England* (Oxford 1962).

[2] Hildesheim, property of Saint Gotthard's Church; New York, Pierpont Morgan MS 736; Cambridge, Corpus Christi College MS 2.

[3] The literature on these books is extensive: full bibliographies are in O. Pächt, C. R. Dodwell and F. Wormald, *The Saint Albans Psalter* (London 1960); E. Parker, "The Scrip-torium of Bury Saint Edmunds in the Twelfth Century," Ph. D. diss. (London University 1965); C. M. Kauffmann, "The Bury Bible," *Journal of the Warburg and Courtauld Institutes* 29 (1966) 60-81; E. Parker, "A Twelfth-Century Cycle of Drawings from Bury St. Edmunds Abbey," *Proceedings of the Suffolk Institute of Archaeology* 21, 1969 (1970) 263-302.

[4] On the continuity of Anglo-Saxon and the influence of Norman illumination in twelfth-century England, see C. R. Dodwell, *The Canterbury School of Illumination, 1066-1200* (Cambridge 1955) chap. 1 and 2. See also now, for Norman influence, J. J. G. Alexander, *Norman Illumination at Mont Saint Michel, 966-1100* (Oxford 1970) esp. the Conclusion, 210-211.

Italy—but also Franco-Flemish and Ottonian.[5] These codices mark the impressive beginnings of the new Romanesque style of manuscript decoration in England, and scholarly attention has thus been closely focused on them since the early years of this century, particularly over the last two decades. Naturally it is of capital importance to establish with reasonable precision the dates and relationships of these books. Sound documentary evidence has placed the Albani Psalter, seemingly the earliest of the group, shortly before 1123,[6] but this degree of exactitude has not so far been reached for the Bury books. The purpose of this essay is, as far as possible, to remedy this defect.

The relationship between the Albani Psalter and the Pierpont Morgan *Vitae* is particularly problematical. No one doubts that the styles of the miniature-cycles in each manuscript are closely related. Otto Pächt would have them to be by the same man, the so-called "Alexis Master," principal artist of the Albani Psalter, responsible for the execution of its full-page miniatures.[7] This view does not seem to have won unqualified acceptance.[8] Of course, if the interval of time between the making of the two manuscripts can be shown to be small, then the possibility that their miniature-cycles are by the same or associated artists is enhanced. Curiously enough, most recent scholars, including Pächt himself, have not been willing to concede a date before the early to mid-1130s for the Morgan manuscript, although earlier writers have offered alternatives from as early as 1125 to as late as 1150.[9] I propose to show that it was, in fact, written and decorated no more than a year or two after the Albani Psalter, about 1124-1125.

The main contents of the manuscript, after the 32 full-page miniatures, are the two *Vitae* of Saint Edmund followed by the *lectiones* and music for his Office.[10] One of the Lives is that by Abbo of Fleury (written ca. 985-987).[11] The other, anonymous, may or may not have some connection with

---

[5] M. Rickert, *Painting in Britain; the Middle Ages* (London 1954) 78-85; C. R. Dodwell, *The Great Lambeth Bible* (London 1959) 9, 38, n. 42; Kauffmann, esp. 73-81; Parker (1970) passim.

[6] Pächt, Dodwell, and Wormald 278-280.

[7] *Ibid.* 141-142 and n. 1.

[8] Cf. Rickert (rev. ed. 1965) 80, Parker (1965) 79-87, and Parker (1970) 264.

[9] *New Palaeographical Society; Facsimiles of Ancient Manuscripts*, 1.4 (London 1907) introduction to plates 113-115 (1125-1150); Rickert (nn. 5, 8 above) 80 and n. 28 (before 1135); Pächt, Dodwell, and Wormald 142 (early 1130s); J. Beckwith, *Early Medieval Art* (London 1964) plate 184 (1130-1133); Parker (1965) 117-119 (ca. 1135); H. Swarzenski, *Monuments of Romanesque Art*, ed. 2 (London 1967) plate 276 (ca. 1140).

[10] Miniatures, fols. 7-22v; anonymous Life, fols. 23-76; Abbo's *Passio sancti Edmundi* fols. 77-86; Office of Saint Edmund, fols. 87-100v, ending imperfectly due to loss of leaves.,

[11] Ed. T. Arnold, *Memorials of Saint Edmunds Abbey*, Rolls Series, 3 vols., 1.3-25. Arnold did not use the text in the Morgan MS, which seems a good one and earlier than most of the MSS that he employed.

the Life known to have been written by Osbert of Clare, prior of Westminster, at the request of Abbot Anselm of Bury (*regn.* 1121-1148).[12] Osbert was in exile from Westminster from 1123 until 1134, during which period he divided his time between Ely and Bury. His Life of Saint Edmund is thought to have been completed mainly after this time, circa 1130-1137, although there seems no reason why it should not have been drafted earlier.[13] In any case the connections between Osbert and the anonymous Morgan Life are so obscure that no certain conclusion can be drawn from them regarding the date of the manuscript. The *lectiones* for the Office are extracted from Abbo's work and from Hermann's *Miracula sancti Edmundi*, written about 1100.[14] These contents are in a single hand, Miss Parker's "scribe A," responsible for several of the finest products of the Bury scriptorium during Anselm's reign.[15] Miss Parker dates his activity to the years between 1130 and 1140. However, one of the books in which his hand appears was commissioned by Prior Baldwin, who held office early in Anselm's abbacy.[16] This man had been an obedientiary since 1112 at least, and I shall shortly demonstrate that he was succeeded as prior by Talbot circa 1125.[17] The paleographical features of scribe A's hand seem to mark him as younger or later than the earliest scribes of the Albani book, although his duct is similar to that of the man who copied the Psalter's Psalms, Canticles, Litanies, and Prayers.[18] On the paleographical evidence, it is highly unlikely that the Morgan book was written before the Psalter; nevertheless, neither the hand nor the authorship of its contents preclude a date soon after the execution of the Saint Albans manuscript.

Preceding the miniature-cycle is a separate quire of six folios containing matter of intrinsic interest and important for dating the manuscript. This quire seems to have been part of the original book, although folios 1 to 4 would then have been blank. Certainly its pricking, ruling, and number of lines per page are the same as in the rest of the manuscript. Folios 5 and 6 contain a set of four alternative *lectiones* for the Vigil of Saint Edmund's

[12] Full discussion in E. W. Williamson, *The Letters of Osbert of Clare* (Oxford 1929) 26ff.

[13] *Ibid.* Cf. *New Pal. Soc.* (n. 9 above), in which it is suggested that the Morgan Life is intermediate between Hermann's and Osbert's. The latest miracle recorded in it took place before 1118. I have begun a detailed investigation of this Life; at present, on historical and stylistic grounds I doubt whether it is Osbert's work. It seems more likely to be the composition of a Bury monk, early in Anselm's reign.

[14] Ed. Arnold (n. 11 above) 26-92, and F. Liebermann, *Ungedruckte Anglo-Normannische Geschichtsquellen* (Strasbourg 1879) 203-281. Neither used the Morgan extracts, which seem to derive from a good exemplar.

[15] Parker (1965) 38-42, 75.

[16] Oxford, Bodleian Library, e Mus 112.

[17] D. C. Douglas, *Feudal Documents from the Abbey of Bury Saint Edmunds* (London 1932) cxxxv and n. 3, 112, 124 n., 154. He was evidently still alive after vacating his office (*ibid.* 117 *bis*).

[18] Parker (1965) 38-42; Pächt, Dodwell, and Wormald (n. 3 above) 6 and chap. 15.

feast, in a hand similar to that of scribe A, and like those in certain other
Bury scriptorium products of Anselm's reign.[19] The presence of these *lectiones*,
condensed from the anonymous Life, is not hard to account for, although
the Office for the Vigil at the end of the manuscript is already supplied with
similar ones drawn from Hermann's *Miracula*. Religious communities perio-
dically felt the need to rework their hagiography solely to modernize or improve its style. This was the motive behind Eadmer of Canterbury's re-
writing of Osbern's Life of Saint Dunstan in the early years of the twelfth
century.[20] Apparently, by the 1120s the Bury monks felt that Hermann's
idiom was a little antiquated or inadequate, and therefore an alternative
was provided. This can only have happened while the book was in course
of manufacture, or shortly after its completion, since the painted initial that
begins the additional *lectiones* is similar to those in the main body of the
manuscript. The less elaborate, foliated initials to *lectiones* 2 and 3 have
no counterpart elsewhere in the book, although they are typical of Bury
work during Anselm's reign.[21] As the years went by more additions were
made on the blank folios 2 to 4, in other hands. Of particular interest for
the dating of the manuscript are the first two items, occupying folios 2 and
3. The first, in two very similar hands,[22] is a letter from Henry I to Abbot
Anselm, forbidding his intended journey abroad, because the monks and
knights of the abbey object. If ill health be the ground, his friends will do
what they can for him.[23] This letter has been dated early in Anselm's reign
by Williamson, and perhaps refers to his projected pilgrimage to Compostella,
from which he was eventually dissuaded.[24] To this assumption, reasonable
enough, I shall return after reviewing further evidence. The second item
is another letter, in the hand of the second scribe,[25] addressed to Anselm
from Prior Talbot and the convent, begging him to return to the house; he
had promised to go no further than Normandy, but now he has, and is
using the plea of royal business as an excuse to delay his return. The
remarkably rhetorical style of this long letter owes much to that of Osbert
of Clare, who while sojourning at the house between 1123 and 1134 could

---

[19] Parker (1965) 75. The quire is preceded by two blank flyleaves.

[20] R. W. Southern, *Saint Anselm and his Biographer* (Cambridge 1962) 281-283.

[21] Parker (1965) 75.

[22] The hands change at line eight; the letter forms in both are very similar, differences
in *g* being the most marked. The first scribe uses Tironian *et*, median point punctuation,
and makes his cedilla in one jagged stroke; the second uses the ampersand, point on the
line, and a looped cedilla.

[23] Summarized in *Regesta regum anglo-normannorum 2, 1100-1135*, ed. C. Johnson and
H. A. Cronne (Oxford 1956) no. 1340.

[24] Williamson (n. 12 above) 195.

[25] On fol. 2v, line 13, the strokes become thinner, but this seems owing to a change of
pen rather than of scribe.

easily have taught grammar in his capacity as a litterateur under obligation to the community for their hospitality.[26] He himself during this time wrote two similar letters to Anselm, beseeching his return from overseas.[27] They may well relate to the same period of absence which called for the writing of the Morgan letter, since there is only one known time between 1123 and 1134 when Anselm was away from Bury. Moreover, on this occasion he was in Normandy on royal business, as specified in Talbot's letter. This was late in 1125, when he witnessed two royal charters at Rouen.[28] The Morgan letter (and both Osbert's) should probably, therefore, be dated early in the following year. If it was copied into the manuscript soon after its original composition, then of course the manuscript would have to be dated before 1126. That it *was* copied in early is strongly suggested by the very reason for so doing.

The Morgan book is a typical liturgical *libellus* intended for use within the church, doubtless at the saint's shrine.[29] It was common practice to copy into the spare leaves of such a service book, more usually an evangeliary, important documents relating to some dearly won or tenaciously defended privilege of the community to which it belonged. Such books, associated with the service of the altar, were especially venerated, and documents included in them were thus endowed with sanctity as well as security.[30] Bury itself furnishes an earlier example in a Gospel book dating from the late-eleventh century.[31] Into its spare leaves were copied, contemporaneously, records of the famous jurisdictional dispute between Abbot Baldwin and the ambitious Bishop Arfast of Thetford, terminated in the abbey's favor in 1081.[32] In the light of this practice, the most likely occasion for the inclusion of the two letters in the Morgan manuscript would be on Anselm's eventual return to the house after his absence of 1125-1126. Doubtless the monks made him promise to stay home more often—possibly even asking him to swear on the Morgan *Vitae*. The presence of the letters in it was to remind him of the sacredness and seriousness of his pastoral responsibility.

[26] I have made a detailed study of the letter, including a comparison of its style with Osbert's, which I hope to publish in the near future.

[27] Williamson (n. 12 above) nos. 5, 6.

[28] *Regesta* (n. 23 above) nos. 1426-1427.

[29] F. Wormald, "Some illustrated Manuscripts of the Lives of Saints," *Bulletin of the John Rylands Library* 35 (1952) 248-266. A similar, although unillustrated *libellus* from Bury (British Museum Cotton Tib. B. ii, late eleventh cent.), is inscribed *Liber feretrariorum*.

[30] F. Wormald, "The Sherborne Chartulary," *Fritz Saxl; a Volume of Memorial Essays*, ed. D. J. Gordon (London 1957) 101-119, esp. 105-107.

[31] London, Brit. Mus. Harl. 76, fols. 137-141. See Douglas (n. 17 above) xxv n. 7, and charters 7 and 8. One wonders whether such service books were deliberately made with plenty of spare leaves for this purpose.

[32] For this dispute see D. Knowles, *The Monastic Order in England*, ed. 2 (Cambridge 1963) 581-582; bibliographical details in accompanying notes.

In support of this it may be noted, firstly, that Anselm was not again away from the house, so far as is known, until 1137, after he was elected bishop of London.[33] Secondly, the two letters do not have the character of casual entries. The hands are those of practised scribes, more or less contemporary with scribe A; the two documents are separated by a space from each other, and gaps have been left for decorated initials at the beginning of each. These were never filled in, suggesting that these additions were made after the initials of the extra *lectiones* and the rest of the manuscript were painted.

To return to the first letter; it does not seem to relate to the same occasion as the second, although the same theme unites them. Williamson's suggestion that it refers to Anselm's intended pilgrimage seems a good one. In the letter Henry states that the monks and knights of Saint Edmunds have besought him to refuse Anselm's journey; similarly, a later account specifies the *sapientes abbatie* as the discouragers of Anselm's Compostella pilgrimage.[34] The same account gives the time of this intended journey as *primo tempore* after his election as abbot, and states that he was persuaded to build the parish church of Saint James instead.[35] We do not, unfortunately, know when the construction of this church commenced; it was apparently dedicated in 1135 or 1136.[36] In 1123 Anselm traveled to Rome to fetch the archbishop of Canterbury's pallium.[37] He seems more likely to have decided on his pilgrimage after rather than before this journey. This is suggested by the date of a royal charter granting Anselm a fair at Bury on the feast of Saint James, almost certainly another compensation for his unperformed pilgrimage. The charter is witnessed at Rouen by Thurstan, archbishop of York, who is known to have passed through Normandy in 1125 and 1129.[38] When it is remembered that Anselm himself was in Rouen in 1125 the earlier date seems the more likely, especially as Thurstan witnessed another charter there along with him in that year.[39] The abbot's pilgrimage must have been conceived not long before, probably in 1124, which would consequently be the date of the first Morgan letter. One might ask why the Morgan manuscript could not have been written before this date, in the light of our earlier reasoning. The

---

[33] Diceto, Rolls Series, 1.248-249.

[34] London, Brit. Mus. Harl. 1005, fol. 218 col. 2.

[35] *Ibid*. fols. 218 col. 2 and 218v col. 1.

[36] *Ibid*. fols. 218v col. 1, where "Willelmus turbius [William de Corbeil] archiepiscopus Cantuariensis" is said to have consecrated it, and fol. 218 col. 2, where "Ricardus de Belfo [Richard de Bella Fago] episcopus Averantensis de Normannia" is given instead. Corbeil reigned 1123-1136, while Bella Fago was bishop of Avranches from 1135 until 1142. If the inference is that they both consecrated the church simultaneously, then the date must be 1135-1136.

[37] *Anglo-Saxon Chronicle*, trans. G. N. Garmonsway (London 1967) 252.

[38] *Regesta* (n. 23 above) no. 1599 and note.

[39] *Ibid*. no 1427.

answer is that the two letters were evidently copied in together, therefore necessarily after the date of the later one. This is logical. It must have taken a little time for the Bury monks to realize that their abbot was afflicted with incurable wanderlust; doubtless his long absence of 1125-1126 was the last straw which prompted the solemn inclusion of the letters in the service book.

On this evidence the Morgan *Vitae* could have been written at any time between the making of the Albani Psalter (ca. 1123), and the sending of Talbot's letter (ca. 1126). Before leaving it, something must be said about the rest of the later entries on folios 3 and 4. These are in no less than five more hands, mostly succeeding one another without a break, and therefore in time as well. The last entry is in a tiny hand, to fill up the bottom of the page. Although the verso is blank, it was evidently thought inappropriate that these more informal entries should be seen opposite the first page of the *lectiones*, the next recto. Because of the chronological succession of these notes, they may provide valuable dating evidence for work on the abbey scriptorium in Anselm's reign. Most of the hands in them are not those of practised scribes, and Miss Parker in her 1965 thesis did not identify any of them in other contemporary Bury manuscripts;[40] but the possibility is always present.[41] It is therefore important to be able to date them as far as possible. The reason for their inclusion, it will be shown, is roughly the same as for the letters. They concern the institution of conventual pittances by Anselm, to be financed from certain of the sacrist's holdings in the vill and elsewhere. The hand which introduces this section, a large, round formal one, supplies, in two groups, a list of the feasts on which the pittances were to be had.[42] Hervey is named as the sacrist concerned. Again, space has been left for a decorated initial, and the fact that this entry was made at about the same time as the two letters is proved by an erasure and alteration by the first scribe of King Henry's letter.[43] This alteration is important additional evidence for the early date that I am proposing for the manuscript. Its effect is to add two more feasts to the list of those for which pittances are prescribed. One of these is the anniversary of Archbishop Anselm, which we would surely expect to be honored with extra pittances early in his nephew's reign. After this, formality is abandoned. Beginning on folio 3v a more pointed charter-hand lists the sacrist's holdings in the vill from which the pittances were to be financed, each identified by its tenant and a witness.

---

[40] Parker (1965) 75-76, 330.

[41] They might, for instance, appear in marginal annotations or flyleaf jottings, etc.

[42] The hand of the second group, although certainly identical with that of the first, seems somewhat more unsteady. This could well be because of age, and might suggest a time lag between the entering of the two groups.

[43] The addition extends from the end of line nine of the first group of feasts to the beginning of line eleven.

Finally, in three informal hands, further feasts are listed. It is reasonable to suppose that these entries, especially the list of *mansi*, are based on documents. The earliest names Anselm "sanctae romanae dignitatis filius," a variant of the title assumed by the abbot himself in some of his charters, one of which is perhaps being paraphrased.[44] Similarly, the list of tenants and witnesses suggests a digest of a series of charters. Fortunately a terminus ante quem for these records is provided by the last, which states: "De reliquis vero xx. solidis stabilivit [Anselmus] x. solidos haberi in sui anniversario et x. in anniversario prefati sacristae Hervei, postquam Deus eos ab hac subtraxerit luce." Evidently both men were still alive when this entry was made. Anselm died in 1148, and Hervey was no longer sacrist ten years before. An original charter in the British Museum, omitted by Douglas from his *Feudal Documents*, supplies important evidence for the date by which Hervey had left office.[45] This is a grant by Abbot Ording to Aubrey de Vere, styled count of Guines, of various fees and services from the abbey lands. The editors of *Facsimiles of Charters in the British Museum* dated it circa 1140; by July 1141 de Vere's principal title was earl of Oxford, and he had been count of Guines in his wife's right since about 1139, when her father is thought to have died.[46] There is, however, a query against this last date, which is only approximate.[47] In 1136 Abbot Anselm of Bury was chosen as bishop-elect of London by some of the Saint Paul's canons, with opposition from some others supporting the candidature of the dean.[48] In 1137 he went to Rome to vindicate his claim, but accomplished nothing because of the schism. Nonetheless, in the following year he was received at Saint Paul's, and Ording made abbot of Saint Edmunds. It is to this period that the charter belongs. Shortly after, Anselm's election was quashed by the pope, and Warner and Ellis, assuming that he returned to Bury shortly before the consecration of Robert de Sigillo as bishop of London in June 1141, dated the charter to the previous year. Dr. Kauffmann, who noticed this neglected document in his recent article on the Bury Bible, dated it circa 1138-1141.[49] But Diceto, from whom much of the above information derives, explicitly states that Anselm was back as abbot of Bury in 1138, when both pope and king concurred in making Henry of Blois, bishop of Winches-

---

[44] Douglas (n. 17 above) cxxxv n. 7; charters 112, 120.

[45] London, Brit. Mus. Cotton charter 21.6.

[46] *Facsimiles of Royal and other Charters in the British Museum*, ed. G. Warner and H. J. Ellis, 1 (London 1903) no. 18. The date of de Vere's assumption of the earldom of Oxford is not, as given by them, 1142, but July 1141. See R. H. C. Davis, *King Stephen* (London 1967) 140-141.

[47] It is thus given by J. H. Round, *Geoffrey de Mandeville* (London 1892), 189, and still accepted by Davis (n. 45 above).

[48] Diceto (n. 33 above) 1.248-249.

[49] Kauffmann (n. 3 above) 65.

ter, custodian of the see of London.[50] The charter, then, can be from one
year only, and that is 1138. In fact it is evidence for Aubrey de Vere assuming the countship of Guines at least a year earlier than has been supposed. Among its witnesses appear Prior William and the sacrist Ralph,
Hervey's successor. These men would most likely have replaced Hervey
and Talbot, the previous sacrist and prior, on Ording's assumption of
the abbacy in that year, if their predecessors did not die in office earlier.
Thus the last entry in the Morgan manuscript may have been made no later
than 1137. But once it is admitted that it could not have been made after
Anselm's abortive promotion to the see of London, it must obviously have
been made before his election by the Saint Paul's canons in 1136. The inclusion of these documents in the service book, given its purpose, would
have been pointless once there was a possibility that Anselm's abbacy at
Saint Edmunds was at an end. They owe their raison d'être solely to the
relations between him end his convent.

This ten-year gap between the time of the first entry describing the newly
instituted pittances, made circa 1126, and the last, circa 1136, is consistent
with the paleography of the hands concerned. It also suggests that after
the original institution about the time of the first entry, the number of occasions on which pittances were to be had was slowly increased. The charter-
hand can be roughly dated by one name in the list of tenants which it supplies: Gilbert the moneyer. Gilbert presided over the abbatial mint in the
vill.[51] His activities can be dated by surviving coins, among which he is represented by one type 15 Henry I and five type 1 Stephen.[52] This gives a
range of six years, from 1135 until 1141, for his tenure of office.[53] Of course
the evidence is fragmentary, and further finds of coins might extend this
period either way. At present it looks as though he took up residence in
the vill late in the last year of Henry's reign. The fact that he appears twice
in the list of holdings, once as a witness and once as the holder of a *mansus*
suggests that he was well established by the time the original record was
compiled. Thus the list of *mansi* could not have been entered before 1136.[54]

[50] Diceto 1.250-252.

[51] The abbots of Bury had had the right to a local mint since the time of Edward the
Confessor. See H. W. C. Davis, "The Liberties of Bury Saint Edmunds," *English Historical
Review* 24 (1909) 417-431, esp. 420.

[52] G. C. Brooke, *A Catalogue of English Coins in the British Museum; The Norman Kings*,
2 vols. (London 1916), 1.cc-cci; 2.318, 335-336. Cf. also 369, now decisively rejected
by Mack (n. 53 below).

[53] M. Dolley, *The Norman Conquest and the English Coinage* (London 1966) 27; R. P.
Mack, "Stephen and the Anarchy, 1135-1154," *British Numismatic Journal* 35 (1966) 38-
112, esp. 41.

[54] It must consequently have been compiled after the first pittances were instituted
before ca. 1126; the whole operation seems to have been carried out gradually, over a period
of at least ten years, so there is no inconsistency here.

As to the later hands, the penultimate has noted Henry I's anniversary among other feasts for which pittances are prescribed. Does this suggest that he was alive or dead at the time? The same hand also lists the anniversaries of Archbishop Anselm and his sister Richeza, Abbot Anselm's mother. The former was dead long before his nephew became abbot or Hervey sacrist of Bury, and the same must be true of Richeza. The king was probably also dead, therefore, before this entry was made.[55] It will be noticed that the entries in the Morgan manuscript relating to Anselm's institution of conventual pittances fall into two groups, the first, in one hand on folio 3, made circa 1126, the rest about ten years later. The early entry is formal; the rest merely add, as it were, detailed notes to its information. The purpose of all the formal entries, including the two letters, is identical: to sanctify two particular aspects of the relationship between the abbot and convent, seen very much from the viewpoint of the latter. Saint Edmund was known preeminently as the saint against tyranny and authoritarianism; it was fitting that his *libellus* should be used to protect the rights of his flock against their active but somewhat capricious pastor.[56] It may be that the letters and the institution of the pittances are connected even more closely than this; could the pittances have been an act of atonement or compensation by Anselm towards his monks for his vexatious absences?

This early dating of the Morgan *Vitae* must involve a similar reassessment for the date of the prefatory miniature-cycle to Pembroke College manuscript 120, another Bury product in the Albani manner.[57] But it prevents the slight embarassment created for themselves by art historians who want to place the Morgan manuscript and the Bury Bible close to each other in time, in spite of their quite different styles. Like the Morgan manuscript, the Bury Bible was until recently assigned by scholars a wide range of dates within the limits of Anselm's reign.[58] In 1966, however, Dr. Kauffmann rediscovered the existence of the Cotton charter mentioned above, which provides a firm terminus ante quem of 1137-1138 for its execution.[59] From the account in the *Gesta sacristarum* it is known that a great Bible was commissioned by

[55] This is the reasoning of Miss Parker (1965) 117-119, against M. Rickert (nn. 5, 8 above) and n. 28. Miss Parker has since returned to the older view (Parker [1970] 264).

[56] For this view of Edmund, see R. H. C. Davis, "The Monks of Saint Edmund, 1021-1148," *History*, n. s. 40 (1955) 227-239, esp. 227-229. This characterization of Bury's patron could be documented very extensively.

[57] Studied most recently and thoroughly in Parker (1970). Miss Parker dates it provisionally a little later than the Morgan MS (264). There is no way of dating this cycle except stylistically, since it was not originally designed for the volume with which it was bound by the fourteenth century.

[58] Rickert (nn. 5, 8 above) 84 (1121-1148); Dodwell (n. 5 above) 9 (shortly before 1148); Beckwith (n. 9 above) 194 (1130-1140); Swarzenski (n. 9 above) plate 302 (ca. 1148).

[59] Kauffmann (n. 3 above) 64-66.

Prior Talbot and his brother Hervey the sacrist.[60] Dr. Kauffmann clinched
M. R. James's already generally accepted identification of this with the extant Bury Bible.[61] Both Talbot and Hervey seem to have come into office
circa 1125-1126,[62] and left it before 1138. On stylistic grounds Kauffmann
placed the execution of the Bury Bible late in this period (ca. 1135). I should
like to propose a more precise date of 1137.

Firstly, the absence of the abbot's interest in or patronage of such an ambitious project is surprising. While the *Gesta* certainly transfers much of
the initiative which rightly belongs to the abbots to their respective sacrists
it usually names the abbot if he is at all involved in a particular project.
Thus Abbot Samson (1182-1211) is mentioned as supplying material for
the building works undertaken in his reign by his sacrist Hugh.[63] Anselm
himself is known as a patron of literary works, interested in painting, and
his influence was undoubtedly present in the design of the nave and western
front of the conventual church, erected in his time.[64] On both counts it is
surprising, therefore, that his name is not connected with the project for
a great Bible. Surely the inference is that he was not at the abbey when the
project was put in hand, and that the prior and sacrist were in charge
of its affairs. It will be recalled that after 1136 Anselm was bishop-elect
of London, and that in 1137 he was in Rome; 1137, then, seems a likely time
for the making of the Bible. Scholars agree that the artist himself, well known
as Master Hugh, was a professional rather than a monk of the house.[65] Hugh
was certainly resident in the vill for some time, since as well as decorating
the Bible he cast a pair of bronze doors for the new west front of the church
and a bell for its crossing-tower, the first work commissioned by Hervey,
the second by Anselm himself.[66] Later he carved a great Cross for the choir

[60] Arnold (n. 11 above) 2.289-296; 2.290.

[61] M. R. James, *A Descriptive Catalogue of the Manuscripts in the Library of Corpus Christi College* (Cambridge 1912) 3-8; Kauffmann (n. 3 above) 62-4.

[62] Baldwin was still prior and Godfrey sacrist ca. 1125 (Douglas, n. 17 above, nos. 110-
111). As evidenced by the second Morgan letter, Talbot had certainly replaced Baldwin
ca. 1126. Probably Anselm replaced both the ageing obedientiaries with younger men
before his protracted absence of 1125-1126.

[63] Arnold (n. 11 above) 291-292.

[64] Williamson (n. 12 above) 26ff.; R. W. Southern, "The English Origin of the Miracles
of the Virgin," *Medieval and Renaissance Studies* 4 (1958) 177-216, esp. 183-200; *idem* and
F. S. Schmitt, *Memorials of Saint Anselm* (Oxford 1969) 25-26; London, Brit. Mus. Harl.
1005, fol. 217v col. 2; A. B. Whittingham, "Bury Saint Edmunds Abbey; the Plan, Design,
and Development of the Church and Monastic Buildings," *Archaeological Journal* 108,
(1951, publ. 1952) 170-171; J. Bony, "The facade of Bury Saint Edmunds; an Additional
Note," *Studies in Western Art* 1 (Princeton 1963) 105-107.

[65] Dodwell (n. 5 above) 9; Kauffmann (n. 3 above) 64.

[66] Arnold (n. 11 above) 2.289; M. R. James, *On the Abbey of Saint Edmund at Bury*,
Cambridge Antiquarian Society, 8vo ser. 28 (1895) 199.

with flanking images of John and Mary.[67] This, his latest known work, was commissioned in the reign of Abbot Ording (1148-1156) by his sacrist Elias. Elias succeeded early as the second of Ording's sacrists, and may have remained in office for the rest of his reign.[68] Probably, then, Hugh made the Cross in the early 1150s. The casting of the bell, by contrast, cannot be dated with any certainty. Another bell for the same tower was cast by one Hailfic for the sacrist Godfrey, who held office from circa 1105 until circa 1125.[69] This may mean that the crossing-tower was already in an advanced stage of construction. The date of Hugh's doors can be determined a little more satisfactorily. The west front must have been nearly complete when the chapel of Saint Faith, in the upper story of the northwestern transept, was dedicated by John, bishop of Rochester.[70] There were two successive bishops of that name, reigning from 1125 to June 1137, and from 1137 to 1142. Two reasons favor the first as the dedicator of the Bury chapel. The record that supplies the information, a brief chronicle of local chapel dedications, usually specifies the presence or absence of the abbot from any particular ceremony. On this occasion it seems that Anselm was present, and it will be remembered that from 1125 until 1136 he was apparently at the house, whereas he was absent at intervals during the period from 1137 to 1142.[71] Secondly, the *Gesta* records that sacrist Hervey built walls around the *atrium* or forecourt of the church.[72] This could only have been done when the western front was nearly finished and, of course, before 1138. Thus the chapel of Saint Faith must have been consecrated before 1137 and Master Hugh's doors cast at about the same time. It is hardly likely that the doors and Bible would have been executed simultaneously, so that the doors were probably made circa 1135. The bell may then be placed even earlier, since work on the church proceeded more or less from east to west. Zarnecki surmised that the fine abbey seal from Bury, dated by him circa 1150 on stylistic grounds, was also Master Hugh's work. The disposition of the drapery folds in the vestments of the seated abbot depicted on it strongly recalls

[67] Arnold 2.290.

[68] Douglas (n. 17 above) no. 134 indicates that Ralph was still sacrist after 1148. The *Gesta* (Arnold 2.290) names Frodo as Elias's successor. He first appears in a charter of Abbot Hugh I (1156-1180), Douglas no. 144, dated 1156-1160.

[69] James (n. 64 above) 200.

[70] Harl. 1005 (n. 64 above) fol. 217v col. 2.

[71] *Ibid.*, in which it is stated that John carried out the dedications "rogatu Anselmi abbatis." Besides his 1137 journey to Rome and 1138 sojourn in London, mentioned above, he apparently went to Rome again towards the end of 1138. Harl. 1005 fol. 218 col. 1 notes that he was there when the papal legate Alberic of Ostia dedicated the altar of Saint Cross in the conventual church at Bury on November 19. Alberic was in England from January, 1138 to January, 1139. Doubtless Anselm's journey was to appeal against the papal decision that had deprived him of the bishopric of London.

[72] Arnold (n. 11 above) 2.290.

the technique of the Bury Bible miniatures.[73] Given Hugh's constant presence at Bury around this time, Zarnecki is surely correct in supposing that this small project could hardly be the work of another artist. But who is the abbot represented on it? Such a seal would normally be made at the beginning of an abbot's reign, and this would rule out Anselm to favour his successor, Ording. The seal would then be datable circa 1148. A possible sequence for Hugh's works at Bury, with approximate dates, then, is as follows: the bell for the central tower, circa 1130; the bronze doors, circa 1135; the Bible, 1137; the seal, 1148, and the Cross, circa 1150.

If this evidence is accepted as proving Hugh's continuous residence at Bury circa 1130-1155, then our early date for the Pierpont Morgan manuscript is further enhanced. Firstly, the Morgan book was almost certainly complete before the Bury Bible on stylistic grounds alone, since Master Hugh appears to have studied its miniatures and learned from them.[74] Secondly, it seems unlikely that the task of decorating the *libellus* would have been given to anyone else while Master Hugh was at the house; certainly he was a much more accomplished artist than the painter of the Morgan miniatures—who himself set a high standard—and later generations of Bury monks regarded his achievement with a kind of awe.[75]

The date (1137) that I have suggested for Hugh's Bible is highly logical seen in relationship to the work on the church, which was virtually completed by that year. At this time funds could be diverted to other projects, and first on the list of priorities would be the provision of new service books consistent with the immense scale and new style of the completed church. The execution of the Bible must therefore be viewed as following on from, and directly related to the construction program for the great Romanesque conventual church and pilgrim shrine. Dr. Kauffmann quoted an unprinted entry from the benefaction list contained in a fifteenth century Bury register.[76] It mentions Talbot's and Hervey's Bible, supplying the added detail that it was in two volumes (as was the Bury Bible originally) and describing it as *de refectorio*. Kauffmann left open the question as to whether this indicated the original or fifteenth century use to which it was put. I think the latter; the volume is much too splendid to have been designed for the monks'

---

[73] G. Zarnecki, *English Romanesque Lead Sculpture* (London 1957) 7, plate 8.

[74] Kauffmann (n. 3 above) 74-75, 80.

[75] Another possible work of Master Hugh's may have been the painting with frescoes of the chapel of Saint Saba commissioned by Anselm (Harl. 1005 fol. 21v col. 2). This chapel, probably the northernmost of the two eastern apsidal chapels in the northeast transept, was dedicated by Bishop John of Rochester on the same occasion as the chapel of Saint Faith (*ibid.*), i.e. shortly before 1137.

[76] Kauffmann 62-63.

meal-time reading.[77] It is a book for the altar par excellence. Why then
did it end up in the refectory? A clue is provided by the same benefaction
list. In it Abbot Hugh II (1215-1229) is remembered as having donated
primam partem Biblie preciosissimam.[78] The Romanesque decoration of Talbot's Bible was probably felt to be antiquated by the early thirteenth century,
and so was replaced (in two stages?) by an equally sumptuous successor,
doubtless in the Gothic style. The older book was then transferred to more
humble service in the refectory. *Habent sua fata libelli.*

The two liturgical books, the Morgan *Vitae* and the Bury Bible were made
in 1124-1125 and 1137 respectively; the first before, the second following
Abbot Anselm's ambitious construction program for the conventual church.
The time interval of ten to fifteen years between them seems to relate satisfactorily to their very different styles of decoration. Certainly it makes more
chronologically intelligible M. Rickert's theory of two waves of Byzantine
influence apparent in English book painting in the first half of the twelfth
century.[79] According to her ideas, the Albani school was influenced by the
earlier, weaker, and less direct of the waves, while the second, more direct
and better assimilated, affected the miniatures of the Bury Bible and related
books. For the Morgan manuscript the abbey was able to use one of its own
scribes, but called in a Saint Albans man for its miniatures, and perhaps
another professional for the initials.[80] For the Bible the process was reversed.
A professional scribe wrote all except the display script, perhaps because
the abbey's best calligraphist, scribe A, was dead; but Master Hugh, by virtue
of his long residence in the vill, the result of mutual satisfaction between
artist and client, may fairly be regarded as a local man, although not an
actual member of the monastic community. The convent's relationship with
him, then, may be described as one of enlightened patronage.

APPENDIX

The information supplied by the second Morgan letter and Cotton charter
21.6 necessitates the redating of most of Abbot Anselm's charters printed
in Douglas, *Feudal Documents.* The two that are witnessed by Prior Talbot
and Baldwin *vetus prior* must be circa 1125-1126, just after Talbot succeeded
to the priorate. Those that are witnessed by Talbot and Hervey must come
before 1138, and therefore before Anselm's journey to Rome in 1137. Those

---

[77] Other surviving books from Bury inscribed *de refectorio* are completely undecorated:
London, Brit. Mus. Egerton 2782; Saint John's Coll. Camb. 35; Wisbech Museum 1.

[78] James (n. 61 above) 181.

[79] Rickert (nn. 5, 8 above) 78-85.

[80] Parker (1965) 75-87, 330-331.

that are witnessed by Prior William and the sacrist Ralph must fall after Anselm's return from his second visit to Rome in 1138-1139.

Number of Charter in Douglas's Edition.	Date given by Douglas.	Corrected Date.
113	1121-1138	1126-1136
114	„ „	„ „
116	„ -1148	1125-1126
117	„ „	„ „
118	„ „	1126-1136
119	„ „	„ „
120	„ „	„ „
121	„ „	„ „
122	„ „	„ „
123	„ „	„ „
124	„ „	1139-1148
128	„ „	„ „
129	„ „	„ „
130	„ „	„ „
131	„ „	„ „
133	1135-1148	„ „

Department of History
University of Sydney
Sydney, New South Wales 2006, Australia

HERMANNUS ALEMANNUS'S RHETORICAL TRANSLATIONS

•

by William F. Boggess

For at least 150 years, medievalists have been generally aware that Hermannus Alemannus (fl. 1240-1256) did some translations related to Aristotle's *Rhetoric*. They have not agreed, however, on how many he did, what originals he used, or when he did them. The most reputable authorities, relying primarily on the translator's prologues, have, after brief and infrequent forays into the no man's land of the translations themselves, brought back reports so varied and contradictory that one might wonder if they had seen the same things or were even serving on the same front. My investigation, employing the translations and, where possible, the originals from which they were made, establishes both the correct interpretation of the prologues and the number, nature, and date of Hermannus's rhetorical translations. Under each of two major headings, Alfarabi and "Averroes," I review previous opinions about the evidence and offer new analyses. A recapitulation of my conclusions vindicates the prologues and they, in turn, furnish the third section on the date of the translations.

I. ALFARABI

Before proceeding to individual analyses of the single Latin manuscript (Bibliothèque Nationale Latin manuscript 16097)[1] and the printed editions (Venice 1481 and 1515) that constitute the major evidence for Hermannus's translation of Alfarabi, we must review the welter of conflicting authorities.

This article was completed at the Gennadius Library, American School of Classical Studies, Athens, Greece, during the tenure of a six-month fellowship awarded by the National Endowment for the Humanities.

[1] A. Jourdain, *Récherches critiques sur l'âge et l'origine des traductions latines d'Aristote*, ed. 2 (1843) 145 n. 1: "J'ai découvert à la Bibliothèque Royale, Fonds de Sorbonne, 954, un petit traité du même Hermann qui est resté inconnu aux auteurs du catalogue et à tous les bibliographes; c'est sous le titre de Didascalion, une introduction à la Rhétorique d'Aristote, composée d'après la glose d'Alfarabius: l'auteur se propose d'y déterminer: 'Quid est rhetorica? in quo differt a facultate oratoria, et quot sunt libri partes, et quot in unaquaque partium tractatus, et quot in unoquoque tractatuum capitula continentur, et circa quod, ad modum introductorium spectare videntur.'"

Jourdain, who discovered the manuscript, gave its title as *Didascalion*, and called it "une introduction à la Rhétorique d'Aristote, composée d'après la glose d'Alfarabius," by which latter term he apparently meant the "Averroes" translation in Bibliothèque Nationale Latin manuscript 16673 (see II below). Renan likewise confused the "gloses d'Alfarabi" with the "Averroes" text and, in a footnote, cited the 1481 edition, but in connection with the *Poetics* rather than the *Rhetoric*.[2] In 1877, Wüstenfeld listed the full contents of the 1481 edition, including the title, *Declaratio compendiosa per viam divisionis Alfarabii super libris rethoricorum Aristotilis*, and the corrector's *explicit*.[3] Steinschneider introduced the 1515 reprint of the *Declaratio compendiosa*, which he identified as the *Glosa* of Alfarabi. Hermannus, claimed Steinschneider, based his *Didascalion* on a "glossary" of Alfarabi that might have been translated from Arabic.[4] In an article devoted entirely to the printed version of 1481 and 1515, Nagy found the *Didascalion* similar in purpose to the *Declaratio compendiosa*, but did not establish their exact relationship. The *Glosa* of Alfarabi, according to Nagy, had been a separate translation now lost.[5] Hermannus's biographer, G. H. Luquet,

---

[2] E. Renan, *Averroès et l'averroïsme, essai historique*, ed. 3 (Paris 1866) 211-212: "En général, Hermann paraît s'être attaché aux textes aristotéliques les plus négligés, la Rhétorique, la Poétique, les Éthiques, la Politique, et comme pour ces ouvrages les abrégés arabes étaient plus répandus ou plus accessibles que le texte d'Aristote, ce fut à ces abrégés que Hermann s'adressa de préférence. Ainsi, comme équivalent de la Rhétorique, il traduit des gloses d'Alfarabi sur cet ouvrage, et comme équivalent de la Poétique, l'abrégé d'Averroès .... Dans le prologue des gloses d'Alfarabi, Hermann nous apprend qu'il avait aussi traduit les Éthiques sur un abrégé arabe, mais que son travail avait été rendu inutile par la traduction de Robert Grosse-Tête, faite sur le grec." Cf. Appendix 2 below.

[3] F. Wüstenfeld, *Die Übersetzungen arabischer Werke in das Lateinische* (Göttingen 1877) 93-94.

[4] M. Steinschneider, *Die arabischen Übersetzungen aus dem Griechischen* (1889, repr. Graz 1960) 49: "Wir besitzen noch eine '*Declaratio compendiosa super libris rhetoricorum Aristotelis* in 2 Ausg., Venedig 1481 und 1515. Der Uebersetzer Hermannus Allemannus (1256) nennt in dem von Jourdain herausgegebenen Vorwort das Buch *Glosa*; Jourdain hat in Ms. Paris, Sorbonne 954, ein *Didascalion* von Hermann entdeckt, nämlich eine Einleitung zur Rhetorik nach dem Glossar des Farabi, welche die Definition und die Einteilung des Buches der Rhetorik behandelt und aus dem Arabischen übersetzt sein könnte. Sie findet sich nicht in den Ausgaben der Rhetorik."

[5] A. Nagy, "Notizie intorno alla retorica d'al-Fārābī," *Rendiconti della Accademia dei lincei* 5.2 (1893) 684-691. After a discussion of the title, *Declaratio compendiosa*, in terms of its Arabic correspondences in catalog descriptions of the lost works of Alfarabi on the *Rhetoric*, he states (689): "Ecco l'origine del nome 'declaratio per viam divisionis' la quale, come vedemmo, comincia di fatto col dividere i tre libri in tanti trattati e capitoli, e quindi indica il contenuto di ciascuno di questi.

"Con essa concorda l'indicazione del *Didascalion*, che appunto tratterebbe della definizione e della divisione del libro."

Of the *Glosa*, he says (690): "Il fatto che l'Herrmann aveva dinanzi a se questa *glosa*, nella quale molti esempî greci erano stati omessi per la loro oscurità, e che non era condotta

mentioned two works: one, an incomplete, lost, *Rhétorique d'Alfarabi*; the other, an extant *Didascalia* or personal commentary, based on the *Glosa* of Alfarabi.[6] Luquet is silent about the 1481 and 1515 editions. In 1939, G. Lacombe described the manuscript that Jourdain discovered as the *Glosa* or *Didascalia* from which the 1481 edition derived.[7] The same year saw D. Salmon noting that the *Declaratio compendiosa* "is only extant in several Renaissance editions" and that Jourdain had discovered and published its introduction.[8] More recently, N. Rescher subscribed to Salmon's view and, in addition, separated the 1481 edition (credited to Dominicus Gundisallinus) by calling the 1515 *Declaratio compendiosa* a reprint of a 1484 *editio princeps* of Hermannus's translation.[9] As this survey suggests, authoritative

---

sino alla fine. L'Herrmann stesso dice di averne voltati in latino più di due quinterni; ma di quest'opera non abbiamo altra notizia."

[6] G. H. Luquet, "Hermann l'Allemand (†1272)," *Revue de l'histoire des religions* 44 (1901) 412: "Avant cette traduction [i. e. the "Averroes" *Rhetoric*], Hermann avait déjà entrepris une traduction, qu'il n'acheva pas, de la *Rhétorique* d'Alfarabi, comme il nous l'apprend à la fin du prologue de sa traduction de la *Rhétorique.*—Peu de temps après la première traduction, qui pour lui correspondait au texte même d'Aristote, il composa sur cet ouvrage un commentaire personnel, en utilisant les gloses d'Alfarabi: *Didascalia in Rhetoricam Aristotelis ex glosa Alfarabii.*"

[7] G. Lacombe *et al.. Aristoteles latinus* (AL) 1 (Rome 1939) 103 n. 3: "De commentario Alpharabii haec dicit Hermannus in prologo: 'Cuius glose plus quam duos quinternos ego quoque transtuli in latinum.' Quae versio in cod. Paris. lat. 16097, ff. 188r-196v nobis servata est, hoc sub titulo: *Incipiunt didascalia in Rethoricam Aristotilis ex glosa Alpharabii;* nec est commentarium ab ipso Hermanno editum ('un commentaire personnel'), ut Luquet censuit. Verbo *'didascalia'* prologus hic denotatur. Ex eadem versione (cap. XLII ss.) fluxisse videtur illa *Declaratio compendiosa per viam divisionis Alfarabii super libris Rethoricorum Aristotilis* 'tabulata et correcta . . . per . . . magistrum Lancillotum de Zerbis (sic),' quae Venetiis a. 1481 impressa est."

Lacombe's otherwise excellent observation is marred for two reasons: 1) the capitulation, which begins with chapter 36 on fol. 192va and ends with chapter 43 on fol. 193vb, has little relation to the content of the manuscript; 2) some parts of the *Declaratio compendiosa* come, as we shall see below, from passages occurring before "chapter 42" in the manuscript.

[8] D. Salmon, "The Mediaeval Latin Translations of Alfarabi's Works," *The New Scholasticism* 13 (1939) 245-261. On 246, Salmon lists: *"Declaratio Compendiosa super Libris Rhetoricorum Aristotelis.* This Commentary was translated by Hermann Alemannus about 1256, and is only extant in several Renaissance editions."

In his footnote to this listing, he adds: "Venetiis, 1481. The introduction has been discovered and published by Jourdain" (citing here the quotation found above, n. 1).

[9] N. Rescher, *Al-Fārābī: An Annotated Bibliography* (Pittsburgh 1962) 37-38: "Venice (1481). *Declaratio compendiosa per viam divisionis Alpharabii super libris rhetoricorum Aristotilis.* Venetiis, 1481. [This work, translated from the Arabic original of F's treatise *Sadr (sic) kitāb al-khaṭābah* by Dominicus Gundisallinus (see *Steinschneider* (1869), p. 59 and *idem* (1904), p. 33), is *not* (italics Rescher's) identical with the *Declaratio compendiosa super libris rhetoricorum* of Venice (1484). Cf. also *Nagy* (1893). For a description of this book see the General Catalogue of the British Museum, vol. VI, col. 175, item 4; or L. Hain, *Repertorium Bibliographicum,* item 821.]

opinions may be invoked to show that Hermannus accomplished at least three works (the *Glosa*, the *Didascalion*, and the *Declaratio compendiosa*); two works (the *Glosa* and the *Didascalion*, or the *Didascalion* and the *Declaratio compendiosa*, or the *Rhetoric of Alfarabi* and the *Didascalion*); or one work variously reported as the *Glosa*, *Didascalia*, or *Declaratio compendiosa*. The manuscript and the printed editions of 1481 and 1515, in other words, may represent two unrelated texts (the *Didascalion* and the *Declaratio compendiosa*); two related texts (the *Didascalion* in manuscript, based on the *Declaratio compendiosa*, that is, *Glosa*, or the manuscript containing the introduction to the *Declaratio compendiosa*); or one text complete in the manuscript and partially printed in 1481 and 1515. The resolution of the problem must begin with the manuscript.

A. THE MANUSCRIPT

Lacombe describes the manuscript as follows:

> *AL* 668: BIBL. NATIONALIS, lat. 16097
> Saec. xiii-xiv, membran., mm. 305 x 205, ff. I + 237, binis columnis. Codex miscellaneus a pluribus librariis exaratus. Tituli in summis paginis litteris rubris alternatim et caeruleis descripti; in ff.226r-237v litterae initiales partim rubrae, partim caeruleae. Nec glossae, nec emendationes; f. 237v: "*Iste liber est collegii pauperum magistrorum de Sorbona, ex legato magistri Jacobi de Padua* († paulo post 1338) *in arcium, medicine et theologie facultatibus professoris. Precii 4 libris*"; f. 1r: "*Incatenetur in magna libraria Sorbone.*" Olim Sorb. 954.

The *Didascalia in Rethoricam Aristotilis ex Glosa Alpharabii* begins on folio 188r. The AL (*Aristoteles latinus*) description gives the *explicit* as *non acquiretur apud ipsum credulitas* on folio 196v, immediately preceding a "treat-

---

"Venice (1484). *Alfarabius*: *Declaratio compendiosa super libris rhetoricorum Aristotillis* (*sic*). Venetiis, 1484. [Latin translation by Hermannus Alemannus (Teutonicus) of F's commentary (*sharḥ*) on Aristotle's *Rhetorica*.]

"Venice (1515). *Rhetorica Aristotelis . . . nec non Alpharabii compendiosa declaratione*: edidit Alexander Achillinus. Venetiis, 1515. [This work contains a reprint of F's *Declaratio compendiosa etc.* first published in *Venice* (1484). For a description of this book see the British Museum catalog (1881-1900 series), vol. 3, col. 10 of entry ARISTOTLE, last item.]"

On p. 43, Rescher credits Jourdain with having published the "introduction only" of the 1484 edition.

The existence of the 1484 edition is founded on C. Brockelmann, *Geschichte der arabischen Litteratur*, ed. 2 (Leiden 1937-1942) p. 1.211, where it is either a misprint or a miscopying of Brockelmann's source (Wüstenfeld). The Steinschneider references cited for the Gundisallinus translation deal exclusively with Hermannus. Finally, the Nagy article that Rescher mentions unequivocally pronounces the 1515 edition to be a reprint of the 1481 version.

ise on the passions." Hermannus's prologue appears below as Appendix 1. The text proper is divided into two parts: the first, folios 188ra-196rb; and the second, folios 196rb-196va. The first part is further subdivided into two segments, the second of which is, in turn, bipartite.

The first section begins (fol. 188ra):
> Inquid Alpharabius. Propositum nostrum est explicare quid contexuit Aristotiles in libro suo quem nominat librum rethorice.

After a general prefatory paragraph, the text continues:

> Incipiemus autem expositionem nostram huius libri a rebus quas consuetum est ponere in prologis glosarum, et sunt viii res numero, scilicet: intentio libri; et conveniencia tituli libri cum ipsius intentione; et partes libri; et utilitas eius que est in libro; et eius proportio sive comparatio; et ordinatio ipsius; et modus doctrine quo proceditur in ipso; et quis auctor ipsius.

Then follows a series of paragraphs concerning Aristotle's rhetorical doctrine, its purpose, elements, and relationships with the other logical works.[10] Some passages here are close paraphrases of the *Rhetoric*, for example, folio 189va:

> Et propter hanc causam dixit Aristotiles in diffinitione rethorice quoniam ipsa est potentia que conatur persuasionem possibile[m]. Et intentio dictionis sue "conatur" est ut perveniatur ad ultimum posse conaminis aut supra ipsum.

Other material, for example, an analogy between the *Organon* (including the *Rhetoric* and the *Poetics*) and Plato's allegory of the cave, has no accepted foundation in the Aristotelian text.[11] The first segment of the first part ends on folio 193ra:

> Verisimile est igitur quod intenderit Plato in prelibato exemplo hanc viam qua processit Aristotiles in traditione logices.

The second segment of the first section is, as we have indicated, bipartite. Its first half begins on folio 193ra:

---

[10] For the place of the *Rhetoric* and the *Poetics* in the late Greek and Islamic tradition, see R. Walzer, "Zur Traditionsgeschichte der aristotelischen Poetik," *Studi italiani di filologia classica* n. s. 11 (1934) 5-14; and *idem, Greek into Arabic* (Oxford 1962) 129-136.

[11] A separate study of this part of the manuscript appeared in *Phronesis* 15 (1971) 86-90.

Liber autem iste et partes eius primo distinguntur in tres tractatus
quorum quilibet continet distinctiones diversas eorum ex quibus perficitur et componitur ars ista.

The end of the first half is on folio 193va:

Hec ergo summa quam enumeravimus sunt partes magne cuiuslibet
tractatus libri.

This half is evidently a division of the *Rhetoric* into three books, each with six
chapters. The contents of each chapter as described here can be readily
identified in the Greek text. The second half of this segment follows immediately (fol. 193va):

Nos ergo non erimus contenti isto modo, sed revertemur et memorabimur capitula que sunt partes minores eius summe quam prestrin-
ximus. Nos ergo incipiemus nunc et adducemus hoc quod est in singulis capitulis primi tractatus ut facile fiat per talem nostram expositione[m] sive glosam ad intelligendum et retinendum totum quod est
in quolibet tractatuum.

Here all twelve chapters of Books A and B of the *Rhetoric* are further subdivided into as many as thirteen sections, each clearly identifiable in the
original Greek. Of the third book, however, the commentator simply states
(fol. 196rb):

Et faciemus ad modum istius in tractatu tertio. Prediximus autem
iam quoniam hic tractatus continet sex differencias et fecimus mentionem earum in precedentibus et determinavimus determinatione
sufficienti de temporis [*leg.* ipsis] dum loqueremur de hiis que continet tractatus iste. Visum ergo nobis est non esse necessarium re-
petere hic que ibi determinata sunt ut videmus libri prolixitatem.

The next passage, a transitional summary, concludes the first part of the
commentary (fol. 196rb):

Nunc ergo declaratum [est] que sit libri intentio et qualiter con-
veniat titulus libri intentioni et que sit operatio libri ad philosophiam et que ordinatio ipsius ad partes sui generis et que sit ipsius
divisio sive partitio. Utilitatem autem eius auctor iste rememorabi-
tur in textu, et nos quoque ibidem exponemus verba ipsius de hac
intentione. Modus autem doctrine est quod ipse utitur in eo modis
omnibus docendi. Verumptamen ut plurimum sequetur modum di-
visivum et modum resolutivum. Istud ergo est postremum eius quod
dictum fuit circa prohemialia et didiscalia huius libri, et sequitur ex-

positio ipsius textus. Dicamus ergo in nomine Dei benedicti et ex-
celsi assumentes verbum ipsius auctoris.

The second section of the commentary is, in Hermannus's translation,
patently truncated. As the first section's summary announces, Alfarabi's
intention in the remainder of the commentary was to quote the text of the
Rhetoric as the basis for his own comments. Only one fragment of this section survives before the *explicit* given in *Aristoteles latinus*. It consists of
that passage of Aristotle (1354a1-4) identified in the preceding detailed analysis as Book A, chapter one, section one (fol. 196rb):

> Inquid Aristoteles. Rethorica quidem convertitur ad artem disputa-
> tivam vel arti disputative, et utreque ipsarum inveniuntur propter
> unam rem et participant in aliquo modorum; et invenitur noticia
> ipsarum circa omnia, cum non sit neque una earum scientiarum sin-
> gulariter. Ideoque inveniuntur omnes scientie participantes ipsius
> in modo.

What follows is Alfarabi's exposition of Aristotle's words:

> Dixit Alpharabius. Hic est sermo quem posuit ad iniciandum per
> ipsum librum suum, et notificavit per ipsum in quo communicent re-
> thorica et dyalectica. Ars quippe rethorice communicat arti dyaletice,
> et intendit per hoc notificare quoniam actus utriusque unus est actus.

According to Lacombe, the text ends with this comment's final sentence
(fol. 196va):

> Quando enim fuerit apud auditorem sermo alius effectivus persua-
> sivus ad oppositum illius rei et fuerit quod apud ipsum est de hoc equa-
> le ei quod propositum est a dictore, non acquiretur apud ipsum cre-
> dulitas.

B. THE PRINTED EDITIONS

The contents of the *Declaratio compendiosa* of 1481 and 1515, as well as their
relationship with the manuscript, may be most conveniently demonstrated
by a comparison of the first and last twenty-five-line passages of the *editio
princeps* with corresponding parts of the Alfarabi commentary. The first
five lines, apparently the corrector's introduction, have no equivalent in
the manuscript:

> Declaratio compendiosa per viam divisionis Alfarabii super libris
> rethoricorum Aristotilis ad formam tamen clariorem et tabule re-

ducta [per infrascriptum d. correctorem.] (The 1515 edition omits the words in brackets.)

Lines 5-10 of folio 1ra, however, closely parallel the opening sentence of the manuscript's first section, second segment, second half (quoted above):

Nos autem erimus contenti isto modo quod memorabimur tractatus et capitula que sunt partes minores eius sume quam perstrinximus.

Similarly, lines 17-23 modify only slightly the manuscript's next sentence (also quoted above):

Nos igitur incipiemus nunc et adducemus quod est in singulis ipsorum summatim ut facile fiat per talem nostram expositionem sive glosam et formam ad intelligendum et retinendum totum quod est in quolibet tractatuum et capitulorum.

Lines 11-17, in contrast, reproduce an earlier part of the manuscript, found in the first section, second segment, first half. The manuscript (fol. 193ra) reads:

ex quibus perficitur et componitur ars ista. Neque est potencia ut comprehendatur quid est in quolibet horum tractatuum sub una aliqua intentione. Ideoque oportet comprehendi per distinctiones que sunt in ipsis.

The *editio princeps* has:

in libris rethoricorum Aristotilis ex quibus perficitur et componinitur ars ista. Neque est possibile ut comprehendatur totum quod est in quolibet horum sub una autem intentione. Ideoque oportet comprehendi per distinctiones tractatuum et capitulorum que sunt in ipsis.

In lines 24-25 of folio 1ra, the sentence, *Iam autem diximus quod liber igitur iste in tres libros dividitur*, seems to have been composed from *iam autem diximus*, the phrase occurring in the manuscript just after the passage reproduced in 1a17-23 (fol. 193va), and from the opening sentence of the second segment (fol. 193ra):

Liber autem iste et partes eius primo distinguntur in tres tractatus.

On the last page of the *Declaratio compendiosa*, almost the same situation prevails. Of the last twenty-five lines, twelve (lines 12-23 of fol. 9vb) are copied from the manuscript's general analysis of the *Rhetoric's* third book (fol. 193va):

> Et universaliter ostenditur qualiter oportet ut sit ars rethorica quando quod adinvenitur ex ipsa usitatur in responsione ad interrogationem, et qualiter oportet ut sit ordo partium ipsius. Deinde ostenditur qualiter oportet ut sit conclusio rethorie et qualiter concludenda sit oratio. Et posuit hunc locum extremum sui libri. Hec ergo summa quam enumeravimus sunt partes magne cuiuslibet tractatus et capitulorum libri rethoricorum Aristotilis.

The last sentence, as we have seen above, closes the first half of the second segment in the commentary's first part, and, in the manuscript, immediately precedes the sentence with which the printed version begins. The *Declaratio compendiosa's* final thirteen lines include the printed version's *explicit* and corrector's own account of his achievement:

> Finis cuius semper Deo gratias agamus sicut sui ordinis celsitudo et ipsius beneficii multitudo meretur cuius misericordie super omnes fideles existunt.
>
> Explicit compendiosa declaratio Alpharabii [tabulata et correcta unaa cum rethorica et poetria sequentibus Aristotilis per nobilem virum et excellentissimum artium et medicine doctorem d. magistrum Lancillotum de Zerlis physicum veronensem magna cum difficultate propter penuriam exemplaris unius tantum et stilum veterem in modernum reductum]. (For the words in brackets the 1515 edition substitutes: *novissime a viro docto optime recognita, cunctisque erroribus castigata. Finis.*)

As the comparison reveals, the printed editions contain a conflated excerpt from the manuscript. The commentary's analysis of the major divisions of the *Rhetoric* has been interwoven with the breakdown into minor segments, *ad formam tamen clariorem et tabule reducta*. Despite his claim, the corrector has made few concessions to comprehensibility in his *pastiche*: he begins with the intention of discussing the *partes minores* and, in the end, says he has enumerated the *partes magne*; also, his farraginous statement at 1ra24-25, *Iam autem diximus quod liber igitur iste in tres libros dividitur*, is, without an antecedent, no more defensible logically than it is syntactically. In some instances, however, the printed version, although freely paraphrased, does afford a better reading than the manuscript, as, for example, at 9ra 14-20:

> Capitulum secundum et ultimum est in quo fit sermo in maneriebus enthimematum qualiter resistitur unicuique ipsarum. Declarat ergo quoniam quibusdam resistitur per instantiam tantum et quibus-

dam non per instantiam sed ostendendo quoniam non sunt necessarie. Et istud est postremum eius quod dicitur in secundo libro.

The corresponding passage in the manuscript is found on folio 196rb as follows:

Pars secunda est sermo in manieriebus enthimematum qualiter resistitur unicuique ipsorum. Declarat ergo quoniam quibusdam resistitur per instanciam tantum et quibus non per instanciam sed ostendendo quoniam non sunt necessarie. [Declarat itaque] [resistitur per instanciam et quibus] [resistitur] [ostendendo quoniam non sunt necessarie.] Et istud est postremum eius quod dicitur in tractatu secundo secundi libri.

In summary, the original Hermannus used was a commentary, attributed to Alfarabi, that included first, an introductory consideration of the nature of rhetoric and a formal analysis of the major and minor divisions of the *Rhetoric*, and second, an alternation of Aristotle's text and Alfarabi's expositions. Hermannus's translation, as preserved in the manuscript, seems to extend just beyond the end of the introduction. A conflated tabulation, sometimes superior in its readings, of the introduction's formal analysis (that is, folios 193ra-196rb of the manuscript) was printed in 1481 and again in 1515 under the title *Declaratio compendiosa per viam divisionis Alfarabii super libris rethoricorum Aristotilis*. Nothing in either the manuscript or the printed version suggests more than one translation of any Alfarabi commentary. That other evidence supports this observation and broadens our knowledge of the commentary and Hermannus's handling of it, will become clear through an investigation of the "Averroes" translation.

II. "AVERROES"

The three manuscripts that contain the "Averroes" translation are:

1. *AL* 706: Cod. Paris., BIBL. NATIONALIS, lat. 16673. Averroes in Rethoricam, *cum Translatoris Prologo*, fols. 65r-147r.[12]

---

[12] AL 1.581: "Saec. xiii, membran., mm. 215 x 145 ,ff. 172, binis columnis. Codex a duobus librariis, ff. 1-61 manu subflava, ff. 65-172 rotundula nigra exaratus. Textus Rethoricae Veteris multis locis deficit, sicut in codice Toletano; defectus tamen erat in exemplari, quia corrector opus castigavit. Tituli nulli in summis paginis. Litterae initiales rubrae aut caeruleae, lineis implicatis alterius coloris ornatae. Emendationes nullae; glossae paucae in secunda parte tantum; f. 172v: '*Explicit Deo gratias anno Domini millesimo ducentesimo quinquagesimo sexto, septimo decimo die Marcii, apud Toletum, urbem nobilem.*' Hic agitur de translatione, non de transcriptione Averrois in Poeticam. Nomen donatoris deest. Codex olim de Sorbona, 1779."

2. *AL* 1234: Cod. Toletanus, BIBL. CAPITULI, 47.15. Averroes in Rethoricam, fols. 36r-53r.[13]

3. *AL* 1343: Cod. Florentinus, BIBL. LAURENT., Gadd., Plut. LXXXX
Sup. 64. Averroes in Rethoricam, fols. 105r-106v (*Sunt excerpta quaedam*;
*titulus est: "Averois. In prohemio rhethoricorum. Ambe enim intendunt unum
finem . . ." ut in Arist. Lat. I, p. 212, lin. 5 . . . ; expl.: "malum inferre ini-
micis et bonum conferre amicis de rebus valde utilibus reputamus."*[14]

The translator's prologue, published first by Jourdain and most recently
by Lacombe, appears below as Appendix 2. After a brief review of previous
opinions about the translation, I shall proceed to my own analysis.

Jourdain and Renan, as we indicated above, referred to the contents of
the Paris manuscript as the "glosses" of Alfarabi, that is, the basis for Hermannus's "*Didascalion*."[15] For Wüstenfeld, the same manuscript was simply
a translation of the *Rhetoric*.[16] Nagy's study of the *Declaratio compendiosa*
made the William of Moerbeke Greco-Latin version of the *Rhetoric* in the
1481 and 1515 printings Hermannus's translation from Hebrew of an Arabic
version of a Syriac translation of the Greek *Rhetoric*.[17] The occurrences of
the name "Averroes" in the Paris manuscript led Luquet to refute Renan.
To Luquet, the translation seemed, albeit conjecturally, rather that of a

[13] AL 1.853-854: "Saec. xiii, membran., mm. 575 x 410, ff. 160 + II. Codex tribus columnis duabus manibus [fols 1-146v; 147-160] satis clare exaratus; litteras initiales nonnul-
las cum personis, in campo quadrato quem turres et arcus in modum castelli coronant (i,
8, 11v, 13v, 55) aut rubras et caeruleas, in principio voluminis tantum exhibet; deinde spa-
tia earum vacua relicta. Neque tituli in summis paginis neque glossae. Foliorum pars
superior humore pessumdata. Textus lacunas et errores multa praebent. In antefolio:
'*do tenie la crus el arçobispo Matheos ferrandes.*'"

[14] AL 1. 925-926: " Saec. xv chart., mm. 280 x 210, ff. ABCDE + 106 scriptura carent
ff. ABCDE), a duobus librariis elegantissime exaratus. In marginibus et in interlineis re-
centior (eiusdem tamen saec. xv) manus scholia et notulas descripsit. Pars prior codicis
praebet Aristotelis Rethoricam ex translatione Georgii Trapezuntii (ff. 1r-97r: *Traductio
Georgii Trapezuntii in Rethorica Aristotelis Stagiritae ad Theodecten. Liber primus.* . .)
ac eorundem librorum *summaria* (ff. 97r-104v). De codice cfr. BANDINI, *Cat.* III, 644-
645."

[15] Jourdain (n. 1 above) 138. On 139-141, however, he prints the prologue under the
title *Aristotelis Rhetorica: Prologus*. Renan (n. 2 above).

[16] Wüstenfeld (n. 3 above) 92-93.

[17] Nagy (n. 5 above) 690-691: "Della versione latina della retorica c'è poco da dire. Se
si prestasse fede alla chiusa essa sarebbe 'a graeco in latinum translata.' Ma gl'indizî ca-
ratteristici delle versioni medievali, nelle quali il termine latino è calcato sopra il termine
originale e le storpiature dei nomi proprî greci, ci attestano che abbiamo dinanzi una delle
tante versioni latine (di traduzioni ebraiche) di versioni arabe di una traduzione siriaca
d'un testo greco, e senza tema d'andar errati, possiamo asserire essere quella già citata
di Hermannus Alemannus, il quale dopo avere tradotto la retorica d'Aristotele e la *Declaratio* di al-Fārābī, v'aggiunse la parafrasi alla poetica d'Averroè. Queste tre opere così
raggrupate nella metà del XIII secolo, corsero insieme manoscritte finchè, come vedemmo,
nel 1481 furono stampate a Venezia 'correctore Domino Lancillotto de Zerlis."

lost work of Averroes in which he challenged Alfarabi's opinions on logic.[18]
Steinschneider, with express uncertainty, referred to Hermannus's original
as Averroes's *Middle Commentary* on the *Rhetoric*.[19] In 1916, Grabmann
dismissed Luquet's evidence, but adopted his conjecture.[20] Twenty-three
years later, Lacombe attempted to clear the air with a fuller, more nearly
accurate description:

> De hac versione ab Hermanno Alemanno († 1272) facta, meliore
> fortasse iure iam superius disserere debuimus, ubi de operibus ip-
> sius Aristotelis in latinum translatis disputavimus; cum tamen com-
> munis opinio sit Hermannum non Aristotelis Rhetoricam, sed po-
> tius tractatum quendam vertisse, in quo Averroes Aristotelis opus

---

[18] Luquet (n. 6 above) 411: "La traduction d'Hermann relative à la *Rhétorique* commence
ainsi: *Rhetorica quidem convertitur arti topicae et utraeque sunt unius rei gratia et communicant in aliquo modorum. . .* et finit: *Et penes vos remanet iudicandi potestas. Ergo digne-
mini iudicare. Explicit rhetorica Aristotelis.*

"Le texte que traduit ici Hermann n'est pas, comme il semble le croire, l'ouvrage même
d'Aristote; ce n'est pas davantage, comme on l'a dit jusqu'ici, le commentaire d'Alfarabi,
car ce texte donne sans cesse la parole à Averroès, qui est de plusieurs siècles postérieur
à Alfarabi; et ce n'est pas davantage le commentaire d'Averroès qui est joint au texte d'Aristote dans les éditions. Ce serait peut-être—mais ceci n'est qu'une pure conjecture—l'ouvrage
perdu d'Averroès que Renan désigne ainsi: *Exposé des opinions d'Alfarabi dans son traité
de Logique et de celles d'Aristote sur le même sujet, avec un jugement sur leurs opinions.*"

[19] M. Steinschneider, "Die europäischen Übersetzungen aus dem Arabischen bis Mitte
des 17. Jahrhunderts," *Sitzungsberichte der philosophisch-historischen Klasse der kaiserlichen
Akademie der Wissenschaften*, Wien 149.4 (1904 repr. Graz 1956) 33: "a) *Averroes* mittl.
Comm. zur Rhetorik (?) und Poetik des Aristoteles (1256), ed. 1481 und 1515 (s. Lasinio
Vorr. zur Poetik des Averroes, p. VII); die Vorbem. zur Poetik s. bei Jourdain p. 155 und
W. 93."

[20] M. Grabmann, *Forschungen über die lateinischen Aristotelesübersetzungen des XIII.
Jahrhunderts*, in Beiträge zur Geschichte der Philosophie des Mittelalters, Texte und Untersuchungen, 17.5-6 (Münster 1916) 242: "Von der aristotelischen Rhetorik besitzen wir
keine Übersetzung aus dem Arabischen ins Lateinische. Wohl ist eine Übertragung der
Aristotelis Rhetorica durch Hermannus Alemannus uns erhalten. Wir haben früher aus
dem Prologus dieser Übersetzung Erkenntnis über die eigene Ethikübersetzung des Hermannus und über die Ehtikübertragung des Robert Grosseteste schöpfen können. In-
dessen handelt es sich hier viel weniger um eine Übersetzung des aristotelischen Textes,
als dies bei der 1240 von Hermannus Alemannus angefertigten Ethikversion der Fall ist.
Bei letzterer ist doch der Hauptsache nach immer der aristotelische Text geboten in der
Regel mit der Einführung: Dixit Aristoteles, wenn es sich auch um eine Paraphrase des
Averroes handelt. Hingegen ist die Rhetorica Aristotelis, welche Hermannus Alemannus
übersetzt hat, nicht der aristotelische Text, auch nicht der Kommentar des Alfarabi, auch nicht
der Rhetorikkommentar des Averroes, sondern vielleicht ein verlorenes Werk des Averroes,
von dem Renan redet. In dieser Weise beurteilt wenigstens Lucquet (*sic*) diese Rhetorik-
übersetzung des Hermannus Alemannus. Der an den Prologus sich anschliessende Text
dieser Rhetorica hat das Initium: 'Rhetorica quidem convertitur arti tropicae (*sic*) et utraeque sunt unius rei gratia et communicant in aliquo modorum.'"

et Alpharabii "glossam" exposuerat, hic locus est, quo hic error radicitus evellatur.

Erroris auctor est G. H. Luquet, vir alioquin de vita operibusque Hermanni Alemanni recensendis non immeritus. Verba eius hic referre inutile nobis visum est, quia eundem codicem Parisinum (lat. 16673) prae manibus habemus, quo Luquet usus est. Sciat ergo lector versionem de qua agitur textum Rhetoricae Aristotelis quasi integrum praebere interpretemque adeo diligentem fuisse, ut complura exemplaria (arabica) laudati operis inter se contulerit. Nihilominus accidit ei quod hic vel illic "sententiam plane intelligibilem ex eis elicere non potuerit" (cod. laud. f. 77r). Coactus igitur est alia insuper versionis subsidia adhibere, videlicet librum Asschiphe ab Avicenna editum ac commentaria quae in Aristotelis librum Alpharabius et Averroes scripserant. Avicennae quidem paraphrasim nonnullis locis textui Aristotelis substituit; ex Alpharabio lectiones tantum varias petiisse videtur. Ex Averrois "determinativa expositione" (quam in prologo et sub finem versionis suae laudat) principium tantummodo transtulit et textui Aristotelis adiunxit (cod. laud. f. 65r-75r).[21]

Most recently, Millás Vallicrosa has described the Toledo manuscript as Averroes's *Middle Commentary* on the *Rhetoric*, observing, however, that folios 49rc-49vc contain a passage of Avicenna.[22] Apart from the translator's prologue, the evidence hitherto considered is primarily internal: Hermannus's own remarks within the text and the names of Aristotle and his Arabic commentators as they appear in the manuscripts. My procedure is to compare Hermannus's interpretation against the commentaries of Averroes and Avicenna, and against the *Rhetoric* itself. The beginning of the translation, published in *Aristoteles latinus*,[23] illustrates my approach and its results.

The first three sentences after the translator's prologue are:

Rethorica quidem convertitur arti topice et utreque sunt unius rei gratia et communicant in aliquo modorum et invenitur utrarumque noticia omnibus. Cum neutra ipsarum sit aliqua scientiarum separatim sive singulariter. Et hinc est quod omnes scientie inveniuntur communicare eis in modo.

These sentences are found neither in Averroes's *Middle Commentary* nor in Avicenna's *kitābu 'š-šifā'i*. There is no claim, in fact, that they are. The

[21] AL 1.102-103.

[22] J. Millás Vallicrosa, *Las Traducciones Orientales en los Manuscritos de la Biblioteca Catedral de Toledo* (Madrid 1942) 55-58. The author's statement about the *Rhetoric*, viz., "La traducción de Hermann acompañaba a las primeras ediciones (1481 y 1515) de la obra, comentada, de Aristóteles" (56 n. 3), has, unfortunately, no basis in fact.

[23] AL 1.212.

opening of the text is rather a translation from the Arabic of the same portion of the *Rhetoric* (1354a1-4) cited by Alfarabi at the beginning of the second part of his commentary. The name *Avenrosd* (*Aristoteles latinus* prints *Averrosd*) occurs next in both the Paris and Toledo manuscripts, immediately preceding a series of eight sentences drawn almost *verbatim* from Averroes's *Middle Commentary* on the *Rhetoric*:[24]

1. a. Ambe enim intendunt unum finem et est sermo ad alterum
   b. 1.1-1.2: wa-ḏālika anna kilaihimā yu'māni [*sic*; tu'matāni?] ġāyatan wāḥidatan wa-hiya muḵāṭabatu 'l-ġairi.
2. a. Non enim utitur eis homo ad se ipsum ut est in demonstrativis, sed tantum ad alterum
   b. 1.3-1.5: laisa yastaʿmiluhumā 'l-insānu bainahu wa-baina nafsihi ka-l-ḥāli fī ṣināʿati 'l-burhāni, bal innamā yastaʿmiluhumā maʿa 'l-ġairi.
3. a. Et conveniunt quodam modo in subiecto uno.
   b. 1.5: wa-taštarikāni bi-naḥwi min al-anḥā'i fī mauḍūʿin wāḥidi.
4. a. Ambiunt enim omnia.
   b. 1.5-1.7: iḏ kāna kullāhumā yataʿāṭā an-naẓara fī jamīʿi 'l-ašyā'i wa-yūjadu 'istiʿmāluhumā muštarakān li-l-jamīʿi.[25]
5. a. Et omnes homines intromittunt se naturaliter de sermonibus thopicis et rethoricis.
   b. 1.7-1.8: aʿnī anna kulla wāḥidin min an-nāsi yastaʿmilu bi-ṭ-ṭabʿi 'l-aqāwīla 'l-jadalīyata wa-l-aqāwīla 'l-ḵuṭbīyata.
6. a. Neutra ergo harum est separatim et singularis scientia.
   b. 1.8-1.9: wa-innamā kāna ḏālika ka-ḏālika li-annahu laisat wāḥidatun minhumā ʿilmān mina'l-ʿulūmi mufradān bi-ḏātihi.
7. a. Quelibet enim scientia certum et proprium habet subiectum et proprium artificem.
   b. 2.1-2.2: wa-ḏālika anna 'l-ʿulūma lahā mauḍūʿātun ḵāṣṣatun wa-yastaʿmiluhumā aṣnāfun min an-nāsi ḵāṣṣatun.
8. a. Et quilibet hominum modo aliquo et usquoque [MSS: usquequo] utitur rethoricalibus, accusatione videlicet et defensione et ceteris que circa particularia existunt.

---

[24] The numbers preceding each Arabic passage are references to page and line in F. Lasinio, *Il Commento medio di Averroe alla Retorica di Aristotele*, Pubblicazioni del R. Istituto di studî superiori in Firenze, sezione di filosofia e filologia, Accademia orientale (Florence 1877). Lasinio's text, containing only 96 pages, is, however, not complete. For the full commentary, see A. Badawī (ed.), *Ibn Rušd: Talḵīṣu ʿl-Kitābati* (Cairo 1960) and, in Ṭōḏrōṣ Ṭōḏrōṣī's Hebrew translation, *Averrois Commentarius in Aristotelis de Arte Rhetorica Libros Tres*, ed. J. Goldenthal (Leipzig 1842).

[25] The Latin sentence is a translation of only one of the two Arabic sentences. A closer investigation of Hermannus's verbatim technique may uncover parallel examples of *ambio* and its Arabic equivalent or, conversely, occurrences of the Arabic verbs found here and Hermannus's usual Latin rendering of them.

b. 1. 2.6-2.7: wa-kullu wāḥidin min an-nāsi yūjadu musta'mi-
lān li-naḥwin mā min anḥā'i 'l-balāġati . . .
2. 2.10-2.11: wa-hiya miṯlu 'š-šikāyati wa-l-i'tiḏāri wa-sā'iri
'l-aqāwīli 'llatī fī 'l-umūri 'l-juz'īyati.

The phrase immediately following, *Aristotiles in sermone de liberatione et
commendatione* should probably read *de deliberatione* and should have, like
Lacombe's *Averrosd*, appeared in italics. This phrase announces the end
of Averroes's comments and the resumption of the Aristotelian text at 1354a4:

Omnes igitur homines modo aliquo et usquoque [MSS: usquequo]
utuntur et accusatione et recusatione et aliqualiter attingunt quod
intendunt. Quidam ergo vulgarium faciunt hec inperspecte. Alii
vero ex assuetudine et habitu stabilito. Cumque sit possibile fieri hoc
utroque istorum modorum, scitum est quoniam modus hic, scilicet
secundus, melior est et rectior, ideo proficiunt qui faciunt hec ex
assuetudine magis proficiunt et qui potentes perspicere causam in
hoc per se ipsos et communiter conceditur istud esse ex opere artis
et pericia ipsius.

Although the section printed in *Aristoteles latinus* stops at 1354a10-11: . . .
τὸ δὲ τοιοῦτον ἤδη πάντες ἂν ὁμολογήσαιεν τέχνης ἔργον εἶναι, the Aristotelian *Rhetoric*, instead of an Arabic commentary, continues, except where
interruptions are indicated in the manuscripts.

The most frequent interruptive device is the name *Avenrosd*. In addition
to the occurrence noted above, the name or its abbreviation appears twelve
times, always introducing one or two sections of the *Middle Commentary*
appended to lengthy passages from the *Rhetoric*, as follows:[26]

1. 66vb (36rc) Avenro. (after 1354a4-54b22) precedes :
a. 1. 66vb Et quoniam nos—66vb de hac arte.
2. 6.12 innā naḥnu—7.2 min al-kitābati.
b. 1. 67ra Habere autem usum—67ra illaudabile est.
2. 7.5 wa-sti'mālu—7.7 fi'lun kasīsun.
2. 67rb (36va) Avenro. (1354b22-55a20):
a. 1. 67rb Et non—67va essentiale rei.
2. 10.10 min ġairi 'an—10.11 'amūdu 'l-balāġati.
b. 1. 67va Et si—67va recta et iusta.
2. 10.14 wa-in kāna qad—10.16 aṣ-ṣawābi wa-l-'adli.[27]

---

[26] In the following examples, the folio numbers refer to the Paris manuscript and, in
parentheses, to the Toledo manuscript. Except where noted, the same passages appear
in the Florence manuscript. The Arabic references are, as above, drawn from Lasinio (n.
24 above).

[27] In the Paris and Florence manuscripts, this passage is followed by an alternate reading: 67va mg, *In alio* [F: *uno*] *exemplari. ut dicant* [F: *dicunt*] *dictionem secundum viam iusti
tantum.*

3. 67va (36va) Avenro. (1355a21-55a24):
   a. 67va Rethorica duas—67va operibus iusticie.
   b. 10.17 wa-l-ḳiṭābatu—10.20 al-afʿāli ’l-ʿādilati.[28]

4. 67vb (36va) Avenro. (1355a24-55a30):
   a. 67vb Peccasse ipsum—67vb modo illud.
   b. 11.18 annahu—12.1 fī waqtin.

5. 72rb (37va) Avenrosd. (1355a30-57a2; 57a3-59a1; 59a2-59b12):[29]
   a. 72rb Res que existunt—72va his assimulantur.
   b. 38.15 wa-l-ašyā’u—39.7 as-sūfisṭāniyati.

6. 72vb (37va) Avenrosd. (1359b12-59b28):
   a. 72vb Et si—72vb consumit.
   b. 40.10 wa-in kāna—40.12 minhu.

7. 75rbmg [Paris MS only] Avenr.:
   a. a potenti[a] sanitatis.
   b. 53.21 ǧaira qūwati ’ṣ-ṣiḥḥati.

8. 75rbmg [Paris MS only] Avenr.:
   a. Et [du]bitatur qualiter stet vi[te] longitudo cum egrit[u]dine
      frequenti.
   b. 53.20 wa-qad yušakku—amrāḍin.

9. 75rb (38ra) Avenrosd. (1359b28-61b39):
   a. 75rb Bona autem fortune—75va periculosa egritudine.
   b. 54.8 wa-ammā—54.16 maraḍun kāna bihi.

10. 75vb (38rb) Avenro. (1361b39-62a17):
    a. 75vb Virtutis [T: Virtutes] enim circa—75vb propter que fiunt
       inhibitiones.
    b. 55.10 wa-ammā—55.17 al-mušīru.

11. 76rb (38rc) Avenros. (1362a17-62b2):
    a. 76rb Bona que—76rb ad bonum.
    b. 57.18 wa-l-ḳairātu—58.3 ḳairun.

12. 76rb (38rc) Avenr. (1362b2-62b10):
    a. 76rb Et quoniam etiam proficiunt ad bonum interdum.
    b. 58.10-11 wa-annahā qad takūnu nāfiʿatan fī ’l-ḳairi.

In sum, up to folio 76rb of the Paris manuscript (38rc of the Toledo manuscript), Hermannus has translated primarily Aristotle's *Rhetoric*, interspersed with quotations, none more than a few lines long, from Averroes's *Middle Commentary*. More of the *Rhetoric*, as well as the longest Averroes passage, hitherto hidden by scribal error, will be revealed through an analysis of another interruptive device, the translator's own remarks.

---

[28] In the Paris and Toledo manuscripts, this selection is followed by an alternate translation: "Inquit interpres. idem. Veritates rerum operandarum pertinentium iusticie sequende sunt et respuende falsitates desideriorum illicitorum. Et ad has veritates conatur rethorica et ad redargutiones et increpationes [P add: et redargutiones et increpationes] propter opposita."

[29] Aristotle's rext is twice interrupted by variant readings, as noted below (pp. 244-245).

In the present text, Hermannus defends omissions from his original, signals substitutions for Aristotle and offers explanations for problems in translation. Accordingly, the Paris and Toledo manuscripts announce, in four places, omissions corresponding to 1375b33-76a8, 1410a9-10a20, 1411a4-11b10, and 1417a13-17a16.[30] In like manner, a significant substitution for 1405a31-07a18 is heralded on folio 128ra (49rc):

> Inquit translator. In hoc passu tot inciderunt exempla extranea et grata vocabula quod nullum nobis consilium fuit prosequendi textum Aristotilis. Unde coacti fuimus [P: fuerimus] sequi illud quod Avicenna [T: Aviscenna] de hoc passu excerpserat et posuerat in libro suo Aschiphe.[31]

Here Hermannus has translated that section of Avicenna's *Kitābu 'š-šifā'i* found in S. Salem's edition,[32] page 206 line 8 to page 212 line 11, and has, moreover, inserted an explanation of difficult terminology (fol. 129ra, b; 49va):

> Usus loquendi arabicus est appellare dictiones frigidas [T: factas] has quarum hic positio subdivisio. Et possunt, ut estimo, in latino dictiones abusive non incongrue nuncupari [T: nuncupare].

By far the most important comment, however, is that on folio 77ra (38va):

> Dixit translator. In hoc passu invenimus textum Aristotilis vel ita corruptum vel decurtatum vel forte in se obscurum quod sententiam [T: sentiam] plane intelligibilem ex eo elicere non potuimus. Unde visum fuit verbum ex verbo transferre et post ipsum ad eius

---

[30] a. 92vb (41vc): "Dixit translator. Circa [T: Contra] hunc locum plures scribebantur [P: scribentes] testes et exempla suorum testimoniorum que propter errorem antiquum scriptorum ita confusa fuerunt in omnibus exemplaribus quod non poterat haberi consilium ad ea transferendum. Ideoque fuerunt relicta."

b. 134va (50vb): "(Pmg add: Sermo translatoris) Plura talia exempla ad idem facientia quia grecam sapiebant sententiam [T: scientiam] non multum usitatam latinis dimissa fuerunt [P: sunt] et subsequitur quasi conclusio auctoris."

c. 135vab (51ra): "Inquit translator. Hic plura exempla dicte rationis confirmativa dimisit Ibiniscena in suo Aschiphe et Avemrosd in sua determinativa expositione huius libri quia penitus grecam sententiam protendebant nec videbatur eis quam magnam [T om.: magnam] habebant utilitatem in arabico eloquio. Hac quoque de causa ego dimisi ipsa. Qui autem magnum habebant adiutorium per ipsa volentes in latino via procedere rethoricandi?"

d. 143ra (52va): "Et inducat probationem ad hoc [Pmg add: Exemplum notum in greco] quemadmodum processit talis in causa quam habuit contra talem."

[31] Previously quoted by Millás Vallicrosa (n. 22 above) 57.

[32] M. Selim Salem (ed.), *Ibn Sīnā. aš-Šifā'u. al-Manṭiq, ṭamāniyatu, al-Ḵaṭābatu* (Cairo 1954).

elucidationem textum Aviscenne ex libro suo Asschiphe subiungere
usque ad finem capituli.

There follows in the Paris manuscript Hermannus's version of 1363a17-63b4,
succeeded in turn (77va-78va) by a rendering of Avicenna (*Kitābu 's̆-s̆ifā'i*
73.7-75.14).[33] A long marginal passage beginning at the translator's remarks
on folio 77ra of the Paris manuscript and, in the Toledo manuscript (38va),
intervening, with the scribe's apology, *Istud est commentum et debebat esse
in margine, set non potuit*, between Hermannus's words and the text of Aristotle, is, in both manuscripts, falsely ascribed to Avicenna. This passage is,
in fact, a translation of Averroes's *Middle Commentary* (62.8-63.3). Our text
thus furnishes three versions here: Aristotle, Avicenna, and Averroes. A
scribal error in an exemplar from which both the Paris and Toledo manuscripts
derive has obscured the final Averroes citation. The Florence manuscript,
however, which contains only those excerpts from the translation credited
to Averroes, that is, generally those listed above, ends with this portion.
Hermannus attempted scrupulously, therefore, to translate Aristotle's *Rhetoric*. Where he could not, he said so. Where he was compelled to substitute
something else, he admitted the substitution and identified its author.

The manuscripts provide still another category of evidence for Hermannus's
rhetorical translations. On folio 69va, the Paris manuscript has *Alfarabius.
idest ordinem artificialem logices*, with the last three words underlined. The
Toledo manuscript (fol. 36vc) has merely *Alpharabius*. The preceding words,
Etenim eius operatio [T: *comparatio*] *fit in eo quod est ut hoc* (P: *hic*) *ex sermone, idest in eo in quo intenditur non esse artem*, correspond to 1357a1-2,
Ἔστιν δὲ τὸ ἔργον αὐτῆς περί τε τοιούτων περὶ ὧν βουλευόμεθα καὶ τέχ-
νας μὴ ἔχομεν. The phrase immediately following, *et in isto modo audi-
torum, idest qui non valent percipere res ab ordinibus pluribus et non faciunt
sillogismum ex longinquo*, represents 1357a3-4, καὶ ἐν τοῖς τοιούτοις ἀκροα-
ταῖς οἳ οὐ δύνανται διὰ πολλῶν συνορᾶν οὐδὲ λογίζεσθαι πόρρωθεν. The i-
solated words *ordinem artificialem logices* are not found in either the *Middle
Commentary* or the *Kitābu 's̆-s̆ifā'i*; Hermannus, furthermore, uses the Greek
genitive, as in *logices*, in his Alfarabi translation (see above at note 11) exclusively; and, finally, Alfarabi's detailed analysis of the *Rhetoric* would
have placed this passage in the sixth and final section (1356b28-58a35) of
Book A's second chapter. We may not unreasonably suggest, therefore,

---

[33] Hermannus also explains difficult terminology in this selection, fol. 78ra (38vb): "Causa huius diversi intellectus fuit quod [T om.: quod] per eosdem karacteres in arabico scri-
bitur debilitas et duplicitas." Translating the terms *ḍuʿfun* or *ḍaʿfun* (weakness, feebleness,
frailty; from the verb *daʿufa*) and *ḍiʿfun* (double, that which is twice as much; from the
verb *ḍaʿʿafa*) with Latin equivalents having approximately the same consonantal pattern,
debilitas and *duplicitas*, is a felicitous achievement worthy of an Arabist with better cre-
dentials than Hermannus ordinarily enjoys.

that this reading is drawn from Alfarabi's quotation of Aristotle or his own exposition in the second half of the same commentary that Hermannus's translation has partially preserved. The same conjecture may also explain folio 88vb (41ra), *Alfarabius. vel in non reddendo vel in* [P add.: *non*] *auferendo* (1372b7); folio 100ra (43rc), *In alio. ipsos amicos esse aut inimicos* (underlined in both manuscripts; 1382a16); folio 71va,b (37rc), *In alio exemplari arabico ita habebatur. Verum ipsi non determinant nisi res per quas fit laus, et sunt virtutes, sive sit hoc dampnosum sive utile, et hoc est factum ipsorum ut plurimum. Sed ipsi quidem conficiunt ea per que fit laus ut plurimum* (1358b37-59a2); and 67rb mg(Paris manuscript only), *probatio quod rethorica sit pars logices* (1355a3), which approximates the "gloss'" (fol. 193vb) *hoc quod hic posuit pars est scientie logices* and the 1481 edition's (1va35-36) *hec quam hic posuit pars est scientie loice.* On folio 94ra (42rb), however, *Alfarabius iurans* (1377a8) and *hoc dimisit Alpharabius* (1377a17) are apparently examples of oaths, inasmuch as both phrases fit neatly into their context and both, including the names, are underlined in each manuscript. Perhaps the most interesting and informative item in this category, however, is a marginal note peculiar to the Paris manuscript 133vb (1409a24): *Huc pervenit glosa Alfarabii.*

We may now, with the aid of the translator's prologues, recapitulate the conclusions provided by the evidence for Hermannus's rhetorical translations.

1. The Alfarabi commentary Hermannus knew consisted of two parts: an introduction described internally as a "gloss" or *didascalion*; and a series of quotations from the *Rhetoric* alternating with Alfarabi's own expositions. That the second part of the commentary did not reach the end of the *Rhetoric* is seen in the Paris *Rhetoric*'s marginal note, *Huc pervenit glosa Alfarabii*, and the translator's remark in his prologue to the *Rhetoric*:

> Ita quod Alfarabius qui primus conatus est ex rethorica aliquem intellectum glosando elicere, multa exempla greca propter ipsorum obscuritatem pertransiens derelinquit. Et propter eandem causam multa dubie exposuit; et ut Avicenna et Avenrosd estimant propter hanc etiam causam glosam usque ad finem negocii non perduxit.

2. Hermannus, furthermore, did not translate all of the Alfarabi commentary he had before him. The demonstrably truncated Latin manuscript and the otherwise superfluous variant readings attributed to Alfarabi in the *Rhetoric* are confirmed by Hermannus's own words in the prologue of the "gloss,"

> visum est michi Hermanno Alamanno transferre inde glose Alpharabii in quantum introducitur in librum rethorice Aristotilis;

and in the prologue of the *Rhetoric*,

> Laborem vero distinguendi tres tractatus libri huius principales in
> suas differentias maiores et illas maiores in suas subdistinctiones mi-
> nores quoad usque ad ultimas particulas perveniatur doctoribus de-
> relinquo. Omnia hec enim in glosa super hunc librum exquisite Al-
> farabius pertractavit. Cuius glose plus quam duos quinternos ego
> quoque transtuli in latinum.

3. As a corollary to the foregoing conclusions about the "gloss," the *Declaratio compendiosa* of 1481 and 1515 should no longer be considered a separate work, except insofar as the corrector, Lancillotus de Zerlis, paraphrased,
improved, or otherwise varied the text of the "gloss" in his conflated excerpt.

4. Hermannus translated Aristotle's *Rhetoric*, rather than a commentary
of Averroes. A comparison of his text against the Greek *Rhetoric* shows
only four omissions, none more than forty-one lines long and all unequivocally
admitted in the translator's remarks. His prologue to this translation, moreover, begins with the statement:

> Opus presentis translationis rethorice Aristotilis et eius poetrie ex
> arabico eloquio in latinum iam dudum intuitu venerabilis patris
> Johannis Burgensis episcopi et regis castelle cancellarii inceperam.
> Sed propter occurrentia inpedimenta usque nunc non potui consum-
> mare.

The prologue to the "gloss" also mentions the

> librum rethorice Aristotilis quem nuper transtuli ex arabico elo-
> quio in latinum.

There is, finally, negative evidence: he nowhere claims to be doing anything
but Aristotle's *Rhetoric*.

5. Hermannus also inserted, as far as 1363b4, explanatory selections from
Averroes's *Middle Commentary* and, from Avicenna's *Kitābu 'š-šifā'i*, an
elucidation of 1363a17-63b4 and a substitution for 1405a31-07a18. The comparison of these selections against the original Arabic confirms, with but
one exception owing to scribal error, the testimony of the commentators'
names in the manuscripts, and, in turn, finds support in Hermannus's prologue:

> Quemadmodum contingit in libro Nichomachie quem latini Ethicam
> Aristotelis appellant. Nam et hunc prout potui in latinum verti
> eloquium ex arabico. Et postmodum reverendus pater magister
> Robertus Grossicapitis sed subtilis intellectus Linkoniensis episcopus

ex primo fonte unde manaverat, greco videlicet, ipsum est completius interpretatus et grecorum commentis proprias annectens notulas commentatus. Sic, si totius scientie largitori placuerit, contingere poterit in his opusculis primordialiter a nobis, etsi debiliter, elaboratis, quod ipse patrare dignetur qui vivit et regnat eternaliter in perfecta trinitate. Amen.

The word *sic*, apparently unnoticed until now, unites Hermannus's description of Grosseteste's *Ethics* with his own present effort. He is, in effect, saying of Aristotle's *Rhetoric*: "Complete interpretatus et arabum commentis proprias annectens notulas commentatus sum." The evidence, in any case, is clear and consistent that this is precisely what he did.

III. THE DATE

Since the "gloss" and the *Rhetoric*, unlike Hermannus's other complete translations, are undated, modern scholars have either declined to speculate on when they were accomplished, proposed that they were done singly between 1243 and 1256, or proposed that they appeared with the *Poetics* in 1256.[34] Once more the translator's own words offer the resolution of the problem.

1. The prologue of the "gloss" treats the translation of the *Rhetoric* as a *fait accompli*: " . . . librum rethorice Aristotilis quem nuper transtuli ex arabico eloquio in latinum." That these words can only mean Aristotle's *Rhetoric* should by now be clear.

2. The prologue of the *Rhetoric* refers to the "gloss" as having been finished previously: "Cuius glose plus quam duos quinternos ego quoque transtuli in latinum." There is, likewise, no evidence for any other "gloss."

---

[34] No one gives a date for the "gloss." Only Salmon (n. 8 above) dates the *Declaratio compendiosa* to "about 1256."

For the *Rhetoric* and *Poetics* together, Jourdain (n. 1 above) 142, gives *septimo die martii*, 1256, but is not sure whether this date follows the common reckoning or refers to the Spanish era. Renan (n. 2 above) 212, dismisses the Spanish era and, following Jourdain rather than the manuscript, says 7 March 1256.

For the *Rhetoric* separately, Wüstenfeld (n. 3 above) 92; Steinschneider, "Die europäischen Übersetzungen" (n. 19 above) 33; and Millás Vallicrosa (n. 22 above) 56, offer, for unspecified reasons, 1256. In like manner, B. L. Ullman, "Hermann the German's translation of Aristotle's Poetics," *Estudis de llatı medieval i de filologia romànica dedicats a la memòria de Lluis Nicolau d'Olwer* 1 (Barcelona 1966) 43-48, says "about 1250."

Luquet (n. 6 above) 411-412, however, observed of the *Rhetoric*: "Nous ne savons pas au juste la date de cette traduction; toutefois Hermann nous apprend, dans le prologue de cette traduction, qu'elle lui coûta beaucoup de temps et de peines et qu'elle était totalement achevée quand, après un essai infructueux pour traduire la *Poétique* d'Aristote il se résigna à traduire le commentaire d'Averroès sur cet ouvrage." Similarly, neither Grabmann nor Lacombe date the *Rhetoric*.

3. Hermannus intended the "gloss" and the *Rhetoric* to be used together. Of the "gloss" he says in the prologue of the *Rhetoric*: "Ex hinc ergo memorata distinctio requiratur et libri marginibus ascribatur."

4. The *Rhetoric*, moreover, is linked closely to the *Poetics*. The prologue of the *Poetics* speaks of the *Rhetoric* as a completed translation and, in turn, the prologue of the *Rhetoric* has abundant references to the *Poetics* as a companion piece.[35]

5. The translation of all three works must, therefore, have antedated the composition of the prologues. The interdependent descriptions of the translations, in addition, argue for the simultaneous appearance of the three texts in a logical arrangement: the "gloss," which, in its prologue, introduces itself and the *Rhetoric*; the *Rhetoric*, which, in its prologue, refers to the "gloss" and looks forward to the *Poetics*; and, lastly, the *Poetics*, which, in its prologue, mentions itself and the *Rhetoric*, but not the "gloss." This arrangement finds partial support in manuscript AL 706, where the *Rhetoric* immediately precedes Hermannus's *Poetics*, and full, albeit qualified, support in the 1481 and 1515 editions, where de Zerlis's version of the "gloss" is followed by a translation of the *Rhetoric* (not, however, Hermannus's), and Hermannus's *Poetics*. If this arrangement was indeed the original order

---

[35] In the *Poetics*, Hermannus says: "Postquam cum non modico labore consummaveram translationem rethorice Aristotilis." See W. F. Boggess, *Averrois Cordubensis Commentarium medium in Aristotelis Poetriam*, diss. (Chapel Hill 1965) 1; *Dissertation Abstracts* 26 (1966) 3933.

In the *Rhetoric*, Hermannus mentions the *Poetics* throughout: "Opus presentis translationis rethorice et eius poetrie ... iam dudum ... inceperam. Sed propter occurrentia inpedimenta usque nunc non potui consummare. Suscipiant ergo ipsum [ipsum = opus presentis translationis rethorice et eius poetrie] latini ... ut sic habeant complementum logici negocii" (i. e. all the logical works, including the *Rhetoric* and the *Poetics*). "Quod autem hi duo libri logicales sint, nemo dubitat. ... Verumptamen dictorum virorum scripta non minimum utilia sunt ad opera presentia intelligendum." The references to Avicenna and Averroes, "Et isti ... sic inquiunt: hoc est quod intelligere et excipere potuimus de translatione que pervenit ad nos horum voluminum Aristotilis," come from their commentaries on the *Poetics* rather than the *Rhetoric*. "Ideoque usque hodie etiam apud arabes hi duo libri quasi neglecti sunt, et vix unum invenire potui qui mecum studendo in ipsis vellet diligentius laborare. ... Sane tamen ipsis consulo ut malint hos codices habere sic translatos," and, finally, "contingere poterit in his opusculis ... a nobis ... elaboratis."

Those who, relying on the pluperfect of *consummaveram* in the prologue of the *Poetics*, date the *Rhetoric* earlier than an incomplete attempt to translate the Aristotelian *Poetics* (for which attempt there is no evidence beyond the tense of *consummaveram*) must decide for themselves whether Hermannus's pluperfect outweighs all other considerations. Hermannus, despite whatever redeeming qualities he may have had as an honest translator, was admittedly not a paragon of stylistic precision.

Inasmuch as the career of Juan Domingues de Medina, bishop of Burgos and chancellor of Castile (for whom see Luquet, n. 6 above) can provide only a *terminus ante quem* for the beginning of Hermannus's project (*iam dudum ... inceperam*), there is no trustworthy evidence opposing the date chosen here for its completion.

of the three translations, Hermannus's date at the end of the *Poetics*, 17 March 1256, should apply to the "gloss" and the *Rhetoric* as well.

The answers to the problems, of date, number, and nature of Hermannus's rhetorical translations have, therefore, been available in his own words since the day he wrote them. After comparing what he did with what he said he was doing, it is difficult to see how he could have expressed himself with any greater clarity. Hermannus's prologues, however, like the words of Cassandra, seem somehow doomed to disbelief.

APPENDIX 1

HERMANNUS'S PROLOGUE TO THE "GLOSS" OF ALFARABI

(Codex Parisiensis, BIBLIOTHECAE NATIONALIS, latinus 16097 folium 188ra) Incipiunt didascalia in Rethoricam Aristotilis ex glossa Alpharabii. Capitulum primum prohemiale.

Quoniam omnis novitas et inusitata edicio suspicate difficultatis honorem indigent lectoribus ac pavorem, visum est michi Hermanno Alamanno transferre inde glose Alpharabii in quantum introducitur in librum rethorice Aristotilis quem nuper transtuli ex arabico eloquio in latinum. Et ea que doctrinalia sunt prelibat determinando quid est rethorica et in quo differt a facultate oratoria et quot sunt libri partes et quot in unaquaque partium tractatus et quot in unoquoque tractatuum capitalia continentur et cetera que ad modum introductorium spectare videntur. Hiis enim habitis familiarior erit via ingrediendi ad ipsum textum. Et si Dominus veri vite concisserit inducias et strepitus impedimentorum submoverit, ad totam gloriam fortassis exequentam finaliter me parabo et forte ad plurima alia que ad totius huius artis intelligentiam suffragantur.

APPENDIX 2

HERMANNUS'S PROLOGUE TO THE "RHETORIC"
(*Aristoteles latinus* 1.211)

Capitulum prohem[i]ale in elucidationem sequentis operis. Inquit Hermannus Alemannus.

Opus presentis translationis rethorice Aristotilis et eius poetrie ex arabico eloquio in latinum iam dudum intuitu venerabilis patris Johannis Burgensis episcopi et regis castelle cancellarii inceperam. Sed propter occurrentia impedimenta usque nunc non potui consummare. Suscipiant ergo ipsum latini precipui inter ceteras nationes secundum statum presentis temporis zelatores et cultores partis philosophie rationalis, ut estimo: ut sic habeant complementum logici negocii secundum Aristotelis intentionem. Quod autem hi duo libri logicales sint, nemo dubitat qui libros perspexerit arabum famosorum, Alfarabii videlicet et Avicenne et Avenrosdi et quorundam aliorum. Imo ex ipso textu manifestius hoc patebit. Neque excusabiles sunt, ut fortassis alicui videbitur, propter Marcii Tullii rethoricam et Oratii poetriam. Tullius namque rethoricam partem civilis scientie posuit et secundum hanc intuitionem eam potissime tractavit. Oratius vero poetriam prout pertinet ad gramaticam potius expedivit. Verumptamen dictorum virorum scripta non minimum utilia sunt ad opera presentia intelligendum. Nec miretur quisquam vel indignetur de difficultate vel quasi ruditate translatonis, nam multo difficilius et rudius ex greco in arabicum est translata. Ita quod Alfarabius qui primus conatus est ex rethorica aliquem intellectum glosando elicere, multa exempla greca propter ipsorum obscuritatem pertransiens derelinquit. Et propter eandem causam multa dubie exposuit; et ut Avicenna et Avenrosd estimant propter hanc etiam causam glosam usque ad finem negocii non perduxit. Et isti quoque duo viri in finibus tractatuum suorum, quos imitantes Aristotilem composuerunt, sic inquiunt. Hoc est quod intelligere et excipere potuimus de translatione que pervenit ad nos horum voluminum Aristotilis. Ideoque usque hodie etiam apud arabes hi duo libri quasi neglecti sunt, et vix unum invenire potui qui mecum studendo in ipsis vellet diligentius laborare. Veniam igitur concedant qui forsitan non immerito poterunt hunc meum laborem de imperfectione redarguere. Et si eis non placuerit quicquam fructus ex eo querere, possunt ipsum deserere redargutum. Sane tamen ipsis consulo ut malint hos codices habere sic translatos, quam penitus derelictos. Nichil enim pura privatione incultius, sed potest quoquomodo habitis per paulatina incrementa finis tandem desiderate perfectionis facilius impertiri. Quemadmodum contingit in libro Nichomachie quem latini Ethicam Aristotelis appellant. Nam et hunc prout potui in latinum verti eloquium ex arabico. Et postmodum reverendus pater magister Robertus Grossicapitis sed subtilis intellectus Linkoniensis episcopus ex primo fonte unde manaverat, greco videlicet, ipsum est completius interpretatus et grecorum commentis proprias annectens notulas commentatus. Sic, si totius scientie largitori placuerit, contingere poterit in his opusculis primordialiter a nobis, etsi debiliter, elaboratis, quod ipse patrare dignetur qui vivit et regnat eternaliter in perfecta trinitate. Amen.

Laborem vero distinguendi tres tractatus libri huius principales in suas differentias maiores et illas maiores in suas subdistinctiones minores quoad usque ad ultimas particulas perveniatur doctoribus derelinquo. Omnia hec enim in glosa super hunc librum exquisite Alfarabius pertractavit. Cuius glose plus quam duos quinternos ego quoque transtuli in latinum. Ex hinc ergo memorata distinctio requiratur et libri marginibus ascribatur.

Department of Classics
Brock University
Saint Catharines, Ontario, Canada

THEOPHRASTUS IN THE MIDDLE AGES

•

by Charles B. Schmitt

Of the Classical authors whose works have survived to the present time some
have exerted a more or less continuous influence on Western thought, while
others seem to have all but completely vanished from the scene during the
Middle Ages. In the first category might be placed Aristotle, Galen, Vergil,
and Cicero; in the second group are many Greek authors, for example, the
dramatists, or philosophical writers such as Sextus Empiricus or Plotinus.
Indeed, much work remains to be done to determine precisely the influence
of the various Classical authors and their individual works during the Middle
Ages. Thus far this has been done for only a few authors, so we do not yet
have a comprehensive picture of the distribution of ancient literature before
the Renaissance, nor do we know in detail the extent of its influence on medieval culture in its various manifestations.

Among the Greek authors whose importance in the Classical world is generally recognized, but who were all but unknown during the Western Middle
Ages, is Theophrastus of Eresos. Here is a figure who seems to substantiate
very well the most far-reaching claims of those scholars who argue that the
Renaissance is a genuine revival of ancient learning and marks a real break
with the Middle Ages. To the best of my knowledge, however, no one has
yet investigated in detail Theophrastus's *fortuna* during the Middle Ages
and Renaissance, nor have they looked into the matter of the distribution
of manuscripts and printed editions of his writings during the period that
divides Antiquity from the modern world. Consequently, in this study, I
would like to investigate in some detail just how much the Middle Ages knew
of Theophrastus and to what extent the medieval view of Theophrastus
is in conformity with ours. What we do, in fact, find is that direct knowledge
of the contribution of Theophrastus was very limited indeed during the
Middle Ages, and it was not until the fifteenth century that some of his more
important writings were recovered. The large majority of his works was

An earlier version of this paper was read before the Post-Graduate Group of the School
of English, the University of Leeds, on 28 January 1969. In addition to those mentioned
in the notes, I would like to thank Mr. Brian S. Donaghey for several helpful suggestions
in connection with its preparation.

never found by the humanists and apparently perished with the ancient world.

This paper is, in large measure, based upon the research of others, although I have been able to add a few bits of new information not generally known. It is hoped that this paper will, at least, bring together more information on Theophrastus's *fortuna* during the Middle Ages than is accessible in a single study.

The historical Theophrastus[1] lived a long life, circa 372 B.C. to 288 B.C., studied with both Plato and Aristotle, and upon the latter's death became both his literary executor and the head of the Peripatetic School. We know little about his life, but we do, at least, have a rather lengthy list of his works from Diogenes Laertius,[2] who names well over 200 separate items, totaling 232,808 lines. Of this, less than ten percent survives. Theophrastus wrote on a very wide range of topics and was considered an important and influential philosopher down to the end of Antiquity. Since a larger portion of his scientific writings have survived than any other group, today he is best known for those, especially the *De historia plantarum* and *De causis plantarum*, by far the most important botanical works extant from Antiquity. He, however, exerted a significant influence on ancient thought even in areas where today we have only the most meager collection of fragments, for example, physics, rhetoric, moral philosophy, and literary theory. From the point of view of pure literature, the most important and best known surviving work is the *Characters*. During the seventeenth and eighteenth centuries this work became one of the most influential and most widely imitated of all writings surviving from Antiquity, particularly in England and France.

We cannot, however, go into detail here with regard to the writings of Theophrastus themselves. Rather we should now turn to a consideration of their influence during the Middle Ages. As I have already mentioned, the works of Theophrastus continued to remain important until the end of Antiquity; they were still known to Latin writers such as Macrobius, Martianus Capella, and Boethius and to Greek writers such as Proclus, Ioannes Philoponus, Simplicius, Olympiodorus, and Priscianus Lydus. His influence di-

---

[1] On Theophrastus see especially O. Regenbogen, "Theophrastos," Pauly-Wissowa, *Real-Encyclopädie der classischen Altertumswissenschaft* Supp. 7 (1940) 1353-1562; E. Zeller and R. Mondolfo, *La filosofia dei Greci nel suo sviluppo storico* 2.6 (Florence 1966) 335-442. A more extensive bibliography is given in my forthcoming article on Theophrastus in the *Catalogus translationum et commentariorum* 2. The standard, but by no means adequate, edition of the works is *Theophrasti Eresii opera quae supersunt omnia*, ed. F. Wimmer (Leipzig 1854-1862). The same text was reprinted by the same editor with a Latin translation in a one-volume edition (Paris 1866). Further references will be to the latter edition.

[2] *De vita et moribus philosophorum* 5.2.36-57. For example, in Loeb Classical Library, ed. R. D. Hicks (London 1925) 1.482-509.

minished sharply, however, after the closing of the schools by Justinian and we find little trace of him during the early Middle Ages in the West.

A good deal of scientific knowledge, ultimately deriving from Theophrastus's writings, passed into the medieval world through Roman intermediaries, who drew upon or summarized his various works. Pliny the Elder's *Natural History*, for example, makes abundant use of several works, of which those on botany and on stones might be singled out for special mention.[3] Nor was Pliny the only writer to plunder the riches of Theophrastus's scientific works. A wide range of late ancient writers made use of Theophrastus and passed his scientific knowledge—in a qualitatively and quantitatively diminished form—on to the Middle Ages, but usually separating the information from the name of its originator. Therefore most medieval authors were not aware of the ultimate source of the information that they were using.

There was a certain continuity of the tradition in the Byzantine and Islamic world. Our general knowledge of many of the details of the intellectual history of the later Byzantine Empire make it difficult to generalize concerning the knowledge of Theophrastus and the influence of his writings to be found there, but we do know that there is some evidence of continuity of the Byzantine literary tradition with that of Antiquity. Stobaeus[4] and Photius[5] knew several Theophrastan works and, indeed, important fragments are preserved in their compilations; Ioannes Tzetzes[6] and Eustathius[7] still referred to the *Characters* in the twelfth century, at a time when there still seems to be no evidence of even knowledge of the work's existence in the

---

[3] For much information on the transmission of Theophrastus's scientific doctrine in Antiquity see P. Steinmetz, *Die Physik des Theophrastos von Eresos* (Bad Homburg 1964) and A. Colonna, "Per una edizione critica del De causis plantarum di Teofrasto," *Bulletino del Comitato per la preparazione della edizione nazionale dei classici greci e latini* N.S. 14 (1966) 1-12. On Theophrastus and Pliny specifically see J. André, "Erreurs de traduction chez Pline l'Ancien," *Revue des études latines* 37 (1959) 203-215; *idem*, "Notes critiques sur le texte de Pline l'Ancien," *Revue de philologie* 87 (1961) 48-66; and D. E. Eichholz, *Theophrastus, de lapidibus* (Oxford 1965) 14-15 and passim. For more detailed information see the bibliography in my forthcoming article (n. 1 above).

[4] For example *Characteres* 1-15 are contained *in toto* in Stobaeus's *Eclogae*.

[5] Fragments 10, 11, 172, 174, 175, 190 in Wimmer's edition are from Photius's *Bibliotheca*. They were first printed, before Photius's work was printed as a whole, in *Aristotelis et Theophrasti scripta quaedam, quae vel nunquam antea vel minus emendata quam nunc edita fuerunt*, ed. Henricus Stephanus (Paris 1557). Fragments 7, 8 and 9 are also preserved in Photius, but were known from an independent textual tradition in the fifteenth century.

[6] Ioannes Tzetzes, *Chiliades*, ed. Kiesslingius (Leipzig 1826, repr. Hildesheim 1963) *ad indicem*.

[7] See, for example, J. Kayser, "Theophrast und Eustathius $\Pi\varepsilon\varrho\grave{\iota}$ $\acute{\upsilon}\pi o\varkappa\varrho\acute{\iota}\sigma\varepsilon\omega\varsigma$" *Philologus* 69 (1910) 327-358.

West; and also in the twelfth century we know that several Theophrastan writings were known to Michael of Ephesus.[8]

Several writings, including at least part of the botanical works, the *Metaphysica*, and the *De sensu et sensibilibus*, were translated into Syriac, Arabic, or both, quite early, that is before the tenth century.[9] In addition, a meteorological work was translated and, indeed, survives, although in fragmentary form, in both Syriac and Arabic versions, despite the fact that the Greek original has not been recovered.[10]

When we come to consider the Western tradition of Theophrastus during the Middle Ages, we find that his works were apparently less well known than in either the Byzantine or Arabic tradition, although better known than in the Hebrew tradition, for no evidence has yet been brought forward to indicate Jewish knowledge of Theophrastus in the Middle Ages, and even the learned Steinschneider failed to disclose any.[11] Theophrastus was one of those Greek authors who essentially disappeared from the scene (others are Plotinus and Sextus Empiricus, among philosophical authors) at the close of Antiquity and who were all but unknown during the early Middle Ages. Moreover, his writings were not recovered during the twelfth and thirteenth centuries, in whole or in significant part, as were those of Aristotle or Themistius. One looks in vain for references to Theophrastus in most of those medieval works where we might expect him to be mentioned, if, indeed, his relevant works were known.[12]

---

[8] *Michaelis Ephesii in parva naturalia commentaria*, ed. P. Wendland, Commentaria in Aristotelem graeca (CAG) 22 (Berlin 1909) 149 (*De plantis*). According to Conrad Gesner, *Bibliotheca universalis* (1574) 498, Maximus Planudes "scripsit commentarios . . . in Theophrasti characteres." No trace of this has been uncovered. Cf. Kayser (n. 7 above) 355. Theophrastus's moral writings are referred to several times by the anonymous Byzantine commentator on the *Ethica nicomachea*. See *Eustratii et Michaelis et Anonyma in Ethica nicomachea commentaria*, CAG 20 (Berlin 1892) 180, 210, 238.

[9] For details see D. S. Margoliouth, "Remarks on the Arabic Version of the *Metaphysics* of Theophrastus," *Journal of the Royal Asiatic Society* (1892) 192-201; M. Steinschneider, *Die arabischen Übersetzungen aus dem Griechischen* (Graz 1960) (129)-(130); and F. Rosenthal, *Das Fortleben der Antike im Islam* (Zurich 1965) 49, 177, 189, 192, 242-248.

[10] See G. Bergsträsser, *Neue meteorologische Fragmente des Theophrast*, Sitzungsberichte der Heidelberger Akademie der Wissenschaften, philos.-hist. Klasse 9 (1918); E. Wagner and P. Steinmetz, *Der syrische Auszug der Meteorologie des Theophrast*, Akademie der Wissenschaften und Literatur, geistes- und sozialwiss. Klasse 1 (Mainz 1964 [date misprinted 1954]); H. J. Drossaart Lulofs, "The Syriac Translation of Theophrastus' Meteorology," *Autour d'Aristote*, Mélanges A. Mansion (Louvain 1955) 433-449. See also H. B. Gottschalk's review of the Wagner and Steinmetz volume in *Gnomon* 37 (1965) 758-762.

[11] Wimmer (n. 1 above) frag. 30 comes from Philo Judaeus, *De aeternitate mundi*, but there is no evidence for knowledge of Theophrastus among later Jewish writers.

[12] There seems to be no evidence whatever, for example, of direct influence of the relevant works of Theophrastus on the numerous medieval lapidaries and works of botany.

What then was the direct and the indirect knowledge of Theophrastus and his doctrines during the Middle Ages in the West? Awareness of Theophrastus and his teachings can be categorized under the four following heads: (1) a few extracts from a work entitled *Peplus* which were known in the ninth century; (2) several minor works translated into Latin in the twelfth century, but which circulated not under his name but under that of Aristotle; (3) a number of individual *sententiae* attributed to him and presumably derived from ancient sources; and (4) one fairly substantial fragment on "Why a wise man should not marry," preserved in Latin translation in Saint Jerome. The last of these is by far the most important and it exerted an enormous influence on a wide range of literatures, both Latin and vernacular. Before turning to this most significant of all aspects of Theophrastus's influence in the Latin Middle Ages, I should like to say at least a few words about the others.

The earliest references to Theophrastus during the Latin Middle Ages are also the most puzzling. Joannes Scotus Eriugena and several other ninth-century figures of the so-called Carolingian Renaissance refer to a work, entitled *Peplus*, which they attribute to Theophrastus.[13] On the one hand, is not really surprising to come across a reference to such a work, since we know that there were several ancient Greek works with the same title, the best known of which is the one attributed to Aristotle and is extant only in fragmentary form. On the other hand, neither Diogenes Laertius nor any other ancient source attributes a work of this title to Theophrastus. Yet the ninth-century references to this work and the extracts quoted from it seem to have some basis in fact, since they are accompanied by quotations in Greek, which would seem to indicate clearly that the Carolingian writers had access to a Greek manuscript of the work or, at least, knew Greek excerpts from it through an intermediary source.[14]

The sum total of the work which has come down to us consists in three brief passages, apparently derived ultimately from the *Peplus*. Two of them are found in commentaries on Martianus Capella's *De nuptiis Philologiae et Mercurii* by Joannes Scotus Eriugena (circa 810 to circa 877), Dunchad (fl. ninth century), and Remigius of Auxerre (circa 841 to circa 908). The first of these is found in all three commentaries[15] and the second seems to

---

[13] On this work, which seems to be known only from the ninth century references discussed here, see especially H. Usener, "Lectiones Graecae 28," *Kleine Schriften* (Leipzig 1912) 1.191-193, and Appendix 2 of *Iohannis Scotti annotationes in Marcianum*, ed. C. Lutz, Mediaeval Academy of America Publication 34 (Cambridge, Mass. 1939) 227-228. Regenbogen (n. 1 above) 1542 gives it bare mention.

[14] All of the manuscripts seem to have some words written in Greek characters.

[15] Iohannes Scottus (n. 13 above) 110; Dunchad, *Glossae in Marcianum*, ed. C. Lutz, American Philological Association, Philological Monograph 12 (Lancaster, Pa. 1944) 40; and *Remigii Autissiordorensis commentum in Marcianum Capellam*, ed. C. Lutz (Leiden 1962-1965) 2.70.

be found only in a different manuscript tradition of Scotus Eriugena's commentary.[16] The third fragment—probably the most interesting and important —occurs in a ninth-century manuscript by Martin of Laon,[17] an Irish contemporary of Scotus Eriugena. This text, nearly as brief as the other two, deals with the invention of the Greek alphabet.

All of these extracts from the *Peplus* seem to be dated uniquely in the ninth century and thus far no information has been uncovered to indicate the sources drawn on by Scotus and his contemporaries. Moreover, I have been unable to find continuing discussion of the *Peplus* in later medieval writers. From the material now at hand the logical conclusion would seem to be that there was a flowering of interest in this work during the Carolingian Renaissance, but that it was as short-lived as that Renaissance itself.

The two Theophrastan works that were actually translated during the Middle Ages, but which passed—as did many other works of relatively minor authors—under the name of Aristotle, are the *De signis*,[18] a meteorological work that often went under the title *De astrologia navale*, and the *Metaphysica*,[19] which was called *De principiis*. Both of these works were translated by Bartolommeo da Messina for King Manfred of Sicily during the years 1258-1266. The former is extant in ten manuscripts, one of which shows significant revisions in the text, but does not represent a separate translation. The *Metaphysica* version survives in a unique manuscript, the famous Padova, Biblioteca Antoniana XVII.370.[20] Both works have appeared in a modern critical edition.[21] Their influence in the Middle Ages seems to have been minimal and, in any case, was integrated within an interpretation of Aristotle to whom the works were attributed.[22] Both works, however, at-

[16] Quoted from MS Oxford Bodleian Auct.T.II.19 fol. 7v by L. Labowsky, "A New Version of Scotus Eriugena's Commentary on Martianus Capella," *Mediaeval and Renaissance Studies* 1 (1941-1943) 187-193, at 189.

[17] Quoted from MS Laon 444 by M. E. Miller, "Glossaire grec-latin de la Bibliothèque de Laon," *Notices et extraits des manuscrits de la Bibliothèque Nationale* 29 (1880) 2. 181. Printed also in Usener (n. 13 above) 192 and Scottus (n. 13 above) 227.

[18] Theophrastus 389-398. Cf. *Aristoteles latinus*, ed. G. Lacombe et al. (Rome 1939) 1.88, 186-187 and passim.

[19] Theophrastus 410-417. See also the better edition by W. D. Ross and F. H. Fobes *Theophrastus, Metaphysics* (Oxford 1929, repr. Hildesheim 1967). For the medieval translation see *Aristoteles latinus* 1.88, 185-186 and passim.

[20] See E. Franceschini, "Le traduzioni latine aristoteliche e pseudo-aristoteliche del codice Antoniano XVII.370," *Aevum* 9 (1935) 3-26.

[21] W. Kley, *Theophrastus metaphysisches Bruchstück und die Schrift Περὶ σημείων in der lateinischen Übersetzung des Bartholomaeus von Messina* (Würzburg 1936).

[22] The medieval translation of the *De signis* was still printed with other Aristotelian or pseudo-Aristotelian works early in the sixteenth century in the collection edited by Alessandro Achillini: *Aristotelis . . . secretum secretorum* (Bologna 1501; repr. Bologna 1516, Paris 1520, Lyons 1528).

tained importance in the fiteenth and sixteenth centuries under the name of Theophrastus.[23]

In the Muslim and Christian civilizations of the Middle Ages there was a vogue for *florilegia* and collections of *sententiae*. Certain doctrines of Theophrastus found their way into some of these collections. In Islam, a number of moral sayings attributed to Theophrastus are to be found in the *Muḫtār al-ḥikam* or *Sayings of the Wise*, compiled by al-Mubaššir b. Fātik.[24]

In the West, various stray fragments and *sententiae* got into works such as the *Speculum historiale* and *Speculum doctrinale* of Vincent of Beauvais (d. 1264);[25] a *Fiori di filosofi* attributed to Brunetto Latini (circa 1220-1294/5),[26] the teacher of Dante; and the *Manipulus florum*,[27] a popular collection of some 3000 extracts from the fathers, the schoolmen, and the ancients, which was compiled by Thomas de Hibernia at the Sorbonne in 1306. If one were to look at other such works one would certainly find other traces of doctrine attributed to Theophrastus. Most of the *sententiae* are short extracts to be found in the works of one or another ancient author. For some reason, a large portion of the opinions attributed to Theophrastus in these works are drawn from his lost treatise on friendship, which was discussed in such ancient works as Aulus Gellius's *Attic Nights*[28] or in Jerome's various writ-

---

[23] The *De signis* was translated by Iacobus Dalechampius (ca. 1574-1575, unpublished); Federicus Bonaventura (printed Urbino 1593), who also wrote an extensive commentary on the work; and Daniel Furlanus (printed Hanau 1605 in Theophrastus, *Opera*). The *Metaphysica* was translated by Ioannes Bessarion (ca. 1447-1450), by Gregorius Tiphernas (between 1453 and 1455, unpublished), and Iacobus Dalechampius (ca. 1574-1575, unpublished). For further information see my paper cited in n. 1 above, and my "Some Notes on Iacobus Dalechampius and His Translation of Theophrastus (Manuscript BN lat. 11, 857)," *Gesnerus* 26 (1969) 36-53.

[24] Rosenthal (n. 9 above) 172-173, 177, 189.

[25] For example, *Speculum historiale* 5.2 (Douai 1624, repr. Graz 1965) 137, and *Speculum doctrinale* 2.5.92, 2.6.14 (Douai 1624, repr. Graz 1965) 456, 490.

[26] This brief treatise seems to have been published for the first time in Vincenzo Nannucci, *Manuale della letteratura del primo secolo della lingua italiana* (Florence 1837-1839). A better and more complete edition is in Antonio Capelli, *Fiori di filosofi a di molti savi attribuito a Brunetto Latini* (Bologna 1865). The Theophrastus section, which gives several brief facts about his life and three *sententiae*, is found on page 15-16 of the latter edition.

[27] A convenient edition is *Flores omnium pene doctorum qui tum in theologia, tum in philosophia hactenus, claruerunt per Thomam Hibernicum* (Paris 1887) 3b. There are about 180 manuscripts of all or part of the work and about fifty editions after the *editio princeps* of Piacenza 1483. Further references will be to the Paris 1887 edition. On Thomas and his work see especially *Histoire littéraire de la France* 30 (Paris 1888), 398-408 and R. H. Rouse, "The List of Authorities Appended to the *Manipulus Florum*," *Archives d'histoire doctrinale et littéraire du Moyen Age* 40 (1965) 243-250, with further bibliography. Professor Rouse is currently working on the *Manipulus florum* and I am indebted to him for much information on the work.

[28] For example, 1.3 (Wimmer, n. 1 above, fragment 81) in *Noctes atticae*, Loeb Library (London 1927-1928) 1.10-22.

ings,[29] which were well known during the later Middle Ages. The precise way in which such collections were compiled is not entirely clear on the basis of the evidence that has thus far been brought forth. They quite evidently have some relation to ancient and Islamic precedents, but just what the connection is, remains somewhat in doubt.[30]

Perhaps the longest section given over to a discussion of Theophrastus, his life, and doctrines is chapter 68 of Walter Burley's *De vita et moribus philosophorum*,[31] a work that dates from the early fourteenth century and which was eventually translated into Spanish, German, and Italian.[32] This work, which has some relation—one that has not yet been entirely clarified— with Diogenes Laertius's writing of a similar title, after giving a brief account of Theophrastus's life and his relation to Aristotle, presents some *sententiae*. Again here we see that a good number of the opinions under Theophrastus's name deal with the question of friendship. For example: "Expedit tam probatos amicos amare quam amaturos probare."[33] This dictum in a slightly different form is found in both the *Manipulus florum*[34] and in the *Speculum doctrinale*[35] and is characteristic of the sort of thing found in these collections. So too, the one that follows it in Burley's work: "Amicicias immortales esse oportet."[36]

---

[29] For example, *Comm. in Osee* 3, proem. and *Comm. in Michaeam* 7.5; in Jerome's *Opera* ed. Vallarsius (Verona 1734f.) 6.110, 517.

[30] The whole problem of the sources of the medieval collections, the way in which they developed, and their relation to Diogenes Laertius is one beyond the scope of this paper. For further information see especially V. Rose, "Die Lücke im Diogenes Laërtius und die alte Übersetzer," *Hermes* 1 (1866) 367-397, and A. Biedl, *Zur Textgeschichte des Laertios Diogenes: Das grosse Excerpte Φ* Studi e Testi 184 (Vatican City 1955) 41-51, where references to further literature will be found.

[31] *Gualteri Burlaei liber de vita et moribus philosophorum*, ed. K. Knust (Tübingen 1886) 282-290.

[32] *Ibid.* 413-416. Knust prints the Spanish translation with the Latin text (pp. 283-291). A number of "lives of philosophers" and similar works date from the thirteenth to the sixteenth century and even later. Several of these contain sections on Theophrastus. One such example is the *Granarium* of Ioannes Whethamstede (d. 1465) and extant in several British Museum manuscripts (for further information see the *Dictionary of National Biography* 60 (1899) 447-449. The section on Theophrastus is to be found in British Museum MS Cotton Tiberius D.5 fols. 168v-169v. It seems to be at least partially dependent upon Walter Burley. Whethamstede 169 refers the reader to Vincent of Beauvais for further information on the *De nuptiis* fragment. See n. 39 below for another example of Theophrastus's material contained in such literature.

[33] Burley (n. 31 above) 282.

[34] "Expedit jam probatos amicos amare, non amatos probare," *Flores* (n. 27 above) 36.

[35] *Speculum doctrinale* (n. 25 above) 490C. The text is the same as the one found in the *Manipulus florum*.

[36] Burley (n. 31 above) 282.

In addition to these and similar *sententiae*, mention is made of Theophrastus's Περὶ πλούτον (*De divitiis*)[37]—no longer extant, but known by name to the Middle Ages through Cicero's *De officiis*[38]—and over half of the brief chapter is devoted to a discussion of the *De nuptiis* fragment of which we shall say more below. The Theophrastus who emerges from this account is a moral philosopher, and we are given no hint whatever that he is one of the most important writers on scientific subjects. Not even the names of his more important works seem to have been known to the author of the treatise.

In short, Burley's work is of a moralizing character, similar to those of John of Wales and of Thomas de Hibernia mentioned previously, and the view of Theophrastus given there illustrates this fact.[39] In it we are given a clearer picture of Theophrastus than appears elsewhere in the Middle Ages, but it is still a far cry from the historical Theophrastus known to the Greeks, or the one that we can reconstruct from the fragmentary works that have survived into the twentieth century.

One doctrine attributed to Theophrastus deserves special mention. This was known to the Middle Ages primarily through Themistius's *Paraphrasis* on the *De anima*, and it attributes to Theophrastus a rather ambiguous position on the "unity of intellect" problem which is quite difficult to interpret. This means that his position was widely discussed during the thirteenth-century debates over this issue, for example in Thomas Aquinas's *De unitate intellectus contra Averroistas*.[40] Theophrastus himself, however, never played a central role in the heated debates over this issue, primarily for the reason that that age never had a significant body of information on Theophrastus's opinion upon which to base a detailed interpretation.[41]

We now come to what is by far the most important Theophrastan text known to the Middle Ages, and the one identified with his name in the minds of historians of medieval literature. This is the antimatrimonial fragment

---

[37] *Ibid.* 286. Cf. Regenbogen (n. 1 above) 1487.

[38] Cicero, *De officiis* 2.16.56.

[39] The same sort of work was still being written in the sixteenth century. At least one of these, *A Treatise of Morall Phylosophie, Contaynyng the Sayings of the Wyse* by William Baldwin, contains a section on Theophrastus, not in the first edition (London 1547), but in the later expanded version: *A Treatise of Morall Phylosophie, Contaynyng the Sayings of the Wyse, Fyrst Gathered and Set Foorthe by Wylliam Baudwin, and Now Againe Augmented and ye Third Tyme Enlarged by Thomas Paulfreyman* (London 1567) 60v-62. See also fols. 78v, 161, 187, 240v for other sayings attributed to Theophrastus. Baldwin's work was one of the most frequently reprinted books in England in the sixteenth century. There seem to be no references to Theophrastus in similar books of the period by William Caxton (fifteenth century), Lodovico Guicciardini, and Gabriel Meurier.

[40] *De unitate* 2.54.55; 3.64, ed. Leo W. Keeler, ed. 2 (Rome 1956) xxi, 35, 41.

[41] E. Barbotin, "Autour de la noétique aristotélicienne: l'interprétation du témoignage de Théophraste par Averroès et Saint Thomas d'Aquin," *Mélanges A. Diès* (Paris 1956) 27-40.

preserved in Latin translation in Saint Jerome's *Adversus Jovinianum*.[42] Before discussing the interest in this work and its influence during the later Middle Ages, I would like to say something about the problem of the preservation of the fragment in Jerome and the nature of its contents.

Most medieval scholars take the work at face value and concern themselves very little with some of the very real problems concerning its authenticity and the way in which it came to Jerome. Some merely say that it is "pseudo-Theophrastan." There seems, however, to be no clear evidence to deny that the doctrine contained in the fragment goes back to Theophrastus himself, although the form in which it is preserved may be several times removed from the original. At least one writer expands one fragment into two, giving separate status to the text preserved in Jerome and the same text that circulated separately under the name of Theophrastus as *An uxor sapienti ducenda sit*, which is nothing more or less than a paraphrase of the *incipit* of the Jerome fragment.[43] The classical scholars who have studied this text and have tried to relate it to the *corpus theophrasteum* have not been very successful in coming to an agreement concerning it, but we should, at least, be aware of some of the problems involved here.[44]

The basic questions are (1) from which lost work of Theophrastus does the fragment derive, and (2) how did it come to Jerome? At the root of the first question is the perplexing situation that, even in what appears to be a very comprehensive list of his works given by Diogenes Laertius, there is nothing that corresponds to Jerome's description: *Theophrasti liber de nuptiis*. That is, there is no work with a title of Περὶ γάμου or of some similar title. This has led scholars to make various conjectures. Some have argued that it is a "lost chapter" of the *Characters*, for the criticism of the wife in the text has some parallels with the savage satire of the flatterer or the loquacious man. It has been argued against this that the fragment has many dissimilarities to the individual characters and is also much longer than any known

---

[42] There is no recent critical edition of this work. One still must use PL 23.215-352. The Theophrastus fragments are in bk. 1, chap. 47 (cols. 289-291). Critical texts of the Theophrastus fragment are to be found in F. Bock, *Aristoteles, Seneca, Theophrastus, de matrimonio*, Leipziger Studien 19.1 (Leipzig 1899) 60-64 and E. Bickel, *Diatribe in Senecae philosophi fragmenta* 1: *Fragmenta de matrimonio* (Leipzig 1915) 388-390. I shall refer to the latter. For a list of 87 manuscripts of Jerome's work see D. S. Silva and J. P. Brennan, "Medieval Manuscripts of Jerome, *Against Jovinian*," *Manuscripta* 13 (1969) 161-166. I have not been able to see the dissertation (University of California, Davis, 1967), J. P. Brennan, "The Chaucerian Text of Jerome, *Adversus Jovinianum*: An Edition Based on Pembroke College Cambridge, MS. 234," as cited in *Dissertation Abstracts* 28A (1967-68) 4622-4623.

[43] J. A. Hiller, *Albrecht von Eyb: Medieval Moralist* (Washington 1939) 115.

[44] See especially Bickel and Bock (n. 42 above); G. Grossgerge, *De Senecae et Theophrasti libris de matrimonio* (Kalingrad 1911); and Regenbogen (n. 1 above) 1487-1488.

chapter of the *Characters*. Other scholars have argued that the fragment
is a rhetorical exercise, a type of work which we know Theophrastus wrote
others have held it to be part of a larger work, perhaps the *Περὶ βίων*; and
still others have held to the position that there was a separate work on marriage, which somehow escaped the inventory of Diogenes Laertius and which
is also not mentioned in any other extant work from Antiquity, save Jerome.
Unfortunately, none of these these seems to compel our acceptance, although
all have points in their favor, as well as others not so favorable to them.

In addition to that thorny problem, however, there is still the second one,
which, of course, cannot really be effectively approached until the first one
is solved. Knowing how works and ideas were transmitted in Antiquity
—or in other ages for that matter—we can raise the problem whether Jerome knew the work of Theophrastus on marriage directly—whatever type
of work or part of a work it might have been—or whether he knew it in a
Latin translation or from another later work that had made use of it and quoted
from it. Since we know that there were other treatises on marriage in Antiquity, it may well be that Jerome derived his information on Theophrastus
from one of those. For example there was a lost treatise of Seneca *De matrimonio* and one by Tertullian *Liber de nuptiarum angustiis*, either of which
may have been a direct source. If this is so, we may presume an unknown
work of Theophrastus used by Seneca, whose work was in turn utilized by
Tertullian, and finally Jerome, drawing upon the latter for his knowledge
of Theophrastus. As we can see, this becomes quite complicated! Other
conjectures have been put forward, but I have mentioned enough to give
some idea of the complexity of the problem involved. In the absence of unambiguous information, the most plausable conclusion is (1) that the treatise
on marriage is a section of a legitimate work of Theophrastus and (2) that
it was translated from Greek into Latin by Jerome himself.[45]

Regardless of the precise way in which the fragment came to the *Adversus
Jovinianum*, it was accepted at face value by the Middle Ages. Let us now
turn to a brief analysis of its contents. The basic question raised in the work
is whether a wise man should marry; and, indeed, it is placed by Jerome
in the midst of a polemical work in which he is attempting to defend the
Christian virtue of virginity against the attacks of Jovinianus. In arguing
against Jovinianus's position, Jerome makes use of much material from Classical pagan sources. Nothing could fit better into his scheme than the text
from Theophrastus. Here is an important and influential Greek pre-Christian
philosopher who argued that a wise man (*sapiens*) should not marry.

---

[45] For a summary of the problem and the various solutions which have been offered
see H. Hagendahl, *Latin Fathers and the Classics*, Göteborgs Universitets Årsskrift 64.2
(Göteborg 1958) 150-156.

In trying to substantiate his major thesis that the wise man should not take a wife, Theophrastus's strategy is primarily to show that the demands of a woman upon the scholar are great and such that he cannot sustain them and yet remain a scholar. The study of philosophy is impeded by a wife, for, as he so aptly says: "nec posse quemquam libris et uxori pariter inservire."[46] That is, one cannot pay attention to both books and a wife. This was perhaps a most fitting comparison in an age when the price of books was high and, as Theophrastus goes on to say, the needs of a wife were many. Even more to the point, however, is Theophrastus's contention that wives are time-consuming. Instead of leaving many leisure hours for the study of books, wives spend whole nights in their chattering complaint: such as "that other woman is dressed more elegantly than I am when she is in public."[47] Theophrastus goes through a long list of the demands of time, money, and energy on the part of the wise man and concludes that although it is possible to find a suitable wife, nevertheless, a "bona . . . et suavis uxor . . . rara avis est."[48] Theophrastus states, however, that the wise man should not be alone, but should have companions and friends who are congenial.[49] The fragment ends with arguments against the reason given by some for taking a wife, namely that by having children one's name will not die with him, but he will be able to leave behind some heirs.[50]

The fragment is not long—it occupies only two or three normal pages, and in many manuscripts it is crammed into one—but the directness and vehemence of its polemic against marriage are striking. This, of course, was made to order for the Christian who was trying to defend the validity of sacerdotal celibacy. To find even a pre-Christian thinker speaking out, in such forthright terms gave a strong case for saying that the Christian position was in accord with the best thought of the philosophers. Indeed the arguments given here by Theophrastus are very similar to the ones still being given by defenders of sacerdotal celibacy within Catholicism: one cannot both serve the needs of his office and those of a wife and family.

There do not seem to be traces of any repercussion from the Theophrastus fragment before the twelfth century, but after that time its influence was widespread.[51] At least three times in the century the fragment was adopted wholesale into supposedly original works. In an era which had a more lax attitude toward plagiarism than ours this should not be taken as unusual.

---

[46] Bickel (n. 42 above) 388 line 16.

[47] 388 lines 19f.

[48] *Ibid.* 389 lines 27-28.

[49] *Ibid.*, 389 line 28; 390 line 3.

[50] *Ibid.* 390 lines 3ff.

[51] Fundamental to any study of the history of the fragment during this period is P. Delhaye, "Le dossier anti-matrimonial de l'*Adversus Jovinianum* et son influence sur quelques écrits latins du xiie siècle," *Mediaeval Studies* 13 (1951) 65-86.

Apparently the first to make significant use of the text was Abelard in his *Theologia christiana*, written about 1124, into which the fragment was incorporated wholesale.[52] It was also taken into two other widely diffused works, the *Policraticus* of John of Salisbury, written about 1159,[53] and Hugo de Folieto's *De nuptiis* of about 1170.[54] The latter sometimes passed under the name of Hugo of Saint Victor, apparently because the two names became confused.[55]

About this time there appeared another important antimatrimonial treatise on the scene, Walter Map's *Dissuasio Valerii ad Ruffinum philosophum ne uxorem ducat*, which later became incoporated into Walter's *De nugis curialium* of about 1180.[56] This work draws on a number of sources and with the Theophrastus text and other antimatrimonial material in the *Adversus Jovinianum* became the basis for later medieval propaganda on the subject. It is these three that are mentioned by name—Valerie, Theofraste, and Saint Jerome—in the prologue to the "wife of Bath's Tale" as being the contents of Jankyn's "book of wikked wyves."[57] But this is getting ahead of my story.

The Theophrastus fragment was apparently widely used throughout the thirteenth century. This is indicated not only by the numerous manuscript copies of the fragment which survive, but also by its inclusion *in toto* again in Vincent of Beauvais's *Speculum historiale*[58] and in John of Wales's *Com-*

---

[52] PL 178.1189-1200.

[53] *Policraticus* 8.9, ed. C. C. J. Webb (Oxford 1909) 2, 296-299.

[54] *De nuptiis* 1.1, PL 176.1203-1204. Other twelfth century writers, who knew and used the work, include Petrus Blesensis, *Epistola* 79, PL 207.243-247, and Ioannes de Alta Silva, *Dolopathos*, ed. A. Hilka (Heidelberg 1913) 88. For a more detailed disussion of the *fortuna* of the fragment in the twelfth century see Delhaye (n. 51 above).

[55] Hugo's works were printed by Migne (PL 176.1017-1218) as an appendix to those of Hugh of Saint Victor. Cf. M. Manitius, *Geschichte der lateinischen Literatur des Mittelalters* (Munich 1911-1931) 3.226, who says: "Er ist öfters mit Hugo von St. Victor verwechselt worden, indem seine Schriften unter dessen Namen abgeschrieben wurden und gedruckt sind."

[56] Walter Map, *De nugis curialium*, ed. M. R. James (Oxford 1914) 143-158. At the end of this passage, the reader is advised to see Theophrastus's book for further information. On Map's letter see Robert A. Pratt, "Jankyn's Book of Wikked Wyves: Medieval Antimatrimonial Propaganda in the Universities," *Annuale mediaevale* 3 (1962) 5-27; Ruth J. Dean, "Unnoticed Commentaries on the *Dissuasio Valerii* of Walter Map," *Mediaeval and Renaissance Studies* 2 (1950) 128-150.

[57] Geoffrey Chaucer, "Wife of Bath's Prologue," *Canterbury Tales* 3 (D) 669f., esp. 669-685. Cf. Pratt (n. 56 above) for the background and also for further literature on this much-studied subject. See also the literature cited in F. N. Robinson, *The Works of Geoffrey Chaucer*, ed. 2 (Boston 1957) 697-698. A useful selection of the background material, including the Theophrastus fragment, is collected in B. J. Whiting, "The Wife of Bath's Prologue," in W. F. Bryan and G. Dempster, *Sources and Analogues of Chaucer's Canterbury Tales* (Chicago 1941) 207-222.

[58] *Speculum historiale* 5.3-4 (n. 25 above) 138-139.

muniloquium.[59] It is also worth noting that it was used in *Roman de la rose* where again Theophrastus is mentioned by name.[60] The Italian protohumanist, Geremia da Montagnone, likewise utilized the work in his *Compendium moralium notabilium*, which was composed at the very beginning of the fourteenth century.[61]

This brings us to the next century, when the Theophrastan fragment gained in popularity, being used by two of the major literary figures of the century Boccaccio and Chaucer, as well as by numerous minor ones.

The manuscript of Boccaccio's *Zibaldone* is still extant in the Biblioteca Laurenziana in Florence[62] and among the items that it contains are the Theophrastus fragment, which is followed here—as in many another manuscript —by Walter Map's letter of Valerius to Ruffinus. Not only did the great Trecento author know the work but he made use of it, as Paget Toynbee pointed out over seventy-five years ago.[63] In a diatribe against marriage in his *Commento sopra la commedia di Dante Alighieri*, he cites the author, the work, and its source by name and goes on to give essentially an Italian paraphrase of the fragment.[64] Chaucer's Prologue to the Wife of Bath's Tale is among the best known sections of the *Canterbury Tales*. As I have already mentioned, he drew on several sources for the antimatrimonial content supposedly found in Jankyn's book. These matters have been abundantly discussed in the extensive literature on Chaucer[65] and, rather than going into further detail, let us pass on to other things that are perhaps less well known.

---

[59] *Communiloquium* 2.4.1: in the first printed edition, *Summa Ioannis Valensis de regimine vite humane* (Venice 1496) 76va-77ra. On John of Wales, who went under various names in medieval manuscripts and in the early printed editions, see A. G. Little, *Studies in English Franciscan History* (Manchester 1917) esp. 174-192; *idem., The Grey Friars in Oxford* (Oxford 1892), especially 144-151 (with list of works and manuscripts and printed editions); W. A. Pantin, "John of Wales and Medieval Humanism," *Medieval Studies Presented to Aubrey Gwynn S. J.* (Dublin 1961) 297-319; and Beryl Smalley, *English Friars and Antiquity in the Early Fourteenth Century* (Oxford 1960) 51-55.

[60] Line 8561 in the *Roman de la Rose* of Guillaume de Lorris et Jean de Meun, ed. E. Langlois (Paris 1914-1924) 3.87.

[61] Remigio Sabbadini, *Le scoperte dei codici latini e greci ne' secoli XIV e XV* (Florence 1905-1914, repr. Florence 1965, ed. E. Garin) 1.219.

[62] Cod. 29.8. For a description of the manuscript see A. M. Bandini, *Catalogus codicum latinorum Bibliothecae mediceae laurentianae* (Florence 1774-1778) 2.9-28. See also V. Branca, *Tradizione delle opere di Giovanni Boccaccio* 1 (Rome 1958) 201-229 (for further literature on the *zibaldone* see 201 n. 1).

[63] "The 'Liber de nuptiis' of Theophrastus in Medieval Literature," *The Academy* 1051 (25 June 1892) 616. Toynbee seems to have been the first to discuss this.

[64] G. Boccaccio, *Il commento alla Divina commedia e gli altri scritti intorno a Dante* ed. D. Guerri (Bari 1918) 3.217-20. This is the *commento* to canto 16 of the Inferno and it refers to the text "E certo la fiera moglie, più ch'altro, mi nuoce" (line 45).

[65] See the literature cited above in n. 57.

Other fourteenth-century users of the fragment against marriage include Francesco da Barberino (circa 1264-1348) and Eustache Deschamps (circa 1345-1406/7). The former cites Theophrastus's work in his *I documenti d'amore*[66] while the latter mentions him often and makes abundant use of his ideas, especially in the *Miroir de mariage*.[67]

Also during the fourteenth century we have evidence that the fragment against marriage found its place in the sermon literature. This is a further line of inquiry which should be pursued at greater length. There is every reason to believe that the content of Theophrastus's tract would have provided good material for a medieval sermon. In a fourteenth century collection of Franciscan sermons preserved in the Vatican, the one listed for the second Sunday after Epiphany begins as follows: "Nuptie facte sunt et cetera . . . Fuerit Oreolus Theophrastes philosophus utrum sapiens ducere debeat uxorem."[68] Here, among other things, we see one of the most common scribal mistakes that occurred in copying the tract. In the original text in Jerome the word *aureolus* is used to describe the book (*De nuptiis*) attributed to Theophrastus: that is, "aureolus Theophrasti liber." Later, however, the *aureolus* is often taken to refer to Theophrastus and even written at times as though it were his first name: Aureolus Theophrastus.[69] At any rate, the

---

[66] *I documemti d'amore di Francesco da Barberino*, ed. F. Egidi (Rome 1905-1927) 3.94. See also 3.194 for *sententiae* of Theophrastus on friendship.

[67] *Œuvres complètes de Eustache Deschamps*, ed. Saint-Hilaire and G. Raynaud (Paris 1878-1903) 5.73-74; 8.11; 9.42, 82, 181. Other French writings of the fourteenth century which indicate a direct or indirect knowledge of Theophrastus's work include the *Lamentations* of Matheolus (*Les lamenations de Matheolus et le livre de Leesce de Jehan le Fèvre, de Resson (Poèmes français du XIVe siècle)*, ed. A. G. van Hamel, Bibliothèque de l'École des Hautes Études (Paris 1892-1905) 2.cxxxii-cxxxv, and several works of Simon de Hesdin (Marcel Lecourt, "Antoine de la Sale et Simon de Hesdin: une restitution littéraire," *Mélanges offerts à M. Émile Chatelain* (Paris 1910) 341-353, esp. 351). Whether or not the author of *Les XV joies de mariage* knew the work directly has been debated. See A. Colville, *Recherches sur quelques écrivains du XIVe et du XVe siècle* (Paris 1935) 158-159 in favor of a direct influence, and Jean Rychner, *Les XV joies de mariage* (Paris 1963) x-xi, esp. xi n. 10, against.

[68] Vat. lat. 11,515. For a description see *Codices vaticani latini* 8, ed. E. Carusi and J. Ruysschaert (1959) 197.

[69] For example, "Liber Aurelli Theofrasti de nupciis," Cambridge, Corpus Christi College MS 177, fol. 83r (M. R. James, *A . . . Catalogue . . . of Corpus Christi College*, Cambridge 1912, 1.407); "Avello [!] Teofasto sommo filosofo," Florence, Biblioteca nazionale MS 2.2.56, fol. 96v, *Inventari* (n. 74 below) 8 (1898) 170; and "Liber Aurelli theofrasti de nupciis," London, British Museum Royal MS 6.E.3. Eustache Deschamps seems to have taken "Aureolus" as the name of a person different from Theophrastus. For example, we read in his *Balade* (contre le mariage; *Œuvres*, n. 67 above, 5.73):

>   Tu qui jadis as les livres leuz
>   De Theophraste et des autres docteurs,
>   Et d'Aureole et de Matheolus

See also 9.42, 182 for other examples of the same mistake. Petrus Blesensis in his *Epistola*

influence of this material on the sermon literature requires further research. We already know that Hugo de Folieto's *De nuptiis* was a work primarily meant for the cloistered, and Professor Pratt has recently argued—successfully I think—that there was a significant amount of anti-matrimonial propaganda in the universities which utilized the Theophrastus fragment.[70] It pemains, however, to show the extent to which it entered into medieval preachrng. Evidence for the use of the fragment for moral and religious purposes is also to be found elsewhere. It played a prominent role in the *Tractatus de matrimonio* of Geert Groot (d. 1384), the Dutch founder of the Brethren of the Common Life.[71]

Of great popularity during the fourteenth and fifteenth centuries in Central Europe was the *Lumen anime*. This work, consisting of a collection of exempla, alphabetically arranged under various moral and dogmatic headings, circulated in three different versions, each compiled by a different person, at a different time, and with different contents. In all there survive about 190 manuscripts of the work among the three versions. Versions A and C each contain twenty to thirty extracts attributed to Theophrastus's *De parte sensitiva* and version B contains exempla attributed to Theophrastus's *De distinctionibus elementorum*. These extracts must be investigated in detail to determine what if any relation they have to the genuine writings of Theophrastus, for many of the extracts contained in the *Lumen anime* have no relation to the legitimate writings of the authors from whom they are said to derive.[72]

---

79 (PL 207.244) seems to convert *aureolus* into the name *Aurelius*, which he then gives to Theophrastus, when he says: "Teste Hieronymo, Aurelius Theophrastus in libro de nuptiis. . . ." Simon de Hesdin considered it to be the name of Theophrastus's work, rather than merely a descriptive adjective given it by Jerome. In his French commentary on Valerius Maximus he says: "Theofrastus fist un livre de noces qui a nom aureole ou quel il monstre que nul sage homme ne doit . . . épouser femme," Lecourt (n. 67 above) 351 citing from Paris, Bibliothèque nationale MS fr. 9749 fol. 77. He makes a similar mistake in his *Salle* (Lecourt 351, citing from Bruxelles, Bibliothèque royale MS 10, 959 fol. 117) The same confusion has been made by modern editors. The recent translators of Walter Map speak of "the Aureolus (Little Golden Book) of Theophrastus," *Master Walter Map's Book De nugis curialium (Courtiers' Trifles)*, trans. F. Tupper and M. B. Ogle (London 1924) 196. The very recent editor of *Les XV joies de mariage* writes in his introduction of "L'*Aureolus* de Théophraste," Rychner (n. 67 above) x.

70 Pratt (n. 56 above).

71 See J. Clarisse, "Over den geest en de denkwijze van Geert Groete (Groot, de Groot) kenbaar uit zijne schriften," *Archief voor kerkelijke Geschiedenis inzonderheid van Nederland* 8 (1837) 1-384. The *Tractatus de matrimonio* is printed on 159-249. See esp. chaps. 4, 18, 22 for reflections of Theophrastus and pp. 170, 244 for mentions of him by name. Cf. Albert Hyma, *The Christian Renaissance: A History of the "Devotio Moderna,"* ed. 2 (Hamden, Conn. 1965) 435 and also 17, 433.

72 For further information see Lynn Thorndike, *A History of Magic and Experimental Science* (New York 1923-1958) 3.546-560. Professor R. H. Rouse, to whom I am indebted for information on this work, is preparing a detailed study of it.

Theophrastus's antimatrimonial tract continued to be read and utilized during the fifteenth and sixteenth centuries and even later, as the numerous manuscript copies of the excerpt—twelve are known to me—made during these centuries indicate. With the help of Professor Pratt, who is primarily interested in the fragment's diffusion in England and in those manuscripts in which it accompanies Walter Map's letter to Ruffinus, I have been able to locate from all periods a total of thirty-one manuscripts.[73] This number excludes those manuscripts in which it is imbedded in a longer work, for example, those of the *Adversus Jovinianum* or of Hugo's *De nuptiis*, and vernacular translations. I have not studied the provenance of these manuscripts in a detailed way, but it is worth noting that of the thirty-one that I have located, sixteen are in English libraries, ten in Italian librarires, three in French libraries, and two in Swiss libraries. Moreover, in addition to this number there are two fifteenth-century manuscripts in Florence which contain an Italian translation of the text.[74] I would be surprised if there were not many more manuscripts that have escaped my attention, for the fragment is quite short and must certainly lie hidden in many uninventoried miscellaneous manuscripts throughout Europe.

The fifteenth century saw the recovery of most of the other writings of Theophrastus which remain extant, including the *Characters* and the *De historia plantarum* and *De causis plantarum*, all of which were known in Italy in the first third of the century and were translated into Latin by 1454 This marks the beginning of a new age of Theophrastan studies and a new epoch of his influence.[75] Although the fifteenth century saw the reintroduction of the "new" Theophrastus there was still a continuity of the "medieval" Theophrastus and the two were sometimes intermingled in a curious way. For example, Guarino da Verona, one of the important initiators of humanist education, still seemed to know only the *De nuptiis* of Theophrastus and referred to it several times in his correspondence.[76]

---

[73] A list is to be found in my article cited in n. 1 above. We will be in a much better position to evaluate the Theophrastus fragment and its relation to Walter Map's treatise in the general context of medieval antimatrimonial literature when "Jankyn's Book of Wikked Wyves," being prepared by Karl Young and Robert A. Pratt, appears. See Pratt (n. 56 above) 12 n. 18. I am indebted to Professor Pratt for much valuable information regarding the diffusion of the Theophrastus fragment in the Middle Ages.

[74] Biblioteca nazionale MS 2.2.56, *Inventari dei manoscritti delle biblioteche d'Italia* 8 (1898) 170; and 2.4.128, *Inventari* 10 (1900) 134-135).

[75] For details see my article cited in n. 1 above.

[76] *Epistolario di Guarino Veronese*, ed. R. Sabbadini (Venice 1915-1919, repr. Turin 1959) 1.215; 3.89.

Among Guarino's students from north of the Alps was a certain Albrecht von Eyb, from a small Bavarian town near Ansbach.[77] While in Italy, Albrecht imbibed a good deal of the new humanistic culture (he quotes Petrarch frequently, as well as many classical authors), although he retained a good deal of the medieval tradition as well. In fact, a protestant scholar saw him as a precursor of the new Reformation ideals,[78] while a Catholic critic emphasized his importance as a "medieval moralist."[79] Albrecht's best known work is a brief *Ehebuchlein*, written about 1470 and extant in nine different incunabular editions, besides numerous later printings.[80] This book is basically promatrimonial—hence one reason for seeing Albrecht as a prereformer —and among those whose position is attacked is Theophrastus, who is mentioned by name near the beginning of Albrecht's booklet.[81]

From all indications, the influence of the *De nuptiis* did not end with the dawn of the Renaissance. Far from it! There still exist at least three sixteenth-century manuscripts of the work[82] and in 1509 there appeared at Prague a printed edition of a Czech translation of the tract.[83] There is some evidence that it continued to be read and used throughout the sixteenth century and, indeed, was still mentioned in 1604 by Thomas Nashe.[84] In France it continued to be cited in feminist and antifeminist literature at least until into the seventeenth century.[85]

---

[77] On Albrecht see especially M. Herrmann, *Albrecht von Eyb und die Frühzeit des deutschen Humanismus* (Berlin 1893) and Hiller (n. 43 above). Hiller gives further bibliography on 204-205.

[78] M. Herrmann (n. 77 above) 331.

[79] J. A. Hiller (n. 43 above).

[80] See Albrecht von Eyb, *Ehebuchlein: Faksimile der Originalausgabe von Anton Koberger, Nürnberg* 1472 (Wiesbaden 1966) esp. 137-138 where the details of the twelve editions by 1540 are to be found.

[81] *Ibid.* fols. 5v, 11v.

[82] Bologna, Biblioteca comunale, MS A.1415 fols. 15v-18, *Inventari* (n. 72 above) 36 (1926) 31-33); Vatican MS lat. 6966 fols. 212-214; Vatican MS lat. 7179 fols. 58-60v. I have examined all three of these manuscripts.

[83] *Ze se müdry ženiti nema. Teophrastus mudrzecz. A že rzydko ktera pocztiwaa gest zena* (Prague 1509). I have examined a photographic reprint (Prague 1928), in four folios, of the first edition (British Museum 11, 900. tt. 3/5[3]).

[84] In quoting Walter Map. See *The Works of Thomas Nashe*, ed. R. B. McKerrow (Oxford 1958) 1.14 (in *The Anatomie of Absurditie*). I have found no evidence of the use of Theophrastus's fragment by George Gascoigne or Joseph Swetnam, although this is asserted to be the case by Katherine M. Rogers, *The Troublesome Helpmate, A History of Misogyny in Literature* (Seattle 1966) 24.

[85] For example, by Jacques Du Bosc, *L'honneste femme* (Paris 1634) 2.296, which reads in part: "Theophrastus vouloit que la femme fut belle, bonne et noble; et que le mary fut sain, rich et sage." Du Bosc's work was enormously popular, being printed at least eight times by 1766, and translated into English, it seems, three separate times (the London editions of 1639, 1692, and 1753) and into Italian (Padua 1742). See the British Museum and Bibliothèque nationale catalogues for further information on the various editions. A very

By this time, however, western Europe had been able to learn much more about Theophrastus and his writings.[86] Diogenes Laertius's work was recovered in the course of the fifteenth century and was widely available in Ambrogio Traversari's Latin translation after about 1430.[87] Early in the same century the *Characteres* was rediscovered and remained a work of major literary influence until at least the eighteenth century. This work went through many editions after the invention of printing, was translated into Latin at least seven times by 1600, and into several vernacular languages as well.

As had been remarked, the writers of the Middle Ages seemed to know nothing whatever of Theophrastus's writings on scientific subjects. This makes the recovery of his two long botanical works, as well as fragments of scientific writings on other subjects, all the more striking. The *De historia plantarum* and *De causis plantarum* apparently re-entered the intellectual heritage of the West when manuscripts were brought back from Constantinople by Giovanni Aurispa in the early years of the fifteenth century. Many manuscript copies were made in the course of the century and Theodore Gaza's Latin translation, which remained standard for several hundred years, was completed in the 1450s.

Other minor works and fragments were also recovered during the fifteenth and sixteenth centuries, so that by the time of Daniel Heinsius's edition of 1613 a substantial *corpus theophrasteum* had been established, although the bulk of it was already available after the *editio princeps* by Aldus at Venice in 1495-1498.

The recovery of Theophrastus's writings, like those of many another Greek author, was accomplished through the work of humanist editors and scholars; and, again—as in many other cases—an abundance of material came to

similar quotation appears in François de Grenaille, *L'honneste mariage* (Paris 1640) 113 I am indebted to Dr. Ian Maclean for calling these references to my attention. He assures me that Theophrastus was still widely used in French feminist and antifeminist literature of the sixteenth and seventeenth centuries. When his research is published we shall be able to evaluate the continuity of this tradition more accurately.

[86] Here and in the paragraphs which follow, I largely rely on my findings as reported in my paper cited in n. 1 above. Further information and bibliography will be found there I plan to treat the question of Theophrastus in the Renaissance in much greater detail in a forthcoming publication.

[87] R. R. Bolgar, *The Classical Heritage and its Beneficiaries* (Cambridge 1954) 472; Richard Hope, *The Book of Diogenes Laertius* (New York 1930) esp. 12-22. There are many incunabular editions of Traversari's translation (*Gesamtkatalog der Wiegendrucke* 8378-8384), beginning with the first one of Rome 1470.

After this article had already been completed, Dr. H. B. Gottschalk kindly called to my attention that some doctrines attributed to Theophrastus were discussed by Barlaam (ca. 1290-1350). See PG 151. 1363-1364. This question must be investigated further elsewhere.

Italy from the East in the early fifteenth century and was slowly diffused throughout western Europe in the next centuries. This process of the study, analysis, and assimilation of the *corpus theophrasteum* required several centuries and the precise way in which it occurred remains to be told. But that story must wait.

My conclusions to this study must be rather modest. Theophrastus— both as a man and as an author—was not widely known during the Middle Ages. What knowledge there was, was based on a very meager acquaintance indeed with his legitimate writings. Even this minimal knowledge was uncommon before the last decades of the thirteenth century. The interest he attracted was largely among humanists, whether of the Carolingian world, the twelfth century, or fourteenth and fifteenth centuries.

Department of Philosophy
University of Leeds
Leeds 2, England

THE INFLUENCE OF GROSSETESTE'S "HEXAEMERON" ON THE "SENTENCES" COMMENTARIES OF RICHARD FISHACRE, O.P. AND RICHARD RUFUS OF CORNWALL, O.F.M.

•

by Richard C. Dales

I

The intellectual history of the early and middle thirteenth century is still known only dimly. The actual channels by which powerful and important ideas entered the mainstream of European thought, to transform and to be transformed by the thoughts of other men in later times, are mapped only in vague outline. This is particularly true concerning the influence of Robert Grosseteste's writings during the thirteenth century.

Most commonly, a great thinker exerts his maximum influence during his own lifetime and during the following generation when his immediate disciples are active. The commonly accepted view of Robert Grosseteste's *fortuna* presents quite a different picture. It is generally conceded that Grosseteste exerted a considerable influence on the fourteenth and fifteenth centuries; his Light Metaphysics, his emphasis on linguistic studies and mathematics, and his ideas on scientific method acted powerfully on later thought. But it has also been generally conceded that he was virtually ignored by his immediate successors during the thirteenth century and was revived only in the fourteenth century when the interests of a new age led men to find more value and pertinence in his works than did those closer to him in time.[1]

There have been some dissenters from this view. Miss Dorothea Sharp saw Grosseteste as the founder of the Franciscan school of philosophy in the

Research for this article was facilitated by grants from the American Philosophical Society and from the University of Southern California.

[1] This is the consensus of most studies of his influence. There are very few references to or quotations from Grosseteste's works during the thirteenth century. About the beginning of the fourteenth century, quotations begin, and his influence remains strong for about 150 years. See Beryl Smalley, "The Biblical Scholar," *Robert Grosseteste, Scholar and Bishop*, ed. D. A. Callus, (Oxford 1955) 80, 83-84; and R. C. Dales, ed. *Roberti Grosseteste Commentarius in VIII libros physicorum Aristotelis* (Boulder 1963) xxi-xxvii.

thirteenth century,[2] although she was able to present very little evidence of direct borrowing. Father Ephraim Longpré argued the same point in a well-known article,[3] but the earliest evidence he could present was a disputation held in the early fourteenth century, during the course of which Henry of Harclay quoted both the *Commentary on the Physics* and the *Hexaemeron*. More recently, A. C. Crombie has pointed out the influence of Grosseteste's scientific works on his successors in the thirteenth century.[4] But even here, the hard evidence is very sparse. Roger Bacon undoubtedly knew and plagiarized Grosseteste's works, and there are a few more bits of direct quotation in the works of other authors, but for the most part, the argument is conjectural, even though probable. For example, Albertus Magnus seemed to have Grosseteste's *De iride* in mind when he was writing his own work on the rainbow; Witelo and Theodoric of Freiberg "must have known" his work. The pseudo-Grosseteste *Summa philosophiae* was clearly written by someone who had imbibed much of Grosseteste's thought.

But the general paucity of citations of or quotations from Grosseteste's works during the thirteenth century has led most Grosseteste scholars to agree that the great bishop's influence was not great until the early fourteenth century. I should like to chart with a little more precision the channels of Grosseteste's influence and to indicate its nature and extent. One of the major works of Grosseteste's long and productive career was his *Hexaemeron*. Although the form in which this work was cast made it old-fashioned almost as soon as it was written, it apparently continued to be read by theological students, and it was plundered for information and arguments by at least two Mendicant students in their commentaries on the *Sentences*. These were Richard Fishacre,[5] the first Dominican to take his degree in Theology at

[2] Dorothea Sharp, *Franciscan Philosophy at Oxford in the Thirteenth Century* (Oxford 1930) 1.

[3] Ephraim Longpré, "Thomas d'York et Matthieu d'Aquasparta," *Archives d'histoire doctrinale et littéraire du moyen âge* 1 (1926) 270.

[4] A. C. Crombie, *Robert Grosseteste and the Origins of Experimental Science, 1100-1700* (Oxford 1953), esp. chap. 7, "Grosseteste and the Oxford School."

[5] On Fishacre, see W. A. Hinnebusch, *The Early English Friars Preachers* (Rome 1951) 364-369, 515; A. B. Emden, *A Biographical Register of the University of Oxford to A. D. 1500* (Oxford 1959) 1.685; and J. C. Russell, *Dictionary of Writers of Thirteenth Century England* (London 1936) 114-115. Selections from his *Commentary on the Sentences* have been printed in A. Landgraf, "Anfänge einer Lehre vom Concursus simultaneus in XIII. Jahrhundert, "*Recherches de théologie ancienne et médiévale* 1 (1929) 202-228, 338-355; and Leo Sweeney, S. J., and Charles J. Ermatinger, "Divine Infinity according to Richard Fishacre," *The Modern Schoolman* 35 (1958) 191-235, where his dependence on Grosseteste concerning divine infinity is noted. Fr. J. R. O'Donnell informs me that the best survey on Fishacre is R. James Long, *The Problem of the Soul in Richard Fishacre's Commentary on the Sentences*, a doctoral dissertation for the University of Toronto. I am indebted to Dr. Long for making his personal copy available to me.

Oxford, and the Franciscan master Richard Rufus of Cornwall,[6] a confidant of Saint Bonaventura.

This type of theological writing is conservative by its very nature. The topics to be treated and the manner of treating them are largely traditional. Authority plays a major part in determining the answers to the questions posed. Consequently the great patristic authorities figure largely in any medieval theological work, and the same quotations from the same authors appear in the works of one writer after another. But there is room for originality. Sometimes the Fathers "seem to disagree." Or they have not answered a certain question definitively, or perhaps have not posed it at all. New authorities complicate the problem, and the role of dialectic becomes larger.

Still, to show that one thirteenth-century theologian borrowed extensively from another is not necessarily to add anything to the history of the transmission of ideas, for the material borrowed is often made up largely of commonplaces. Grosseteste himself had an enormous respect for authority, and when he added anything that he realized was his own, he characteristically cautioned the reader that his remarks were not to be taken as authoritative. In spite of this, there is a great deal of "originality" in his works of which he seems to be unconscious. A large part of this results from what Father J. T. Muckle considered a wilful misuse of his authorities,[7] but which I prefer to interpret as a habit of understanding his authorities in such a way as to make them support his own ideas. He also read more widely than the average theologian and had a greater interest and competence in linguistic studies than most. There is contained in the *Hexaemeron*, therefore, a significant body of material whose entry into the mainstream of European thought is of considerable importance, and whose influence during the thirteenth century has been largely overlooked.

---

[6] On Rufus, see Emden (n. 5 above) 1604-1605; and Russell (n.5 above) 119-121. His use of Grosseteste's *Hexaemeron* was first noted by Gedeon Gál, O. F. M., in a review of Callus (n. 1 above) in *Archivum franciscanum historicum* 48 (1955) 435: "Citationes ex *Hexaemeron* inveniri possunt non solum initio saeculi XIV, ut dicitur p. 80, sed iam circa 1250; nam in *Commentario in Sent.* Richardi Rufi circa hoc tempus Oxonii confecto (cod. Oxford, Balliol 62), lib. II, d. 12, f. 128a [*recte* 127a] in margine legimus: 'Basilius. In scripto episcopi Lincolniensis super opera 6 dierum. D. 1a'; et in eodem libro, d. 15, f. 140c [*recte* 139c] in textu, ubi agitur de numero dierum septenario, dicitur: 'Et habetur de hoc ab episcopo Lincolniensi super hunc locum.'"

[7] See especially J. T. Muckle, C. S. B., "The Hexameron of Robert Grosseteste: The First Twelve Chapters of Part Seven," *Mediaeval Studies* 6 (1944) 151-174, and "Robert Grosseteste's Use of Greek Sources in His Hexameron," *Medievalia et humanistica* 3 (1945) 33-48, in both of which he continually complains that Grosseteste reads meanings into his authorities, especially the Greek Fathers, which the text will not bear.

II

A comparison of the texts of Grosseteste's *Hexaemeron* with the *Sentences* commentaries of Fishacre and Rufus will make clear beyond any doubt that this borrowing did in fact take place on a large scale.[8] Although the total amount of material taken nearly verbatim from Grosseteste's *Hexaemeron* by Fishacre and Rufus is very large, not all of it is of equal importance. Among the most important of Grosseteste's doctrines appropriated by our two friars are: (1) the noneternity of the world; (2) the heretical nature of astrology; (3) the way in which man is the image of God; (4) the active as well as passive potency in matter; (5) the metaphysics of light.

1. It was one of Robert Grosseteste's most strongly held convictions that the world was not eternal and that time was limited in both directions, past and future. He had written a separate opuscule on this subject, which circulated in two redactions, and the longer of these two redactions was appended to the end of his *Commentary on the Physics*.[9] His treatment of the same question in the *Hexaemeron* is even longer than his separate treatise and is written from the standpoint of a theologian rather than a philosopher. His argument may be summarized as follows:

In the one phrase, *In the beginning*, Moses destroys the errors of the philosophers who said that the world did not have a beginning in time, as Aristotle tries to prove in Book 8 of the *Physics* and Plato in the *Timaeus*. Those moderns who try to show that Aristotle did not teach this only make heretics of themselves, for, in addition to the evidence of the text of the *Physics* itself, all its commentators, Greek and Arab, agree that he taught the eternity of the world. To illustrate this, Augustine, Ambrose, Basil, and Pliny are cited. "We have adduced these authorities," he says, "against those presumtuous moderns who have tried to make a Catholic of Aristotle on the basis of corrupt Latin translations, contrary to the testimony of those, both Catholic and gentile, who have had access to the original Greek."

What deceived the ancients, so that they posited a world without beginning, was a false imagining that forced them to imagine another time before all time, as men falsely imagine another space beyond the limit of space, to

---

[8] For Grosseteste, I use the principal manuscript, Bodley, lat. th. C. 17. This manuscript, first described by R. W. Hunt in the *Bodleian Library Record* 2 (1948) 226, was carefully corrected by Grosseteste himself, and contains *graeca*, chapter headings, and concordantial signs in Grosseteste's own hand. It and the other manuscripts of Grosseteste's *Hexaemeron* are described in Richard C. Dales and Servus Gieben, O.F.M. Cap., "The Prooemium to Robert Grosseteste's *Hexaemeron*," *Speculum* 43 (1968) 452-453. For Fishacre and Rufus, I use Balliol College manuscripts 51 and 62, respectively.

[9] Richard C. Dales, "Robert Grosseteste's Treatise 'De Finitate Motus et Temporis,'" *Traditio* 19 (1963) 245-266; and Dales (n. 1 above) xii-xiii, 144-155.

eternity. This error can only be purged when the mind's desire is purged of the love of temporal things, so that the mind's gaze can transcend time and understand simple eternity. They were also deceived by the argument that holds that an effect must be coeval with its full and complete cause. They do not understand that this is true only when the cause and effect are measures of the same kind. Also, it is false to say that every change is preceded by another change, and that an instant is the boundary between past and future. Plato and Aristotle erred in positing something other than God as the beginning (*principium*). First matter and first form were created from nothing at the beginning of time. Ambrose, Jerome, Bede, Augustine, and Basil are then cited to support his argument.[10]

Fishacre paraphrases this quite freely and omits most of the patristic quotations except for Ambrose's *Hexaemeron*. Rufus, however, has taken over considerable portions of it and cites many of the same authorities.

Grosseteste, Part 1 (fol. 9c)	Rufus, Part 2, distinction 1 (fol. 103c)
Primum itaque verbum, videlicet: *In principio*, resonat temporis inicium et mundum a temporis principio esse factum, et non esse ex parte anteriori interminatum et infinitum. Unde in hoc unico verbo quod dicit: *In principio*, elidit errorem philosophorum qui dixerunt mundum non habuisse temporis inicium, quemadmodum dixit et probare nisus est Aristoteles in octavo *Physicorum*, similiter Plato in *Thimeo* inducit quemdam qui infinitas inundaciones diluviorum asserit precessisse.... (196d) Expositores quoque omnes eiusdem loci Aristotelis, tam Greci quam Arabes, dictum locum de perpetuitate motus et temporis et mundi ... concorditer exponunt. Boecius quoque in libro *De consola-*	Errores philosophorum circa creacionem mundi qui hic tanguntur in prima parte distinccionis, et 2ª breviter, universalius in principio notandi sunt. Ait ergo Ambrosius, *Exameron*, in principio: Plato cum discipulis eius tria principia posuit esse increata ac sine inicio, Deum et exemplar et materiam.... Et cito post, ipsum mundum semper fuisse et fore, Aristoteles usurpat dicere. Contra autem Plato non semper fuisse et semper fore presumit astruere. Istud nititur Aristoteles probare in 8 *Phisicorum*.... Et testantur qui viderunt quod omnes expositores eiusdem loci Aristotelis exponunt dictum locum de duracione motus et temporis et mundi ex utraque parte in infinitum. Et Boecius in libro *De con-*

---

[10] Portions of the Latin text paraphrased in the foregoing have been printed in the following works: R. C. Dales, "A Note on Robert Grosseteste's *Hexaemeron*," *Medievalia et humanistica* 15 (1963) 69-70; Longpré (n. 3 above) 270; Dales (n. 1 above) xiv 146, 151; Sharp (n. 2 above) 43-44; Smalley (n. 1 above) 87-88; L. Baur, *Die philosophischen Werke des Robert Grosseteste, Bischofs von Lincoln* (Münster i.W. 1912), 95*.

cione philosophie evidenter asserit tam Aristotelem quam Platonem censuisse mundum inicio caruisse. . . . Augustinus autem in XI° libro *De civitate Dei* asserit quosdam philosophos sensuisse mundum eternum sine ullo inicio, qui ideo volunt nec a Deo factum videre, "nimis," ut ipse ait, "aversi a veritate et letali morbo impietatis insanientes." . . . In libro quoque *De civitate Dei XII°* refert Augustinus Apuleum cum multis aliis credidisse mundum et hominem semper fuisse. . . .

[197a] In libro quoque XIII *De civitate Dei* refert Platonem sensisse mundum esse animal beatissimum maximum et sempiternum. Ambrosius quoque in libro *Exameron* ait: Ipsum mundum semper fuisse et fore Aristoteles usurpat dicere; contra autem Plato non semper fuisse sed semper fore presumit astruere, plurimi vero alii nec fuisse semper nec semper fore scriptis suis testificantur. Plato igitur videtur sibi ipsi contrarius, quia, ut patet ex superioribus, alicubi affirmat mundum carere inicio, alibi vero insinuat mundum habuisse inicium. . . .

[197b] Nec intelligunt quod verbum coexistencie simul pleni effectus cum plena causa, implicat causam et effectum sub eiusdem generis cadere mensuram, utpote quod ambo sunt temporalia, vel ambo eterna. Et in hiis quidem que participant eiusdem generis mensuram necessaria est argumentacio supra dicta. Si autem causa et causatum non

solacione philosophie plane asserit tam Aristotelem quam Platonem sensisse mundum incio caruisse. Et Augustinus *De civ. Dei* li.13, refert Platonem sensisse mundum esse animal beatissimum, maximum, sempiternum. Refert eciam idem Augustinus li.12 ca. 10 Aculeum [*sic*!] cum multis aliis credidisse mundum et hominem semper fuisse. Idem eciam, li.XI ca. 4, refert quod quidam posuerunt mundum eternum sine ullo inicio, et immo nec a Deo factum volunt; et hii nimis aversi sunt a veritate, et letali morbo impietatis insaniunt.

[103d] Hic solvunt aliqui quod hec racio necessaria est in hiis que participant mensuram eiusdem generis. . . .

Si autem causa et causatum non

participent eiusdem generis essendi mensura, non potest eis coaptari illa regula, ut dicatur, existente causa, necessario coexistit causatum. Cum igitur Deus sit eternus, mundus quoque et motus et tempus sint temporales, tempus vero et eternitas non sint eiusdem generis mensure; non habet in hiis locum illa regula de cause et causati coexistencia. Habet autem locum, ut dictum est, cum causa et causatum participant eadem mensura, quapropter Pater et Filius quorum uterque eternus et Pater causa Filii, secundum Iohannem Crisostomum et Damascenum et Augustinum, et principium Filii coeterni sunt. Deus autem eternus causa est mundi temporalis et temporis, nec precedit ista tempore, sed simplici eternitate.

participent eiusdem generis essensendi mensuram, non potest eis coaptari illa regula, ut dicatur, existente causa, necessario coexistet creatum. Tempus vero et eternitas non sunt eiusdem generis mensure, et immo in hiis non tenet. Sed in Patre et Filio, quorum uterque eternus, et Pater causa Filii, secundum Augustinum, Damascenum et Crisostomum, ambo coeterni sunt. Sed Deus eternus causa est mundi temporalis, et precedit mundum non tempore, sed simplici eternitate.

Rufus then continues the discussion by quoting verbatim a passage from Grosseteste's *De finitate motus et temporis* in the long redaction, which is identical to the end of his *Physics* commentary. This is the only thirteenth-century citation of this work which I have been able to find, and it invalidates my earlier assertion that there is no evidence that it was known before about 1300.[11]

2. Grosseteste also came to believe in his later life that astrology was the work of the devil and was completely false and heretical because it degraded the image of God, denied free will, and was scientifically unsound, since it pretended to an accuracy that was not in fact obtainable.[12] His treatment of this matter in the *Hexaemeron* takes the form of a gloss on the text: *et sint in signa.* He first shows that there are some signs in the heavens which it is lawful to consider, since they are firmly based on truth. Basing his case

---

[11] It is identical with *De finitate motus et temporis* (Dales, n. 9 above) 256-261 and *Comm. in Phys.* (Dales, n. 1 above) 148-151. See my remarks in *De finitate*, 250-251 and *Comm. in Phys.*, xxi, xxiii.

[12] See R. C. Dales, "Robert Grosseteste's Views on Astrology," *Mediaeval Studies* 29 (1967) 357-363. Much of what follows is substantially the same as appeared in that article and it is used here with the kind permission of the editor of *Mediaeval Studies*, the Rev. T. P. McLaughlin. See also Dales and Gieben (n. 8 above) 460.

largely on Matthew 16.1-3 and on Augustine and Basil, he argues that since the
heavenly bodies do in fact cause changes in the air, they are reliable indexes
of winds, rain, snow, thunderstorms, of the direction the winds will come
from, and whether it will be stormy or calm. "But", he goes on, "there are
other signs which the astrologers pretend exist in the heavenly bodies. These
are completely empty and false, and it is profane to consider them; and even
if it were not profane, it would nevertheless be fruitless and vain." He then
presents a series of arguments, based on human dignity, the freedom of the
will, and the omnipotence of God, to show that the claims of the astrologers
are false. Rufus bases his own discussion of the same question on Grosseteste's treatment, often using Grosseteste's own words and using the same
authorities.

Grosseteste, Part 5 (fol. 214c-216c)

Rufus, Part 2, distinction 14 (fol. 136a-c)

Et sint in signa. Secundum Augustinum *Ad Ianuarium*, luminaria quoque facta sunt in signa quadruplicia. Sunt enim in signa qualitatum aeris, quod eciam ipse Dominus manifestat cum dicit: *Facto vespere dicitis*: *Serenum erit, rubicundum est enim celum. Et mane: Hodie erit tempestas, rutilat enim triste celum. Faciem ergo celi diiudicare nostis.* Ex sitibus igitur luminarium et ex ortu et occasu eorum, et ex visibilibus impressionibus quas faciunt in superioribus, certa possunt sumi signa qualitatum aeris, ventorum, et pluviarum, grandinum, nivium, et tonitruorum, tempestatis quoque et serenitatis. Sunt eciam luminaria in signa viarum, tam nautis per mare, quam viatoribus per arenas et vastas solitudines. Ad luminaria enim aspicientes, iter suum directe dirigunt usque ad destinatum locum conferentes situm loci quo tendunt in terra, ad situs et vias luminarium in celo. Sunt quoque luminaria signa dis-

Et sint in signa. . . . pluribus modis sunt astra in signa. Sunt enim in signa qualitatum aeris. Unde Lucas 12 et Mattheus 16; *Facto vespere dicitis: Serenum erit, rubicundum est enim celum. Et mane: Hodie erit tempestas, rutilat enim triste celum. Faciem ergo celi diiudicare nostis.*

Ex sitibus igitur stellarum et ortu et occasu earum, et ex visibilibus impressionibus quas faciunt in superioribus certa sumuntur signa qualitatum aeris.

Sunt eciam in signa viarum, tam nautis quam viatoribus, aspicientes enim in mari vel in desertis ad sydera, vias suas dirigunt usque ad destinatum locum conferentes situm loci quo tendunt in terra, ad situs et vias stellarum in celo.

Sunt quoque signa distinccionis

tinccionis et numeracionis determinatarum mensurarum temporis. Sunt eciam in signa spiritualium similitudinum, sed hoc quartum genus existendi in signum quod insinuat Augustinus, quasi speciale celi luminaribus, commune est creaturis omnibus. Ut enim ipse Augustinus testatur, ex omni creatura est per aliquem similitudinem significacio mistica trahenda. Sed forte istud quadam speciali prerogativa inter corporalia assignatur celi luminaribus, quia in hiis est signacio spiritualium maior et evidentior, et in scriptura celebrior, quam in ceteris corporalibus.

Sunt eciam quinto modo luminaria in signum consummacionis seculi. Unde ipse Dominus requirentibus discipulis signum adventus eius in maiestate, inter cetera signa hoc connumeravit, dicens: *Erunt signa in sole et luna et stellis.* Ioel quoque propheta ait: *Sol convertetur in tenebras et luna in sanguinem antequam veniat dies Domini, magnus et horribilis.* Et Marcus ait: *Sol contenebrabitur et luna non dabit splendorem suum et stelle celi erunt decidentes.* In hec igitur V signorum genera, facta sunt celi luminaria. Et propter hec omnes artifices quorum opera proficiunt, aut detrimentum paciuntur per aeris qualitates aut per temporum mutaciones, a luminaribus signa con-[214d]- siderant et recipiunt. Unde Basilius ait: "Necessarias igitur humane vite ... *dabit lucem suam.*" Hec igitur signa licita sunt considerandum, quia soliditatem habent veritatis. Alia autem signa ple-

et numeracionis determinatarum mensurarum temporis. Sunt item in signa spiritalium similitudinum, sed hoc 4^{m} genus existendi in signum quasi speciale est stellis, commune vero creaturis omnibus, quod ex omni creatura per aliquam similitudinem significacio mistica est trahenda. ...

Sunt adhuc 5 modo in signum consummacionis seculi. Unde Lucas, 21: *Erunt signa in sole et luna et stellis.*

Et Ioel 3: *Sol convertetur in tenebras et luna in sanguinem antequam veniat dies Domini magnus.* Et hec accipe ab Augustino *Ad Ianuarium.* ...

Hec igitur signa licita sunt ad considerandum, verbi gracia, "quod aer terre proximus ... transquillitatis tempus expectat" Hec signa, ut dixi, licita sunt ad considerandum, quia soliditatem habent veritatis. Sunt autem alia signa plena inanitatis et falistatis que

na inanitatis et falsitatis, que
fingunt matematici in luminaribus consistere, profanum est con-
siderare; et si non esset profanum,
esset tamen infructuosum et va-
num.

. . . [215b] Nec est verum nec nisi
disputacionis gracia conceden-
dum, quod stelle habeant effectum super liberum arbitrium, vel
super mores et actus voluntarios
hominum. Liberum enim arbitrium mentis racionalis in ordine rerum naturali nulli sibicitur
nisi soli Deo, sed omnibus corporalibus creaturis prelatum est.
Unde cum agens nobilius sit paciente, non potest corporalis natura in arbitrii libertatem per suam accionem passiones inprimere,
esset enim natura corporalis li-
bertate arbitrii nobilior et superior si eidem passiones imprime-
ret. Qui igitur ponunt astris efficienciam in liberum arbitrium,
naturam anime racionalis et dignitatem humane condicionis sub-
iciunt nature corporali; et inimici sunt humane nature, cum eam
subiciant sibi naturaliter subiecto, auferantque ei esse ymaginem
Dei. Ymago enim est summa et
propinquissima similitudo. Blas-
phemi quoque sunt in Deum, quia
detrahunt Deo suam diginitatem,
cum mentem racionalem quam
concedunt esse Dei ymaginem,
ponant corporibus inferiorem. Si
enim corpus vel aliquid vilius
corpore esset Dei ymago et summa similitudo, non esset Deus hoc
quod ipse, est sed aliquid minus
quam est; et ita non esset Deus.
Sed forte aliqui matematici dicent quod stelle habent spiritus
incorporeos viventes et raciona-

fingunt mathematici dicentes a
stellis causari mores et fortunas
subdentes eciam liberum stellis.

Obicitur eciam contra istos, nichil
ignobilius agit in nobilius. Ergo
corpus celeste non agit in spiritum racionalem. Qui ergo ponunt
hec habere efficienciam in liberum
arbitrium inimici sunt humane nature, subicientes dignitatem condicionis humane nature corporali,
auferentesque ei ymaginem Dei;
ymago enim est propinquissima
similitudo.

Sed forte dicent stellas esse anima-
tas, et animas earum agere in nos-
tras animas, sicut corpora earum

les, et per spiritus suos agunt in spiritus hominum, et per corpora sua in corpora hominum. Sed hec eorum diccio omnino vana est, quia eciam si concederemus eis hoc quod ipsi temerarie asserunt, nullo tamen modo verum esset quod spiritus stelle superior esset natura spiritu hominis, cum homo secundum spiritum suum sit Trinitatis ymago. Convincit quoque eos scripture auctoritas que in Deuteronomio dicit: *Solem et lunam et omnia sidera creata a Deo in ministerium cunctis sentibus que sub celo sunt.* Si enim creata sunt in ministerium homini, magis naturale est quod ipsa agantur et imperentur et recipiant ab homine, quam econtra agant vel imperent vel imprimant homini. . . .

Sed forte adhuc dicent huiusmodi vanitatis professores quod sidera faciunt in corporibus humanis multas et manifestas impressiones, et paciente corpore necesse est animam compati. Corpus enim, ut dicunt medici, sequitur animam in accionibus anime, et anima sequitur corpus in passionibus corporis. Hoc est, cum patitur corpus, ipsa compatitur, non quia corpus agat in ipsam, sed quia ipsamet movet se ipsam comproporcionaliter motibus corporis cui unitur; quemadmodum moto speculo super quod reflectitur radius solis, commovetur et reflexus radius, non quia speculum moveat radium, sed quia radius per naturam propriam generat se in directum et continuum vel ad angulum equalem angulo incidenti super politum obstaculum. Quia igitur sidera im-

agunt in corpora nostra. Sed hoc nichil est; si enim haberent animas, non possent esse nobiliores animabus nostris, quia spiritu racionali nichil creatum est melius. Ergo aut bone sunt anime stellarum, aut male. Si male, sunt impotenciores ad cogendum ad malum. Si bone, nolunt cogere ad malum.

Dicitur eciam Deuteronomio 4 quod create sunt stelle propter nos. Ergo sunt ignobiliores.

Sed tunc dicent: sicut si radius solaris continuetur ad aquam, mota aqua, necesarsio et radius movetur, non quod aqua ipsum moveat, sed quia ipse radius necessario se movet ad motum aque motu consimili; sic ad motum corporum celestium consequitur necessario mutacio in corporibus nostris. Ad quam consequitur necessario ut animam seipsam moveat motu consimili. Paciente enim corpore, necesse est animam compati. Corpus enim, ut dicunt medici, sequitur animam in accionibus anime, et anima sequitur corpus in passionibus corporis. Hoc est, cum corpus patitur, ipsa compatitur, non quia corpus agat in ipsam, sed quia ipsa movet seipsam proporcionaliter motibus corporis cui ipsa unita est, sicut universaliter moto speculo super quod reflectitur radius solis, movetur et remutant corpora, et mutatis corporibus compaciuntur et anime, dicent huiusmodi astrologi quod ad [215c] scienciam iudiciorum pertineat iudicare et pronunciare de omnibus motibus et passionibus anime, quas habet ex compassione cum suo corpore. Sed eciam istis dicendum est, quod corpus humanum velud duobus subiacet motoribus. Recipit enim multas passiones et impressiones a sideribus, et recipit eciam motus et impressiones ab anime proprie accionibus. Et cum anima secundum vim racionabilem subiecta est Deo, potens est secundum eandem vim impetrare virtutibus inferioribus, et potencior est in afficiendo corpus proprium, quam sint corpora celestia. Unde quantumcumque moveat saturnus vel mars corpus, sive hic sanguinem constringendo, sive ille sanguinem accendendo, ut proveniat tristicia vel ira in anima, plus potest racio bene ordinata in contrarium operando, ut sit in anima gaudium et mansuetudo et per hoc nulla aut parva et imminuta sit in sanguine et corporeis spiritibus ab accione saturni vel martis, constrictio vel inflammacio. Plus enim potest vera animi mansuetudo in temperanciam et quietacionem sanguinis et spirituum, quam possit aliqua vis marcialis in eorundem perturbacionem; et plus potest verum gaudium in dilatacionem sanguinis et spirituum, quam possit saturnus in eorum constrictionem. Quod facile patere potest ex contrario, quia videmus quod tristicia vel ira mentis plus et magis subito immutat et con-

flexus radius, non quia speculum moveat radium, sed quia radius per naturam propriam generat se in directum et continuum, vel ad angulum equalem angulo incidenti super politum obstaculum.

Sed ad hoc respondetur quod corpus duobus modis subiacet motoribus, scilicet corporibus celestibus et anime racionali. Et cum anima secundum vim racionalem subiecta est Deo, potencior est ipsa in afficiendo corpus proprium quam sydera, anima enim omni sydere potencior est.

Unde quantumcumque moveat saturnus vel mars corpus, sive hic sanguinem constringendo, sive ille sanguinem accendendo, ut proveniat tristicia vel ira in anima, plus potest racio bene ordinata in contrarium operando, ut sit in anima gaudium et mansuetudo; plus enim potest vera animi mansuetudo in temperanciam et quietacionem sanguinis quam aliqua vis martis in perturbacionem; quod patet eciam ex contrario. Plus enim proficiet in anima inordinata, quod ira multo magis sanguinem perturbat et inflammat, non cooperante marte, quam faciat syderum vel aeris vel alterius corporis continentis accio.

stringit, vel perturbat et inflammat sanguinem et spiritus, quam faciat aliqua siderum vel aeris vel alterius continentis accio.
[Preterea natura libertatis arbitrii est quod ipsa est in sui ipsius potestate potens sponte proficere, adiutrice sola divina gracia. A nullo autem cogi potest in defectum.][13]

[Hec tamen in cacle volumus admonere, quod huiusmodi iudices seducti sunt et seductores, et eorum doctrina impia est et profana, diabolo dictante conscripta.]
Unde Augustinus super Psalmum nonagessimum primum: "Forte quidem tunc videntur . . . quam anima tua?"[14] Exposito quoque ad populum Psalmo sexagesimo primo, introduxit Augustinus quendam matematicum penitentem, ut in populo monstraretur; quo ostenso, sub hiis verbis ad populum de eodem locutus est; "Illa ecclesie sitis . . . transeat ad refrigerium."[15]
Item Augustinus *Super Iohannem*, loquens de matematicis et de hiis qui eos consulunt ait: "Dant isti nummos . . . domina cupiditas traxit."[16] In eadem omelia quoque super Iohannem insinuat Augustinus se combussisse libros matematicorum, sicut apostolorum temporibus factum est. . . . [et non solum isti, sed eciam qui consulunt tales sunt perditi.]

Item si hec vera essent iudicia, periret liberum arbitrium. Cuius natura est quod ipsa est in sui ipsius potestate potens sponte proficere, adiutrice sola divina gracia. A nullo autem cogi in defectum. . . . De hiis signis ait Damascenus 21: "Hec signa sunt ymbris. . . existimus actuum." . . . Sciendum ergo quod ista doctrina impia est et prophana, et diabolo dictante conscripta.

Unde Augustinus super Psalmum 91: "Forte quidam tunc videntur . . . quam anima tua?"

Item Augustinus, exposito ad populum Psalmo 61 vel 63, introduxit quendam mathematicum penitentem, ut in populo monstraretur; quo ostenso, sub hiis verbis ad populum loquitur: "Seductus ab inicio . . . et queritis mendacium?"[15]
Item Augustinus *Super Iohannem*, omelia 8, loquens de matematicis et de hiis qui eos consulunt, ait: "Dant isti nummos . . . domina cupiditas traxit." Et in eadem omelia insinuat Augustinus se combussisse libros mathematicorum, sicut temporibus apostolorum factum est. Ex hiis patet quod et ipsi et qui tales consulunt perditi sunt.

---

[13] Words in square brackets are not in the same order as Grosseteste has them.
[14] Augustine, *Enarratio in Psalmum* 91.7, PL 37.1175.
[15] *Ibid.* 61.23, PL 36.746-747.
[16] Augustine, *In Ioannis Evangelium* 9.2, 11, PL 35.1457.

Fishacre is much more selective and does not seem convinced by all of Grosseteste's arguments. In discussing the distinctions among magi, astrologers, and prophets, he says:

> cum omnes futura predicunt, quod magi predicunt que ex demonibus revelantibus didicerunt. Astrologi vero quod ex cursu naturali stellarum experti sunt, et tales magi eciam vocantur, quales fuerunt, ut creditur a quibusdam, illi 3 qui Christum adoraverunt. Matt. 2. Prophete vero quod revelante Deo didicerunt.[17]

And a little later in the same distinction, he shows that he fully accepts the reality and power of the demons who aid the magi, although it is wrong to worship them as gods.[18]

But in distinction 14 he simply repeats much of what Grosseteste had written, leaving out some, but emphasizing the freedom of man's will and the dignity of the human condition. He begins copying at the beginning of Grosseteste's discussion (*Hexaemeron* 5, 214c) with the quotation from Augustine's Epistle 55 *Ad Ianuarium* 6.11-8.14. He then paraphrases until he reaches the quotation from Basil, *Hexaemeron* 6.6, which he copied *in toto*. Then come several important quotations:

> Item, nichil ignobilius agit in nobilius. Sed omne corpus est spiritu ignobilius. Ergo nullum corpus agere potest in spiritum. Ergo nec corpus celeste in spiritum racionalem. Igitur qui ponunt hoc habere efficienciam in liberum arbitrium inimici sunt humane nature, subicientes dignitatem condicionis humane nature corporali, auferentesque ei ymaginem Dei. Ymago enim est propinquissima similitudo.[19]
>
> Sed forte dicent stellas esse animatas, et animas earum in nostris agere animabus, sicut corpora in nostris corporibus. Sed hoc nichil est. Si enim eciam haberent animas, non tamen possent esse nobiliores animabus nostris, cum spiritu racionali nichil creatum sit nobilius.[20], . .
>
> Dicitur eciam Deu. 4 quod create sunt stelle propter nos. Igitur sunt nobiliores. Sed tunc dicent: sicut si radius solis continuentur ad aquam, mota aqua, necessario et radius movetur, non quidem quod aqua ipsum moveat, sed pocius ipse radius necessario se movet ad motum aque motu consimili; sic ad motum corporum celestium consequitur necessario mutacio in corporibus nostris. Ad quam consequitur necessario ut anima se ipsam moveat motu consimili,

---

[17] Fishacre 2.7 (fol. 92a).
[18] *Ibid.* (fol. 93d).
[19] *Ibid.* 2.14 (fol. 109b-c).
[20] *Ibid.* (fol. 109c).

et sic ad mocionem celestium consequitur neccessario mocio in animabus nostris. Set contra hoc sic dicendum: corpus nostrum duobus subiacet motoribus, sc. corporibus celestibus et anime racionali. Cum ergo corpus et a corporibus celestibus recipiat passiones et impressiones ab anima patet quod potencior erit anima in efficiendo corpus proprium quam sidera, anima enim omni sideri potencius est. Unde quantumcumque moveat saturnus vel mars corpus, hic sanguinem constringendo sive ille sanguinem accendendo, ut proveniat vel ira vel accidia, plus potest anima bene ordinata in temperanciam et quietacionem sanguinis contra operando, ut sit gaudium et mansuetudo quam aliqua vis martis in perturbacionem. Quod patet eciam ex contrario, in anima enim inordinata ira multo magis sanguinem perturbat et inflammat, non cooperante marte, quam faciat siderum vel aeris vel cuiuslibet alterius corporis continentis accio.[21]

Fishacre repeats much of this in Part 2, distinction 24 (fol. 130c). He also takes over the entire last part of Grosseteste's discussion, including the authorities:

Item, si vera sunt talia iudicia, perirent liberum arbitrium, providencia, consilium, pietas. Sciendum igitur quod talium iudiciorum doctrina impia est et prophanata, eciam diabolo dictante conscripta. Unde Augustinus super Ps. 91: "Forte quidam . . . anima tua?" Item de eisdem Augustinus super Iohannem dicit: "Dant isti nummos . . . cupiditas traxit." Et ibidem insinuat se libros mathematicorum combussisse, sicut temporibus apostolorum factum est. Item Augustinus, exposito ad populum Ps. 61, introduxit Augustinus quemdam mathematicum penitentem ut in populo monstraretur quo ostenso sub hiis verbis ad populum loquitur: "Seductus ab inimico . . . queritis mendacium?"[22]

It is interesting that in the above quotations, Rufus is clearly often citing Grosseteste through Fishacre, although he must necessarily have had the *Hexaemeron* himself, since he makes more extensive use of it than does Fishacre.

3. Closely related to this is Grosseteste's teaching on how we should understand man to be the image of God.[23] Allegedly basing his views on Augustine's *De trinitate*, he asserts that the text: *Faciamus hominem ad imaginem et similitudinem nostram* contains the most secret things of God and the most holy things of man. It points out the trinity of the one God and the dignity of the human condition, for it says that man was made to the image of the

---

[21] Fishacre 2.14 (fol. 109c).

[22] Augustine, *Enarratio in Psalmum* 61.23, PL 36.746-747.

[23] This is discussed by Grosseteste in *Hex.* 8 (fol. 224-a-227a). It has been studied and edited by Muckle (n. 7 above) 151-174.

highest Trinity. An image, he says is the most perfect likeness. But a likeness can be either of equality or of inequality, and an image can be similarly distinguished. In the first sense, the Son alone is the image of God the Father. Man, however, is the image of God the Trinity through imitation, for a creature cannot be compared univocally to its creator. It can, however, imitate its creator in a certain fashion. Therefore, since man is, on the authority of Scripture, the image of God the Trinity, he is also the highest imitative likeness of the Trinity. But he would not be this unless he were able to imitate the Trinity in everything. Therefore, insofar as man is the image of God, he is, in a sense, all things. The most nearly accurate example of the trinity of God is memory, understanding, and love in the highest face of reason, by which supreme force alone God the Trinity remembers, understands, and loves without any cloud of fantasms or any corporeal instrument. And thus, according to this one supreme and simple power of remembering, understanding, and loving, man is the greatest likeness, and thus the image, of the one Trinity. "Image" used in this fashion can be understood in three ways. According to his natural power of thus remembering, understanding, and loving, man is naturally the image of God the Trinity. When this power becomes active, then man is the renewed image of the Trinity, deiform, and renewed in the spirit of his mind, and a new creature. Through sin it becomes a deformed image. The natural is never lost; the renewed image is lost through sin; the deformed image is destroyed by the grace of the Holy Spirit.

Fishacre begins his borrowing right at the beginning of the chapter, abridging somewhat:

Grosseteste, Part 8 (fol. 224a-b)	Fishacre, Part 2, distinction 16 (fol. 113b)
Valde brevis est istud verbum, sed tamen profundissimis et amplissimis sensibus fecundissimum; cuius fecunditas si esset explicanda et scribenda per singula, non arbitror mundum posse capere eos qui scribendi essent libros. Comprehendit enim Dei secretissimum et hominis sacratissimum. Ostendit unius Dei trinitatem et humane condicionis summam dignitatem; dicit enim hominem factum ad imaginem summe Trinitatis. Imago autem, ut dicit Augustinus in libro *De trinitate*, est summa similitudo. Similitudo autem dupliciter est, aut equalita-	De primo, sciendum quod licet breve sit hoc verbum, tamen est profundissimum et amplissimum et fecundissimum sensibus; cuius fecunditas si esset explicanda, scio mundum non posse capere, immo nec omnes lingue tot temporis spacio loquendo eam loqui sufficerent. Hominem enim esse Dei imaginem est eum esse summam Dei imitatoriam similitudinem. [Est autem ymago, ut dicit Augustinus in libro *De trinitate*, summa similitudo. Summa autem similitudo dupliciter est, scilicet vel

tis et paritatis, aut imparitatis et imitacionis. Quapropter et imago dupliciter est, aut summa videlicet similitudo secundum paritatem, aut summa similitudo secundum imitacionem. Secundum primam accepcionem ymaginis, solus Filius est imago Dei Patris. Omnia enim que habet Pater, habet equaliter et Filius. Et quecumque facit Pater, hec eadem et similiter Filius operatur. *Et sicut habet Pater vitam in semetipso, sic dedit et Filio habere vitam in semetipso,* vitam, inquam, hoc est, divinitatis plenam et totam substanciam, non multiplicatam neque divisam nec imminutam. Ideoque Patris est similitudo secundum equalitatem. Homo vero similitudo est Dei Trinitatis per imitacionem. Non enim potest creatura factori suo comparari, nec cum eo in aliquo univocari; potest tamen per modum aliquem imitari. Cum igitur homo testante scriptura imago sit Dei Trinitatis et ita sit Dei Trinitatis summa similitudo imitativa. Summa autem similitudo imitativa non esset, nisi secundum omnia eum cuius est summa similitudo imitari posset, ut videlicet omnia haberet in imitacione. Et quasi vestigii impressione que ille habet in substanciale possessione, explicacio huius verbi exigeret ut evolverentur omnia que habet in se Trinitas Deus; et singulis que sunt in Deo, invenirentur singula imitatorie aptata in homine. Deus autem est omnia in omnibus, vi-

paritatis et equalitatis, aut imparitatis et imitacionis. Et immo summa similitudo vel imago dupliciter est, aut summa similitudo secundum paritatem, aut summa similitudo secundum imitacionem Primo modo solus Filius est ymago Patris. Secundo modo est homo ymago Dei Trinitatis.]²⁴

Summa autem imitatoria similitudo non esset nisi secundum omnia eum, cuius est summa similitudo, imitaretur, ut scilicet omnia haberet in imitacione que Deus habet in substanciali possessione, sicut cera et sigillum. Igitur explicacio huius verbi (exigeret) ut evolverentur omnia que habet Trinitas Deus et eis singulis singula invenirentur in homine aptata imitatorie.
Sed Deus est omnia in omnibus. ...

²⁴ The words in brackets are omitted in this place by Fishacre and repeated near the end of the column.

ventium vita, formosorum forma, speciosorum species; et homo in omnibus eius propinquissima similitudo imitatoria. Quapropter et homo, in hoc quod ipse est imago Dei, est quodammodo omnia. Quapropter et dicti verbi explicacio exigit plus quam formarum et specierum et rerum omnium explicacionem, quia cum hoc Dei et hominis et illarum adinvicem coaptacionem. Huius igitur explicacio non est expectanda ab homine. Quanto magis a me imperito homine? Quantumcumque enim de hoc explicabit homo, neque tantum est quantum punctus ad lineam, aut calculus unus ad maris harenam, aut una stilla pluvie ad maris aquam, aut una athomus [224b] ad tocius mundi machinam.

Igitur dicti verbi explicacio exigeret plus quam rerum omnium explicacionem, quia cum hac Dei et hominis et illorum adinvicem coaptacionem. . . . Quod si omnes homines hunc sermonem explicare non sufficerent, et eius explicacio ab uno homine ́non expectetur, quanto magis nec a me imperito homine? Hinc eciam patet quecumque de hiis explicavit natura, vel eciam omnes homines, non maius est quam punctus ad lineam, nec quantum calculus unus ad totam harenam, aut minima roris stilla ad maris aquam, aut minima athomus ad totam mundi machinam.

Rufus omits the opening remarks and keeps the order of Grosseteste:

> Ymago est perfecta et summa similitudo. Sed est similitudo duplex: aut equalitatis et paritatis, aut imparitatis et imitacionis. Quare et ymago dupliciter est: summa similitudo secundum paritatem, aut summa similitudo secundum imitacionem. Primo modo solus Filius est imago Dei Patris. Secundo modo homo est Dei Trinitatis similitudo per imitacionem. Summa autem similitudo imitativa non est nisi secundum omnia eum, cuius est similitudo summa, imitari possit, ut secundum omnia haberet in imitacione que Ille habet in substanciali possessione. Ergo sufficiens exposicio huius sermonis ut evolverentur omnia que habet in se Trinitas Deus, et singulis que sunt in Deo invenirentur singula imitatorie aptata in homine. Deus autem est omnia in omnibus, ita quod nichil singularum, et homo in omnibus eius propinquissima similitudo imitatoria, quare et homo in hoc quod ipse est ymago Dei, est quodammodo omnia. Quis ergo sufficiet explicare hunc sermonem?[25]

He also takes over Grosseteste's teaching of the natural, reformed and deformed image, although he attributes it to Augustine (whom Grosseteste

---

[25] Rufus 2.16 (142b).

does not cite here), and the scribe has added a diagram in the margin to illustrate it:

Grosseteste, Part 8 (fol. 225c)
Potest quoque considerari a summo bono aversa, et ad inferiora
conversa, et deformata. Naturalis itaque imago, numquam am-
mittitur; renovata vero imago,
amittitur per peccatum; deformata vero, tollitur per Spiritus
Sancti graciam.

Rufus, Part 2, distinction 16 (fol. 192c)
Satis patet differencia ymaginis
et similitudinis. Sed notandum
quod ymago tripliciter intelligi-
tur in anima, scilicet naturalis
imago, et renovata, et deformata.
. . . Naturalis numquam amittitur; renovata amittitur per peccatum; deformata vero tollitur
[*cod.* totaliter] per Spiritus Sancti
graciam.

Both men borrow freely from the works of the Greek Fathers included in this
section of Grosseteste's work.

4. Grosseteste's basically Augustinian habits of thought often influenced
profoundly his understanding of other authors. This is notably true of the
way he interpreted Aristotle's works, and one of the major modifications
of Aristotelian concepts to arise in this way was Grosseteste's conflation
of Augustine's seminal reasons with Aristotle's potency. This view had been
elaborated in other works[26] and was used by Grosseteste in the *Hexaemeron*
to account for the different words used by God to bring different kinds of
things into being. As was often the case, he started with a text of Augustine
but went far beyond it in his interpretation.

Grosseteste, Part 3 (fol. 205c)
Potest quoque et per triplica-
cionem verbi fiendi notari, ut primo fiat res materialiter ex pure
nichilo; deinde in racionibus cau-
salibus et seminalibus inditis in
ipsa materia et in elementis respectu elementatorum; tercio vero
ut fiat res secundum formacionem
in specie perfecta. Verumtamen
an omnia post primum diem condita habeant huiusmodi condi-
cionem triplicem, non facile di-
xerim. Forte enim quod firmamentum et luminaria non habue-

Rufus, Part 2, distinction 14 (fol. 134d)
Potest eciam per triplex verbum
fiendi notari rem fieri materialiter ex pure nichilo, demum in
racionibus seminalibus inditis in
ipsa materia, 3º in suo specie perfecta.

Sed forte non omnia condita erant
in racionibus seminalibus, quia ce-

[26] *De potentia et actu*, ed. L. Baur (n. 10 above) 128 and *Comm. in Phys.* (n. 1 above)
29-30. See also Sharp (n. 2 above) 15.

runt in materia aut in elementis raciones causales et seminales inditas, secundum quas horum materia de qua fiebant, habebat inclinacionem et naturalem aptitudinem motivam et activam ut firmamentum et luminaria inde in esse prodirent. Sed solum hoc forte habuit illorum materia in potencia, ut hec inde fieri possent, sicut es habet in potencia passiva solum et inde fiat statua; granum vero habet ut ex eo sit planta, non solum in potencia passiva, sed eciam in racione causali seminali inclinante ad hoc, ut granum fiat planta. Hoc itaque universaliter dicere possumus quod in triplicacione verbi fiendi notatur; primo quid res est in potencia activa Dei efficientis omnia ex nichilo, eciam antequam creetur materia ex nichilo; secundo quod creata materia sit res in potencia materiali, sive illa sit potencia solum passiva ut in ere, sive eciam activa ut in grano; [205d] tercio quod res sit in se perfecta specie

Part 4 (fol. 207b)

Queritur hic primo cur mutato loquendi modo dicit: *Congregentur aque*, et: *Appareat arida*; et non dicit observato superiori modo loquendi: "Fiat aquarum congregacio," et: "Fiat aride apparicio." Et est hec questio validior contra sentenciam expositorum qui dicunt hoc die factam aque speciem et terre. Ad quam questionem respondit Augustinus dicens: "Quoniam per enumeracionem . . . terra stabiliter fixa." Summa igitur dicte racionis est quod quia hee infime species minus imitantur formam di-

lum et stelle sic tantum erant in potencia in sua natura, ut statua in ere, scilicet in potencia passiva tantum. Sed hoc universaliter est verum, quod res primo est in potencia activa Dei efficientis omnia ex nichilo et antequam sit materia; secundo in potencia materie communiter activa et passiva, sicut in ere et in grano differenter est potencia materie; tercio est res in sua specie perfecta.

Et queritur hic quare mutato loquendi modo dicit: *Congregentur aque*, et: *Appareat arida*, et non dicit: "Fiat aquarum congregacio," et: "Fiat aride apparicio"? Quam questionem movet et solvit Augustinus *Super genesim ad litteram*, lib. 2.,

Et est summa solucionis quod hoc verbum "est" propriisime dicitur de Deo. Hec autem inter verba,

centis verbi quam species lucis et celi, informiora enim sunt illis, non dictum est de hiis: "Dixit Deus: fiat." Is enim loquendi modus insinuat propinquam imitacionem rei facte ad verbum per quod fit. Habere enim fieri et esse velud proximo impressum et sigillatum a verbo quod est ipsum esse, et vere per se ens, nec aliud aliquid est quam esse et ens. Quicquid enim nominando de Deo dixeris in hoc verbo quod est esse instauratur, formacius est quam aliquid quod post esse potest dici. Ideo in luce et celo, et luminaribus quorum esse formacius est, et quorum forma ad esse propinquius est, dictum est: Dixit Deus: Fiat." In inferioribus vero formandis, ut terra et aqua et terrenascentibus, et irracionalibus animantibus, dictum est verbum a verbo essendi remocius, ut "congregentur," "germinet," "producat." In homine vero faciendo quasi hiis utrisque maius aliquid insinuatur, cum dicitur: *Dixit Deus*: *Faciamus hominem* et cetera.

Et forte in hiis verborum et modorum loquendi distinctionibus, potest aliud quid notari, videlicet quid ubi exprimenda erat sola creantis potencia, nulla adhuc preexistente potencia materiali passiva, dictum est: "Creavit Deus." Ubi vero exprimenda erat solummodo materialis potencia passiva receptiva solum cum potencia Creatoris activa, dictum est: "Dixit Deus: Fiat." Ubi vero exprimenda erat potencia in materia non passiva et receptiva solum, sed eciam [207c] inclinativa et motiva ad actum essendi, dic-

quod ei est propinquius est verbum fiendi. Cetera, sicut "congregare." "producere," "germinare," sunt ad esse remociora. Volens igitur ostendere a quo terrenascencia et bruta esse minus conformia verbo per quod facta sunt omnia, quam lux et firmamentum et stelle, et per consequens respectu illorum difformia, in hiis utitur scriptura verbis magis conformibus verbo essendi; in aliis vero verbis remocioribus, ut "germinet," "producat," et cetera. Summa igitur responsionis est quod hee species infime minus imitantur formam verbi eterni quam species lucis et celi, et immo de hiis dictum est: *Dixit Deus*: *Fiat*; de illis vero: "germinet," "producat," "congregentur." Sed hiis utrisque magis aliquid insinuatur cum dicitur: *Faciamus hominem ad ymaginem.*

Alia racio eiusdem est quod ubi exprimenda erat potencia activa creantis sola, nulla adhuc existente potencia materiali, dixit: "Creavit Deus," ut in creacione materie corporalium et spiritualium, et merito in hiis usus est verbo creandi, quia omnino ex nichilo fiebant; hoc autem significat verbum creandi. Ubi vero exprimenda erat potencia materie non activa, sed passiva tantum, merito usus est verbo fiendi, ut patet in faccione lucis sive corporalis sive spiritualis, et celi et stellarum, quorum omnium materia erat res-tum est: "Dixit Deus: Congregentur, Germinet, Producat." Materia namque prima et spiritalis natura designate per terram et celum in principio creata, ex nichilo facte sunt; nec precessit eas potencia, nisi sola activa potencia creatrix. Verbum autem creandi signat "fieri ex nichilo." Lux vero, si corporalis intelligatur, et celum et luminaria, ex materia facta sunt habente potenciam passivam, ut inde fierent ista. Sed non videtur quod fuerit in eorum materia aliqua vis inclinativa ad hoc ut hec specialiter prodirent de sua materia. Omnis enim vis in materia motiva et inclinativa materie ad aliquid melius et formacius, a superiori virtute impressa est. Que, cum impressa est, nititur redire pro modo suo in suum principium, et renovare materiam cui imprimitur, prout potest ad sui principii conformitatem. Est enim in impressionibus virtutum talium quasi humiliacio maioris ad minus ut humiliatum maius, reducat quod est minus ad suam maioritatem secundum receptibilitatem eius quod reducitur. Vis igitur imprimens se materia et cum impressa est inclinativa materie ad melius, prius est separata in univoco vel analogo; igitur cum non fuerit ante celum et lucem corporalem et luminaria, forma corporalis nobilior istis formatis, non fuit, ut videtur corporale creatum quod se posset imprimere materie horum, ut impressum inclinaret materiam ad esse istorum. Forma enim prima concreata in materia, licet videatur inclinare materiam ad perfec-

pectu forme eorum in potencia passiva tantum. Quod volens insinuare scriptura, dixit: *Fiat.* Si enim verbum artificis esset eius facere, diceret artifex eri: "Fiat es statua," et non diceret: "Producat es statuam." Ubi autem exprimenda erat virtus materie non passiva tantum, scilicet ad recipiendum, sed pocius inclinativa et motiva ad actum essendi, dixit: "Producat, Germinet, Congregentur." Facto autem celo et dirigente radios ad celi medium, scilicet ad terram, forte ex impressione luminis indita fuit aquis vis inclinativa ad congregacionem, et terre ablatis aquis ad germinacionem. Factis vero luminaribus ex eorum luminibus imprimebatur aquis et terre vis inclinativa ad sensibilium produccionem. In corporali vero materia non potuit esse vis inclinativa in hominis racionis consummacionem.

cionem, non tamen videtur quod
unde forma prima est, inclinet
materiam ad hoc vel illud esse
speciale. Si igitur lux et celum
et luminaria facta sunt ex materia
habente solum potenciam recep-
tivam, ut hec de illa fierent, con-
venienter est hoc insinuatum per
hunc loquendi modum: *Fiat lux*;
Fiat firmamentum: *Fiant luminaria*. Si enim locucio artificis
esset vis operatoria, diceret eri:
"Fiat ex te statua"; et non diceret: "Producas statuam." Grano autem diceret: "Producas plan-
tam," quasi "quod habes in te
virtutem enitentem ad hoc, ut
fit ex te planta." Facto autem
celo et dirigente lumen ad celi
medium quod idem est mundi et
terre medium, forte ex impressione luminis indita fuit aquis,
sive fuerint aque secundum speciem, sive materialiter, vis inclinativa ad congregacionem, et terra ablatis aquis ad germinacionem. Factis vero luminaribus, ex
eorum luminibus imprimebatur
aquis et terre vis inclinativa ad
sensibilium produccionem. In corporali tamen materia non potuit
esse vis inclinativa in hominis racionalis consummacionem.

5.   The best known of all of Grosseteste's doctrines is his Metaphysics of Light;
indeed this is the only thing for which he is mentioned in most histories of philosophy.   No doctrine more thoroughly permeates and gives coherence to his
thought.   In view of this, it is surprising how slight an impact it made on
Fishacre and Rufus. Both men copied from the *Hexaemeron* material containing
this teaching, and both on occasion repeated phrases from it, but neither accepted
it as Grosseteste had worked it out, if indeed they comprehended his remarks.

In Fishacre's commentary we find such phrases as "Omnis forma lux est"[27]
and "multiplicacio specierum,"[28] which come from Grosseteste, but the ex-

---

[27] Fishacre 2.34 (fol. 144a).
[28] *Ibid.* 2.28 (fol. 137c); 30 (fol. 190d).

tended treatments of light are thoroughly Aristotelian and show little or no influence of Grosseteste.[29]

Rufus too uses the characteristic phrases,[30] but the context in which they appear shows that he either does not accept or does not understand them, probably the latter. He makes one extensive quotation from the *Hexaemeron*, very slightly abridged, which contains the quintessence of the Light Metaphysics and includes material that Grosseteste had developed in *De luce*, *De lineis*, and *De natura locorum*:

> Omne corpus luminosum a quolibet sui puncto undique circa se lumen dirigit, et omnium linearum luminosarum ab eodem puncto luminosi corporis directarum, illa maioris est virtutis et forcius agens operacionem luminis que a corpore luminoso procedit ad angulos undique equales super corporis luminosi superficiem. Et quelibet linea luminosa alia, quanto propinquior est linee exeunti ad angulos equales, tanto eidem in fortitudine accionis magis accedit; et quanto ab illa remocior est, tanto minoris est virtutis. Omne quoque corpus luminosum spericum concavum, a quolibet puncto sui dirigit unam lineam radiosam in centrum suum ad angulos equales super superficiem concavam illius corporis sperici. Ad aliud vero punctum preter centrum signatum non possunt concurrere nisi due linee radiose ad angulos equales exeuntes a superficie concava illius corporis, ille videlicet due linee que veniunt a punctis oppositis per diametrum spere transeuntem per punctum extra centrum signatum. Que due linee non sunt nisi una diameter spere, secta in duas partes in puncto preter centrum signato. Item ad quodlibet punctum intra corpus spericum luminosum, pervenit unica linea radiosa a quolibet puncto superficiei sperice corporis luminosi. Unde in quolibet puncto intra concavum spere luminose, aggregantur tot linee luminose quot in alio; hoc est, quot sunt puncta in concava superficie corporis sperici luminosi. Quoad numerositatem igitur luminis, quodlibet punctum intra speram luminosam equaliter habet de lumine. Sed quoad fortitudinem virtutis luminis, centrum recipit maximum de lumine, et quodlibet punctum preter centrum, quanto est centro propinquius, tanto recepit de virtute luminis maius; et quanto est a centro remocius, tanto recipit minus, quia in puncto propinquiori centro, aggregantur plures radii minus oblique egredientes a superficie concava circumdantis luminosi, et in puncto remociori a centro, congregantur plures radii magis oblique egressi. Ex hiis patet quod

---

[29] See especially Fishacre 2.26 (fol. 136a ff.).

[30] Rufus 2.13: "Unus enim punctus lucis subito tocius mundi spacium replet" (fol. 129b.) "Item, lux naturaliter diffundit se in omnem partem, et tamen non incedit nisi secundum rectum" (fol. 131d). "Lux diffundit se undique naturaliter et secundum rectum" (fol. 132a). In the same distinction, he says that light propagates itself by multiplication of species (fol. 131c-d).

cum terra respectu celi non optineat nisi vicem puncti, quod in terra est aggregatio maxima virtutis luminis celi et stellarum, et immo ipsa maxime congruit generacioni et provectui vegetabilium et sensibilium. Unde si haberet terra quantitatem respectu celi, non caperet sufficienter de virtute luminis ad generacionem et provectum illorum. Quapropter oportuit et celum esse quantitate magnum et terram parvam.[31]

He makes this quotation with approval, as though he accepted it. But in his separate discussion of light, which occupies five columns, he is unable to decide whether light is matter and form, only form, only matter (he does not entertain this notion very seriously), or whether it is active or passive, and ends by saying: "Non tamen multum curo de hoc."[32]

Much the same is true of Grosseteste's key epistemological doctrine that the gaze of the mind (*aspectus mentis*) cannot rise higher than the mind's desire (*affectus mentis*), and that the mind must be purged of the corporeal phantasms that cloud its view before it can see things as they really are.[33] Although the key terms, *aspectus et affectus mentis* or *animae*, occur many times in Fishacre's commentary,[34] they are never coupled with the term *purgatio mentis* and are never given the fundamental importance that Grosseteste assigns to them. In fact, both he and Rufus conspicuously omitted the expression of this teaching in the material they copied from the *Hexaemeron* about the finitude of the world (see above, II.1). Rufus too sometimes uses the words but never with Grosseteste's meaning. The closest he comes to accepting Grosseteste's teaching on the soul is in his quotation of a discussion of the relationship between soul and body:

Anima secundum racionem et intelligenciam est aspectus rectus in se reflexus. Et vita a quibusdam diffinitur quod ipsa est spiritus reciprocus. Quapropter ipse vitalis tocius anime motus est quedam de se spiritalis egressio, et in se reciproca reversio, et est ista perfecta circulacio simili tempore in ipso spiritu incorporeo. Et quia substancia anime unita est corpori in unitatem persone, corpus humanum necessario sequitur ipsam animam pro modo et possibilitate sua in mocionibus naturalibus. Ex reciprocacione igitur spiritalis motus anime in se sequitur motum cordis, qui in se reciprocatur. Movetur enim cor continue per dilatacionem corporalem secundum

---

[31] Rufus 2.17 (fol. 146d); Grosseteste 3 (fol. 206d-207b).

[32] Rufus 2.13 (fol. 131a-132b).

[33] This doctrine of Grosseteste's is investigated by Callus (n. 1 above) 16, 21-22; Dales, *De Finitate* (n. 9 above) 251-253; and Lawrence E. Lynch, "The Doctrine of Divine Ideas and Illumination in Robert Grosseteste, Bishop of Lincoln," *Mediaeval Studies* 3 (1941) 168-170.

[34] Fols. 95d, 96b, 104b, 121c, 125a, 128c, 130a (twice), 135a, 135d.

extensionem virtutis anime vitalis, et per constriccionem corporalem secundum reciprocacionem spiritalem. Et sequitur naturaliter ex motu cordis motus inspiracionis. Et forte omnis motus animalis qui incedit secundum rectum, provenit a motu nervorum et musculorum qui fit per constriccionem et dilatacionem.[35]

It seems quite clear that both Fishacre and Rufus took the terms from Augustine (*De genesi ad litteram, Soliloquia. De spiritu et anima*) and were consciously unwilling to give them the expanded significance that Grosseteste did.

III

Of less general interest than the transmission of original ideas, but still of considerable importance in the history of ideas, is the transmission of authorities by way of Grosseteste's *Hexaemeron*. Grosseteste apparently led Fishacre and Rufus to several other sources that were not commonly used; he provided them with their only access to the Septuagint and linguistic matters in general; and he furnished them with a ready-made marshaling of authorities on many points.

1. There are four works among the common sources of these three men which deserve special mention. The first two are pseudo-Augustinian: Gennadius's *De ecclesiasticis dogmatibus* is cited as Augustine's *De diffinicione recte fidei*;[36] and a work known as *De mirabilibus divine scripture* is attributed to Augustine by all three men.[37] A marginal note in one manuscript of the *Hexaemeron* reads: "Lincolniensis considerat librum de mirabilibus scripture fuisse Augustini."[38] Both friars quote these works much more extensively than Grosseteste did.

A third work, cited by all three men as "Rabani de ligno vite," is actually Radbertus of Corbie's *De corpore et sanguine Domini*.[39]

[35] Rufus 2.17 (fol. 143a); Grosseteste 10 (fol. 236b).

[36] PL 58.979-1054. Fr. Servus Gieben informs me that a work entitled, "Liber Rabbani de diffinicionibus recte fidei" is contained in manuscript Douai 350 (thirteenth century), fols. 104-118. And in fact an abridgement of Gennadius's work appears under the title *De definitionibus recte fidei* in Rabanus's *De universo* 4.10, PL 111.98ff.

[37] Printed in PL 35.2152ff.

[38] Oxford, Queen's College manuscript 312 fol. 46b.

[39] Fishacre 2.17: "Rabanus dicit de ligno vite quia non erat ei hoc in natura ut ex usu eius subsisteret hominis immortalitas. Solucio: Potest intelligi dupliciter illud lingum non habere hanc vim naturaliter, sc. vel quia non habuit hanc vim ex natura communi lignorum—et hoc verum est, et hoc intendit Rabanus. Habuit tamen eam naturaliter, id est simul sibi cum sua natura collatam, et sic intelligere alios expositores" (fol. 116b).

Rufus 2.17: "Sed Rabanus dicit econtra de ligno vite, sc. quod non erat ei hoc in natura, ut ex eius esu subsisteret hominis immortalitas. Respondetur quod dupliciter potest intelli-

The most serious of the source problems is a *Hexaemeron* attributed to Saint Jerome. Grosseteste cites this frequently, often coupling Jerome's name with Bede's when he does so. Several of these citations can be found in authentic works of Jerome. Most can be found, though not always verbatim, in pseudo-Bede's *Commentary on the Pentateuch*, in Bede's *Hexaemeron*, or in the *Glossa ordinaria*. Father J. T. Muckle has tried to show that Grosseteste mistakenly attributed Bede's *Hexaemeron* to Jerome, and that his citations of Bede were taken from the *Glossa ordinaria*.[40] But this is not possible, since on many occasions Grosseteste makes specific verbatim quotations from Bede's *Hexaemeron*. Furthermore he was well acquainted with the *Glossa ordinaria*, which he always cites as "Strabus." The most that can be said at present is that the book Grosseteste refers to was probably a compilation of statements on hexameral questions attributed to Jerome; the book probably contained some authentic material from Jerome's works as well as material from a variety of other sources, much of which also appeared in Bede's *Hexaemeron* and the *Glossa ordinaria*. The only "first-hand" citations of pseudo-Jerome's *Hexaemeron* I know of are in Grosseteste's *Hexaemeron*. Fishacre and Rufus cite the work only through Grosseteste,[41] as does Henry of Harclay in the early fourteenth century.[42]

2. Neither Fishacre nor Rufus was particularly interested in linguistic matters. Grosseteste's *Hexaemeron* fairly teems with Hebrew and Greek etymologies, discussions of Greek syntax, vocabulary and pronunciation. The greater part of this was overlooked by both friars. They borrowed several etymologies through Grosseteste, and their knowledge of the Septuagint seems limited to what Grosseteste had said about it.[43] Borrowing of this

---

gi illud lignum non habere hanc vim naturaliter: vel quia non habuit hanc vim ex natura communi lignorum, et hoc intendit Rabanus; habuit tamen eam naturaliter, i. e. simul sibi cum sua natura collatam, et sic intelligunt alii" (fol. 143b).

Both of these are a conflation of Grosseteste 11 (fols. 238c and 239c). "Rabanus" is Paschaius Radbertus, *De corpore et sanguine Domini* 1.6, PL 120.1272A.

[40] J. T. Muckle, C. S. B., "Did Robert Grossesteste Attribute the Hexameron of St. Venerable Bede to St. Jerome?" *Mediaeval Studies* 13 (1951) 242-244.

[41] Rufus 2.12 (fols. 127b, 128a), Fischacre, 2.12 (fol. 102c), Grosseteste 1 (fol. 200d); Rufus 2.13 (fol. 130a), Fishacre 2.13 (fol. 103d), Grosseteste 2 (fol. 201cd); Rufus 2.13 (fol. 130c), Fishacre 2.13 (fol. 104a), Grosseteste 2 (fol. 202ab); Rufus 2.14 (fol. 133d), Grosseteste 3 (fol. 204d); Fishacre 2.14 (fol. 108ab), Grosseteste 4 (fol. 207d); Rufus 2.15 (fol. 139b), Fishacre 2.15 (fol. 112d), Grosseteste 9 (fol. 233b).

[42] Henrici de Harclay, *Quaestio disputata* "*Utrum mundus potuit fuisse ab eterno*," manuscript Assisi, Bibl. Com. 172 fol. 150: "Ieronimus et Beda super Genesim eosdem philosophos [Platonem et Aristotelem] reprehendunt." Grosseteste 1 (fol. 197c).

[43] Fishacre 2.14 (fol. 108a), Rufus 2.14 (fol. 134d), Grosseteste 3 (fol. 205d); Fishacre 2.14 (fol. 108b), Rufus 2.14 (fol. 135b), Grosseteste 4 (fol. 208cd); Fishacre 2.14 (fol. 108b), Rufus 2.14 (fol. 135c), Grosseteste 4 (fol. 208d), citing Basil, *Hex.* 4.5 PG 30.909a; Rufus 2.15 (fol. 188cd), Grosseteste 9 (fol. 231d).

sort, limited though it is, is important, since Grosseteste's remarks, whether he was borrowing from Saint Jerome, Saint Basil, or Priscian, or speaking from personal knowledge, were usually far superior to what was contained in the standard handbooks. Both men copied Grosseteste's information on the derivation of "abyssus"[44] and several of Jerome's remarks; Fishacre includes Grosseteste's explanation of *ge*;[45] and Rufus takes over a discussion of the words "firmamentum" and "celum."[46]

3. By far the most extensive type of borrowing by Fishacre and Rufus was the taking over of whole discussions, including the authorities, of many standard hexameral questions. In this way, Grosseteste's formulation of these questions passed into the *Sentences* commentaries of the thirteenth century.

One of the points of sharpest contrast between the classical philosophical tradition and the commonly accepted Christian view was the nature of creation itself. This topic was widely discussed during the twelfth and thirteenth centuries, and in his *Hexaemeron* as in his *Physics* commentary Grosseteste insisted that creation was "ex nichilo." This argument was incorporated into the *Sentences* commentaries of both Fishacre and Rufus.[47]

Few things fascinated Grosseteste so much as the light of the first three days, and his discussions of this were taken over by both friars,[48] as was his treatment of the related question concerning the visiblility and color of the earth during the first three days.[49]

The matter of which the heavens were made was discussed at great length by Grosseteste and was copied by Rufus.[50] Closely connected with this was the way in which the terms "heaven" and "earth" should be understood,[51]

---

[44] "Basilius [*Hex.* 2.4, PG 30.885b]: Abyssus, inquit, est aqua nimia in infinitum habens profunditatem. Est autem abyssus grecum nomen, et secundum derivacionem grecam dicitur abyssus quasi nimium et inpertransibile sive infirmum. *Bio* enim verbum grecum a quo derivatur abyssus duo signat. Est enim idem quod 'in eo' et idem quod 'firmo', a quo verbo et ab 'a' privativa preposicione derivatur abyssus." Fishacre 2.12 (fol. 102b); Rufus 2.12 (fol. 128a) Grosseteste (fol. 200d).

[45] "Huic concordat nomen terre in greco, sc. *ge*, a verbo sc. *geo*, quod sonat 'capio' vel 'recipio', quia ipsa est receptaculum animalium et terrenascencium." Fishacre 2.14 (fol. 108b), Grosseteste 4 (fol. 209a).

[46] Rufus 2.14 (fol. 132c), Grosseteste 3 (fol. 204c), based on Augustine, *De Gen. ad litt.* 2.10, Corpus scriptorum ecclesiasticorum latinorum 28.1.48 and Basil, *Hex* 3.7, PG 30.899B; 3.8, PG 30.900CD).

[47] Grosseteste 1 (fol. 198b); Fishacre, 2.12 (fol. 102a); Rufus 2.12 (fol. 127d).

[48] Grosseteste 2 (fol. 202b); Rufus 2.13 (fol. 130c). Grosseteste 2 (fol. 201d); Fishacre 2.13 (fol. 103d); Rufus 2.12 (fol. 130a). Grosseteste 2 (fol. 202b); Fishacre 2.13 (fol. 103d); Rufus 2.13 (fol. 130a).

[49] Grosseteste 4 (fol. 208cd); Fishacre 2.14 (fol. 108b); Rufus 2.14 (fol. 135b).

[50] Grosseteste 3 (fol. 204d); Rufus 2.14 (fol. 133c).

[51] Grosseteste 1 (fol. 198b); Rufus 2.12 (fol. 127a). Grosseteste 1 (fol. 200d); Fishacre 2.12 (fol. 102c); Rufus 2.12 (fol. 128a).

and whether the "heaven" created on the first day was the same as the "firmament" created on the second day.[52] This firmament and the waters above and below it were also discussed at some length,[53] and the troublesome phrase, "the one place of waters," was carefully explained by Grosseteste.[54]

Both friars took from Grosseteste's *Hexaemeron* discussions of the four seasons and the different kinds of years;[55] why the sun and the moon are called "two great luminaries," when in fact the moon is smaller than the earth and stars;[56] why fish are called reptiles;[57] and how the earth could bring forth a living soul.[58] In addition, Rufus borrowed Grosseteste's treatment of God's resting on the seventh day[59] and on the mystery of the number seven;[60] on the location and climate of Paradise;[61] the assertion that time passed before Eve was created from Adam's rib;[62] and finally Grosseteste's summary of the six days of creation.[63]

Rufus was sufficiently conscientious that he nearly always tracked down Grosseteste's sources (except for the troublesome Jerome citations) and added title, book, and chapter references if these were missing in Grosseteste. He sometimes added material from these sources just before or just after the extracts that Grosseteste had made. In this way, he was led to read very carefully the works of John Damascene, John Chrysostom, Basil, Gregory of Nyssa, and Josephus, in addition to the more widely read works of the Latin Fathers.

Fishacre, however, seems to have been content just to copy, although he too made wider use of the works of these Greek authors than the quotations contained in Grosseteste's *Hexaemeron.*

IV

There is not the slighest doubt that Robert Grosseteste's *Hexaemeron* was thoroughly pillaged by Fishacre and Rufus in their commentaries on the *Sentences,* and that among the material appropriated by them were some

---

[52] Grosseteste 1 (fol. 199a-d); Rufus 2.12 (fol. 127a).

[53] Grosseteste 3 (fol. 204a-c); Rufus 2.14 (fols. 132 d-133a).

[54] Grosseteste 4 (fols. 207d-208b); Fishacre 2.14 (fol. 108b); Rufus 2.14 (fol. 135a-b).

[55] Grosseteste 5 (fol. 216b-c); Fishacre 2.14 (fol. 110b); Rufus 2.14 (fols. 136c-137a).

[56] Grosseteste 5 (fol. 216 d); Fishacre 2.14 (fol. 110b); Rufus 2.14 (fol. 137a).

[57] Grosseteste 6 (fols. 218d-219d); Fishacre 2.14 (fol. 110c-d); Rufus 2.14 (fol. 137c).

[58] Grosseteste 7 (fol. 221a-c); Fishacre 2.15 (fols. 110d-111a); Rufus 2.15 (fol. 138a).

[59] Grosseteste 9 (fol. 232b-233a); Rufus 2.15 (fol. 138a-c).

[60] Grosseteste 9 (fol. 234b); Rufus 2.15 (fol. 139b-c). See above n. 6.

[61] Grosseteste 11 (fol. 238b); Rufus 2.17 (fol. 146c).

[62] Grosseteste 10 (fol. 237b); Rufus 2.16 (fol. 142d).

[63] Grosseteste 1 (fol. 195c-198a); Rufus 2.12 (fol. 126d-127c).

of Grosseteste's more important ideas. Still, they were far from being blind followers or members of a "school of Robert Grosseteste." They took from him only what they found useful, and they rather arbitrarily ceased following him along a certain line of thought if they did not like where it was leading. Grosseteste's use of the Greek Fathers also seems to have led to their playing a larger part in the works of our two mid-century friars than would otherwise have been the case. Each of these friars was an important influence on the thought of his own order. They were both renowned in their own day, and their works were widely copied during the 150 years after their deaths.

This study, I believe, has laid the groundwork and provided the justification for searching more thoroughly for traces of Grosseteste's influence in the works of thirteenth-century authors. Certainly we must modify the prevailing view that it was only from the beginning of the fourteenth century that Grosseteste exerted any significant influence on European thought.

Department of History
University of Southern California
Los Angeles, California 90007, U.S.A.

THE METAMORPHOSES OF THE EDEN SERPENT DURING THE MIDDLE AGES AND RENAISSANCE

•

by Henry Ansgar Kelly

The varied appearances of the Eden serpent in medieval and renaissance literature, drama, and art have caused a good deal of interest among students of these periods; it is particularly mystifying to see the tempting reptile take on the head and other features of a woman. There has, however, been comparatively little formal study of these developments. The subject first received extended scholarly treatment in the early part of this century, from Hugo Schmerber and J. K. Bonnell,[1] but these pioneering works are frequently neglected, and their findings quite incomplete.

I. Eastern Traditions

Curiosity about the nature of the serpent who tempted the first parents of mankind developed early. That the serpent's curse entailed its crawling on its belly thenceforward suggested, of course, that it had previously had legs and feet, of which it was ever after deprived. Such was the rabbinic tradition, witnessed to by the Midrash and Targum,[2] as well as by Josephus, who adds that it also lost its voice.[3] It was said to look like a camel in its original state.[4]

As for the serpent's sex, apart from the fact that the Hebrew word for serpent (*nahash*) is in the masculine gender, the Eden serpent was thought

---

[1] Hugo Schmerber, *Die Schlange des Paradieses*, Zur Kunstgeschichte des Auslandes 31 (Strassburg 1905); J. K. Bonnell, "The Serpent with a Human Head in Art and in Mystery Play," *American Journal of Archaeology* 2.21 (1917) 255-291. See also Alice Kemp-Welch, "The Woman-headed Serpent in Art," *The Nineteenth Century and After* 52 (Dec. 1902) 983-991.

[2] *Bereshith Rabbah* 19.1: "Rabbi Hoshaya the Elder said: 'He stood out distinguished (erect) like a reed, and he had feet.'" —*Midrash Rabbah: Genesis*, trans. H. Freedman (London 1939, repr. 1951) 1.149. The Palestinian Targum expands God's curse to read, "Upon thy belly thou shalt go, and thy feet shall be cut off." —J. W. Etheridge, *The Targums of Onkelos and Jonathan ben Uzziel on the Pentateuch, with the Fragments of the Jerusalem Targum* (London 1862-1865) 1.166.

[3] Josephus, *Jewish Antiquities* 1.1.4, Loeb Library (London 1930) 22-24.

[4] *Bereshith Rabbah* 19.1. This opinion is ascribed to Rabbi Simeon ben Eleazar.

to have been very *male*, since it actually lusted after Eve,[5] thus maintaining (for us post-Freudians) its reputation as a phallic symbol.

As is well known, there is no devil or Satan figure in the Genesis account of the temptation of Eve, but Jewish as well as Christian tradition came to associate such a figure with the serpent. Most often the serpent was not taken to be a symbol of Satan, but an animal that was simply used by the devil to carry forward his determination to destroy mankind.

According to the ninth-century compiler of the *Chapters of Rabbi Eliezer the Great*, Sammael, the great prince in heaven, who had twelve wings to the seraphim's six, took his band and descended to earth and saw all the creatures that God had made; "and he found among them none so skilled to do evil as the serpent. . . . Its appearance was something like that of the camel, and he [Sammael] mounted and rode upon it. . . . Like . . . a man in whom there was an evil spirit, . . . all the deeds which it did, and all the words which it spake, it did not speak except by the intention of Sammael." After the sin of Adam and Eve was effected by this unholy team-work, God "cast down Sammael and his troop from their holy place in heaven, and cut off the feet of the serpent."[6]

About the same time that Pseudo-Eliezer was at work with his *Chapters*, Pseudo-Ben Sirach came up with the story of Lilith as Adam's first wife,[7] but Bonnell rightly dismisses Lilith as a possible influence upon the feminized Eden serpent, since there is no evidence that she was ever regarded as serpentine in form in the Middle Ages.[8]

The tradition that the Eden serpent originally had feet that were cut off when it was cursed found its way into the Eastern tradition of the Christian church at an early date. A treatise on paradise among the spurious works of Saint Basil the Great assures us that in the beginning the serpent had nothing horrible about it, but was rather a mild and gentle creature that did not crawl on its belly in a wild and savage manner but carried itself high upon feet.[9] We see the tradition illustrated in the Byzantine Octateuchs

---

[5] *Ibid.* 18.6 (147): "Said R. Joshua ben Karhah: 'It teaches you through what sin that wicked creature inveigled them; viz., because he saw them engaged in their natural functions, he [the serpent] conceived a passion for her.'"

[6] *Pirḳê de Rabbi Eliezer*, trans. Gerald Friedlander (London 1916, repr. New York 1965) 92-93, 99.

[7] Israel Lévi, "Lilit et Lilin," *Revue des études juives* 68 (1914) 15-21, puts the *Sepher* or *Alphabet* of "Ben Sirach" in the ninth or tenth century, and believes that it comes from Persia.

[8] Bonnell (n. 1 above) 290 n. 2. Jeffrey M. Hoffeld, "Adam's Two Wives," *The Metropolitan Museum of Art Bulletin* 26 (June 1968) 430-440, asserts that Lilith is definitely the basis for the woman-headed Eden serpent, but he offers no proof.

[9] Pseudo-Basil, *De paradiso* 7 (PG 30.67-68).

of the twelfth century,[10] where in fact the serpent looks like a camel. The outline of the serpent's future shape can be seen in its neck, backbone, and tail, so that God had simply to curse away the camelian understructure, and the modern serpent was ready for action.

II. EARLY TRADITIONS IN THE WEST

In the West the Jewish traditions were preserved and enlarged by European rabbis; those who lived in northern France are particularly important. Rashi (Rabbi Solomon ben Isaac of Troyes, circa 1040-1105), for instance, repeated the Midrash interpretations of the serpent's passion for Eve and the idea that "it had feet but they were cut off."[11]

Andrew of Saint Victor (who died in 1175) was the first Christian exegete in the Middle Ages to draw systematically upon the works of the Jewish commentators. In his commentary on the Octateuch, which he finished by about 1147,[12] he seems to accept the reading that the serpent once had feet,[13] but not that it was inflamed with desire for Eve. Andrew acknowledges that the serpent was not speaking by itself but was possessed by the devil;[14] this was the traditional Western interpretation. Andrew takes it as a sign of Eve's great simplicity that she was not dumbfounded or startled when a hitherto mute brute started to speak to her.

Before the time of Andrew of Saint Victor, the usual iconographic representation of the Eden temptation featured an ordinary serpent twined about the fatal tree of knowledge, with Adam on one side and Eve on the other. At times, however, the devil was illustrated separately from the serpent, as in the Old English Junius manuscript (circa A.D. 1000). Here Satan himself is bound in hell, but he sends a subordinate to paradise who transforms

---

[10] T. Ouspensky, *L'octateuque de la bibliothèque du Sérail à Constantinople*, Bulletin de l'Institut archéologique russe à Constantinople 12 (Sofia 1907; pls., Munich 1907) 115, pl. 11 fig. 25 (f. 43v); D. C. Hesseling, *Miniatures de l'octateuque grec de Smyrne*, Codices graeci et latini, ed. Scatone de Vries, Supplement 6 (Leiden 1909) 6-7 figs. 19, 21. Cf. Sigrid Esche, *Adam und Eva*; *Sündenfall und Erlösung*, Lukas-Bücherei zur christlichen Ikonographie 8 (Düsseldorf 1957) 13-14, 28.

[11] See M. Rosenbaum et al., *Pentateuch with Targum Onkelos, Haphtaroth, and Rashi's Commentary: Genesis* (New York n.d.) 12, 15.

[12] Beryl Smalley, *The Study of the Bible in the Middle Ages*, ed. 2 (Oxford 1952, repr. Notre Dame 1964) 112.

[13] Andrew of Saint Victor, *Comm. in Gen.* 3, Bibl. Vat. Barb. lat. 693 fol. 109v: The curse is that only the serpent among the beasts of the earth goes upon its belly: "Maledicionem dicit serpenti & dampnacionis sentenciam infligit inter cetera animancia & bestias terre que pedibus gradiuntur super terram; cum enim cetera pedibus gradiantur & tibiis & cruribus se subleuent a terra & terre graminibus uescantur, ipse solus uentre & pectore repperit [*sic*] & terram in cibum sumit."

[14] *Ibid.* 109: "Esto quod in serpente diabolus illum suo instinctu replens eique suum spiritum miscens eo more quo vates demoniorum inplere solet repleretur [*sic*] loqueretur."

himself into a serpent, shown in the branches of the tree. Later the demon appears as an angel of light and continues his temptation.[15]

Something similar happens in the mid-twelfth-century Anglo-Norman *Play of Adam*, though the sequence is reversed; the devil first appears in person —in what guise we are not told, except that he affects a friendly approach with a cheerful countenance in his attempt to persuade Eve. Later an artificially constructed serpent (supposedly a normally appearing one) ascends the tree and Eve pretends to be listening to it.[16] Though the devil does not now appear, it is understood that he is engineering the conversation.

In the *Saint Albans Psalter* (executed before the year 1123) the devil himself, in a typically horrible humanoid form, is in the tree, and the serpent issues from his mouth; in the serpent's own mouth is an apple, which Eve is taking.[17]

Eventually in Western art the Eden serpent appears with feet (and with wings). A striking example can be found in the *Huntingfield Psalter*, an English manuscript dated around 1170. Here, in the temptation scene, the serpent is twined around the tree as usual, but is equipped with a small pair of legs and a small set of wings, as well as doglike ears.[18] This development has nothing to do, it seems, with the tradition of the Eden serpent first having feet and then being cursed by their removal. Andrew of Saint Victor's lead in accepting this reading was not followed up. Rather it reflects a tendency in medieval iconography to represent all kinds of serpents as winged, footed, and dog-headed. Eden serpents with doglike heads appear in some of the earliest representations of the temptation.[19] This trait in medieval iconography may, however, be an independently developed tradition. The notion of flying serpents (and therefore, presumably, serpents with wings) was not a new one, but was known in antiquity. Isidore in his *Etymologies* has a nuber of them, including the dragon, which he defines as the largest of the ser-

---

[15] Oxford, Bodleian MS Junius 11, ed. Israel Gollancz, *The Caedmon Manuscript* (Oxford 1927).

[16] *Le mystère d'Adam* (*Ordo representacionis Ade*), ed. Paul Aebischer, Textes littéraires français (Geneva 1963) 44, 52: "Tunc tristis et vultu demisso recedet ab Adam et ibit usque ad portas inferni. . . . De hinc ex parte Evae accedet ad paradisum, et Evam laeto vultu blandiens sic alloquitur." "Tunc serpens artificiose compositus ascendit iuxta stipitem arboris vetitae. Cui Eva proprius adhibebit aurem, quasi ipsius auscultans consilium."

[17] Otto Pächt, C. R. Dodwell, and Francis Wormald, *The St. Albans Psalter*, Studies of the Warburg Institute 25 (London 1960) pl. 14.

[18] *Huntingfield Psalter*, Pierpont Morgan Library MS 43 fol. 8v, reproduced in Walter W. S. Cook, "The Earliest Painted Panels of Catalonia" 5, *Art Bulletin* 10 (1927-1928) 152-204 (p. 165 fig. 20).

[19] Three examples are given in Theodor Ehrenstein, *Das alte Testament im Bilde* (Vienna 1923) 37-38 figs. 5, 7, 16.

pents, if not of all land animals.[20] Although according to Isidore dragons and other serpents by definition do not have feet, they did come to acquire them in the course of time, as can be seen from the illuminated manuscripts of the *Physiologus*, or bestiary. In the oldest surviving illustrated bestiary, the ninth-century Bern manuscript, none of the serpents have appendages.[21] The vipers, which have arms in virtue of being half human in form, do not count (I shall deal with them later). In the only tenth-century illustrated bestiary that has come down to us, the Brussels manuscript, the serpents are footless.[22] No eleventh-century illustrated bestiaries are extant, but many survive from the twelfth century, and in them there is an abundance of footed and winged serpents of various kinds, including amphisbenas, asps, basilisks, dragons, and hydruses.

This is not the place to attempt to trace all the factors that contributed to this development, but as far as the devil in his role of serpent is concerned, the raw material for the transformation can be found in the *Stuttgart Psalter*, which is dated between 820 and 830.[23] The Eden serpent in this work is limb-less (fols. 28v, 121v), as are the larger serpents or dragons, except that some have wings (fols. 69v, 107v). But we find a creature tormenting the damned in hell which has the head and forequarters, including the legs, of a dog, and a body that tapers into the tail of a serpent (fol. 10v). The whale that swallows Jonah is somewhat similar, except that its serpentine body ends in a fish's tail (fols. 79, 147v). The whale came to be identified with "Leviathan the twisting serpent" of Isaiah 27.1, and the whole verse was read as referring to the devil.

It is likely too that the dragon-devil of the Apocalypse would be influenced by his colleague, the beast from the sea, which shared with him the attributes of seven heads and ten horns, but which had in addition the feet of a bear. The ninth-century *Valenciennes Apocalypse* shows this creature to have only two feet, with the rest of its body being that of a sea serpent like the whale of the *Stuttgart Psalter*. The dragon, in contrast, is still limbless in this early work.[24]

When we come to the *Bamberg Apocalypse* at the beginning of the eleventh century, we see that a good deal of interchange has occurred among several

[20] Isidore, *Etymologiae, sive Origines* 12.4.4, ed. W. M. Lindsay (Oxford 1911). Other flying serpents are the jaculus and the siren serpent (12.4.29).

[21] *Physiologus bernensis* (Codex bongarsianus 318, Bern Burgerbibliothek), ed. Christoph von Steiger and Otto Homburger (Basel 1964). This manuscript represents the C tradition.

[22] *Physiologus* (A tradition), Brussels, Bibliothèque Royale 10074 fols. 141v, 143; given in Richard Stettiner, *Die illustrierten Prudentiushandschrifte* (Berlin 1905) pl. 177 figs. 2, 5.

[23] Wilhelm Hoffmann et al., *Der stuttgarter Bilderpsalter* (Stuttgart 1965-1968).

[24] See Amédée Boinet, *La miniature carolingienne* (Paris 1913) pl. 159a. I wish to thank Ruth Mellinkoff and Barbara Abou-El-Haj for drawing my attention to these Carolingian whales and apocalyptic beasts, respectively.

of the evil monsters, including the beast from the earth and the red beast of Babylon. The dragon-devil now has a pair of wings and a pair of feet, and his "angels," when engaging in battle with Michael and his angels, resemble him, except that they have only one head apiece instead of seven.[25]

A serpent of this sort, that is, one having two wings and two feet, appears in the Eden scenes of the bronze doors of Saint Michael's Church, Hildesheim (A.D. 1015). In the panel portraying the temptation, this elaborate serpent, which obviously represents the devil or a delegated demon, looks on from one tree, while an ordinary limbless serpent with fruit in its mouth is coiled around the forbidden tree, tempting Eve. In the next panel it is the limbed serpent, now breathing fire, that Eve accuses when called to account by God, and the simple serpent has disappeared from the scene (or perhaps we are meant to think that the limbed serpent transformed itself into a limbless form, and then resumed its original shape.)[26] The next logical step would be to have a limbed serpent do the actual tempting, as in the *Huntingfield Psalter*.[27]

There was another traditional concept of the Eden serpent which I have not yet mentioned, namely, that before it was cursed it was able to hold itself erect, not by means of legs, but simply by standing on the tip of its tail. We see an example of this in the ninth-century *Grandval Bible*.[28]

Some scholars began to identify the Eden serpent as a particular species of serpent, especially the free-standing pareas, mentioned by Lucan in his *Pharsalia* and followed by Isidore. This tendency was objected to by Alexander Neckham, an Englishman (born at Saint Albans in 1157) who was a distinguished professor at Paris as early as 1180. In his *De naturis rerum* he says that he is not prepared to say whether the serpent used by Satan to deceive Eve was a viper. "Nor," he goes on, "will you wring from me the assertion that it was a pareas that appeared to the first parent, although some try to prove this to have been the case. Now they take their argument from what is said in Genesis::'Upon your belly shall you go.' For they conjecture from this that that serpent was erect, according to what Lucan says: 'And the pareas, tensed to plow his way with his tail.'"[29]

Neckham does not describe the viper. If, as seems likely, he was familiar only with Isidore or the most common form of medieval bestiary, which

[25] Heinrich Wölfflin, *Die bamberger Apokalypse* (Munich 1921) pl. 30.

[26] See Francis J. Tschan, *Saint Bernward of Hildesheim* 3, Publications in Mediaeval Studies 13 (Notre Dame 1952) pls. 118-119.

[27] Above, n. 18.

[28] Wilhelm Koehler, *Die karolingischen Miniaturen* 1.3 (Berlin 1930, repr. 1963) pl. 50.

[29] Alexander Neckham, *De naturis rerum* 2.105, ed. Thomas Wright, Rolls Series 34 (London 1863) 188. See Lucan, *Pharsalia* 9.721; Isidore 12.4.27.

simply repeated Isidore's entry,[30] he would have no definite picture in mind, since no description is given. If, however, he knew the definition of the Greek *Physiologus* in one of its Latin versions (the *Y*, *A*, and *C* traditions), he would have been thinking of a creature whose lower half was crocodilian and whose upper half was human in appearance, either male or female, depending on its own sex. The illustration in the Bern manuscript, however, provides the creatures with the lower extremities of a simple limbless serpent, and not those of a crocodile. The male has a triple fin at the end, like that of a fish.[31] This description of the viper may have been influential in the development of the tradition to which this essay is primarily directed.[32]

Those who believed the Eden serpent to be a particular kind of serpent that continued to exist after the fall did not regard God's curse as hereditary (at least not in all serpents), unlike those who held that the serpent had feet which were cut off. For they maintained that other serpents of the same kind remained erect after the curse, since a breed of this sort could be so described by Lucan and Isidore. Some authorities, by the way, following the lead of Saint Augustine, interpreted the curse as applying to the devil; and in the twelfth century Rupert of Deutz and Hugh of Saint Victor went further and exempted the serpent from it. Rupert was even able to prove from Genesis that the serpent had its legless nature and reptilian crawl from the beginning, before the fall.[33]

---

[30] Isidore, *Etymologiae* 12.4.10, and the various bestiaries in the expanded *B* tradition of the *Physiologus*; see Florence McCulloch, *Medieval Latin and French Bestiaries*, University of N. Carolina Studies in the Romance Languages and Literatures 33 (Chapel Hill 1960) 28ff. Neckham's initial characterization of the viper (p. 187) corresponds closely to Isidore's.

[31] *Physiologus bernensis* fol. 111. Francis J. Carmody gives what he takes to be the *Physiologus's* original description of the viper in his *Physiologus; the Very Ancient Book of Beasts, Plants, and Stones* (San Francisco 1953) chap. 13: "The Physiologus tells of the viper that the male has a man's face, the female a woman's face; from head to navel they have the form of men, thence to the tail the form of the crocodile." His edition of the *Y* text reads: "Physiologus dicit de vipera quoniam faciem habet hominis masculus, femina autem mulieris, usque ad umbilicum; ab umbilico autem usque ad caudam corcodrilli habet figuram." *Physiologus latinus versio Y* 12, University of California Publications in Classical Philology 12 (Berkeley 1941) 110.

[32] Schmerber (n. 1 above) 12-15 notes that in late Hellenistic times sarcophagi (especially Roman ones) showed Hercules fighting with a Hydra that was half woman and half serpent; he points out that Hydra here has the form of Echidna, her mother, who, according to Hesiod, "is half a nymph with glancing eyes and fair cheeks, and half again a huge snake, great and awful, with speckled skin" (*Theogony* 297-299, trans. H. G. Evelyn White, Loeb Classical Library). It was obviously this description that inspired the *Physiologus* notion of the viper, which in Greek is none other than *echidna*. The Latin form, *vipera*, is, like the Greek, in the feminine gender, and the female of the species therefore has denotative primacy over the male.

[33] Augustine, *De Genesi ad litteram* 11.36; Rupert of Deutz, *De Trinitate et operibus eius* in Gen. 3.18 (PL 167.303-304); Hugh of Saint Victor, *Adnotat. elucid. in Pent.* in Gen. (PL 174.42). I owe these references to an article on "The Lintel Fragment Representing Eve

III. Peter Comestor's Virginal Serpent

About the year 1170 a new tradition was born, that of the maiden-faced
serpent in the Garden of Eden. It was fathered by the celebrated "Peter
the Eater"—Petrus Comestor or Manducator (circa 1100-circa 1180), who
was known as "the Master of the Histories," the histories being the chapters
of his *Historia scholastica*, a paraphrase of the Bible, supplemented from
various sacred and profane sources. He began this work around the time
that he became a canon regular of Saint Victor in Paris.

In his "Story of the Book of Genesis," Peter speaks of the serpent as follows:

> "The serpent was more cunning than all other animals," both by
> nature and by accident—by accident, because it was filled with the
> demon. For when Lucifer had been cast out of the paradise of
> spirits, he envied man, because he was in the paradise of bodies.
> He knew that if he made him transgress he too would be cast out.
> Because he was afraid of being found out by the man, he approached
> the woman, who had less foresight and was "wax to be twisted into
> vice"[34] and this by means of the serpent; for the serpent at that
> time was erect like a man, since it was laid prostrate when it was
> cursed; and even now the pareas is said to be erect when it moves.
> He also chose a certain kind of serpent, as Bede says, which had
> the countenance of a virgin, because like favors like; and he moved
> its tongue to speak, though it knew nothing itself, just as he speaks
> through the frenzied and possessed.[35]

Peter does believe, however, that the serpent that Lucifer used had a voice
of its own, since he says that part of the serpent's punishment was to have
its voice taken away, and poison put in its mouth.[36]

Even though Peter's career began in Troyes, the chief center of rabbinical
exegesis in the North, he does not follow the Jewish tradition of giving the

---

from Saint-Lazare at Autun," which Professor O. K. Werckmeister of UCLA is preparing
for publication.

[34] Cf. Horace, *Ars poetica* 163.

[35] Peter Comestor, *Historia scholastica* 1.21, PL. 198.1072: "'Serpens erat callidior cunctis animantibus' et naturaliter et incidenter. Incidenter, quia plenus erat daemone. Lucifer enim deiectus a paradiso spirituum invidit homini, quod esset in paradiso corporum,
sciens si faceret eum transgredi, quod et ille eiceretur. Timens vero deprehendi a viro,
mulierem minus providam et certam [*sic*; *lege* ceream] in vitium flecti aggressus est, et
hoc per serpentem, quia tunc serpens erectus est ut homo, quia in maledictione prostratus
est; et adhuc, ut tradunt, phareas erectus incedit. Elegit etiam quoddam genus serpentis,
ut ait Beda, virgineum vultum habens, quia similia similibus applaudunt, et movit ad lo-
quendum linguam eius, tamen nescientis, sicut et per fanaticos et energumenos loquitur."

[36] *Ibid.* 1.23 (PL 198.1074).

serpent feet in its pristine state, but apparently accepts the "upright but legless" tradition of the West. At any rate, when speaking of the serpent's fate, to go on its belly thenceforward, he does not speak of any loss of "footage."[37] But since he acknowledges that some serpents, like the pareas, remain in their upright position, he does not seem to think that God laid a curse upon all serpents, but only upon the individual one that was employed in Eden by the devil. If so, he presumably believed that there still existed venomless serpents with virginal faces and voices, which could move in an upright position.

Peter seems to cite the Venerable Bede as his source for the idea of a maiden-headed serpent, and his statement was interpreted in this way by many of his readers. An example is Stephen Langton, who glossed the *Historia* shortly after Peter's death.[38] But Bonnell appears to be correct when he says that the concept is foreign to Bede, and that perhaps Peter is attributing to Bede only what goes before "ut ait Beda," namely, "elegit etiam quoddam genus serpentis," and not what follows (virgineum vultum habens); but he also suggests a possible misreading of a phrase in a work attributed to Bede.[39]

IV. "A Certain Kind of Serpent"

Whether or not we are inclined to grant that a "misprint" may have led Peter to his conclusion that the serpent that deceived Eve had a virginal countenance, we must remain puzzled by the Master of the Histories' willingness to accept what should have struck him (I feel) as a most unlikely suggestion. What is the psychological explanation for his adoption of the idea?

We may be able to throw some light upon this problem by citing an earlier precedent of the very same notion; it is all the more remarkable in that it

[37] *Ibid.* For Peter's Jewish connections, see Esra Shereshevsky, "Hebrew traditions in Peter Comestor's *Historia scholastica*," *Jewish Quarterly Review* 59 (1969) 268-289.

[38] Stephen Langton, *Expositio litteralis in Hist. schol.*, Paris Bibliothèque Nationale MS lat. 14417 fol. 129v: "Dicit Beda uirgineum uultum habuisse." This gloss was written before 1187. In an *Expositio moralis*, composed in 1193 (MS 14414) Langton does not take up the subject of the maiden's head when speaking of the serpent (fol. 116v). Cf. F. Stegmüller, *Repertorium biblicum medii aevi* 5 (Madrid 1955) 235, 239. Nor does he refer to this interpretation in his own commentary on the Heptateuch (I have consulted only Cambridge Peterhouse MS 112 fols. 7v-8v), which was written also during his Paris period (i.e., before 1206); see Beryl Smalley, in G. Lacombe and B. Smalley, "Studies on the Commentaries of Cardinal Stephen Langton," *Archives d'histoire doctrinale et littéraire du moyen âge* 5 (1930) 5-220, esp. 163-169.

[39] Bonnell (n. 1 above) 257 n. 3. He quotes this sentence from the Pseudo-Bede *Quaestiones super Genesim*: "Serpens per se loqui non poterat . . . nisi nimirum illum diabolus utens, et velut organum per quod articulatum sonum emitteret" (PL 93.276), and asks if *velut organum* could have been corrupted into *vultum virgineum*.

seems highly unlikely for it to have influenced Comestor's work, for it appears only in an ancient Syrian biblical history called *The Cave of Treasures*.[40] This work, fictitiously ascribed to Ephraem the Syrian, says that Satan, filled with jealousy and wrath, "took up his abode in the serpent, and he raised him up and made him to fly through the air to the skirts of Mount (Eden), whereon was Paradise." Satan hid in the serpent because his own appearance was so foul that Eve would have fled from him if she had seen how he really looked; therefore just as a man who teaches a bird to speak Greek hides behind a mirror and makes the bird think that a fellow bird is speaking to it, Satan entered the serpent and called Eve by name. "And when she turned round towards him, she saw her own form [reflected] in him, and she talked to him; and Satan led her astray with his lying words, because the nature of woman is soft [or, yielding]."[41]

From this account I conclude either that Eve looked like a serpent or that the serpent looked like a woman! Budge's interpretation seems to be that Eve herself was somehow mirrored in the serpent. Luise Troje conjectures that the *Cave of Treasures* passage is a polemic against the Hellenistic goddess Isis-Thermutis, an erect serpent with the breasts and head of a woman.[42] The *Cave* serpent, however, seems to have been the usual legged masculine serpent of Eastern tradition; God says, "I have fettered his legs in his belly, and I have given him the dust of the earth for food."[43]

If we accept Mrs. Troje's reading of the motivation of the author of *The Cave of Treasures*, we should seek a similar movement in Peter Comestor's mind. We can hardly think of him as being exercised against a serpentine deity with a woman's face, nor are we able to see a polemic against Eve for any serpentine qualities she might have possessed; rather we must simply think that he accepted the idea of a woman-faced serpent because he knew

---

[40] E. A. Wallis Budge, *The Book of the Cave of Treasures* (London 1927) xi-xiv, puts the original work in the fourth century, but says that the form in which we have it is no older than the sixth century. Cf. Albrecht Götze, "Die Schatzhöhle," *Sitzungsberichte der Heidelberger Akademie der Wissenschaften*, philosophisch-historische Klasse 13 (1922) 4.38, who postulates a Syriac archetype of which two recensions survive: 1) a Nestorian Syriac edition, made after A. D. 500, and 2) a Monophysite Arabic translation, made circa 750-760. There is also an Ethiopic version, based on the Arabic.

[41] Budge 63-64.

[42] L. Troje, "*ΑΔΑΜ* und *ΖΩΗ*; eine Szene der altchristlichen Kunst in ihrem religionsgeschichtlichen Zusammenhange," *Sitzungsberichte der Heidelberger Akademie der Wissenschaften*, philos.-hist. Klasse 7 (1916) 17.43 n. 3. Mrs. Troje also calls attention to a Gnostic principle, conceived of as a virgin above and serpent below. Alice Kemp-Welch (n. 1 above) 987-989 attempted, with no evidence, to bring the Gnostic Serpent-Sophia to bear upon the maiden-headed Eden serpent of the medieval West by way of the Albigensians.

[43] Budge 67.

that such serpents existed. I have mentioned the viper as one example. Were there others?

The siren is an obvious candidate. The classical form of this creature was half virginal, half birdlike.[44] Hyginus specifies that the upper part is that of a woman,[45] and no doubt the common view was that it had the head, arms, and torso of a woman, and the lower body, legs, and tail of a bird.

The *Physiologus*, in the chapter on the siren and onocentaur, says that the siren has the figure of a human being to the navel, and in the other half the figure of a bird.[46] Isidore follows this tradition in general, but adds that it has wings and talons.[47]

The *Physiologus* is commenting on the Septuagint version of Isaiah 13.21-22. Jerome, however, in his comentary on the same text says that the word that is translated by "sirens" he interpreted to mean either demons, or a kind of monster, or large flying dragons with crests.[48] Perhaps Isidore was inspired by Jerome when he included in his treatment of serpents the note that "in Arabia there are serpents with wings, which are called sirens; they run faster than horses, but they are also said to fly."[49]

Somewhat after Isidore's time, beginning with the *Liber monstrorum* (ascribed to Aldhelm, Bishop of Sherborne), the siren became half fish instead of half bird, and thus the mermaid was born.[50] But the tradition of the bird-siren lived on, and so apparently did that of the serpent-siren, for they are obviously combined in the scene of the siren and onocentaur sculpted on one of the capitals in the choir (right side) of the twelfth-century cathedral of Autun (fig. 1). Here the siren has only a woman's head, with a rather scaly body, a serpent's tail, and a bird's wings and feet.[51]

[44] See Edmond Faral, "La queue de poisson des sirènes," *Romania* 74 (1953) 433-506, esp. 439-440.

[45] Hyginus, *Fabulae* 125, ed. H. J. Rose (Leyden 1933, repr. 1963) 91.

[46] *Physiologus* Y 15 (113-114): "Dimidiam partem usque ad umbilicum hominis habent figuram, dimidio autem volatilis."

[47] Isidore, *Etym.* 11.3.30.

[48] Jerome, *Comm. on Is.* (PL 24.163): "Sirenae autem *thennim* vocantur, quas nos aut daemones, aut monstra quaedam, aut certe dracones magnos interpretabamur, qui cristati sunt et volantes."

[49] Isidore, *Etym.* 12.4.29.

[50] Faral (n. 42 above); see below, n. 51.

[51] There is a similar scene on a capital in the church at Vézelay, but the onocentaur (if such it be) is female, and there is a three-headed bird between it and the siren. Denis Grivot and George Zarnecki, *Gislebertus, Sculptor of Autun* (New York 1961) 66 (cf. pl. B 12-16), think that the three-headed bird belongs to the original scene. The coupling of onocentaur and siren by themselves, however, is obviously more primitive. Grivot and Zarnecki do not place the scene in the *Physiologus* tradition, perhaps because they consider the humanoid figure to be a faun. But as is pointed out by Richard Hamann, "Diana and the Snake-tongued Demon," *The Burlington Magazine for Connoisseurs* 61.2 (July-Dec. 1932) 207, centaurs and fauns are portrayed alike. Furthermore, the ordinary *Physiologus* description

Similar creatures can be found in another twelfth-century cathedral, that of Sens, not far from Peter's home city of Troyes; on one capital (in the left nave), there are two sirens of the Autun type; on another (in the right nave), one such siren is with a male of the species—he has the same attributes as his partner, except that he is endowed with a beard.

The maiden-faced scorpion is another medieval invention that antedates the *Historia scholastica*. Isidore, who wrote in the seventh century, says simply that the scorpion is a worm (that is, *vermis*, a word that he applies chiefly to insects and arachnids and not to serpents) with a sting in its tail.[52] He speaks of another kind of scorpion, however, which is a type of *virga*, that is, a "switch" or whip.[53] This coincidence may have inspired an etymological explanation of the Isidorean type, according to which the scorpion was characterized as a *virga* because it had the face of a *virgo*, as is implied in Holy Writ (though it is obvious that a *virga* was called a scorpion because of the scorpionlike wounds that it inflicted).

One of the scriptural bases for representing scorpions with female faces is the description of the hellish locusts in the Apocalypse; they had the power like that of the scorpions of the earth, and the torment they inflicted was like that of a scorpion; they looked like horses prepared for battle; they wore crowns on their heads, had faces like those of human beings and hair like that of women, and tails like those of scorpions, with stings in them. Furthermore, in the Greek text they are he-locusts, but they were transformed into she-locusts because of the gender of *locusta*.[54] We see an illustration of these creatures in the mid-eleventh-century Saint-Sever copy of Beatus of Liébana's *Commentary on the Apocalypse*, in which some have the bodies of lions and others the bodies of locusts, or grasshoppers.[55]

Another scriptural indication of the woman-headed scorpion occurs in the Book of Ecclesiasticus, where Jesus the son of Sirach warn that "a wicked woman is like a loose ox-yoke; a man who holds her is like one who grasps

---

of the onocentaur does not demand a complete ass's body; its lower part is simply said to "exceedingly wild," or, as the *Y* version says, "like an ass." See McCulloch (n. 30 above) 166.

[52] Isidore, *Etymologiae* 12.5.4: "Scorpio vermis terrenus, qui potius vermibus ascribitur, non serpentibus; animal armatum aculeo, et ex eo graece vocatum quod cauda figat et arcuato vulnere venena diffundat."

[53] *Ibid.* 5.27.18: "Virgae sunt summitates frondium arborumque, dictae quod virides sint, vel quod vim habeant arguendi; quae si lenis fuerit, virga est; si certe nodosa vel aculeata, scorpio rectissimo nomine vocatur, qui arcuato vulnere in corpus infigitur."

[54] Rev. 9.3, 5, 7-8, 10. In classical Greek locust (*akris*) is feminine but it is treated as masculine in this text of the New Testament.

[55] Paris Bib. Nat. MS lat. 8878 fol. 145; Jean Porcher, *Medieval French Miniatures* (New York [1960]) 27 (and pl. 18).

a scorpion."[56] The author of the *Ancrene Riwle*, who seems to have flourished somewhat later than Comestor,[57] applies the text to woman in general and attributes the sentiment to Solomon: "The man who grasps a woman is like one who grasps a scorpion." The scorpion is taken as a symbol of lechery in the *Ancrene Riwle*, and is described as "a type of worm that is said to have a head something like a woman's but behind this it is a serpent. It puts forth a fair countenance and flatters with its head but stings with its tail. Such then is lechery, the devil's beast."[58]

The *Ancrene Riwle* therefore describes a scorpion as a woman-headed serpent, a symbol of lechery, the animal used by the devil. If this work was written after Peter Comestor's *Historia*, it is barely possible that the latter work influenced this description. But it is obvious that the *Riwle* does not have the Eden serpent in mind at all, but is drawing on a tradition independent of it. The characterization of the scorpion as part serpent was obviously due to the fact that the Germanic cognate of *vermis* means not only "worm" but primarily "serpent" or "dragon" (that is, "large serpent").

V. The Sphinx in Eden

One other fabulous monster from classical times must be mentioned as a possible influence on the womanized Eden serpent, and that is the Sphinx, who according to Hesiod is both daughter and granddaughter of Echidna. By Typhaon (another serpent-type) Echidna bore the hounds Orthus and Cerberus, as well as Hydra and Chimaera. Then she (Echidna, though Hesiod could possibly mean Chimaera) "was subject in love to Orthus and brought forth the deadly Sphinx which destroyed the Cadmeans."[59] Hesiod does not describe the Sphinx, but since she is found in such serpentine company, it is not surprising that she sometimes is thought to have something of the serpent about her. This characteristic, however, is mentioned, so far as I know, in only one classical literary source (which alludes to another written source), namely, a scholion on the *Phoenissae* of Euripides: "The Sphinx, as it is written, had the tail of a she-dragon" (δράκαινα).[60]

---

[56] Ecclus. 26.10: "Sicut boum iugum quod movetur, ita et mulier nequam; qui tenet illam quasi qui apprehendit scorpionem."

[57] C. H. Talbot, "Some Notes on the Dating of the *Ancrene Riwle*," *Neophilologus* 40 (1956) 38-50, suggests that the work may have been composed even in the first part of the thirteenth century.

[58] *The English Text of the Ancrene Riwle*, London British Museum Cotton MS Nero A XIV, ed. Mabel Day, Early English Text Society 225 (London 1952) 92.

[59] Hesiod, *Theogony* 306-327 (Loeb 100-103). Hesiod's word for Sphinx is Phix.

[60] W. Dindorf, *Scholia graeca in Euripidis tragoedias* (Oxford 1863) 3.407 (*Scholia in Phoenissas* 1760). Dindorf cites the twelfth-century San Marco manuscript and the fourteenth-century Munich manuscript as reading δράκαινα, whereas the thirteenth-century Paris manuscript and the Venice 1534 edition read the masculine form, δράκω. But ac-

The only ancient examples of the serpent-tailed sphinx that I have seen, however, have tails that end with a serpent's head.[61] This is a fashion popularized by the Chimaera,[62] and continued in the lion-headed, fire-breathing horses of the Apocalypse.[63] The ancient sphinxes of this sort could hardly have come to the attention of the people of the Middle Ages. But somehow or other the image made its appearance in the medieval West (whether or not it was identified as a sphinx), as in one of the capitals in the crypt of the Duomo of Modena (fig. 2). The work was done in the time of Wiligelmo (early twelfth century), and it shows a creature, repeated four times, with a woman's head covered by a flat hat; it has a heavy horse's body and hooves, the wings of a bird, and a (serpentine?) tail ending in a laughing head.[64]

From further south in Italy, in Terracina, comes a wooden chest tentatively dated in the eleventh century,[65] in which a sphinxlike creature is brought into conjunction with what is apparently a depiction of the fall of Adam and Eve (fig. 3). The serpent is erect between Adam and Eve where the tree is normally placed, and it seems to be speaking in Eve's ear, though Adam and Eve both hold foliage in front of them, which would indicate that they have already fallen. But this is the traditional stylized way of portraying the unfortunate couple. Above these three figures is what looks like a winged lion with a human face. Perhaps we are meant to think of the devil —we recall that in the eleventh-century door from Hildesheim a winged and footed serpent looked on as an ordinary serpent (or the same serpent simplified) did the actual tempting; and in the Junius manuscript and the

---

cording to the edition of Eduard Schwartz, *Scholia in Euripidem* (Berlin 1887) 1.414, not only the San Marco manuscript but the Paris manuscript as well (and a thirteenth-century Vatican manuscript) have δράκαινα.

[61] A. Dessenne, *Le sphinx: étude iconographique*: vol. 1, *Des origines a la fin du second millénaire*, Bibliothèque des écoles françaises d'Athènes et de Rome 186 (Paris 1957) 204-205, says that the serpent-headed tail is encountered among nearly all the neo-Hittite sphinxes of the ninth and eighth centuries before Christ; he shows a sample from Perachora, Corinth (pl. 38.6). An Etruscan example is in the museum at Palermo (coll. Casuccini no. 103), in Gustavo Körte, *I rilievi delle urne etrusche*, Imperiale istituto archeologico germanico (Berlin 1916) 3.222 pl. 150.15. An ancient Greek bronze statuette of a sphinx in the Berlin museum (no. 8266) has a tail that ends in a bearded serpent's head (*Archäologischer Anzeiger* 8 [1893] 96).

[62] According to the *Iliad* 6.181 the Chimaera is a lion in front, a goat in the middle, and a serpent behind. This description was also interpolated into Hesiod, after his statement that the Chimaera has three heads, a lion's, a goat's, and a snake's (*Theog.* 321-323).

[63] Rev. 9.17-19.

[64] Arturo Carlo Quintavalle, *Wiligelmo e la sua scuola*, I diamanti dell' arte 28 (Florence 1967) 37. Cf. the *Bamberger Apocalypse* (n. 25 above) p. 23, where similar creatures result from combining the locusts and serpent-tailed horses of Rev. 9.3-19.

[65] The chest is now in the Palazzo Venezia, Rome. See Federico Hermanin, *Il Palazzo di Venezia* (Bologna 1925) 28; *Roma e dintorni*, Touring club italiano (Milan 1965) 94.

Saint Albans Psalter the devil in human (angelic) form is pictured along-side the serpent or the same devil in his serpentine form. But it could also represent the cherub stationed before the garden of Eden,[66] or indeed the cherub (understood as Satan or one of the other sinful angels) who like Adam and Eve was cast out of Eden.[67] It is conceivable that the artist or his source would think of a cherub as a sphinx, from the various descriptions given in the Bible.[68]

It has sometimes been doubted, however, whether the scene deals with the garden of Eden at all, since it is difficult to recognize any other biblical or Christian motif on the chest. But we may point to the scene of the eagle fighting the serpent immediately above the scene that I have been discussing. This struggle was taken as an allegory of Christ's defeat of Satan, and it becomes very common in Italy from the eleventh century on.[69] Most of the other panels also represent scenes of struggle, and it seems that serpents are the chief enemies of the men, centaurs, birds, and other beasts. Perhaps the scenes are illustrations of the consequences of original sin.

An unequivocal designation of the Eden serpent as a sphinx comes in the *Chester Plays*, which could not have been composed in English before the last quarter of the fourteenth century.[70] The play of the Fall, however, may have been based on an earlier Latin play, since fragments of Latin dialogue appear in the best manuscript.[71] At the place where the devil disguises himself as a serpent there occurs this marginal notation:

Versus: Sphinx: volucris penna, serpens pede, fronte puella.

The devil's account of the serpent in the play corresponds to this description:

> A manner of an adder is in this place,
> That wings like a bird she has,
> Feet as an adder, a maiden's face;
> Her kind I will take.[72]

---

[66] Gen. 3.24; the Latin reads *cherubim*, which was often understood as singular in the Middle Ages.

[67] Ezek. 28.12-19 (Vulgate).

[68] Ex. 25.19-20; Ezek. 41.18-19; cf. Ezek. 1.5-11.

[69] Rudolf Wittkower, "Eagle and Serpent; a Study in the Migration of Symbols," *Journal of the Warburg Institute* 2 (1938-1939) 293-325 esp. 318.

[70] F. M. Salter, *Medieval Drama in Chester* (Toronto 1955) 33-42; Glynne Wickham, *Early English Stages* 1 (London 1959, repr. 1966) 133-137.

[71] *The Chester Plays* 1, ed. Hermann Deimling, Early English Text Society extra series 62 (London 1892, repr. 1959) 30: At the point where Eve takes the apple: "Vah! Quam dulcis est! Impertiendum est marito." When she suggests that Adam eat, and he agrees: "Quando ita vis, faciam." —B. M. Harl. 2124, A. D. 1607.

[72] *Ibid.* 28. The variants in the Latin verse in the four less authentic manuscripts are proved false by their lack of agreement with Ausonius.

The Latin hexameter is based upon a line in the *Riddle of the Number Three*
of the fourth-century poet Ausonius of Bordeaux, who follows a common
Greco-Latin tradition characterizing the Sphinx as having the wings of a
bird, the body of a lioness, and the face of a girl:

Sphinx: volucris pennis, pedibus fera, fronte puella.[73]

The author of the *Chester Plays* or the author of his source cleverly substituted serpent's feet for those of the lioness; he kept the meter by avail-
ing himself of the poetic option of using the singular for the plural—necessarily, for the feet, but for good measure for the wings. The questions arise
(and I must leave them unanswered for the present): How did the author of
this verse know Ausonius? And how did he know (if he did not simply impro-
vise it) that the Sphinx was sometimes characterized as partly serpentine?

VI. Species of Womanized Serpents

We cannot tell with certainty how the author of the *Chester Plays* envisaged
his adder, nor specify the kind of costume used by the actor who played the
devil when he assumed the adder's form. Presumably the devil's ordinary
(that is, nonserpentine) costume included feathers, since the banns for the
play of the temptation of Jesus promise the customary appearance of "the
devil in his feathers, all ragger [*lege* ragged] and rent."[74] The author of the
Chester Plays, however, may have been inspired by another, more common
way of portraying the Eden serpent, that is, as a traditional winged and footed
serpent like the one in the *Huntingfield Psalter*, but with a woman's head.
Winged serpents of this kind were not given reptilian or batlike wings, such
as demons in their humanoid forms usually possess, but rather feathered,
birdlike ones.

The earliest instance of a woman-headed Eden serpent of this kind that
has come to my attention occurs in a copy made in 1220 of Beatus's *Commentary on the Apocalypse*, which is now in the Pierpont Morgan Library.[75]

---

[73] Ausonius, *Griphus ternarii numeri* 41, ed. Rudolf Peiper, *Decimi Magni Ausonii Bur-
digalensis Opuscula* (Leipzig 1886) 202.

[74] *Chester Plays* 6. M. D. Anderson, *Drama and Imagery in English Medieval Churches*
(Cambridge 1963) 169-170 (and pl. 24a), suggests that a feathered fiend that appears on
a misericord in the church at Gayton in Northamphire could have been inspired by a
play. It could conceivably double as the Chester serpent without further transformation,
although we might object that the feet of this creature have talons like those of a bird of
prey; but since it was anyone's guess what the feet of a serpent looked like, such ones as
these might have been considered perfectly satisfactory.

[75] Morgan MS 429 fol. 6. The colophon is dated 1258 of the Spanish era, which is the
equivalent of A. D. 1220. It is interesting to see that in the same manuscript there is another
depiction of the Eden temptation (a detail of the *Mappa mundi* page, fol. 32), where the
tempter is just an ordinary serpent twined around the tree. See Cook (n. 18 above) 165
fig. 19.

The serpent in the temptation scene (fol. 6v) has only the tail of a serpent, with the body and wings of a bird and a vulturelike (or, if one insists, serpentine) neck topped by the tiny head of a woman (fig. 4).[76]

A slightly different version of the woman-headed serpent appeared a short time after the Beatus version. On a pillar of the Virgin portal of the Cathedral of Notre Dame in Amiens there is a statue of the Virgin (dating from circa 1230) crushing a sphinxlike serpent under her feet in fulfillment of the prophecy made in the curse of the Eden serpent (fig. 5). It is wingless, however, and has only one pair of legs (with paws), in front, and a serpentine tail in back; and the beast has what looks like a wimpled woman's head. In the panel below, where the temptation of Eve is depicted, the serpent is of the same type, except that it has no headcovering, and the hair is visible (fig. 6).[77]

These species of serpent tended toward extinction after the fourteenth century. It is evident that some modifications would have had to be made in these types before an actor could easily assume their form. Another, more adaptable, kind of serpent, which would better allow for stage use, is suggested in William Langland's *Piers the Plowman*. He has it that Satan disguised himself "ylyke a lusarde with a lady visage."[78] If a lizard is to be considered a serpent, then there is a precedent in nature for the serpent's feet. The celebrated picture of the fifteenth-century Dutch painter Hugo van der Goes

[76] Another early example of this kind of illustrated serpent-lady appears in *Queen Blanche's Psalter*, which was executed about 1230. See Porcher (n. 55 above) pl. 42. Another instance can be seen in the *Holkham Bible*, an English work with a French text, which seems to have been produced in the London area about 1330; see W. O. Hassall, *The Holkham Bible Picture Book* (London 1954) 65. Another example is the *Bible historiale* in the Geneva library (MS fr. 2 fol. 7), which dates from the second half of the fourteenth century; see Hippolyte Aubert, "Les principaux manuscrits à peintures de la bibliothèque publique et universitaire de Genève," *Bulletin de la Société française de reproductions de manuscrits à peintures* 2 (1912) 61-62 (pl. 31). But here the serpent is given two pairs of feet.

[77] Somewhat similar Eden serpents appear in two Jewish manuscripts executed at the end of the thirteenth century (thereby showing that, even though the tradition of the lady serpent did not originate with the Jews, it eventually found its way to them). One is in a Cologne manuscript discussed by Elisabeth Moses, "Über eine kölner Handschrift der Mischneh Thora des Maimonides," *Zeitschrift für bildenden Kunst* 60 (1926-1927) 71-76, fig. on p. 74. The other is in the British Museum (Add. 11,639 fol. 520v) and is available on postcard; it is likewise in the style of northern France. The *Queen Mary's Psalter*, ed. George Warner (London 1912) pl. 5, has a similar serpent; this work is dated in the beginning of the fourteenth century. All three of these serpents have an enlarged body, between the woman's head and the serpent's tail, where the legs issue on each side much like a mammal's hind limbs. The *Queen Mary's Psalter* miniature is also noteworthy in showing conventional demons nearby aiding in the temptation.

[78] *Piers the Plowman* B 18.335, ed. W. W. Skeat (London 1869) 338. Cf. the four-footed winged serpent of the *Bible historiale* (n. 76 above) and the figure on the Terracina chest (fig. 3).

in Vienna has a serpent that looks like a child dressed in a salamander suit;[79] all four of her limbs are reptilian. In another Dutch picture, painted around the turn of the sixteenth century, that in the *Breviarium Grimani*, van der Goes's example has inspired a similar depiction, except that here the upper limbs and torso are human (the sex, however, is obscured).[80]

Arnoul Gréban no doubt had a lizardlike serpent in mind, for the devil in his biblical play (written around 1452) says that he will take on a virginal face and the feet and body of a serpent; and the stage direction says that he goes on four feet, like a serpent.[81] The sixteenth-century Lucerne plays are similar, and Bonnell attempts to deduce the same for other plays.[82]

Other portrayals of the Eden serpent have no problem with serpents' feet at all, since they use realistic legless snakes, and simply cap them with tiny human heads. An early example of this type occurs in the *Peterborough Psalter*, dated about 1250 (fig. 7).[83] In the fourteenth century a similar serpent was fashioned in the temptation fresco of the Upper Church of the Basilica of Saint Francis at Assisi.[84] Perhaps the most famous instance of this kind occurs in the temptation scene by Masolino in the Brancacci Chapel of the Chiesa del Carmine at Florence (circa 1428). Other examples are numerous.[85]

---

[79] Cf. Anderson (n. 74 above) 144.

[80] Both the van der Goes painting and the Breviary picture (fol. 286v) are reproduced in Ehrenstein (n. 19 above) 58 fig. 89-90, and in Robert A. Koch, "The Salamander in van der Goes' Garden of Eden," *Journal of the Warburg and Courtauld Institutes* 28 (1965) 323-326 pls. 47a and 48c. Herbert Leon Kessler in an appendix to Koch's note ("The Solitary Bird in van der Goes' *Garden of Eden*," 326-229) gives two more examples of Eden serpents influenced by van der Goes: in one, formerly in the Hirsch collection (pl. 49c), the salamander-serpent has been given female breasts; in the other, a *Garden of Paradise* by a follower of Bosch, now in the Chicago Art Institute (pl. 50ab), the serpent seems to be completely human, except that a serpentine tail descends from its back.

[81] Arnoul Gréban, *Le mystère de la passion*, ed. Omer Jodogne, Académie royale de Belgique, classe des lettres, mémoires 10.12.3 (Brussels 1965) 1.18.

[82] Bonnell (n. 1 above) 281-288. We may add to his list the *Passion of Semur*, which survives in a manuscript dated 1488; it has a serpent with the breast of a woman and the feet and tail of a serpent, and it goes upright. See the ed. of mile ÉRoy, *Le mystère de la Passion en France du XIVe au XVIe siècle*, Revue bourguignonne 13.3-4 (Dijon 1903) 13: "Habeat pectus feminae, pedes et caudam serpentis, et vadat totus directus, et habeat pellem de quodam penno [*lege* panno] rubro." Cf. Grace Frank, *The Medieval French Drama*, ed. 2 (Oxford 1960) 176.

[83] *Le psautier de Peterborough*, ed. J. van den Gheyn (Haarlem [1906]) pl. 15 (Bibl. royale de Belgique MS 9961-62 fol. 25).

[84] Beda Kleinschmidt, *Die Wandmalereien der Basilika San Francisco in Assisi* (Berlin 1930) pl. 7a.

[85] See, for instance, Ehrenstein (n. 19 above) 18 fig. 57 (Ghiberti), 54 fig. 75 (della Quercia), 56 fig. 81 (Lippi), 60 fig. 90 (School of Raphael). There is a crowned serpent-lady of this type on the enameled altar of the Stiftskirche in Klosterneuburg, which Ehrenstein dates as 1186 (46 fig. 46), but according to Schmerber (n. 1 above) 8 this part is a fourteenth-century restoration. Bonnell (n. 1 above) 266 fig. 1 shows Didron's sketch of a double-

The Eden serpent was also often adorned with more features of a woman than just her face or head. A very early example (circa 1220) occurs in the base of the statue of the Virgin in the door decoration in the cathedral of Notre Dame in Paris, where the serpent has not only the head but the breasts, shoulders, and arms of a woman, above a serpentine body that tapers so severely that the creature looks like a mermaid. The arms, however, end in clawlike hands, and there is a pair of wings issuing from her back (fig. 8).

Another serpent with the upper part of a woman's torso (but without claws or wings) occurs in a Paris psalter of the middle of the thirteenth century.[86] Later examples of the type can be seen in Bosch's *Haycart* triptych and in Raphael's Vatican Stanze. Michelangelo's celebrated representation in the Sistine Chapel goes much further, so that even the upper legs of a woman appear, both of which turn into serpentine bodies that twine around the tree; the end of one of them is visible, and presumably the end of the other is hidden behind the tree. As Bonnell suggests,[87] it seems clear that Michelangelo was primarily influenced by the classical giant, with its human body and serpentine legs. Titian's painting of the temptation, now in the Prado, has an infant version of the same type, that is, a serpent that has two distinct tails, while the upper part is a torso of a very young child—and therefore one of indeterminable sex.

VII. The Reaction of the Learned

What effect did Comestor's novel conception of the Eden serpent have upon the scholarly and literary world? Not much, it seems. But in the realm of theology, Saint Bonaventure, writing at the middle of the thirteenth century, accepts the notion as a solution to a problem raised in his commentary on the *Sentences* of Peter Lombard. He admits that if the devil had appeared in human form it would have been easier for him to have engaged Eve in conversation; but divine providence was unwilling to permit him so advantageous a strategy, and he had to be content with a compromise, namely, the body of a serpent, which nevertheless had a virgin's face, as the Venerable Bede asserts. As a result he could be concealed from one end, but was left open to discovery from the other.[88]

Later in the century (1287) the concept was introduced into a literary history by Guido delle Colonne. In his prosaic retelling of Benoît de Sainte-Maure's *Roman de Troie*, he inserts a long explanation of the beginnings of

---

headed serpent, and is no doubt correct in his surmise that the head is repeated to indicate motion, or rather progressive action.

[86] Paris Bib. Nat. MS lat. 10.434 fol. 10; Porcher (n. 55 above) pl. 44.

[87] Bonnell (n. 1 above) 275.

[88] Bonaventure, *In 2 Sent.* 21.1.2 ad 2, *Opera omnia* 2 (Quaracchi 1885) 495.

idolatry. From the time that Lucifer fell, he says, "God changed him into a brute animal, that is, a twisting serpent, and since he is of a huge size he is called a dragon." Guido goes on to indicate, however, that this description is purely allegorical:

> For he is said to be twisting and to be in this sea [the ocean, where he was seen by Saint Brendan] because the devil acts with shifty cunning in the sea of this world in his effort to deceive the souls of wretched men. He is that Leviathan who from the very outset of his fall became a serpent, and, envying the glory of our first parents, had the daring to enter into the paradise of delights; and going erect like a man, he infected them with the vice of prevarication by means of his blind temptations, so that they lost their fear of God's commandment, and by their transgression deserved to be cast down from the glory of that paradise, just as he had deserved by his own fault to be cast down from the glory of heaven.
>
> In spite of what we read in the beginning of the Book of Genesis, according to the Mosaic tradition (where it is said: "But the serpent was more cunning than all the animals that God had made, and he said to the woman, 'Why did God command you?'" and so on), nevertheless according to the tradition of the sacred writings of the catholic and universal Church it is confirmed that, as Bede has written, the devil at that time chose a certain serpent from a certain type of serpents, one that had a virgin's face, and moved its tongue to say what it did, though with no knowledge on its part, just every day the devil still speaks through unknowing fanatics and energumens, that is, through men whose bodies are possessed by these demons; this is discussed in the book *Scholastic Histories*, near the beginning, where the author sets out a history and explanation of the Book of Genesis. Therefore, whatever we Catholics know through these writings, it is certain that that Leviathan, that is, the prince of devils, once cast down from the heavenly heights, either transformed himself into a material serpent or entered into a real one and by his cunning temptations brought about the fall of our wretched parents and their descendants into everlasting ruin.[89]

Peter's theory also appeared in the encyclopedias of natural history—for instance, in Vincent of Beauvais's great *Mirror of Nature*, the final form of which appeared just after the midpoint of the thirteenth century. But in addition to quoting Peter's comments directly,[90] Vincent also records

[89] Guido de Columnis, *Historia destructionis Troiae* 10, ed. Nathaniel Edward Griffin, Mediaeval Academy of America Publications 26 (Cambridge, Mass. 1936) 96-97.

[90] Vincent of Beauvais, *Speculum naturale* 30.68, in *Speculum quadruplex* (Douai 1624) 2265-2266.

the modification of the theory produced by Thomas of Cantimpré (or of Brabant) in his *De natura rerum*,[91] a work composed during the 1220s and 1230s,[92] the time in which the first iconographic representations of maiden-headed Eden serpents began to appear.

In his discussion of serpents Thomas comes to one called dracontopod, which is described in the *Book of Monsters*, a work that he ascribes (perhaps accurately) to Aldhelm, the English bishop (d. 709).[93] Aldhelm (if we may, for the moment, accept his authorship of the book as established), in turn, draws on the Pseudo-Clementine *Recognitions* in Rufinus's Latin translation. The author of the *Recognitions* simply mentions the dracontopods of Greek legend to deny that they were the giants mentioned in the sixth chapter of Genesis.[94] Aldhelm improvises a description from the etymology of the word and says: "Greek fables tell of men with enormous bodies, who in spite of such great size were similar to the human race, except that they had tails of dragons, so that they were called dracontopods in Greek."[95] This description occurs in the part of his work dedicated to monstrous types of men, and not in his section on serpents; but he does regard the viper as a

---

[91] *Ibid.* 20.33 (1478). Vincent does not cite Thomas by name but by his work: *Ex libro de natura rerum* or *Ex libro de naturis rerum.*

[92] Cf. C. Ferckel, *Die Gynäkologie des Thomas von Brabant, ausgewählte Kapitel aus Buch I de naturis rerum, beendet um 1240*, Alte Meister der Medizin und Naturkunde 5, ed. G. Klein (Munich 1912) 3; and Lynn Thorndike, *A History of Magic and Experimental Science During the First Thirteen Centuries of Our Era* 2 (New York 1923, repr. 1947) 373.

[93] Beowulf scholars have assigned the *Liber monstrorum* to England; see Dorothy Whitelock, *The Audience of Beowulf* (Oxford 1951, repr. 1958) 47-53; Kenneth Sisam, *Studies in the History of Old English Literature* (Oxford 1953, repr. 1962) 75-77, 288-290. Edmond Faral, "La queue de poisson des sirènes," *Romania* 74 (1953) 433-506 esp. 441-470, discusses the possibility of Aldhelm's authorship, on the basis of Thomas's ascription.

[94] *Recog.* 1.29.3, ed. Bernhard Rehm and Franz Paschke, *Rekognitionen in Rufins Übersetzung*, Die Pseudoklementinen 2, Griechischen christlichen Schriftsteller 51 (Berlin 1965) 25: "Exin nona generatione nascuntur gigantes illi qui a saeculo nominantur, non dracontopedes, ut Graecorum fabulae ferunt, sed immensis corporibus editi, quorum adhuc ad indicium in nonnullis locis ossa immensae magnitudinis ostenduntur." This passage may also have been the source for Aldhelm's description of Hygelac's bones, or at least it may have influenced his expressions. He says: "Et fiunt monstra mirae magnitudinis, ut rex Hugilaicus, qui imperavit Getis et a Francis occisus est, quem equus a duodecimo aetatis anno portare non potuit. Cuius ossa in Rheni fluminis insula, ubi in Oceanum prorumpit, reservata sunt et de longinquo venientibus pro miraculo ostenduntur." *Liber monstrorum* 1.3, ed. Moritz Haupt in his *Opuscula* 2 (Leipzig 1876) 218-252 (Index lectionum aestivarum 1863) 223.

[95] *Liber monstrorum* 1.49 (234-235): "Ferunt fabulae Graecorum homines immensis corporibus fuisse et in tanta mole tamen humano generi similes, nisi quod draconum caudas habuerunt, unde et graece dracontopedes dicebantur." Haupt emends *dracontopedes* to *dracontopodes.*

serpent, in spite of the fact that its upper part is very human in appearance.[96]

As we saw, however, Thomas of Cantimpré considers the dracontopod to be a serpent; it has, according to him, not only a dragon's tail but a dragon's body, and apparently only its face has a human appearance. He believes it likely that it was this breed of serpent that the devil used in deceiving Eve, even though he himself describes two other possible candidates for the role, namely, the viper with its half-human, half-crocodilian appearance,[97] and the scorpion, a serpent (and not a worm) with a flattering and virginlike countenance and a poisoned sting in its knotty tail.[98]

Thomas's entry on dracontopods can be translated as follows:

> Dracontopods are serpents, and the Greeks say, according to Aldhelm, that they are large and powerful. They have virginal faces like those of human beings, but they end in the body of dragons. It can be believed that the serpent by which Eve was deceived was from this class of serpents. For Bede says that that serpent had a virginal countenance, so that the devil allured her with a form similar to hers, for every animal loves what is similar to it. But he hid the remaining serpentlike part in the fruits of the trees. But we do not see how the devil could bring it about that the serpent could form articulated words, unless perhaps we should wish to say that, as the serpent has a human countenance, it also had the windpipe and organs arranged for uttering human sounds, just as we see birds imitating human sounds in speaking.[99]

---

[96] *Ibid.* 3.18 (250-251): "Vipera autem eo quod vi pariat ita nuncupatur. De qua scribunt physici quod ignotum genus quoddam humanae formae simillimum usque ad umbilicum habeat et semen ore concipiat, et fracto latere moriens pariat." If one did not know of the *Physiologus* specification that it was like a crocodile below, one would gather that it was serpentine, since it is after all a serpent. We have already noted that in spite of the *Physiologus* account, the ninth-century Bern manuscript illustrates vipers with serpentine lower extremities.

[97] Thomas, *De natura rerum* (British Museum MS Egerton 1984) 96v: "Dicit philosophus [*sic*] quod uipera faciem habet humanum usque ad umbilicum; ab umbilico uero usque ad caudam figuram cocodrilli." Royal 12 E XVII (a copy of the anonymous expanded version) reads correctly "Physiologus" (fol. 129). But Konrad von Megenberg, in his German adaptation of Thomas's work, obviously followed a manuscript with the reading of "Philosophus," since he attributes the statement to Aristotle. —*Das Buch der Natur* 3 E 37, ed. Franz Pfeiffer (Stuttgart 1861, repr. Hildesheim 1962) 285. For a modern German translation of Konrad, see the edition of Hugo Schulz (Greifswald 1897).

[98] Thomas, *De natura rerum* (Egerton 1984) 95v: "Scorpio serpens est, ut dicit Solinus, qui blandum et quasi virgineum wltum habere dicitur, sed habet utique in cauda nodosa aculeum venenatum quo pungit et inficit proximantem."

[99] *Ibid.* 93rv: "De drantopedibus [*sic*]. Drrantopedes [*sic*] serpentes sunt, et referente Adelino Greci dicunt, magni et potentes. Hii facies habent virgineas, faciebus humanis similes, sed in draconum corpus desinunt. De hoc genere serpencium credi potest fuisse ser-

If we are mystified at how Thomas was able to create this kind of a creature out of Aldhelm's description, we need only glance at some of his other entries, and we will realize that he had "more than Circean powers of transformation."[100]

It is not altogether clear that Thomas means his dracontopod to be girl-like only in its "face," in the narrow sense of that word, since he speaks of the viper as having "a human face down to the navel." But he was later understood to be speaking restrictively because of a misreading of the name of the serpent as *draconcopes* instead of *dracontopes*. This mistake appears already in Albert the Great[101] and Vincent of Beauvais,[102] and was the reading of the manuscript used by Konrad von Megenberg in the middle of the fourteenth century for his German adaptation of Thomas's work; he accordingly etymologizes the word, which really means "dragon-foot," as *Drachenkopf*, "dragon-head,"[103] that is, "dragon with a human head."

Albert the Great does not suggest that this serpent, which had "the virginal face of a beardless human being," was the kind used by the devil in Eden, but he does say that he has heard from reliable witnesses that such a serpent had been killed in a German forest, and its body could be seen by whoever wanted to do so for a long time, until it finally decayed.[104] He strongly denies, however, that the viper is like a man in its foreparts,[105] and he does not even mention the tradition that the scorpion had a virginal face; furthermore, he classifies it among the worms.[106]

It seems to have been Thomas of Cantimpré's dracontopod, probably in its mutated draconcopedal form, that inspired the first illustrator of the

pentem quo Eua decepta est. Dicit enim Beda quod serpens ille wltum virginalem habuit, ut forma consimili dyabolus eam alliceret. Omne enim diligit simile sibi. Partem uero reliquam serpenti similem arborum fructibus occultauit. Quomodo autem dyabolus potuerit efficere ut serpens articulata uerba formaret non videmus, nisi forte uelimus dicere quod sicut serpens habebat wltum humanum, ita et arterias et officia disposita habuerit ad proferendum uoces humanas, sicut aues uidemus voces humanas loquendo imitari." The Royal manuscript gets the name correctly: "Dracontopedes" (fol. 125).

[100] See Pauline Aiken, "The Animal History of Albertus Magnus and Thomas of Cantimpré," *Speculum* 22 (1947) 205-225, esp. 209.

[101] Albertus Magnus, *De animalibus* 25.29, ed. Hermann Stadler from the Cologne autograph; Beiträge zur Geschichte der Philosophie des Mittelalters 15-16 (Münster 1916-1920) 1567.

[102] Vincent of Beauvais, *Speculum naturale* 20.33 (n. 90 above) 1478. I have checked only this printed text.

[103] Konrad von Megenberg, *Buch von Natur* 3 E 11 (Pfeiffer 270, Schulz 228).

[104] Albertus Magnus (n. 101 above): "Draconcopodes dicunt Graeci serpentem magnum de ordine tertio et genere draconum, quem dicunt vultum virgineum imberbis hominis habere; et talem serpentem a fide dignis audivi interfectum esse in silva Germaniae et diu monstratum nostris temporibus omnibus volentibus eum videre donec computruit."

[105] *Ibid.* 25.61 (1577).

[106] *Ibid.* 26.39 (1595-1596).

Speculum humanae salvationis, since his serpent is a huge two-legged dragon, with wings, whose womanlike head towers above Eve; and we may note that it does not have its body hidden in foliage (fig. 9).[107] The text of the *Speculum* itself, however, which was composed around 1324, reflects only Peter Comestor's account.[108]

VIII. Masculinization and Extinction

The serpent in the text of the *Speculum humanae salvationis* retains its masculine gender in spite of its virginal face. Such was not the case in the *Chester Plays*, where Eve tells God, "This adder, Lord, she was my foe."[109] The serpent in William Jordan's Cornish play, *The Creation of the World*, written in 1611, is also feminine. The English stage direction reads: "A fine serpent with a virgin face and yellow hair upon her head."[110]

In other English plays it is not so, however. In the York pageant of the fall "the worme" whose likeness Satan takes upon himself is not described, but he is definitely masculine. Eve says of him, "With tales untrue he me betrayed."[111]

In the Lincoln (N. Town) play, the *Serpens* is described as "a fair angel," "the false angel," and "a worm with an angel's face." Eve says of him, "He hight us to be full of grace the fruit if that we eat. I did his bidding, alas, alas! . . . I suppose it was Sathanas."[112]

In the 1565 text of the Norwich play, the serpent appears and says, "Angel of light I show myself to be," and alludes to "my voice so small." Eve later tells Adam, "The heavenly king most strong to eat of this apple his angel

---

[107] MS of Selestat, now at Munich, Staatsbibliothek lat. 146 fol. 4v. Cf. the similar serpent in the version of the *Speculum* in Brussels Bibl. Roy. MS 281-283 fol. 5 (circa 1350), in Cook (n. 18 above) 163 fig. 21. Cf. also the woodcut in the Dutch 1483 edition, ed. Ernst Kloss (Munich 1925).

[108] *Speculum humanae salvationis* 1.11-16, ed. J. Lutz and P. Perdrizet (Mulhouse 1907-1909) 1.4:

> Quapropter diabolus, homini invidens, sibi insidiabatur
> Et ad praecepti transgressionem ipsum inducere nitebatur.
> Quoddam ergo genus serpentis sibi diabolus eligebat,
> Qui tunc erectus gradiebatur et caput virgineum habebat.
> In hunc fraudulosus deceptor mille artifex intrabat,
> Et per os eius loquens, verba deceptoria mulieri enarrabat.

[109] *Chester Plays* 32.

[110] William Jordan, *Gwreans an Bys*; the *Creation of the World*, ed. Whitley Stokes, in *Transactions of Philological Society* (1863), cited in E. K. Chambers, *The Medieval Stage* (Oxford 1903, repr. 1963) 2.142, 435.

[111] *York Plays* 5.12.122-123, ed. Lucy Toulmin Smith (Oxford 1885, repr. New York 1963) 26.

[112] *Ludus Coventriae, or the Plaie Called Corpus Christi*, ed. K. S. Block, Early English Text Society extra series 120 (London 1922, repr. 1960) 23-25, cf. 182.

hath prepare," and she confesses to God, "The serpent deceived me with that his fair face."[113]

According to the inventory of the players, the actor who plays the serpent was to wear a white wig and colored tights and tail.[114] It seems, then, that his legs would be showing as such. It is not clear whether the white hair that he puts on is meant to make him look like a woman; it would not seem so, to judge from Eve's mention of "his fair face." It is true that "his" can be neuter as well as masculine, but it cannot be feminine.

M. D. Anderson suggests that the bosses in the Norwich Cathedral, which were made early in the sixteenth century, were influenced by earlier portrayals of the biblical plays. The Temptation boss shows a serpent with the upper torso of a young man or boy; of course, it could also be that of a very young girl. The point is that there has been no attempt to emphasize its femininity by giving it a woman's breasts, such as Eve has.[115] We may recall that Titian's cherubic serpent was also too young for its sex to be determined. The serpent of the *Breviarium Grimani* was also of indistinct sexuality.

Miss Anderson also draws attention to the Creation scene in the stained glass in the church of Saint Neot in Cornwall (it was worked on from 1400 to 1532, and is partially restored), where the serpent has the face of a man with a bulging body—which looks as if an actor has slipped on a sacklike disguise.[116] His hair is somewhat like that of the serpent of the Norwich boss.

Another definitely masculine portrayal of the human-headed serpent can be seen in the painting of the German artist Georg Penz (1500-1550), now in the Ferdinandeum at Innsbruck. Here the serpent has the upper torso, arms, and bearded and horned head of a satyr![117] Finally, in the church of Santa Maria della Pace in Rome, the fresco by Girolamo Siciolante da Sermoneta portraying the sin of Adam and Eve (circa 1560-1565) has a male version of the two-legged variety of serpent immortalized by Michelangelo and Titian (fig. 10).

The reasoning of Peter Comestor which demanded a woman's head, was obviously lost upon such artists. And in fact, the need for any kind of human head disappeared among the artists of the seventeenth century and later, though no doubt one can find a number of revivals of the old tradition of the lady serpent.

---

[113] *The Creation of Eve, with the Expelling of Adam and Eve out of Paradise,* acted by the Grocers of Norwich; ed. Joseph Quincy Adams, *Chief Pre-Shakespearean Dramas* (Boston 1924) 90-91.

[114] *Ibid.* 89 n. 1: "A coat with hosen and tail for the serpent, stained, with a white hair."

[115] M. D. Anderson (n. 74 above) 87, 143 (and pl. 13b).

[116] *Ibid.* 144 (and pl. 15b). *Blue Guide to England,* ed. L. Russell Muirhead and Stuart Rossiter (London 1965) 194.

[117] Ehrenstein (n. 19 above) 67 fig. 117.

Peter's bizarre notion of a lady-faced Eden serpent did not find widespread support among scripture scholars and theologians, and it appears to have been abandoned by them much earlier than by the iconographers. It is instructive to read what Nicholas of Lyre had to say upon the subject early in the fourteenth century in his postill on Genesis 3:

> The demon's entering into the serpent for this purpose was not a thing chosen by him, but rather was arranged by God, who did not allow man to be tempted by the devil in a pleasing and noble appearance, through which he could be more easily deceived, but rather in a horrible appearance, in which the demon's fallaciousness could be more quickly perceived. Nevertheless some say that that serpent had a pleasing and virginal face; but this has no scriptural authority, and therefore the first interpretation seems better.[118]

Three hundred years later the same conclusion was reached by painters, sculptors, and playwrights.

IX. Conclusion

The Jewish and Byzantine tradition of the Eden serpent was, as we have seen, fairly straightforward. The serpent had feet to begin with, since he could walk, and they were cut off from him and from all his race as a punishment for tempting Eve. In the West, serpents had no feet to begin with, but by a miraculous iconographic mutation some of them acquired feet in the course of time, and the Eden serpent was at times included among their number.

A further complication was introduced in the West, this time perhaps because of a simple graphic mutation (like the one that transformed Thomas of Cantimpré's *dracontopes* into a *Drachenkopf*); according to Peter Comestor the devil used a serpent with a woman's face in order to gain Eve's confidence more easily. Peter may have honestly thought that the venerable Bede supported this view, but he was no doubt also more easily inclined to accept the view because he was familiar with some variety or varieties of serpent-woman combination; I suggested as possibilities the viper of *Physiologus*, the sphinx, the siren, and the scorpion, and I stated that the author of *The Cave of Treasures* before Peter's time may have been influenced in a similar way in creating an Evelike serpent.

---

[118] Nicholas de Lira, *Postilla*, in *Biblia sacra cum glossa ordinaria* (Douai 1617) 90: "Quod autem ad hoc serpentem intravit, non fuit ex electione, sed magis ex divina dispensatione, quae non permisit hominem tentari per diabolum in specie gratiosa et nobili, per quam posset facilius decipi, sed magis in specie horribili, in qua fallacia daemonis citius poterat deprehendi. Aliqui tamen dicunt quod ille serpens habebat faciem gratiosam et virgineam, sed hoc de scriptura nullam habet auctoritatem, et ideo primum melius videtur."

It might be thought that Peter had a deeply misogynic view of woman to have postulated a serpent with a woman's countenance in the Garden of Eden. It is true that he had a low opinion of woman, but he was not saying that the first woman was like a snake, but rather that the snake was like a woman. It is doubtless true that some of the serpent-ladies of the past were thought of as *femmes fatales*—the siren and the scorpion are obvious examples. But Peter gives as the reason for the woman-headed serpent's appearance in the garden the simple consideration that since one approves of what is similar to oneself the devil sought to win Eve's confidence in this way. He approached her because she was weaker and more suggestive than Adam. Far from considering Eve serpentine herself, Peter specifies that women in such situations are weak, and they are baleful only because of their malleability, and not because they are actively dangerous. There is nothing reptilian about Eve's successful efforts to convince Adam to follow her course.

Though relatively few scholars of the Middle Ages were ready to accept Peter's new serpent, it made a decided impact upon the visual and dramatic arts, beginning, in the former, about fifty years after Peter introduced the idea. It opened up for the artists intriguing new possibilities in an old scene, and they rose to the challenge with great inventiveness. Yet they did not simply visualize the monster with the abandon of the grotesque-drawers and misericord-makers, for they were not dealing with a whimsical creature of the imagination, but with a very real and painfully authentic beast. They therefore combined the features of a woman with the characteristics of real serpents. The fact that serpents had attained many forms accounts for the variegated results of their efforts. The dramatists were able to choose from among these offerings the types that were most suited for representation upon the stage. The solutions that were arrived at in all the media assured for Peter's odd notion an important and lasting place in the monuments of medieval and renaissance culture, before the fundamental absurdity of the concept could raze the strong walls of tradition that had been erected around it.

Department of English
University of California
Los Angeles, California, 90024, U.S.A.

FIG. 1. Onocentaur and siren. Capital of the arch in front of the south apse, Cathedral of Autun. Early twelfth century

FIG. 2. Capital in the crypt of the Duomo of Modena. Early twelfth century

FIG. 3. Terracina chest, Palazzo Venezia. Eleventh century?

Fig. 4. Beatus of Liébana's *Commentary on the Apocalypse*, Pierpont Morgan Library MS 429, fol. 6v. A.D. 1220

Fig. 5a. Portal of the Virgin, Cathedral of Notre Dame, Amiens. Circa 1230

Fig. 6. Panel in the base of the middle pillar of the door of the Virgin, Cathedral of Notre Dame, Amiens. Circa 1230

Fig. 7. Peterborough Psalter, Brussels (Bibl. Roy. MS 9961–9962, fol. 25). Circa 1250

FIG. 8. Base of pillar, Virgin's door. Cathedral of Notre Dame, Paris. Circa 1220

FIG. 9. *Speculum humanae salvationis*. Munich (Bayerische Staatsbibliothek MS lat. 146 fol. 4v). Middle of fourteenth century

Fig. 10. "Peccato originale" by Girolamo Siciolante da Sermoneta, in the church of Santa Maria della Pace, Rome. Circa 1560–1565

SOME REMARKS ON THE CONCEPT OF IMPETUS AND THE DETERMINATION OF SIMPLE MOTION

•

by Amos Funkenstein

I. The Problem

Recent discussions of the medieval concept of *impetus* have generally suffered from the wish either to establish or to disprove its approximation to the law of inertia. The scholastic term is, indeed, untranslatable into the vocabulary of early modern physics.[1] "Impetus" is a quality somewhat analogous to heat. It is a motive *power* accounting for motion and thus still conceived on the basis of the assumption that "omne quod movetur ab alio movetur,"[2] and hence on the distinction between rest and movement. Inertia, on the contrary, is not a force, but a state under which both rest and uniform motion are subsumed, and distinguished from change of either velocity or direction.[3] In regard to them only the quest for immediate causes is meaningful.

The concept of impetus was introduced to save the essential features in the theory of motion of the Philosopher, which early modern physics since Galileo was very conscious of destroying. At best, one could refer to some genetic and semantic links leading back to the medieval concept; one might prove that Galileo was well acquainted with the concept and that, by modi-

---

[1] So repeatedly argued by A. Maier, "Die aristotelische Theorie und die impetus Hypothese," *Zwei Grundprobleme der scholastischen Naturphilosophie* (Rome 1951) 113ff., esp. 126; 217ff.; 223ff., etc.; *idem*, "Die naturphilosophische Bedeutung der scholastischen Impetustheorie," *Ausgehendes Mittelalter; gesammelte Aufsätze zur Geistesgeschichte des 14. Jahrhunderts* 1 (Rome 1964) 353ff., esp. 376f.; *idem*, "Ergebnisse der scholastischen Naturphilosophie," *ibid.* 431ff. Cf. also A. Koyré, *Metaphysics and Measurement: Essays in the scientific revolution*, (Cambridge, Mass. 1968) 28-32: "Galileo and Plato," *Journal for the History of Ideas* 4 (1943) 400ff. For different recent interpretations, cf. nn. 5 and 6 below.

[2] Aristotle, *Physica* 7.1, 241b34: Ἅπαν τὸ νινούμενον ὑπό τινος ἀνάγκῃ κινεῖσθαι. That this includes "natural movement" by virtue of an intrinsic principle is shown in the following sentence.

[3] The relative nature also of this distinction became thematic only in the general theory of relativity. Cf. also the logical analysis of Newton's first law by Bertrand Russell, *Principles of Mathematics* (New York 1902) 482ff.

fying it, he showed how to overcome the impediments that both the Aristotelian interpretation of forced movement and its correction by the *moderni*
imposed on the way towards a quantified dynamics.[4] The same objections
could be raised against any of the other alleged progressive aspects of the
impetus hypothesis: Though it is true, for example, that Buridan considered
a mechanical explanation of celestial movement,[5] he abolished neither the
gap between celestial and terrestial matter nor the distinction between forced
and natural motion.[6]

The resemblance of the impetus theory to certain definite postgalilean
terms thus has served as almost the sole criterion to evaluate its role in the
foundation of modern dynamics. With such a criterion any substantial approximation of the two had to be denied.[7] The impetus hypothesis had,
instead, to be replaced into its genuine Aristotelian, or at least medieval,
context. The quest for a term-to-term translation is meaningless in the case of
two different interpretations of the same set of phenomena, interpretations that
can not be mediated through one comprehensive theory. Yet these inevitable
conclusions do not exclude another criterion of approximation, based on
methodological and epistemological considerations rather than on a review
of possible similar contents. The aim of the following discussion is to show
that the concept of impetus, at least as used since Buridan, introduced a
subtle methodological change in the meaning of simple motion and in the
modes of determining them. The schoolmen themselves were perhaps una-
ware of this change or of its impact: Galileo recognized it clearly.

The outline of my argument is this. Simple motion in the Aristotelian
frame of reference meant, and had to mean, the natural motion in its to-

---

[4] A. Maier, "Die aristotelische Theorie" (n. 1 above) 291ff., esp. 306-311; against P.
Duhem, *Études sur Léonard da Vinci*, 3 vols., (Paris 1906-1913) passim; A. Koyré, *Études
Galiliennes* (Paris 1939) vol. 3, esp. 70ff.; for further literature see M. Clagett, *The Science
of Mechanics in the Middle Ages* (London 1961) 628ff., esp. 666-671.

[5] In ascribing the celestial movement to an indefatigable impetus. Cf. Maier, "Die na-
turphilos. Bedeutung" 378f.; Clagett (n. 4 above) 523f. Clagett, like Ernest Moody, "Laws
of Motion in Medieval Physics," *Scientific Monthly* 72.1 (1951) 18-23, repr. in: *Towards
Morden Science*, ed. R. M. Packer (New York 1969) 220ff., esp. 231, and the much more
radical E. J. Dijksterhuis, *Die Mechanisierung des Weltbildes* (Berlin 1956) 111-115, considers the principle of perpetuation as well as Buridan's analysis of falling bodies (acceleration) to be an approximation to the concept of momentum. Yet Buridan does not extend
his principle to horizontal motions.

[6] Against H. Blumenberg, *Die kopernikanische Wende* (Frankfurt 1965) 31ff. As a matter
of fact, it is rather the equation of "simple "with "perfect" movement, and not the distinction between natural and forced movements, which was abandoned in modern physics;
see below.

[7] In another article, A. Maier draws attention to the fact that impetus, although the
quest for its nature has been given up, remained nevertheless an analogy for quantifiable
forces to the seventeenth century: "Die Mechanisierung des Weltbildes im 17. Jahrhundert,"
Zwei Untersuchungen zur nachscholastischen Philosophie (Rome 1968) 23f.

tality—an actually existing motion and, for some simple bodies, one immediately discernible through the senses. In modern dynamics, simple motion
became an abstraction. For Descartes, inertia was merely a "tendency,"
a "clear and distinct" idea, not something perceived: all actual motions were,
by necessity, mixed motions.[8] The validity of the idea relied totally on its
rational evidence and its success in rescuing the phenomena. In the last
consequence, it relied on the epistemological certainty that "ordo rerum idem
est ordo idearum." Buridan's concept of impetus was a good step towards
this insight into the abstract character of necessary physical key terms, of
course without the demand for actual quantification. Simple motion, to
him, was no longer the motion of a naturally moving body in its totality,
but only one aspect of this motion, an aspect which may only abstractly
be separated from others. The introduction of impetus forced him to assume that (at least) all sublunar movements are mixed. The terministic
background of such points of view is transparent.

II. THE ARISTOTELIAN BACKGROUND

Cessante movente, what is it that keeps a thrown body in its (forced) motion?
Not an inner principle inherent to the moving body, since such a principle
can be attributed to the movement towards the οἴκεος τόπος only, to the
"natural" movement. A body moving by its nature is such that has "*a* cause
of movement in itself."[9] Nor indeed can the cause be attributed to the original
mover, since it lost its immediate physical contact with the moved body.
Aristotle then takes recourse to the medium in its capacity of being "both

---

[8] "Harum [i.e., causae secundariae ac particulares diversorum motuum] prima est, unamquamque rem, quatenus est simplex et indivisa, manere, *quantum in se est*, in eodem semper statu." And even clearer: "Altera lex naturae est: unamquamque partem materiae,
seorsim spectatam, non *tendere* unquam ut secundum ullas lineas obliquas pergat moveri,
sed tantummodo secundum rectas, etsi multae saepe *cogantur deflectere* propter occursum
aliarum." since the cosmos is rather a material continuum. Descartes, *Principia philosophiae* 2.37, 39, *Œuvres*, ed. C. Adam and P. Tannery, 8.1 (Paris 1964) 62-63. A. C. Crombie,
Augustin to Galileo; *Science in the later Middle Ages and Early Modern Times* (London
1961) 2.160, in neglecting the cogent epistomological character of these laws, does injustice
to Descartes when he maintains that "Descartes based his complete principle on an entire
metaphysical assumption of God's power to conserve movement." This, as we shall see,
applies not to the validity of these (clear and distinct) laws, but to their actual imposition
on the *ordo rerum*. Crombie's interpretation would have rather served to explain the validity
of natural laws in the Kalam.

[9] For the importance of distinguishing between a "self mover" and "having a cause of
movement within itself," see W. Wieland, *Die aristotelische Physik; Untersuchungen über
die Grundlegung der Naturwissenschaften und die sprachlichen Bedingungen der Prinzipienforschung bei Aristoteles* (Göttingen 1962) 231ff.

light and heavy at the same time":[10] The original mover imparts on the air layer next to the moved body (and to itself) both movement and the capacity to act as a mover, that is, to impart movement on the air-layer next to it. Aristotle assumes this force to be actualized a short interval after the cessation of the movement of each layer: the movement of the body carried by all the successive layers would otherwise be instantaneous, which is impossible. The projectile movement is thus not continuous, "but only seems so." This capacity to act as a mover of both the object and (after a pause) of the next layer of air is thus carried forth, with decreasing intensity, from one layer to the next until the capacity to act as a mover fades; the object, then, is carried only to the end of the last layer, and drops down by its own "heaviness."

Undoubtedly this was a most oblique and complicated solution. Later adherents to other explanations found it easy to marshal a good many arguments "from experience" against it. In Aristotele's own terms, it must have had grave methodological faults. For once Aristotle set aside his reluctance "to explain by many principles what might be explained by few":[11] here he assumes a multiplicity of quasi elements in order to explain a seemingly simple, or rather continuous, phenomenon. In this arbitrary dissection of the medium into layers he takes counsel *ab hoste*, his language suspiciously resembles Atomistic patterns of interpretation. Much as Leucippus and Democritus replaced the misleading appearance of material continuity with the assumption of spatial gaps and likewise imperceptible material elements, so Aristotle also resolves the "misleading" appearance of the continuity of projectile movement into a series of instantaneous shifts and imperceptible gaps. Thus, he also sets aside his insistence on our ability to form immediate abstraction from sense perception, "to explicate what everybody knows, but clearer."[12] Again, the Democritian mistrust of sense perception was attacked by Aristotle in other contexts. This distrust led the Atomists, on the one hand, to assume that the truth, or the elements, are hidden and imperceptible, pure abstractions. On the other hand, the Atomists take slight differences in the perception of the same object by different persons as a guideline: such differences hint at a material difference underlying them; it means that a real "more or less" subsists in the image of the object as dif-

---

[10] The following after Aristotle, *Physica* 4.8, 215a14-17; 8.10, 266b27-267a20; *De caelo*, 301b17-31. Cf Clagett (n. 4 above) 505-508; Maier, "Die aristotelische Theorie" (n. 1 above) 114-119.

[11] *De caelo* 3.4, 302b25-29 (against Anaxagoras).

[12] *De caelo* 4.1, 308a24; *Ethica Nicomachea* 7.1, 1145b2-6. Cf., also on the ἐπαγογή G. E. L. Owen, "Tithenai ta phainomena," *Aristote et les problèmes de la méthode, Symposium aristotelicum* (Louvain 1961) 83-103.

ferently presented.[13] The Atomists thus contradict the sense data[14] and are at
the same time radical sensualists. Aristotle's position may be elicited from
these pieces of epistemological criticism as being in the middle. Sense perceptions are indeed reliable as far as they are common experience. Deviations
and small irregularities may be neglected. And yet the impression of the
continuity of projected motion is indeed common experience. To regard
it as deceptive, to substitute for it an abstract model, is not comparable with
other examples of Aristotelian ἐπαγογή. Even where he corrects common
opinion for example, by relativizing "up" and "down,"[15] he preserves the
sense data underlying it. The concept of movement, with its continuity
as an inseparable constituent, is not formed by "opinion." Aristotle's interpretation of projectile movement is one of the very few cases in which he
knowingly rejects the data of experience. Besides all that, Aristotle did
not, as already indicated by the Ancients, really avoid ascribing an intrinsic
principle to the projectile movement. He merely shifted it from the body
moved to the moving medium.[16]

It is, then, by no means difficult to account for the emergence of the concept of *impetus*, either in Antiquity or in the Middle Ages. It is likewise
needless to look for the transmission of some vague recollections of Philo-
ponos into the Middle Ages. To assume the continuation of the moving force
in the moved body was actually the only remaining, and certainly the most
obvious escape. Such an assumption must not have meant abandoning the
principle that whatever moves is moved by another; the δύναμις or *impetus*
through which the object continues its forced movement had not necessarily
to be regarded as a principle inherent to the moving body as such; it could
be called accidental and be conceived as accompanying the body as "something
else" within itself. It has been observed that as a matter of fact Aristotle
implies a similar force when describing the behavior of the medium.[17] Be it
as it may, the question why and how the concept of impetus emerged is far
easier to answer than the question why Aristotle took refuge in such a complicated and unsatisfactory[18] theory. With less trouble he could have ac-

---

[13] *Metaphysica* 3.5, 100b7ff.; cf. *De generatione et corruptione* 1.2, 315b7-15. As to the
authenticity of the first reference cf. E. Zeller, *Die Philosophie der Griechen in ihres Entwicklung dargestellt*, ed. W. Nestle, 1 (Leipzig 1919) 1132. As to the atomistic methoodlgy
see also S. Samburski, *Das physikalische Weltbild der Antike* (Zurich 1965) 144ff.

[14] *De caelo* 3.7, 305b1 ff.; also 3.4, 303a23.

[15] For the Platonic origin, *Timaios* 62c-63e, cf. F. M. Cornford, *Plato's Cosmology; the
Timaeus of Plato* (New York 1937) 262ff.

[16] Simplicius, *in Aristotelis Physicorum Libros... commentaria* 1349.26 (ed. H. Diels, Berlin
1882-1895); quoted by Samburski (n. 13 above) 465.

[17] Samburski 463.

[18] I find it odd that Koyré (n. 1 above) 27 praises Aristotle's solution as if in it he gives
us "the measure of his genius." Samburski (n. 13 above) rightly calls it a "desperate" attempt.

cepted the phenomenon at its face value and constructed a specific modus of forced movement to account for it. The answer seems to be that by introducing such a third modus of motion, though it would in no way challenge the *theoretical* distinction between forced and natural movement,[19] it would nevertheless render this distinction undiscernable in actual experience. A short analysis of *De caelo* 3.2, 301a21-b33 might clarify this point.

Here Aristotle proves that all sublunar bodies are either heavy or light; that is, if they are conceived as moving, they necessarily move also up or down. In this context he introduces, at the end, his explanation of movement seemingly without an external agent. In the preceding passage (300a20-301a20) Aristotle demonstrates that all bodies must have a natural movement if constrained movement has any meaning, if they are at all to be conceived as movable. The movement upwards or downwards is now to be inductively recognized as this natural movement in all cases, for all moving bodies. The proof proceeds in two parts. He shows first (301a21-301b1) that whatever moves without force, or rather without an extrinsic cause, either upwards or downwards, performs one of these opposite movements necessarily. Aristotle then proceeds to show (301b2-17) also that bodies moving by force either sidewards or opposite to their natural inclination, must possess the same inclination upwards or downwards. In both parts Aristotle uses an imaginary experiment that reduces the notion of a weightless body A *ad absurdum* if compared to a heavy body B (or a part of it) traversing the same distance at the same time. Aristotle starts in both parts with certain postulates, some of them manifest, some latent. He (1) assumes the proportional equation

$$\frac{\text{weight}_1}{\text{weight}_2} = \frac{\text{size}_1}{\text{size}_2}$$

He (2) assumes in the first part of the proof that Distance=Gravity (or levity) x time. If time is constant, any heavy body must traverse a longer distance than an imaginary wieghtless body A falling or rising a given distance, which is absurd. He further (3) assumes in the second part of the proof that

$$\text{Distance} = \frac{\text{time}}{\text{gravity or levity}}.$$

Any body with weight or lightness must traverse a smaller distance than the imaginary weightless A. A weightless body must therefore continue

---

[19] Cf. for example, *De caelo* 1.2, 268b15-20. The analysis of perfect, simple motions follows here the concept of the perfect geometrical figures. It is, therefore, false to relieve Aristotle of any share in the "geometrization" of physics altogether; see below, 346.

its motion infinitely, which is absurd. It has been remarked that with this sentence (301b16) Aristotle fas formulated the principle of inertia in order to reject it.[20] Certainly if we ask for approximations, Aristotle's formulation comes nearer to the principle of inertia than even Buridan's indefatigable celestial impetus—and Buridan might indeed have been inspired by this remark of the Stagirite.[21] Aristotle, it seems, draws here the utmost conclusions from the (Platonic) assumption of elements as geometrical planes[22] and the mere relativity of heaviness and lightness. He, on the contrary, assumes that bodies maintain their gravity or levity even in their proper places.

In the context of Aristotle's insistence on the absolute character of gravity and levity we must also consider his further (4), and tacit, assumption: that there are at least *some* bodies that are heavy and light to begin with. Without this assumption all he would have proved in both parts of the demonstration would be that either gravity and levity *or* weightlessness, but not both, are universal properties. Since we are supposed to decide as a matter of course in favor of the former Aristotle assumes that in the case of at least some bodies gravity or levity are obvious, which allows us to draw conclusions on another group of bodies which also contain these properties, though less manifestly. Evidently Aristotle thinks of earth and fire on the one hand, of air and water (with their relative behavior) on the other. This interpretation gains probability when comparing our text with *De caelo* 4.4, 311a20-29; 311b21, where Aristotle discusses the problem of relative movements. That earth moves naturally downwards, fire upwards, without constraint—this needs no proof, this "we see with our eyes." It is the basis for further proofs.

We may now be able to determine Aristotle's attitude towards sense perception somewhat further. It is characterized neither by absolute trust nor by systematic mistrust. At least in our case, Aristotle uses sense-data as a principle of falsification almost in the sense of recent methodologies,[22a] i.e. as an instance to "decide" between two "theories", and no more. The atomists, we can now reformulate his criticism, lacked such a principle.

---

[20] S. Samburski, חוקות שמים וארץ (Jerusalem 1954) 97, on the similar idea in *Physics* 215a16.

[21] See below.

[22] Cf. *De caelo* 4.2, 308b36f.; Plato, *Timaeus* 53c-55c.

[22a] K. R. Popper, *The Logics of scientific Discovery* (2nd ed., New York 1968) 39-42 and *passim*. As a *methodological* principle, Popper's criterion has at least drawn attention to a most important feature of universal synthetic judgements *in praxi*. As an explanation of historical processes leading towards a new system, the principle is most contestable, as I hope to show on another occasion. Popper at times confuses the methodological and the historical heuristic value of his thesis; but so do all the critics who only accuse him of misrepresenting historical processes.

Some cases of levity and gravity are thus immediate data of experience. It is especially this postulate of immediacy which concerns us here. The postulate of immediacy might be the ultimate reason why Aristotle excluded the possibility of a third modus of movement, movement by *concealed* force; such a possibility would destroy the immediate evidence of some bodies moving up or downwards without any *apparent* cause involved. The fundamental distinction between forced and natural movement would still remain valid; but the possibility of actually recognizing and determining which movement is natural would become severely affected,[23] a matter of probability rather than of certainty.

Aristotle, then, stood between two unpleasant interpretations of projected movements. He had either to deny the absolute certainty by which we recognize the most apparent natural movements as such, or he had to deny the equally apparent continuity of projectile movements. He chose the lesser evil. Lesser it was, since, compared to the sum total of movements occurring, he could perhaps have regarded projectile motions as relatively rare.

Even if one maintains that these last conclusions were neither drawn nor implied by Aristotle, one point becomes clear. Simple motions are simple in every aspect; natural motions are under no point of view mixed. Inasmuch as a heavy body moves downwards, it moves so by gravity only. Gravity explains its motion and acceleration alike. The medium only accounts for the body moving in time, that is, for the motion not being instantaneous, in the case of natural movements. With forced movement the medium helps —through its relative lightness—to move the object, at times even *cessante movente*.

III. The Medieval Theory of Impetus

It is not my task to write the history of the concept of impetus either in Antiquity or in the Middle Ages. Some of the existing studies are both cautions and comprehensive. My attention is mainly restricted to the epistemological aspect of the new dynamics of the *moderni*.

At the very outset of the reception of Aristotle, even before the concept of impetus was used (or revived) and became rapidly popular, it was clearly rejected by Thomas Aquinas. This again proves how natural and unavoi-

---

[23] This would not be the only place where Aristotle distinguishes between the theoretical and the factual discernibility of natural states. In another context altogether, having postulated slavery by nature, he is confronted with a similar problem: "Nature would like to distinguish between the bodies of freemen and slaves . . . but the opposite often happens, that some have the souls and others have the bodies of freemen." In actual societies, one could add, "conventional" slavery (which Aristotle discusses in the following lines) adds to the difficulty (*Politics* 1.5, 1254b 25-32). Actual slavery, of course, can be also "conventional" through the law of the victor (1.6, 1255a3ff.).

dable it was to conceive the theory, if only in order to reject it: "Non est autem intelligendum quod virtus violenti motoris imprimat lapidi qui per violentiam movetur aliquam virtutem per quam moveatur, sicut virtus generantis imprimit genito formam, quam consequitur motus naturalis: nam sic motus violentus esset a principio intrinseco, quod est contra rationem motus violenti. Sequeretur etiam quod lapis, ex hoc ipso quod movetur localiter per violentiam, alteratur: quod est contra sensum."[24] Both reasons are needed since the first alone could be contested by refering to the accidental character of this hypothetical *virtus aliqua*. Thomas thus calls for the testimony of sense-perception, albeit he does not seem to recognize the difference between distinguishing natural from forced movements theoretically and the problem of discerning this distinction by the sense. Yet we had to admit that it is doubtful whether Aristotle reflected on this difference. Thomas raises and rejects the concept of *vis interior* in passing.

In the following passage, however, Thomas contributes a good deal towards the clarification of what is meant by a "natural" movement. He polemized against Averroes who accepted the medium as a necessary agent, that is, an efficient (or active) cause of natural movements.[25] Thomas understands and explicates Aristotle more accurately in holding that when we speak of "forms" as the "cause" of gravity or levity we do not refer to it as a *movens*, as an active source of movement. We rather articulate a methodological principle that says that, when encountering natural movement, we may abandon the search for causes. The form (that is, the proper place) of a body is but a passive cause.

In Thomas's analysis the immediate evidence of simple motion is again stressed against all attempts to obscure it. Simplicity is not one aspect of gravity or levity, but the total motion of these bodies.

At about the same time that the suggestion of a *vis derelicta* was raised[26] and started its long career, William of Ockham rejected it as strongly as did Thomas—although for altogether different reasons. Ockham not only regarded the impetus hypothesis as explaining the unknown by the less known ("a quo causatur illa virtus?")[27] but moreover the question underlying this

---

[24] Thomas Aquinas, *In libros Aristotelis de caelo et mundo expositio* 3.2 lectio 7, *Opera* 3 (Roma 1952) 252; cf. Clagett (n. 4 above) 516f. As to the question whether Thomas accepted this *virtus* in other contexts, cf. Maier, "Die aristotelische Theorie" (n. 1 above) 134-140.

[25] Averroes, *Physica* 8, summa 4 text 82, *Opera* 4.195vb-196va; *De caelo* 3 summa 3.2 text 28, *Opera* 5.91vb-92va; Maier, "Die aristotelische Theorie" 119.

[26] On Olivi and Franciscus of Marchia cf. Maier, "Die aristotelische Theorie" 142ff.; Clagett 517ff; Blumenberg (n. 6 above) 23ff.

[27] *Sent.* 2.26 (Lyons 1495); Maier, "Die aristotelische Theorie" 154ff., pp. Böhner, *Ockham: Philosophical Writings* (Edingburgh 1957) 139-141; Clagett 520f.; cf. S. Moser, *Grundbegriffe der Naturphilosophie bei Wilhelm von Ockham* (Innsbruck 1932) 91-111 (Moser sees

or other solutions[28] he regarded as superflous. The term "movement" de-
notes an object and connotes a series of places which this body occupies consecutively. We need only one cause to explain why the body A left l_1 and
why it reached l_n through $l_2 \ldots l_{n-1}$; if it left l_1, it necessarily occupies
another *ubi*, say l_2. The *ubi* is not a new quality which the body acquired
recently; rather, change of places is considered to be a part of the concept
of motion. Both the movement from l_1 and the conservation of this movement
through $l_2 \ldots l_n$ are two expressions for one and the same phenomenon.
To introduce a further cause would mean to separate the concept of "the
motion of this body" from that of "this body, moving", that is to raise motion
to an independent ontological status. Yet the term signifies only the moving
body and (connotatively) the places it occupies; the concept of motion includes *a limine* the concept of its conservation.

Here, as in his entire philosophical work, Ockham concentrates mainly
on the analysis of our concepts and terms. Since connotative terms such as
motion, extension, quantity, or time are complex notions, the duty of a philosopher is to isolate and distinguish the components of a complex term in
such a way that it may not lead us to mistake aspects of objects as being
absolute qualities or things, but rather enable us to discern what the term
signifies *in recto*, what *in obliquo*.[29] Such terms are far from being, as the crude
nominalism of earlier periods used to say, *nudae denominationes*; nor do they
stand for mere concepts. If well construed, they represent a valid reference-
structure *in rebus*, or even, as one modern interpreter argued: "Man könnte
eine solche Bestimmung als intentio dahin auffassen, daß eine Beziehung
zwar in den Dingen existiert, daß sie aber, wenn sie aufgefaßt werden soll,
als Vorstellung muß vorgestellt werden."[30] Even if we accept, with Martin,
that Ockham recognized some connotative terms as establishing a valid,

---

Ockham too much as a mere interpreter of Aristotle; see the next note), and H. Shapiro
"Motion, Time and Place according to William Ockham", *Franciscan Studies* 16 (1956)
213-303, 319-372.

[28] In his commentary on Aristotle's *Physics* (MS Berlin Lat. 2°41 fol. 202 va-rb) he ven-
tures another explanation: that the air as such has slower or quicker parts which help carrying the body. That is, he replaces Aristotle's "layers" by "air currents," divided, so to
say, not vertically, but horizontally. Yet this would make the movement of a body *cessante
movente* unpredictable. Ockham makes it very clear that this is not his own interpretation,
but the only way to rescue the model of Aristotle.

[29] On the role of connotative terms in Ockham's logic and epistemology cf. Ernest Moody,
The Logic of William of Ockham (New York 1935) 53ff.; G. Martin, *Wilhelm von Ockham,
Untersuchungen zur Ontologie der Ordnungen* (Berlin 1947) 221-227; and, a more recent
work (an application of Martin's thesis), J. Miethke, *Ockham's Weg zur Sozialphilosophie*
(Berlin 1969) 201-227.

[30] Martin 227. J. Miethke (note 9 above) has shown the heuristic possibilities of this
approach for the understanding of Ockham's political philosophy.

though transcendental, unity between objects, properties, and events, it remains that the main intention of Ockham's criticism was to reduce such concepts to the real elements they connote, that is, subjects and their absolute qualities. In many cases he stops after having achieved this goal, after having destroyed any false elevation of mutual aspects of things to the dignity of distinct entities. So also in his analysis of motion.

Undoubtedly, here lies the unbridgeable gap between Ockham's reduction of complex concepts into their elements and, for example, Descartes's *regulae ad directionem ingenii* or, for that matter, the epistemology underlying the modern *metodo risolotivo e compositivo* from Galileo onward. For both of them, for Ockham as for Descartes, motion is an abstract term. Yet for Ockham this connotative term draws its validity from, and is directly caused by, the successive intuitive cognitions of a singular body being first "here" and then "not here any more, but elewhere" (the *ubi* being also materially determinable). Not so for Descartes: It is the concept itself, and not its empirical foundation, which must be "clear and distinct." Our perceptions are mixed and confused; conceptualization is imposed on them by the spontaneous work of the mind. Although elicited from and corroborated by experience, they do not depend for their validity on the senses. Indeed, for Descartes and more so for Spinoza the degree of reality of objects is measured by their rationality: matter *is* extension, and extension can be understood "by itself." It is therefore that extension and motion are, for Ockham, *complexa*; for Descartes, they are simple concepts, *intuitive* cognitions—a term reserved, in Ockham's analysis of knowledge, to the immediate cognition of the singulars.[31] Implicity or explicitly, this principle of the spontaneity, or rather self-sufficiency, of simple concepts characterizes modern scientific methodologies; for a clear elaboration of this aspect it suffices to refer to the considerations of Cassirer and Koyré;[32] with some of its implications I will deal later on.

These considerations might also help us to understand the inadequacy in Ockham's interpretation of forced movements. He stopped exactly at the point where he could have reached the principle underlying the law of inertia—the distinction namely between uniform motion or rest and change

[31] Cf. Descartes, *Regula ad directionem ingenii* 12 *Œuvres*, ed. C. Adam and P. Tannery 10 (Paris 1966) 418: "tales [i.e., of the kind of cognition that is *perspicua et distincta*] sunt figura, extensio, motus, etc; reliquas autem omnes quodam modo compositas exhisesse conscipimus."

[32] E. Cassirer, *Das Erkenntnisproblem in der Philosophie und Wissenschaft der Neuzeit* (Berlin 1911) 1.8ff., 31ff., 138ff., 377ff., 349ff. (471: "Die Erfahrung vermag uns über die Natur eines verwickelten und komplexen Vorganges niemals vollständig aufzuklären; ist doch die Antwort, die sie zu erstatten vermag, selbst mehrdeutig und bedarf erst der Erläuterung und der Interpretation durch den reinen Begriff"). Also Koyré (n. 1 above) More than Cassirer, Koyré tends towards a contraposition of "medieval" and "modern" science, both imagined as monolithic, coherent sytems; see below, 347.

of motion or direction, as replacing the Aristotelian contraposition of rest and movement.[33] For once, rest and movement had to remain separated. Rest signifies the singular body A being at the same place in consecutive times; movement connotes with the body A two different places, which it occupies in different imes. Both uniform and difform movements—supposing Ockham had chosen to operate with these notions—signify, if one refers to the method by which the *calculatores* elicited them, the same body, the same places, the same "times." The *calculatores* only showed the way to reduce uniformly difform motions (constant acceleration and deceleration) into terms of uniform motion and vice versa;[34] they were much nearer than Ockham to the interpretation of uniform motion as a "state," only they did not aim at the formulation of laws: they were merely interested in convenient mathematical descriptions. And of course neither they nor Ockham paid any attention to friction as a *variable* factor. The distinction between rest and movement pertained, for Ockham, more closely to the aspects of a moving body than the distinction between uniform and difform movement In any other consideration of the difference between uniform and accelerated motion (other than that of the *calculatores*), "acceleration" remains hardly distinguishable from "movement by greater force" or simply "greater velocity." To say that Ockham could not have reached the distinction between movement and change of movement is, of course, nonsensical; this is not the same as saying, as we do, that his concentration on the proper way in which to speak about single objects and their qualities seems to explain why he could easily disregard a distinction that if he considered it at all, must have appeared to him as a *mere* abstraction.

On the other hand, the terministic analysis of concepts did pave the way towards a greater flexibility in conceptualizing experiences, inasmuch as it stressed the significatory functions and levels of concepts; their operative function became more important than their ontological status.

IV. Buridan and the Impetus Hypothesis

I will, then, refrain from the attempt to determine how close Buridan's concept of impetus came to the law of inertia; and ask instead for its contribution to the process which led from an intuitive towards an analytical concept of motion.

---

[33] "Rest" as a privation of motion and hence its opposite: Aristotle, *Physics* 5, 229b25. The circular, celestial movements are in a way a *coincidentia oppositorum*: in respect to the center, the spheres' state is that of rest, in respect to the circumference, movement.

[34] A selection of texts in Clagett (n. 4 above) 199ff., 255ff.; cf. also, for Ockham's contribution towards a distinction between kinematic and dynamic analysis, Ernest Moody," "Ockham and Aegidius of Rome," *Franciscan Studies* 9 (1949) 417-442.

Buridan introduced the impetus hypothesis[35] almost as a concept won by induction. From his predecessors he inherited a list of "arguments from experience" against the Aristotelian interpretation of projectile movements; he adds to them some of his own; and after having introduced his owns interpretation he returns to "experience" and points at a group of movements which, although they were explainable by the displaced theory of the active air layers, are better explainable by the new one. From there he goes even further to consider the celestial movements as conserved by their impetus. Once introduced to explain one group of movement in which it seems manifest, "impetus" soon becomes a key concept to explain every movement as one of its aspects. The universality of impetus is a logical consequence of its postulation. There can be no sufficient reason why it should be confined to projectile bodies only. It has rather to be conceived as a universal factor in every movement.

Buridan is thus led to understand all movements as an interaction of impetus and the natural inclination of the body: (1) The gravity (or levity) of a body, together with the resistance of the air, is a retarding factor in the case of forced movements. Buridan gives no detailed analysis of these movements, though we have every reason to believe that they can be described as an inverted analogy to the natural movements. The impetus of forced movement decreases constantly owing to gravity (or levity), if left to itself. Only if force continued to be exerted on the body, it would presumably continue its motion indefinitely, since its impetus is renewed. For a physicist operating without a clear notion of friction, this is the most logical interpretation of continuous movements. (Buridan, it is true, recognizes the resistance of the air as a factor in movements; but it is a constant, not a variable that can be abstractly reduced towards zero). Note that, all of a sudden, projectile movements become the rule, continuously forced movements the exception, or rather a secondary phenomenon. (2) The gravity (or levity) of a body is an accelerating factor in the case of natural terrestial movements This is not to say that impetus is not always the cause for the *preservation* of motion; but rather that gravity acts as an intrinsic force imparting to a body both movement and impetus. Since "movement" is steadily imparted to the body, its impetus (determined by force and *quantitas materiae*) must also increase. Movement as such never produces impetus, but rather the force causing movement is also the force causing impetus—in falling bodies as in reflexive motions.[36] (3) The natural inclination of celestial bodies neither

[35] *Questiones super libris physicorum* 8.12 (Paris 1509) quoted by Maier, "Die aristotelische Theorie" (n. 11 above) 207-214; and the later *Questiones super libris quattuor de caelo et mundo* 2.12, 13; 3.2; ed. Ernest Moody (Cambridge, Mass. 1942) 180-184, 240-243.

[36] Moody, "Laws" (n. 5 above) interprets Buridan with the help of a model seemingly more exact than Buridan's.

retards nor accelerates their motion; it does not interfere with their impetus at all, since this inclination means nothing else than potential circular movement. Given the initial impetus, the celestial bodies will continue to move *uniformiter* indefinitely. Buridan could thus discharge the "intelligences" as the efficient cause moving the spheres.[37] That he intended a "mechanical" interpretation of the universe is, however, an exaggeration. His celestial impetus is entirely hypothetical; he did not want to link the celestial and terrestial impetus to the point where the rejection of the former would mean the rejection of the latter. Consequently, this aspect is not discussed in the *later* questions on Aristotle's book on heaven and earth. It might well be that Buridan, in considering the perpetuity of the celestial impetus, was inspired by the remark of Aristotle: "Again, a body which is in motion but has neither wieght nor lightness, must be moved by constraint, and must continue its constrained movement indefinitely."[38]

In short, Buridan describes terrestial motions as impetus $\pm$ gravity (or levity), celestial motions as impetus $+$ O. The methodological revolution underlying this analysis of motion is considerable. *All* terrestial motions. including natural movement, are complex motions, a product of the interaction between the natural inclination of the body moving and the impetus it acquired either by external force or by its very inclination. Gravity and levity are but one factor of all movement. Even natural movements are not "simple" in their totality. Their simplicity is but one aspect of them, isolated not in the immediate observation, but as a mental concept.

---

[37] On the history of this problem cf. H. Wolfson, "The Problems of the Souls of the Spheres from the Byzantine Commentaries on Aristotle through the Arabs and St. Thomas to Kepler", *The Dumberton Oaks Papers* (1961) 67-93. For Blumenberg (n. 6 above) 33 Buridan's cosmos, in eliminating the intelligences, ceased to be "ein zuschuβsystem," as was the Aristotelian and medieval cosmos. But never would Buridan have conceived excluding nonmechanical factors (souls,, intelligence, will) from his system altogether, as did Descartes.

[38] Ἔτι δ᾽εἰ ἔσται τὶ σῶμα κινούμενον μήτε κουφότητα μήτε βάρος ἔχον, ἀνάγκη τοῦτο βίᾳ κινεῖσθαι, βίᾳ δὲ κινούμενον ἄπειρον ποιεῖν τὴν κίνησιν .(301b1-4; trans. R. Mc Keon, *The basic works of Aristotle*, New York 1941, 443); and even more clearly in *Physica* 4.8,215a19-22: ἔτι οὐδεὶς ἂν ἔχοι εἰπεῖν διὰ τί κινηθὲν στήσεταί που · τί γὰρ μᾶλλον ἐνταῦθα ἢ ἐνταῦθα ; ὥστε ἢ ἠρεμήσει ἢ εἰς ἄπειρον ἀνάγκη φέρεσθαι, ἐαν μή τι ἐμποδίσῃ κρεῖττον. See above, 335. On several occasions, S. Drake (*Galileo Studies*, Ann Harbor: The University of Michigan Press, 1970, 240-256; *Galileo Galilei on Motion and Mechanics* [together with I. E. Drabkin], Madison: The University of Wisconsin Press 1960, 170 n. 25) chose to see in the "recognition of a special kind of motion", namely a motion neither violent nor natural but rather "indifferent", Galileo's "original" contribution to the emerging inertial concept. Yet whether decisive or not, the concept of a "neutral" motion is by no means original. It his clearly envisioned (as an absurdity) in the above quoted passages of Aristotle; furthermore, as we have tried to prove, the concept of impetus introduced a healthy uncertainty as to the actual discernment of the distinction between natural (simple) and violent motion.

If my interpretation is correct, it should find some corroboration in Buridan's views on simple movements. He deals with the subject *in extenso* in the fifth *quaestio* of the first book of his *Quaestiones super libris quattuor de caelo et mundo*.[39] The question is whether there are more than three *motus simplices*, a difficult question, as he concedes, "quia difficile est videre quid debeamus intelligere per motum simplicem et motum compositum." He sets out therefore to distinguish between several possible meanings of simplicity as attached to Aristotle's concept of motion. He has to exclude, among other features, regularity; either regularity in time, since natural motions are "velociores in fine quam in principio," or regularity of space, since the geometrical figure of movements downwards is the same as that of lateral movements; or indeed the regularity of the body moved, which might have any shape. Two different connotations remain. One refers to the geometrical structure of natural movements; they are "simplices respectu medii, scilicet centri." The other refers to the moving cause: "ita quod motus dicatur simplex qui est ab unico simplici motore . . . ut grave movetur naturaliter deorsum a sola gravitate . . . et caelum ab intelligentia." This last connotation, the uniformity of cause, is given in total disregard of the theory of impetus. Not so much because of the intelligences; as noted above, the removal of the intelligences, although it gives the theory of impetus its universality and elegance, does not seem to be for Buridan the *condito sine qua non* for the acceptance of impetus. The contradiction rather lies in the condition of unity. If the unity of moving cause is the meaning of simplicity in natural movements, then at least the actual movement of heavy and light bodies is complex. This should be the immediate consequence of 2.12:[40] "suppono quod gravitas naturalis ipsius lapidis manet semper eadem et consimilis ante motum et post motum et in motu, unde aeque gravis invenitur lapis post motum sicut erat ante. Suppono etiam quod resistentia quae est ex parte medii remanet eadem vel consimilis . . . Tertio suppono quod si mobile sit idem, et movens etiam totale sit idem, et resistentia etiam sit eadem vel consimilis, motus remanebit aeque velox": and yet falling bodies accelerate. "Ex quibus concluditur, quod ad illum motum *concurrit aliud movens* praeter gravitatem naturalem quae a principio movebat et quae semper manet eadem." Impetus, thus, is an *additional* cause. In the second meaning of simplicity mentioned above, the natural movement of heavy and light bodies can hardly be called simple. Their distinction from forced movements is not total, but only in one of their aspects. Once this aspect is isolated, there can be nothing relative in it: "potentiae . . . et virtutes cognoscuntur per motus et operationes"[41] because Buridan's cognition of simple motion does not refer to

---

[39] Ed. Moody (n. 35 above) 20-57.
[40] *Ibid.*, 176-181, here 179f.
[41] *Questiones super libris IV de caelo et mundo* 4.1, ed. Moody 245.

the motion in its totality, he can assume, as he does, that all four simple sublunar motions, including that of water and earth, are absolute, not relative, *virtutes*.[42] In contrast, natural movements, even those of earth and fire, can not remain what they were for Aristotle—definable as such in their immediate givenness. They, also, are a product of a factoral analysis, and thus are mental concepts.

V. On the Emergence of the Inertial Law

The further variations and transformations of the impetus hypothesis, until and after Benedetti and Galileo, need no discussion here. Some methodological remarks, however, are needed as to the role of ancient and medieval concepts in the historical process which led towards the formulation of the inertial laws of Gassendi and Descartes. Four aspects can be discerned in this process.

(1) The epistemological aspect. Aristotle's determination of simple, natural movements was partly based on immediate evidence. Aristotle, in the words of Galileo, "assumed it as known and manifest that the motions directly upward and downward correspond to fire and earth."[43] Slowly and almost inadvertently, the Middle Ages replaced this intuitive identification with a factoral analysis of all motions, natural and forced. The natural inclination of a body became, after Buridan, merely one aspect of all movements; an aspect that is only mentally isolated from others.[44]

Buridan and his followers were hardly aware of the grave epistemological implications of this shift. Since the key concepts of Aristotle's physics were preserved, there was no urgency for such an awareness. It became a dominant theme in the methodology of science for natural philosophers after the seventeenth century. If my simple concepts, albeit "clear and distinct," are unobservable abstractions, what guarantees the validity of the ideas in regard to the *res*? Of necessity, the synthesis of the ideas supplies a proof—which must, however, remain rather on the level of probability unless one assumes a metaphysical principle to guarantee that "ordo rerum idem est ordo idea-

---

[42] *Ibid.* 4.6, Moody 261-264. Again Buridan believes that he has "rescued the appearances" better with his theory of the four absolute *virtutes*, which means that he was well aware of its distance from the text. If we are to ask in what sense movements are simple, only the first of Buridan's above mentioned determinations would make sense: in respect to the place they aspire to achieve.

[43] *Dialogo sopra i due massimi sistemi* (first day), trans. S. Drake (Berkeley 1962) 18; cf. *ibid.* 32: "Now who is there so blind as not to see that earthly and watery parts, as heavy things, move naturally downward."

[44] Although referring to a real force, or *virtus*, in the body.

rum." For Descartes, God's will and goodness are such a guarantee.[45] For Spinoza, the finite and infinite number of attributes must correspond as aspects of one and the same "substance."[46] For Leibnitz, these infinite aspects, hypostatized into monads, are guaranteed by the preestabilized harmony that again is nothing else than God's comprehensive appreciation of the totality.[47] The monad is a spontaneous principle of order. The principle of the spontaneity of our notions acquires an ever more prolific formulation; its problematics becomes ever sharper, until given a new turn in the Kantian philosophy. The principle was not a product of a rationalistic hybris, but rather the methodical foundation of the new science.

The readiness to admit that all actual motions are mixed, necessitated the growing awareness that natural or simple movement is an abstraction gained by the *metodo risolotivo*. This was the only aspect of the inertial law we have dealt with. In his respect we have claimed that the impetus hypothesis as used by and since Buridan was of decisive importance. It was by no means simply "a return to common sense."[48]

(2) The definitory aspect: It is indicated by Descartes's "first law."[49] In Aristotle's definition of motion as "the movable in activity."[50] Locomotion, much like other kinds of motion, was regarded as finite (or the actualization of a potentiality). It is terminated either by its goal or by its constant place

[45] This he could accept all the more easily, since he assumed God already as a guarantee for the coherence, or synthesis, of clear and distinct ideas: as a methodical guarantee of scientific memory.

[46] An object is thus *omnimodo determinatum* in (theoretically) infinite ways; in each of them it occupies the same functional position. To regard these attributes as comprehensive theories, universal explanatory formulas, as done recently by E. M. Curley, *Spinoza's Metaphysics; an Essay in Interpretation* (Cambridge, Mass. 1969) esp. 119ff., means to disregard their epistemological basis. It would mean that a known attribute (e.g., *extensio*), though useful to explain a group of phenomena known to us, is not yet explaining all phenomena or determining every single given object *omnimodo*, and might be replaced, with the progress of science, by another, better hupothesis. But the attribute is valid not on behalf of its explanatory merits but rather as perfectly evident by and in itself; no other attribute can be conceived to replace it. Suppose we came to know a third attribute A_3, it would not replace A_2 or A_1, but (as Curley rightly explains) supply a new "aspect," or organizing principle, for the whole of the world much as extension and thinking do it now, everyone of them independently. As to its inner order, A_3 will also correspond in its modes to A_2 and A_1 totally. If Leibnitz's monads are also to be understood as such spontaneous organizing principles (or an infinity of "Seinsgründe"), their *exigentia existentiae* becomes a most natural assumption.

[47] The "prestabilized harmony" is convincingly interpreted as a reference structure within every monad t all other monads in A. Gurwitsch, "An Apparent Paradox in the Leibnizian System" in: *Iyyun: A Hebrew Philosophical Quarterly* 14-15 (1963-1964) 145-156: I hope to discuss these questions on another occasion.

[48] S. Koyré *"Galileo an Plato"* (n. 1 above) 30.

[49] See n. 8 above.

[50] *Physics* 5.1, 224b10; 25f.; cf. 3.1, 201a10.

(the circle), not only or necessarily by the resistance of the medium; and therefore an immediate cause must be found for every forced movement. At its outset, the law of inertia subsumes rest and uniform movement under the category of the "state": its preservation needs no immediate cause; instead it distinguishes between uniform motion and change of either motion or direction. This distinction does not, however, indicate as such what the natural direction (or path) is. What it does imply is that even without a medium (be its removal possible or merely an ideal experiment), a body with no other forces acting on it moves in a given velocity. It is interesting to note that in his systematic critique of Aristotle's physics, Hasdai Crescas not only restored the possibility of empty space, but also (following, Avempace, whose doctrine he knew through Averroes's refutation) revised Aristotle's concept of movement in space: it is not instantaneous, but a movement in a given velocity זמן שרשי.[51] The Italian Platonists knew these arguments. We have seen, however, that Aristotle himself had already conceived of this possibility in order to refute it.[52] A more direct avenue was the combination of the impetus hypothesis with the descriptive tools of the *calculatores*— a synthesis that Oresme started and which was completed in Galileo's work. That this aspect can be logically and historically separated from the one to be discussed in the following, is demonstrated again by Galileo, who conceived of both circular and rectilinear impetus.

(3) The geometrical determination. This third aspect is formulated in Descartes's "second law." The only adequate geometrical description of natural movements is the straight (infinite) line. Only at this point was the "geometrization" of the universe achieved. Aristotle's cosmos was based on geometrical considerations, but these belonged to the geometry of figures, while the geometry underlying Descartes's universe was that of pure spatial dimensions, of relations renderable to quantification. The "perfection" of the geometrical circle ceased to be a criterion for natural movements.[53]

---

[51] Hasdai Crescas, *Or Adonai* 1, 2.1 (Vienna 1859) 16ff: וזה שלמה שאי אפשר לתנועה אלא בזמן הוא מן ההכרח שיהיה לו לתנועה זמן שרשי אם נניח התנועה באנה.
He wants to prove the possibility of infinite motion, circular or straight. Cf. H. Wolfson, *Crescas' Critique of Aristotle*; *Problems of Aristotle's Physics in Jewish and Arabic Philosophy* (Cambridge, Mass. 1929) 183, 205, 403ff.

[52] Above, 335, 342 n. 38.

[53] The abandonment of the circle as a pattern of perfect movement was, in a certain sense, the abandonment of an aesthetic ideal. Here, as in the acceptance of the "void" or in the cosmogonic hypothesis of the vortex, modern science might have had (in this case without knowing it) a forerunner in the Atomists. "Admirabor eorum tarditatem qui animantem immortalem et eundem beatum rotundum esse velint, quod ea forma neget ullam esse pulchriorem Plato: at mihi vel cylindri vel quadrati vel coni vel pyramidis videtur esse formosior": we hear Cicero's Epicurean arguing against the *anima mundi*. Cicero, *De natura deorum* 1.10.24 (Vellius), ed. Plasberg (Stuttgart 1959).

(4) The rejection of *language* as a legitimate instrument for the interpretation of experience went hand in hand with the ideal of a quantified science of nature. Mathematical entities became the only "language of nature"; Aristotle and the Aristotelian tradition were condemned for their dependence on language as a guideline for understanding nature.[54] With good reasons later scholasticism was included in this early modern critique. The "idea" of the seventeenth century, if clear and distinct, was detached from the verbal concept; this detachment enabled early modern philosophy to set aside the terministic insistence that abstract concepts should always be related to singulars.

Obviously, the second of the considered aspects is conditioned (though not strictly implied) by the first, and so the third by the second. These aspects are, then, at least theoretical phases of the idea, although never separately formulated. To distinguish between the elements of either the Aristotelian or the later medieval or again the modern concept of motion, to ask for their degree of independence and interdependence both logically and historically, is a task as much neglected as it is methodologically important. It has been more or less taken for granted that the assumptions on which the Aristotelian theory of motion were based (and likewise its modern counterpart) formed a coherent system of mutually implied sentences. This, indeed, was what many commentators of the philosopher and all his modern opponents felt: that none of his ἀϱχαί is exchangeable, that all of them form a well ordered cosmos that must be either accepted or rejected totally. Koyré's masterful contraposition of the "old cosmos" and the "new universe" reflects without reservation the self-understanding of most anti-Aristotelian natural philosophers in the seventeenth century. But their self-consciousness should not become our only guide for historical investigations. A recent examination has made it very plausible that Aristotle himself was by no means a constructor of a "system" in Zeller's (or the general modern) understanding of the word, that Aristotle rather accepted a plurality of principles.[55] Many of the medieval "Aristotelians" were well aware of this, and not only because of the incompatibility of some of the Master's principles with theological assumptions. Were it not so, it would be astonishing enough that many of the natural philosophers between the Averroists and Descartes, including Galileo, could live with some of the elements of Aristotlian dynamics altered, but some others still unchallenged, without feeling highly uncomfortable.

---

[54] Cf., for example, Gassendi, *Exercitationes paradoxicae adversus Aristoteleos* 1.14, ed. B. Rochot (Paris 1959) 45f.: "Postremo, ut coarguantur verba magis curare, quam sensus, efficere ut cum Seneca exclamare merito liceat, 'Nostra, quae erat Philosophia, facta Philologia est, ex quo disputare docemus, non vivere,' non memoro quod quaestiones omnes apud Aristoteleos de nomine fere sint."

[55] W. Wieland (n. 9 above) 1ff.

We should, therefore, systematically ask what elements in the Aristotelian theory of motion were replaced by early modern mechanics and whether these elements are logically and historically separable. Only then can we proceed to determine whether, and how, dynamical concepts in Antiquity and in the Middle Ages—either those opposed by Aristotle (such as Atomism) or those meant to save his interpretations from inconsistencies (such as the concept of impetus), or even those opposing Aristotle, but not yet identifiable with Newtonian laws—paved the way towards the first formulation of these Laws.

Department of History
University of California
Los Angeles, California 90024, U.S.A.

MEHMED II THE CONQUEROR AND
HIS PRESUMED KNOWLEDGE OF GREEK AND LATIN

•

by Christos G. Patrinelis

The personality of Mehmed II the Conqueror (1432-1481) is portrayed with considerable variations in the chronographies, the histories, and the multifarious other texts that pertain to the conquest of Constantinople and to the establishment of the Turks as the dominant power in the Balkan peninsula. Theologians saw in the young conqueror the new Sennacherib, the precursor of Antichrist who was to destroy the Church of Christ[1], while several humanists, historians, and scholars adopted a milder and often ambivalent attitude. They described the Turks as "Asiatic barbarians" who might destroy the ongoing rebirth of the Greco-Roman culture, but at the same time—evidently reflecting the Renaissance concept of the ideal prince—they did not hide their admiration for Mehmed's strong personality, his administrative ability, his religious tolerance, and his military genius. In this spirit they did not hesitate to connect him with the Classical tradition and draw parallels between the young sultan and Alexander the Great or Julius Caesar. Sometimes Mehmed was even portrayed as an exemplary leader, a "philosopher king" surrounded by artists and men of letters, a prince who divided his time between victorious campaigns and leisurely academic pursuits reaching so far afield as to embrace Greek and Latin literature.[2]

---

[1] See such a description of Mehmed by pope Nicholas V in F. Babinger, *Mahomet II le Conquérant et son temps, 1432-1481*, French translation from the German supervised by the author (Paris 1954) 147-148; for a similar dark picture of Mehmed painted by Aeneas Sylvius Piccolomini and other leading ecclesiastics of the time see in G. Voigt, *Enea Silvio Piccolomini* 2 (Berlin 1862) 95.

[2] On the attitude of these Italian humanists towards Mehmed II, and on their tendency to idealize him, see F. Babinger, "Mehmed II, der Eroberer, und Italien," *Byzantion* 21 (1951) 127-170, reprinted in a revised from in F. Babinger, *Aufsätze und Abhandlungen zur Geschichte Südosteuropas und der Levante* 1, Südosteuropa 3 (Munich 1962) 172-200, esp. 178-184. See also F. Babinger, "Mehmed der Eroberer in östlicher und westlicher Beleuchtung," *Südost-Forschungen* 22 (1963) 281-298, and *idem, Mahomet le Conquérant* 106, 433, 606, 608, 616-617.

The same romantic attitude is reflected in the tendency of some humanists to consider the Ottoman Turks as descendants of the Trojans; see Steven Runciman, *The Fall of Constantinople* (Cambridge 1965) 167-168. It is pertinent to recall here that several other personali-

This romantic portrait of Mehmed II was completed through oft-repeated assertions about his extraordinary linguistic competence. He has been credited with knowledge of two, three, or even five languages in addition to Turkish.

Thus, Giacomo de Langusco, a mid-fifteenth century chronicler of dubious reliability,[3] in describing Mehmed with an obvious desire to idealize him, tells us that he "usa tre lingue: turcho, greco, et schiavo [Slavonic]."[4] Theodoros Spandones or Spandugino (1455—post 1538), a Greek who wrote in Italian, asserts that Mehmed "fu dottissimo in lettere arabe et grece."[5] Martino Barletio, in his chronicle printed in 1504, increases to five the number of languages that Mehmed was presumably able to speak: "havea imparato à fauellar' in greco, in latino, in arabo, in caldeo [Hebrew] et alla persiana."[6] The same information is repeated by Francesco Sansovino (1521-1583), who most likely drew on Barletio. Sansovino, whose works enjoyed wide popularity in the sixteenth century, states that Mehmed "sapeva oltre a ciò cinque lingue oltre alla sua naturale, perch' egli parlava sicuramente nella lingua greca, nella latina, nell' arabica, nella caldea e nella persiana."[7] Finally, the

---

ties (such as the Albanian hero Skanderbeg, the Hungarian leader John Hunyadi, sultans Bayezit I and Selim I) were also occasionally exalted as "New Alexanders" by historians of the time; see G. Veloudis, *Der neugriechische Alexander Tradition in Bewahrung und Wandel*, Micellanea byzantina monacensia 8 (Munich 1968) 196-197. Greek contemporary historians, such as Kritovoulos and Doucas, also viewed Mehmed II as the new Alexander the Great. It is worth noting, however, that all these pretentious Classical reminiscences are absent in the Turkish chronographers of the same period; they preferred to extol Mehmed II as new Cyrus, Xerxes, or Chosroes and generally in terms more fitting to their Turco-Persian cultural tradition.

[3] On Langusco's dubious trustworthiness, see F. Babinger, *Johannes Darius (1414-1494), Sachwalter Venedigs im Morgenland, und sein griechischer Umkreis*, Sitzungsberichte der bayer. Akademie der Wissenschaften, philos.-hist. Kl. 5 (Munich 1961) 15 n. 2; and *idem*, "Nikolaos Sagoundinos, ein griechisch-venedischer Humanist des 15. Jhdts.," Χαριστήριον εἰς 'Α.' Ὀρλάνδον 1 (Athens 1965) 202 n. 9. See also my recent article "Κυριακὸς ὁ Ἀγκωνίτης. Ἡ δῆθεν ὑπηρεσία του εἰς τὴν αὐλὴν τοῦ σουλτάνου Μωάμεθ τοῦ Πορθητοῦ καὶ ὁ χρόνος τοῦ θανάτου του" in Ἐπετηρὶς τῆς Ἑταιρείας Βυζαντινῶν Σπουδῶν 36 (1968) 155-157.

[4] Giacomo de Langusco's brief chronicle was edited by G. M. Thomas, *Die Eroberung Constantinopels im Jahre 1453 aus einer venetianischen Chronic*, in Sitzungsberichte der Kgl. bayer. Akademie der Wissenschaften, philos.-hist. Kl. 2, Jahrg. 1866 (Munich 1868) 5-6. The same passage is cited and discussed by Babinger (n. 2 above) 182.

[5] Theodoro Spandugnino, *De la origine deli imperatori Ottomani*, ed. Const. Sathas, *Documents inédits relatifs à l'histoire de la Grèce au Moyen Age* 9 (Paris 1890) 168 lines 38-39.

[6] Martino Barletio, *Dell'assedio di Scutari*, republished by F. Sansovino in *Historia universale dell'origine et imperio de' Turchi* (Venice 1654) 303.

[7] F. Sansovino, *Gl'annali turcheschi overo vite de principi della casa othomana* (Venice 1573) 151. See also a Greek chronicle edited by G. Th. Zoras, Χρονικὸν περὶ τῶν Τούρκων σουλτάνων (Athens 1958) 121 lines 25-26: Ἤξερε πέντε γλῶσσες καλά· τούρκικα, ῥωμέικα, φράγκικα, ἀράπικα, χαλδέικα, περσικά. This chronicle is largely dependent on

Greek *Chronicon majus* of Pseudo-Sphrantzes, relying probably on Western
sources, informs us that Mehmed spoke correctly five languages beside his
mother tongue: Greek, Latin, Arabic, Hebrew, and Persian.[8]

Modern historians have generally accepted the testimony of the above
sources without much questioning.[9] The distinguished Turcologist F. Babinger, however, has taken a more cautious view. Although in his monumental
book on Mehmed II he left out the problem, he had discussed it briefly in
an earlier work.[10] He noted there the disagreement of the sources as to the
number of languages that Mehmed spoke and concluded that the evidence
is more reliable where Arabic and Persian are concerned. With regard to
Greek and Slavic, Babinger speculates that if Mehmed's mother was indeed
either a Greek or a Serbian—a matter still under dispute—then one should
conclude that Mehmed would know his mother's tongue.

There is, however, substantial evidence from reliable sources that allows
us to eliminate certainly Greek and most probably Latin from the list of
languages in which Mehmed may have been competent in any way. Kritovoulos, the well-known Greek historian and personal aquaintance of Mehmed,
in discussing the young sultan's education states explicitly that Mehmed
knew Greek literature solely from translations: "He was extremely well-
versed in Arabic and Persian [literature] and in as much of Greek as had been
translated into Arabic and Persian."[11]

Sansovino; see Eliz. Zachariadou, *Τὸ Χρονικὸ τῶν Τούρκων Σουλτάνων καί τὸ ἰταλικό του
πρότυπο* (Thessaloniki 1960) 43.

[8] Pseudo-Sphrantzes, *Chronicon Majus*, ed. V. Grecu, *Georgios Sphranzes, Memorii,
1401-1477: Ȋn anexâ Pseudo-Phranzes: Macarie Melissenos Cronica, 1258-1481*, Scriptores
byzantini 5 (Bucharest 1966) 234 lines 16-17.

[9] See for example, J. F. von Hammer-Purgstall, *Geschichte des osmanischen Reiches* 2
(Pest 1828) 210, and Runciman (n. 2 above) 56.

[10] Babinger (n. 2 above) 182-183.

[11] Kritovoulos, *Ξυγγραφὴ Ἱστοριῶν*, ed. V. Grecu, *Critobul din Imbros, Din domnia
lui Mahomed al II-lea anii 1451-1467*, Scriptores byzantini 4 (Bucharest 1963) 43 lines 11-12:
Ἤσκητο γὰρ ἐς ἄκρον πᾶσαν τὴν Ἀράβων καὶ Περσῶν καὶ ὅση τῶν Ἑλλήνων ἐς τὴν
Ἀράβων τε καὶ Περσῶν γλῶσσαν μεθηρμηνεύθη; see also *ibid*. 335 lines 28-29: Ἐσχόλαζε
δὲ καὶ φιλοσοφίᾳ, ὅση τε Ἀράβων καὶ Περσῶν καὶ Ἑλλήνων μάλιστα ἐς τὴν Ἀράβων με-
τενεχθεῖσα. Similar information about ancient Greek and Latin works translated into
Turkish on Mehmed's order is provided also by Nicholas Sekoundinos (or Sagoundino), a
Greek in the service of Venice, who was sent on a diplomatic mission to Constantinople
in the autumn of 1453. In his *Report* Sekoundinos says that Mehmed "Alexandrum Mace-
donem et Gaium Cesarem precipue imitandos delegit, quorum res gestas in linguam suam
traduci effeci"; see his *Report* partly published in N. Iorga, *Notes et extraits pour servir
à l'histoire des Croisades au XVe siècle*, 3 (Paris 1902) 318. Sekoundinos's testimony is
corroborated by Barletio (n. 6 above) 303: "[Mehmed] havea letto i fatti illustri de gli huo-
mini grandi, et spetialmente dei Cesari e di Alessandro Magno dal quali ardentemente
infiammato, s'era proposto imitargli."

An incident that took place shortly after the capture of Constantinople sheds more light on the problem. Some time between January 1454 and the spring of 1456 Mehmed visited the monastery of Pammakaristos, which was the seat of the patriarchate at the time, and held several lengthy discussions on Christianity with the patriarch Gennadios Scholarios. Afterwards the contents of the discussion were put into writing by the patriarch at the request of the sultan. Gennadios's treatise bears the title: *On the Only Way for Man's Salvation; Composed, Translated into Arabic* [Turkish] *and Submitted to Those Who Requested it after the Second Conversation in the Patriarchate.*[12] Mehmed and his advisors found Gennadios's treatise to be too lengthy and difficult to understand. Therefore, Gennadios was asked to rewrite the text in a more concise and clear form. This was the occasion that prompted the patriarch to compose his well-known *Confession of Faith*, now preserved in three manuscripts written in his own hand. On one of those manuscripts Gennadios wrote the following note: "This was submitted to those who, on behalf of the sultan, requested something brief and clear on the main doctrines of our faith which had been the subject of our conversation; this, too, was translated into Arabic along with the previous one."[13] At the end of his composition Gennadios noted that he wrote this *Confession* in a way that would facilitate the translator's work, and remarked that "indeed, it was well translated into Arabic [Turkish]."[14] It is clear from the above incident that Mehmed could not read Gennadios's Greek treatise and had to have the text translated into Turkish.

Moreover, even during his conversations with the patriarch, Mehmed had to rely on an interpreter, as we are explicitly told by Theodosios Zygomalas in his *Political History of Constantinople*, compiled on the basis of older sources in 1578. Referring to the discussions between the sultan and the patriarch, Zygomalas states that Mehmed "questioned the patriarch exten-

---

[12] Gennadios's treatise is included in the edition of his works by L. Petit, X. A. Siderides, M. Jugie, *Œuvres complètes de Gennade Scholarios* 3 (Paris 1930) 434 lines 2-5: Περὶ τῆς μόνης ὁδοῦ πρὸς τὴν σωτηρίαν τῶν ἀνθρώπων. Συνεγράφη δὲ καὶ ἀρραβικῶς ἡρμηνεύθη καὶ ἐδόθη ζητήσασι, μετὰ τὰς διαλέξεις ἐν τῷ πατριαρχείῳ τὰς δευτέρας.

[13] *Ibid.* 453 note: Ἐδόθη τοῦτο ἀπαιτήσασι παρὰ τοῦ Ἀμηρᾶ σύντομόν τι καὶ σαφὲς περὶ τῶν κεφαλαίων τῆς ἡμετέρας πίστεως, περὶ ὧν καὶ ἡ διάλεξις γέγονε. καὶ ἡρμηνεύθη καὶ τοῦτο ἀρραβικῶς.

[14] *Ibid.* 458 lines 6-7: Ἵνα καὶ δυνηθῶσι ῥᾷον μεταγλωττισθῆναι, ὥσπερ καὶ ἡρμηνεύθη καλῶς ταῦτα ἀρραβικῶς. On these two texts and their Turkish translations as well as on the meetings of the sultan with Gennadios in general, see *ibid.*, reprinted from M. Jugie, "Ecrits apologétiques de Gennadios Scholarios à l'adresse des musulmans," *Byzantion* 5 (1929) 295-314; also T. Halasi Kun, "Gennadios török hitrvallása" [Gennadios's Turkish Confession] in *Körösi Csoma-Archivum*, supp. 1.2 (Budapest 1936) 139-247, and A. Decei, "Versiunea turcească a confesiunii patriarhului Ghenadie II Scholarios, scrisă la cererea sultanului Mehmet II," *Omagiu Nicolae Bălan* (Sibiu 1940) 372-410.

sively through an interpreter on everything relating to the christian faith."[15] Zygomalas further notes that Mehmed instructed the patriarch "to put into writing the entire discussion, organize it into chapters and give it to him; this was done, indeed, as evidenced by the very existence of the treatise which was translated into the Turco-Arabic language by Ahoumat, kadi of Veria, and was given to the sultan himself who read it in its entirely."[16]

Another incident reported by Zygomalas in the same work confirms further the view that Mehmed did not know Greek. Commenting on patriarch Maxim III (1476-1482), Zygomalas remarks that "his erudition and wisdom reached the ears of the sultan of the Agarenes [Turks] who sent for him and demanded that he [the patriarch] prepare an exegesis of the Creed and hand it in to him. [The patriarch] composed forthrightly an exegesis of the Creed and gave it to him; and when it was carefully translated into Arabic, he [the sultan] read it thoroughly."[17]

Significant and entirely trustworthy evidence on the subject is also offered by the notable Greek scholar Georgios Trapezountios, who was closely connected with Sultan Mehmed and had aspired to become his political counselor. Trapezountios conceived the strange utopian plan of the creation of a Turco-Christian empire by reconciling the doctrinal differences between Islam and Christianity. To achieve this aim he composed a lengthy treatise entitled *On the Truth of the Christian Faith*,[18] which he addressed to Mehmed himself shortly after the fall of Constantinople. From what Trapezountios says in the preface of this work we may infer that he did not expect a response from Mehmed before his treatise was translated into Turkish (mainly from the Greek original but also with the aid of a Latin translation on which Trapezountios was working at the time.)[19] Further on Trapezountios adds:

---

[15] Theodosios Zygomalas, Ἰστορία Πολιτικὴ Κωνσταντινουπόλεως, ed. I. Bekkeri, *Historia Politica et Patriarchica Constantinopoleos*, in the Corpus scriptorum historiae byzantinae (Bonn 1849) 29 lines 19-21: Ἠρώτησε πολλὰ δι᾿ ἑρμηνέως τὸν πατριάρχην περὶ πίστεως πάντα τὰ χριστιανῶν.

[16] *Ibid.* 30 lines 16-20 : Ἐνετείλατο αὐτῷ, ἵνα συγγράψῃ πᾶσαν τὴν διάλεξιν καὶ ἐν κεφαλαίοις καταστρώσῃ καὶ δώσῃ αὐτῷ, ὃ καὶ ἐγένετο, ὡς φαίνεται τὸ σύγγραμμα, καὶ μετεγλωττίσθη καὶ εἰς τὴν τουρκοαραβόγλωσσαν ὑπὸ Ἀχουμὰτ καδῆ Βεροίας, καὶ ἐδόθη αὐτῷ τῷ σουλτάνῳ καὶ ἀνέγω ἅπαν.

[17] *Ibid.* 47 lines 21ff. : Ἡ λογιότης αὐτοῦ καὶ ἡ σοφία ἔφθασε καὶ τὰ τοῦ σουλτάνου τῶν Ἀγαρηνῶν ὦτα · καὶ ἔπεμψε καὶ ἠξίωσεν αὐτὸν ἵνα ποιήσηται ἐξήγησιν εἰς τὸ ἅγιον σύμβολον τῆς πίστεως τῶν χριστιανῶν καὶ δώσῃ αὐτῷ ταύτην. Ποιησάμενος οὖν τὴν ἐξήγησιν τοῦ συμβόλου ἀνυποστόλως ... δέδωκεν αὐτῷ · καὶ μεταγλωττίσαντες πάντα καλῶς ἐν Ἀράβων γλώσσῃ ἀνέγνω κατὰ ἀκρίβειαν.

[18] Georgios Trapezountios, Περὶ τῆς ἀληθείας τῆς τῶν χριστιανῶν πίστεως, ed. G. T. Zoras, Γεώργιος ὁ Τραπεζούντιος καὶ αἱ πρὸς ἑλληνοτουρκικὴν συνεννόησιν προσπάθειαι αὐτοῦ. Ἡ περὶ τῆς τῶν Χριστιανῶν πίστεως ἀνέκδοτος πραγματεία (Athens 1954).

[19] *Ibid.* 94 lines 28-31 : Διὰ τοῦτο δέομαί σου ... ποίησον μεταγλωττισθῆναι τὸν λόγον τοῦτον εἰς τὴν τουρκικὴν γλῶτταν, νῦν μὲν παρὰ γραικικοῦ, ὕστερον δὲ καὶ παρὰ λατινικοῦ, ὅταν πέμψω κἀκεῖνο. See also *ibid.* lines 33-35.

"O king of kings . . . listen to me with favor and have this treatise translated, and then examine it with the aid of the wise men in your court, and see
whether it agrees with the Koran."[20] It is evident, therefore, that Mehmed
was not able to read Trapezountios's work, either in the Greek original or
in the Latin translation, a fact hardly compatible with his presumed knowledge of Greek and Latin.[21]

In conclusion I observe that, contrary to the Italian panegyrists of Mehmed
the Conqueror, the Greek authors who provide evidence that the young sultan did not know Greek and Latin were personally acquainted with him.

---

[20] *Ibid.* 99 lines 179-181 : Ἀλλ', ὦ βασιλεῦ βασιλέων . . . εὐμενῶς ἄκουσον, καὶ τὸν
λόγον τοῦτον μεταγλωττισθέντα ἐξέτασον διά τῶν αὐτόθι σοφῶν, εἰ συμφωνεῖ τό κοράν.
Some other passages of Trapezountios's treatise also indicate clearly Mehmed's ignorance
of Greek ; see e.g. *ibid.* 94 lines 21-22 : Σὺ δέ, ὦ πάγχρυσε ἀμιρᾶ, δέξαι ἀσμένως ταῦτά
μου τὰ γράμματα, ἁπλούστερόν μοι γεγραμμένα, ἵν'εὐκολώτερον μεταγλωττισθῇ παρὰ
τῶν αὐτόθι εἰς τὴν . . . τῶν Τουρκῶν διάλεκτον. Also *ibid.* 132 lines 1121-1124 : ἀλλὰ
μόνον διὰ τὸ ἀγνοεῖν ἡμᾶς τοὺς χριστιανοὺς τήν γλῶτταν τῶν μουσουλμάνων καὶ ὑμᾶς
τοὺς μουσουλμάνους μὴ εἰδέναι πῶς λέγομεν οἱ χριστιανοί, ὑποπτεύομεν ἀλλήλους καὶ
μισοῦμεν.

[21] It is true that Mehmed's personal library numbered several manuscripts or maps in
many different languages including Greek and Latin (see A. Deissmann, *Forschungen und
Funde im Serai, mit einem Verzeichnis der nichtislamischen Handschriften im Topkapu
Serai zu Istanbul* [Berlin-Leipzig 1933]; E. Jacobs, "Mehemmed II., der Eroberer, seine
Beziehungen zur Renaissance und seine Büchersammlung," *Oriens* 2 [1949] 6-29). The
mere possession by Mehmed, however, of such works in Western languages as well cannot be used as evidence that he knew any Western tongue.

Research Center for Medieval and Modern
Hellenism of the Academy of Athens
14 Anagnostopoulou St.
Athens (136), Greece

Reflections on
Medieval Anti-Judaism: 1*

ASPECTS OF PATRISTIC ANTI-JUDAISM

•

by Gerhart B. Ladner

Anti-Judaism in early Christian and medieval history raises the grave question: How was it possible that some of the greatest figures of these ages should have demonstrated in deed and word extreme lack of Christian charity toward Jews? How, for instance, can one explain that Saint Louis IX of France, a man of great justice as well as piety, should according to Joinville, who is on the whole a trustworthy source, have remarked to him that a layman should never defend the Christian law against the Jews, "unless it be with his sword, and with that he should pierce the detractor in the midriff, so far as the sword will enter"?[1]

A few texts and events concerning three of the greatest Fathers of the Church—Saint Ambrose, Saint John Chrysostom, and Saint Augustine—will perhaps lay bare some of the roots of the negative attitude of Christians toward Jews in the patristic period, an attitude that oscillated between regretful disapproval and hostile aversion.

It was Saint Ambrose who made famous an anti-Jewish incident of which we might not even have known, had he not involved himself in it.[2] In 388

* These five papers were prepared for a colloquium organized by Prof. Amos Funkenstein.

[1] Joinville, *Histoire de Saint Louis* 53, ed. N. de Wailly (Paris 1874) 30. The king admits, however, that an expert cleric might hold disputations with Jews. Also, M. de Wailly rightly reminds the reader that Louis IX's practical conduct toward Jews differed from his theoretical attitude, as reported by Joinville.

[2] The principal sources are Ambrose's Letters 40 (to Theodosius the Great) and 41 (to his own sister), PL 16.1148ff. and 1160ff. See also Paulinus, *Vita S. Ambrosii* 22f., PL 14.36Dff. Cf., for instance, H. Dudden, *The Life and Times of Saint Ambrose* 2 (Oxford 1935) 371ff.; J. R. Palanque, *Saint Ambroise et l'empire romain* (Paris 1933) 205ff.; W. Ensslin, "Die Religionspolitik des Kaisers Theodosius d. Gr.," *Sitzungsberichte der Bayerischen Akademie der Wissenschaften*, Philos.-histor. Kl. (1953) 2.60ff.

the Synagogue of Callinicum on the Euphrates was burned down upon the instigation of the local bishop. Far from concurring with the command of the emperor Theodosius the Great that the synagogue be rebuilt at the expense of the bishop, Ambrose declared his solidarity with the latter's action, and finally forced the emperor's hand by refusing to celebrate Mass in the presence of a protector of the Jews. During the time of the persecution of the Christians by the Roman Empire their status had been defined by the cutting sentence *non licet esse vos*.[3] A post-persecution Christian bishop in this case advocates not, it is true, the destruction of the Jews, but what amounts to the termination or at least the diminution of the public worship of God by them. For he says in so many words : "I claim that *I* would have burned that synagogue . . . so that there may be no place in which Christ be denied."[4]

This then is the principal reason for Ambrose's stand: those who deny Christ have no right to demand a place for the worship of God, and even less are they entitled to force Christians to reconstruct what Christian righteous zeal has destroyed.

The only other serious argument that Ambrose sets forth concerns the alleged demolition of churches by Jews in several cities of Syria and in Alexandria during the reign of the emperor Julian, who as is well known, was not only hostile to the Christians but also relatively friendly toward the Jews. According to Ambrose—and he is our only source—no indemnification was ever paid by the Jews for these destructions.[5]

One might pass over in silence the veiled threats of divine punishment uttered by Ambrose against Theodosius,[6] were it not that one must see his action not merely from the point of view of anti-Judaism, but also as part and parcel of his more general role in the relationship between Church and empire. For Ambrose challenged Theodosius and his imperial colleagues not only on the occasion of the affair of Callinicum and not only when he protested against equal rights of Jews and Christians before the law. He likewise vigorously denounced the rights of heretics—for instance of the Valentinian Gnostics in Callinicum itself[7] and of the Arians in Milan, who were protected by the empress Justina;[8] likewise the rights of pagans—for instance in the famous affair of the statue of the Goddess of Victory in the

---

[3] Cf. Tertullian, *Apologeticum* 4.4, Corpus Christianorum, ser. lat. 1.93. For the question whether, and if so, how early, this sentence was actually contained in imperial legislation (the question of the "Institutum Neronianum"), cf. H. Leclercq, "Droit persécuteur," *Dictionnaire d'archéologie chrétienne et de liturgie* 4.2 (1921) 1618ff.

[4] *Epist.* 40.8, PL 16.1151B: "Proclamo quod ego synagogam incenderim, certe quod ego illis mandaverim; ne esset locus in quo Christus negaretur."

[5] *Epist.* 40.15, PL 16.1154Af.

[6] Cf. *Epist.* 40.22, PL 16.1156Aff., *Epist.* 41.26, *ibid.* 1168Aff.

[7] Cf. *Epist.* 40.16, PL 16.1154B.

[8] Cf. Dudden (n. 2 above) 1.271ff.

Roman Senate building, the removal of which he obtained from the emperors.[9] Most important, he confronted Theodosius with the same intransigence that he had shown in Callinicum, after the wholesale massacre of Salonika, where religion was not directly involved, but where the emperor had thrown all counsels of Christian forgiveness to the winds.[10] In this instance, and not only in this instance, Ambrose acted as a representative of spiritual freedom against the omnipotence of a theocratic state, and chiefly for this reason was he remembered in future ages.

Saint Ambrose's unconcern about Jewish rights to their synagogues, though far from unique,[11] did not become the general rule of ecclesiastical practice, whether during the time when Roman law was in force or later.[12] Gregory the Great, for instance, emphatically followed the tracks of Theodosius and not of Ambrose in such matters.[13] Ambrose's attitude appears less extraordinary, though not more palatable, if one reads Saint John Chrysostom's sermons against the Jews.[14] For it is the main gist of these sermons, which were given at Antioch about 386-387,[15] that the synagogues are not truly places of religious worship at all. According to him, since the destruction of the Temple of Jerusalem, the Jews can never again have a temple, a priesthood, sacrifices, and meaningful religious rites. Chrysostom tries to prove

[9] On this affair cf. Dudden 1.256ff.; Palanque (n. 2 above) 118ff., 277ff.; L. Malunovicz, *De ara victoriae in curia Romana quomodo certatum sit* (Milano 1937); H. Bloch, "A New Document of the Last Pagan Revival in the West," *Harvard Theological Review* 38 (1945) 214ff.; F. Paschoud, "Réflexions sur l'idéal religieux de Symmaque," *Historia* 14 (1965) 215ff., *idem*, *Roma Aeterna* (Rome 1967) 71ff.

[10] Cf. Dudden 2.381ff.; Palanque 277ff.; also H. v. Campenhausen, *Ambrosius von Mailand als Kirchenpolitiker*, Arbeiten zur Kirchengeschichte 12 (Berlin 1929) 236ff.; Ensslin (n. 2 above) 67ff.

[11] Cf. M. Simon, *Verus Israel: Étude sur les relatiosns entre Chrétiens et Juifs dans l'empire romain (135-425)* (Paris 1964) 264ff.

[12] Cf. A. H. M. Jones, *The Later Roman Empire 284-602* 2 (Oklahoma University Press 1964) 949 and 1392f.; B. Blumenkranz, *Juifs et chrétiens dans le monde occidental 430-1096* (Paris 1960) 309ff.

[13] Cf. *Gregorii I Registrum, Epistolae* 1.34, 2.6, 9.38, 9.195, MGH Epist. 1.47f., 104f., 2.67, 182f. In these letters the pope prevents certain bishops, and (in *Epist.* 9.195) a Jewish convert to Christianity, from attempting to deprive Jewish communities of their synagogues or to convert them into churches. Cf. also the statement on Christian toleration of the Jewish cult, addressed to Bishop Pascasius of Naples, *Epist.* 13.15 (2.383): it would be unreasonable to prohibit their age old ceremonies; this would most certainly not lead to their conversion, which might be achieved only by reasoning and mild persuasion.

[14] *Orationes VIII adversus Judaeos*, PG 48.843ff.

[15] Cf. E. Schwartz, "Christliche und jüdische Ostertafeln," *Abhandlunger der Königl. Gesellschaft der Wissenschaft zu Göttingen*, Phil.-histor. Kl., N. S. 8.6 (1905) 169ff.; M. Simon, *Verus Israel* (Paris 1964) 256ff.; also *idem*, "La polémique anti-juive de S. Jean Chrysostome et le mouvement judaïsant d'Antioche," *Annuaire de l'Institute de philologie et d'histoire orientales et slaves, Université Libre de Bruxelles* 4, *Mélanges Franz Cumont* (1936) 403ff.

this by extensive exegesis of those Old Testament passages that restrict the
public worship of God to the Temple at Jerusalem. This line of thought
is the main rationale of his sermons against the Jews.[16] But the immediate
cause for his attack against them and for the highly emotional and aggressive
tone which he uses is a different one. It is none other but the very real attraction that the synagogues of the Jews of Antioch, with their feasts and
fasts and other rites, had for the Christians of that city. John Chrysostom
makes it appear as if Christians were attracted to the feasts of the Jews,
such as their New Year, their Feast of Tabernacles, their Passover, merely
by comparatively external paraphernalia and customs, especially by the
sound of their tubas, by their fasting, followed by festive dancing and singing,[17] and last but not least by certain magic aspects connected with the
synagogues. Oaths sworn there were believed to have a special binding
power, and cures of diseases were attempted with the help of amulets and
other devices, and at times, it would seem, with apparent success.[18]

From the point of view of John Chrysostom Christian participation in
these things amounted almost to apostasy, but Marcel Simon and others
have shown that we are actually confronted with a late survival in Antioch
of the strong trend of Judaizing tendencies in early Christendom.[19] That
Chrysostom should have considered the very real evidence of Judaizing and
the more remote threat of conversion to Judaism a danger to his church,
one can well understand. One can also not forget that he himself, less successful than Ambrose in his opposition to imperial theocracy, died as a martyr
for Christian ethical principles, in resistance to an unholy alliance of corrupt
Church dignitaries with the irresponsible heirs of Theodosius the Great.

Yet there is something very repellent in his anti-Jewish polemical method
when he applies the vituperations of Israel by its prophets to the Jews of
his own time. So, to mention just one example, Chrysostom wants to prove
that the synagogues because of their festivities are really not places of wor-

---

[16] Cf., for instance, *Oratio* 4.6, PG 48.880f.: "Ἰερουσαλὴμ ἄβατος γέγονεν, ἔνθα μόνον
θύειν ἐξῆν . . . ὁ Θεός, καθάπερ τινά σύνδεσμον λατρείας τὴν πόλιν ποιήσας, εἶτα ταύτην ἀνατρέψας, καὶ τὴν λοιπὴν τῆς πολιτείας ἐκείνης οἰκοδομὴν κατέλυσεν ἄπασαν."
For Chrysostom's scriptural demonstration of the definitive loss by the Jews of their temple
and religious "Politeia," cf. especially *Oratio* 5.4-12, PG 48.889ff. For the abrogation of
the Jewish rites and priesthood, cf. *Oratio* 6.1f., *ibid.* 916f.: "Οὔτε ἀναστήσεται λοι-
πὸν ἡ πόλις, οὔτε ἀπολήψονται τὴν ἑαυτῶν πολιτείαν. Τούτου δὲ ἀποδειχθέντος, καὶ τὰ
λοιπὰ ἅπαντα συνωμολόγητο, οἷον ὡς οὔτε θυσίας εἶδος, οὔτε ὁλοκαυσώσεως, οὐχ ἡ τοῦ
νόμου δύναμις, οὐκ ἄλλο τι τῆς πολιτείας ἐκείνης στῆναι δυνήσεται . . . (2) . . . οὔτε τὸν
ἱερέα δύνατον εἶναι, τῆς πόλεως οὐκ οὔσης."

[17] Cf. *Oratio* 1.1 and 2, PG 48.844 and 846f.; *Oratio* 4.7, *ibid.* 881; *Oratio* 7.1, *ibid.* 915.

[18] For the superstitious use of oaths sworn in synagogues, cf. *Oratio* 1.3, PG 48.847f.;
for magical cures in synagogues, cf. *Oratio* 8.5-8, *ibid.* 935-941.

[19] Cf. Simon, *Verus Israel* 379f., also see Simon, n. 15 above; furthermore, S. Krauss,
"Antioche," *Revue des études juives* 45 (1902) 43f.

ship but theaters—and we know how the Fathers of the Church hated theaters as dens of iniquity and placed them on the same moral level as houses of ill repute.

Chrysostom argues as follows: he quotes one of the castigations of Israel by Jeremiah: "Thy appearance has become that of a harlot." He does not add the next verse: "Wilt thou not from now on call me as father and guide of your virginity?" (Jer. 3.3-4). Instead he continues: "But where a harlot dwells, there is a whorehouse."[20] So the synagogue is a theater and a bordello, but that is not all. Jeremiah had also spoken of the Jewish Temple as a "den of robbers" and as a "den of the hyena" (Jer. 7.11 and 12.9, Septuagint); the synagogue for John Chrysostom therefore has become a resting place of wild and impure animals.[21] Finally Jeremiah had made God say to Israel "I have forsaken my house, I have left my heritage" (12.7). Chrysostom concludes: A place abandoned by God is the habitation of demons.[22] The outcome of the whole diatribe—reinforced by accusations of gluttony, drunkenness, and lasciviousness—is simply that all Jews are impure animals and demons.[23]

One might well ask: How could Christianity, a religion of love, produce in one of its most eminent figures such vehemence of anti-Judaism? We all know that there are historical antecedents[24] as well as socioeconomic, anthropological, and psychological preconditions, but I do not know of any one reason that will serve as a general explanation. The suggestion that anti-Semitism—also Christian anti-Semitism—is at least in part the externalization of the need for a scapegoat[25] would be too simple an explanation as far as the Fathers of the Church are concerned, for it is old and inescapable Christian doctrine that every Christian sinner crucifies Christ anew. Norman Cohn, in a lecture given at Los Angeles a few years ago, proposed a theory in which he suggested that anti-Semitism is the expression of an oedipal

---

[20] *Oratio* 1.3, PG 48.847 : *"Τί οὖν ὁ προφήτης φησίν ; ʽ Ὄψις πόρνης ἐγένετό σοι. . . .ʼ Ἔνθα δε πόρνη ἔστηκεν, πορνεῖόν ἐστιν ὁ τόπος."*

[21] *Ibid.* : *"Μᾶλλον δὲ οὐχὶ πορνεῖον καὶ θέατρον μόνον ἐστὶν ἡ συναγωγή, ἀλλὰ καὶ σπήλαιον λῃστῶν καὶ καταγώγιον θηρίων. ʽΣπήλαιονʼ γαρ, φησίν, ʽὑαίνης ἐγένετό μοι ὁ οἶκος ὑμῶνʼ· οὐδε ἁπλῶς θηρίου, ἀλλὰ θηρίου ἀκαθάρτου."*

[22] *Ibid.* : *"Καὶ πάλιν : ʽΑφῆκα τὸν οἶκόν μου, ἐγκαταλέλοιπα τὴν κληρονομίαν μουʼ . . . Ὅταν ὁ Θεὸς ἀφῇ, δαιμόνων κατοικητήριον γίνεται ἐκεῖνο τὸ χωρίόν."*

[23] *Oratio* 1.4, *ibid.* 848f. : *"Ἐκεῖνοι . . . τῇ γαστρὶ ζῶντες, πρὸς τὰ παρόντα κεχηνότες, ὑῶν καὶ τράγων οὐδὲν ἄμεινον διακείμενοι, κατὰ τὸν τῆς ἀσελγείας λόγον καὶ τὴν τῆς ἀδηφαγίας ὑπερβολήν · ἓν δὲ ἐπίστανται μόνον: γαστρίζεσθαι καὶ μεθύειν. . . τὸ τῆς συναγωγῆς χωρίον . . . δαιμόνων ἐστὶ καταγώγιον, μᾶλλον δὲ οὐχ αἱ συναγωγαὶ μόνον, ἀλλὰ καὶ αὐταὶ αἱ ψυχαὶ τῶν Ἰουδαίων."*

[24] For pre-Christian (as well as Christian) anti-Judaism in the Roman Empire, cf. J. Juster, *Les Juifs dans l'empire romain* (Paris 1914).

[25] Cf., for instance, R. M. Loewenstein, *Christians and Jews*, Delta Book edition, (New York 1963) 190f.

wish to kill one's own father in the guise of the Jewish Father God and of every Jew. If that be so, it is even harder to understand how the anti-Semite could identify himself with a Son who had said "I and the Father are one"[26] and who was born from a Jewish mother. Assertion of identity has perhaps some bearing here, however; for all through history groups of men seem to have found it very difficult to gain and maintain their own identity merely by loving those within the group without hating those on the outside. The warmth of the nest is a great generator of cold hatred.

To return to John Chrysostom, he did not always condemn the Jews in the violent manner described. Also he was too intelligent to ignore the objections that they could raise against the wholesale applicability of prophetic condemnations to all of Israel for all times. His most forceful argument therefore is that the eclipse of the validity of the Jewish law was *not* because of the sins of the Jews but because of its own inherent imperfection which required the new dispensation of Christ.[27] If the Jews—lacking a temple and a priesthood—can no longer offer a true sacrifice to God, this is owing ultimately to the fact that a new order of sacrifice exists, it, too, rooted in the Old Testament, but transformed in the New Testament: this is the order of Melchizedek mentioned in a Psalm verse, which is the order of Christ according to the Epistle to the Hebrews.[28]

The real Jewish-Christian problem then for Chrysostom as for all the Fathers of the Church was the relation between the Old and the New Testament. We can see this perhaps most clearly in Saint Augustine's treatise against the Jews, really a sermon, written probably between 425 and 430, which has been interpreted very competently by Bernhard Blumenkranz.[29]

The Jews, Augustine must see to his distress, still refuse to believe that the prophecies of the Old Testament, which Christianity refers to Christ, really refer to Him. Why do they refuse? "Quoniam quod legunt non intelligunt."[30] Augustine is convinced that if they did understand what they read, "they would not be so blind, so sick, that they would not recognize in the Lord Christ the light and the salvation" of which for instance Isaiah 49.6 had spoken.[31] The cause for Jewish obstinacy according to Augustine is their failure to understand the Old Testament spiritually rather than me-

---

[26] John 10.30.

[27] *Oratio* 7.4f., PG 48.921ff.

[28] Psalm 109 (110). 4; Hebrews 5.6.

[29] Bernhard Blumenkranz, *Die Judenpredigt Augustins*, Basler Beiträge zur Geschichtswissenschaft 25 (Basel 1946).

[30] *Tractatus adversus Judaeos* 1.2, PL 42.51. Cf. Blumenkranz 162ff.

[31] *Ibid.* 51f.: "Nam utique si intelligerent, de quo praedixerit propheta, quem legunt, 'Dedi te in lucem gentium, ita ut sit salus mea usque in fines terrae,' non sic caeci essent, non sic aegroti, ut in Domino Christo nec lucem agnoscerent nec salutem."

rely literally.[32] In his treatise against the Jews Augustine exemplified the Christian interpretation of the Old Testament by an elaborate exegesis of those Psalms that in the Septuagint, and in the Latin translations derived from it, according to their very titles expressly speak of those things or men that will be transformed.[33] But how did Augustine imagine that the Jews would accept the transformation of the Old Testament in the New? His answer is included in his comment on a Psalm verse (in a translation derived from the Septuagint) at the end of the treatise: "Accedite ad eum et illuminamini"—"Come ye to Him and be enlightened." What does "Come ye" mean, he asks: nothing other but to believe.[34] It would seem to me that Augustine here applies his famous principle *crede ut intellligas*[35] to the problem of the conversion of the Jews, as he saw it. The Jews read the prophecies concerning Christ but do not understand them; to do so, they must first believe. Let us therefore, Augustine says, preach to them in love, whether they hear us willingly or not, let us preach to them "non cum praesumptione insultando, sed cum tremore exultando," for, he says, we Christians, too, owe what we are only to the grace and mercy of God.[36]

This is a tone very different from that of Ambrose and Chrysostom. In another sermon, Augustine compares the sincere and just Jew, who keeps the Law, to the older son in the Gospel parable of the lost younger son, whom in turn he compares to the gentile converted to Christianity. If the older, the Jewish, son will only accept Christ, the Father will say to him as he did in the parable: "Omnia mea tua sunt."[37] It is interesting to note that in the twelfth century Hildegard of Bingen and Joachim of Flora interpreted

---

[32] *Ibid.* 7.9 (57ff).

[33] *Ibid.* 3-6 (53ff.). Augustine treats here of Psalms 44 (45), 68 (69), 79 (80). These titles are the result of a misunderstanding of the Hebrew text; cf. C. A. and E. G. Briggs, *A Critical and Exegetical Commentary on the Book of Psalms* 1 (Edinburgh 1952) lxxv n. 1c. The beginning of the title of Psalm 44 (45), for instance, reads in the Vulgate as follows: "In finem, pro iis qui commutabuntur," which is a translation from the Septuagint: Εἰς τὸ τέλος, ὑπὲρ τῶν ἀλλοιωθησομένων." My colleague, Professor Amos Funkenstein, kindly explains that the Hebrew text reads here: "To the conductor of the 'Lilies,'" that the title therefore contained instructions to the musical director of the choirs—probably called after flowers—who sang the Psalms, and that the Hebrew words for "conductor" and "lilies" are not unlike those signifying "end" and "change".

[34] *Tractatus adversus Iudaeos* 9.14, PL 42.62: "Quid est 'Accedite' nisi: 'Credite.'" He is citing Psalm 33.6 (34.5).

[35] Cf., for instance, his *Sermo* 43.3, 4, PL 38.255: "Dicit mihi homo: 'Intelligam ut credam.' Respondeo: 'Crede, ut intelligas.'"

[36] *Tractatus adversus Judaeos* 10.15, PL 42.63f.

[37] Cf. *Sermo Caillau* 2.11, 8-14, *Miscellanea agostiniana* 1: *Sancti Augustini sermones post Maurinos reperti*, ed. G. Morin, O.S.B. (Rome 1930) 260-264. See also F. van der Meer, *Augustine the Bishop* (New York 1961) 77f.

this Gospel parable in the same rather irenic manner by identifying the older son with the Jews.[38]

Of course all this does not make Augustine a friend of the Jews as a people.[39] He is convinced that the reason why they could not believe in Christ was that they freely willed not to believe.[40] That this unwillingness of theirs was a necessity for the redemption of mankind[41] is part of the inscrutable mystery of divine grace and predestination which forms such an important part of Augustine's theology and anthropology. The Jews for him can never lose the stigma of having disbelieved and killed Christ;[42] in their dispersion and misery they remain as testimony of a negative attitude toward the grace of redemption, and of its consequences.[43]

Both the relatively mild tone of Saint Augustine and the harsh tones of Saint Ambrose and Saint John Chrysostom were left to the Middle Ages as a legacy from the patristic age. As we have seen, even Saint Augustine did not for a moment consider that the Jews might be justified by their subjective conscience in denying what to him was objective truth. Nor did he doubt that the Jews were collectively guilty for the death of Christ. This question of conscience began to be perceived in its whole magnitude only much later, perhaps from the age Abelard onward,[44] and this question

[38] Cf. Hildegard of Bingen's Letter to Guibert of Gembloux, ed. J. B. Pitra, *Analecta sacra spicilegio solesmensi parata* 8 (Monte Cassino 1882) 419f.; Joachim of Flora, *Adversus Judaeos*, ed. A. Frugoni, Fonti per la storia d'Italia 95 (Rome 1957) 101 and n. 1, where Professor Frugoni noted the similarity of Joachim's interpretation with that of Hildegard.

[39] Blumenkranz (n. 29 above) 186ff., quotes a considerable number of Augustinian texts, in which the Jews are treated harshly (though by no means as spitefully as by Chrysostom).

[40] *De dono perseverantiae* 9.23, PL 45.1005f.: "Facile est quippe, ut infidelitatem accusemus Judaeorum de libera voluntate venientem, qui factis apud se tam magnis virtutibus credere noluerunt." Cf. Blumenkranz (n. 29 above) 190.

[41] Cf. Blumenkranz 190. For the concept of *felix culpa* in patristic thought and in the liturgy, cf. for instance my book *The Idea of Reform* (Cambridge, Mass. 1959) 146 (with bibliography).

[42] Cf. especially *Tractatus adversus Judaeos* 8.11, PL 42.60: "Occidistis Christum in parentibus vestris."

[43] Cf. Blumenkranz 175ff.

[44] Cf. for instance, Abelard, *Dialogus inter philosophum, Judaeum et Christianum*, PL 178, 1617C, where the Jew says to the pagan philosopher: "Sit denique dubium mihi sicut et tibi, quod hanc Deus legem [the law of the Old Testament] instituerit . . ., cogeris tamen secundum suppositae similitudinis inductionem id mihi consulere, ut ipsi obediam, maxime cum ad hoc propria me invitet conscientia." See also Étienne Gilson's characterization of the dialogue, which was interrupted by Abelard's death and therefore does not tell us as much, as one would like to know, about the point of view of the *Christianus*. According to Gilson, *Christian Philosophy in the Middle Ages* (New York 1955) 163, "we see the Christian exerting himself to convince the Jew and the pagan, not by denying the truths they themselves lay claim to, but by bringing all of them into the richer and more comprehensive truth of Christian faith." For the rest, I can on this occasion only refer to the more general process of the development of an incipient "ethics of intention" rather than "deed,"

of collective guilt is being effectively refuted, one may hope, in our own day.

———

an ethics according to which the moral value of an act lies in the intention and not necessarily in the resulting deed, which may be objectively bad and even lead to damnation; cf. Gilson 160ff., and R. Pouchet, O.S.B., *La rectitudo chez saint Anselme*, Études Augustiniennes (Paris 1964), especially 85ff., on Saint Anselm of Canterbury's concept of the *rectitudo propter se servata*, which nevertheless is in no way separated from the divine, salvific, will and order—in other words, the mystery remains also in that later phase of Christian thought.

Department of History
University of California
Los Angeles
California 90024, U.S.A.

Reflections on
Medieval Anti-Judaism: 2

EASTERN JEWRY UNDER ISLAM

•

by G. E. von Grunebaum

Generalizing somewhat sweepingly, one may perhaps characterize the position of Jewry in classical Islam on the basis of seven factors, four of them belonging to the Near Eastern tradition preceding Islam and three of them introduced by Islam. The distinction is of necessity a bit tenuous but may be of help for this particular presentation.

1. The Near East has been accustomed since time immemorial to religious and ethnic pluralism within larger political units. Rarely has there been an attempt to strive for the kind of unity that Justinian saw it his mission to accomplish in his empire. The Persians, not to mention earlier reigns, and after them the Romans made no attempt at religious equalization. It was in fact taken for granted that as you are born to a language so are you born to a religion and to an ethnic affiliation; thus the habituation to pluralism has been indigenous to the area from time out of mind. It bears mention, however, that the immediate predecessor of Islam in the Iranian highlands and in Iraq, the Sassanian Empire, did endeavor to establish if not religious homogeneity at least strict superiority of the Zoroastrian religion of the dynasty and consequently limited participation of non-Zoroastrians in the body politic.

2. There was a certain fluctuation between religious and national, religious and ethnic identification. Ethnic unity seems frequently to have been welded or consecrated by adhesion to the same ritual, the same theological assumptions; in contrast, groups that for some reason, usually political, came to deviate from the standard religion of their masters tended to isolate themselves, become castes, to speak loosely, and finally set themselves up separately as what in French is called an *ethnie*. Instances are fairly numerous. The last one, or at any rate the one that has especially caught the imagination of Orientalists, is the formation of the Druzes. In their case there gra-

dually arose out of certain sectarian deviations that can be linked to political opposition in the ninth and tenth centuries something like an ethnic unit which in this particular case happened to keep the language of its environment, namely Arabic, but nevertheless isolated itself and refrained from intermarriage; it has come to be considered a sect or a heresy by itself and an isolated ethnic unit by those who share with it the loyalty to the same state.

3. The conception of personal rather than territorial law has tended to prevail in the Middle East for a very long time and has certainly been carried over by or carried into Islam without any hesitation. The unification of "imperial" law and of the legal status of the subjects occasionally proposed to the Caliphs has always been rejected as a thoroughgoing, all-inclusive policy and, if one can speak of a unified imperial law in the larger Muslim-dominated units, it is an imperial law that takes the personal status, the personal law of the religious community into which the individual was born, into consideration and gives it as wide a range as compatible with the "religious sociology" of Islam.

4. Finally, it should be recalled that the religious units in the Roman and the Persian, as before in the Hellenistic empires, to single out three points of reference, were always accorded a certain autonomy, in fact a rather generous measure of self rule. The policy of the imperial power was to reach the religious and ethnic units through their own authorities and with as little upset of their traditional laws and customs as was politically possible. We are aware of the deviations from this political style, such as the attempt of Antiochus IV to interfere with the Jewish community, but we are aware of them precisely because they broke the rules. It should be borne in mind however, that both the Byzantine and the Sassanian predecessors of the Muslims had insisted on political dominance retaining a particular religion identified with the imperial house; so members of other religions or of sectarian movements within the state religion would be barred in varying degrees from full participation in the body politic.

Islam, although only in part formally ratifying the tradition, did in fact accept untouched and without significant modification the pluralistic conception of society and empire. It did, however, develop its own rationale and its own legal systemization. This rationale must be counted the principal of the three factors Islam added to the situation as inherited.

First, from the very beginning Islam, or better, the Prophet Muhammad, has seen the validation of his mission in the conviction that that mission was in all essentials identical with the missions entrusted in earlier days to other prophets and more specifically to those on whose initiative the communities of the Jews and the Christians had come into existence. It is only natural that the truth of God must be one and the same to whomsoever it be vouchsafed and that such adjustments of the Word as were dictated by

the necessities of time and place do not on the whole play an important part
when measured against the basic oneness of revelation. Consequently the
identity of essential dogma becomes a principal truth of the later Envoy's
mission. The identity of essential dogma among Islam, Judaism, and Christianity is offered as one of the strongest arguments for the veracity of the Prophet. In a very different sense from the concept developed by the Fathers
of the Christian Church to whom the dissenters were first of all a *skandalon*,
a stumbling block, the existence of the Jewish and Christian communities is to
Islam a necessary foil, half needed contrast, half needed confirmation, of the le-
gitimacy and of the necessity of the final revelation that is Islam and was sent
down from heaven through Muhammad. Islam, therefore, makes specific al-
lowances for and accords specific privileges to those religions it feels are in the
deeper sense of the term within Islam, proclaiming that they constitute a necessary stage that has preceded Islam and been overtaken and overcome by it. At
the same time that this concept assures toleration and indeed a measure
of privilege for such communities, it identifies them as inferior because obsolete, made obsolete specifically by the final, better, more perfect, more
complete revelation brought by Muhammad.

Second, Islam, precisely like those religions it felt most definitely to have absorbed within itself and superseded, views itself as a universal message, as a
message that is not only applicable to all, but sooner or later actually will convince and conquer the whole world. There is, however, a big difference between the concept of Islam's obtaining the commanding position on the globe
and, for example, the idea Christianity has developed of its universal mission. In principle, Islam is not interested in converting every individual
soul. Islam is interested in making the world safe for Islam, in getting Islam
into the controlling position and making it possible for Islam to be practiced
perfectly, completely, and without any danger of controversion or subversion
wherever Islam wishes to be practiced. Whether individuals or communities elect to stay outside and to continue their own error is no concern for
Islam. If they wish to carry their obstinacy so far as to forego the privilege
of salvation, the false judgment is theirs. Consequently the spread of Islam
does not necessarily bring about a corresponding pressure for the conversion
of the non-Muslim community, let alone all non-Muslim individuals, provided, of course, they accept the position that stems in direct logical sequence
from the basic assumptions just outlined.

Third, this outlook, combined with the general pluralistic expectations and
organization patterns of the Near East and with the preference accorded
to personal over territorial legal status, creates a concept of integration or,
to use another anachronistic expression, citizenship that makes for an attitude that with some stretching of the term may be designated as tolerance.
Its application is almost a matter of quantification. This is the rationale
of the spiritual and legal gradation: If your community possesses the last,

the best, and the most perfect truth, it is clearly a reflection of the divine will that this particular community be distinguished by unmatchable excellence. Simple logic permits concluding that having the better truth implies a richer and fuller participation in being and hence that the chosen community by essence and value must be superior to essence and value of all other communities. There really is no escaping the realization that the best community, morally best in terms of its possession of truth and ontologically best in terms of its essential structure, should rule. Since adherence to Islam is open to everyone and, in fact, rather easy to obtain by means of a unilateral declaration on the part of the non-Muslim expressing his wish to join by declaring openly his acceptance of the fundamental verities of Islam, there is no excuse whatever for the non-Muslims not to convert, and whatever excuse there once might have been has long since disappeared considering that with time the non-Muslims have been exposed for an ever longer period to the perfections of Islam in actual operation. Consequently, it is no more than just that the non-Muslim communities be integrated in the *dār al-Islām*, the domain of Islam, that is to say in that part of the world already controlled by Islam, as citizens of circumscribed right. The term may be somewhat misleading. What is meant is that they will be tolerated, they may follow those pursuits that seem to be more important to them than ultimate salvation—in other words their own religious beliefs, their own religious law, to some extent their traditional internal organization; in return, however, they must accept exclusion from what would today be called the policy-making bodies. They must be barred from the truly important executive positions. They cannot be allowed in the army, of course, and they have to pay in the most literal sense for their toleration and for their exemption from armed duty by offering the state a tax over and above what the Muslim subjects of the state will have to pay. Historically speaking, the ensuing socio-political order is but a continuation of Near Eastern custom, as should be clear by what has been said before; but the structure is also the inevitable transfer onto the plane of social organization of the basic premises behind the Muslim's outlook on himself and his community and on the remaining enclaves of the nonconverted.

From a practical point of view Islam has had every interest in stabilizing the non-Muslim communities. Islam did, in fact, become the majority religion after three or four centuries in most of the areas of the Middle East, but it has continued into the modern age a policy of making the non-Muslim or the sectarian Muslim communities politically innocuous by stabilizing them not only against Islam, return from which to an earlier community was legally impossible, but also by banning or at least discouraging transfers from one unbelieving community to another because of the (remote) possibility that by a union of all Christian communities, let alone by the highly improbable occurrence of a union of all the Jewish and all the Christian communities, the minorities would become politically too powerful for the principles of an Islamic policy to be implemented.

There is no need here to dwell on specific distinctions between the actual position of Christians and Jews. There are periods in which Christians were more favored by the central government and others where Jews were preferred. Polemical writings, of which we have a great many, and occasional references in other kinds of literature allow the retracing in large measure of the oscillations in time and place of the vicissitudes befalling these communities. It would not be difficult to put together the names of a very sizable number of Jewish subjects or citizens of the Islamic area who have attained to high rank, to power, to great financial influence, to significant and recognized intellectual attainment; and the same could be done for Christians. But it would again not be difficult to compile a lengthy list of persecutions, arbitrary confiscations, attempted forced conversions, or pogroms. What must be retained from such tribulations is the coexistence of a strong and solid community life and a precarious dependence on circumstances never under community control. Nerve-wracking as this ambivalent situation may have been, on the whole and exception made for times of special stress, the religious communities were able to pursue their life as they felt it should be lived, though within statutory and customary limits, under their own laws and under their own leaders so long as there was no direct interference or connection with Muslim affairs in which case the power of decision passed to the Muslim authorities. Yet their lack of political weight did relegate them to a corner and in terms of large-scale decisions to political irrelevance.

Political irrelevance does not entail intellectual irrelevance, of course, although being kept on the sidelines tends to estrange from central issues. It is known that for more than three centuries between 900 and 1250 the Jews experienced a great intellectual upsurge. The Jewish contribution was recognized by Muslim statesmen as well as by Muslim intellectuals; the influence of Jewish professionals and of Jewish thinkers was a fact of life with which the Muslim intellectual and politician would reckon. But acceptance remained limited, not so much because of legal restrictions but because this acceptance was always confined to sectors of Muslim society; the religious classes and the masses behind them never ceased to see in the preferment of the nonbelievers an abnormality that had to be rectified at the first opportunity.

Let me illustrate the peculiar ambivalence of Jewish success and its pride, and its coexistence with a sense of endangerment and brutal discrimination, by quoting from three letters written by Maimonides. To use Maimonides as an example is of course to distort the situation. Maimonides is one of the great figures of the Middle Ages and his Muslim contemporaries were fully aware of his intellectual and professional importance. The average man, however, has not left us this kind of documentation nor is he in the eyes of his community as representative. The texts are too long to be offered in full but this is their gist. Maimonides was among other things a highly successful physician, the sultan of Egypt was aware of his attainments, and in fact he made him his court physician. We have a letter addressed to R. Samuel ibn Tibbon of Lunel, Provence (1160-1230) in which Maimonides describes the intensity with which the sultan and his family availed themselves of his services, and it is difficult not to see that Maimonides was rather flattered and proud; there is even a little of that peculiar fussiness and boisterousness and a tendency to show off his position in the larger dominant society which people in his situation tend to display. In the same letter and at even greater length he gives advice to his correspondent about the books R. Samuel should or should not consult. The books are works belonging exclusively to the Greek tradition.[1] This part of the letter could have been written by a Muslim intellectual of the period or, better, it could have been written by any Muslim intellectual about fifty or sixty years before Maimonides because within Islam the decline of this sharply Hellenizing tendency seems to have set in somewhat earlier. My emphasis here is not on coincidence in time. My emphasis is on the shared intellectual material. It could be shared insofar as it was Greek. It could be shared insofar as it represented method, intellectual procedure: the questions asked, the solutions acquiesced in. There could of course be no identity with respect to the sacred texts to which the Greek works and their import had to be reconciled; but the primary problems, of faith and reason, the problem of finding an adequation between the Greek tradition and the inherited sacred tradition were the same, and the methods to arrive at such conciliation were the same too.

But next to these statements of personal satisfaction at being accepted, however tenuously, and at being influential in the society of the ruling unbelievers there comes to the fore the hatred of this very unbelieving ruling society which stands quite unreconciled and abrupt beside it. Thus we read in another letter the following: "And after him [meaning Christ] a madman arose [meaning Muhammad] and acted after his pattern, that is, to change our religion . . . and added to all this another intention: he looked for reign [political power] and wanted all to be his subjects."[2] Or in a third letter: "And you, brethren [this is written to the Jewish community in the Yemen], it is kown to you that because of the profusion of our sins the Holy One—blessed be He—dropped us in the midst of this nation [meaning the Muslims], the nation of Ishmael whose tyranny has hardened upon us and they are taking counsel to injure and degrade us, according to the decree against us.

[1] The letter was translated by H. Adler, *Miscellany of Hebrew Literature* 1 (London 1872) 219ff.

[2] *Igrot*, ed. M. D. Rabinovitz (Jerusalem 1954) 121 (trans. A. Funkenstein).

. . . And its is known to you that no nation stood against Israel more hostile than they [meaning the Muslims], that no nation did evil to perfection in order to weaken us and belittle us and degrade us like them."[3] The letter goes on for some length but I need not continue. The precariousness of the position is evident: high repute, high financial rewards, considerable standing and influence at court and at that period at least a community autonomy never infringed upon— are accompanied by the realization that all these attainments are on sufferance. The happiness of being integrated into what was at that time the greatest culture in the world known to him is marred by the feeling that this integration and the toleration it presupposes can change any day, not perhaps culturally but politically, socially and economically.

Let me conclude by pointing out that this ambivalence felt by spokesmen for minorities, and the reference is to minority not in the numerical sense, but rather to a group of people that are politically in the position of a minority, a position in which they are discriminated against or at least could be discriminated against at the ruler's pleasure and without notice, is fairly frequent. One document of such ambiguous response which has not been sufficiently noted are the novels of a South African Zulu woman, Noni Jabavu, which are not only extremely well written but extremely interesting from our point of view. In two books, *Drawn in Colour* (London 1960) and *The Ochre People: Scenes from a South African Life* (London 1963), she speaks on the whole about her own life and the life of her family. Her father appears to have been a chieftain in a Zulu tribe. She leaves South Africa not as a refugee but to travel to visit her married sister in independent Uganda; when she reaches Uganda she feels relieved of the pressures that South African legislation exposes her to, and she feels very happy. But then she develops a truly nineteenth-century sense of superiority with regard to the Negroes in Uganda and their distressing cultural backwardness measured against the cultural advancement which the South African blacks are willy-nilly sharing with the South African whites. I am perfectly aware of the great differences in the situation of Jews and Christians within medieval Islam and of the situation of the blacks in the Republic of South Africa. There is, however, this similarity, that cultural identification and, in fact, pride to be caught up in what is obviously the greatest culture within reach or perhaps the greatest culture altogether accessible at the time, is accompanied disharmoniously by the sharp pain of social discrimination suffered or feared or, as in the case of a Maimonides, only by the threat of potential social discrimination.

This ambivalence of being as of right within, but only on sufferance of, the cultural structure of Islam is the dominant fact in the life of the educated

---

[3] *Ibid.* pp. 183-185, with omissions (trans. J. Eliash).

Christian or Jew of the period—along with the peculiar gradation and double-facedness of his existence: full status but restricted effectiveness in the community of his birth, restricted status but (during long stretches of time) full effectiveness in the dominant community that extended to him its tolerance.

Department of History
University of California
Los Angeles
California 90024, U.S.A.

Reflections on
Medieval Anti-Judaism: 3

BASIC TYPES OF CHRISTIAN ANTI-JEWISH POLEMICS
IN THE LATER MIDDLE AGES[1]

•

by Amos Funkenstein

The destructive effect of the public religious disputations, so often enforced on the Jews of Western Europe since the thirteenth century, are well known. Modern considerations hardly confirm the idyllic picture drawn in Heine's famous poem of a chivalrous duel between the representatives of the contesting religions under the supervision and neutral arbitration of the Spanish queen, who is much bored by the exposure of theological emotions in the proceeding of the disputation and at its end neither knows nor cares "wer hier Recht hat." Religious polemics, written and oral, public and private, became sharper and more dangerous after the twelfth century than ever before in the Middle Ages. Both in its functions and in its cardinal types it became radically different from religious polemics up to that time, reflecting, on the one hand, the growing alienation of the Jewish image and its dehumanization in the Christian consciousness on all levels, and on the other hand, a growing understanding of each other's theological position and even growing influence on it.

The varieties of anti-Jewish polemics after the twelfth century may be subsumed under four patterns: (1) the older pattern of *Dailogi cum Judaeis* or *Tractatus contra Judaeos*—a stereotype repetition of arguments usually going back to Tertullian, Cyprian and Augustine. (2) The rationalistic polemics, attempting a deduction of the Christian dogma or a demonstration of the philosophical superiority of Christianity. (3) The attack against the

[1] Parts of this article appeared in Hebrew, in an extended form, in: *Zion, Quaterly for Research in Jewish History*, 33.3-4 (1968) 126-144. The reader will find there detailed references and discussion of modern literature.

Talmud, or, more exactly, against the totality of postbiblical Jewish religious literature: the accusation that it is heretical even in the terms of Judaism proper. This, I believe, was the most dangerous part of the Talmud-trials since the thirteenth century, by far more detrimental than the accusation of blasphemous *topoi* in the Talmud. (4) The attempt to demonstrate, with the help of the Talmud, that even postbiblical Jewish literature, especially the Midrash, contains explicit hints of the veracity of the Christian dogma. With such arguments, even Reuchlin still tried to protect the Talmud.

It is my aim here to describe these patterns, to prove that all of them may be traced to the twelfth century, and to give an idea of the Jewish response.

* * *

1. The older pattern of Western religious polemics was essentially a stereotyped enumeration of proofs taken from the Bible for the truth of Christianity, and the detection of prophecies and prefigurations that were enriched with arguments taken from the present status of the Jews in "servitude" and dispersion. This polemical literature, prevalent in Antiquity and in the early Middle Ages, had long ceased to be missionary, that is, to appeal to Jews directly, or even to be based on real experience. Perhaps Avi-Yona and others are right in assuming that Justin Martyr's *Dialogue with Trypho* was the last piece of the genre to be at least partially based on the reminiscence of real contests, for all later disputations are literary fictions. When the missionary competition, mainly perhaps over the θεοσεβεῖς, faded, Christian anti-Jewish polemics became internalized. Its content became admonitory (against the *iudaizantes*) and homiletic; its function was both to assist the self-interpretation of Christianity and to supply the community with an explanation for the existence of the Jews and for the relative tolerance they enjoyed—or were supposed to enjoy. The arguments, as mentioned above, were seldom original.

The doctrine of relative tolerance as expressed in this early medieval phase of polemics has often been described in modern literature, though its basic assumption were seldom recognized. The "blindness" of the Jews is due to the "stubbornness" with which they stick to the *sensus literalis* of the Old Testament; they refuse to perceive the fulfillment and termination of the Mosaic law in the times *sub gratia*; and thus they prefer rather to remain "children" and "servants" than to be free from the burden of the law, which was meant to be but a παιδαγωγὸς εἰς Χριστόν. The continuity of Jewish existence in Christian times had to be explained. In the prevailing interpretation, developed not without contradictions up to the fifth century, the dispersion and survival of the Jews assumed a threefold teleological meaning —besides its retrospective justification as collective punishment for the collective guilt of the crucifixion. In and through dispersion, the Jews are witnesses for the antiquity of the Old Testament to the pagans who suspected Christianity of introducing novelties and of being a revolutionary *collegium illicitum*. Moreover, their permanent humiliation is a libing testimony for the Christians that the scepter had departed from Judah when *shiloh* came, and that the election has been transferred from Israel "in the flesh" to the spiritual Israel, that is, the gentiles. Finally, at the end of history, the remnant of Israel will dramatically accept the hitherto rejected Christian faith, perhaps even help decisively in reviving it, thus completing and crowning the labor of the *militans ecclesia*.

With the aid of this position, the Church could either justify relative tolerance towards Jews, or, when suitable, justify depravation of their condition on the grounds that the actual social and political status of the Jews did not befit their de jure servitude.

The basic assumption of such theological formulas, dominant until the twelfth century, was that neither Jews nor Judaism had changed since the emergence of Christianity. *Secundum carnem*, ethnically as well as in their literal exegesis and its erroneous juridical consequences, the Jews remained the same as they had been then, a living anachronism. Joachim of Fiore formulated this assumption pregnantly: "noluerunt ipsi Judaei mutari cum tempore."[2] That alleged lack of change was sometimes understood very literally, we can learn from a casual remark made in quite a different context, in Rimbert's *Vita Anskari*. The hagiographer narrates a vision in which Christ appeared to the missionary and, as a matter of course, appeared "more judaico vestitus."[3] If, then, a radical change in Judaism, to say nothing of a *nova lex*, could be detected—this would alter the basis of the relative tolerande practiced, or even demand its revocation.

The certainty of the Jewish ethnic continuity was not subject to polemics —neither side ever doubted it; the essence of this phase of polemics was rather the evaluation of this certainty. Under the force of the polemical situation, Judaism was compelled to stress the positive meaning of its ethnical continuity far more than it did in the times when, as a missionary religion, it appealed to the "fearers of heaven." Judah Halevi developed the biological criterion of Jewish self-understanding almost *ad absurdum* in determining that the superhuman sense of the divine and its succession among men was dependent upon, and guaranteed by, the biological succession only—even converts are excluded from it.

[2] Joachim de Fiore, *Super quattuor Evangelia* 105 from: H. de Lubac, *Exégèse Médiévale, les quatre sens de l'écriture*, Études publiées sous la direction de la faculté de Théologie S. J. de Lyons-Fourvière 42 (Lyons 1961) 3.144 n. 2. For a similar definition of the Christian position by Albo, see my article in *Zion* (above n. 1) 128 n. 12.

[3] Rimbert, *Vita Anskari* 4, ed. G. Waitz, MGH in usum scholarum (Hannover 1884) 24.

The Jewish answer to the Christian interpretation of the Diaspora was complex. A response was not merely a polemical demand but vital for their own self-estimation. Few questions were as urgent as that of the discrepancy between the certainty of being God's chosen people and the present humiliation in dispersion. The answers given were mostly of three kinds—the cathartic, the missionary, and a combination of both, the soteriological. The cathartic theodicy was the oldest and remained the prevailing one. Shlomo ben R. Shime'on, chronicler during the Crusader pogroms, understood the sudden catastrophe of the Rheinish communities to be one step within the process of completing the punishment for sins as old as the *originale peccatum* of the nation, the adoration of the golden calf.[4] He stood within a long tradition. In the sixteenth century, this view of *Galut* as a catharsis found its profoundest expression in Lurianic *kabbalah*: here it became a symbol for the alienation of God from himself for the sake of his own self-purification from his hidden "seeds of sternness"—by means of emanation and creation; and more than a symbol, the dispersion of Israel was seen as the last step in the cosmo-historical process of reparation (*tikkun*).[5] As an argument against Christians, the cathartic view stresses the totally immanent course of Jewish history: dispersion and sufferings have no relation with any external event, political (such as the Roman empire) or religious (such as the emergence of Christianity). Jewish history, similar to the *procursus* of the *Civitas Dei peregrinans in teris* in the Augustinian interpretation, was independent of-external secular events. There hardly exists a reflection of historical causality between Josephus and Shlomo ben Verga.

The "missionary" justification of dispersion was brought up in times of increasing cultural assimilation of the Jews with their environment. Here the positive meaning of dispersion was projected to the outside: the Jews were scattered in order to be a paradigm to other nations and to carry monotheism—the seeds of the Logos in a similar Christian argument in Antiquity—all over the world. The Alexandrian, the Spanish, and the modern Jewish Enlightenment used this argument alike, seldom to repudiate Christianity or Islam, more often (by the nature of the argument) to show the relative historical value of those "daughter religions" over mere polytheism. The third, "soteriological" theodicy is the only argument really developed under the impact of Christianity. It demonstrates the intensity both of the influence and of the rejection of Christian theology on Jewish thought. It is expressed in some interpretations of the "Servant of God" in Deutero-Isaiah as a personification of the whole of Israel which, through its sufferings,

---

[4] A. M. Habermann (ed.), *Sefer geserot ashkenas ve'tsorfat* (Jerusalem 1946) 25.

[5] G. Scholem, *Major Trends in Jewish Mysticism* (New York 1961), 246ff., 286; J. Tishby, *The Doctrine of Evil and the 'Kelippah in Lurianic Kabbalism* (Hebrew, Jerusalem 1952) 41-43. 52-61, 134ff.

redeems the world and is a ransom even for those nations which persecute it.[6]

That Christian polemics evoked doubts within Jewish ranks is self-evident. "You gave the heretic an evasive answer; how will you answer us on the same question?" R. Simlai was asked by his pupils.[7]

* * *

2. The radical changes in contents and in function of medieval Christian polemics during the twelfth century resulted both from the changes in western theology and, far more important, from the changes in the social, economic, and legal status of the Jews after the twelfth century. It was a complicated process that can hardly be interpreted by a monocausal reduction, not even in one land.[8] From one minority among many, in the Carolingian (or even Ottonian) empire, possessing privileges (*libertates*) similar to other comparable minorities, they became conspicuous, a minority par excellence. Under these circumstances, polemics against Jews became at times more aggressive than even in Antiquity. The patterns now created were to last until the seventeenth and eighteenth centuries, though the Reformation again brought a renewed emphasis on the missionary function of polemics whenever it needed this particular missionary success for the sake of its own *certitudo salutis*.

Two formal factors became decisive in the twelfth century: first, the rationalization of religious polemics and second, the growing awareness among Christian theologians of the existence of an extensive body of postbiblical Jewish literature besides mere exegesis. The invocation of reason was characteristic of the twelfth century; naturally it stood for a variety of tendencies and positions. In one sense, it meant the attempt to derive dogmatic principles *sola ratione*. Such experiments were shared by only a few, and were entirely discredited after the thirteenth century. They provided, among other things, an opportunity to rethink afresh the function, and perhaps limitations, of controversies about principles. Anselm of Canterbury's *Cur Deus homo*, though itself not a polemical treatise, had considerable influence on the polemical literature of the twelfth century. His demonstration of

---

[6] H. H. Ben-Sasson, *On Jewish History in the Middle Ages* (Hebrew, Tel-Aviv 1962) 258.

[7] *Talmud Jerushalmi, Berachot* 9.1, fol. 12b.

[8] Recently, L. Dasberg, *Untersuchungen über die Entwertung des Judenstatus im 11. Jahrhundert*, École practique des hautes études—Sorbonne, 16me section: sciences économique et sociales, Études Juives 11 (Paris 1965) esp. 115-193, has attempted such a causal reduction by exaggerating the importance of the growing self-consciousness of Jewish communities in the West ("aggressivity") and by likewise exaggerating the role of apocalyptic trends in the eve of the Crusades.

the necessity of the Incarnation is well known. It is based on the assumption that God, by wanting creation, wanted also its definite order; by the creation of man, he wanted the fulfillment of the *civitas Dei*. Thus, if the *debitum satisfactionis* of humanity after the Fall had to be paid only by man who is unable to change the corrupted disposition of his will in order to do so, God had to become man. This necessity can not be compared to the *'akl* of the Kalam. In fact, Anselm was one of the first medieval thinkers to have formulated clearly the question of the relation between the (later so-called) *potestas dei ordinata* and the *potestas dei absoluta*. The implicit negation of Peter Damian's concept of God's omnipotence is very thematic in this treatise. God cannot act *contra naturam* if this means self-contradiction, for such omnipotence, Anselm says elsewhere, is in reality weakness,[9] since it implies the possibility of self-negation; similarly, God cannot want an order and negate its necessary consequences. The objects of his will must remain compatible.

Anselm's treatise is an example of the possibilities of rational tolerance—possibilities which were seldom subsequently actualized. Anselm is aware that his demythologization of former theological concepts (like that of the devil's share of the human soul since the Fall) leaves no room for the concept of collective guilt of crucifixion: "Deum enim occidere nullus homo umquam scienter saltem velle posset."[10] His imitators in the twelfth century not only forgot such arguments, but forgot also the epistemological basis for tolerance which might have lead Anselm to doubt the efficacy of polemic altogether. *Necessariae rationes* do not necessitate subjective evidence; to be understood and accepted, the argument presupposes faith, that is illumination. There is no point in comparing Anselm's objective principle of evidence with the subjective principle of notions "clear and distinct" in Cartesian philosophy.

In other cases, rationalism contributed rather to the justification of intolerance. Peter the Venerable presented the following syllogism: since man is an *animal rationale*, and the Jews would not listen to reason, there is no conclusion left but that they are beasts. The considerate position of Anselm, Abelard, Raymund Lull, are the exceptions, not the rule.

Still another type of rationalism had an important role in the self-justification of converts. Polemical literature written by converts begins with the twelfth century, and the importance that Petrus Alfonsi attributes to "philosophy" in the process of his "rebirth" is indicative of the mood of that class of intellectuals, officials, and merchants which was the main source

---

[9] In addition to the literature quoted in *Zion* (n. 1 above) 130 nn. 18, 19, cf. D. P. Henry, *The Logic of Saint Anselm* (Oxford 1967) 134-180, esp. 151ff.

[10] Anselm of Canterbury, *Cur Deus homo?* 2.15, ed. Schmitt, *Anselmi opera omnia* (Edinburgh 1946) 2.115.

of the later "Taufwellen" in Spain. Alfunsi's main argument against his older Jewish self, represented in his dialogue by the bearer of his former name, Moses, amounts to the accusation that neither *Halakha* nor exegesis are compatible with reason, that is, philosophy. Nor is Islam, a religion accommodated to the primitive mentality of desert dwellers, a religion without accord with the norms of enlightenment. Interesting enough is the fact that he draws heavily from Jewish philosophy, and in a peculiar manner. He quotes[11] almost verbatim Sa'adia's distinction between the three main sources of evidence—the sense perception, immediate intuition, and deductive knowledge. Alfunsi omits the fourth source, tradition: for in that he implied the superiority of Christianity; that it had no need for irrational precepts, "commandments of obedience," in Sa'adia's terminology. Alfunsi is an early prototype of the later, and far more subtle, Abner of Burgos and of many average converts for similar reasons. He enables us to understand better Halevi's awareness of the dangers of a mere philosophical foundation of religion. Alfunsi's conversion seems to have been a very sincere one; his dialogue contains no defamation. Though introducing many examples and demonstrations from the Talmud and the Midrash, he never takes refuge in the accusation, which was later to become pernicious that they contain deliberate blasphemies against Christianity.

* * *

3. It was also through him that Peter the Venerable, a generation later, became aware of the postbiblical Jewish literature, and only in the subsequent centuries did Christian theology begin a systematic study of this literature. Two main attitudes were possible, and both were already taken in the twelfth century. The one attitude goes from Peter the Venerable to Eisenmenger, and amounts to a systematic alienation of the Jew even from the position he had in Christian consciousness before, an alienation based on the hidden assumption that he is not a Jew any more in the Classical sense, that the Jews have changed. The other possible attitude was the one indicated by Alanus ab Insulis and developed in the Disputation of Barcelona and in the *Pugio fidei* of Raymundus Martini; it was still the basis for Reuchlin's demand for the preservation of the Talmud, as it contains christological traditions and thus serves to refute the Jews from within.

---

[11] Petrus Alfunsi, *Dialogi* 1 (PL 157.555C). In the meantime, M. Merchavia, *The Church Versus Talmudic and Midrashic Literature* (Hebrew, Jerusalem 1970) 93-127, esp. 128, has confirmed my impression. In subsequent chapters, he adds important material concerning the acquaintance with the postbiblical Jewish literature up to the trial of the Talmud, but remains rather descriptive than analytical.

Sporadic knowledge of legal and homiletic Jewish traditions is to be found before, particularly in Origen and Jerome, but also in the early Middle Ages (Agobard of Lyon). The demonstration of Jerome (to which one finds parallel formulations in Epiphanius and Augustine), that on behalf of their δευτερώσεις the Jews were preferring "doctrinae hominum" to "doctrina Dei,"[12] became especially famous and might have inspired Justinian's Novella 146. Even the most aggressive attitude, however, towards Jewish Halakah, aggadah, or fragments of speculative literature (Agobard) never denied the subjective dependence of this literature on the Bible, that is, its exegetical character from the standpoint of Judaism. Paradigmata of "errores et superstitiones" were presented as an example of the harm which literal exegesis can do, but not more.

The treatise of Peter the Venerable *Against the Old Stubbornness of the Jews*, if analyzed cautiously, already shows the new turn. The Talmud, fragments of which he knew through Alfunsi, is not only an "error"; it is, even from the Jewish standpoint as he wants it, a heresy. It is the "secret" of the Jews: "Pugnasti tanto tempore contradivos libros diabolicis libris."[13] It is the Jewish equivalent to the New Testament—a heretical, diabolical aberration from the Bible. It is a tradition that begins here and ends with the "Conspiracy of the Elders of Zion," and the accusation that the Talmud was a heresy, played a far more decisive role in the trials of the Talmud in the thirteenth century (though not afterwards) than the mere accusation of defamation of Christianity. On a more primitive level, this fear of the Jews having a "secret tradition" found its expression, about the same time in the blood accusation. Thomas of Monmouth, referring to the Norwich case, quotes a converted Jew:[14] there are stipulations in "the old scriptures of the Jews," that redemption would be achieved only through continuous bloodshed. He implies the secrecy of such traditions. On both levels, we are faced with a revification of one motive in pagan anti-Judaism in the Graeco-Roman antiquity: the accusation of *odium humani generis* due to esoteric ways. Their *arcana* are directed against the surrounding world, against the "political" *religio*. Christianity changed this polemic: it was unable to use it because it claimed a share in these *arcana*. It only claimed that the Jews did not correctly understand their own traditions. In the later Middle Ages, the Jews again became mysterious and incomprehensible, alienated and demonized in the Christian consciousness; a process reflecting itself on the popular as well as on the theological level.

[12] Hieronymus, *Epistulae* 121.10, ed. I. Hilberg, *Corpus Scriptorum Ecclesiasticorum Latinorum* 61.3 (1918) 4879.

[13] Petrus Venerabilis, *Tractatus adversus Judaeorum inveteratam duritiem* 5, PL 189.602; Merchavia (n. 11 above) 128-152.

[14] Thomas of Monmouth, *De vita et passione sancti Wilhelmi martyris norwicensis* 2.9, ed. A. Jessop and M. R. James (Cambridge 1896) 93.

The condemnation of the rabbinical oral tradition as a postbiblical inno-vation and therefore heresy was by far the most detrimental theological argument the Jews were to confront in the Middle Ages. Their answer, as documented in the Hebrew protocol of the disputation of Paris, was evasive. It had to be evasive, since the Jewish Halakah was not conceived as mere conservation and explication of the revealed law, but as its adaptation to the *necessitas temporum*: the law is submitted to the interpretative ingenuity of men, so that even the divine inspiration counts less than the *consensus scholarum*. Yet is was just this fundamental understanding of the Halakah which was chosen already by Peter the Venerable to prove his point.

Why, then, did the Church avoid this path of argumentation in later cen-turies—though by no means the attack against the Talmud? Why did cen-sors look so meticulously for the scattered alleged blasphemies, if theologians could easily demonstrate that the whole Talmud surpassed the realm of errors permitted to the Jews? Perhaps because this line of argument was dangerous for the Church itself. To insist that the Jews, erring as they might be, have to stick to *sola scriptura*, to insist that the body of tradition means, by definition, mutation of the original revelation, was, once translated into the context of Catholic self-understanding and the increasing challenge it had to face in the later Middle Ages, a most suspicious argument, perhaps even if applied to Jews only. As to the charge of blasphemies against the Christian religion, Jacob Katz has shown us that, if compelled to, Jews were able to revise their interpretation of Christians as heathens.[15] Katz stresses the role of the disputation of Paris in the process leading to Hameiri's dis-tinction between the "peoples defined by the ways of religions" and the real heathens. Thus, the polemical situation sometimes aided to modify the Jewish self-definition as the only true monotheistic religion.

* * *

4. The fourth pattern of anti-Jewish polemics was to use the Jewish tra-dition, even the postbiblical tradition, against the Jews. Alanus ab Insulis, by the end of the twelfth century, uses one of the Talmudic apocalyptic spe-culations to prove that even according to later Jewish tradition, "manifestum est legem transiisse et messiam venisse."[16] This *vaticinium Elliae*, as it was

---

[15] J. Katz, *Exclusiveness and Tolerance* [Hebrew: *Between Jews and Gentiles*] (Jerusa-lem 1960) 115-128. A similar term with similar connotations can be found in Maimonides, *More Nebuchim* 3.51, trans. S. Pines, *The Guide of the Perplexed* (Chicago 1963) 618-619.

[16] Alanus ab Insulis, *De fide catholica libri quattuor* 4.3, PL 210.410. Alanus introduced this tradition with the reference "in Sehale dicitur," which I suggested be read either as a metathesis of *Chasal* (ḥsl-shl) or, less probably, as a contraction of the name of the treatise *Sanhedrin* with the name of the chapter, *Chelek* (s-hl). See Funkenstein (n. 1 above) 142.

called later, postulating that the world is to endure six thousand years, of
which two thousand are chaos, two thousand Torah, and two thousand the
days of the Messiah, remained a *locus communis et classicus* for the pattern
of polemics I am discussing; even Reuchlin quoted it as an example of Talmudic teachings which make it well worthwhile to conserve the Talmud.
The most comprehensive elaboration of this polemical type, which was exercised first in the disputation of Barcelona in 1263, was done by Raymundus
Martini in his *Pugio fidei*. Though less dangerous than the total condemnation of the Talmud, it nevertheless led to the habit of discerning "genuine"
and worthless traditions within Jewish literature; the Midrash, and later
especially the Kabbalah, were sometimes declared to be the only parts of
Jewish tradition worth conserving.

The Jewish answer was given already by Nachmanides, the leading Jewish disputant at Barcelona. The Aggadah has no authoritative legitima-
tization compared to the legal tradition; it is the Jewish equivalent to a Christian sermon. Another Nachmanides—and this is again characteristic of the
Jewish polemical situation—meets us in his biblical exegesis: there he demonstrates in almost every page the necessity of the Kabbalah, which is
expressed in the old Midrashim and which bring them into concordance,
for the real understanding of every biblical sentence: "the Torah speaking
of the lower regions and hints at the upper regions." In the same way, he
and later polemists, as an answer to this polemical pattern, at times minimized the role of messianism among the "principles of faith"—perhaps against
their genuine conviction.

Learned men, since knowledge is their domain, like to believe that intolerance
originates in ignorance. The beginning of the *Wissenschaft vom Judentum*
in the nineteenth century was founded on this cliché. What we know about
anti-Judaism in the later Middle Ages confirms the opposite impression.
Christian and Jewish polemics during that period are characterized by increase of knowledge of the antagonists' theological literatures and modes
of thinking. It is true indeed that there was mutual influence and that many
parallel movements may be found. Even in their polemics, Christians and
Jews used a common theological language. Yet subjectively, the increase
of mutual knowledge was accompanied by a growing awareness of, and stress
upon, the gap. If there existed a mutual cultural language it served for contradictory assertions.

Merchavia, (n. 11 above) 216 n. 15, seems to have noticed only the second suggestion; he
adds further remote possibilities. (He implies, but does not name, earlier references to
this passage in modern literature).

Department of History
University of California
Los Angeles, California 90024 U.S.A.

Reflections on
Medieval Anti-Judaism: 4

ANTI-JUDAISM AS THE NECESSARY PREPARATION
FOR ANTI-SEMITISM

•

by Gavin Langmuir

Anti-Judaism I take to be a total or partial opposition to Judaism—and to Jews as adherents of it—by men who accept a competing system of beliefs and practices and consider certain genuine Judaic beliefs and practices as inferior. Anti-Judaism, therefore, can be pagan, Christian, communist, or what you will, but its specific character will depend upon the character of the specific competing system. Voltaire's anti-Judaism differed from that of Augustine, as Augustine's differed from that of Tacitus. Of all forms of anti-Judaism, the Christian has been the most intense because of the intimate dependence of Christianity on Judaism.

Classical pagan anti-Judaism was neither universal nor homogeneous Throughout the Roman Empire there was considerable objection to Jewish exclusiveness and peculiar customs, as these were imperfectly understood. In addition, in the east there was intense hostility provoked by violent military, political, and economic intergroup competition. None of this, however, led Romans to attempt to suppress Judaism or degrade the social status of Jews. For paganism shared few fundamental premises with Judaism, and therefore did not recognize Judaism as a vital challenge, but saw it rather as an alien alternative which attracted proselytes from the lower orders. Precisely because the character of pagan anti-Judaism depended on the character of classical polytheistic culture, it could not be transmitted to Christianity to any serious degree.[1]

---

[1] Jean Juster, *Les Juifs dans l'Empire romain*, 2 vols. (Paris 1914); Bernhard Blumenkranz, "Tacite, antisémite ou xenophobe?" *Revue des Études Juives* n.s 11 (1951-1952) 187-191 ; A. N. Sherwin-White, *Racial Prejudice in Imperial Rome* (Cambridge 1967); Victor Tcherikover, *Hellenistic Civilization and the Jews* (Philadelphia 1959); Marcel Simon, *Verus Israel*, ed. 2 (Paris 1964) 273.

Christianity, by contrast, grew out of Judaism amidst a conflict with non-Christian Jews, and that birth trauma was enshrined in Christian revelation and central to Christian theology. The Christian acceptance of Jewish scripture and the Christian claim to be the true Israel meant that for Christians Jews were a central element of God's providential plan. Moreover the continued existence of Judaism after Jesus was the physical embodiment of doubt about the validity of Christianity. Unlike pagan anti-Judaism, Christian anti-Judaism was a central and essential element of the Christian system of beliefs. The elaboration of anti-Judaic doctrine and polemics and the effort to prove that Christianity was foreshadowed in the Old Testament would be a major theological enterprise for centuries.[2]

Christian anti-Judaism can be separated into three aspects: the doctrinal, the legal, and the popular. Doctrinal anti-Judaism attempted to prove that Christians were the true Israel and that most adherents of Judaism before Jesus and all of its adherents thereafter were at the least inferior to Christians and, at the strongest, the polar enemies of Christianity. I need not rehearse the basic elements of the doctrine about the willful rebels who disobeyed God, killed Christ, persecuted his followers, and obdurately persisted in their blindness, thereby serving as witness to the truth of Christian scripture and to the punishment imposed on Jews by God. Nor need I comment on the strongly defensive tone that marks the initial elaboration of the doctrine, even in Chrysostom.[3]

The legal aspect of anti-Judaism was the effort of Christians to order society legally according to the implications of the doctrine, to reinforce argument by physical sanctions. Foreshadowed within the pre-Constantinian Christian communities, that aspect only became prominent when Christians were able to influence or control secular authority. From the time of Constantine, and particularly from that of Theodosius I, ecclesiastical influence was successfully exerted to obtain secular legislation that would inhibit contact between Christians and Jews, diminish Jewish social status, and, in the extreme policy of Ambrose and some other ecclesiastics, extirpate Judaism. Legal anti-Judaism had little impact in the early Middle Ages but

---

[2] *Ibid.* passim; Bernhard Blumenkranz, *Les auteurs latins du moyen âge sur les Juifs et le Judaisme* (Paris 1963).

[3] James Parkes, *The Conflict of the Church and the Synagogue* (Philadelphia 1961); Jules Isaac, *Genèse de l'antisémitisme* (Paris 1956); John Chrysostom, "Homilies against the Jews," PG 48.875: "Or is it but a small distance that separates us from the Jews? Or is controversy between us about light and everyday things, so that you believe that our practices and theirs are one and the same? Why do you confuse that which is not to be confused? They crucified the Christ whom you adore. Do you see how great the separation? How then does it happen that you, professing to adore the crucified, run to those who crucified Christ?"

one of its principles exerted gradual pressure even though there was little feeling against Jews.[4]

A central proposition of legal anti-Judaism from the earliest days had been that no Jew should be in a position to exercise control over Christians, whether through public office, the institution of slavery, or otherwise. Motivated by the desire to prevent Jewish proselytism and manifest God's punishment of Jews, it also provided a useful justification for self-interested Christians who desired to monopolize social and economic advantages and to deprive Jews of the advantages they possessed. The prohibition of Jewish possession of Christian slaves on that basis made Jewish involvement in large-scale agriculture difficult. The same principle made exclusion of Jews from the feudal network almost axiomatic, and, by the twelfth century, it was serving to exclude Jews from membership in merchant gilds and other activities in the developing towns.[5]

Yet the legal implications of Christian anti-Judaism could not be fully developed until the bulk of the population identified profoundly with Christianity and accepted its cosmology in such a way as to desire to attack Judaism and degrade Jews. That condition did not obtain in the Christian Roman Empire or the early Middle Ages and was not reached in western Europe, I would argue, until the eleventh century. The failure of Agobard and Amulo's effort to win promulgation of a rigorous legal anti-Judaism in the Carolingian Empire indicates how slowly broad anti-Judaic feeling developed.[6] Only by the eleventh century, after nominally Christian Europe had repulsed the second wave of pagan invasions, does a profound identification with Christianity—as then understood—seem to have developed, and Europe to have cloaked itself in a new mantle of white churches and set a broad movement of religious reform in motion.[7] And only in the eleventh century is there indisputable evidence of broad, popular anti-Judaism.

At this point it becomes essential to distinguish northern from Mediterranean Europe and popular from legal anti-Judaism. Up to the eleventh century, the effort to implement anti-Judaism had been primarily episcopal and Mediterranean. But in the eleventh century, intense popular anti-Judaism emerged only in northern Europe, and it was not officially incited. Although Christianity was longer and more deeply rooted in Mediterranean

---

[4] Parkes 166-168, 174-182, 187-189, 199-206; Bernhard Blumenkranz, *Juifs et Chrétiens dans le monde occiental, 430-1096* (Paris 1960) 291-371.

[5] Guido Kisch, *The Jews in Medieval Germany* (Chicago 1949) 32, 318.

[6] Blumenkranz (n.2 above) 152-168, 195-200.

[7] See Jeffrey B. Russell, *Dissent and Reform in the Early Middle Ages* (Berkeley 1965). I would argue that the appearance in the north only of peasant heresy of the type that Russell styles extravagant, including the popular crusade of 1096, demonstrates that the bulk of the population in the north had finally identified firmly with Christianity—however they interpreted it.

Europe, and although the Jewish population was densest there, there was little violent popular anti-Judaism, possibly because a significant, diversified Jewish population had existed there as long as Christianity, the sense of Christian identity had developed more gradually, and the disruption of social institutions had been less, particularly of urban centers. In the north, major social institutions were in the formative stage, the revival of commerce was stimulating the reappearance of town life, Christianity was more recent, identification with it was more abrupt, and the less diversified and in many cases very recent Jewish population was a very small—and strange— minority. Moreover the sudden intensification of Christian consciousness here was paralleled by the great development of Jewish consciouness from Gershom to Rashi.

Whatever the reasons, the massacres of 1096 were almost entirely limited to the north, were perpetrated by lower levels of the population, and were overwhelmingly anti-Judaic.[8] Jews were killed because they had adhered to Judaism and rejected Christianity. Indoctrination in Christianity and its attendant anti-Judaism had here proved more explosive than its propagators had intended. And after 1096 and through most of the twelfth century, most ecclesiastical and secular authorities were more concerned to check than to develop popular anti-Judaic feeling. Papal bulls of protection, while reiterating basic anti-Judaic doctrine, reemphasized the obligation to protect Jews and Judaism; and secular authorites on the same basis took further measures to protect—and also to control—Jews.[9] Yet all these efforts were explicitly based on official anti-Judaic doctrine; they increased awareness of it, and brought a further implementation of legal anti-Judaism.

In the twelfth century, the pressure of popular anti-Judaism, the implementation of legal anti-Judaism, and anti-Judaism's long appeal to Christian self-interest combined to set in motion the process known as the self-fulfilling prophecy whereby a group already assumed to be inferior is forced by the majority to engage in conduct which seems further confirmation of the minority's inferiority.[10] By the middle of the twelfth century in northern

---

[8] E. L. Dietrich, "Das Judentum im Zeitalter der Kreuzzüge," *Saeculum* 3 (1952) 94-129; Salo W. Baron, *A Social and Religious History of the Jews*, ed. 2 (New York 1952) 4.97-102; Hans Liebeschutz, "The Crusading Movement in its Bearing on the Christian Attitude toward Jewry," *Journal of Jewish Social Studies* 10 (1959) 97-111. Norman Golb, "New Light on the Persecution of French Jews at the Time of the First Crusade," *Proceedings of the American Academy of Jewish Research* 34 (1966) 1-63, while interesting, does not significantly alter the accepted views of the geography of the massacres.

[9] Solomon Grayzel, "The Papal Bull *Sicut Judeis*," *Studies and Essays in Honor of A. A. Neuman* (Leiden 1952) 243-280; Gavin I. Langmuir, "'Judei nostri' and the Beginning of Capetian Legislation," *Tradiito* 16 (1960) 203-239; "The Jews and the Archives of Angevin England," *Traditio* 19 (1963) 196-202, 208-209; Kisch (n. 5 above) 107-153.

[10] Robert K. Merton, *Social Theory and Social Structure*, ed. 2 (Glencoe, Ill. 1957) 421-436.

Europe, Jews were becoming stereotyped as usurers in addition to the older stereotype of Christ-killers.[11] The gradual exclusion of Jews from many social roles and the danger of participation in long-distance commerce because of violent popular anti-Judaism drastically reduced the choices available to literate people who had heretofore enjoyed most of the privileges of freemen. And the need for credit in a rapidly expanding economy, the self-interested support by secular authorities of Jewish moneylending which made that occupation temporarily profitable, and the desire of the minority to come together behind the relative safety of town walls, all encouraged a disproportionate participation of Jews in the single social role of providers of the lesser and more unpopular kind or credit.[12]

That concentration was not intended by those who had propagated anti-Judaism, any more than it was dictated by Judaism, and by the beginning of the thirteenth century, the Church was trying to reverse the undesired development. Nonetheless, it was the pressure of anti-Judaism which had restricted Jews to a specific and degrading role. That Jews were forced into a role that the Church officially desired to eliminate was owing to the specific character of medieval society, not to ecclesiastical intention, but the general principle that Jews should occupy a degraded social position had long been inherent in Christian anti-Judaism.

Because of these developments, Jews, by the beginning of the thirteenth century, were no longer simply dispersed adherents of an inferior religion but had been assigned a definite, collective, religious, legal, and social status in the organization of medieval society. They had become an institutionalized inferior minority, symbolized ecclesiastically by the distinctive clothing commanded by the Fourth Lateran Council, secularly by their legal status as serfs of secular authorities, and socially by their prominence in moneylending. And now, as a defenseless and institutionalized minority, Jews in northern Europe could be manipulated by the majority not only physically but also mentally. The way was open for the development of a false, irrational conception of the Jew.

Norwich, Pontoise, Blois, Fulda, Valréas, Lincoln, Oberwesel, Röttingen, Chinon, the Armleder, the Black Death, Trent—the sequence symbolizes the appearance and development, chronological and geographical, of a new and deadly kind of persecution of Jews, and one very different from that

[11] Georg Caro, *Sozial- und Wirtschaftsgeschichte der Juden*, 2 vols. (Frankfurt 1920-1924) 1.220-223.

[12] R. Génestal, *Rôle des monastères comme établissements de crédit* (Paris 1901); H. van Wervecke, "Le mort-gage et son rôle économique en Flandre et en Lotharingie," *Revue belge de philologie et d'histoire* 8 (1929) 53-91; Jean Lestocquoy, "Les usuriers au début du moyen âge," *Studi in onore di Gino Luzzatto*, 2 vols. (Milan 1949-1950) 1.67-77; H. G. Richardson, *The English Jewry under Angevin* Kings (London 1960).

in Alexandria or in 1096. Whereas the old accusations that Jews were responsible for the death of Christ (as they acknowledged), that they obdurately rejected Christianity, and that they were peculiarly involved in moneylending had been faulty overgeneralizations reflecting a central core of truth, the new accusations of ritual murder, host desecration, and well-poisoning were not faulty and inflexible generalizations but false fantasies unsupported by evidence. In addition to anti-Judaism, anti-Semitism now appears, developing slowly until 1300 and then intensifying rapidly, starting in the north and only gradually spreading to the south of Europe.[13] It starts where the Jewish population was smallest and most defenseless, and where the pressure of majority anti-Judaism—doctrinal, legal, and popular—had most restricted diversity within the minority.

In the north by about 1200, Jews had become an ideal focus for all those individuals whose personal need to displace and project guilt and hatred[14] sought a socially acceptable outlet. There was a wide audience predisposed to accept accusations against a little-known group whose evil deviance had been so institutionally defined, and there were self-interested individuals who sought calculated profit from purveying the rumors. And Jews no longer had the power to act as they wished, to demonstrate the falsity of stereotypes about their character and potential, or to disprove the specific irrational accusations against them.

These projections of ritual muder, host desecration, and well-poisoning inevitably assumed a religious coloration, but in fact they owed more to tensions within majority society and the psychological problems of individuals than to the real conflict between Christianity and Judaism. They were not a necessary or predictable result of anti-Judaism as a body of ideas but rather a social and psychological reaction to the institutionalization of the inferior minority in a rapidly developing society whose stresses increased dramatically at the end of the thirteenth century.

Henceforth and for centuries, however, anti-Judaism and anti-Semitism would coexist and be mutually reinforcing. And anti-Semitism could persist even when social norms were non-Christian or anti-Christian, for anti-Semitism was neither a logical extension nor a simple vulgarization of Christian anti-Judaic doctrine[15] but an expression of darker and less ideate needs generated by the oppression of a minority. To the extent that Christian anti-Judaism was initially responsible for making Jews an oppressed minority, it helped to create beliefs and attitudes that Christianity could not con-

---

[13] Léon Poliakov, *Histoire de l'antisémitisme*, 3 vols. (Paris 1955-1968) 1.115-139.

[14] Gordon W. Allport, *The Nature of Prejudice* (Cambridge, Mass. 1954) 343-392.

[15] Cf. Cecil Roth, "The Medieval Conception of the Jew," *Essays and Studies in Memory of Linda R. Miller* (New York 1938) pp. 171-190; Isaac (n. 2 above) 319-320.

trol. They contaminated Christianity itself and were only generally condemned as unchristian in the second half of the twentieth century. A problem that yet remains to be solved is how Christians can remain Christians
and avoid anti-Judaism.[16]

[16] See, for example, Edward H. Flannery, *The Anguish of the Jews* (New York 1965).

Department of History
Stanford University
California 94305, U.S.A.

Reflections on
Medieval Anti-Judaism: 5

THE WANDERING JEW:
THE ALIENATION OF THE JEWISH IMAGE
IN CHRISTIAN CONSCIOUSNESS[1]

•

by Adolf F. Leschnitzer

The concept of "The Wandering Jew" or, in German, "Der Ewige Jude," the eternal, that is, the everlasting Jew, can be traced to a German chapbook entitled: *Kurze Beschreibung und Erzählung von einem Juden mit Namen Ahasver.* What do the two phrases "The Wandering Jew" and "Der Ewige Jude" mean?

Generally, both English and German dictionaries give two meanings.[2] First, there is the medieval legendary figure of a man who treated Christ mockingly or with contempt on his way to the crucifixion and who is condemned to wander upon the earth until the return of Christ. Second, there is an obviously ironical variant of the first definition: a man who never settles down, a figure of a restlessly roving person.

Let us now consider popular usage: In Gottfried Keller's novella *Das Fähnlein der sieben Aufrechten* there is a passage that sheds clear light upon the use of the phrase in everyday language. A citizen of Zurich, around 1860, says the following in the course of a chat in an inn:

---

[1] Some of the ideas that are set forth in this paper, but not the conclusion, also appear in my article "Der Gestaltwandel Ahasvers," in: *In zwei Welten; Siegfried Moses zum 75. Geburtstag.* (Tel Aviv 1962) 470-505. Of the older literature on the subject, L. Neubaur, *Die Sage vom Ewigen Juden* (Leipzig 1884) is still indispensable. Recently, the problem of origin and career of the legend has been dealt by G. K. Anderson, *The Legend of the Wandering Jew* (Providence 1965); S. Baron, *A Social and Religious History of the Jews* 11 (New York 1967) 180-182, 374-375 (nn. 80-81).

[2] See for instance *The Concise Oxford Dictionary of Current English.* ed. 3 (Oxord 1934) 1390; and *Deutsches Wörterbuch von Jacob und Wilhelm Grimm.*, ed. Moritz Heyne (Leipzig 1877) 4.2.2353.

Just as it is proper, at times, for a man to think of death in the midst of the best years of his life so, in an hour of reflection, he might concern himself with the inevitable end of his fatherland so that he might love it all the more devoutly in the present; for everything in this world is transitory and subject to change. Or have not far bigger nations than ours perished? Or do you wish one day to drag on an existence like that of the Eternal Jew who cannot die, bowing before all newly risen peoples, this man who stood at the grave of the Egyptians, the Greeks and the Romans? No! A people that knows that one day it will no longer exist, makes all the more vital use of its days, lives all the longer and leaves behind it a glorious heritage; for it will not rest until it has fully developed the potentialities that are latent within it, like a diligent and provident man who sets his house in order before his inevitable demise. This, in my opinion, is the crux of the matter. Once a destiny of a people has been fulfilled, a few days more or less do not matter. New events wait impatiently on the threshold of their time.[3]

The concept of the Eternal Jew is clearly delineated here. Normally— and this is the underlying idea—a people is born, lives, achieves, and dies. Jewry, on the other hand, is something abnormal, as if it were a living corpse, a specter. It has survived the great peoples of ancient history and reaches into our time, a mystery, an enigma. Jewry lives on and on, although it has lived up to its destiny, has accomplished its task. For what purpose, one must ask, does it still live? But beyond all these considerations Keller's words conjure up a mythical image of compulsive force, the weird figure of the Eternal Wanderer who cannot die, forever dragging on an existence without aim or purpose.

What is the relation between the meaning of the phrase as I have just developed it and the definitions of the dictionaries? The second, the ironic meaning, " a person who never settles down" or "figure of a restlessly roving person" is not relevant. The first definition seems to be appropriate, but one is struck by the fact that there is absolutely no reference to the cause of the eternal wandering nor is there any reference to Christ. This may be accidental. Since all reference to Christ, however, seems to be omitted in very many, probably most, mentions of the Eternal Jew in the nineteenth century, one gains the impression that this is the rule rather than the exception.

Is it possible that in nineteenth century Germany a third meaning may have developed, which has not yet received lexical definition, namely that of a mythical figure not unlike the Flying Dutchman or the Wild Huntsman ("Der wilde Jaeger")? Be that as it may, this figure, whether called the

---

[3] Gottfried Keller, *Gesammelte Werke*, 6 (Berlin 1889) 277.

Wandering Jew, the Eternal Jew, or Ahasverus, has been considered ancient, precisely because he has a mythical character, as ancient as the Jewish diaspora itself. If he has been considered somewhat younger then, at best, a figure of late Antiquity or of medieval times. These assumptions are wrong. The figure is actually much younger and was not yet known in the sixteenth century. The first edition of the German chapbook *Brief Description and Story of a Jew named Ahasverus* from which the first meaning given by the dictionaries stems, was published in 1602.

The figure has no genuine precursors. A figure such as the Christian penitent Kartaphilus in the thirteenth century writings of Roger of Wendover and Matthew of Paris, which may have been known to the writer of the chapbook, lacks all the essential characteristics of the figure of Ahasverus: he does not wander around, he is no Jew, to mention only two deviations.

But is our first impression really all wrong? Does not this early modern figure perhaps still present certain medieval traits? To answer this question we must keep in view how diaspora Jewry looked to people in the Middle Ages. We must arrive at the basic characteristics of the image that has remained the same throughout the centuries despite certain nuances and shadings and which, to a certain extent, is still in effect, particularly among Roman Catholics.

We can summarize this Jewish image in Christian consciousness, as known since the days of Saint Augustine, in the following manner: First, the Jews have lost their claim to being the Chosen People, but on the Day of Judgment or shortly before it they will be converted and will gain entry into the Kingdom of Heaven. Second, as punishment for having killed Christ and for refusal to believe in him, the Jews have been scattered and, through their writings, bear witness to the fact that the Christians did not invent their prophecies concerning Christ.

The first dictum dates from early Christian times and can be traced to Saint Paul: Branches—the converted Gentiles—have been cut from the wild olive tree—paganism—and have been grafted upon the cultivated olive tree —the true faith; the old branches—the Jews—have been cut off because they did not believe in Christ; but they will surely be grafted back; after the full number of Gentiles has come in, all Israel will gain salvation; the Israelites had to become enemies for the sake of the Gentiles, but for the sake of their forefathers they are beloved of God; God's grace and call are irrevocable.

This teaching is, above all, perhaps the strongest neutralization of anti-Judaism in Christian thinking that has ever occurred. *Populus Israel*, once the Chosen People, will in the fullness of time be chosen again and will belong to the *populus christianus*. The history of the world from Creation to the Day of Judgment is conceived of as an all-embracing continuum, one in which Israel plays a significant part.

The second teaching, developed later and retained by Saint Augustine, about the Jews bearing witness through their Scriptures, gained meaning only with the ever increasing allegorical exegesis of those very Scriptures on the part of the Christians. In effect this obviously rendered the Old Testament nothing but a prelude to the New.

Both teachings resulted in an image of the diaspora Jews who had to live on so that at the end of time the salvation of all mankind might become a reality. This explains the self-imposed restraint on the part of the Christian majority which perhaps partly accounts for the very existence of Jewish communities in medieval Europe.

Quite opposed to the concept embodied in the Eternal Jew, *Jewish* existence according to medieval concepts was, therefore, neither enigmatic nor meaningless. Jewry was a living community that, though it had gone astray, would one day find the right path and become the keystone of the edifice of the Christian church. This was the meaning of the Jewish diaspora, this was the reason why Jewry had to survive up to the end of all time.

Far from being a "living corpse," a weird, meaningless spectral being, to whom all that was left was to wait until it was allowed to go to its eternal rest, Jewry was a living community meaningfully fitting into the course of universal history as an indispensable entity. Its survival up to the end of history and its final conversion in the last moment of history, or shortly before it, was a condition sine qua non for the salvation of mankind, the second advent of the Lord, and the dawn of a new day, of the Kingdom of Heaven.

The medieval image of the Jew was the result of partial neutralization of anti-Judaism. It is true, the Jew continued to be an alien, did not belong to the majority group, was an outsider. There was a vague feeling, however, which for many centuries never ceased to exist: even if he was an alien, he would, or rather could, not remain so forever.

To summarize: It was beyond doubt that the Lord would return at the end of all time; and the conversion of the Jews, their incorporation into the *corpus christianum*, likewise taking place at the end of all time, was hardly less certain than the second advent of the Lord. Jews might be discriminated against, humiliated, persecuted, expelled. They might be considered the pariahs of Christendom, the most wretched, lowest people of this world. But they were part of this world. They belonged to it. Their survival was indispensable for the salvation of mankind.

It is already apparent why the mythical figure of the nineteenth century is mysterious, leads an existence devoid of meaning, and lacks all relation to Christ. In the mind of the people for whom our citizen of Zurich speaks there are only *gentes* left. The concept of the *populus christianus* which has already partially absorbed and which is to absorb the *gentes* still more, has vanished. It has become as nonexistent as the concept of a *populus Israel*.

The Jews, too, are only a *gens* or, more properly, were one once upon a time like the peoples of Antiquity.   However, the disappearance of those escha-tological considerations which were connected with the concepts of *populus Israel* and of *populus christianus* results in much more than the mere mys-teriousness ans senselessness of the Eternal Jew's existence.   The uninter-rupted rise and fall of peoples, of the *gentes*, becomes an endless repetition, likewise lacking all sense and purpose for want of any kind of all-embracing universal historical conception.

This total disappearance of eschatological considerations was, a long time before, preceded by a partial one in the chapbook of 1602. The story of Ahas-verus has a decidedly theological meaning if it is read in the light of certain theological teachings of its time.   In early Protestant theology the eschato-logy of the end of the world was theoretically still retained but, practically speaking, lost its importance when compared with the eschatology of the individual, that is, the fate of the individual after death.[4] It is for this reason that Lutheran care of the soul was concerned primarily with blissful dying. The soul is judged directly after death, and believers are immediately granted perfect and eternal bliss by God and by Christ.[5] The chapbook is based on the assumption of the validity of this conception.   The fate of Ahasverus, to whom the portal leading to bliss was forever closed, must have seemed the most horrible punishment conceivable to people who were versed in Lu-theran ways of thinking.

But we must keep in mind that eternal life is generally regarded as a re-ward and not as punishment.   The thought processes that were basic for an understanding of the chapbook were so subtle, so sophisticated that they were far beyond the capacity of the average reader to understand.   As a result, later reprints or versions of the book, a great many of which appeared in the course of a century and a half, contained appendices depicting count-less blood-curdling details of the punishment to be meted out to each of the Jewish tribes.

The chapbook documents the beginning of the disappearance in early modern times of eschatological concepts—a process that had to result in an intensification of the alienation of the Jewish image in Christian conscious-ness.   A quarter of a millenium after the appearance of the chapbook, in the nineteenth century, Ahasverus underwent a metamorphosis and became

[4] Paul Althaus, in *Religion in Geschichte und Gegenwart* 2, ed. 2; (Tübungen 1928) "Die Erwartung des Reiches verkümmert, das Denken ist ganz auf das Anliegen der persoen-lichen Heilsgewissheit gesammelt.   Die endgeschichtliche Eschatologie wird theoretisch behauptet, verliert aber den Ton. . . Die Hoffnung ist in der Hauptsache individualistisch und jenseitig eingestellt."

[5] Althaus: "Der Tod hat den Ernst des letzten Kampfes mit dem Satan, der endgueltigen Entscheidung.   Daher gilt die Seelsorge auf lutherischem Boden ueberwiegend dem *seligen Sterben*.   Die Seele erlebt das Gericht unmittelbar nach dem Tode."

the mythical figure of the Eternal Jew whose spectral image is completely isolated from everything that is Christian.

The mythical figure of the Eternal Jew as it appears in nineteenth century colloquial German is a product of a mode of thinking that has become progressively secularized. Those people who conceived of the Eternal Jew in the same way as Keller described him in 1860 were not prone to indulge in eschatological considerations, regardless of whether these concerned the end of all human history or the salvation of the individual's soul. For decades, the mythical figure is referred to, but in a tone of ever increasing animosity and hatred. In the Keller passage that has been cited, the alienation is still neutralized because in the Switzerland of the 1860s, in a country where the emancipation of the Jews was just having a rather belated start, compassion and condescension were probably often extended to the underprivileged group. In the last third of the nineteenth century the mythical figure that was isolated because it had been detached from all Christian concepts was incorporated into a newly evolving mythology, the mythology of so-called "modern" anti-Semitism. Thus the figure, having been devoid of meaning for some time, gained a new meaning but, unfortunately, one that portended evil.

That consciousness, in which the alienation of the Jewish image now began to grow apace, was no longer a Christian one but rather un-Christian, or even anti-Christian. It had just become a fad in the German literature of those days to contrast shining, glorified and idealized German hero-types with dark, sinister Jewish villains.[6] Soon demagogic, anti-Semitic agitators began to conjure up the fantastic figure of a Jewish demon of darkness as a contrast to the Germanic Siegfried- or Baldur-type. They equated this demon with the eternal enemy of the Nordic race, the Eternal Jew. The victor in this mortal combat had to be the glorified Nordic type. This was the core of the new anti-Semitic mythology which began nationalistic and ended up by being racist. It soon gave rise to a new misshapen concept of universal history: the goal of history was no longer the Kingdom of Heaven, the realm of the world to come. Now the goal was, after the triumph of the allegedly noblest of races over all its sinister antagonists, the Nordic-Germanic *Reich* of this world in which there was room neither for Jews nor for Christianity.

[6] Ernst Kohn-Bramstedt, *Aristocracy and the Middle Classes in Germany; Social Types in German Literature* (London 1937) 133-149.

Free University
Berlin
Federal Republic of Germany

VIATOR Style Sheet

1. All contributions must be typewritten in double space, with ample margins. This applies to text, quoted material, and footnotes. Please do *not* use corrasible paper.

2. Footnotes should be typed in double space on separate sheets at the end of the article and numbered consecutively.

3. Bibliographical references ordinarily belong in the notes rather than in the text; the first reference to an item should contain the complete data:

Book: J. K. Brown, *Book Title* (City 1879) 234-236.
           Title, 3 vols. (City 1870) 2.45ff.
           Title [Translation of title] (City 1877) 34.
           Title, ed. John Doe and Jane Doe (City [etc.].
           ed. 2 (City [etc.].
           trans. John Doe (City 1876) fol. 15v.

Monograph: John G. Brown, *Monograph*, Title of Series (ABBRV) 21 (1786) 34.
           C. J. Smith, *Monograph in Same Series*, ABBRV 22 (1787) 345-346.

Article: John Doe, "Article," *Journal* 76 (1879) 1-22, 34ff., 50.
           Undated Journal 76.1-22.

Manuscript: Augustine, *De musica* 3.4, Paris, Bibliothèque Nationale lat. MS 9320, fols. 4, 5v, 6rv.

4. Subsequent references may be shortened as follows, always with a view to brevity without ambiguity.

    a. Smith 24-25. (Only one Smith is cited, in a recent footnote, and there can be no possible ambiguity.)

    b. Jones (n. 2 above) 245-246. (Complete reference is in n. 2 above.)

    c. Jones, "The Blue Book" (n. 2 above) 34. (Jones has more than one reference in n. 2, so short title is necessary.)

    d. Augustine 3.6 (7v).

5. Sigla: *Acta sanctorum*: AS Apr. 3.420.
    Patrologia graeca: PG 37.96A.
    Patrologia latina: PL 129.432.
    Monumenta Germaniae historica: MGH Auctores antiquiores 5.1 (Berlin 1882) 130.

6. Titles of foreign books and articles should be capitalized according to the usages of the respective languages. In Latin and the Romance languages, only the first word and proper nouns should be capitalized.